Essentials of
Contemporary
Management

Ninth Edition

Gareth R. Jones

Jennifer M. George
Rice University

ESSENTIALS OF CONTEMPORARY MANAGEMENT, NINTH EDITION

Published by McGraw-Hill Education, 2 Penn Plaza, New York, NY 10121. Copyright © 2021 by McGraw-Hill Education. All rights reserved. Printed in the United States of America. Previous editions © 2019. No part of this publication may be reproduced or distributed in any form or by any means, or stored in a database or retrieval system, without the prior written consent of McGraw-Hill Education, including, but not limited to, in any network or other electronic storage or transmission, or broadcast for distance learning.

Some ancillaries, including electronic and print components, may not be available to customers outside the United States.

This book is printed on acid-free paper.

1 2 3 4 5 6 7 8 9 LWI 24 23 22 21 20

ISBN 978-1-260-26153-0 (bound edition)
MHID 1-260-26153-0 (bound edition)
ISBN 978-1-260-68157-4 (loose-leaf edition)
MHID 1-260-68157-2 (loose-leaf edition)

Director: *Michael Ablassmeir*
Product Development Manager: *Kelly Delso*
Product Developer: *Haley Burmeister*
Executive Marketing Manager: *Debbie Clare*
Content Project Managers: *Maria McGreal, Keri Johnson*
Buyer: *Laura Fuller*
Design: *David Hash*
Content Licensing Specialist: *Ann Marie Jannette*
Compositor: *SPi Global*

All credits appearing on page or at the end of the book are considered to be an extension of the copyright page.

Library of Congress Cataloging-in-Publication Data

Names: Jones, Gareth R., author. | George, Jennifer M., author.
Title: Essentials of contemporary management / Gareth R. Jones, Jennifer M. George.
Description: 9th Edition. | New York : McGraw-Hill Education, 2020. |
  Revised edition of the authors' Essentials of contemporary management, [2019]
Identifiers: LCCN 2019026657 (print) | LCCN 2019026658 (ebook) |
  ISBN 9781260261530 (paperback) | ISBN 1260261530 (bound edition) |
  ISBN 9781260681574 (loose-leaf edition) | ISBN 9781260681420 (ebook)
Subjects: LCSH: Management.
Classification: LCC HD31 .J5974 2020 (print) | LCC HD31 (ebook) | DDC 658—dc23
LC record available at https://lccn.loc.gov/2019026657
LC ebook record available at https://lccn.loc.gov/2019026658

The Internet addresses listed in the text were accurate at the time of publication. The inclusion of a website does not indicate an endorsement by the authors or McGraw-Hill Education, and McGraw-Hill Education does not guarantee the accuracy of the information presented at these sites.

mheducation.com/highered

Brief Contents

Authors

Courtesy of Gareth Jones

Gareth Jones currently offers pro bono advice on solving management problems to non-profit organizations in Houston, Texas. He received his BA in Economics Psychology and his PhD in Management from the University of Lancaster, UK. He was formerly Professor of Management in the Graduate School of Business at Texas A&M University and earlier held teaching and research appointments at Michigan State University, the University of Illinois at Urbana–Champaign, and the University of Warwick, UK.

He continues to pursue his research interests in strategic management and organizational theory and his well-known research that applies transaction cost analysis to explain many forms of strategic and organizational behavior. He also studies the complex and changing relationships between competitive advantage and information technology in the 2010s.

He has published many articles in leading journals of the field and his research has appeared in the *Academy of Management Review,* the *Journal of International Business Studies,* and *Human Relations.* He published an article about the role of information technology in many aspects of organizational functioning in the *Journal of Management.* One of his articles won the *Academy of Management Journal'*s Best Paper Award, and he is one of the most cited authors in the *Academy of Management Review.* He is, or has served, on the editorial boards of the *Academy of Management Review,* the *Journal of Management,* and *Management Inquiry.*

Gareth Jones has used his academic knowledge to craft leading textbooks in management and three other major areas in the management discipline: organizational behavior, organizational theory, and strategic management. His books are widely recognized for their innovative, contemporary content and for the clarity with which they communicate complex, real-world issues to students.

Courtesy of Jennifer George

Jennifer George is the Mary Gibbs Jones Professor of Management and Professor of Psychology in the Jesse H. Jones Graduate School of Business at Rice University. She received her BA in Psychology/Sociology from Wesleyan University, her MBA in Finance from New York University, and her PhD in Management and Organizational Behavior from New York University. Prior to joining the faculty at Rice University, she was a professor in the Department of Management at Texas A&M University.

Professor George specializes in organizational behavior and is well known for her research on mood and emotion in the workplace, their determinants, and their effects on various individual and group-level work outcomes. She is the author of many articles in leading peer-reviewed journals such as the *Academy of Management Journal,* the *Academy of Management Review,* the *Journal of Applied Psychology, Organizational Behavior and Human Decision Processes, Journal of Personality and Social Psychology,* and *Psychological Bulletin.* One of her papers won the Academy of Management's Organizational Behavior Division Outstanding Competitive Paper Award, and another paper won the *Human Relations* Best Paper Award. She is, or has been, on the editorial review boards of the *Journal of Applied Psychology, Academy of Management Journal, Academy of Management Review, Administrative Science Quarterly, Journal of Management, Organizational Behavior and Human Decision Processes, Organization Science, International Journal of Selection and Assessment,* and *Journal of Managerial Issues;* was a consulting editor for the *Journal of Organizational Behavior;* was a member of the SIOP *Organizational Frontiers Series* editorial board; and was an associate editor of the *Journal of Applied Psychology.* She is a fellow in the Academy of Management, the American Psychological Association, the Association for Psychological Science, and the Society for Industrial and Organizational Psychology and a member of the Society for Organizational Behavior. She also has coauthored a textbook titled *Understanding and Managing Organizational Behavior.*

Preface

In this ninth edition of *Essentials of Contemporary Management,* we continue to focus on providing the most up-to-date account of the changes taking place in the world of management and management practices while maintaining our emphasis on making our text relevant and interesting to students. And we know from feedback from instructors and students that the text does engage them. Our increased focus on the challenges and opportunities facing businesses large and small and integrated timely examples bring management issues to life for students.

The number and complexity of strategic, organizational, and human resource challenges facing managers and employees continue to rise. In most companies, managers at all levels address these challenges by implementing new and improved management techniques and practices. Today, relatively small differences in performance between companies, such as in the speed at which they bring new products or services to market or in the ways they motivate their employees to find ways to reduce costs or improve performance, can combine to give a company a significant competitive advantage. Managers and companies that utilize proven management techniques and practices in their decision making and actions increase their effectiveness over time.

The issues facing managers continue to intensify as changes in the global environment, such as tightening of the U.S. labor market, rising wages in China and other countries, and increasing political and economic instability, impact organizations large and small. In addition, increasing globalization means that managers must be quick to respond to major differences in the legal rules and regulations and ethical values and norms that prevail in countries around the globe.

Moreover, the ongoing revolution in technology continues to transform how managers make decisions across all levels of a company's hierarchy and across its functions and global divisions. This new edition addresses these ongoing challenges as technology continues to change at breakneck speed, especially in the areas of artificial intelligence, data analytics, and cybersecurity.

Other major challenges we continue to expand on in this edition include the impact of the steadily increasing diversity of the workforce on companies and how this increasing diversity makes it imperative for managers to understand how and why people differ so that they can effectively manage and reap the performance benefits of diversity. Similarly, across all functions and levels, managers and employees must continually seek ways to work smarter and increase performance. Using new technologies to improve all aspects of an organization's operations to enhance efficiency and customer responsiveness is a vital part of this process. So too is the continuing need to innovate and improve the quality of goods and services, and the ways they are produced, to allow an organization to compete effectively. We significantly revised and updated this edition of *Essentials of Contemporary Management* to address these challenges to managers and their organizations.

Major Content Changes

Once again, encouraged by the number of instructors and students who use each new edition of our book, and based on the reactions and suggestions of both users and reviewers, we revised and updated our book in many ways. However, the organization and sequence of chapters remain the same in this new edition. Instructors tell us that they like the way the chapters flow, and the way they build up a picture of management part by part, to provide an excellent learning experience and a comprehensive coverage of management. As examples of the changes we made, this new edition expands the coverage of ways to encourage high motivation, creativity, and innovation in organizations and the importance of managers' and organizations' taking steps to stay ahead of technological changes that may impact daily business operations.

CHAPTER-BY-CHAPTER CHANGES We made the following specific changes to this edition.

Chapter 1

- New "Management Snapshot" on how Microsoft CEO Satya Nadella has brought a fresh vision to the technology giant.
- New "Manager as a Person" on how an ER director is helping make visits to the emergency room as painless as possible.
- New content and table have been added that describe Mintzberg's typology and the various roles managers perform in an organization.
- New "Management Insight" on using managerial skills as a city manager in the public sector.
- New section of text discusses the differences between managers and entrepreneurs.
- New "Ethics in Action" on giving employees a nudge to increase ethical behavior in the workplace.
- New end-of-chapter case on GE spinning off its railroad business.
- Appendix A: New discussion on the Gilbreths and their important contributions to management theory.

Chapter 2

- New "Management Snapshot" on how the CEO of Carnival Cruise Lines uses his personal attitudes to steer the company in the right direction.
- New section describes the Myers-Briggs Type Indicator and DiSC Inventory Profile personality assessments.
- New "Ethics in Action" on how to promote ethical values in the hotel industry.
- New discussion of job satisfaction levels among U.S. workers today.
- New "Managing Globally" on emotional intelligence across borders.
- New end-of-chapter case on Google's ongoing challenge to maintain a strong company culture.

Chapter 3

- New "Management Snapshot" on Intel's diversity and inclusion efforts.
- New "Ethics in Action" on how Accenture is using a chatbot to provide ethical guidance for employees.

- Updated in-text statistics on age, and men's and women's participation rates in the U.S. workforce and median weekly earnings.
- New discussion on the lack of women CEOs in S&P 500 companies.
- Updated statistics on the increasing diversity of the U.S. workforce.
- New "Focus on Diversity" describing SodaStream's diversity efforts in its business operations.
- Updated discussion and statistics on sexual harassment.
- New "Management Insight" on providing effective anti-harassment training in the workplace.
- New end-of-chapter case on Chevron's efforts to stay on the high road in Venezuela amid political and economic unrest.

Chapter 4

- New "Management Snapshot" on Walmart's global expansion by investing in Flipkart, the Indian e-commerce giant that competes with Amazon.
- New "Ethics in Action" on how Levi Strauss motivates its global suppliers to treat their employees well.
- New "Management Insight" on the impact of tariffs on auto companies' supply chains.
- Updated discussion on the new trade agreement that will replace NAFTA.
- New discussion on the GLOBE project that extends Hofstede's work on national culture by looking at additional cultural dimensions and how they impact the ways in which business is conducted in a variety of cultures and countries.
- New "Manager as a Person" that describes some of the rewards and pitfalls of being an expat working in a foreign country.
- New end-of-chapter case on Foxconn's decision to build a manufacturing facility in Wisconsin.

Chapter 5

- New "Management Snapshot" on how creativity and the ability to learn helped the management of 23andMe, an online genetic screening service, adapt its business when roadblocks almost derailed the company.
- New "Manager as a Person" about the CEO of an online beauty start-up who was unafraid to

seek expert advice about making strategic business decisions that helped grow her company.

- An updated discussion about continuous learning and attaining personal mastery.
- New "Managing Globally" on how management at Western Union embraces continuous learning, which has helped the company stay relevant in this high-tech, global business environment.
- New end-of-chapter case on the U.S. Marines logistics unit and how it is teaching military personnel in the field to use various computer-aided technologies to think creatively in their everyday job activities.

Chapter 6
- New "Management Snapshot" on Marriott International's CEO and strategies he put in place to expand the company's growth over the next few years.
- A new discussion about how General Mills and its management team devise and implement planning strategies at various levels of the organization.
- New "Manager as a Person" that describes how the CEO of Los Angeles World Airports plans for and oversees various projects at the nation's second-busiest airport.
- A new discussion about SWOT analysis factors experienced by both Amazon and Walmart as they compete head-to-head in the exploding e-commerce sector.
- New "Management Insight" on how Comcast is rethinking the customer experience.
- A new discussion that points out some of the missteps by toy retailer Toys "R" Us as they pertain to Porter's five forces framework.
- New "Managing Globally" on how transportation company FourKites uses technology and real-time data to help its customers with on-time deliveries.
- New end-of-chapter case on how Best Buy tweaks its strategies to stay relevant and compete in an ever-changing business environment.

Chapter 7
- New "Management Snapshot" on how Alaska Airlines's organizational structure is designed with customers in mind.

- New "Managing Globally" on how IKEA is redesigning new stores on a smaller scale now that many consumers shop online.
- New "Ethics in Action" about Pfizer changing its organizational structure to help improve business and marketing efforts.
- New "Manager as a Person" about how McDonald's CEO continues to shake things up by streamlining the company's structure to increase efficiency, productivity, and sales.
- New end-of-chapter case about restructuring and rebranding efforts at Ogilvy's U.S. advertising operations.

Chapter 8
- Discussion of entrepreneurship has been moved to Chapter 1 to provide a framework for highlighting the differences between managers and entrepreneurs.
- New "Management Snapshot" about Procter & Gamble's efforts to control expenditures for digital ads.
- New "Management Insight" on the skills employers are looking for in recent college graduates.
- New "Managing Globally" on the growing trend of companies using zero-based budgeting as a way of controlling expenses.
- New section on the balanced scorecard and its increasing use by organizations to evaluate various measures of a company's performance.
- New "Ethics in Action" on Volkswagen's continuing efforts to implement top-down change to regain consumers' confidence after an emissions scandal.
- New end-of-chapter case on how Stitch Fix controls inventory and the customer experience.

Chapter 9
- New "Management Snapshot" on the 90-something owner of the Detroit Lions and her ability to motivate the management team as well as her NFL players.
- New "Focus on Diversity" on the importance of equity in a diverse workforce.
- New "Ethics in Action" on United Airlines and how a recent attempt backfired to make merit pay more motivating.

- New end-of-chapter case on DTE Energy and company efforts to reenergize its workforce with a shared sense of purpose to cut costs and avoid layoffs.

Chapter 10
- New "Management Snapshot" on effective leadership strategies at the Dana-Farber Cancer Institute.
- New section on the traits of servant leadership.
- New "Managing Globally" on international differences in leadership.
- New "Management Insight" on the effectiveness of leaders with high levels of emotional intelligence.
- New end-of-chapter case on how the CEO of Levi Strauss uses effective leadership strategies to help the company and its employees succeed.

Chapter 11
- New "Management Snapshot" on how the U.S. Army's use of teamwork helps in the battle against bureaucracy.
- New "Management Insight" on the importance of team members developing soft skills.
- New discussion on the skills and abilities of successful virtual teams and the technology they use to help with their long-distance work activities.
- New "Focus on Diversity" that provides strategies for using team members' diversity as a competitive advantage.
- New discussion on recent research about high-performing teams and the factors that contribute to their success.
- New end-of-chapter case on how Adient, the world's largest supplier of automotive seating, uses high-performance teams to maintain its competitive edge.

Chapter 12
- New "Management Snapshot" on Unilever's chief human resource officer and how she manages workforce planning and development at the global consumer products company.
- New "Management Insight" on Home Depot's CEO and his competitive strategy of using economic slowdowns to invest in employee training

and development, as well as improving customers' online shopping experiences.
- New "Focus on Diversity" on using recruiting practices that promote diversity.
- New section that discusses recent trends in performance appraisal strategies.
- New end-of-chapter case on how Salesforce sets itself apart in a tight labor market.

Chapter 13
- Chapter content has been streamlined to focus on the key components of effective communication at all levels of the organization. Technology discussion has moved to Chapter 14.
- New "Management Snapshot" on ways Boston Consulting Group encourages its employees to engage in short, informal interactions with colleagues as way of increasing communication and reducing the need for lengthy meetings.
- New "Manager as a Person" profiles the cofounders of Hyphen, a technology platform that lets businesses gather and analyze anonymous communications from employees.
- New "Ethics in Action" on how the use of questions can foster effective communication.
- New "Management Insight" on how to make a positive first impression.
- New end-of-chapter case on how Netflix aims to keep communication honest throughout the organization.

Chapter 14
- Chapter has been revised to include a discussion of how information and technology help managers make better decisions, linking this content to the discussion of operations management.
- New "Management Snapshot" on Kraft Heinz's efforts to make sure managerial decisions add value to the company.
- New "Management Insight" on the use of artificial intelligence to help identify situations within an organization that require more active leadership on the part of managers.
- New "Ethics in Action" on why Facebook users are quitting the social networking platform over privacy issues.

- New "Managing Globally" feature on Happy OrNot—a Finnish company that captures customer sentiments about their shopping experiences via in-store terminals labeled with four different happy or sad faces.
- New end-of-chapter case on how Brooks Brothers redesigned its processes to make the clothing retailer more relevant and more efficient.

We feel confident that the changes to the ninth edition of *Essentials of Contemporary Management* will stimulate and challenge students to think about their future in the world of organizations.

Emphasis on Applied Management

We went to great lengths to bring the manager back into the subject matter of management. That is, we wrote our chapters from the perspective of current or future managers to illustrate, in a hands-on way, the problems and opportunities they face and how they can effectively meet them. For example, in Chapter 3, we provide an integrated treatment of ethics and diversity that clearly explains their significance to practicing managers. In Chapter 6, we provide an integrated treatment of planning, strategy, and competitive advantage, highlighting the crucial choices managers face as they perform the planning function. Throughout the text, we emphasize important issues managers face and how management theory, research, and practice can help them and their organizations be effective.

The last two chapters cover the topics of communication, operations management, and technology, subjects that tend to be difficult to teach to new management students in an interesting way. We have streamlined the chapters in an effort to highlight the key concepts students need to know and understand when it comes to how managers address these important processes.

Flexible Organization

We designed the grouping of chapters to allow instructors to teach the chapter material in the order that best suits their needs. Instructors are not tied to the planning, organizing, leading, and controlling framework, even though our presentation remains consistent with this approach.

You're in the driver's seat.

Want to build your own course? No problem. Prefer to use our turnkey, prebuilt course? Easy. Want to make changes throughout the semester? Sure. And you'll save time with Connect's auto-grading too.

65%

Less Time Grading

Laptop: McGraw-Hill; Woman/dog: George Doyle/Getty Images

They'll thank you for it.

Adaptive study resources like SmartBook® 2.0 help your students be better prepared in less time. You can transform your class time from dull definitions to dynamic debates. Find out more about the powerful personalized learning experience available in SmartBook 2.0 at **www.mheducation.com/highered/connect/smartbook**

Make it simple, make it affordable.

Connect makes it easy with seamless integration using any of the major Learning Management Systems— Blackboard®, Canvas, and D2L, among others—to let you organize your course in one convenient location. Give your students access to digital materials at a discount with our inclusive access program. Ask your McGraw-Hill representative for more information.

Padlock: Jobalou/Getty Images

Solutions for your challenges.

A product isn't a solution. Real solutions are affordable, reliable, and come with training and ongoing support when you need it and how you want it. Our Customer Experience Group can also help you troubleshoot tech problems— although Connect's 99% uptime means you might not need to call them. See for yourself at **status.mheducation.com**

Checkmark: Jobalou/Getty Images

SUPPORT AT *every step*

FOR STUDENTS

Effective, efficient studying.

Connect helps you be more productive with your study time and get better grades using tools like SmartBook 2.0, which highlights key concepts and creates a personalized study plan. Connect sets you up for success, so you walk into class with confidence and walk out with better grades.

Study anytime, anywhere.

Download the free ReadAnywhere app and access your online eBook or SmartBook 2.0 assignments when it's convenient, even if you're offline. And since the app automatically syncs with your eBook and SmartBook 2.0 assignments in Connect, all of your work is available every time you open it. Find out more at **www.mheducation.com/readanywhere**

"I really liked this app—it made it easy to study when you don't have your text-book in front of you."

- Jordan Cunningham, Eastern Washington University

Calendar: owattaphotos/Getty Images

No surprises.

The Connect Calendar and Reports tools keep you on track with the work you need to get done and your assignment scores. Life gets busy; Connect tools help you keep learning through it all.

Learning for everyone.

McGraw-Hill works directly with Accessibility Services Departments and faculty to meet the learning needs of all students. Please contact your Accessibility Services office and ask them to email accessibility@mheducation.com, or visit **www.mheducation.com/about/accessibility** for more information.

Top: Jenner Images/Getty Images, Left: Hero Images/Getty Images, Right: Hero Images/Getty Images

create **CREATE** Instructors can now tailor their teaching resources to match the way they teach! With McGraw-Hill Create, **www.mcgrawhillcreate.com**, instructors can easily rearrange chapters, combine material from other content sources, and quickly upload and integrate their own content, such as course syllabi or teaching notes. Find the right content in Create by searching through thousands of leading McGraw-Hill textbooks. Arrange the material to fit your teaching style. Order a Create book and receive a complimentary print review copy in three to five business days or a complimentary electronic review copy via e-mail within one hour. Go to **www.mcgrawhillcreate.com** today and register.

TEGRITY: LECTURES 24/7 Tegrity in Connect is a tool that makes class time available 24/7 by automatically capturing every lecture. With a simple one-click start-and-stop process, you capture all computer screens and corresponding audio in a format that is easy to search, frame by frame. Students can replay any part of any class with easy-to-use, browser-based viewing on a PC, Mac, iPod, or other mobile device.

Educators know that the more students can see, hear, and experience class resources, the better they learn. In fact, studies prove it. Tegrity's unique search feature helps students efficiently find what they need, when they need it, across an entire semester of class recordings. Help turn your students' study time into learning moments immediately supported by your lecture. With Tegrity, you also increase intent listening and class participation by easing students' concerns about note-taking. Using Tegrity in Connect will make it more likely you will see students' faces, not the tops of their heads.

Campus **MCGRAW-HILL CAMPUS** McGraw-Hill Campus is a new one-stop teaching and learning experience available to users of any learning management system. This institutional service allows faculty and students to enjoy single sign-on (SSO) access to all McGraw-Hill Higher Education materials, including the award-winning McGraw-Hill *Connect* platform, from directly within the institution's website. With McGraw-Hill Campus, faculty receive instant access to teaching materials (e.g., eTextbooks, test banks, PowerPoint slides, animations, learning objectives, etc.), allowing them to browse, search, and use any instructor ancillary content in our vast library at no additional cost to instructor or students. In addition, students enjoy SSO access to a variety of free content (e.g., quizzes, flash cards, narrated presentations, etc.) and subscription-based products (e.g., McGraw-Hill *Connect*). With McGraw-Hill Campus enabled, faculty and students will never need to create another account to access McGraw-Hill products and services. Learn more at **www.mhcampus.com**.

ASSURANCE OF LEARNING READY Many educational institutions today focus on the notion of *assurance of learning,* an important element of some accreditation standards. *Essentials of Contemporary Management* is designed specifically to support instructors' assurance of learning initiatives with a simple yet powerful solution. Each test bank question for *Essentials of Contemporary Management* maps to a specific chapter learning objective listed in the text.

 **AACSB TAGGING** McGraw-Hill Education is a proud corporate member of AACSB International. Understanding the importance and value of AACSB accreditation, *Essentials of Contemporary Management* recognizes the curricula guidelines detailed in the AACSB standards for business accreditation by connecting selected questions in the text and the test bank to the eight general knowledge and skill guidelines in the AACSB standards. The statements contained in *Essentials of Contemporary Management* are provided only as a guide for the users of this product. The AACSB leaves content coverage and assessment within the purview of

individual schools, the mission of the school, and the faculty. While the *Essentials of Contemporary Management* teaching package makes no claim of any specific AACSB qualification or evaluation, we have within *Essentials of Contemporary Management* labeled selected questions according to the eight general knowledge and skills areas.

MCGRAW-HILL CUSTOMER EXPERIENCE GROUP CONTACT INFORMATION At McGraw-Hill Education, we understand that getting the most from new technology can be challenging. That's why our services don't stop after you purchase our products. You can e-mail our Product Specialists 24 hours a day to get product training online. Or you can search our knowledge bank of Frequently Asked Questions on our support website. For Customer Support, call **800-331-5094** or visit **www.mhhe.com/support**. One of our Technical Support Analysts will be able to assist you in a timely fashion.

Acknowledgments

Finding a way to integrate and present the rapidly growing literature on contemporary management and make it interesting and meaningful for students is not an easy task. In writing and revising the various editions of *Essentials of Contemporary Management,* we have been fortunate to have had the assistance of several people who have contributed greatly to the book's final form. First, we are grateful to Michael Ablassmeir, our executive brand manager, for his support and commitment to our project, and for always finding ways to provide the resources that we needed to continually improve and refine our book. Second, we are grateful to Haley Burmeister, our product developer, for so ably coordinating the book's progress, and to her and Deb Clare, our marketing manager, for providing us with concise and timely feedback and information from professors and reviewers that have allowed us to shape the book to the needs of its intended market. We also thank David Hash for executing an awe-inspiring design and Maria McGreal for coordinating the production process. We are also grateful to the many colleagues and reviewers who provided us with useful and detailed feedback, perceptive comments, and valuable suggestions for improving the manuscript.

Producing any competitive work is a challenge. Producing a truly market-driven textbook requires tremendous effort beyond simply obtaining reviews on a draft manuscript. Our goal behind the development of *Essentials of Contemporary Management* has been clear-cut: to be the most customer-driven essentials of management text and supplement package ever published! The favorable reception that our book has received from its users suggests that our thorough product development plan did lead to a book that has met the expectations of both faculty and students. For the new edition, we have continued to add new reviewers to the more than 200 faculty who originally took part in developmental activities ranging from regional focus groups to manuscript reviews and surveys. Consequently, we're confident that the changes we have made to our book and its excellent support package will even more closely meet your expectations and needs.

We extend our special thanks to the faculty who gave us detailed chapter-by-chapter feedback during the development of the ninth edition:

Joseph Aranyosi, *University of Phoenix*
William Belcher, *Troy University*
Cydna Bougae, *Montclair State University*
Marcia Simmering Dickinson, *Louisiana Tech University*
Carla C. Flores, *Ball State University*
Dana Frederick, *Missouri State University*
Shahbaz Gill, *University of Illinois at Urbana–Champaign*
Terry A. Girdon, *Pennsylvania College of Technology*
Joanne Hartsell, *East Carolina University*
Anne Kelly Hoel, *University of Wisconsin–Stout*
Tammy G. Hunt, *University of North Carolina, Wilmington*
Tiffany Maldonado, *University of Houston Downtown*
Marina Sebastijanovic, *University of Houston*
Joanna Shaw, *Tarleton State University*
Brandi L. Ulrich, *Anne Arundel Community College*

Our thanks to these faculty who have contributed greatly to previous editions of *Essentials of Contemporary Management:*

Garry Adams, *Auburn University*
M. Ruhul Amin, *Bloomsburg University of Pennsylvania*
Fred Anderson, *Indiana University of Pennsylvania*
Jacquelyn Appeldorn, *Dutchess Community College*
Barry Armandi, *SUNY–Old Westbury*
Dave Arnott, *Dallas Baptist University*
Debra Arvanites, *Villanova University*
Douglas E. Ashby, *Lewis & Clark Community College*
Joe Atallah, *Devry University*
Kenneth E. Aupperle, *The University of Akron*
Barry S. Axe, *Florida Atlantic University*
Andrea D. Bailey, *Moraine Valley Community College*

Jeff Bailey, *University of Idaho*
Robert M. Ballinger, *Siena College*
Moshe Banai, *Bernard M. Baruch College*
Frank Barber, *Cuyahoga Community College*
Reuel Barksdale, *Columbus State Community
College*
Sandy Jeanquart Barone, *Murray State University*
Lorraine P. Bassette, *Prince George's Community
College*
Gene Baten, *Central Connecticut State University*
Myra Jo Bates, *Bellevue University*
Josephine Bazan, *Holyoke Community College*
Hrach Bedrosian, *New York University*
William Belcher, *Troy University*
Omar Belkhodja, *Virginia State University*
James Bell, *Texas State University–San Marcos*
Ellen A. Benowitz, *Mercer County Community
College*
Stephen Betts, *William Paterson University*
Jack C. Blanton, *University of Kentucky*
David E. Blevins, *University of Arkansas at Little
Rock*
Mary Jo Boehms, *Jackson State Community College*
Karen Boroff, *Seton Hall University*
Jennifer Bowers, *Florida State University*
Barbara Boyington, *Brookdale Community College*
Dan Bragg, *Bowling Green State University*
Charles Braun, *Marshall University*
Dennis Brode, *Sinclair Community College*
Gil Brookins, *Siena College*
Murray Brunton, *Central Ohio Technical College*
Patricia M. Buhler, *Goldey-Beacom College*
Judith G. Bulin, *Monroe Community College*
David Cadden, *Quinnipiac College*
Thomas Campbell, *University of Texas–Austin*
Thomas Carey, *Western Michigan University*
Barbara Carlin, *University of Houston*
Daniel P. Chamberlin, *Regents University–CRB*
Larry Chasteen, *Stephen F. Austin State University*
Raul Chavez, *Eastern Mennonite University*
Nicolette De Ville Christensen, *Guilford College*
Anthony A. Cioffi, *Lorain County Community
College*
Sharon F. Clark, *Lebanon Valley College*
Sharon Clinebell, *University of Northern Colorado*
Dianne Coleman, *Wichita State University*
Elizabeth Cooper, *University of Rhode Island*
Anne Cowden, *California State
University–Sacramento*
Thomas D. Craven, *York College of Pennsylvania*

Kent Curran, *University of North Carolina*
Arthur L. Darrow, *Bowling Green State University*
Tom Deckelman, *Walsh College*
D. Anthony DeStadio, *Pittsburgh Technical
Institute*
Ron DiBattista, *Bryant College*
Thomas Duening, *University of Houston*
Charles P. Duffy, *Iona College*
Steve Dunphy, *The University of Akron*
Subhash Durlabhji, *Northwestern State University*
Robert A. Eberle, *Iona College*
Karen Eboch, *Bowling Green State University*
Robert R. Edwards, *Arkansas Tech University*
Susan Eisner, *Ramapo College of New Jersey*
William Eldridge, *Kean College*
Pat Ellsberg, *Lower Columbia College*
Stan Elsea, *Kansas State University*
Scott Elston, *Iowa State University*
Joseph Eshun, *East Stroudsburg University*
Judson Faurer, *Metro State College of Denver*
Dale Finn, *University of New Haven*
Joseph Fitzgerald, *Siena College*
Charles Flaherty, *University of Minnesota*
Alisa Fleming, *University of Phoenix*
Lucinda Fleming, *Orange County Community
College*
Robert Flemming, *Delta State University*
Jeanie M. Forray, *Eastern Connecticut State
University*
Marilyn L. Fox, *Minnesota State University*
Mankato Ellen Frank, *Southern Connecticut State
University*
Tracy Fulce, *Oakton Community College*
Joseph A. Gemma, *Providence College*
Neal Gersony, *University of New Haven*
Donna H. Giertz, *Parkland College*
Leo Giglio, *Dowling College*
Camille Girardi-Levy, *Siena College*
David Glew, *Texas A&M University*
Carol R. Graham, *Western Kentucky University*
Matthew Gross, *Moraine Valley Community
College*
John Hall, *University of Florida*
Eric L. Hansen, *California State University–Long
Beach*
Justin U. Harris, *Strayer College*
Allison Harrison, *Mississippi State University*
Sandra Hartman, *University of New Orleans*
Brad D. Hays, *North Central State College*
Gary Hensel, *McHenry Community College*

Robert A. Herring III, *Winston-Salem State University*

Eileen Bartels Hewitt, *University of Scranton*

Stephen R. Hiatt, *Catawba College*

Tammy Bunn Hiller, *Bucknell University*

Adrienne Hinds, *Northern Virginia Community College*

Anne Kelly Hoel, *University of Wisconsin–Stout*

Eileen Hogan, *Kutztown University*

Jerry Horgesheiner, *Southern Utah State*

Gordon K. Huddleston, *South Carolina State University*

John Hughes, *Texas Tech University*

Larry W. Hughes, *University of Nebraska at Kearney*

Tammy Hunt, *University of North Carolina–Wilmington*

Gary S. Insch, *West Virginia University*

Charleen Jaeb, *Cuyahoga Community College*

Velma Jesser, *Lane Community College*

Richard E. Johe, *Salem College*

Gwendolyn Jones, *The University of Akron*

Kathy Jones, *University of North Dakota*

Marybeth Kardatzke, *North Harris Montgomery Community College District*

Jim Katzenstein, *California State University–Dominguez Hills*

Jehan G. Kavoosi, *Clarion University of Pennsylvania*

Robert J. Keating, *University of North Carolina at Wilmington*

Frank Khoury, *Berkeley College*

Peggi Koenecke, *California State University–Sacramento*

Donald Kopka, *Towson University*

Dennis Lee Kovach, *Community College of Allegheny County–North Campus*

Mark Kunze, *Virginia State University*

Ken Lehmenn, *Forsyth Technical Community College*

Lianlian Lin, *California State Polytechnic University*

Grand Lindstrom, *University of Wyoming*

John Lipinski, *Robert Morris University*

Mary Lou Lockerby, *College of DuPage*

Esther Long, *University of Florida*

E. Geoffrey Love, *University of Illinois*

George S. Lowry, *Randolph–Macon College*

George E. Macdonald Jr., *Laredo Community College*

Bryan Malcolm, *University of Wisconsin*

Z. A. Malik, *Governors State University*

Mary J. Mallott, *George Washington University*

Christine Marchese, *Nassau Community College*

Jennifer Martin, *York College of Pennsylvania*

Lisa McCormick, *Community College of Allegheny County*

Reuben McDaniel, *University of Texas*

Robert L. McKeage, *The University of Scranton*

John A. Miller, *Bucknell University*

Richard R. J. Morin, *James Madison University*

Don Moseley, *University of South Alabama–Mobile*

Behnam Nakhai, *Millersville University of Pennsylvania*

Robert D. Nale, *Coastal Carolina University*

Daniel F. Nehring, *Morehead State University*

Thomas C. Neil, *Clark Atlanta University*

Brian Niehoff, *Kansas State University*

Judy Nixon, *University of Tennessee*

Cliff Olson, *Southern Adventists University*

Karen Overton, *HCC–Northeast College*

Audrey Parajon, *Wilmington University*

Ralph W. Parrish, *University of Central Oklahoma*

Dane Partridge, *University of Southern Indiana*

Sheila J. Pechinski, *University of Maine*

Marc Pendel, *Ball State University*

Fred Pierce, *Northwood University*

Mary Pisnar, *Baldwin Wallace College*

Laynie Pizzolatto, *Nicholls State University*

Eleanor Polster, *Florida International University*

Paul Preston, *University of Texas–San Antonio*

Samuel Rabinowitz, *Rutgers University–Camden*

Gerald Ramsey, *Indiana University Southeast*

Charles Rarick, *Transylvania University*

Deana K. Ray, *Forsyth Technical Community College*

Robert A. Reber, *Western Kentucky University*

Bob Redick, *Lincoln Land Community College*

Douglas Richardon, *Eastfield College*

Michael Riley, *Gateway Community and Technical College*

Tina L. Robbins, *Clemson University*

Deborah Britt Roebuck, *Kennesaw State University*

Harvey Rothenberg, *Regis University*

Catherine Ruggieri, *St. John's University*

George Ruggiero, *Community College of Rhode Island*

Kathleen Rust, *Elmhurst College*

Robert Rustic, *University of Findlay*

Cyndy Ruszkowski, *Illinois State University*
Nestor St. Charles, *Dutchess Community College*
Lynda St. Clair, *Bryant College*
Michael Santoro, *Rutgers University*
John L. Schmidt Jr., *George Mason University*
Gerald Schoenfeld Jr., *James Madison University*
Don Schreiber, *Baylor University*
Robert Schwartz, *University of Toledo*
Marina Sebastijanovic, *University of Houston*
Amit Shah, *Frostburg State University*
Joanna Shaw, *Tarleton State University*
Michael Shapiro, *Dowling College*
Raymond Shea, *Monroe Community College*
Richard Ray Shreve, *Indiana University Northwest*
Sidney Siegel, *Drexel University*
Thomas D. Sigerstad, *Frostburg State University*
Roy L. Simerly, *East Carolina University*
Randi L. Sims, *Nova Southeastern University*
Sharon Sloan, *Northwood University*
Erika E. Small, *Coastal Carolina University*
Andrea Smith-Hunter, *Siena College*
Brien Smith, *Ball State University*
Marjorie Smith, *Mountain State University*
Nayrie Smith, *Miami Dade College*
Raymond D. Smith, *Towson State University*
William A. Sodeman, *University of Southern Indiana*
Carl J. Sonntag, *Pikes Peak Community College*
Robert W. Sosna, *Menlo College*
William Soukup, *University of San Diego*
Rieann Spence-Gale, *Northern Virginia Community College–Alexandria Campus*
H. T. Stanton Jr., *Barton College*
Jerry Stevens, *Texas Tech University*
William A. Stoever, *Seton Hall University*
Charles I. Stubbart, *Southern Illinois University at Carbondale*
James K. Swenson, *Moorhead State University*
Karen Ann Tarnoff, *East Tennessee State University*

Scott Taylor, *Moberly Area Community College*
Jerry L. Thomas, *Arapahoe Community College*
Joe Thomas, *Middle Tennessee State University*
Kenneth Thompson, *DePaul University*
John Todd, *University of Arkansas*
Thomas Turk, *Chapman University*
Isaiah Ugboro, *North Carolina A & T University*
Brandi Ulrich, *Anne Arundel Community College*
Linn Van Dyne, *Michigan State University*
Jaen Vanhoegaerden, *Ashridge Management College*
Barry L. Van Hook, *Arizona State University*
Gloria Walker, *Florida Community College*
Stuart H. Warnock, *University of Southern Colorado*
Tommy Lee Waterson, *Northwood University*
Philip A. Weatherford, *Embry-Riddle Aeronautical University*
Ben Weeks, *St. Xavier University*
Emilia S. Westney, *Texas Tech University*
Donita Whitney-Bammerlin, *Kansas State University*
Robert Williams, *University of North Alabama*
W. J. Williams, *Chicago State University*
Shirley A. Wilson, *Bryant College*
Robert H. Woodhouse, *University of St. Thomas*
Michael A. Yahr, *Robert Morris College*
D. Kent Zimmerman, *James Madison University*

Finally, we are grateful to two incredibly wonderful children, Nicholas and Julia, for being all that they are and for the joy they bring to all who know them.

Gareth R. Jones

Jennifer M. George
*Jesse H. Jones Graduate School of Business
Rice University*

Contents

Part Two The Environment of Management

CHAPTER THREE

Managing Ethics and Diversity 78

Sam Edwards/age fotostock RF

Management Snapshot

Inclusion for Women Engineers at Intel 79

Overview

CHAPTER FOUR

Managing in the Global Environment 120

Polka Dot Images/Jupiterimages

Management Snapshot

Walmart Takes on Amazon in India 121

Overview

Part Three   Planning, Decision Making, and Competitive Advantage

CHAPTER FIVE

Decision Making, Learning, and Creativity   154

Robert Nicholas/Ojo Images/age fotostock

CHAPTER SIX

Planning, Strategy, and Competitive Advantage   182

Tom Merton/AGE Fotostock RF

Management Snapshot

Creativity and Ability to Learn Keep 23andMe Strong   155

Management Snapshot

Sorenson Plans for Continued Growth at Marriott   183

Part Four Organizing and Change

CHAPTER SEVEN
Designing Organizational Structure 218

@Jacob Lund/Shutterstock

CHAPTER EIGHT
Organizational Control and Change 252

Image Source/Getty Images

Part Five Leading Individuals and Groups

CHAPTER ELEVEN

Effective Team Management 352

El Nariz/Shutterstock

Management Snapshot
Leading the Army's Battle against Red Tape 353

Overview

CHAPTER TWELVE

Building and Managing Human Resources 386

David Lees/Digital Vision/Getty Images

Management Snapshot
Unilever CHRO Makes Talent Development Count 387

Overview

Part Six Controlling Essential Activities and Processes

Tom Merton/age fotostock

CHAPTER THIRTEEN

Effective Communication 422

Management Snapshot

Tom Merton/age fotostock

CHAPTER FOURTEEN

Operations Management: Managing Operations and Processes 448

Management Snapshot

Essentials of
Contemporary
Management

Ninth Edition

PART 1

Sam Edwards/age fotostock RF

1 The Management Process Today

Learning Objectives

After studying this chapter, you should be able to:

LO 1-1 Describe what management is, why management is important, what managers do, and how managers use organizational resources efficiently and effectively to achieve organizational goals.

LO 1-2 Distinguish among planning, organizing, leading, and controlling (the four principal managerial tasks), and explain how managers' ability to handle each one affects organizational performance.

LO 1-3 Differentiate among three levels of management, and understand the tasks and responsibilities of managers at different levels in the organizational hierarchy.

LO 1-4 Distinguish among three kinds of managerial skill, and explain why managers are divided into different departments to perform their tasks more efficiently and effectively.

LO 1-5 Contrast the differences between managers, entrepreneurs, and intrapreneurs.

LO 1-6 Discuss the principal challenges managers face in today's increasingly competitive global environment.

Management Snapshot

Microsoft Soars with Nadella at the Helm

What Difference Can a Manager Make?

After the success of its Windows operating system and Office software suite, Microsoft struggled to find a source of new growth. While earnings continued to rise, an unmoving stock price suggested that investors no longer saw a rosy future for the company.[1] This changed when Microsoft made Satya Nadella its third chief executive officer (CEO).

Nadella brought a fresh vision. Microsoft had defined its mission as a personal computer on every desk and in every home, running Microsoft's software. By the end of the millennium in most of the world, that mission had been accomplished. It no longer illuminated a way forward. Nadella introduced a new mission: to "create technology so that others can create more technology," enabling people and organizations to accomplish more.[2] This is a view of technology being beneficial—for example, opening ways for people with disabilities to participate in the world more fully.

Nadella brought Microsoft a new kind of leadership, based on empathy. Empathy includes listening carefully to customer needs—information essential for providing relevant products and services.[3] Nadella asks employees to use empathy with one another, too. Leading by example, he conducts town-hall meetings online, inviting employees to give live feedback by submitting anonymous emojis, which he reviews to gauge employee concerns.[4] He is also known for listening attentively to employees' ideas.

Nadella instructs employees to avoid a fixed mind-set, using existing skills to reach some endpoint and then staying put. He teaches a growth mind-set, based on learning and constantly improving. Nadella exemplifies this with his open-mindedness toward his own performance. He has said that reflecting on his mistakes inspires him, as it motivates him to change.[5] He shares this spirit in each of the leadership team's weekly meetings by scheduling a presentation by employees who are working on something exciting. When employees try for growth but fall short, Nadella encourages them to push on and fix the problem.

Nadella values diversity. High-tech companies have been criticized as unfriendly to some employees, particularly women. In contrast, Nadella's drive for a culture of empathy fosters an environment that recognizes all employees' contributions. His goal is that Microsoft will not merely hire a diverse workforce but enable employees to participate and thrive. Nadella is particularly committed to providing opportunities for persons with disabilities.

What prepared Nadella for all this? He knows the business well, having worked for Microsoft since age 25. Raised in India, he earned a master's degree in computer science from the University of Wisconsin–Madison and joined Microsoft after a few years with Sun Microsystems. He accepted tough assignments and guidance from mentors, including a Netflix executive who

Microsoft CEO Satya Nadella has brought a new perspective and vision to the tech giant. His leadership and focus on empathy and diversity are a winning combination.
Matt Winkelmeyer/Getty Images

took him to board meetings so Nadella could see that company's agile decision making. He reads widely and is skillful at making connections among ideas. Being the father of three children, two with disabilities, has taught him the value of empathy and a desire to empower people to make change.[6]

Under Nadella's leadership, Microsoft is exceeding expectations. It is getting involved in today's cutting-edge technology. Employee morale and product quality have risen, and the market value of its stock continues to climb.[7]

Overview

Managing a company is a complex activity, and effective managers like Satya Nadella face many challenges from within and outside their organizations. Management is an unpredictable process. Making the right decision is often difficult, and even successful managers often make mistakes. But the most effective managers learn from their mistakes and continually try to find ways to improve their companies' performance.

In this chapter we look at what managers do and what skills and abilities they must develop to manage their organizations successfully. We also identify the different kinds of managers that organizations need and the skills and abilities they must develop to succeed. Finally, we identify some challenges managers must address if their organizations are to grow and prosper.

organizations
Collections of people who work together and coordinate their actions to achieve a wide variety of goals or desired future outcomes.

What Is Management?

When you think of a manager, what kind of person comes to mind? Do you think of an executive like Satya Nadella, who helps direct his company? Or do you see a manager at a fast-food restaurant, who deals directly with employees and customers, or the person you answer to if you have a part-time job? What do all these people have in common? First, they all work in organizations. Organizations are collections of people who work together and coordinate their actions to achieve a wide variety of goals or desired future outcomes. Second, as managers, they are the people responsible for supervising and making the most of an organization's human and other resources to achieve its goals.

Management, then, is the planning, organizing, leading, and controlling of human and other resources to achieve organizational goals efficiently and effectively. An organization's *resources* include assets such as people and their skills, know-how, and experience; machinery; raw materials; computers and information technology; and patents, financial capital, and loyal customers and employees.

LO 1-1
Describe what management is, why management is important, what managers do, and how managers use organizational resources efficiently and effectively to achieve organizational goals.

management The planning, organizing, leading, and controlling of human and other resources to achieve organizational goals efficiently and effectively.

Achieving High Performance: A Manager's Goal

One of the most important goals that organizations and their members try to achieve is to provide some kind of good or service that customers value or desire. Satya Nadella's principal goal is to manage Microsoft so that the company continues to innovate with new products and services for the global marketplace. Likewise, the principal goal of fast-food managers is to produce tasty and convenient food that customers enjoy and come back to buy again and again.

organizational performance
A measure of how efficiently and effectively a manager uses resources to satisfy customers and achieve organizational goals.

efficiency A measure of how well or how productively resources are used to achieve a goal.

effectiveness
A measure of the appropriateness of the goals an organization is pursuing and the degree to which the organization achieves those goals.

Organizational performance is a measure of how efficiently and effectively managers use available resources to satisfy customers and achieve organizational goals. Organizational performance increases in direct proportion to increases in efficiency and effectiveness (see Figure 1.1). What are efficiency and effectiveness?

Efficiency is a measure of how productively resources are used to achieve a goal. Organizations are efficient when managers minimize the amount of input resources (such as labor, raw materials, and component parts) or the amount of time needed to produce a given output of goods or services. For example, Burger King develops ever more efficient fat fryers that not only reduce the amount of oil used in cooking, but also speed up the cooking of french fries. UPS develops new work routines to reduce delivery time, such as instructing drivers to leave their truck doors open when going short distances.

To encourage efficiency, Satya Nadella has led Microsoft in a comprehensive retooling of the company's products and services since he became CEO in 2014. He has eliminated unsuccessful product lines while expanding others and continues to foster a collaborative environment in which he encourages employees to be fearless in their efforts to transform the company into a digital powerhouse.[8]

Effectiveness is a measure of the *appropriateness* of the goals that managers have selected for the organization to pursue and the degree to which the organization achieves those goals. Organizations are effective when managers choose appropriate

Figure 1.1
Efficiency, Effectiveness, and Performance in an Organization

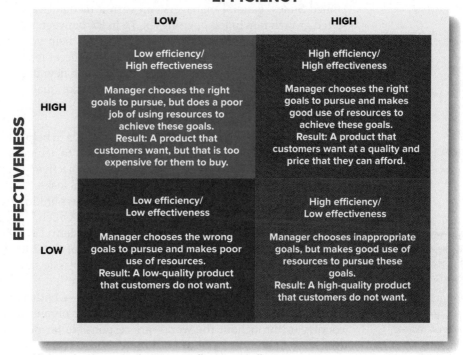

High-performing organizations are efficient *and* effective.

goals and then achieve them. Some years ago, for example, managers at McDonald's decided on the goal of providing breakfast service to attract more customers. The choice of this goal proved smart. Shortly thereafter, McDonald's management made the decision to offer the breakfast menu all day long, a strategy that has been successful and well received by consumers. Recently, the fast-food giant announced it would be adding more items to its breakfast menu, in an effort to attract more customers.[9]

High-performing organizations, such as Apple, Marriott, Walmart, Home Depot, Accenture, and Habitat for Humanity are simultaneously efficient and effective. Effective managers are those who choose the right organizational goals to pursue and have the skills to utilize resources efficiently.

Why Study Management?

The dynamic and complex nature of modern work means that managerial skills are in demand. Organizations need individuals like you who can understand this complexity, respond to environmental contingencies, and make decisions that are ethical and effective. Studying management helps equip individuals to accomplish each of these tasks.

In a broader sense, individuals generally learn through personal experience (think the "school of hard knocks") or through the experiences of others. By studying management in school, you are exposing yourself to the lessons others have learned. The advantage of such social learning is that you are not bound to repeat the mistakes others have made in the past. Furthermore, by studying and practicing the behaviors of good managers and high-performing companies, you will equip yourself to help your future employer succeed.

The economic benefits of becoming a good manager are also impressive. In the United States, general managers can earn a median wage of $100,410 with a projected growth rate in job openings of 5% to 9% between now and 2026.[10]

Finally, learning management principles can help you make good decisions in nonwork situations. If you're coaching a child's soccer team, organizing a charity 5K run, planning your financial budget, or starting a new business, good management principles will help you understand others, make quality decisions, and improve your overall personal success.

Essential Managerial Tasks

The job of management is to help an organization make the best use of its resources to achieve its goals. How do managers accomplish this objective? They do so by performing four essential managerial tasks: *planning, organizing, leading, and controlling.* The arrows linking these tasks in Figure 1.2 suggest the sequence in which managers typically perform them. French manager Henri Fayol first outlined the nature of these managerial activities around the turn of the 20th century in *General and Industrial Management,* a book that remains the classic statement of what managers must do to create a high-performing organization.[11]

LO 1-2
Distinguish among planning, organizing, leading, and controlling (the four principal managerial tasks), and explain how managers' ability to handle each one affects organizational performance.

Managers at all levels and in all departments—whether in small or large companies, for-profit or not-for-profit organizations, or organizations that operate in one country or throughout the world—are responsible for performing these four tasks, which we look at next. How well managers perform these tasks determines how efficient and effective their organizations are.

Figure 1.2
Four Tasks of
Management

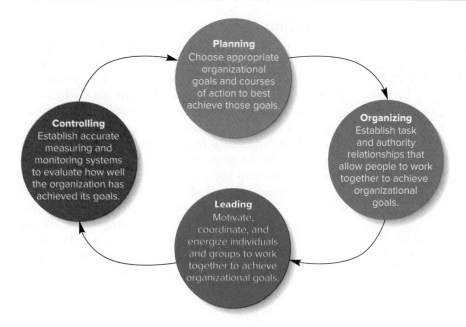

Planning
Choose appropriate organizational goals and courses of action to best achieve those goals.

Organizing
Establish task and authority relationships that allow people to work together to achieve organizational goals.

Controlling
Establish accurate measuring and monitoring systems to evaluate how well the organization has achieved its goals.

Leading
Motivate, coordinate, and energize individuals and groups to work together to achieve organizational goals.

Planning

planning Identifying and selecting appropriate goals; one of the four principal tasks of management.

To perform the planning task, managers identify and select appropriate organizational goals and courses of action; they develop *strategies* for how to achieve high performance. The three steps involved in planning are (1) deciding which goals the organization will pursue, (2) deciding what strategies to adopt to attain those goals, and (3) deciding how to allocate organizational resources to pursue the strategies that attain those goals. How well managers plan and develop strategies determines how effective and efficient the organization is—its performance level.[12]

As an example of planning in action, consider Microsoft's recent innovation in artificial intelligence (AI) with its app, Seeing AI, which uses computer vision to audibly help people who are blind and visually impaired "see" the world around them through narration on an iOS device. Users can customize the voice it uses to verbalize observations and set how fast the voice talks. In addition, the app boasts currency recognition (e.g., U.S. dollars, British pounds, Euros), can detect the color of specific objects like clothing, recognizes handwriting, and includes a musical detector to alert users with an audible tone to light in a specific environment. Microsoft says this last feature will save users from touching a hot bulb or LED battery to check if it's working. To date, the app has been downloaded more than 100,000 times and is now available in 35 countries.[13] This AI innovation helps Microsoft shape its planning into an effective business strategy, which is a cluster of decisions about what organizational goals to pursue, what actions to take, and how to use resources to achieve these goals.

strategy A cluster of decisions about what goals to pursue, what actions to take, and how to use resources to achieve those goals.

Planning strategy is complex and difficult, especially because planning is done under uncertainty when the result is unknown so that either success or failure is a possible outcome of the planning process. Managers take major risks when they commit organizational resources to pursue a particular strategy.

Organizing

Organizing is structuring working relationships so organizational members interact and cooperate to achieve organizational goals. Organizing people into departments according to the kinds of job-specific tasks they perform lays out the lines of authority and responsibility between different individuals and groups. Managers must decide how best to organize resources, particularly human resources.

The outcome of organizing is the creation of an **organizational structure**, a formal system of task and reporting relationships that coordinates and motivates members so they work together to achieve organizational goals. Organizational structure determines how an organization's resources can be best used to create goods and services. For example, as Microsoft shifts its focus from PCs and software to cloud services and other innovations, management continues to face the issue of how best to structure or reorganize different groups within the organization. The company recently implemented a major reorganization of its sales group, including a massive retraining effort, which has helped the company's stock hit an all-time high.[14] We examine the organizing process in detail in Chapter 9.

Leading

An organization's *vision* is a short, succinct, and inspiring statement of what the organization intends to become and the goals it is seeking to achieve—its desired future state. In **leading**, managers articulate a clear organizational vision for the organization's members to accomplish, and they energize and enable employees so everyone understands the part he or she plays in achieving organizational goals. Leadership involves managers using their power, personality, influence, persuasion, and communication skills to coordinate people and groups so their activities and efforts are in harmony. Leadership revolves around encouraging all employees to perform at a high level to help the organization achieve its vision and goals. Another outcome of leadership is a highly motivated and committed workforce. Microsoft's more than 120,000 employees appreciate the core values of their leadership, especially CEO Nadella's refreshing focus on collaboration and innovation, which contributes to their success as a workforce. Likewise, Nadella's lengthy association with the tech giant gives him a competitive edge in knowing what works, what doesn't, and how better to relate to his employees. We discuss the issues involved in managing and leading individuals and groups in Chapters 9 through 12.

Controlling

In **controlling**, the task of managers is to evaluate how well an organization has achieved its goals and to take any corrective actions needed to maintain or improve performance. For example, managers monitor the performance of individuals, departments, and the organization as a whole to see whether they are meeting desired performance standards. Microsoft's CEO learned early in his career about the importance of monitoring performance to ensure that his organization realized its profit objectives. When these goals fall short, Nadella and Microsoft's management team must find ways to improve performance.

The outcome of the control process is the ability to measure performance accurately and regulate organizational efficiency and effectiveness. To exercise

organizing Structuring working relationships in a way that allows organizational members to work together to achieve organizational goals; one of the four principal tasks of management.

organizational structure A formal system of task and reporting relationships that coordinates and motivates organizational members so they work together to achieve organizational goals.

leading Articulating a clear vision and energizing and enabling organizational members so they understand the part they play in achieving organizational goals; one of the four principal tasks of management.

controlling Evaluating how well an organization is achieving its goals and taking action to maintain or improve performance; one of the four principal tasks of management.

control, managers must decide which goals to measure—perhaps goals pertaining to productivity, quality, or responsiveness to customers—and then they must design control systems that will provide the information necessary to assess performance—that is, determine to what degree the goals have been met. The controlling task also helps managers evaluate how well they themselves are performing the other three tasks of management—planning, organizing, and leading—and take corrective action. For an example of a manager who excels at controlling, see the "Manager as a Person" feature.

The four managerial tasks—planning, organizing, leading, and controlling—are essential parts of a manager's job. At all levels in the managerial hierarchy, and across all jobs and departments in an organization, effective management means performing these four activities successfully—in ways that increase efficiency and effectiveness.

Manager as a Person

Making ER Visits as Painless as Possible

If you've ever had the misfortune of visiting a hospital's emergency room, you know the hardest part can be waiting for a doctor to see you. And on the hospital's side, ERs have their own challenges serving patients who are often in desperate situations. The best case, then, is to have a manager like Erin Daley, the ER director for Mercy Medical Center in Massachusetts.

Daley says that since her days as a nursing student, she has loved "everything" about working in an emergency room.[15] She sees an exciting challenge in the way each patient's arrival can require the staff to restructure all their activities to meet the most pressing need. Thriving in that environment, Daley spent a decade in Mercy's ER, moving up from staff nurse to charge nurse to clinical nurse supervisor. The supervisory position gave her experience in hiring and scheduling. From there, she moved up to the nurse manager position, adding duties related to the productivity of the nursing staff.[16]

In her role as ER director, Daley focuses on improving the department's performance in meeting objectives for efficiency and quality of care. While keeping costs within her $65 million budget, she has found ways her staff can move patients through the system faster while improving survey scores for patient satisfaction. Under her watch, Mercy's ER has also cut the rate of patients who leave before they have been seen by a doctor. In a further measure of quality performance, Mercy has won awards for superior care of patients who experience strokes.[17]

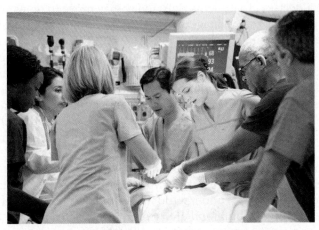

Working closely with employees can help managers control daily operations and increase efficiencies, even in a busy ER department. monkeybusinessimages/Getty Images

Daley's approach involves working with her team to study exactly what steps occur to take a patient through the process of getting care. Team members look for any wasted steps they can cut to improve efficiency. They set up a process that sorts patients who have less severe conditions in which they don't need a bed from those with more serious conditions. Those in the first group are seen in one room and then discharged, while the others follow a separate process. Before this process was implemented, beds were too often filled with patients who didn't really need them. The team also set up systems for treating ER patients as a "whole person," not just a broken leg or a drug overdose. This means educating patients about their conditions, planning what will happen after their release, and following up to help manage their recovery.[18] ●

Performing Managerial Tasks: Mintzberg's Typology

So far, our discussion of management has presented it as an orderly process in which individuals carefully weigh information before making the best possible decision. Henry Mintzberg was one of the first to show that management is often chaotic, marked by quick decisions in a tense and sometimes emotional environment. Quick, immediate reactions to situations, rather than deliberate thought and reflection, are an important aspect of managerial action. Mintzberg, a professor at McGill University, has spent most of his life researching management in an attempt to help organizations better achieve their goals in an ethical manner.

Some of his most important research examined the different roles that managers play in organizations, and directly informs our discussion in this chapter. Often managers are overloaded with responsibilities and do not have time to analyze every nuance of a situation. They make decisions in uncertain conditions, not knowing which outcomes will be best.[19] Moreover, top managers face constantly changing situations, and a decision that seems right today may prove to be wrong tomorrow. The range of problems that managers face is enormous; managers usually must handle many problems simultaneously; and they often must make snap decisions using the intuition and experience gained through their careers to perform their jobs to the best of their abilities.[20] Henry Mintzberg, by following managers and observing what they actually *do* hour by hour and day by day, identified 10 kinds of specific roles, or sets of job responsibilities, that capture the dynamic nature of managerial work.[21] He grouped these roles according to whether the responsibility is primarily decisional, interpersonal, or informational; they are described in Table 1.1.

Given the many complex, difficult job responsibilities managers have, it is no small wonder that many claim they are performing their jobs well if they are right just half of the time.[22] And it is understandable that many experienced managers accept their employees' failure and shortcomings as a normal part of the learning experience and a rite of passage to becoming an effective manager. Managers and their direct reports learn from both their successes and their failures.

Table 1.1

Managerial Roles Identified by Mintzberg

Type of Role	Specific Role	Role Activity Examples
Decisional	Entrepreneur	Commit organizational resources to develop innovative goods and services; decide to expand internationally to obtain new customers.
	Disturbance handler	Move quickly to take action to deal with unexpected problems facing the organization from the external environment, such as dealing with a crisis like an oil spill, or from the internal environment, such as producing faulty goods or services.
	Resource allocator	Allocate organizational resources among different tasks and departments of the organization; set budgets and salaries of middle and first-level managers.
	Negotiator	Work with suppliers, distributors, and labor unions to reach agreements about the quality and price of input, technical, and human resources; work with other organizations to establish agreements to pool resources to work on joint projects.
Interpersonal	Figurehead	Outline future organizational goals to employees at company meetings; state the organization's ethical guidelines and principles of behavior employees are to follow in their dealings with customers and suppliers.
	Leader	Provide an example for employees to follow; give them direct commands and orders; make decisions about the use of human and technical resources; mobilize employee support for specific organizational goals.
	Liaison	Coordinate the work of managers in different departments; establish alliances between different organizations to share resources to produce new goods and services.
Informational	Monitor	Evaluate the performance of managers in different tasks and take corrective action to improve their performance; watch for changes occurring in the external and internal environments that may affect the organization in the future.
	Disseminator	Inform employees about changes taking place in the external and internal environments that will affect them and the organization; communicate to employees the organization's vision and purpose.
	Spokesperson	Launch a national media campaign to promote new goods and services; give a speech to inform the local community about the organization's future intentions.

Levels of Managers

To perform the four managerial tasks efficiently and effectively, organizations group or differentiate their managers in two main ways—by level in hierarchy and by type of skill. First, they differentiate managers according to their level or rank in the organization's hierarchy of authority. The three levels of managers are first-line managers, middle managers, and top managers—arranged in a hierarchy. Typically first-line managers report to middle managers, and middle managers report to top managers.

Second, organizations group managers into different departments (or functions) according to their specific job-related skills, expertise, and experiences, such as a manager's engineering skills, marketing expertise, or sales experience. A department, such as the manufacturing, accounting, engineering, or sales department, is a group of managers and employees who work together because they possess similar skills and experience or use the same kind of knowledge, tools, or techniques to perform their jobs. Within each department are all three levels of management. Next we examine why organizations use a hierarchy of managers and group them, by the jobs they perform, into departments.

department A group of people who work together and possess similar skills or use the same knowledge, tools, or techniques to perform their jobs.

Levels of Management

Organizations normally have three levels of management: first-line managers, middle managers, and top managers (see Figure 1.3). Managers at each level have different but related responsibilities for using organizational resources to increase efficiency and effectiveness.

LO 1-3
Differentiate among three levels of management, and understand the tasks and responsibilities of managers at different levels in the organizational hierarchy.

At the base of the managerial hierarchy are first-line managers, often called *supervisors.* They are responsible for daily supervision of the nonmanagerial employees who perform the specific activities necessary to produce goods and services. First-line managers work in all departments or functions of an organization.

Examples of first-line managers include the supervisor of a work team in the manufacturing department of an auto plant, the head nurse in the obstetrics department of a hospital, and the chief mechanic overseeing a crew of mechanics in the service function of a new car dealership.

Supervising the first-line managers are middle managers, responsible for finding the best way to organize human and other resources to achieve organizational goals. To increase efficiency, middle managers find ways to help first-line managers and nonmanagerial employees better use resources to reduce manufacturing

first-line manager A manager who is responsible for the daily supervision of nonmanagerial employees.

Figure 1.3
Levels of Managers

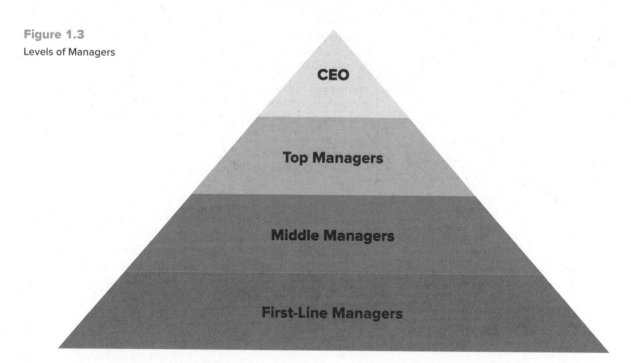

CEO

Top Managers

Middle Managers

First-Line Managers

middle manager A manager who supervises first-line managers and is responsible for finding the best way to use resources to achieve organizational goals.

costs or improve customer service. To increase effectiveness, middle managers evaluate whether the organization's goals are appropriate and suggest to top managers how goals should be changed. Often the suggestions that middle managers make to top managers can dramatically increase organizational performance. A major part of the middle manager's job is developing and fine-tuning skills and know-how, such as manufacturing or marketing expertise, that allow the organization to be efficient and effective. Middle managers make thousands of specific decisions about the production of goods and services: Which first-line supervisors should be chosen for this particular project? Where can we find the highest-quality resources? How should employees be organized to allow them to make the best use of resources?

Behind a top-notch sales force, look for the middle managers responsible for training, motivating, and rewarding the salespeople. Behind a committed staff of high school teachers, look for the principal who energizes them to find ways to obtain the resources they need to do outstanding and innovative jobs in the classroom.

top manager A manager who establishes organizational goals, decides how departments should interact, and monitors the performance of middle managers.

In contrast to middle managers, top managers are responsible for the performance of *all* departments. They have *cross-departmental responsibility.* Top managers establish organizational goals, such as which goods and services the company should produce; they decide how the different departments should interact; and they monitor how well middle managers in each department use resources to achieve goals.[23] Top managers are ultimately responsible for the success or failure of an organization, and their performance is continually scrutinized by people inside and outside the organization, such as other employees and investors.[24]

top management team A group composed of the CEO, the COO, and the vice presidents of the most important departments of a company.

The *chief executive officer (CEO)* is a company's most senior and important manager, the one all other top managers report to. Today the term *chief operating officer (COO)* refers to the company's top manager, such as Tim Cook, who was groomed by Steve Jobs to take over as Apple's CEO. Together the CEO and COO are responsible for developing good working relationships among the top managers of various departments (manufacturing and marketing, for example); usually these top managers have the title "vice president." A central concern of the CEO is the creation of a smoothly functioning top management team, a group composed of the CEO, the COO, and the vice presidents most responsible for achieving organizational goals.[25]

The relative importance of planning, organizing, leading, and controlling—the four principal managerial tasks—to any particular manager depends on the manager's position in the managerial hierarchy.[26] The amount of time managers spend planning and organizing resources to maintain and improve organizational performance increases as they ascend the hierarchy (see Figure 1.4).[27] Top managers devote most of their time to planning and organizing, the tasks so crucial to determining an organization's long-term performance. The lower managers' positions in the hierarchy, the more time they spend leading and controlling first-line managers or nonmanagerial employees.

Mary Barra, pictured here, is the chairman and CEO of General Motors. The first female CEO of a global automaker, Barra climbed the managerial ranks at GM thanks to her unrelenting drive and her ability to cultivate strong relationships with colleagues at every level of the organization. Bill Pugliano/Getty Images

Figure 1.4

Relative Amount of Time That Managers Spend on the Four Managerial Tasks

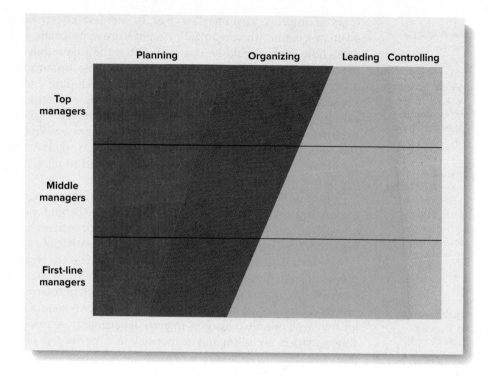

Types of Managerial Skills

Both education and experience enable managers to recognize and develop the personal skills they need to put organizational resources to their best use. Research has shown that education and experience help managers acquire and develop three types of skills: *conceptual, human,* and *technical.*[28]

Conceptual skills are demonstrated in the general ability to analyze and diagnose a situation and to distinguish between cause and effect. Top managers require the best conceptual skills because their primary responsibilities are planning and organizing.[29] Managers like Satya Nadella must constantly identify new opportunities and mobilize managers and other resources to take advantage of those opportunities.

Formal education and training are important in helping managers develop conceptual skills. Business training at the undergraduate and graduate (MBA) levels provides many of the conceptual tools (theories and techniques in marketing, finance, and other areas) that managers need to perform their roles effectively. The study of management helps develop the skills that allow managers to understand the big picture confronting an organization. The ability to focus on the big picture lets managers see beyond the situation immediately at hand and consider choices while keeping in mind the organization's long-term goals.

Today continuing management education and training, including training in advanced technology, are an integral step in building managerial skills because theories and techniques are constantly being developed to improve organizational effectiveness, such as total quality management, benchmarking, and cloud computing and virtual business-to-business (B2B) networks. A quick scan through a magazine such as *Bloomberg Businessweek* or *Forbes* reveals a host of seminars on topics such as advanced marketing, finance, leadership, and human resource management that are offered to managers at many levels in the organization, from the most senior corporate executives to middle managers. Microsoft, IBM, and many other organizations designate a portion of each manager's personal budget to be used at the manager's discretion to attend management development programs.

In addition, organizations may wish to develop a particular manager's abilities in a specific skill area—perhaps to learn an advanced component of departmental skills, such as international bond trading, or to learn the skills necessary to implement total quality management. The organization thus pays for managers to attend specialized programs to develop these skills. Indeed, one signal that a manager is performing well is an organization's willingness to invest in that manager's skill development. Similarly, many nonmanagerial employees who are performing at a high level (because they have studied management) are often sent to intensive management training programs to develop their management skills and to prepare them for promotion to first-level management positions.

human skills The ability to understand, alter, lead, and control the behavior of other individuals and groups.

Human skills include the general ability to understand, alter, lead, and control the behavior of other individuals and groups. The ability to communicate, to coordinate, and to motivate people, and to mold individuals into a cohesive team distinguishes effective from ineffective managers. Skills such as these are especially significant for successful management in the public (government) sector, as described in the "Management Insight" feature.

Management Insight

Success as a City Manager

Businesses are not the only organizations that need people with management skills. Governments are an important sector of the economy that also employs managers. Many cities, for example, have a government structure in which an elected city council hires a manager to oversee the work of the city government.

A city manager faces the challenge of serving a diverse group of citizens while also maintaining productive relationships with the elected officials who hired him or her. Jim Schutz recalls that when he became city manager of San Rafael, California, he faced a steep learning curve.[30] On any given day, the issues he faced included personnel matters, budget shortfalls, emergencies involving the police and fire departments, and publicly aired complaints from unhappy residents. He has faced those concerns with a service-oriented approach to providing government services and a growing appreciation of the community's many strengths. Keeping his approach positive has helped him succeed in the job.

As Schutz discovered, a key part of the city manager's necessary skills involves the ability to work with other people. The council members who hire and fire a city manager are necessarily concerned with the political impact of actions taken by the city government.[31] Therefore, the manager needs to plan for residents' and politicians' reactions to any new policy or new spending. The manager also has to build support from and cooperation with other members of the local government, such as judges and administrators of the public schools. And the city manager is usually the one to carry out personnel decisions, such as hiring and firing.

To bring these skills to the job, a city manager needs experience in working for a local government. Many managers seek education beyond a bachelor's degree, such as a master's in public administration.[32] A group of public managers in Massachusetts determined that city managers could bring more skills to the job if they had a training program. They pooled their experience to create a boot camp for new managers and administrators, which focuses on human skills such as working effectively with government colleagues, taking a leadership role in the community, and developing a network for career support.[33] City managers have found that sharing experiences at the boot camp is a valuable way to build skills for their complex jobs. ●

Like conceptual skills, human skills can be learned through education and training, as well as be developed through experience.[34] Organizations increasingly utilize advanced programs in leadership skills and team leadership as they seek to capitalize on the advantages of self-managed teams.[35] To manage personal interactions effectively, each person in an organization needs to learn how to empathize with other people—to understand their viewpoints and the problems they face. One way to help managers understand their personal strengths and weaknesses is to have their superiors, peers, and employees provide feedback about their job performance. Thorough and direct feedback allows managers to develop their human skills.

technical skills
The job-specific knowledge and techniques required to perform an organizational role.

Technical skills are the *job-specific* skills required to perform a particular type of work or occupation at a high level. Examples include a manager's specific manufacturing, accounting, marketing, and increasingly, technological skills. Managers need a range of technical skills to be effective. The array of technical skills managers need depends on their position in their organization. The manager of a restaurant, for example, may need cooking skills to fill in for an absent cook, accounting and bookkeeping skills to keep track of receipts and costs and to administer the payroll, and aesthetic skills to keep the restaurant looking attractive for customers.

As noted earlier, managers and employees who possess the same kinds of technical skills typically become members of a specific department and are known as, for example, marketing managers or manufacturing managers.[36] Managers are grouped into different departments because a major part of a manager's responsibility is to monitor, train, and supervise employees so their job-specific skills and expertise increase. Obviously this is easier to do when employees with similar skills are grouped into the same department because they can learn from one another and become more skilled and productive at their particular job.

Figure 1.5 shows how an organization groups managers into departments on the basis of their job-specific skills. It also shows that inside each department, a managerial hierarchy of first-line, middle, and top managers emerges. These managers work together on similar tasks. For example, middle and front-line managers may specialize in areas such as marketing and sales, human resource management, accounting, engineering, or production. When the head of manufacturing finds that she has no time to supervise computer assembly, she may recruit experienced manufacturing middle managers from other companies to take on this responsibility.

core competency
The specific set of departmental skills, knowledge, and experience that allows one organization to outperform another.

Today the term core competency is often used to refer to the specific set of departmental skills, knowledge, and experience that allows one organization to outperform its competitors. In other words, departmental skills that create a core competency give an organization a *competitive advantage.* Dell, for example, was the

Figure 1.5

Types and Levels of
Managers

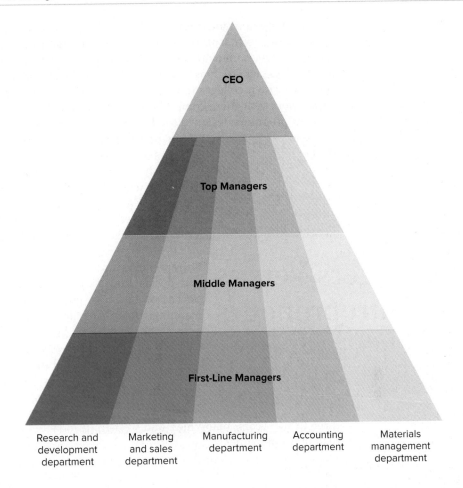

first PC maker to develop a core competency in materials management that allowed it to produce PCs at a much lower cost than its competitors—a major source of competitive advantage. Google is well known for its core competency in research and development (R&D) that allows it to innovate new products at a faster rate than its competitors. From artificial intelligence (AI) to self-driving cars, Google continues to pioneer the development of technology for the masses.

Effective managers need all three kinds of skills—conceptual, human, and technical—to help their organizations perform more efficiently and effectively. The absence of even one type of managerial skill can lead to failure. One of the biggest problems that people who start small businesses confront, for example, is their lack of appropriate conceptual and human skills. Someone who has the technical skills to start a new business does not necessarily know how to manage the venture successfully. Similarly, one of the biggest problems that scientists or engineers who switch careers from research to management confront is their lack of effective human skills. Ambitious managers or prospective managers are constantly in search of the latest educational contributions to help them develop the conceptual, human, and technical skills they need to perform at a high level in today's changing and increasingly competitive global environment.

Developing new and improved skills through education and training has become a priority for both aspiring managers and the organizations they work for. As we discussed earlier, many people are enrolling in advanced management courses; but many companies, such as Walgreens, Enterprise, and Goldman Sachs, have established their own colleges to train and develop their employees and managers at all levels. Every year these companies put thousands of their employees through management programs designed to identify the employees whom the company believes have the competencies that can be developed to strengthen its future top managers. Most organizations closely link promotion to a manager's ability to acquire the competencies that a particular company believes are important.[37] At Apple and 3M, for example, the ability to successfully lead a new product development team is viewed as a vital requirement for promotion; at Accenture and IBM, the ability to attract and retain clients is viewed as a skill their consultants must possess. We discuss the various kinds of skills managers need to develop in most of the chapters of this book.

Managers Versus Entrepreneurs

LO 1-5
Contrast the differences between managers, entrepreneurs, and intrapreneurs.

entrepreneur
An individual who notices opportunities and decides how to mobilize resources necessary to start a new business venture.

Entrepreneurs are individuals who notice opportunities and decide how to mobilize the resources necessary to start a new business venture. Entrepreneurs make all of the planning, organizing, leading, and controlling decisions necessary to start new business ventures. However, they may not be successful actually running the day-to-day operations of their new business and hire managers to oversee the business and supervise employees. Although some entrepreneurs, such as Google founders Larry Page and Sergey Brin, make vast fortunes when their businesses succeed, others may lose their life savings when their new business fails. Despite the fact that many small businesses fail in the first three to five years, many men and women in today's workforce still want to start their own companies.[38]

Characteristics of Entrepreneurs

Entrepreneurs are likely to possess a particular set of personality characteristics, which we discuss in Chapter 2. First, they are likely to be high on the personality trait of *openness to experience,* meaning they are predisposed to be original, to be open to a wide range of stimuli, to be daring, and to take risks. Entrepreneurs also are likely to have an *internal locus of control,* believing that they are responsible for what happens to them and that their own actions determine important outcomes such as the success or failure of a new business. People with an external locus of control, in contrast, would be unlikely to leave a secure job in an organization and assume the risk associated with a new venture.

Entrepreneurs are likely to have a high level of *self-esteem* and feel competent and capable of handling most situations—including the stress and uncertainty surrounding a plunge into a risky new venture. Entrepreneurs are also likely to have a high *need for achievement* and have a strong desire to perform challenging tasks and meet high personal standards of excellence.

Entrepreneurship and Management

Given that entrepreneurs may be predisposed to activities that are somewhat adventurous and risky, in what ways can people become involved in entrepreneurial ventures? One way is to start a business from scratch. However, when people who go it alone succeed, they frequently need to hire other people to help them run the business. Michael Dell, for example, began his computer business as a college student and within weeks hired several people to help him assemble computers from the components he bought from suppliers. From his solo venture grew Dell Computer.

Some entrepreneurs who start a new business have difficulty deciding how to manage the organization as it grows; entrepreneurship is *not* the same as management. Management encompasses all the decisions involved in planning, organizing, leading, and controlling resources. Entrepreneurship is noticing an opportunity to satisfy a customer need and then deciding how to find and use resources to make a product or service that satisfies that need. When an entrepreneur has produced something customers want, entrepreneurship gives way to management because the pressing need becomes providing the product both efficiently and effectively. Frequently, a founding entrepreneur lacks the skills, patience, and experience to engage in the difficult and challenging work of management. Some entrepreneurs find it hard to delegate authority because they are afraid to risk their company by letting others manage it. As a result, they become overloaded and the quality of their decisions declines. Thus, to succeed, it is necessary to do more than create a new product or service; an entrepreneur must hire managers who can create an operating system that will help a new venture survive and prosper.

Many employees, including managers, scientists, and researchers, who are employed by companies engage in entrepreneurial activity, and they are an important source of organizational creativity and success. They are involved in innovation, developing new and improved products and ways to make them. Such employees identify opportunities for product creation or product improvements and may be responsible for managing the product development process. These individuals are known as intrapreneurs to distinguish them from entrepreneurs, who start their own businesses.

There is an interesting relationship between entrepreneurs and intrapreneurs. Many employees with intrapreneurial talents become dissatisfied if their superiors decide not to support or fund new product ideas and development efforts that the employees think will succeed. What do intrapreneurs within an organization do when they feel they are getting nowhere? Often they decide to leave their current organizations and start their own companies to take advantage of their new product ideas. In other words, intrapreneurs become entrepreneurs and start companies that often compete with the companies they left. To avoid losing these talented individuals, top managers must find ways to facilitate the entrepreneurial spirit of their most creative employees.

entrepreneurship
The mobilization of resources to take advantage of an opportunity to provide customers with new or improved goods and services.

intrapreneur
An employee who works inside an organization who notices opportunities to develop new or improved products and services and mobilizes the organization's resources to try to create them.

Post-it Notes were invented by accident at 3M by an intrapreneur who was trying to develop a super-strong adhesive for use in the aerospace industry. Instead, the brightly colored sticky note became one of the top-selling office products of all time.
Wavebreak Media Ltd/123RF

Challenges for Management in a Global Environment

Because the world continues to change more rapidly than ever before, managers and other employees throughout an organization must perform at higher and higher levels. In the last 20 years, rivalry between organizations competing domestically (in the same country) and globally (in countries abroad) has increased dramatically. The rise of global organizations, organizations that operate and compete in more than one country, has pressured many organizations to identify better ways to use their resources and improve their performance. The successes of German pharmaceutical conglomerate Bayer, Italian furniture manufacturer Natuzzi, Korean electronics companies Samsung and LG, Brazilian plane maker Embraer, and Europe's Airbus Industries are putting pressure on companies in other countries to raise their level of performance to compete successfully against these global organizations.

Even in the not-for-profit sector, global competition is spurring change. Schools, universities, police forces, and government agencies are reexamining their operations because looking at how activities are performed in other countries often reveals better ways to do them. For example, many curriculum and teaching changes in the United States have resulted from the study of methods that Japanese and European school systems use. Similarly, European and Asian hospital systems have learned much from the U.S. system—which may be the most effective, though not the most efficient, in the world.

Today managers who make no attempt to learn from and adapt to changes in the global environment find themselves reacting rather than innovating, and their organizations often become uncompetitive and fail. Four major challenges stand out for managers in today's world: building a competitive advantage, maintaining ethical standards, managing a diverse workforce, and utilizing new technologies.

LO 1-6
Discuss the principal challenges managers face in today's increasingly competitive global environment.

global organizations
Organizations that operate and compete in more than one country.

Building Competitive Advantage

What are the most important lessons for managers and organizations to learn if they are to reach and remain at the top of the competitive environment of business? The answer relates to the use of organizational resources to build a competitive advantage. Competitive advantage is the ability of one organization to outperform other organizations because it produces desired goods or services more efficiently and effectively than its competitors. The four building blocks of competitive advantage are superior *efficiency, quality, innovation,* and *responsiveness to customers* (see Figure 1.6).

Organizations increase their efficiency when they reduce the quantity of resources (such as people and raw materials) they use to produce goods or services. In today's competitive environment, organizations continually search for new ways to use their resources to improve efficiency. Many organizations are training their workforces in the new skills and techniques needed to operate heavily computerized assembly plants. Similarly, cross-training gives employees the range of skills they need to perform many different tasks; and organizing employees in new ways, such as in self-managed teams, lets them make good use of their skills. These are important steps in the effort to improve productivity. Japanese and German companies invest far more in training employees than do American or Italian companies.

competitive advantage
The ability of one organization to outperform other organizations because it produces desired goods or services more efficiently and effectively than they do.

Figure 1.6

Building Blocks of Competitive Advantage

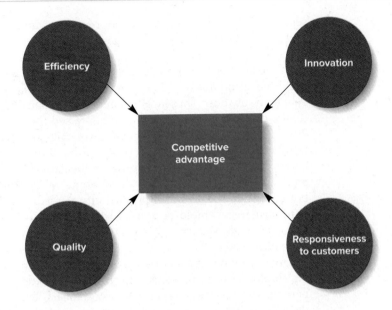

Managers must improve efficiency if their organizations are to compete successfully with companies operating in Mexico, Malaysia, and other countries where employees are paid comparatively low wages. New methods must be devised either to increase efficiency or to gain some other competitive advantage—higher-quality goods, for example—if outsourcing and the loss of jobs to low-cost countries are to be prevented.

The challenge from global organizations such as Korean electronics manufacturers, Mexican agricultural producers, and European design and financial companies also has increased pressure on companies to develop the skills and abilities of their workforces in order to improve the quality of their goods and services. One major thrust to improving quality has been to introduce the quality-enhancing techniques known as *total quality management (TQM)*. Employees involved in TQM are often organized into quality control teams and are responsible for finding new and better ways to perform their jobs; they also must monitor and evaluate the quality of the goods they produce. We discuss ways of managing TQM successfully in Chapter 14.

Today companies can win or lose the competitive race depending on their *speed*—how fast they can bring new products to market—or their *flexibility*—how easily they can change or alter the way they perform their activities to respond to actions of their competitors. Companies that have speed and flexibility are agile competitors: Their managers have superior planning and organizing abilities; they can think ahead, decide what to do, and then speedily mobilize their resources to respond to a changing environment. We examine how managers can build speed and flexibility in their organizations in later chapters. Agile companies are adept at responding to changes in their environments. For example, companies like Microsoft are seeking ways to produce their products more economically amid tightening margins and increased competition. One way Microsoft is responding to this pressure is by expanding its portfolio of products and services and its business partnerships, which will help support the company's other endeavors.[39]

Innovation, the process of creating new or improved goods and services that customers want or developing better ways to produce or provide goods and

innovation The process of creating new or improved goods and services or developing better ways to produce or provide them.

services, poses a special challenge. Managers must create an organizational set-ting in which people are encouraged to be innovative. Typically innovation takes place in small groups or teams; management decentralizes control of work activi-ties to team members and creates an organizational culture that rewards risk tak-ing. Innovation doesn't happen by itself; companies have to devote resources that enable innovation. These investments are a balancing act. Consider Google. More than a decade ago, the company was praised for its 80/20 work allocation, where 20% of an employee's time was spent working on individual "pet projects." Innova-tions such as Gmail came from this program. But the company recently announced it was suspending the 80/20 program because of productivity concerns. Google had banked on the idea that "down" time would enable individuals to innovate, but economic realities and productivity needs meant a change in how the com-pany structured employee work. Instead of a more autonomous approach to inno-vation, Google is now relying on its X lab as a formal means of maintaining a competitive edge.[40]

Organizations compete for customers with their products and services, so train-ing employees to be responsive to customers' needs is vital for all organizations, but particularly for service organizations. Retailers, banks, and hospitals, for example, depend entirely on their employees to perform behaviors that result in high-quality service at a reasonable cost. As many countries (the United States, Canada, and Switzerland are just a few) move toward a more service-based economy (in part because of the loss of manufacturing jobs to Vietnam, Malaysia, and other coun-tries with low labor costs), managing behavior in service organizations is becoming increasingly important. Many organizations are empowering their customer service employees and giving them the authority to take the lead in providing high-quality customer service. As noted previously, empowering nonmanagerial employees and creating self-managed teams change the role of first-line managers and lead to more efficient use of organizational resources.

Sometimes the best efforts of managers to revitalize their organization's for-tunes fail; and faced with bankruptcy, the directors of these companies are forced to appoint a new CEO who has a history of success in rebuilding a company. Turnaround management is the creation of a new vision for a struggling company using a new approach to planning and organizing to make better use of a com-pany's resources and allow it to survive and eventually prosper—something Apple's Steve Jobs excelled at. It involves developing radical new strategies such as how to reduce the number of products sold or change how they are made and distributed, or close corporate and manufacturing operations to reduce costs. Organizations that appoint turnaround CEOs are generally experiencing a crisis because they have become inefficient or ineffective; sometimes this is because of poor management over a continuing period, and sometimes it occurs because a competitor introduces a new product or technology that makes their own products unattractive to custom-ers. For example, fast-casual food chain Chipotle was flying high until food safety scares in recent years caused the company to lose customers, market share, and consumers' confidence in the chain's reputation for quality. Founder and CEO Steve Ells, who ran the chain since its start in 1993, stepped aside as CEO in 2018 and shifted into the chairman's role focusing on innovation. Ells was replaced by Brian Niccol, former CEO of Taco Bell.[41]

Achieving a competitive advantage requires that managers use all their skills and expertise, as well as their companies' other resources, to find new and improved ways to improve efficiency, quality, innovation, and responsiveness to customers.

turnaround management The creation of a new vision for a struggling company based on a new approach to planning and organizing to make better use of a company's resources and allow it to survive and prosper.

We revisit this theme often as we examine the ways managers plan strategies, organize resources and activities, and lead and control people and groups to increase
efficiency and effectiveness.

Maintaining Ethical and Socially Responsible Standards

Managers at all levels are under considerable pressure to make the best use of
resources to increase the level at which their organizations perform.[42] For example,
top managers feel pressure from shareholders to increase the performance of the
entire organization to boost its stock price, improve profits, or raise dividends. In turn,
top managers may pressure middle managers to find new ways to use organizational
resources to increase efficiency or quality and thus attract new customers and earn
more revenues—and then middle managers pressure their department's supervisors.

Pressure to increase performance can be healthy for an organization because
it leads managers to question how the organization is working, and it encourages
them to find new and better ways to plan, organize, lead, and control. However,
too much pressure to perform can be harmful. It may induce managers to behave
unethically, and even illegally, when dealing with people and groups inside and outside the organization.[43]

A purchasing manager for a nationwide retail chain, for example, might buy
inferior clothing as a cost-cutting measure or ignore the working conditions under
which products are made to obtain low-priced products. These issues faced the managers of companies that make footwear and clothing in the 1990s, when customers
learned about the sweatshop conditions in which garment and shoe workers around
the world labored. Today companies such as Nike, Walmart, and Apple are trying
to stop sweatshop practices and prevent managers abroad from adopting work practices that harm their workers. They now employ hundreds of inspectors who police
the factories overseas that make the products they sell and who can terminate contracts with suppliers when they behave in an unethical or illegal way.[44]

Similarly, to secure a large foreign contract, a sales manager in a large company,
such as in the defense or electronics industry, might offer bribes to foreign officials
to obtain lucrative contracts—even though this is against the law. For example, cosmetics giant Avon recently paid $135 million to settle a bribery probe into its devel-
opment of new markets. Other companies such as Siemens, Teva Pharmaceutical,
and Brazil-based Odebrecht SA have paid billions in penalties to resolve international bribery charges.[45]

The temptation to gain from practices such as these can get companies into legal
trouble. Harmful and illegal actions also can hurt a company's reputation with its
suppliers and customers, as well as with the communities in which it operates. Furthermore, people of good character do not want to manage or work for such organizations. For all of these reasons, organizations need managers who will uphold
ethical standards, as will be described in Chapter 3. One way they do so is by promoting ethics at all levels of the organization. The "Ethics in Action" box describes
ways that organizations are trying to promote ethics.

The issue of social responsibility, discussed in Chapter 3, centers on deciding what
obligations a company has toward the people and groups affected by its activities—
such as employees, customers, or the cities in which it operates. Some companies
have strong views about social responsibility; their managers believe they should
protect the interests of others. Socially responsible companies put this view into
action when they set goals for reducing wasted resources and pollution, treating
workers with dignity, and promoting community development.

Ethics in Action

Giving Employees a Nudge

Why would employees behave unethically? Do they lack knowledge about what is ethical, or do they prefer unethical options? Many companies promote ethics via training, which assumes employees require knowledge about ethical behavior. However, if you think most people already know that lying, cheating, stealing, and hurting people are unethical, you are not alone.

Scientists who study how people make decisions are applying their field to ethics. According to their studies of behavioral ethics, people generally do not set out to make unethical decisions. Rather, they might overlook the ethical dimensions, or they might downplay the ethical issues—say, by thinking an unethical action will not hurt anyone or is what everyone else does. After the bubble burst in the real estate market in 2007, evidence emerged that Wells Fargo employees had been working under intense pressure to increase sales. Falsifying loan applications seemed insignificant relative to sales targets.[46]

Seeing that context affects decision making, organizations that foster ethics are looking at ways to shape the context. An increasingly popular idea is the "nudge." A nudge involves changing the context in a way that makes a particular decision more likely without forcing that option. Some companies, including Google, have hired behavioral scientists to help them design nudges. Virgin Atlantic tried nudging with regard to fuel conservation. The airline told pilots it was studying fuel use, and with that, pilots reduced fuel consumption—cutting 20,000 tons of carbon dioxide emissions. Similarly, the British government reduced overuse of antibiotics by identifying doctors who were prescribing far more than their peers and sending them the data.[47]

To nudge, organizations can make ethical options easier, more convenient, or more socially acceptable. Ford made ethics guidelines handy by creating an app for employees to use when making decisions. In a study, taxpayers tended to comply with the law when they received a statement that most taxpayers comply (evidence of a social norm). Changing the language the organization uses about ethical issues can signal that ethical behavior is the standard. A consulting firm previously called its ethics hotline the "whistleblowing facility," a term that could suggest disloyalty as much as anything admirable. The firm renamed it the Speak Up Line, and employees became much more willing to raise concerns.[48]

Nudges show promise as a tool for ethical behavior, but employers must be careful to nudge ethically. In particular, employees should know they are being nudged, and they should have some degree of freedom to make their own choices within the job requirements.[49]

Protesters outside Wells Fargo headquarters in New York City draw attention to some of the ethical missteps by the organization. Some companies are now giving employees a nudge to redirect their behavior in a more ethical manner.
Erik McGregor/Pacific Press/LightRocket/Getty Images

Managing a Diverse Workforce

A major challenge for managers everywhere is to recognize the ethical need and legal requirement to treat employees fairly and equitably. Today the age, gender, race, ethnicity, religion, sexual preference, and socioeconomic composition of the workforce presents new challenges for managers. To create a highly trained and motivated workforce, as well as to avoid lawsuits, managers must establish human resource management (HRM) procedures and practices that are legal and fair and do not discriminate against any organizational members.[50] Today most organizations understand that to motivate effectively and take advantage of the talents of a diverse workforce, they must make promotion opportunities available to each and every employee. Managers must recognize the performance-enhancing possibilities of a diverse workforce, such as the ability to take advantage of the skills and experiences of different kinds of people from different generations.[51] Accenture provides a good example of a company that has leveraged the potential of its diverse employees.

Accenture is a global management consulting company that serves the needs of thousands of client companies located in more than 120 countries around the world. A major driving force behind Accenture's core organizational vision is to manage and promote diversity in order to improve employee performance and client satisfaction. At Accenture, managers at all levels realize consultants bring distinct experiences, talents, and values to their work, and a major management initiative is to take advantage of that diversity to encourage collaboration between consultants to improve the service Accenture provides to each of its clients. Because Accenture's clients are also diverse by country, religion, ethnicity, and so forth, it tries to match its teams of consultants to the attributes of its diverse clients.

Accenture provides hundreds of diversity management training programs to its employees each year. Several years ago, Accenture became the first large consulting firm to publish its race and gender statistics in an effort to increase transparency when it comes to diversity and inclusion among its employees. Almost 40% of its workforce are women, and a little more than half of its employees are white and a third Asian. Julie Sweet, CEO of Accenture North America, believes the company needs to make progress in hiring more African Americans, Latinos, and military veterans. Accenture also works to accommodate individuals with disabilities, as well as promoting an inclusionary environment for lesbian, gay, bisexual, and transgender (LGBT) employees.[52] The firm also provides diversity training programs to its suppliers and prospective suppliers around the world to show them how diversity can increase their efficiency and effectiveness. In all these ways, Accenture uses its expertise in managing diversity to promote individual and organizational performance—one reason it has become the most successful and fast-growing consultancy company in the world.

Global management consulting firm Accenture provides hundreds of diversity programs to its employees each year in an effort to promote individual and organizational performance.
Lisette Le Bon/Purestock/SuperStock RF

Managers who value their diverse employees not only invest in developing these employees' skills and capabilities but also succeed best in promoting performance over the long run. Today more organizations are realizing that people are their most important resource and that developing and protecting human resources is the most important challenge for managers in a competitive global environment. For the first time ever in 2018, *Forbes* released a list of America's best employers for diversity, based on a survey of more than 30,000 U.S. employees working for firms or institutions with 1,000 or more employees. The top five employers on this inaugural list were Northern Trust, a banking and financial services firm in Chicago; the Smithsonian Institution in Washington, DC; Levy Restaurants, head-quartered in Chicago; Intuit, a technology, Internet, and software services company located in Mountain View, California; and Harvard University in Cambridge, Massachusetts.[53] We discuss the many issues surrounding the management of a diverse workforce in Chapter 3.

Utilizing New Technologies

As we have discussed, another important challenge for managers is to continually utilize efficient and effective new technologies that can link and enable managers and employees to better perform their jobs—whatever their level in the organization. One example of how technology has changed the jobs of people at all organizational levels comes from UPS, where the average UPS driver makes 120 deliveries a day and figuring out the quickest way to navigate all of these stops is a challenge with economic implications for the global shipping company. UPS estimates that a driver with 25 packages could choose from 15 *trillion* different routes! To help navigate these difficult roads, UPS relies on ORION—its On-Road Integrated Optimization and Navigation system. ORION is designed to blend GPS navigation and learning to help drivers optimize driving along their routes. Of course, UPS drivers must also balance promised delivery times, traffic, and other factors into their driving decisions, meaning ORION is a critical technological competency helping the company work effectively and efficiently. According to the company, now that ORION has been fully implemented, the system helps reduce 100 million miles driven annually and saves UPS upwards of $300 million to $400 million each year.[54]

Increasingly, new kinds of technology enable not just individual employees but also self-managed teams by giving them important information and allowing virtual interactions around the globe using the Internet. Increased global coordination helps improve quality and increase the pace of innovation. Most companies now search for new technologies that can help them build a competitive advantage. The importance of technology is discussed in detail in Chapter 14.

Using ORION and other types of technology, UPS drivers plan the most efficient delivery route each day, which saves the company time, money, and fuel. David Goldman/AP Images

Summary and Review

WHAT IS MANAGEMENT? A manager is a person responsible for supervising the use of an organization's resources to meet its goals. An organization is a collection of people who work together and coordinate their actions to achieve a wide variety of goals. Management is the process of using organizational resources to achieve organizational goals effectively and efficiently through planning, organizing, leading, and controlling. An efficient organization makes the most productive use of its resources. An effective organization pursues appropriate goals and achieves these goals by using its resources to create goods or services that customers want. [LO 1-1]

MANAGERIAL TASKS The four principal managerial tasks are planning, organizing, leading, and controlling. Managers at all levels of the organization and in all departments perform these tasks. Effective management means managing these activities successfully. [LO 1-2]

LEVELS AND SKILLS OF MANAGERS Organizations typically have three levels of management. First-line managers are responsible for the day-to-day supervision of nonmanagerial employees. Middle managers are responsible for developing and utilizing organizational resources efficiently and effectively. Top managers have cross-departmental responsibility. Three main kinds of managerial skills are conceptual, human, and technical. The need to develop and build technical skills leads organizations to divide managers into departments according to their job-specific responsibilities. Top managers must establish appropriate goals for the entire organization and verify that department managers are using resources to achieve those goals. [LO 1-3, 1-4]

MANAGERS, ENTREPRENEURS, AND INTRAPRENEURS Entrepreneurs are individuals who notice opportunities and decide how to mobilize resources necessary to start a new business venture. Unlike entrepreneurs, who start new ventures, managers typically supervise the daily operations of a business and manage the workforce. Intrapreneurs work inside organizations and typically manage the product development process. Organizations need to encourage intrapreneurship because it leads to organizational innovation. [LO 1-5]

CHALLENGES FOR MANAGEMENT IN A GLOBAL ENVIRONMENT Today's competitive global environment presents many interesting challenges to managers. One of the main challenges is building a competitive advantage by increasing efficiency, flexibility, innovation, and customer responsiveness. Other challenges include behaving in an ethical and socially responsible manner; managing a diverse workforce; and utilizing new technologies. [LO 1-6]

Management *in Action*

Topics for Discussion and Action

Discussion

1. Describe the difference between efficiency and effectiveness, and identify real organizations that you think are, or are not, efficient and effective. [LO 1-1]

2. In what ways can managers at each of the three levels of management contribute to organizational efficiency and effectiveness? [LO 1-3]

3. Identify an organization that you believe is high-performing and one that you believe is low-performing. Give five reasons why you think the performance levels of the two organizations differ so much. [LO 1-2, 1-4]

4. What are the key differences between managers and entrepreneurs? [LO 1-5]

5. In what ways do you think managers' jobs have changed the most over the last 10 years? Why have these changes occurred? [LO 1-6]

Action

6. Choose an organization such as a school or a bank; visit it; then list the different organizational resources it uses. How do managers use these resources to maintain and improve the organization's performance? [LO 1-2, 1-4]

7. Visit an organization, and talk to first-line, middle, and top managers about their respective management roles in the organization and what they do to help the organization be efficient and effective. [LO 1-3, 1-4]

8. Ask a middle or top manager, perhaps someone you already know, to give examples of how he or she performs the managerial tasks of planning, organizing, leading, and controlling. How much time does he or she spend performing each task? [LO 1-3]

9. Try to find a cooperative manager who will allow you to follow him or her around for a day. List the roles the manager plays, and indicate how much time he or she spends performing them. [LO 1-3, 1-4]

Building Management Skills

Thinking about Managers and Management [LO 1-2, 1-3, 1-4]

Think of an organization that has provided you with work experience and the manager to whom you reported (or talk to someone who has had extensive work experience). Then answer the following questions:

1. Think about your direct supervisor. Of what department is he or she a member, and at what level of management is this person?

2. How do you characterize your supervisor's approach to management? For example, which particular management tasks and roles does this person perform most often? What kinds of management skills does this manager have?

3. Are the tasks, roles, and skills of your supervisor appropriate for the particular job he or she performs? How could this manager improve his or her task performance? How can technology affect this?

4. How did your supervisor's approach to management affect your attitudes and behavior? For example, how well did you perform as an employee, and how motivated were you?

5. Think about the organization and its resources. Do its managers use organizational resources effectively? Which resources contribute most to the organization's performance?

6. Describe how the organization treats its human resources. How does this treatment affect the attitudes and behaviors of the workforce?

7. If you could give your manager one piece of advice or change one management practice in the organization, what would it be?

8. How attuned are the managers in the organization to the need to increase efficiency, quality, innovation, or responsiveness to customers? How well do you think the organization performs its prime goals of providing the goods or services that customers want or need the most?

Managing Ethically [LO 1-1, 1-3]

Think about an example of unethical behavior that you observed recently. The incident could be something you experienced as an employee or a customer or something you observed informally.

Questions

1. Either by yourself or in a group, give three reasons why you think the behavior was unethical. For example, what rules or norms were broken? Who benefited or was harmed by what took place? What was the outcome for the people involved?

2. What steps might you take to prevent such unethical behavior and encourage people to behave in an ethical way?

Small Group Breakout Exercise [LO 1-2, 1-3, 1-4]

Opening a New Restaurant

Form groups of three or four people, and appoint one group member as the spokesperson who will communicate your findings to the entire class when called on by the instructor. Then discuss the following scenario:

You and your partners have decided to open a restaurant in your local community; it will be open from 7 a.m. to 3 p.m. daily to serve breakfast and lunch. Each of you is investing $50,000 in the venture, and together you have secured a bank loan for $300,000 to begin operations. You and your partners have little experience in managing a restaurant beyond serving meals or eating in restaurants, and you now face the task of deciding how you will manage the restaurant and what your respective roles will be.

1. Decide what each partner's managerial role in the restaurant will be. For example, who will be responsible for the necessary departments and specific activities? Describe your managerial hierarchy.

2. Which building blocks of competitive advantage do you need to establish to help your restaurant succeed? What criteria will you use to evaluate how successfully you are managing the restaurant?

3. Discuss the most important decisions that must be made about (a) planning, (b) organizing, (c) leading, and (d) controlling to allow you and your partners to use organizational resources effectively and build a competitive advantage.

4. For each managerial task, list the issues to solve, and decide which roles will contribute the most to your restaurant's success.

Be the Manager [LO 1-2, 1-5]

Rapid Growth Causes Problems

You have just been called in to help managers at Achieva, a fast-growing Internet software company that specializes in business-to-business (B2B) network software. Your job is to help Achieva solve some management problems that have arisen because of its rapid growth.

Customer demand to license Achieva's software has boomed so much in just two years that more than 50 new employees have been added to help develop a new range of software products and to improve customer service. Achieva's growth has been so swift that the company still operates informally, its organizational structure is loose and flexible, and employees are encouraged to find solutions to problems as they go along. Although this structure worked well in the past, you have been told that problems are arising.

There have been increasing complaints from employees that good performance is not being recognized in the organization and that they do not feel equitably treated. Moreover, there have been complaints about getting managers to listen to their new ideas and to act on them. A bad atmosphere is developing in the company, and recently several talented employees left. Your job is to help Achieva's managers solve these problems quickly and keep the company on the fast track.

Questions

1. What kinds of organizing and controlling problems is Achieva suffering from?
2. What kinds of management changes need to be made to solve them?

Case in the News [LO 1-1, 1-2, 1-3, 1-6]

GE Drives Away from Transportation

When John Flannery took over as CEO of General Electric, he brought a vision of a company that would be simpler and leaner. For years, GE had wowed managers around the globe as a high-performing conglomerate engaged in everything from electricity-generating equipment to entertainment (NBC Universal) to financial services to its iconic lighting division. But as the economy has changed, GE has been unable to sustain solid profits in some of those areas. Flannery determined that GE would focus on its three most profitable lines of business: aviation (making jet engines), power generation, and health care (especially imaging equipment).

Flannery's first big moves included spinning off GE's railroad business, one of North America's leading makers of locomotives for freight trains. The business unit, GE Transportation, has been owned by GE since 1907 and became less profitable in recent years. Flannery negotiated a deal with the Wabtec Corporation (formerly Westinghouse Air Brake Technologies), which produces equipment for freight railways and mass-transit operations. The deal combines the two companies into one; roughly 50 percent is owned by Wabtec shareholders, 40 percent by GE shareholders, and 10 percent by GE itself. Wabtec's CEO was selected to run the business, and GE was to receive $2.9 billion in cash when the deal closed.

The combined company should be a powerhouse in the transportation business. Based on the merging companies' sizes at the time the deal was announced, it has $8 billion in revenues and about 27,000 employees. Combining the companies allows management to cut costs, perhaps as much as $250 million a year. And it gives GE extra cash at a time when the company has a heavy load of debt.

While Flannery and his recent successor, Larry Culp, have been asking themselves which businesses GE should be engaged in, the managers of the former GE Transportation facilities have faced their own set of decisions. GE Transportation not only built a locomotive factory in Lawrence Park, Pennsylvania, a century ago; it also designed and built the community in which its workers would live. Generations of Lawrence Park residents took jobs in the factory and earned a comfortable living at wages negotiated by their union. GE was a key part of the community, and being a GE employee was a significant part of many community members' identities.

For managers, being part of GE's high-performance culture meant they had to keep looking for ways to be more efficient. One way to save money was to have more of the work done by employees who would work for a lower wage. Like many other manufacturers in the Northeast and Midwest, GE Transportation opened a facility in the southern United States. The company chose Fort Worth, Texas, and built its largest plant there. Employment at the Lawrence Park facility has dwindled from about 5,000 in 2013 (the year the Fort Worth facility opened) to fewer than 2,000 today. That does not mean the factory cut production by the same amount, however. Many of the remaining jobs at Lawrence Park are high-tech positions in advanced manufacturing, which lets companies produce greater output with fewer workers.

Meanwhile, at the million-square-foot Fort Worth facility, the non-union workers are busy assembling locomotives. A high-demand area of business is refurbishing locomotives. A 25-year-old locomotive is considered "middle-aged"—far from ready for the scrap heap if it can be cleaned up and modernized with new parts. When locomotives arrive at the facility, workers remove major components and send them through separate production lines that meet up at the opposite end of the facility to be reassembled into a rejuvenated locomotive. The whole process takes roughly two months. Renovating a locomotive allows its owner not only to extend its life but to make it more efficient. Installing high-tech sensors and software can increase the locomotive's efficiency and power. A train that once required three locomotives might run with two—a considerable savings for the railroad, especially considering that each locomotive's fuel consumption might have fallen by 10%. Demand for this service is so great that the company even works on locomotives outside its factory; it has dispatched workers with supplies to customers' own depots.

Some observers expect that the move of production from Pennsylvania to Texas is one step in a process that will lead to building facilities in Mexico or other lower-wage countries. If that happens, it will be a decision made not by GE Transportation, but by the management under Wabtec CEO Raymond Betler.

Questions for Discussion

1. What kinds of decisions and actions were taken by GE and the managers at Lawrence Park and Fort Worth? Categorize these as planning, organizing, leading, and controlling.

2. How have new technologies utilized at the Lawrence Park facility help save local jobs?

3. In your opinion, what responsibilities do GE and Wabtec have toward their employees and the communities in which they operate?

Sources: M. J. Belvedere, "Jim Cramer: 'Everything Is on the Table' under New GE CEO to Revive the Fallen Giant," *CNBC*, www.cnbc.com, October 1, 2018; J. Martin, "GE Transportation Receives Order for 60 Locomotives," www.goerie.com, September 6, 2018; S. Lohr, "G.E. Spins Off Railroad Business," *The New York Times*, www.nytimes.com, May 21, 2018; M. Egan, "GE's Latest Sale: Its 111-Year-Old Rail Business," *CNNMoney*, https://money.cnn.com, May 21, 2018; E. Beras, "General Electric Built This Town, but Its Presence Is Shrinking," *Marketplace*, www.marketplace.org, January 19, 2018; T. Kellner, "Forever Young: This Texas Plant Gives Middle-Aged Locomotives Extreme Makeovers," *GE Reports*, www.ge.com, March 26, 2018.

Endnotes

1. A. Carr and D. Bass, "The Nadellaissance," *Bloomberg Businessweek*, May 6, 2019, 36–41; K. Ryssdal and B. Bodnar, "CEO Satya Nadella on Why He's Hitting Refresh at Microsoft," *Marketplace*, www.marketplace.org, September 27, 2017; H. McCracken, "Satya Nadella Rewrites Microsoft's Code," *Fast Company*, www.fastcompany.com, September 18, 2017.

2. McCracken, "Satya Nadella Rewrites Microsoft's Code"; M. Murphy, "Satya Nadella on AI, Sexual Harassment, and Microsoft's Soul," *Bloomberg Businessweek*, www.bloomberg.com, December 21, 2017; K. Ryssdal and B. Bodnar, "CEO Satya Nadella Explains His Vision for Microsoft and the Future," *Marketplace*, www.marketplace.org, September 28, 2017.

3. Murphy, "Satya Nadella on AI, Sexual Harassment, and Microsoft's Soul"; McCracken, "Satya Nadella Rewrites Microsoft's Code."

4. Ryssal and Bodnar, "CEO Satya Nadella Explains His Vision."

5. Ryssdal and Bodnar, "CEO Satya Nadella on Why He's Hitting Refresh"; Murphy, "Satya Nadella on AI, Sexual Harassment, and Microsoft's Soul."

6. J. Francisco, "Satya and Anu Nadella Open Up about Their Family Life," *Good Housekeeping,* www.goodhousekeeping.com, September 27, 2017.

7. Carr and Bass, "The Nadellaissance"; McCracken, "Satya Nadella Rewrites Microsoft's Code"; J. Fortt, "Microsoft's CEO Satya Nadella Broke Unspoken Rules on His Rise to CEO," *CNBC,* www.cnbc.com, October 2, 2017.

8. B. Evans, "10 Powerful Examples of Microsoft CEO Satya Nadella's Transformative Vision," *Forbes,* www.forbes.com, July 26, 2017.

9. D. Wiener-Bronner, "McDonald's Is Changing Its Breakfast Menu to Draw More Customers," *CNN Business,* www.cnn.com, October 23, 2018.

10. "Summary Report: 11-1021.00—General and Operations Managers," *O*NET OnLine,* www.onetonline.org, accessed November 30, 2018.

11. H. Fayol, *General and Industrial Management* (New York: IEEE Press, 1984). Fayol actually identified five different managerial tasks, but most scholars today believe these four capture the essence of Fayol's ideas.

12. P. F. Drucker, *Management Tasks, Responsibilities, and Practices* (New York: Harper & Row, 1974).

13. "See AI," www.microsoft.com, accessed November 1, 2018; M. Wilson, "A Phone App for the Visually Impaired," *Fast Company,* www.fastcompany.com, September 10, 2018; S. Shah, "Microsoft's Seeing AI App for the Blind Now Reads Handwriting," *Engadget,* www.engadget.com, December 14, 2017.

14. J. Novet, "Microsoft's Sales Overhaul Has Led to All-Time High Stock Price and Continuing Cloud Growth," *CNBC,* www.cnbc.com, July 16, 2018.

15. G. O'Brien, "ER Manager Creates Efficiencies—and a True 'Front Door,'" *BusinessWest,* http://businesswest.com, accessed November 8, 2018.

16. "New Responsibilities for Members of Mercy's Nursing Leadership," *SPHS Journal* (Sisters of Providence Health System), June 2015, 3.

17. A. G. Flynn, "Mercy Medical Center Earns Top Honors for Stroke Care," *MassLive,* www.masslive.com, accessed November 8, 2018.

18. O'Brien, "ER Manager Creates Efficiencies"; "Mercy's Healthcare Heroes," *Journal* (Trinity Health of New England/Mercy Medical Center), www.mercycares.com, September 26, 2017.

19. L. Hill, *Becoming a Manager: Mastery of a New Identity* (Boston: Harvard Business School Press, 1992).

20. Ibid.

21. H. Mintzberg, "The Manager's Job: Folklore and Fact," *Harvard Business Review,* July–August 1975, 56–62.

22. H. Mintzberg, *The Nature of Managerial Work* (New York: Harper & Row, 1973).

23. A. K. Gupta, "Contingency Perspectives on Strategic Leadership," in D. C. Hambrick, ed., *The Executive Effect: Concepts and Methods for Studying Top Managers* (Greenwich, CT: JAI Press, 1988), 147–78.

24. D. G. Ancona, "Top Management Teams: Preparing for the Revolution," in J. S. Carroll, ed., *Applied Social Psychology and Organizational Settings* (Hillsdale, NJ: Erlbaum, 1990); D. C. Hambrick and P. A. Mason, "Upper Echelons: The Organization as a Reflection of Its Top Managers," *Academy of Management Journal* 9 (1984), 193–206.

25. T. A. Mahony, T. H. Jerdee, and S. J. Carroll, "The Jobs of Management," *Industrial Relations* 4 (1965), 97–110; L. Gomez-Mejia, J. McCann, and R. C. Page, "The Structure of Managerial Behaviors and Rewards," *Industrial Relations* 24 (1985), 147–54.

26. W. R. Nord and M. J. Waller, "The Human Organization of Time: Temporal Realities and Experiences," *Academy of Management Review* 29 (January 2004), 137–40.

27. R. L. Katz, "Skills of an Effective Administrator," *Harvard Business Review,* September–October 1974, 90–102.

28. Ibid.

29. P. Tharenou, "Going Up? Do Traits and Informal Social Processes Predict Advancing in Management," *Academy of Management Journal* 44 (October 2001), 1005–18.

30. J. Schutz, "Tales from a City Manager's Freshman Year," *Public Management,* October 2017, 18–21.

31. M. Roberts, "Government Job Profile: City Manager," *The Balance Careers,* www.thebalancecareers.com, accessed November 29, 2018.

32. Ibid.

33. K. Fitzpatrick, J. Nutting, and J. Petrin, "Massachusetts' Boot Camp for Managers," *Public Management,* December 2017, 10–13.

34. C. J. Collins and K. D. Clark, "Strategic Human Resource Practices, Top Management Team Social Networks, and Firm Performance: The Role of Human Resource Practices in Creating Organizational Competitive Advantage," *Academy of Management Journal* 46 (December 2003), 740–52.

35. R. Stewart, "Middle Managers: Their Jobs and Behaviors," in J. W. Lorsch, ed., *Handbook of Organizational Behavior* (Englewood Cliffs, NJ: Prentice-Hall, 1987), 385–91.

36. S. C. de Janasz, S. E. Sullivan, and V. Whiting, "Mentor Networks and Career Success: Lessons for Turbulent Times," *Academy of Management Executive* 17 (November 2003), 78–92.

37. K. Labich, "Making Over Middle Managers," *Fortune,* May 8, 1989, 58–64.

38. T. Monosoff, "So You Want to Be Your Own Boss. . .," *Entrepreneur,* www.entrepreneur.com, accessed November 30, 2018; B. Green, "Why Do People Become Entrepreneurs If It's So Difficult to Succeed? Here's the Honest Truth," *INC.,* www.inc.com, accessed November 30, 2018.

39. McCracken, "Satya Nadella Rewrites Microsoft's Code."

40. M. Karch, "Google X, the Secret Google Lab," *Lifewire,* www.lifewire.com, accessed November 28, 2018.

41. D. Klein, "Chipotle Surges in CEO Brian Niccol's First Report," *QSR Magazine,* www.qsrmagazine.com, accessed November 28, 2018.

42. T. Donaldson, "Editor's Comments: Taking Ethics Seriously—A Mission Now More Possible," *Academy of Management Review* 28 (July 2003), 363–67.

43. W. H. Shaw and V. Barry, *Moral Issues in Business,* 6th ed. (Belmont, CA: Wadsworth, 1995);

T. Donaldson, *Corporations and Morality* (Englewood Cliffs, NJ: Prentice-Hall, 1982).

44. "Supplier Responsibility," www.apple.com, accessed December 1, 2018.

45. M. Rosenberg and N. Raymond, "Brazilian Firms to Pay Record $3.5 Billion Penalty in Corruption Case," Reuters, www.reuters.com, December 21, 2016; P. Wahba, "Avon Settles Justice Department Charges of China Bribery for $135 Million," *Fortune,* http://fortune.com, December 17, 2014.

46. Institute of Business Ethics, "Using Behavioural Ethics to Improve Your Ethics Programme," *Business Ethics Briefing,* no. 61, www.ibe.org.uk, April 2018; Todd Hough, "Nudging Corporate Compliance," *American Business Law Journal* 54, no. 4 (Winter 2017), 683–741.

47. Hough, "Nudging Corporate Compliance"; Carsten Tams, "Small Is Beautiful: Using Gentle Nudges to Change Organizations," *Forbes,* www.forbes.com, February 22, 2018.

48. Tams, "Small Is Beautiful"; Ben DiPietro, "Companies Try Nudging Their Way to Better Ethics," *The Wall Street Journal,* https://blogs.wsj.com, May 24, 2018.

49. Hough, "Nudging Corporate Compliance."

50. S. Jackson et al., *Diversity in the Workplace: Human Resource Initiatives* (New York: Guilford Press, 1992).

51. D. Jamieson and J. O'Mara, *Managing Workforce 2000: Gaining a Diversity Advantage* (San Francisco: Jossey-Bass, 1991).

52. "Inclusion & Diversity," www.accenture.com, accessed December 3, 2018; E. Fry, "How the Heads of Accenture and Girls Who Code Are Tackling Diversity," *Fortune,* http://fortune.com, November 30, 2016; K. Bellstrom, "Exclusive: Accenture Is the First Big Consulting Firm to Publish Race and Gender Stats," *Fortune,* http://fortune.com, February 8, 2016.

53. "Forbes Releases First-Ever List of America's Best Employers for Diversity," *Forbes,* www.forbes.com, accessed December 1, 2018.

54. E. Woyke, "How UPS Delivers Faster Using $8 Headphones and Code That Decides When Dirty Trucks Get Cleaned," *MIT Technology Review,* www.technologyreview.com, February 16, 2018; R.V. Zicari, "Big Data at UPS: Interview with Jack Levis," *ODBMS Industry Watch,* www.odbms.org, August 1, 2017.

History of Management Thought

The systematic study of management began in the closing decades of the 19th century, after the Industrial Revolution had swept through Europe and America. In the new economic climate, managers of all types of organizations—political, educational, and economic—were increasingly turning their focus toward finding better ways to satisfy customers' needs. Many major economic, technical, and cultural changes were taking place at this time. With the introduction of steam power and the development of sophisticated machinery and equipment, the Industrial Revolution changed the way goods were produced, particularly in the weaving and clothing industries. Small workshops run by skilled workers who produced hand-manufactured products (a system called *crafts production*) were being replaced by large factories in which sophisticated machines controlled by hundreds or even thousands of unskilled or semiskilled workers made products. For example, raw cotton and wool that in the past families or whole villages working together had spun into yarn were now shipped to factories where workers operated machines that spun and wove large quantities of yarn into cloth.

Owners and managers of the new factories found themselves unprepared for the challenges accompanying the change from small-scale crafts production to large-scale mechanized manufacturing. Moreover, many of the managers and supervisors in these workshops and factories were engineers who had only a technical orientation. They were unprepared for the social problems that occur when people work together in large groups (as in a factory or shop system). Managers began to search for new techniques to manage their organizations' resources, and soon they began to focus on ways to increase the efficiency of the worker–task mix. They found help from Frederick W. Taylor and others.

scientific management
The systematic study of relationships between people and tasks to increase efficiency.

F. W. Taylor and Scientific Management

Frederick W. Taylor (1856–1915) is best known for defining the techniques of scientific management, the systematic study of relationships between people and tasks for the purpose of redesigning the work process to increase efficiency. Taylor was a manufacturing manager who eventually became a consultant and taught other managers how to apply his scientific management techniques. Taylor believed that if the amount of time and effort that each worker expends to produce a unit of output (a finished good or service) can be reduced by increasing specialization and the division of labor, the production

Frederick W. Taylor, founder of scientific management, and one of the first people to study the behavior and performance of people in the workplace. Source: Frederick Taylor, 1856–1915

process will become more efficient. Taylor believed the way to create the most efficient division of labor could best be determined by using scientific management techniques, rather than intuitive or informal rule-of-thumb knowledge. Based on his experiments and observations as a manufacturing manager in a variety of settings, he developed four principles to increase efficiency in the workplace[1]:

- Principle 1: *Study the way workers perform their tasks, gather all the informal job knowledge that workers possess, and experiment with ways of improving the way tasks are performed.*

To discover the most efficient method of performing specific tasks, Taylor studied in great detail and measured the ways different workers went about performing their tasks. One of the main tools he used was a time-and-motion study, which involves the careful timing and recording of the actions taken to perform a particular task. Once Taylor understood the existing method of performing a task, he then experimented to increase specialization; he tried different methods of dividing up and coordinating the various tasks necessary to produce a finished product. Usually this meant simplifying jobs and having each worker perform fewer, more routine tasks. Taylor also sought to find ways to improve each worker's ability to perform a particular task—for example, by reducing the number of motions workers made to complete the task, by changing the layout of the work area or the type of tool workers used, or by experimenting with tools of different sizes.

- Principle 2: *Codify the new methods of performing tasks into written rules and standard operating procedures.*

Once the best method of performing a particular task was determined, Taylor specified that it should be recorded so that the procedures could be taught to all workers performing the same task. These rules could be used to further standardize and simplify jobs—essentially, to make jobs even more routine. In this way efficiency could be increased throughout an organization.

- Principle 3: *Carefully select workers so that they possess skills and abilities that match the needs of the task, and train them to perform the task according to the established rules and procedures.*

To increase specialization, Taylor believed workers had to understand the tasks that were required and be thoroughly trained in order to perform a task at the required level. Workers who could not be trained to this level were to be transferred to a job where they were able to reach the minimum required level of proficiency.[2]

- Principle 4: *Establish a fair or acceptable level of performance for a task, and then develop a pay system that provides a reward for performance above the acceptable level.*

To encourage workers to perform at a high level of efficiency, and to provide them with an incentive to reveal the most efficient techniques for performing a task, Taylor advocated that workers benefit from any gains in performance. They should be paid a bonus and receive some percentage of the performance gains achieved through the more efficient work process.

By 1910, Taylor's system of scientific management had become nationally known and in many instances faithfully and fully practiced.[3] However, managers in many organizations chose to implement the new principles of scientific management selectively. This decision ultimately resulted in problems. For example, some managers using scientific management obtained increases in performance, but rather than sharing performance gains with workers through bonuses as Taylor had advocated, they simply increased the amount of work that each worker was expected to do. Many workers experiencing the reorganized work system found that as their performance increased, managers required them to do more work for the same pay. Workers also learned that increases in performance often meant fewer jobs and a greater threat of layoffs because fewer workers were needed. In addition, the specialized, simplified jobs were often monotonous and repetitive, and many workers became dissatisfied with their jobs.

From a performance perspective, the combination of the two management practices—(1) achieving the right mix of worker–task specialization and (2) linking people and tasks by the speed of the production line—resulted in huge savings in costs and huge increases in output that occur in large, organized work settings. For example, in 1908, managers at the Franklin Motor Company using scientific management principles redesigned the work process, and the output of cars increased from 100 cars a month to 45 cars a day; workers' wages, however, increased by only 90%.[4]

Taylor's work has had an enduring effect on the management of production systems. Managers in every organization, whether it produces goods or services, now carefully analyze the basic tasks that workers must perform and try to create a work environment that will allow their organizations to operate most efficiently. We discuss this important issue in Chapter 7.

The Gilbreths

Two prominent followers of Taylor were Frank Gilbreth (1868–1924) and Lillian Gilbreth (1878–1972), who refined Taylor's analysis of work movements and made many contributions to time-and-motion study.[5] Their aims were to (1) analyze every individual action necessary to perform a particular task and break it into each of its component actions; (2) find better ways to perform each component action; and (3) reorganize each of the component actions so that the action as a whole could be performed more efficiently—in less time and with less effort.

The Gilbreths often filmed a worker performing a particular task and then separated the task actions, frame by frame, into their component movements. Their goal was to maximize the efficiency with which each individual task was performed so that gains across the tasks would add up to substantial savings of time and effort. Their attempts to develop management principles were captured—at times quite humorously—in the movie *Cheaper by the Dozen*,

This scene from the 2003 version of Cheaper by the Dozen illustrates how "efficient families" such as the Gilbreths use formal family meetings to solve problems, such as assigning chores to different family members. Collection Christophel/Alamy Stock Photo

which depicts how the Gilbreths with their 12 children tried to live their own lives according to these efficiency principles and apply them to daily actions such as cooking, cleaning, and even raising a family.[6]

Eventually the Gilbreths became increasingly interested in the study of fatigue. They studied how physical characteristics of the workplace contribute to job stress that often leads to fatigue and poor performance. They isolated factors that result in worker fatigue, such as lighting, heating, the color of walls, and the design of tools and machines. Their pioneering studies paved the way for new advances in management theory.

In workshops and factories, the work of the Gilbreths, Taylor, and many others had a major effect on the practice of management. In comparison with the old crafts system, jobs in the new system were more repetitive, boring, and monotonous as a result of the application of scientific management principles, and workers became increasingly dissatisfied. Frequently, the management of work settings became a game between workers and managers: Managers tried to implement work practices to increase performance, and workers tried to hide the true potential of the more efficient work setting to protect their own well-being.

Weber's Bureaucratic Theory

Side by side with scientific managers studying the person–task mix to increase efficiency, other researchers were focusing on how to increase the efficiency with which organizations were managed. Max Weber, a German professor of sociology, outlined his famous principles of bureaucracy—a formal system of organization and administration designed to ensure efficiency and effectiveness—and created bureaucratic theory. A bureaucratic system of administration is based on five principles:

bureaucracy
A formal system of organization and administration designed to ensure efficiency and effectiveness.

- Principle 1: *In a bureaucracy, a manager's formal authority derives from the position he or she holds in the organization.*

    Authority is the power to hold people accountable for their actions and to make decisions concerning the use of organizational resources. Authority gives managers the right to direct and control their employees' behavior to achieve organizational goals. In a bureaucratic system of administration, obedience is owed to a manager, not because of any personal qualities—such as personality, wealth, or social status—but because the manager occupies a position that is associated with a certain level of authority and responsibility.[7]

authority The power to hold people accountable for their actions and to allocate organizational resources.

- Principle 2: *In a bureaucracy, people should occupy positions because of their performance, not because of their social standing or personal contacts.*

    This principle was not always followed in Weber's time and is often ignored today. Some organizations and industries are still affected by social networks in which personal contacts and relations, not job-related skills, influence hiring and promotion decisions.

- Principle 3: *The extent of each position's formal authority and their responsibilities, and their relationship to other positions in an organization, should be clearly specified.*

Max Weber developed the principles of bureaucracy during Germany's burgeoning industrial revolution to help organizations increase their efficiency and effectiveness. Source: Max Weber, 1864–1920

When the tasks and authority associated with various positions in the organization are clearly specified, managers and workers know what is expected of them and what to expect from each other. Moreover, an organization can hold all its employees strictly accountable for their actions when they know their exact responsibilities.

• Principle 4: *Authority can be exercised effectively in an organization when positions are arranged hierarchically, so employees know whom to report to and who reports to them.*[8]

Managers must create an organizational hierarchy of authority that makes it clear who reports to whom and to whom managers and workers should go if conflicts or problems arise. This principle is especially important in the military, FBI, CIA, and other organizations that deal with sensitive issues involving possible major repercussions. It is vital that managers at high levels of the hierarchy be able to hold employees accountable for their actions.

• Principle 5: *Managers must create a well-defined system of rules, standard operating procedures, and norms so that they can effectively control behavior within an organization.*

Rules are formal written instructions that specify actions to be taken under different circumstances to achieve specific goals (for example, if A happens, do B). **Standard operating procedures (SOPs)** are specific sets of written instructions about how to perform a certain aspect of a task. A rule might state that at the end of the workday employees are to leave their machines in good order, and a set of SOPs specifies exactly how they should do so, itemizing which machine parts must be oiled or replaced. **Norms** are unwritten, informal codes of conduct that prescribe how people should act in particular situations. For example, an organizational norm in a restaurant might be that servers should help each other if time permits.

Rules, SOPs, and norms provide behavioral guidelines that increase the performance of a bureaucratic system because they specify the best ways to accomplish organizational tasks. Companies such as McDonald's and Walmart have developed extensive rules and procedures to specify the behaviors required of their employees, such as "Always greet the customer with a smile."

Weber believed that organizations that implement all five principles establish a bureaucratic system that improves organizational performance. The specification of positions and the use of rules and SOPs to regulate how tasks are performed make it easier for managers to organize and control the work of employees. Similarly, fair and equitable selection and promotion systems improve managers' feelings of security, reduce stress, and encourage organizational members to act ethically and further promote the interests of the organization.[9]

If bureaucracies are not managed well, many problems can result. Sometimes managers allow rules and SOPs, "bureaucratic red tape," to become so cumbersome that decision making becomes slow and inefficient and organizations are unable to change. When managers rely too much on rules to solve problems and not enough on their own skills and judgment, their behavior becomes inflexible. A key challenge for managers is to use bureaucratic principles to benefit, rather than harm, an organization.

rules Formal written instructions that specify actions to be taken under different circumstances to achieve specific goals.

standard operating procedures (SOPs) Specific sets of written instructions about how to perform a particular task.

norms Unwritten, informal codes of conduct that prescribe how people should act in particular situations and that are considered important by most members of a group or an organization.

The Work of Mary Parker Follett

If F. W. Taylor is considered the father of management thought, Mary Parker Follett (1868–1933) serves as its mother.[10] Much of her writing about management and the way managers should behave toward workers was a response to her concern that Taylor was ignoring the human side of the organization. She pointed out that management often overlooks the multitude of ways in which employees can contribute to the organization when managers allow them to participate and exercise initiative in their everyday work lives.[11] Taylor, for example, never proposed that managers involve workers in analyzing their jobs to identify better ways to perform tasks, or even ask workers how they felt about their jobs. Instead, he used time and motion experts to analyze workers' jobs for them. Follett, in contrast, argued that because workers know the most about their jobs, they should be involved in job analysis and managers should allow them to participate in the work development process.

Follett proposed, "Authority should go with knowledge . . . whether it is up the line or down." In other words, if workers have the relevant knowledge, then workers, rather than managers, should be in control of the work process itself, and managers should behave as coaches and facilitators—not as monitors and supervisors. In making this statement, Follett anticipated the current interest in self-managed teams and empowerment. She also recognized the importance of having managers in different departments communicate directly with each other to speed decision making. She advocated what she called "cross-functioning": members of different departments working together in cross-departmental teams to accomplish projects—an approach that is increasingly utilized today.[12] She proposed that knowledge and expertise, not managers' formal authority deriving from their position in the hierarchy, should decide who would lead at any particular moment. She believed, as do many management theorists today, that power is fluid and should flow to the person who can best help the organization achieve its goals. Follett took a horizontal view of power and authority, rather than viewing the vertical chain of command as being most essential to effective management. Thus, Follett's approach was very radical for its time.

Mary Parker Follett, an early management thinker who advocated, "Authority should go with knowledge . . . whether it is up the line or down." ©Regina A. Greenwood, from the Ronald G. Greenwood Collection

The Hawthorne Studies and Human Relations

Probably because of its radical nature, Follett's work went unappreciated by managers and researchers until quite recently. Most continued to follow in the footsteps of Taylor, and to increase efficiency, they studied ways to improve various characteristics of the work setting, such as job specialization or the kinds of tools workers used. One series of studies was conducted from 1924 to 1932 at the Hawthorne Works of the Western Electric Company.[13] This research, now known as the Hawthorne studies, was initiated as an attempt to investigate how characteristics of the work setting—specifically the level of lighting or illumination—affect worker fatigue and performance. The researchers conducted

Workers in a telephone manufacturing plant, in 1931. Around this time, researchers at the Hawthorne Works of the Western Electric Company began to study the effects of work setting characteristics—such as lighting and rest periods—on productivity. To their surprise, they discovered that workers' productivity was affected more by the attention they received from researchers than by the characteristics of the work setting—a phenomenon that became known as the Hawthorne effect. Fox Photos/Hulton Archive/Getty Images

an experiment in which they systematically measured worker productivity at various levels of illumination.

The experiment produced some unexpected results. The researchers found that regardless of whether they raised or lowered the level of illumination, productivity increased. In fact, productivity began to fall only when the level of illumination dropped to the level of moonlight, a level at which presumably workers could no longer see well enough to do their work efficiently.

As you can imagine, the researchers found these results very puzzling. They invited a noted Harvard psychologist, Elton Mayo, to help them. Mayo proposed another series of experiments to solve the mystery. These experiments, known as the relay assembly test experiments, were designed to investigate the effects of other aspects of the work context on job performance, such as the effect of the number and length of rest periods and hours of work on fatigue and monotony.[14] The goal was to raise productivity.

During a two-year study of a small group of female workers, the researchers again observed that productivity increased over time, but the increases could not be solely attributed to the effects of changes in the work setting. Gradually, the researchers discovered that, to some degree, the results they were obtaining were influenced by the fact that the researchers themselves had become part of the experiment. In other words, the presence of the researchers was affecting the results because the workers enjoyed receiving attention and being the subject of study and were willing to cooperate with the researchers to produce the results they believed the researchers desired.

Subsequently, it was found that many other factors also influence worker behavior, and it was not clear what was actually influencing the Hawthorne workers' behavior. However, this particular effect—which became known as the Hawthorne effect—seemed to suggest that the attitudes of workers toward their managers affect the level of workers' performance. In particular, the significant finding was that a manager's behavior or leadership approach can affect performance. This finding led many researchers to turn their attention to managerial behavior and leadership. If supervisors could be trained to behave in ways that would elicit cooperative behavior from their employees, then productivity could be increased. From this view emerged the human relations movement, which advocates that supervisors be behaviorally trained to manage employees in ways that elicit their cooperation and increase their productivity.

The importance of behavioral or human relations training became even clearer to its supporters after another series of experiments—the bank wiring room experiments. In a study of workers making telephone-switching equipment, researchers Elton Mayo and F. J. Roethlisberger discovered that the workers, as a group, had deliberately adopted a norm of output restriction to protect their jobs. Other group members subjected workers who violated this informal production norm to

Hawthorne effect Workers' productivity is affected more by observation or attention received than by physical work setting.

human relations movement Advocates behavior and leadership training of supervisors to elicit worker cooperation and improve productivity.

sanctions. Those who violated group performance norms and performed above the norm were called "ratebusters"; those who performed below the norm were called "chiselers."

The experimenters concluded that both types of workers threatened the group as a whole. Ratebusters threaten group members because they reveal to managers how fast the work can be done. Chiselers are looked down on because they are not doing their share of the work. Work-group members discipline both ratebusters and chiselers in order to create a pace of work that the workers (not the managers) think is fair. Thus, the work group's influence over output can be as great as the supervisors' influence. Since the work group can influence the behavior of its members, some management theorists argue that supervisors should be trained to behave in ways that gain the goodwill and cooperation of workers so that supervisors, not workers, control the level of work-group performance.

informal organization The system of behavioral rules and norms that emerge in work groups.

One of the main implications of the Hawthorne studies was that the behavior of managers and workers in the work setting is as important in explaining the level of performance as the technical aspects of the task. Managers must understand the workings of the informal organization, the system of behavioral rules and norms that emerge in a group, when they try to manage or change behavior in organizations. Many studies have found that, as time passes, groups often develop elaborate procedures and norms that bond members together, allowing unified action either to cooperate with management in order to raise performance or to restrict output and thwart the attainment of organizational goals.[15] The Hawthorne studies demonstrated the importance of understanding how the feelings, thoughts, and behavior of work-group members and managers affect performance. It was becoming increasingly clear to researchers that understanding behavior in organizations is a complex process that is critical to increasing performance.[16] Indeed, the increasing interest in the area of management known as organizational behavior, the study of the factors that have an impact on how individuals and groups respond to and act in organizations, dates from these early studies.

organizational behavior The study of factors that impact how workers respond to and act in an organization.

Theory X and Theory Y

Several studies after the Second World War revealed how assumptions about workers' attitudes and behavior affect managers' behavior. Douglas McGregor developed the most influential approach. He proposed that two different sets of assumptions about work attitudes and behaviors dominate the way managers think and affect how they behave in organizations. McGregor named these two contrasting sets of assumptions *Theory X* and *Theory Y*.[17]

Theory X The assumption that workers will try to do as little as possible and avoid further responsibility unless rewarded or punished for doing otherwise.

According to the assumptions of Theory X, the average worker is lazy, dislikes work, and will try to do as little as possible. Moreover, workers have little ambition and wish to avoid responsibility. Thus, the manager's task is to counteract workers' natural tendencies to avoid work. To keep workers' performance at a high level, the manager must supervise them closely and control their behavior by means of "the carrot and stick"—rewards and punishments.

Managers who accept the assumptions of Theory X design and shape the work setting to maximize their control over workers' behaviors and minimize workers' control over the pace of work. These managers believe that workers must be made to do what is necessary for the success of the organization, and they focus on developing rules, SOPs, and a well-defined system of rewards and punishments to control behavior. They see little point in giving workers autonomy to solve their own problems because they think that the workforce neither expects nor desires cooperation. Theory X managers see their role as to closely monitor workers to ensure that they contribute to the production process and do not threaten product quality. Henry Ford, who closely supervised and managed his workforce, fits McGregor's description of a manager who holds Theory X assumptions.

Theory Y The assumption that workers will do what is best for an organization if given the proper work setting, opportunity, and encouragement.

In contrast, Theory Y assumes that workers are not inherently lazy, do not naturally dislike work, and, if given the opportunity, will do what is good for the organization. According to Theory Y, the characteristics of the work setting determine whether workers consider work to be a source of satisfaction or punishment; and managers do not need to closely control workers' behavior in order to make them perform at a high level, because workers will exercise self-control when they are committed to organizational goals. The implication of Theory Y, according to McGregor, is that "the limits of collaboration in the organizational setting are not limits of human nature but of management's ingenuity in discovering how to realize the potential represented by its human resources."[18] It is the manager's task to create a work setting that encourages commitment to organizational goals and provides opportunities for workers to be imaginative and to exercise initiative and self-direction.

When managers design the organizational setting to reflect the assumptions about attitudes and behavior suggested by Theory Y, the characteristics of the organization are quite different from those of an organizational setting based on Theory X. Managers who believe that workers are motivated to help the organization reach its goals can decentralize authority and give more control over the job to workers, both as individuals and in groups. In this setting, individuals and groups are still accountable for their activities, but the manager's role is not to control employees but to provide support and advice, to make sure workers have the resources they need to perform their jobs, and to evaluate them on their ability to help the organization meet its goals.

These same kinds of debates continue today as managers seek to increase both the efficiency and effectiveness of their organizations.

Endnotes

1. F. W. Taylor, *Shop Management* (New York: Harper, 1903); F. W. Taylor, *The Principles of Scientific Management* (New York: Harper, 1911).

2. L. W. Fry, "The Maligned F. W. Taylor: A Reply to His Many Critics," *Academy of Management Review* 1 (1976), 124–29.

3. J. A. Litterer, *The Emergence of Systematic Management as Shown by the Literature from 1870–1900* (New York: Garland, 1986).

4. D. Wren, *The Evolution of Management Thought* (New York: Wiley, 1994), 134.

5. F. B. Gilbreth, *Primer of Scientific Management* (New York: Van Nostrand Reinhold, 1912).

6. F. B. Gilbreth Jr. and E. G. Gilbreth, *Cheaper by the Dozen* (New York: Crowell, 1948).

7. C. Perrow, *Complex Organizations*, 2nd ed. (Glenview, IL: Scott, Foresman, 1979).

8. M. Weber, *From Max Weber: Essays in Sociology*, ed. H. H. Gerth and C. W. Mills (New York: Oxford University Press, 1946), 331.

9. See Perrow, *Complex Organizations*, Ch. 1, for a detailed discussion of these issues.

10. L. D. Parker, "Control in Organizational Life: The Contribution of Mary Parker Follett," *Academy of Management Review* 9 (1984), 736–45.

11. P. Graham, *M. P. Follett—Prophet of Management: A Celebration of Writings from the 1920s* (Boston: Harvard Business School Press, 1995).

12. M. P. Follett, *Creative Experience* (London: Longmans, 1924).

13. E. Mayo, *The Human Problems of Industrial Civilization* (New York: Macmillan, 1933); F. J. Roethlisberger and W. J.

Dickson, *Management and the Worker* (Cambridge, MA: Harvard University Press, 1947).

14. D. W. Organ, "Review of *Management and the Worker,* by F. J. Roethlisberger and W. J. Dickson," *Academy of Management Review* 13 (1986), 460–64.

15. D. Roy, "Banana Time: Job Satisfaction and Informal Interaction," *Human Organization* 18 (1960), 158–61.

16. For an analysis of the problems in distinguishing cause from effect in the Hawthorne studies and in social settings in general, see A. Carey, "The Hawthorne Studies: A Radical Criticism," *American Sociological Review* 33 (1967), 403–16.

17. D. McGregor, *The Human Side of Enterprise* (New York: McGraw-Hill, 1960).

18. Ibid., 48.

2 Values, Attitudes, Emotions, and Culture: The Manager as a Person

Learning Objectives

After studying this chapter, you should be able to:

LO 2-1 Describe the various personality traits that affect how managers think, feel, and behave.

LO 2-2 Explain what values and attitudes are, and describe their impact on managerial action.

LO 2-3 Appreciate how moods and emotions influence all members of an organization.

LO 2-4 Describe the nature of emotional intelligence and its role in management.

LO 2-5 Define organizational culture, and explain how managers both create and are influenced by organizational culture.

Management Snapshot

Success Is No Accident for Carnival's CEO

How Do a Manager's Personal Qualities Affect His or Her Success?

If you have taken a cruise, there's a good chance you were on a Carnival ship. Carnival Corporation & PLC is the largest leisure travel company in the world. Its nine brands—including Carnival, Costa, Cunard, Holland America Lines, and Princess Cruises—operate more than 100 ships, serving 12 million travelers annually, almost half of the world's cruise passengers.[1] Despite its dominant position in the market, Carnival has not always enjoyed smooth sailing. In 2012, one of its ships wrecked near Italy, leaving 32 passengers dead; another ship experienced a fire that disabled the vessel with passengers onboard. Vacationers questioned Carnival's reputation and the value of taking a cruise.[2]

The following year, Carnival replaced its CEO with Arnold Donald, a member of its board of directors since 2001. He launched a mission to restore the public image of cruising and to consistently exceed customers' expectations. In addition, Donald observed that Carnival's business units were failing to collaborate effectively, so he insisted that unit leaders share revenue and cost information and ideas to improve operations across the entire organization. The resulting improvements were as basic as negotiating unified contracts for salad greens and as powerful as identifying best practices for exceeding passenger expectations. Profits, revenues, and the company's stock price all began rising at a healthy clip under Donald's guidance.[3]

Donald's background instilled attitudes that have propelled his success. As a teenager in New Orleans' Ninth Ward, Donald attended a Catholic high school where the following announcement came over the public-address system three times a day: "Gentlemen, prepare yourselves. You're going to run the world." He set a goal to become a general manager of a large, global science-based corporation. Then he mapped out a plan to get there. To improve his chances of admission into an MBA program, he double-majored in engineering and economics. In his first job, at the agricultural-products giant Monsanto, his manager disrespected him, but Donald stayed focused on his plan. He figured out how to tackle difficult assignments and deliver the greatest value to Monsanto's shareholders; the manager was impressed and became a mentor. Besides perseverance and discipline, Donald has optimism. As Carnival CEO, he reacts to economic and political issues such as trade wars, armed conflicts, and economic uncertainty by noting that although tensions and risks always exist somewhere in the world, there are always locations where cruise travel remains attractive to many travelers.[4]

Values are important to Arnold Donald, CEO of Carnival Corporation. From embracing diversity and inclusion to showing concern for the well-being of others, Donald's upbringing in New Orleans' Ninth Ward instilled attitudes that have helped him succeed both personally and professionally. Lars Niki/Getty Images

Donald's values include concern for the well-being of others. He embraces the idea that when crew members are happy, they make passengers (Carnival's "guests") happy. Further, when the communities where ships dock are happy, the locals make guests happy. Donald therefore sees social responsibility as a way to foster great customer experiences. On a personal level, he prioritizes listening to others, making sure their needs are understood and respected. Because he believes that "everyone you encounter has something to offer and something you can learn from,"[5] he tries to listen patiently and ask questions to draw out the other person—even when he believes he already knows the answers.[6]

Donald places a high value on diversity and inclusion. He says business success requires innovation and that diverse groups with a shared objective will outperform homogeneous groups when it comes to innovation. He also notes the importance of not merely hiring diverse employees, but also ensuring that people are enabled to contribute. Donald, who is Carnival's first African American CEO, hired the heads of seven of Carnival's nine business units. Of those, four are women and another is the first African American president of a cruise line; they come from Australia, Britain, Germany, and Italy, as well as the United States. Donald takes care to listen to all of them.[7]

Overview

LO 2-1
Describe the various personality traits that affect how managers think, feel, and behave.

Like people everywhere, Arnold Donald has his own distinctive personality, values, and ways of viewing situations, meeting challenges, and getting along with others. In this chapter we focus on the manager as a feeling, thinking human being. We start by describing enduring characteristics that influence how managers work and how they view other people, their organizations, and the world around them. We also discuss how managers' values, attitudes, and moods play out in organizations, shaping organizational culture. By the end of this chapter you will appreciate how the personal characteristics of managers influence the process of management in general—and organizational culture in particular.

Enduring Characteristics: Personality Traits

personality traits Enduring tendencies to feel, think, and act in certain ways.

All people, including managers, have certain enduring characteristics that influence how they think, feel, and behave both on and off the job. These characteristics are personality traits: particular tendencies to feel, think, and act in certain ways that can be used to describe the personality of every individual. It is important to understand the personalities of managers because their personalities influence their behavior and their approach to managing people and resources.

Some managers are demanding, difficult to get along with, and highly critical of other people. Other managers may be as concerned about effectiveness and efficiency as highly critical managers but are easier to get along with, are likable, and frequently praise the people around them. Both management styles may produce excellent results, but their effects on employees are quite different. Do managers deliberately decide to adopt one of these approaches to management? Although they may do so part of the time, in all likelihood their personalities account for their different approaches. Indeed, research suggests that the way people react to different conditions depends, in part, on their personalities.[8]

The Big Five Personality Traits

We can think of an individual's personality as being composed of five general traits or characteristics: extraversion, negative affectivity, agreeableness, conscientiousness, and openness to experience. Researchers often consider these the Big Five personality traits.[9] Each of them can be viewed as a continuum along which every individual or, more specifically, every manager falls (see Figure 2.1).

Some managers may be at the high end of one trait continuum, others at the low end, and still others somewhere in between. An easy way to understand how these traits can affect a person's approach to management is to describe what people are like at the high and low ends of each trait continuum. As will become evident as you read about each trait, no single trait is right or wrong for being an effective manager. Rather, effectiveness is determined by a complex interaction between the characteristics of managers (including personality traits) and the nature of the job and organization in which they are working. Moreover, personality traits that enhance managerial effectiveness in one situation may impair it in another. Recent studies suggest that personality traits may even predict job performance in certain situations. For example, researchers found that extraversion better predicted performance in jobs requiring social skills, while agreeableness was less positively related to job performance in competitive environments.[10]

extraversion
The tendency to experience positive emotions and moods and to feel good about oneself and the rest of the world.

EXTRAVERSION Extraversion is the tendency to experience positive emotions and moods and to feel good about oneself and the rest of the world. Managers who are high on extraversion (often called *extraverts*) tend to be sociable, affectionate, outgoing, and friendly. Managers who are low on extraversion (often called *introverts*) tend to be less inclined toward social interactions and to have a less positive outlook. Being high on extraversion may be an asset for managers whose jobs entail

Figure 2.1
The Big Five
Personality Traits

Managers' personalities can be described by determining which point on each of the following dimensions best characterizes the manager in question:

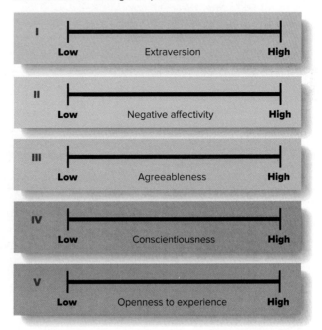

especially high levels of social interaction. Managers who are low on extraversion may nevertheless be highly effective and efficient, especially when their jobs do not require much social interaction. Their quieter approach may enable them to accomplish quite a bit of work in limited time. See Figure 2.2 for an example of a scale that can be used to measure a person's level of extraversion.

Figure 2.2

Measures of Extraversion, Agreeableness, Conscientiousness, and Openness to Experience

Listed below are phrases describing people's behaviors. Please use the rating scale below to describe how accurately each statement describes *you*. Describe yourself as you generally are now, not as you wish to be in the future. Describe yourself as you honestly see yourself, in relation to other people you know of the same sex as you are and roughly your same age.

1	2	3	4	5
Very inaccurate	Moderately inaccurate	Neither inaccurate nor accurate	Moderately accurate	Very accurate

_____ 1. Am interested in people.

_____ 2. Have a rich vocabulary.

_____ 3. Am always prepared.

_____ 4. Am not really interested in others.*

_____ 5. Leave my belongings around.*

_____ 6. Am the life of the party.

_____ 7. Have difficulty understanding abstract ideas.*

_____ 8. Sympathize with others' feelings.

_____ 9. Don't talk a lot.*

_____ 10. Pay attention to details.

_____ 11. Have a vivid imagination.

_____ 12. Insult people.*

_____ 13. Make a mess of things.*

_____ 14. Feel comfortable around people.

_____ 15. Am not interested in abstract ideas.*

_____ 16. Have a soft heart.

_____ 17. Get chores done right away.

_____ 18. Keep in the background.*

_____ 19. Have excellent ideas.

_____ 20. Start conversations.

_____ 21. Am not interested in other people's problems.*

_____ 22. Often forget to put things back in their proper place.*

_____ 23. Have little to say.*

_____ 24. Do not have a good imagination.*

_____ 25. Take time out for others.

_____ 26. Like order.

_____ 27. Talk to a lot of different people at parties.

_____ 28. Am quick to understand things.

_____ 29. Feel little concern for others.*

_____ 30. Shirk my duties.*

_____ 31. Don't like to draw attention to myself.*

_____ 32. Use difficult words.

_____ 33. Feel others' emotions.

_____ 34. Follow a schedule.

_____ 35. Spend time reflecting on things.

_____ 36. Don't mind being the center of attention.

_____ 37. Make people feel at ease.

_____ 38. Am exacting in my work.

_____ 39. Am quiet around strangers.*

_____ 40. Am full of ideas.

* Item is reverse-scored: 1 = 5, 2 = 4, 4 = 2, 5 = 1
Scoring: Sum responses to items for an overall scale.
        Extraversion = sum of items 6, 9, 14, 18, 20, 23, 27, 31, 36, 39
        Agreeableness = sum of items 1, 4, 8, 12, 16, 21, 25, 29, 33, 37
        Conscientiousness = sum of items 3, 5, 10, 13, 17, 22, 26, 30, 34, 38
        Openness to experience = sum of items 2, 7, 11, 15, 19, 24, 28, 32, 35, 40

Source: International Personality Item Pool, Oregon Research Institute, October 8, 2012.

negative affectivity
The tendency to experience negative emotions and moods, to feel distressed, and to be critical of oneself and others.

NEGATIVE AFFECTIVITY Negative affectivity is the tendency to experience negative emotions and moods, feel distressed, and be critical of oneself and others. Managers high on this trait may often feel angry and dissatisfied and complain about their own and others' lack of progress. Managers who are low on negative affectivity do not tend to experience many negative emotions and moods and are less pessimistic and critical of themselves and others. On the plus side, the critical approach of a manager high on negative affectivity may sometimes spur both the manager and others to improve their performance. Nevertheless, it is probably more pleasant to work with a manager who is low on negative affectivity; the better working relationships that such a manager is likely to cultivate also can be an important asset.

agreeableness The tendency to get along well with other people.

AGREEABLENESS Agreeableness is the tendency to get along well with others. Managers who are high on the agreeableness continuum are likable, tend to be affectionate, and care about other people. Managers who are low on agreeableness may be somewhat distrustful of others, unsympathetic, uncooperative, and even at times antagonistic. Being high on agreeableness may be especially important for managers whose responsibilities require that they develop good, close relationships with others. Nevertheless, a low level of agreeableness may be an asset in managerial jobs that actually require that managers be antagonistic, such as drill sergeants and some other kinds of military managers. See Figure 2.2 for an example of a scale that measures a person's level of agreeableness.

conscientiousness
The tendency to be careful, scrupulous, and persevering.

CONSCIENTIOUSNESS Conscientiousness is the tendency to be careful, scrupulous, and persevering.[11] Managers who are high on the conscientiousness continuum are organized and self-disciplined; those who are low on this trait might sometimes appear to lack direction and self-discipline. Conscientiousness has been found to be a good predictor of performance in many kinds of jobs, including managerial jobs in a variety of organizations.[12] Entrepreneurs who found their own companies often are high on conscientiousness, and their persistence and determination help them overcome obstacles and turn their ideas into successful new ventures. Figure 2.2 provides an example of a scale that measures conscientiousness.

openness to experience
The tendency to be original, have broad interests, be open to a wide range of stimuli, be daring, and take risks.

OPENNESS TO EXPERIENCE Openness to experience is the tendency to be original, have broad interests, be open to a wide range of stimuli, be daring, and take risks.[13] Managers who are high on this trait continuum may be especially likely to take risks and be innovative in their planning and decision making. Arnold Donald, discussed in this chapter's opening story, continues to explore new ways for his company Carnival Corporation & PLC to grow, innovate, and succeed—a testament to his high level of openness to experience. Managers who are low on openness to experience may be less prone to take risks and more conservative in their planning and decision making. In certain organizations and positions, this tendency might be an asset. The manager of the fiscal office in a public university, for example, must ensure that all university departments and units follow the university's rules and regulations pertaining to budgets, spending accounts, and reimbursements of expenses. Figure 2.2 provides an example of a measure of openness to experience.

Successful managers occupy a variety of positions on the Big Five personality trait continuum. One highly effective manager may be high on extraversion and negative affectivity; another equally effective manager may be low on both these traits; and still another may be somewhere in between. Members of an organization must understand these differences among managers because they can shed light on how managers behave and on their approach to planning, leading, organizing, or controlling. If employees realize, for example, that their manager is low on extraversion, they will not feel slighted when the manager seems to be aloof because they will realize that by nature he or she is simply not outgoing.

Managers themselves also need to be aware of their own personality traits and the traits of others, including those of their employees and fellow managers. A manager who knows that he has a tendency to be highly critical of other people might try to tone down his negative approach. Similarly, a manager who realizes that her chronically complaining employee tends to be so negative because of his personality may take all his complaints with a grain of salt and realize that things probably are not as bad as this employee says they are.

In order for all members of an organization to work well together and with people outside the organization, such as customers and suppliers, they must understand each other. Such understanding comes, in part, from an appreciation of some fundamental ways in which people differ from one another—that is, an appreciation of personality traits.

Other Personality Traits That Affect Managerial Behavior

Many other specific traits in addition to the Big Five describe people's personalities. Here we look at traits that are particularly important for understanding managerial effectiveness: locus of control; self-esteem; and the needs for achievement, affiliation, and power.

internal locus of control The tendency to locate responsibility for one's fate within oneself.

LOCUS OF CONTROL People differ in their views about how much control they have over what happens to and around them. The locus of control trait captures these beliefs.[14] People with an internal locus of control believe they themselves are responsible for their own fate; they see their own actions and behaviors as being major and decisive determinants of important outcomes such as attaining levels of job performance, being promoted, or being turned down for a choice job assignment. Some managers with an internal locus of control see the success of a whole organization resting on their shoulders. One example is Arnold Donald in the "Management Snapshot." An internal locus of control also helps ensure ethical behavior and decision making in an organization because people feel accountable and responsible for their own actions.

external locus of control The tendency to locate responsibility for one's fate in outside forces and to believe one's own behavior has little impact on outcomes.

People with an external locus of control believe that outside forces are responsible for what happens to and around them; they do not think their own actions make much of a difference. As such, they tend not to intervene to try to change a situation or solve a problem, leaving it to someone else.

Managers need an internal locus of control because they *are* responsible for what happens in organizations; they need to believe they can and do make a difference. Moreover, managers are responsible for ensuring that organizations and their members behave in an ethical fashion, and for this as well they need an internal locus of control—they need to know and feel they can make a difference.

SELF-ESTEEM Self-esteem is the degree to which individuals feel good about themselves and their capabilities. People with high self-esteem believe they are

self-esteem The degree to which individuals feel good about themselves and their capabilities.

competent, deserving, and capable of handling most situations. People with low self-esteem have poor opinions of themselves, are unsure about their capabilities, and question their ability to succeed at different endeavors.[15] Research suggests that people tend to choose activities and goals consistent with their levels of self-esteem. High self-esteem is desirable for managers because it facilitates their setting and keeping high standards for themselves, pushes them ahead on difficult projects, and gives them the confidence they need to make and carry out important decisions.

NEEDS FOR ACHIEVEMENT, AFFILIATION, AND POWER Psychologist David McClelland has extensively researched the needs for achievement, affiliation, and power.[16] The need for achievement is the extent to which an individual has a strong desire to perform challenging tasks well and to meet personal standards for excellence. People with a high need for achievement often set clear goals for themselves and like to receive performance feedback. The need for affiliation is the extent to which an individual is concerned about establishing and maintaining good interpersonal relations, being liked, and having the people around him or her get along with one another. The need for power is the extent to which an individual desires to control or influence others.[17]

need for achievement The extent to which an individual has a strong desire to perform challenging tasks well and to meet personal standards for excellence.

Research suggests that high needs for achievement and for power are assets for first-line and middle managers and that a high need for power is especially important for upper-level managers.[18] One study found that U.S. presidents with a relatively high need for power tended to be especially effective during their terms of office.[19] A high need for affiliation may not always be desirable in managers because it might lead them to try too hard to be liked by others (including their employees) rather than doing all they can to ensure that performance is as high as it can and should be. Although most research on these needs has been done in the United States, some studies suggest that these findings may also apply to people in other countries such as India and New Zealand.[20]

need for affiliation The extent to which an individual is concerned about establishing and maintaining good interpersonal relations, being liked, and having other people get along.

Taken together, these desirable personality traits for managers—an internal locus of control, high self-esteem, and high needs for achievement and power—suggest that managers need to be take-charge people who not only believe their own actions are decisive in determining their own and their organizations' fates but also believe in their own capabilities. Such managers have a personal desire for accomplishment and influence over others.

need for power The extent to which an individual desires to control or influence others.

Additional Personality Assessments

In addition to the Big Five personality factors discussed earlier, several other personality assessments can be effective in helping managers and others identify positive and negative behaviors demonstrated by individuals in the workplace.

The Myers-Briggs Type Indicator (MBTI) is the most widely used personality instrument around the world—an estimated 3.5 million assessments are administered annually. Based on the theories of psychologist Carl Jung, MBTI measures a person's preferences for introversion versus extroversion, sensation versus intuition, thinking versus feeling, and judging versus perceiving. Various combinations of these four preferences result in 16 unique personality types, which can be helpful to individuals who seek to understand not only how they make decisions but also how they manage their time, problem solve, and deal with stress. In addition, recent research suggests that the four personality dimensions can be linked to various job-related components including job satisfaction, job performance, motivation, and promotion. More than 80% of *Fortune* 100 companies use this type of assessment to build stronger and healthier organizations.[21]

Another personality measure that can be useful to managers and others in an organization is the DiSC Inventory Profile, which many companies use to assess the personality characteristics of their employees. DiSC is based on the work of William Marston, a psychologist who attempted to characterize normal behavior patterns. A person taking the DiSC inventory receives a profile describing his or her behavioral style, preferred environment, and strategies for effectiveness. Behavior style is described in terms of **d**ominance, **i**nfluence, **s**teadiness, and **c**onscientiousness (DiSC).[22]

Information from these types of assessments help companies better understand their employees' strengths and weaknesses and how people perceive and process information—all factors that contribute to the success of an organization.

Values, Attitudes, and Moods and Emotions

What are managers striving to achieve? How do they think they should behave? What do they think about their jobs and organizations? And how do they actually feel at work? We can find some answers to these questions by exploring managers' values, attitudes, and moods.

Values, attitudes, and moods and emotions capture how managers experience their jobs as individuals. *Values* describe what managers are trying to achieve through work and how they think they should behave. *Attitudes* capture their thoughts and feelings about their specific jobs and organizations. *Moods and emotions* encompass how managers actually feel when they are managing. Although these three aspects of managers' work experience are highly personal, they also have important implications for understanding how managers behave, how they treat and respond to others, and how, through their efforts, they help contribute to organizational effectiveness through planning, leading, organizing, and controlling.

LO 2-2
Explain what values and attitudes are, and describe their impact on managerial action.

terminal value
A lifelong goal or objective that an individual seeks to achieve.

instrumental value A mode of conduct that an individual seeks to follow.

norms Unwritten, informal codes of conduct that prescribe how people should act in particular situations and that are considered important by most members of a group or an organization.

Values: Terminal and Instrumental

The two kinds of personal values are *terminal* and *instrumental.* A terminal value is a personal conviction about lifelong goals or objectives; an instrumental value is a personal conviction about desired modes of conduct or ways of behaving. Terminal values often lead to the formation of norms, which are unwritten, informal codes of conduct, such as behaving honestly or courteously, that prescribe how people should act in particular situations and that are considered important by most members of a group or an organization.

Milton Rokeach, a leading researcher in the area of human values, identified 18 terminal values and 18 instrumental values that describe each person's value system. By rank ordering the terminal values from "1 (most important as a guiding principle in one's life)" to "18 (least important as a guiding principle in one's life)" and then rank ordering the instrumental values from 1 to 18, people can give good pictures of their value systems—what they are striving to achieve in life and how they want to behave.[23]

Although Rokeach's research is more than 40 years old, some of his findings are still applicable today.[24] Several terminal values seem to be especially important for managers, such as a sense of accomplishment, equality, and self-esteem. For example, a manager who thinks a sense of accomplishment is particularly important

value systems
The terminal and instrumental values that are guiding principles in an individual's life.

might focus his or her energies on making a lasting contribution to an organization by developing a new product or by opening a new foreign subsidiary.

Several of Rokeach's instrumental values are also important modes of conduct for managers, such as being ambitious, open-minded, competent, responsible, and self-disciplined.[25] A manager who considers being honest to be of paramount importance may be a driving force for taking steps to ensure that all members of an organization behave ethically, as described in the following "Ethics in Action" feature.

All in all, managers' value systems signify what managers as individuals are trying to accomplish and become in their personal lives and at work. Thus, managers' value systems are fundamental guides to their behavior and efforts at planning, leading, organizing, and controlling.

Ethics in Action

Promoting Ethical Values in the Hotel Industry

Hotels aim to operate at a profit, but actions that give an immediate boost to earnings may not serve a hotel's best interests in the long run. For example, overbooking might ensure that every room is occupied on any given night, but if the hotel is turning away guests, the practice can hurt the hotel's reputation. The problem is worse if the company tries to keep costs low by staffing the front desk with untrained employees who lack the skills and authority to handle unhappy guests. Managers with an eye on long-term success value not just efficiency, but also integrity, honesty, and empathy.[26]

Another ethical norm for working in a hotel is to be respectful in handling interactions with customers and coworkers. This includes staying calm and pleasant in difficult situations, as well as respecting privacy and keeping promises.[27] Experiencing such behavior turns first-time guests into loyal customers, and employees who are treated respectfully are more apt to be dedicated workers.

Judi Brownell, a professor at Cornell University, explored the challenges managers face in promoting ethical values among hotel employees. She found that many managers value ethical behavior, but they need to teach the values because they have a diverse workforce of people with a wide range of values concerning desirable behavior at work.[28] This calls for personal feedback and face-to-face discussions of ethical situations that arise. Brownell also has investigated the practice of listening, which plays an important role in respectful treatment of others. Brownell identified particular skills a person can learn in order to listen well; examples include focus, comprehension, and

Managers in the hotel industry can encourage ethical values by having face-to-face discussions with employees about situations that may arise and providing personal feedback about how best to handle the situation. Gabriel Georgescu/Shutterstock

interpretation. But she found that training in these skills affects behavior only when people value listening.[29]

Scott Nadel, through his experience as a manager for DMC Hotels/Dhillon Management, has identified ways a manager can promote ethical values among hotel employees.[30] He values ethical behavior and makes it a part of hiring decisions and employee training. He connects ethical principles to employees' own lives and ambitions, so that employees don't merely know ethical standards but also embrace the value that ethics matter. To help employees work respectfully with others, he encourages patience and compassion, along with the use of deep-breathing techniques during difficult encounters. Nadel's experience convinced him that creating a climate of ethical conduct also creates a welcoming atmosphere for hotel customers. ●

Attitudes

attitude A collection of feelings and beliefs.

An attitude is a collection of feelings and beliefs. Like everyone else, managers have attitudes about their jobs and organizations, and these attitudes affect how they approach their jobs. Two of the most important attitudes in this context are job satisfaction and organizational commitment.

job satisfaction The collection of feelings and beliefs that managers have about their current jobs.

JOB SATISFACTION Job satisfaction is the collection of feelings and beliefs that managers have about their current jobs. Managers who have high levels of job satisfaction generally like their jobs, feel they are fairly treated, and believe their jobs have many desirable features or characteristics (such as interesting work, good pay and job security, autonomy, or nice coworkers). Figure 2.3 shows sample items from two scales that managers can use to measure job satisfaction. Levels of job satisfaction tend to increase as one moves up the hierarchy in an organization. Upper managers, in general, tend to be more satisfied with their jobs than entry-level employees. Managers' levels of job satisfaction can range from very low to very high.

One might think that in tough economic times, when unemployment is high and layoffs are prevalent, people who have jobs might be relatively satisfied with them. However, this is not necessarily the case. For example, in 2009 in the middle of a global recession, the U.S. unemployment rate was 10%, thousands of jobs were lost from the economy, and the underemployment rate (which includes people who have given up looking for jobs and those who are working part-time because they can't find a full-time position) was 17.3%. During these recessionary conditions, job satisfaction levels in the United States fell to record lows.[31]

The Conference Board has been tracking levels of U.S. job satisfaction since 1987, when 61.1% of workers surveyed indicated that they were satisfied with their jobs. In 2009 only 45% of workers surveyed indicated that they were satisfied with their jobs, an all-time low for the survey.[32] In 2018, more than 50% of U.S. workers indicated they were satisfied with their jobs according to the Conference Board's annual survey. This was the seventh year in a row that job satisfaction among U.S.

Figure 2.3

Sample Items from
Two Measures of Job
Satisfaction

Sample items from the Minnesota Satisfaction Questionnaire:

People respond to each of the items in the scale by checking whether they are:

[ ] Very dissatisfied   [ ] Satisfied
[ ] Dissatisfied   [ ] Very satisfied
[ ] Can't decide whether satisfied or not

On my present job, this is how I feel about . . .

_____ **1.** Being able to do things that don't go against my conscience.

_____ **2.** The way my job provides for steady employment.

_____ **3.** The chance to do things for other people.

_____ **4.** The chance to do something that makes use of my abilities.

_____ **5.** The way company policies are put into practice.

_____ **6.** My pay and the amount of work I do.

_____ **7.** The chances for advancement on this job.

_____ **8.** The freedom to use my own judgment.

_____ **9.** The working conditions.

_____ **10.** The way my coworkers get along with each other.

_____ **11.** The praise I get for doing a good job.

_____ **12.** The feeling of accomplishment I get from the job.

The Faces Scale

Workers select the face which best expresses how they feel about their job in general.

    11   10   9   8   7   6   5   4   3   2   1

Source: D. J. Weiss et al., *Manual for the Minnesota Satisfaction Questionnaire.* Copyrighted by the Vocational Psychology Research, University of Minnesota; copyright ©1975 by the American Psychological Association. Adapted by permission of R.B. Dunham and J.B. Brett.

organizational citizenship behaviors (OCBs) Behaviors that are not required of organizational members but that contribute to and are necessary for organizational efficiency, effectiveness, and competitive advantage.

workers improved. The increase in job satisfaction is largely due to a strong labor market in which layoff rates were at an all-time low. In addition to overall satisfaction, the survey also looks at other components that contribute to job satisfaction. The report indicates that more than 62% of workers are satisfied with their colleagues at work. On the downside, workers are least satisfied with their companies' performance review process (32%), bonus plans (27%), and promotion policies (26%).[33]

In general, it is desirable for managers to be satisfied with their jobs, for at least two reasons. First, satisfied managers may be more likely to go the extra mile for their organizations or perform organizational citizenship behaviors (OCBs)—behaviors that are not required of organizational members but that contribute to and are necessary for organizational efficiency, effectiveness, and competitive advantage.[34] Managers who are satisfied with their jobs are more likely to perform these "above and beyond the call of duty" behaviors, which can include putting in long hours when needed to coming up with truly creative ideas and overcoming obstacles to implement them (even when doing so is not part of the manager's job) or going out of one's way to help a coworker, subordinate, or superior (even when doing so entails considerable personal sacrifice).[35]

A second reason it is desirable for managers to be satisfied with their jobs is that satisfied managers may be less likely to quit. A manager who is highly satisfied may never even think about looking for another position; a dissatisfied manager may always be on the lookout for new opportunities. Turnover can hurt an organization because it causes the loss of the experience and knowledge that managers have gained about the company, industry, and business environment.[36]

A growing source of dissatisfaction for many lower-level and middle managers, as well as for nonmanagerial employees, is the threat of unemployment and increased workloads from organizational restructurings, including layoffs. Organizations that try to improve their efficiency through restructurings and layoffs often eliminate a sizable number of first-line and middle management positions. This decision obviously hurts the managers who are laid off, and it can reduce the job satisfaction levels of managers who remain. They might fear being the next to be let go. In addition, the workloads of remaining employees often increase dramatically as a result of restructuring, and this can contribute to dissatisfaction.

How managers and organizations handle layoffs is of paramount importance, not only for the employees let go but also for employees who survive the layoff and keep their jobs. Showing compassion and empathy for layoff victims, giving them as much advance notice as possible about the layoff, providing clear information about severance benefits, and helping them in their job search efforts are a few of the ways in which managers can humanely manage a layoff.[37]

organizational commitment The collection of feelings and beliefs that managers have about their organization as a whole.

ORGANIZATIONAL COMMITMENT Organizational commitment is the collection of feelings and beliefs that managers have about their organization as a whole.[38] Managers who are committed to their organizations believe in what their organizations are doing, are proud of what these organizations stand for, and feel a high degree of loyalty toward their organizations. Committed managers are more likely to go above and beyond the call of duty to help their company and are less likely to quit.[39] Organizational commitment can be especially strong when employees and managers truly believe in organizational values; it also leads to a strong organizational culture.

Organizational commitment is likely to help managers perform some of their figurehead and spokesperson roles (see Chapter 1). It is much easier for a manager to persuade others, both inside and outside the organization, of the merits of what the organization has done and is seeking to accomplish if the manager truly believes in and is committed to the organization.

Do managers in different countries have similar or different attitudes? Differences in the levels of job satisfaction and organizational commitment among managers in different countries are likely because these managers have different kinds of opportunities and rewards and because they face different economic, political, and sociocultural forces in their organizations' general environments. Levels of organizational commitment from one country to another may depend on the extent to which countries have legislation affecting firings and layoffs and the extent to which citizens of a country are geographically mobile.

Moods and Emotions

LO 2-3
Appreciate how moods and emotions influence all members of an organization.

mood A feeling or state of mind.

emotions Intense, relatively short-lived feelings.

Just as you sometimes are in a bad mood and at other times are in a good mood, so are managers. A mood is a feeling or state of mind. When people are in a positive mood, they feel excited, enthusiastic, active, or elated. When people are in a negative mood, they feel distressed, fearful, scornful, hostile, jittery, or nervous.[40] People who are high on negative affectivity are especially likely to experience negative moods. People's situations or circumstances also determine their moods; however, receiving a raise is likely to put most people in a good mood regardless of their personality traits. People who are high on negative affectivity are not always in a bad mood, and people who are low on extraversion still experience positive moods.[41]

Emotions are more intense feelings than moods, are often directly linked to whatever caused the emotion, and are more short-lived.[42] However, once whatever has triggered the emotion has been dealt with, the feelings may linger in the form of a less intense mood.[43] For example, a manager who gets very angry when an employee has engaged in an unethical behavior may find his anger decreasing in intensity once he has decided how to address the problem. Yet he continues to be in a bad mood the rest of the day, even though he is not directly thinking about the unfortunate incident.

Research has found that moods and emotions affect the behavior of managers and all members of an organization. For example, research suggests that the employees of managers who experience positive moods at work may perform at somewhat higher levels and be less likely to resign and leave the organization than the employees of managers who do not tend to be in a positive mood at work.[44] Other research suggests that under certain conditions creativity might be enhanced by positive moods, whereas under other conditions negative moods might push people to work harder to come up with truly creative ideas.[45] Recognizing that both mood states have the potential to contribute to creativity in different ways, recent research suggests that employees may be especially likely to be creative to the extent that they experience both mood states (at different times) on the job and to the extent that the work environment is supportive of creativity.[46]

Other research suggests that moods and emotions may play an important role in ethical decision making. For example, researchers at Princeton University found that when people are trying to solve difficult personal moral dilemmas, the parts of their brains that are responsible for emotions and moods are especially active.[47]

More generally, emotions and moods give managers and all employees important information and signals about what is going on in the workplace.[48] Positive emotions and moods signal that things are going well and thus can lead to more expansive, and even playful, thinking. Negative emotions and moods signal that there are problems in need of attention and areas for improvement. So when people are in negative moods, they tend to be more detail-oriented and focused on the facts at hand.[49] Some studies suggest that critical thinking and devil's advocacy may be promoted by a negative mood, and sometimes especially accurate judgments may be made by managers in negative moods.[50]

Emotions and moods affect the behavior of managers and other members of any organization. Katarzyna Bialasiewicz/123RF

Figure 2.4

A Measure of Positive and Negative Mood at Work

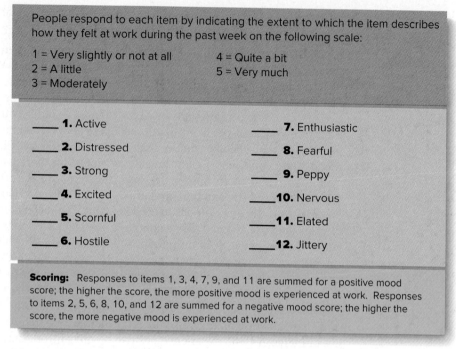

People respond to each item by indicating the extent to which the item describes how they felt at work during the past week on the following scale:

1 = Very slightly or not at all   4 = Quite a bit
2 = A little   5 = Very much
3 = Moderately

_____ **1.** Active   _____ **7.** Enthusiastic

_____ **2.** Distressed   _____ **8.** Fearful

_____ **3.** Strong   _____ **9.** Peppy

_____ **4.** Excited   _____**10.** Nervous

_____ **5.** Scornful   _____**11.** Elated

_____ **6.** Hostile   _____**12.** Jittery

Scoring: Responses to items 1, 3, 4, 7, 9, and 11 are summed for a positive mood score; the higher the score, the more positive mood is experienced at work. Responses to items 2, 5, 6, 8, 10, and 12 are summed for a negative mood score; the higher the score, the more negative mood is experienced at work.

Sources: A. P. Brief, M. J. Burke, J. M. George, B. Robinson, and J. Webster, "Should Negative Affectivity Remain an Unmeasured Variable in the Study of Job Stress?" *Journal of Applied Psychology* 72 (1988), 193–98; M. J. Burke, A. P. Brief, J. M. George, L. Roberson, and J. Webster, "Measuring Affect at Work: Confirmatory Analyses of Competing Mood Structures with Conceptual Linkage in Cortical Regulatory Systems," *Journal of Personality and Social Psychology* 57 (1989), 1091–102.

Managers and other members of an organization need to realize that how they feel affects how they treat others and how others respond to them, including their employees. For example, an employee may be more likely to approach a manager with a somewhat unusual but potentially useful idea if the employee thinks the manager is in a good mood. Likewise, when managers are in very bad moods, their employees might try to avoid them at all costs. Figure 2.4 is an example of a scale that can measure the extent to which a person experiences positive and negative moods at work.

Emotional Intelligence

In understanding the effects of managers' and all employees' moods and emotions, it is important to take into account their levels of emotional intelligence. Emotional intelligence is the ability to understand and manage one's own moods and emotions and the moods and emotions of other people.[51] Managers with a high level of emotional intelligence are more likely to understand how they are feeling and why, and they are more able to effectively manage their feelings. When managers are experiencing stressful feelings and emotions such as fear or anxiety, emotional intelligence lets them understand why and manage these feelings so they do not get in the way of effective decision making.[52]

Emotional intelligence also can help managers perform their important functions such as their interpersonal roles (figurehead, leader, and liaison).[53] Understanding how your employees feel, why they feel that way, and how to manage these feelings is central to developing strong interpersonal bonds with them.[54] For work that involves encounters with people from different cultures, this effort is more complex

LO 2-4

Describe the nature of emotional intelligence and its role in management.

emotional intelligence The ability to understand and manage one's own moods and emotions and the moods and emotions of other people.

but just as important, as described in the "Managing Globally" feature. More generally, emotional intelligence has the potential to contribute to effective leadership in multiple ways.[55]

For example, emotional intelligence helps managers understand and relate well to other people.[56] It also helps managers maintain their enthusiasm and confidence and energize employees to help the organization attain its goals.[57] Recent theorizing and research suggest that emotional intelligence may be especially important in awakening employee creativity.[58] Managers themselves are increasingly recognizing the importance of emotional intelligence. An example of a scale that measures emotional intelligence is provided in Figure 2.5.

Managing Globally

Emotional Intelligence across Borders

Although definitions of emotional intelligence are based on the work of U.S. researchers, the idea has attracted the interest of managers, psychologists, and educators around the world.[59] Thus, although managing and reading emotions is important globally, the specific emotional information tends to vary by culture.

For example, in the United States, people express enthusiasm openly; this is considered both normal and desirable. Hiring managers tend to look favorably on job candidates who express enthusiasm, and people who act excited about a new project or product are admired for being devoted to the company's vision. In other countries, this outward enthusiasm is seen as odd or even annoying or offensive. British businesspeople tend to tone down their emotions, and Chinese people might interpret enthusiastic behavior as showing off rather than fitting in.[60]

Smiling also differs by culture. In North America, people smile often to signal they are friendly and well intentioned. This looks odd in northern Europe, where smiles have the more limited purpose of signaling happiness. In Japan, a smile is more often a way to cover up embarrassment or unhappiness.[61]

Evidence suggests that differences such as these are less about what people feel (feelings are similar across cultures) and more about what they learn to express around others. Those differences in expression are tied to cultural values.[62] For example, British people value mature self-control, so they don't broadcast enthusiasm. In the United States, enthusiasm is more compatible with the high value placed on individual success and happiness. In much of Asia, group harmony is valued over individuality, so open celebration of personal success can seem inappropriate. Further, as people practice different culture-based behaviors, they tend to develop different areas of strength in emotional intelligence. Travis Bradberry, president of TalentSmart, compared test scores of U.S. and Chinese managers and found that the Chinese managers scored higher in aspects of emotional intelligence focused on the feelings of others.[63]

Recognizing that emotional expressions vary by culture can build emotional intelligence.[64] A good starting point is to recognize that unexpected behavior might indicate that emotions are being expressed differently. For example, if a U.S. manager notices that a Chinese employee seems unenthusiastic about a new project, the manager should check the assumption that absence of enthusiastic behavior signals lack of interest. Follow-up questions can be an effective way to find out. Also, whenever situations involve interacting with people from different cultures, it's worthwhile to learn each culture's emotional norms. ●

Figure 2.5

A Measure of
Emotional Intelligence

Please indicate the extent to which you agree or disagree with each of the following items using the 1–7 scale below:

1	2	3	4	5	6	7
Totally disagree	Disagree	Somewhat disagree	Neither agree nor disagree	Somewhat agree	Agree	Totally agree

_____ **1.** I have a good sense of why I have certain feelings most of the time.

_____ **2.** I always know my friends' emotions from their behavior.

_____ **3.** I always set goals for myself and then try my best to achieve them.

_____ **4.** I am able to control my temper so that I can handle difficulties rationally.

_____ **5.** I have a good understanding of my own emotions.

_____ **6.** I am a good observer of others' emotions.

_____ **7.** I always tell myself I am a competent person.

_____ **8.** I am quite capable of controlling my own emotions.

_____ **9.** I really understand what I feel.

_____ **10.** I am sensitive to the feelings and emotions of others.

_____ **11.** I am a self-motivating person.

_____ **12.** I can always calm down quickly when I am very angry.

_____ **13.** I always know whether or not I am happy.

_____ **14.** I have good understanding of the emotions of people around me.

_____ **15.** I would always encourage myself to try my best.

_____ **16.** I have good control of my own emotions.

Scoring: Self-emotions appraisal = sum of items 1, 5, 9, 13
Others-emotions appraisal = sum of items 2, 6, 10, 14
Use of emotion = sum of items 3, 7, 11, 15
Regulation of emotion = sum of items 4, 8, 12, 16

Sources: K. Law, C. Wong, and L. Song, "The Construct and Criterion Validity of Emotional Intelligence and Its Potential Utility for Management Studies," _Journal of Applied Psychology_ 89, no. 3 (June 2004), 496; C. S. Wong and K. S. Law, "The Effects of Leader and Follower Emotional Intelligence on Performance and Attitude: An Exploratory Study," _Leadership Quarterly_ 13 (2002), 243–74.

Organizational Culture

Personality is a way of understanding why all managers and employees, as individuals, characteristically think and behave in different ways. However, when people belong to the same organization, they tend to share certain beliefs and values that lead them to act in similar ways.[65] Organizational culture comprises the shared set of beliefs, expectations, values, norms, and work routines that influence how members of an organization relate to one another and work together to achieve organizational goals. In

LO 2-5
Define organizational culture, and explain how managers both create and are influenced by organizational culture.

organizational culture The shared set of beliefs, expectations, values, norms, and work routines that influence how individuals, groups, and teams interact with one another and cooperate to achieve organizational goals.

essence, organizational culture reflects the distinctive ways in which organizational members perform their jobs and relate to others inside and outside the organization. It may, for example, be how customers in a particular hotel chain are treated from the time they are greeted at check-in until they leave; or it may be the shared work routines that research teams use to guide new product development. When organizational members share an intense commitment to cultural values, beliefs, and routines and use them to achieve their goals, a *strong* organizational culture exists.[66] When organizational members are not strongly committed to a shared system of values, beliefs, and routines, organizational culture is weak.

The stronger the culture of an organization, the more one can think about it as being the "personality" of an organization because it influences the way its members behave.[67] Organizations that possess strong cultures may differ on a wide variety of dimensions that determine how their members behave toward one another and perform their jobs. For example, organizations differ in how members relate to each other (formally or informally), how important decisions are made (top-down or bottom-up), willingness to change (flexible or unyielding), innovation (creative or predictable), and playfulness (serious or serendipitous). In an innovative design firm like IDEO in Silicon Valley, employees are encouraged to adopt a playful attitude toward their work, look outside the organization to find inspiration, and adopt a flexible approach toward product design that uses multiple perspectives.[68] IDEO's culture is vastly different from that of companies such as Citibank and ExxonMobil, in which employees treat each other in a more formal or deferential way, employees are expected to adopt a serious approach to their work, and decision making is constrained by the hierarchy of authority.

IDEO employees brainstorming—informal communication, casual attire, and flexibility are all hallmarks of this successful organization. ©IDEO

Managers and Organizational Culture

While all members of an organization can contribute to developing and maintaining organizational culture, managers play a particularly important part in influencing organizational culture[69] because of their multiple and important roles (see Chapter 1). How managers create culture is most vividly evident in start-ups of new companies. Entrepreneurs who start their own companies are typically also the start-ups' top managers until the companies grow and become profitable. Often referred to as the firms' founders, these managers literally create their organizations' cultures.

The founders' personal characteristics play an important role in the creation of organizational culture. Benjamin Schneider, a well-known management researcher, developed a model that helps explain the role that founders' personal characteristics play in determining organizational culture.[70] His model, called the attraction–selection–attrition (ASA) framework, posits that when founders hire employees for their new ventures, they tend to be attracted to and choose employees whose personalities are similar to their own.[71] These similar employees are more likely to stay with the organization. Although employees who are dissimilar in personality might be hired, they are more likely to leave the organization over time. As a result of these attraction, selection, and attrition processes, people in the organization tend to have similar personalities, and the typical or dominant personality profile of organizational members determines and shapes organizational culture.[72]

For example, when David Kelley became interested in engineering and product design challenges in the late 1970s, he realized that who he was as a person meant he would not be happy working in a typical corporate environment. Kelley is high on openness to experience, driven to go where his interests take him, and not content to follow others' directives. Kelley recognized that he needed to start his own business, and with the help of other Stanford-schooled engineers and design experts, IDEO was born.[73]

From the start, IDEO's culture has embodied Kelley's spirited, freewheeling approach to work and design—from colorful and informal workspaces to an emphasis on networking and communicating with as many people as possible to understand a design problem. No project or problem is too big or too small for IDEO; the company designed the Apple Lisa computer and mouse (the precursor of the Mac), the Palm, and more recently PillPack, a prescription home-delivery system for consumers' medications.[74] Kelley hates rules, job titles, big corner offices, and all the other trappings of large, traditional organizations that stifle creativity. Employees who are attracted to, are selected by, and remain with IDEO value creativity and innovation and embrace one of IDEO's mottos: "Everyone is creative."[75]

Although ASA processes are most evident in small firms such as IDEO, they also can operate in large companies.[76] According to the ASA model, this is a naturally occurring phenomenon to the extent that managers and new hires are free to make the kinds of choices the model specifies. However, while people tend to get along well with others who are similar to themselves, too much similarity in an organization can impair organizational effectiveness. That is, similar people tend to view conditions and events in similar ways and thus can be resistant to change. Moreover, organizations benefit from a diversity of perspectives rather than similarity in perspectives (see Chapter 3). At IDEO, Kelley recognized early on how important it is to take advantage of the diverse talents and perspectives that people with different personalities, backgrounds, experiences, and education can bring to a design team. Hence, IDEO's design teams include not only engineers but others who might have

attraction–selection–attrition (ASA) framework
A model that explains how personality may influence organizational culture.

a unique insight into a problem, such as anthropologists, communications experts, doctors, and users of a product. When new employees are hired at IDEO, they meet many employees who have different backgrounds and characteristics; the focus is not on hiring someone who will fit in but, rather, on hiring someone who has something to offer and can "wow" different kinds of people with his or her insights.[77]

In addition to personality, other personal characteristics of managers shape organizational culture; these include managers' values, attitudes, moods and emotions, and emotional intelligence.[78] For example, both terminal and instrumental values of managers play a role in determining organizational culture. Managers who highly value freedom and equality, for example, might be likely to stress the importance of autonomy and empowerment in their organizations, as well as fair treatment for all. As another example, managers who highly value being helpful and forgiving might not only tolerate mistakes but also emphasize the importance of organizational members' being kind and helpful to one another.

Managers who are satisfied with their jobs, are committed to their organizations, and experience positive moods and emotions might also encourage these attitudes and feelings in others. The result would be an organizational culture emphasizing positive attitudes and feelings. Research suggests that attitudes like job satisfaction and organizational commitment can be affected by the influence of others. Managers are in a particularly strong position to engage in social influence, given their multiple roles. Moreover, research suggests that moods and emotions can be contagious and that spending time with people who are excited and enthusiastic can increase one's own levels of excitement and enthusiasm.

The Role of Values and Norms in Organizational Culture

Shared terminal and instrumental values play a particularly important role in organizational culture. *Terminal values* signify what an organization and its employees are trying to accomplish, and *instrumental values* guide how the organization and its members achieve organizational goals. In addition to values, shared norms also are a key aspect of organizational culture. Recall that norms are unwritten, informal rules or guidelines that prescribe appropriate behavior in particular situations. For example, norms at IDEO include not being critical of others' ideas, coming up with multiple ideas before settling on one, and developing prototypes of new products.[79]

Managers determine and shape organizational culture through the kinds of values and norms they promote in an organization. Some managers, like David Kelley of IDEO, cultivate values and norms that encourage risk taking, creative responses to problems and opportunities, experimentation, tolerance of failure in order to succeed, and autonomy.[80] Top managers at organizations such as Microsoft and Google encourage employees to adopt such values to support their commitment to innovation as a source of competitive advantage.

Other managers, however, might cultivate values and norms that tell employees they should be conservative and cautious in their dealings with others and should consult their superiors before making important decisions or any changes to the status quo. Accountability for actions and decisions is stressed, and detailed records are kept to ensure that policies and procedures are followed. In settings where caution is needed—nuclear power stations, oil refineries, chemical plants, financial institutions, insurance companies—a conservative, cautious approach to making decisions might be appropriate. In a nuclear power plant, for example, the catastrophic consequences of a mistake make a high level of supervision vital. Similarly, in a bank or mutual fund company, the risk of losing investors' money makes a cautious approach to investing appropriate.

Managers of different kinds of organizations deliberately cultivate and develop the organizational values and norms that are best suited to their task and general environments, strategy, or technology. Organizational culture is maintained and transmitted to organizational members through the values of the founder, the process of socialization, ceremonies and rites, and stories and language (see Figure 2.6).

VALUES OF THE FOUNDER From the ASA model just discussed, it is clear that founders of an organization can have profound and long-lasting effects on organizational culture. Founders' values inspire the founders to start their own companies and, in turn, drive the nature of these new companies and their defining characteristics. Thus, an organization's founder and his or her terminal and instrumental values have a substantial influence on the values, norms, and standards of behavior that develop over time within the organization.[81] Founders set the scene for the way cultural values and norms develop because their own values guide the building of the company, and they hire other managers and employees who they believe will share these values and help the organization attain them. Moreover, new managers quickly learn from the founder what values and norms are appropriate in the organization and thus what is desired of them. Employees imitate the style of the founder and, in turn, transmit their values and norms to their employees. Gradually, over time, the founder's values and norms permeate the organization.[82]

A founder who requires a great display of respect from employees and insists on proprieties, such as formal job titles and formal dress, encourages managers to act in this way toward their employees. Often a founder's personal values affect an organization's competitive advantage. For example, McDonald's founder Ray Kroc insisted from the beginning on high standards of customer service and cleanliness at McDonald's restaurants; these became core sources of McDonald's competitive advantage. Similarly, Bill Gates, the cofounder of Microsoft, pioneered certain cultural values in Microsoft. Employees are expected to be creative and to work hard, but they are encouraged to dress informally and to personalize their offices. Gates also established a host of company events such as cookouts, picnics, and sports events to emphasize to employees the importance of being both an individual and a team player.

SOCIALIZATION Over time, organizational members learn from each other which values are important in an organization and the norms that specify appropriate

Figure 2.6

Factors That Maintain and Transmit Organizational Culture

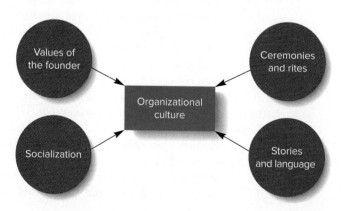

and inappropriate behaviors. Eventually, organizational members behave in accordance with the organization's values and norms—often without realizing they are doing so.

organizational socialization The process by which newcomers learn an organization's values and norms and acquire the work behaviors necessary to perform jobs effectively.

Organizational socialization is the process by which newcomers learn an organization's values and norms and acquire the work behaviors necessary to perform jobs effectively.[83] As a result of their socialization experiences, organizational members internalize an organization's values and norms and behave in accordance with them, not only because they think they have to but because they think these values and norms describe the right and proper way to behave.[84]

At Texas A&M University, for example, all new students are encouraged to go to "Fish Camp" to learn how to be an "Aggie" (the traditional nickname of students at the university). They learn about the ceremonies that have developed over time to commemorate significant events or people in A&M's history. In addition, they learn how to behave at football games and in class and what it means to be an Aggie. As a result of this highly organized socialization program, by the time new students arrive on campus and start their first semester, they have been socialized into what a Texas A&M student is supposed to do, and they have relatively few problems adjusting to the college environment.[85]

Most organizations have some kind of socialization program to help new employees learn the ropes—the values, norms, and culture of the organization. The military, for example, is well known for the rigorous socialization process it uses to turn raw recruits into trained soldiers. Organizations such as The Walt Disney Company also put new recruits through a rigorous training program to teach them to perform well in their jobs and play their parts in helping visitors have fun in the company's theme parks. New recruits at Disney are called "cast members" and attend Disney University to learn the Disney culture and their parts in it. Disney's culture emphasizes the values of safety, courtesy, entertainment, and efficiency, and these values are brought to life for newcomers at Disney University. Newcomers also learn about the attraction area they will be joining (such as Adventureland or Fantasyland) at Disney University and then receive on-the-job socialization in the area itself from experienced cast members.[86] Through organizational socialization, founders and managers of an organization transmit to employees the cultural values and norms that shape the behavior of organizational members. Thus, the values and norms of founder Walt Disney live on today as newcomers are socialized into the Disney way.

CEREMONIES AND RITES Another way in which managers can create or influence organizational culture is by developing organizational ceremonies and rites—formal events that recognize incidents of importance to the organization as a whole and to specific employees.[87] The most common rites that organizations use to transmit cultural norms and values to their members are rites of passage, of integration, and of enhancement (see Table 2.1).[88]

Table 2.1

Organizational Rites

Type of Rite	Example of Rite	Purpose of Rite
Rite of passage	Induction and basic training	Learn and internalize norms and values
Rite of integration	Office holiday party	Build common norms and values
Rite of enhancement	Presentation of annual awards	Motivate commitment to norms and values

Rites of passage determine how individuals enter, advance within, and leave the organization. The socialization programs developed by military organizations (such as the U.S. Army) or by large accountancy and law firms are rites of passage. Likewise, the ways in which an organization prepares people for promotion or retirement are rites of passage.

Rites of integration, such as shared announcements of organizational successes, office parties, and company cookouts, build and reinforce common bonds among organizational members. IDEO uses many rites of integration to make its employees feel connected to one another and special. In addition to having wild "end-of-year" celebratory bashes, groups of IDEO employees periodically take time off to go to a sporting event, movie, or meal or sometimes go on a long bike ride or for a sail. These kinds of shared activities not only reinforce IDEO's culture but also can be a source of inspiration on the job (for example, IDEO has been involved in making movies such as *The Abyss* and *Free Willy*). One 35-member design studio at IDEO led by Dennis Boyle has bimonthly lunch fests with no set agenda—anything goes. While enjoying great food, jokes, and camaraderie, studio members often end up sharing ideas for their latest great products, and the freely flowing conversation that results often leads to creative insights.[89]

A company's annual meeting also may be used as a ritual of integration, offering an opportunity to communicate organizational values to managers, other employees, and shareholders.[90] Walmart, for example, makes its annual stockholders' meeting an extravagant ceremony that celebrates the company's success. The company often flies thousands of its highest-performing employees to its annual meeting at its Bentonville, Arkansas, headquarters for a huge weekend entertainment festival complete with star musical performances. Walmart believes that rewarding its supporters with entertainment reinforces the company's high-performance values and culture. The proceedings are shown live over closed-circuit television in all Walmart stores so all employees can join in the rites celebrating the company's achievements.[91]

Rites of enhancement, such as awards dinners, press releases, and employee promotions, let organizations publicly recognize and reward employees' contributions and thus strengthen their commitment to organizational values. By bonding members within the organization, rites of enhancement reinforce an organization's values and norms.

STORIES AND LANGUAGE *Stories and language* also communicate organizational culture. Stories (whether fact or fiction) about organizational heroes and villains and their actions provide important clues about values and norms. Such stories can reveal the kinds of behaviors that are valued by the organization and the kinds of practices that are frowned upon.[92] At the heart of the rich culture at McDonald's are hundreds of stories that organizational members tell about founder Ray Kroc. Most of these stories focus on how Kroc established the strict operating values and norms that are at the heart of McDonald's culture. Kroc was dedicated to achieving perfection in McDonald's quality, service, cleanliness, and value for money (QSC&V), and these four central values permeate McDonald's culture. For example, an often retold story describes what happened when Kroc and a group of managers from the Houston region were touring various restaurants. One of the restaurants was having a bad day operationally. Kroc was incensed about the long lines of customers, and he was furious when he realized that the products

Stories about McDonald's founder, Ray Kroc (pictured here), permeate the company's organizational culture. Bettmann/Getty Images

customers were receiving that day were not up to his high standards. To address the problem, he jumped up and stood on the front counter to get the attention of all customers and operating crew personnel. He introduced himself, apologized for the long wait and cold food, and told the customers they could have freshly cooked food or their money back—whichever they wanted. As a result, the customers left happy; and when Kroc checked on the restaurant later, he found that his message had gotten through to its managers and crew—performance had improved. Other stories describe Kroc scrubbing dirty toilets and picking up litter inside or outside a restaurant. These and similar stories are spread around the organization by McDonald's employees. They are the stories that have helped establish Kroc as McDonald's "hero."

Because spoken language is a principal medium of communication in organizations, the characteristic slang or jargon—that is, organization-specific words or phrases—that people use to frame and describe events provides important clues about norms and values. "McLanguage," for example, is prevalent at all levels of McDonald's. A McDonald's employee described as having "ketchup in his or her blood" is someone who is truly dedicated to the McDonald's way—someone who has been completely socialized to its culture. McDonald's has an extensive training program that teaches new employees "McDonald's speak," and new employees are welcomed into the family with a formal orientation that illustrates Kroc's dedication to QSC&V.

The concept of organizational language encompasses not only spoken language but how people dress, the offices they occupy, the cars they drive, and the degree of formality they use when they address one another. For example, casual dress reflects and reinforces IDEO's entrepreneurial culture and values. Formal business attire supports the conservative culture found in many banks, which emphasizes the importance of conforming to organizational norms such as respect for authority and staying within one's prescribed role. When employees speak and understand the language of their organization's culture, they know how to behave in the organization and what is expected of them.

At IDEO, language, dress, the physical work environment, and extreme informality all underscore a culture that is adventuresome, playful, risk-taking, egalitarian, and innovative. For example, when designing products at IDEO, employees refer to taking the consumers' perspective as "being left-handed." Employees dress in T-shirts and jeans, the physical work environment continually evolves and changes depending on how employees wish to personalize their workspace, no one "owns" a fancy office with a window, and rules are almost nonexistent.[93]

Culture and Managerial Action

While founders and managers play a critical role in developing, maintaining, and communicating organizational culture, the same culture shapes and controls the behavior of all employees, including managers themselves. For example, culture influences how managers perform their four main functions: planning, organizing, leading, and controlling. As we consider these functions, we continue to distinguish between top managers who create organizational values and norms that encourage creative, innovative behavior and top managers who encourage a conservative, cautious approach by their employees. We noted earlier that both kinds of values and norms can be appropriate depending on the situation and type of organization.

PLANNING Top managers in an organization with an innovative culture are likely to encourage lower-level managers to participate in the planning process and develop a flexible approach to planning. They are likely to be willing to listen to new ideas and to take risks involving the development of new products. In contrast, top managers in an organization with conservative values are likely to emphasize formal top-down planning. Suggestions from lower-level managers are likely to be subjected to a formal review process, which can significantly slow decision making. Although this deliberate approach may improve the quality of decision making in a nuclear power plant, it can have unintended consequences. In the past, at conservative IBM, the planning process became so formalized that managers spent most of their time assembling complex slide shows and overheads to defend their current positions rather than thinking about what they should do to keep IBM abreast of the changes taking place in the computer industry. When former CEO Lou Gerstner took over, he used every means at his disposal to abolish this culture, even building a brand-new campus-style headquarters to change managers' mind-sets. IBM's culture underwent further changes initiated by its next CEO, Samuel Palmisano. IBM's current CEO, Ginni Rometty, has changed the company's culture in her own way, including bringing back thousands of remote workers to IBM regional offices in an effort to improve collaboration and accelerate the pace of work and innovation at the global tech giant. In addition, Rometty recently announced IBM's acquisition of software company Red Hat, the world's leading provider of open-source cloud software.[94]

ORGANIZING What kinds of organizing will managers in innovative and in conservative cultures encourage? Valuing creativity, managers in innovative cultures are likely to try to create an organic structure—one that is flat, with few levels in the hierarchy, and one in which authority is decentralized so employees are encouraged to work together to solve ongoing problems. A product team structure may be suitable for an organization with an innovative culture. In contrast, managers in a conservative culture are likely to create a well-defined hierarchy of authority and establish clear reporting relationships so employees know exactly whom to report to and how to react to any problems that arise.

LEADING In an innovative culture, managers are likely to lead by example, encouraging employees to take risks and experiment. They are supportive regardless of whether employees succeed or fail. In contrast, managers in a conservative culture are likely to use management by objectives and to constantly monitor employees' progress toward goals, overseeing their every move. We examine leadership in detail in Chapter 10, when we consider the leadership styles that managers can adopt to influence and shape employee behavior.

CONTROLLING The ways in which managers evaluate, and take actions to improve, performance differ depending on whether the organizational culture emphasizes formality and caution or innovation and change. Managers who want to encourage risk taking, creativity, and innovation recognize that there are multiple potential paths to success and that failure must be accepted for creativity to thrive. Thus, they are less concerned about employees' performing their jobs in a specific, predetermined manner and in strict adherence to preset goals and more concerned about employees' being flexible and taking the initiative to come up with ideas for improving performance. Managers in innovative cultures are also more concerned about long-term performance than short-term targets because they recognize that real innovation entails much uncertainty that necessitates flexibility. In contrast, managers in cultures that emphasize caution and maintenance of the status quo often set specific, difficult goals for employees, frequently monitor progress toward these goals, and develop a clear set of rules that employees are expected to adhere to.

The values and norms of an organization's culture strongly affect the way managers perform their management functions. The extent to which managers buy into the values and norms of their organization shapes their view of the world and their actions and decisions in particular circumstances. In turn, the actions that managers take can have an impact on the performance of the organization. Thus, organizational culture, managerial action, and organizational performance are all linked together.

While our earlier example of IDEO illustrates how organizational culture can give rise to managerial actions that ultimately benefit the organization, this is not always the case. The cultures of some organizations become dysfunctional, encouraging managerial actions that harm the organization and discouraging actions that might improve performance. Corporate scandals at large companies such as Enron, Tyco, and WorldCom show how damaging a dysfunctional culture can be to an organization and its members. For example, Enron's arrogant, "success at all costs" culture led to fraudulent behavior on the part of its top managers.[95] Unfortunately, hundreds of Enron employees paid a heavy price for the unethical behavior of these top managers and the dysfunctional organizational culture. Not only did these employees lose their jobs, but many also lost their life savings in Enron stock and pension funds, which became worth just a fraction of their value before the wrongdoing at Enron came to light. We discuss ethics in depth in the next chapter.

Summary and Review

ENDURING CHARACTERISTICS: PERSONALITY TRAITS Personality traits are enduring tendencies to feel, think, and act in certain ways. The Big Five general traits are extraversion, negative affectivity, agreeableness, conscientiousness, and openness to experience. Other personality traits that affect managerial behavior are locus of control, self-esteem, and the needs for achievement, affiliation, and power. Several other personality assessments can be effective in helping managers and individuals identify positive and negative behaviors in themselves and others. These include the Myers-Briggs Type Indicator (MBTI) and the DiSC Inventory Profile. [LO 2-1]

VALUES, ATTITUDES, AND MOODS AND EMOTIONS A terminal value is a personal conviction about lifelong goals or objectives; an instrumental value is a personal conviction about modes of conduct. Terminal and instrumental values have an impact on what managers try to achieve in their organizations and the kinds of behaviors they engage in. An attitude is a collection of feelings and beliefs. Two attitudes important for understanding managerial behaviors include job satisfaction (the collection of feelings and beliefs that managers have about their jobs) and organizational commitment (the collection of feelings and beliefs that managers have about their organizations). A mood is a feeling or state of mind; emotions are intense feelings that are short-lived and directly linked to their causes. Managers' moods and emotions, or how they feel at work on a day-to-day basis, have the potential to impact not only their own behavior and effectiveness but also those of their employees. Emotional intelligence is the ability to understand and manage one's own and other people's moods and emotions. [LO 2-2, 2-3, 2-4]

ORGANIZATIONAL CULTURE Organizational culture is the shared set of beliefs, expectations, values, norms, and work routines that influence how members of an organization relate to one another and work together to achieve organizational goals. Founders of new organizations and managers play an important role in creating and maintaining organizational culture. Organizational socialization is the process by which newcomers learn an organization's values and norms and acquire the work behaviors necessary to perform jobs effectively. [LO 2-5]

Management *in Action*

Topics for Discussion and Action

Discussion

1. Discuss why managers who have different types of personalities can be equally effective and successful. [LO 2-1]

2. Can managers be too satisfied with their jobs? Can they be too committed to their organizations? Why or why not? [LO 2-2]

3. Assume that you are a manager of a restaurant. Describe what it is like to work for you when you are in a negative mood. [LO 2-3]

4. Why might managers be disadvantaged by low levels of emotional intelligence? [LO 2-4]

Action

5. Interview a manager in a local organization. Ask the manager to describe situations in which he or she is especially likely to act in accordance with his or her values. Ask the manager to describe situations in which he or she is less likely to act in accordance with his or her values. [LO 2-2]

6. Watch a popular television show, and as you watch it, try to determine the emotional intelligence levels of the characters the actors in the show portray. Rank the characters from highest to lowest in terms of emotional intelligence. As you watched

the show, what factors influenced your assessments of emotional intelligence levels? [LO 2-4]

7. Go to an upscale clothing store in your neighborhood, and go to a clothing store that is definitely not upscale. Observe the behavior of employees in each store as well as the store's environment. In what ways are the organizational cultures in each store similar? In what ways are they different? [LO 2-5]

Building Management Skills

Diagnosing Culture [LO 2-5]

Think about the culture of the last organization you worked for, your current university, or another organization or club to which you belong. Then answer the following questions:

1. What values are emphasized in this culture?
2. What norms do members of this organization follow?
3. Who seems to have played an important role in creating the culture?
4. In what ways is the organizational culture communicated to organizational members?

Managing Ethically [LO 2-1, 2-2]

Some organizations rely on personality and interest inventories to screen potential employees. Other organizations attempt to screen employees by using paper-and-pencil honesty tests.

Questions

1. Either individually or in a group, think about the ethical implications of using personality and interest inventories to screen potential employees. How might this practice be unfair to potential applicants? How might organizational members who are in charge of hiring misuse it?

2. Because of measurement error and validity problems, some relatively trustworthy people may "fail" an honesty test given by an employer. What are the ethical implications of trustworthy people "failing" honesty tests, and what obligations do you think employers should have when relying on honesty tests for screening?

Small Group Breakout Exercise [LO 2-2, 2-3, 2-4, 2-5]

Making Difficult Decisions in Hard Times

Form groups of three or four people, and appoint one member as the spokesperson who will communicate your findings to the whole class when called on by the instructor. Then discuss the following scenario:

You are on the top management team of a medium-size company that manufactures cardboard boxes, containers, and other packaging materials. Your company is facing increasing levels of competition for major corporate customer accounts, and profits have declined significantly. You have tried everything you can to cut costs and remain competitive, with the exception of laying off employees. Your company has had a no-layoff policy for the past 20 years, and you believe it is an important part of the organization's culture. However, you are experiencing mounting pressure to increase your firm's performance, and your no-layoff policy has been questioned by shareholders. Even though you haven't decided whether to lay off employees and thus break with a 20-year tradition for your company, rumors are rampant in your organization that something is afoot, and employees are worried. You are meeting today to address this problem.

1. Develop a list of options and potential courses of action to address the heightened competition and decline in profitability that your company has been experiencing.

2. Choose your preferred course of action, and justify why you will take this route.

3. Describe how you will communicate your decision to employees.

4. If your preferred option involves a layoff, justify why. If it doesn't involve a layoff, explain why.

Be the Manager [LO 2-1, 2-2, 2-3, 2-4, 2-5]

You have recently been hired as the vice president for human resources in an advertising agency. One problem that has been brought to your attention is the fact that the creative departments at the agency have dysfunctionally high levels of conflict. You have spoken with members of each of these departments, and in each one it seems that a few members of the department are creating all the problems. All these individuals are valued contributors who have many creative ad campaigns to their credit. The high levels of conflict are creating problems in the departments, and negative moods and emotions are much more prevalent than positive feelings. What are you going to do to both retain valued employees and alleviate the excessive conflict and negative feelings in these departments?

Case in the News [LO 2-1, 2-2, 2-5]

Google Searches for a Way to Maintain a Strong Culture

As an employer, Google enjoys the advantage of being widely considered a great place to work. The company carefully screens job applicants to select people who are extremely intelligent but also humble about what they don't know. It gives them big problems to solve and a significant mission: providing Google's users with access to information, which is potentially the world's most valuable resource. Google employees are excited about interacting with smart coworkers and collaborating on difficult, significant projects. They are encouraged to think like entrepreneurs, which entails taking thoughtful risks to build the business.

Employees also are expected to follow a code of conduct that includes participating in a "supportive work environment, where employees have the opportunity to reach their fullest potential." This includes employment decisions based on merit and skills. It also means creating a workplace where people can thrive free of harassment, bullying, and any level of violence. And employees who meet the requirements of the company's Dog Policy can even bring their canine companions to work.

The values that Google advocates are consistent with being an innovative, high-performance company. Google employees are expected to constantly learn and improve. One way they do this is by communicating: asking questions, arguing viewpoints, and challenging ideas. Google enables this by inviting employees to provide questions for executives to answer at weekly meetings. Employees also can set up internal online discussion groups on topics of their choice. Topics can be as whimsical as juggling, but employees also sign up for groups like Activists at Google (who organized a rally protesting policies of President Trump) and Militia at Google (who have advocated for permitting employees to bring guns to work).

At best, Google's values contribute to a stimulating environment much like a university at which students engage in passionate debates. Google has investigated the factors associated with its teams' performance and found that "psychological safety" is important for employee retention, creative decision making, and effective team performance. Psychological safety means team members feel they can try out their ideas without feeling embarrassed or insecure.

But this ideal is realized only when employees' freewheeling self-expression is grounded in mutual respect. In its early years, the company was smaller, and coworkers debated with people they knew well and worked with on shared projects and goals. As the company has grown to 80,000 employees, discussions are more often deteriorating into the kinds of name-calling, ridicule, and intimidation that take place in the wider world of social media.

As unwelcome opinions, rumors, and hostile comments circulate, employees are complaining, and Google's managers—who are used to giving employees wide latitude—are struggling to police the behavior. For example, a white male engineer shared a memo saying that the company's efforts to promote diversity ignore that men are better suited than women to some high-tech jobs. Other employees complained that his view created a hostile work environment for women. The employee was relieved of his employment and later sued on the grounds that the company was discriminating against conservative white men. At the same time, some female employees observed pay data and filed a suit alleging pay discrimination. Yet another lawsuit by a male engineer says he was fired for advocating diversity. The company found that some of his posts on mailing lists and message boards crossed a line; the engineer says he was merely responding to attacks by others. He and others maintain that some employees are baiting them with offensive content, waiting for them to get angry and then reporting them to human resources. Google's investigation of these problems included a survey question to employees; results indicate that employees see a decline in respect and an increase in rudeness in internal communications.

The company's response to this culture of conflict is to insist on some behavioral standards while continuing to maintain that open debate is possible. Employees are free to air their views but not to engage in bullying, harassment, or discrimination. The company provided employees with guidelines to help them identify behavior that crosses a line, as well as to help them communicate respectfully. Employees are encouraged to focus on understanding others and keeping an open mind.

Questions for Discussion

1. Review the personality traits described in this chapter and identify which ones you think would make it easiest for a person to succeed at Google. Explain your choices.

2. What are some values that Google tries to encourage? What challenges have arisen with putting these values into practice?

3. Do you think you would thrive in Google's organizational culture? Why or why not? If you could change its culture, what changes would you make?

Sources: Alphabet, "Google Code of Conduct," https://abc.xyz, accessed December 3, 2018; M. Sun and E. Minaya, "Google Workers' Walkout Signals Crisis of Faith in Company," *The Wall Street Journal*, www.wsj.com, November 2, 2018, www.wsj.com; J. Wingard, "Conflict as a Catalyst for Corporate Success," *Forbes*, www.forbes.com, September 28, 2018; K. Conger, "Google Rolls Out New Internal Rules in an Effort to Fix Its Culture," *Gizmodo*, https://gizmodo.com, June 27, 2018; K. Grind and D. MacMillan, "Google vs. Google: How Nonstop Political Arguments Rule Its Workplace," *The Wall Street Journal*, www.wsj.com, May 1, 2018; K. Conger, "Google Isn't Listening, So Its Employees Are Suing," *Gizmodo*, https://gizmodo.com, March 26, 2018; Forbes Technology Council, "13 Reasons Google Deserves Its 'Best Company Culture' Award," *Forbes*, www.forbes.com, February 8, 2018; J. Nicas, "Two Suits Catch Google in Middle of Gender Debate," *The Wall Street Journal*, www.wsj.com, January 8, 2018.

Endnotes

1. Carnival Corporation, "Our Brands," http://phx.corporate-ir.net, accessed February 19, 2019.

2. M. Sorrells, "In the Big Chair: Arnold Donald of Carnival Corporation," *PhocusWire*, www.phocuswire.com, January 9, 2019; V. Fuhrmans, "Carnival's CEO on Steering a Turnaround: Listen to Your Employees," *The Wall Street Journal*, www.wsj.com, June 13, 2018.

3. M. Juliano, "Cruise Control: How Arnold Donald Turned Carnival Around," *TradeWinds*, www.tradewindsnews.com, September 13, 2018.

4. R. Umoh, "The One Sentence That Took Carnival's CEO from Poverty to Running a $48 Billion Company," *Make It* (CNBC), www.cnbc.com, May 24, 2018; K. Gilchrist,

"Carnival's CEO Overcame a Common Career Dilemma to Run a $48 Billion Company," *Make It* (CNBC), www.cnbc.com, October 24, 2018; C. Gallo, "The Nine Words That Took This CEO from Poverty to the Top of a $48B Company," *Forbes*, www.forbes.com, May 13, 2018.

5. Sorrells, "In the Big Chair."

6. S. J. Young, "10 Key Takeaways from Arnold Donald's Cruise360 Keynote," *Travel Agent Central*, www.travelagentcentral.com, April 23, 2018.

7. Sorrells, "In the Big Chair"; Fuhrmans, "Carnival's CEO on Steering a Turnaround."

8. E. Larson, "Here's How Your Personality Type Affects Your Decision Making at Work,"

Forbes, www.forbes.com, accessed November 8, 2018.

9. J. M. George, "Personality, Five-Factor Model," in S. Clegg and J. R. Bailey, eds., *International Encyclopedia of Organization Studies* (Thousand Oaks, CA: Sage, 2007); J. M. Digman, "Personality Structure: Emergence of the Five-Factor Model," *Annual Review of Psychology* 41 (1990), 417–40.

10. T. A. Judge and C. P. Zapata, "The Person–Situation Debate Revisited: Effect of Situation Strength and Trait Activation on the Validity of the Big Five Personality Traits in Predicting Job Performance," *Academy of Management Journal* 58, no. 4 (2015), 1149–79.

11. L. A. Witt and G. R. Ferris, "Social Skills as Moderator of

Conscientiousness–Performance Relationship: Convergent Results across Four Studies," *Journal of Applied Psychology* 88, no. 5 (2003), 809–20; M. J. Simmering, J. A. Colquitte, R. A. Noe, and C. O. L. H. Porter, "Conscientiousness, Autonomy Fit, and Development: A Longitudinal Study," *Journal of Applied Psychology* 88, no. 5 (2003), 954–63.

12. M. R. Barrick and M. K. Mount, "The Big Five Personality Dimensions and Job Performance: A Meta-Analysis," *Personnel Psychology* 44 (1991), 1–26; S. Komar, D. J. Brown, J. A. Komar, and C. Robie, "Faking and the Validity of Conscientiousness: A Monte Carlo Investigation," *Journal of Applied Psychology* 93 (2008), 140–54.

13. Digman, "Personality Structure."

14. J. B. Rotter, "Generalized Expectancies for Internal versus External Control of Reinforcement," *Psychological Monographs* 80 (1966), 1–28; P. Spector, "Behaviors in Organizations as a Function of Employees' Locus of Control," *Psychological Bulletin* 91 (1982), 482–97.

15. J. Brockner, *Self-Esteem at Work* (Lexington, MA: Lexington Books, 1988).

16. D. C. McClelland, *Human Motivation* (Glenview, IL: Scott, Foresman, 1985); D. C. McClelland, "How Motives, Skills, and Values Determine What People Do," *American Psychologist* 40 (1985), 812–25; D. C. McClelland, "Managing Motivation to Expand Human Freedom," *American Psychologist* 33 (1978), 201–10.

17. D. G. Winter, *The Power Motive* (New York: Free Press 1973).

18. M. J. Stahl, "Achievement, Power, and Managerial Motivation: Selecting Managerial Talent with the Job Choice Exercise," *Personnel Psychology* 36 (1983), 775–89; D. C. McClelland and D. H. Burnham, "Power Is the Great Motivator," *Harvard Business Review* 54 (1976), 100–10.

19. R. J. House, W. D. Spangler, and J. Woycke, "Personality and Charisma in the U.S. Presidency: A Psychological Theory of Leader Effectiveness," *Administrative Science Quarterly* 36 (1991), 364–96.

20. G. H. Hines, "Achievement, Motivation, Occupations and Labor Turnover in New Zealand," *Journal of Applied Psychology* 58 (1973), 313–17; P. S. Hundal, "A Study of Entrepreneurial Motivation: Comparison of Fast- and Slow-Progressing Small Scale Industrial Entrepreneurs in Punjab, India," *Journal of Applied Psychology* 55 (1971), 317–23.

21. "MBTI® Basics," www.myersbriggs.org, accessed November 8, 2018; Elena Bajic, "How the MBTI Can Help You Build a Stronger Company," *Forbes,* www.forbes.com, September 28, 2015; A. Furnham and J. Crump, "The Myers-Briggs Type Indicator (MBTI) and Promotion at Work," *Psychology* 6, no. 12 (September 2015), 1510–15.

22. "What Is DiSC?," http://discprofile.com, accessed November 8, 2018.

23. M. Rokeach, *The Nature of Human Values* (New York: Free Press 1973).

24. K. Tuulik, T. Ounapuu, K. Kuimet, and E. Titov, "Rokeach's Instrumental and Terminal Values as Descriptors of Modern Organisation Values," *International Journal of Organizational Leadership* 5 (2016), 151–61.

25. Rokeach, *The Nature of Human Values.*

26. S. Nadel, "Increasing the Role of Ethics in the Hospitality Industry," *Hotel Business Review,* www.hotelexecutive.com, accessed November 8, 2018; J. Brownell, "Ethics from the Bottom Up," *Cornell Hospitality Report* 17 (April 3, 2017), 3–13.

27. Brownell, "Ethics from the Bottom Up"; Nadel, "Increasing the Role of Ethics."

28. G. Witham, "A Strong Strategy Is Required When Talking about Ethics," *Hotel Management,* June 1, 2017, 30.

29. "Cornell's Judi Brownell: Listening to Women Business Travelers," GlassCeiling.com, accessed November 8, 2018.

30. Nadel, "Increasing the Role of Ethics."

31. L. Saad, "Job Security Slips in U.S. Worker Satisfaction Ratings," https://news.gallup.com, August 27, 2009.

32. The Conference Board, "U.S. Job Satisfaction at Lowest Level in Two Decades," www.conference-board.org, January 5, 2010.

33. The Conference Board, "Labor Day Survey: 51% of U.S. Employees Overall Satisfied with Their Job," www.conference-board.org, accessed November 9, 2018.

34. D. W. Organ, *Organizational Citizenship Behavior: The Good Soldier Syndrome* (Lexington, MA: Lexington Books, 1988).

35. J. M. George and A. P. Brief, "Feeling Good—Doing Good: A Conceptual Analysis of the Mood at Work—Organizational Spontaneity Relationship," *Psychological Bulletin* 112 (1992), 310–29.

36. W. H. Mobley, "Intermediate Linkages in the Relationship between Job Satisfaction and Employee Turnover," *Journal of Applied Psychology* 62 (1977), 237–40.

37. C. Hymowitz, "Though Now Routine, Bosses Still Stumble during Layoff Process," *The Wall Street Journal,* June 25, 2007, B1; J. Brockner, "The Effects of Work Layoffs on Survivors: Research, Theory and Practice," in B. M. Staw and L. L. Cummings, eds., *Research in Organizational Behavior,* vol. 10 (Greenwich, CT: JAI Press, 1988), 213–55.

38. N. Solinger, W. van Olffen, and R. A. Roe, "Beyond the Three-Component Model of Organizational Commitment," *Journal of Applied Psychology* 93 (2008), 70–83.

39. J. E. Mathieu and D. M. Zajac, "A Review and Meta-Analysis of the Antecedents, Correlates, and Consequences of Organizational Commitment," *Psychological Bulletin* 108 (1990), 171–94.

40. D. Watson and A. Tellegen, "Toward a Consensual Structure of Mood," *Psychological Bulletin* 98 (1985), 219–35.

41. J. M. George, "The Role of Personality in Organizational Life: Issues and Evidence," *Journal of Management* 18 (1992), 185–213.

42. H. A. Elfenbein, "Emotion in Organizations: A Review and Theoretical Integration," in J. P. Walsh and A. P. Brief, eds., *The Academy of Management Annals*, vol. 1 (New York: Erlbaum, 2008), 315–86.

43. J. P. Forgas, "Affect in Social Judgments and Decisions: A Multi-Process Model," in M. Zamma, ed., *Advances in Experimental and Social Psychology*, vol. 25 (San Diego, CA: Academic Press, 1992), 227–75; J. P. Forgas and J. M. George, "Affective Influences on Judgments and Behavior in Organizations: An Information Processing Perspective," *Organizational Behavior and Human Decision Processes* 86 (2001), 3–34; J. M. George, "Emotions and Leadership: The Role of Emotional Intelligence," *Human Relations* 53 (2000), 1027–55; W. N. Morris, *Mood: The Frame of Mind* (New York: Springer-Verlag, 1989).

44. J. M. George and K. Bettenhausen, "Understanding Prosocial Behavior, Sales Performance, and Turnover: A Group Level Analysis in a Service Context," *Journal of Applied Psychology* 75 (1990), 698–709.

45. George and Brief, "Feeling Good—Doing Good"; J. M. George and J. Zhou, "Understanding When Bad Moods Foster Creativity and Good Ones Don't: The Role of Context and Clarity of Feelings," paper presented at the Academy of Management Annual Meeting, 2001; A. M. Isen and R. A. Baron, "Positive Affect as a Factor in Organizational Behavior," in B. M. Staw and L. L. Cummings, eds., *Research in Organizational Behavior*, vol. 13 (Greenwich, CT: JAI Press, 1991), 1–53.

46. J. M. George and J. Zhou, "Dual Tuning in a Supportive Context: Joint Contributions of Positive Mood, Negative Mood, and Supervisory Behaviors to Employee Creativity," *Academy of Management Journal* 50 (2007), 605–22; J. M. George, "Creativity in Organizations," in J. P. Walsh and A. P. Brief, eds., *The Academy of Management Annals*, vol. 1 (New York: Erlbaum, 2008), 439–77.

47. J. D. Greene, R. B. Sommerville, L. E. Nystrom, J. M. Darley, and J. D. Cohen, "An FMRI Investigation of Emotional Engagement in Moral Judgment," *Science*, September 14, 2001, 2105–08; L. Neergaard, "Brain Scans Show Emotions Key to Resolving Ethical Dilemmas," *Houston Chronicle*, September 14, 2001, 13A.

48. George and Zhou, "Dual Tuning in a Supportive Context."

49. George and Zhou, "Dual Tuning in a Supportive Context;" J. M. George, "Dual Tuning: A Minimum Condition for Understanding Affect in Organizations?" *Organizational Psychology Review*, no. 2 (2011), 147–64.

50. R. C. Sinclair, "Mood, Categorization Breadth, and Performance Appraisal: The Effects of Order of Information Acquisition and Affective State on Halo, Accuracy, Informational Retrieval, and Evaluations," *Organizational Behavior and Human Decision Processes* 42 (1988), 22–46.

51. D. Goleman, *Emotional Intelligence* (New York: Bantam Books, 1994); J. D. Mayer and P. Salovey, "The Intelligence of Emotional Intelligence," *Intelligence* 17 (1993), 433–42; J. D. Mayer and P. Salovey, "What Is Emotional Intelligence?" in P. Salovey and D. Sluyter, eds., *Emotional Development and Emotional Intelligence: Implications for Education* (New York: Basic Books, 1997); P. Salovey and J. D. Mayer, "Emotional Intelligence," *Imagination, Cognition, and Personality* 9 (1989–1990), 185–211.

52. S. Epstein, *Constructive Thinking* (Westport, CT: Praeger, 1998).

53. "Leading by Feel," *Inside the Mind of the Leader*, January 2004, 27–37.

54. P. C. Early and R. S. Peterson, "The Elusive Cultural Chameleon: Cultural Intelligence as a New Approach to Intercultural Training for the Global Manager," *Academy of Management Learning and Education* 3, no. 1 (2004), 100–15.

55. George, "Emotions and Leadership"; S. Begley, "The Boss Feels Your Pain," *Newsweek*, October 12, 1998, 74; D. Goleman, *Working with Emotional Intelligence* (New York: Bantam Books, 1998).

56. "Leading by Feel."

57. George, "Emotions and Leadership."

58. J. Zhou and J. M. George, "Awakening Employee Creativity: The Role of Leader Emotional Intelligence," *Leadership Quarterly* 14 (2003), 545–68.

59. See Daniel Goleman, "Emotional Intelligence," www.danielgoleman.info, accessed November 15, 2018.

60. A. Molinsky, "Emotional Intelligence Doesn't Translate across Borders," *Harvard Business Review*, https://hbr.org, April 20, 2015.

61. P. Surana, "Is Emotional Intelligence Culture Specific?," *LinkedIn*, www.linkedin.com, May 4, 2017.

62. Surana, "Is Emotional Intelligence Culture Specific?,"; Molinsky, "Emotional Intelligence Doesn't Translate."

63. P. Gaul, "Travis Bradberry, *TD*, May 2017, pp. 60–61.

64. Molinsky, "Emotional Intelligence Doesn't Translate"; Surana, "Is Emotional Intelligence Culture Specific?"

65. H. M. Trice and J. M. Beyer, *The Cultures of Work Organizations* (Englewood Cliffs, NJ: Prentice-Hall, 1993).

66. J. B. Sørensen, "The Strength of Corporate Culture and the Reliability of Firm Performance," *Administrative Science Quarterly* 47 (2002), 70–91.

67. "Personality and Organizational Culture," in B. Schneider and D. B. Smith, eds., *Personality and Organizations* (Mahway, NJ: Erlbaum, 2004), 347–69; J. E. Slaughter, M. J. Zickar, S. Highhouse, and D. C. Mohr, "Personality Trait Inferences about Organizations: Development of a Measure and Assessment of Construct Validity," *Journal of Applied Psychology* 89, no. 1 (2004), 85–103.

68. A. Ferrara, "Why Workplace Culture Matters (and How to Build a Good One)," www.ideo.com, accessed December 3, 2018; T. Kelley, *The Art of Innovation: Lessons in Creativity from IDEO, America's Leading Design Firm* (New York: Random House, 2001).

69. "Personality and Organizational Culture."

70. B. Schneider, "The People Make the Place," *Personnel Psychology* 40 (1987), 437–53.

71. "Personality and Organizational Culture."

72. B. Schneider, H. B. Goldstein, and D. B. Smith, "The ASA Framework: An Update," *Personnel Psychology* 48 (1995), 747–73; J. Schaubroeck, D. C. Ganster, and J. R. Jones, "Organizational and Occupational Influences in the Attraction–Selection–Attrition Process," *Journal of Applied Psychology* 83 (1998), 869–91.

73. Kelley, *The Art of Innovation.*

74. "Launching an Online Pharmacy Startup," www.ideo.com, accessed December 3, 2018.

75. "Who We Are," www.ideo.com, accessed December 3, 2018.

76. "Personality and Organizational Culture."

77. Kelley, *The Art of Innovation.*

78. George, "Emotions and Leadership."

79. Kelley, *The Art of Innovation.*

80. Ibid.

81. G. R. Jones, *Organizational Theory, Design, and Change* (Upper Saddle River, NJ: Prentice-Hall, 2003).

82. H. Schein, "The Role of the Founder in Creating Organizational Culture," *Organizational Dynamics* 12 (1983), 13–28.

83. J. M. George, "Personality, Affect, and Behavior in Groups," *Journal of Applied Psychology* 75 (1990), 107–16.

84. J. Van Maanen, "Police Socialization: A Longitudinal Examination of Job Attitudes in an Urban Police Department," *Administrative Science Quarterly* 20 (1975), 207–28.

85. Texas A&M University, "Fish Camp," www.tamu.edu, accessed December 3, 2018.

86. www.intercotwest.com/Disney; M. N. Martinez, "Disney Training Works Magic," *HRMagazine,* May 1992, 53–57.

87. P. L. Berger and T. Luckman, *The Social Construction of Reality* (Garden City, NY: Anchor Books, 1967).

88. H. M. Trice and J. M. Beyer, "Studying Organizational Culture through Rites and Ceremonies," *Academy of Management Review* 9 (1984), 653–69.

89. Kelley, *The Art of Innovation.*

90. H. M. Trice and J. M. Beyer, *The Cultures of Work Organizations* (Englewood Cliffs, NJ: Prentice-Hall, 1993).

91. B. Ortega, "Walmart's Meeting Is a Reason to Party," *The Wall Street Journal,* June 3, 1994, A1.

92. Trice and Beyer, "Studying Organizational Culture through Rites and Ceremonies."

93. Kelley, *The Art of Innovation.*

94. B. Peterson, "It's Official: IBM Is Acquiring Software Company Red Hat for $34 Billion," *Business Insider,* www.businessinsider.com, accessed November 15, 2018; N. Cameron, "IBM's Ginni Rometty: Comfort and Growth Will Never Co-Exist," *CMO,* www.cmo.com, accessed November 15, 2018; C. K. Goman, "Why IBM Brought Remote Workers Back to the Office—and Why Your Company Might Be Next," *Forbes,* www.forbes.com, accessed November 15, 2018.

95. B. McLean and P. Elkind, *The Smartest Guys in the Room: The Amazing Rise and Scandalous Fall of Enron* (New York: Penguin Books, 2003); R. Smith and J. R. Emshwiller, *24 Days: How Two* Wall Street Journal *Reporters Uncovered the Lies That Destroyed Faith in Corporate America* (New York: HarperCollins, 2003); M. Swartz and S. Watkins, *Power Failure: The Inside Story of the Collapse of ENRON* (New York: Doubleday, 2003).

PART 2

3 Managing Ethics and Diversity

Learning Objectives

After studying this chapter, you should be able to:

LO 3-1 Illustrate how ethics help managers determine the right way to behave when dealing with different stakeholder groups.

LO 3-2 Explain why managers should behave ethically and strive to create ethical organizational cultures.

LO 3-3 Describe the increasing diversity of the workforce and of the organizational environment.

LO 3-4 Explain the central role that managers play in the effective management of diversity.

LO 3-5 Understand why effective management of diversity is both an ethical and a business imperative.

LO 3-6 Understand the two major forms of sexual harassment and how they can be eliminated.

Management Snapshot

Inclusion for Women Engineers at Intel

What Steps Can an Organization Take to Ensure Diversity among Its Workforce?

The U.S. high-tech industry has a reputation for being dominated by white (and sometimes Asian) males—and an often-unconscious expectation that this is what computer experts look like. The numbers support this view: women and people of color are underrepresented in college computer programs and even more so in the big tech companies.[1] Companies tend to blame the problem on a shortage of women and minorities with technical skills, but some industry insiders observe companies limiting their recruiting to top-tier universities and managers failing to recognize the contributions of women and minorities.

Intel's former CEO Brian Krzanich realized this criticism could apply to the tech company. Of Intel's U.S. workforce, more than 6 in 10 were white and Asian males, with single-digit percentages of employees who were black, Hispanic, or Native American.[2] Krzanich doubted that such a workforce could fully identify with and serve the needs of its more diverse customers. He decided to make a public commitment to diversifying Intel's workforce. In 2015, he announced that the company would commit $300 million to a diversity initiative.[3] The goal: by 2020, the composition of Intel's workforce by race and sex would match these groups' percentages in the U.S. labor supply for Intel's job categories.

Krzanich appointed Danielle Brown to lead Intel's diversity initiative. As chief diversity and inclusion officer, Brown reported directly to the CEO, signaling that diversity was to become a companywide issue. She determined that to meet the 2020 targets, Intel needed to bring in 2,300 female and/or minority employees. She launched a program based on accountability, transparency, data-based decisions, and a holistic view of the issue.[4] Managers have goals for their group's diversity, and part of their pay depends on meeting those goals. Twice yearly, Intel publishes a report of its performance on the diversity goal, including data for hiring, pay levels, rate of employees leaving, and rate being promoted. To support decision making based on data, rather than comfort with similarity, managers receive data on their people's performance.

As the program began delivering results, Google recruited Brown, and Intel promoted Barbara Whye to continue the effort in Brown's place.[5] As a black engineer with more than two decades at Intel in various roles, Whye has firsthand experience with the challenges involved. So far, Whye's efforts are bearing fruit.

Senior management at Intel continues to work toward closing the gap when it comes to diversity and inclusion in its workforce.
Shutterstock/Robert Kneschke

Intel is ahead of its time line for hiring diverse workers. One productive technique has been ensuring that each slate of candidates for a position includes at least two qualified people who meet criteria for diverse hiring.[6] Intel expanded the pool of candidates by recruiting at a wider variety of schools and publicly posting all job openings. For interviews, it brings together a diverse group into a panel, rather than relying on one manager alone. In October 2018, Intel announced it had achieved "full representation," meaning the company's workforce now reflects the available talent pool.[7]

Retention has been a stickier problem, but Intel has reduced its exit rates for minority employees to near the rates for whites and Asians—and the rates for women are below the rates for men.[8] This progress came after the company introduced a program called WarmLine, a number employees can use to contact the diversity team if they feel dissatisfied with conditions. The diversity and inclusion team provides a personal response to problems such as managers being "too busy" to help new employees develop a career path. The results yield data Intel uses in preventing such problems in the first place—for example, training managers to fully engage with all of their employees. WarmLine has opened more than 20,000 cases, and Whye reports a success rate above 80 percent.[9]

Overview

While a strong code of ethics can influence the way employees behave, what causes people to behave unethically in the first place? Moreover, how do managers and employees determine what is ethical or unethical? In this chapter, we examine the nature of the obligations and responsibilities of managers and the companies they work for toward the people and society that are affected by their actions. First, we examine the nature of ethics and the sources of ethical problems. Second, we discuss the major groups of people, called *stakeholders*, who are affected by the way companies operate. Third, we look at four rules or guidelines that managers can use to decide whether a specific business decision is ethical or unethical and why it is important for people and companies to behave in an ethical way.

We then turn to the issue of the effective management of diversity. This first requires that organizations, their managers, and all employees behave ethically and follow legal rules and regulations in the ways diverse employees are hired, promoted, and treated. Second, effectively managing diversity means learning to appreciate and respond appropriately to the needs, attitudes, beliefs, and values that diverse employees bring to an organization and finding ways to use their skills and talents to benefit them and the company they work for. Finally, we discuss steps managers can take to eradicate sexual harassment in organizations. By the end of this chapter, you will understand the central role that the effective management of ethics and diversity plays in shaping the practice of business and the life of a people, society, and nation.

The Nature of Ethics

Suppose you see a person being mugged. Will you act in some way to help even though you risk being hurt? Will you walk away? Perhaps you might not intervene, but will you call the police? Does how you act depend on whether the person being mugged is a fit male, an older person, or a homeless person? Does it depend on whether other people are around so you can tell yourself, "Oh, well, someone else will help or call the police. I don't need to"?

Ethical Dilemmas

ethical dilemma The quandary people find themselves in when they have to decide if they should act in a way that might help another person or group even though doing so might go against their own self-interest.

The situation just described is an example of an ethical dilemma, the quandary people find themselves in when they have to decide if they should act in a way that might help another person or group and is the right thing to do even though doing so might go against their own self-interest.[10] A dilemma may also arise when a person has to choose between two different courses of action, knowing that whichever course he or she selects will harm one person or group even though it may benefit another. The ethical dilemma here is to decide which course of action is the lesser of two evils.

People often know they are confronting an ethical dilemma when their moral scruples come into play and cause them to hesitate, debate, and reflect upon the rightness or goodness of a course of action. Moral scruples are thoughts and feelings that tell a person what is right or wrong; they are a part of a person's ethics. Ethics are the inner guiding moral principles, values, and beliefs that people use to analyze or interpret a situation and then decide what is the right or appropriate way to behave. Ethics also indicate what is inappropriate behavior and how a person should behave to avoid harming another person.

ethics The inner guiding moral principles, values, and beliefs that people use to analyze or interpret a situation and then decide what is the right or appropriate way to behave.

The essential problem in dealing with ethical issues, and thus solving moral dilemmas, is that no absolute or indisputable rules or principles can be developed to decide whether an action is ethical or unethical. Put simply, different people or groups may dispute which actions are ethical or unethical depending on their personal self-interest and specific attitudes, beliefs, and values—concepts we discussed in Chapter 2. How are we and companies and their managers and employees to decide what is ethical and, so, act appropriately toward other people and groups?

Ethics and the Law

The first answer to this question is that society as a whole, using the political and legal process, can lobby for and pass laws that specify what people can and cannot do. Many different kinds of laws govern business—for example, laws against fraud and deception and laws governing how companies can treat their employees and customers. Laws also specify what sanctions or punishments will follow if those laws are broken. Different groups in society lobby for which laws should be passed based on their own personal interests and beliefs about right and wrong. The group that can summon the most support can pass laws that align with its interests and beliefs. Once a law is passed, a decision about what the appropriate behavior is with regard to a person or situation is taken from the personally determined ethical realm to the societally determined legal realm. If you do not conform to the law, you can be prosecuted; and if you are found guilty of breaking the law, you can be punished. You have little say in the matter; your fate is in the hands of the court and its lawyers.

In studying the relationship between ethics and law, it is important to understand that *neither laws nor ethics are fixed principles* that do not change over time. Ethical beliefs change as time passes; as they do so, laws change to reflect the changing ethical beliefs of a society. It was seen as ethical, and it was legal, for example, to acquire and possess slaves in ancient Rome and Greece and in the United States until the late 19th century. Ethical views regarding whether slavery was morally right or appropriate changed, however. Slavery was made illegal in the United States when those in power decided that slavery degraded the meaning of being human. Slavery makes a statement about the value or worth of human beings and about their right to life, liberty, and the pursuit of happiness. And if we deny these rights to other people, how can we claim to have any natural rights to these things?

Moreover, what is to stop any person or group that becomes powerful enough to take control of the political and legal process from enslaving us and denying us the right to be free and to own property? In denying freedom to others, one risks losing it oneself, just as stealing from others opens the door for them to steal from us in return. "Do unto others as you would have them do unto you" is a common ethical or moral rule that people apply in such situations to decide what is the right thing to do.

Changes in Ethics over Time

There are many types of behavior—such as murder, theft, slavery, rape, and driving while intoxicated—that most people currently believe are unacceptable and unethical and should therefore be illegal. However, the ethics of many other actions and behaviors are open to dispute. Some people might believe a particular behavior—for example, smoking tobacco or possessing guns—is unethical and, so, should be made illegal. Others might argue that it is up to the individual or group to decide if such behaviors are ethical and thus whether a particular behavior should remain legal.

As ethical beliefs change over time, some people may begin to question whether existing laws that make specific behaviors illegal are still appropriate. They might argue that although a specific behavior is deemed illegal, this does not make it unethical and thus the law should be changed. In 17 states, for example, it is illegal to possess or use marijuana (cannabis). To justify this law, it is commonly argued that smoking marijuana leads people to try more dangerous drugs. Once the habit of taking drugs has been acquired, people can get hooked on them. More powerful drugs such as heroin and other narcotics are addictive, and most people cannot stop using them without help. Thus, the use of marijuana, because it might lead to further harm, is an unethical practice.

It has been documented medically, however, that marijuana use can help people with certain illnesses. For example, for cancer sufferers who are undergoing chemotherapy and for those with other diseases who are on potent medications, marijuana offers relief from many treatment side effects, such as nausea and lack of appetite. Yet in the United States it is illegal in some states for doctors to prescribe marijuana for these patients, so their suffering continues. Since 1996, however, 33 states have made it legal to prescribe marijuana for medical purposes; nevertheless, the federal government has sought to stop such state legislation. The U.S. Supreme Court ruled in 2005 that only Congress or the states could decide whether medical marijuana use should be made legal, and people in many states are currently lobbying for a relaxation of state laws against its use for medical purposes.[11] Initiatives are under way in several states to decriminalize the possession of small amounts of marijuana for personal use as well as to make it more widely available to people legally for medical purposes. A major ethical debate continues to rage over this issue in many states and countries.

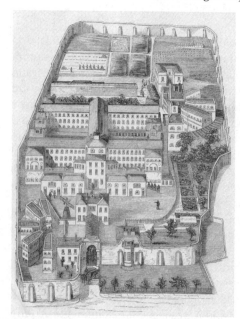

Coldbath Fields Prison, London, circa 1810. The British criminal justice system around this time was severe: A person could be executed for 350 different crimes, including sheep stealing. As ethical beliefs change over time, so do laws.
Hulton Archive/Getty Images

The important point to note is that while ethical beliefs lead to the development of laws and regulations to prevent certain behaviors or encourage others, laws themselves change or even disappear as ethical beliefs change. In Britain in 1830 a person could be executed for over 350 different crimes, including sheep stealing. Today the death penalty is no longer legal in Britain. Thus, both ethical and legal rules are *relative:* No absolute or unvarying standards exist to determine how we should behave, and people are caught up in moral dilemmas all the time. Because of this, we have to make ethical choices.

The previous discussion highlights an important issue in understanding the relationship among ethics, law, and business. Throughout the 2010s many scandals plagued major companies such as JPMorgan Chase, HSBC, Standard Chartered Bank, ING, Barclays, and Wells Fargo. Managers at some of these companies engaged in risky trades, interest rate manipulation, illegal trade facilitation, drug money laundering, and deception of customers.

In other cases no laws were broken, yet outrage was expressed over perceptions of unethical actions. One example of this is the anti-gun movement, a protest that has been growing over the last several years as a result of multiple instances of gun violence. In February 2018, 14 students and 3 coaches and teachers were gunned down inside Marjory Stoneman Douglas High School in Parkland, Florida, by a former student who purchased an AR-15 assault rifle legally.[12] The friends and schoolmates of the slain students started the #marchforourlives protest, which included a national walk on Washington, DC. The ongoing protest, spearheaded by students on social media, continues across the country today and has caused several major companies to end their business relationships with the National Rifle Association (NRA) and eliminate discounts to NRA members. In addition, major retailers such as Walmart, Dick's Sporting Goods, and Kroger have changed their policies with regard to gun sales.[13]

Stakeholders and Ethics

Just as people have to work out the right and wrong ways to act, so do companies. When the law does not specify how companies should behave, their managers must decide the right or ethical way to behave toward the people and groups affected by their actions. Who are the people or groups that are affected by a company's business decisions? If a company behaves in an ethical way, how does this benefit people and society? Conversely, how are people harmed by a company's unethical actions?

The people and groups affected by how a company and its managers behave are called its stakeholders. Stakeholders supply a company with its productive resources; as a result, they have a claim on and a stake in the company.[14] Because stakeholders can directly benefit or be harmed by the company's actions, the ethics of a company and its managers are important to them. Who are a company's major stakeholders? What do they contribute to a company, and what do they claim in return? Here we examine the claims of these stakeholders—stockholders; managers; employees; suppliers and distributors; customers; and community, society, and nation-state as Figure 3.1 depicts.

stakeholders The people and groups that supply a company with its productive resources and, so, have a claim on and a stake in the company.

Stockholders

Stockholders have a claim on a company because when they buy its stock or shares they become its owners. When the founder of a company decides to publicly

Figure 3.1

Types of Company
Stakeholders

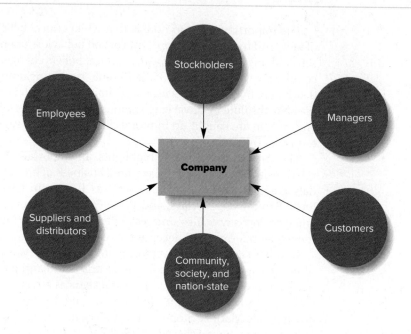

incorporate the business to raise capital, shares of the stock of that company are issued. This stock grants its buyers ownership of a certain percentage of the company and the right to receive any future stock dividends. For example, in 2005 Microsoft decided to pay the owners of its 5 billion shares a special dividend payout of $32 billion. Bill Gates received $3.3 billion in dividends based on his stockholding, and he donated this money to the Bill and Melinda Gates Foundation, to which he has reportedly donated over $50 billion to date, with the promise of much more to come. In 2017, for example Gates gave the Foundation $4.6 billion worth of his Microsoft stock shares.[15] Gates's friend and fellow billionaire, Warren Buffett, committed to donate at least $30 billion of his fortune to the Gates Foundation over the next decade. Two of the richest people in the world have decided to give away a large part of their wealth to serve global ethical causes—in particular to address global health concerns such as malnutrition, malaria, tuberculosis, and AIDS.

Stockholders are interested in how a company operates because they want to maximize the return on their investment. Thus, they watch the company and its managers closely to ensure that management is working diligently to increase the company's profitability. Stockholders also want to ensure that managers are behaving ethically and not risking investors' capital by engaging in actions that could hurt the company's reputation. No company wants the reputation described by the #marchforourlives protesters, who alleged that some organizations value money over people. Experts warn businesses not to ignore the movement. They warn that the growing voice and influence of the anti-gun violence movement may continue to single out politicians, companies, and other organizations that continue to associate or do business with the NRA and its millions of members.[16]

Managers

Managers are a vital stakeholder group because they are responsible for using a company's financial, capital, and human resources to increase its performance

Layoff decisions are always difficult. General Motors recently announced plans to reduce both its corporate and manufacturing workforce by thousands in response to consumers' changing taste in automobiles. Steve Debenport/iStock/Getty Images

and thus its stock price. Managers have a claim on an organization because they bring to it their skills, expertise, and experience. They have the right to expect a good return or reward by investing their human capital to improve a company's performance. Such rewards include good salaries and benefits, the prospect of promotion and a career, and stock options and bonuses tied to company performance.

Managers are the stakeholder group that bears the responsibility to decide which goals an organization should pursue to most benefit stakeholders and how to make the most efficient use of resources to achieve those goals. In making such decisions, managers frequently must juggle the interests of different stakeholders, including themselves.[17] These sometimes difficult decisions challenge managers to uphold ethical values because some decisions that benefit certain stakeholder groups (managers and stockholders) harm other groups (individual workers and local communities). For example, in economic downturns or when a company experiences performance shortfalls, layoffs may help cut costs (thus benefiting shareholders) at the expense of the employees laid off. Many U.S. managers have recently faced this difficult decision. Until the 2009 financial crisis sent unemployment soaring over 10%, on average about 1.6 million U.S. employees out of a total labor force of 140 million were affected by mass layoffs each year; and over 3 million jobs from the United States, Europe, and Japan have been outsourced to Asia since 2005. Layoff decisions are always difficult: They not only take a heavy toll on workers, their families, and local communities but also mean the loss of the contributions of valued employees to an organization. In late 2018, General Motors announced plans to cut roughly 8,000 white-collar positions as well as more than 6,000 factory jobs in an effort to address the shifting consumer demand from traditional passenger cars to sport-utility vehicles (SUVs) and trucks. GM's CEO Mary Barra said these actions would help the automaker stay ahead of changing marketing conditions and position the company for long-term success.[18]

As we discussed in Chapter 1, managers must be motivated and given incentives to work hard in the interests of stockholders. Their behavior must also be scrutinized to ensure they do not behave illegally or unethically, pursuing goals that threaten stockholders and the company's interests. Unfortunately, we have seen in the 2010s how easy it is for top managers to find ruthless ways to pursue their self-interest at the expense of stockholders and employees because laws and regulations are not strong enough to force them to behave ethically.

In a nutshell, the problem has been that in many companies corrupt managers focus not on building the company's capital and stockholders' wealth but on maximizing their own personal capital and wealth. In an effort to prevent future scandals, the Securities and Exchange Commission (SEC), the government's top business watchdog, has begun to rework the rules governing a company's relationship with its auditor, as well as regulations concerning stock options, and to increase the power of outside directors to scrutinize a CEO. The SEC's goal is to outlaw many actions that were previously classified as merely unethical. For example, companies are now forced to reveal to stockholders the value of the stock options they give their top executives and directors and when they give them these options; this shows how much such payments reduce company profits. Managers and directors can now be prosecuted if they disguise or try to hide these payments. In the 2010s the SEC announced many new rules requiring that companies disclose myriad details of executive compensation packages to investors; already the boards of directors of many companies have stopped giving CEOs perks such as free personal jet travel, membership in exclusive country clubs, and luxury accommodations on "business trips." Also, in 2010 Congress passed new laws preventing the many unethical and illegal actions of managers of banks and other financial institutions that led to the 2009 financial crisis. One of these regulations, the "Volcker Rule," seeks to reduce the chances that banks will put depositors' money at risk. Recently, however, Wall Street and U.S. banks asked federal regulators to revisit the Volcker Rule in an effort to loosen some of the stricter requirements of the legislation, which could lessen the financial burden put on banking institutions nationwide.[19]

Indeed, many experts argue that the rewards given to top managers, particularly the CEO and COO, grew out of control in the 2000s. Top managers are today's "elites," and through their ability to influence the board of directors and raise their own pay, they have amassed personal fortunes worth hundreds of millions of dollars. For example, according to a study by the Federal Reserve, U.S. CEOs now get paid about 300 times what the average worker earns, compared to about 40 times in 1980—a staggering increase. In 2018, the median reported total compensation for CEOs was nearly $19 million.[20] We noted in Chapter 1 that besides their salaries, top managers often receive tens of millions in stock bonuses and options—even when their companies perform poorly.

Is it ethical for top managers to receive such vast amounts of money from their companies? Do they earn it? Remember, this money could have gone to shareholders in the form of dividends. It could also have reduced the huge salary gap between those at the top and those at the bottom of the hierarchy. Many people argue that the growing disparity between the rewards given to CEOs and to other employees is unethical and should be regulated. CEO pay has skyrocketed because CEOs are the people who set and control one another's salaries and bonuses; they can do this because they sit on the boards of other companies as outside directors. Others argue that because top managers play an important role in building a company's capital and wealth, they deserve a significant share of its profits. Some recent research has suggested that the companies whose CEO compensation includes a large percentage of stock options tend to experience big share losses more often than big gains, and on average, company performance improves as stock option use declines.[21] The debate over how much money CEOs and other top managers should be paid is still raging, particularly because the financial crisis beginning in 2009 showed how much money the CEOs of troubled financial companies earned even as their companies' performance and stock prices collapsed.

Employees

A company's employees are the people who work in its various departments and functions, such as research, sales, and manufacturing. Employees expect to receive rewards consistent with their performance. One principal way that a company can act ethically toward employees and meet their expectations is by creating an occupational structure that fairly and equitably rewards employees for their contributions. Companies, for example, need to develop recruitment, training, performance appraisal, and reward systems that do not discriminate against employees and that employees believe are fair.

Suppliers and Distributors

No company operates alone. Every company is in a network of relationships with other companies that supply it with the inputs (such as raw materials, components, contract labor, and clients) that it needs to operate. It also depends on intermediaries such as wholesalers and retailers to distribute its products to the final customers. Suppliers expect to be paid fairly and promptly for their inputs; distributors expect to receive quality products at agreed-upon prices. Once again, many ethical issues arise in how companies contract and interact with their suppliers and distributors. Important issues concerning safety specifications are governed by the contracts a company signs with its suppliers and distributors, for example; however, lax oversight can have tragic consequences.

Many other issues depend on business ethics. For example, numerous products sold in U.S. stores have been outsourced to countries that do not have U.S.-style regulations and laws to protect the workers who make these products. All companies must take an ethical position on the way they obtain and make the products they sell. Commonly, this stance is published on a company's website.

Customers

Customers are often regarded as the most critical stakeholder group because if a company cannot attract them to buy its products, it cannot stay in business. Thus, managers and employees must work to increase efficiency and effectiveness in order to create loyal customers and attract new ones. They do so by selling customers quality products at a fair price and providing good after-sales service. They can also strive to improve their products over time and provide guarantees to customers about the integrity of their products.

Community, Society, and Nation-State

The effects of the decisions made by companies and their managers permeate all aspects of the communities, societies, and nation-states in which they operate. *Community* refers to physical locations like towns or cities or to social milieus like ethnic neighborhoods in which companies are located. A community provides a company with the physical and social infrastructure that allows it to operate; its utilities and labor force; the homes in which its managers and employees live; the schools, colleges, and hospitals that serve their needs; and so on.

Through the salaries, wages, and taxes it pays, a company contributes to the economy of its town or region and often determines whether the community prospers or declines. Similarly, a company affects the prosperity of a society and a nation-state and, to the degree that a company is involved in global trade, all the countries it operates in and thus the prosperity of the global economy. We have already discussed the many issues surrounding global outsourcing and the loss of jobs in the United States, for example.

Although the individual effects of the way each McDonald's restaurant operates might be small, for instance, the combined effects of how all McDonald's and other fast-food companies do business are enormous. In the United States alone, more than 3.5 million people work in the fast-food industry, and many thousands of suppliers, like farmers, paper cup manufacturers, and builders, depend on it for their livelihood. Small wonder, then, that the ethics of the fast-food business are scrutinized closely. This industry was the major lobbyer against attempts to raise the national minimum wage (which was raised to $7.25 an hour in 2009, where it remains today, up from $5.15—a figure that had not changed since 1997), for example, because a higher minimum wage would substantially increase its operating costs. However, responding to protests about chickens raised in cages where they cannot move, McDonald's—the largest egg buyer in the United States—issued new ethical guidelines concerning cage size and related matters that its egg suppliers must abide by if they are to retain its business. What ethical rules does McDonald's use to decide its stance toward minimum pay or minimum cage size?

Business ethics are also important because the failure of a company can have catastrophic effects on a community; a general decline in business activity affects a whole nation. The decision of a large company to pull out of a community, for example, can threaten the community's future. Some companies may attempt to improve their profits by engaging in actions that, although not illegal, can hurt communities and nation-states. One of these actions is pollution. For example, many U.S. companies reduce costs by trucking their waste to Mexico, where it is legal to dump waste in the Rio Grande. The dumping pollutes the river from the Mexican side, but the U.S. side of the river is increasingly experiencing pollution's negative effects.

Rules for Ethical Decision Making

When a stakeholder perspective is taken, questions on company ethics abound.[22] What is the appropriate way to manage the claims of all stakeholders? Company decisions that favor one group of stakeholders, for example, are likely to harm the interests of others.[23] High prices charged to customers may bring high returns to shareholders and high salaries to managers in the short run. If in the long run customers turn to companies that offer lower-cost products, however, the result may be declining sales, laid-off employees, and the decline of the communities that support the high-priced company's business activity.

When companies act ethically, their stakeholders support them. For example, banks are willing to supply them with new capital, they attract highly qualified job applicants, and new customers are drawn to their products. Thus, ethical companies grow and expand over time, and all their stakeholders benefit. The results of unethical behavior are loss of reputation and resources, shareholders selling their shares, skilled managers and employees leaving the company, and customers turning to the products of more reputable companies.

When making business decisions, managers must consider the claims of all stakeholders. To help themselves and employees make ethical decisions and behave in ways that benefit their stakeholders, managers can use four ethical rules or principles to analyze the effects of their business decisions on stakeholders: the *utilitarian, moral rights, justice,* and *practical* rules (Figure 3.2).[24] These rules are useful guidelines that help managers decide on the appropriate way to behave in situations where it is

Figure 3.2

Four Ethical Rules

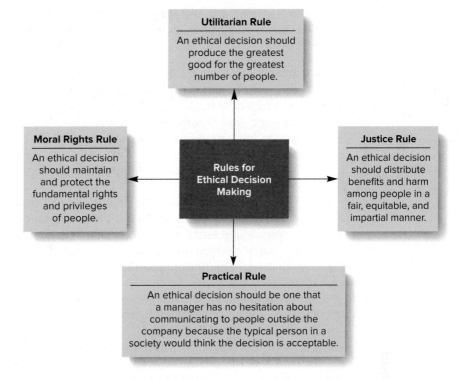

Utilitarian Rule

An ethical decision should produce the greatest good for the greatest number of people.

Moral Rights Rule

An ethical decision should maintain and protect the fundamental rights and privileges of people.

Rules for Ethical Decision Making

Justice Rule

An ethical decision should distribute benefits and harm among people in a fair, equitable, and impartial manner.

Practical Rule

An ethical decision should be one that a manager has no hesitation about communicating to people outside the company because the typical person in a society would think the decision is acceptable.

necessary to balance a company's self-interest and the interests of its stakeholders. Remember, the right choices will lead resources to be used where they can create the most value. If all companies make the right choices, all stakeholders will benefit in the long run.

utilitarian rule An ethical decision is a decision that produces the greatest good for the greatest number of people.

UTILITARIAN RULE The utilitarian rule is that an ethical decision is a decision that produces the greatest good for the greatest number of people. To decide which is the most ethical course of business action, managers should first consider how different possible courses of business action would benefit or harm different stakeholders. They should then choose the course of action that provides the most benefits, or, conversely, the one that does the least harm, to stakeholders.[25]

The ethical dilemma for managers is this: How do you measure the benefit and harm that will be done to each stakeholder group? Moreover, how do you evaluate the rights of different stakeholder groups, and the relative importance of each group, in coming to a decision? Because stockholders own the company, shouldn't their claims be held above those of employees? For example, managers might face a choice of using global outsourcing to reduce costs and lower prices or continuing with high-cost production at home. A decision to use global outsourcing benefits shareholders and customers but will result in major layoffs that will harm employees and the communities in which they live. Typically, in a capitalist society such as the United States, the interests of shareholders are put above those of employees, so production will move abroad. This is commonly regarded as being an ethical choice because in the long run the alternative, home production, might cause the business to collapse and go bankrupt, in which case greater harm will be done to all stakeholders.

MORAL RIGHTS RULE Under the moral rights rule, an ethical decision is one that best maintains and protects the fundamental or inalienable rights and privileges of the people affected by it. For example, ethical decisions protect people's rights to freedom, life and safety, property, privacy, free speech, and freedom of conscience. The adage "Do unto others as you would have them do unto you" is a moral rights principle that managers should use to decide which rights to uphold. Customers must also consider the rights of the companies and people who create the products they wish to consume.

> **moral rights rule** An ethical decision is one that best maintains and protects the fundamental or inalienable rights and privileges of the people affected by it.

From a moral rights perspective, managers should compare and contrast different courses of business action on the basis of how each course will affect the rights of the company's different stakeholders. Managers should then choose the course of action that best protects and upholds the rights of *all* stakeholders. For example, decisions that might significantly harm the safety or health of employees or customers would clearly be unethical choices.

The ethical dilemma for managers is that decisions that will protect the rights of some stakeholders often will hurt the rights of others. How should they choose which group to protect? For example, in deciding whether it is ethical to snoop on employees, or search them when they leave work to prevent theft, does an employee's right to privacy outweigh an organization's right to protect its property? Suppose a coworker is having personal problems and is coming in late and leaving early, forcing you to pick up the person's workload. Do you tell your boss even though you know this will probably get that person fired?

JUSTICE RULE The justice rule is that an ethical decision distributes benefits and harms among people and groups in a fair, equitable, or impartial way. Managers should compare and contrast alternative courses of action based on the degree to which they will fairly or equitably distribute outcomes to stakeholders. For example, employees who are similar in their level of skill, performance, or responsibility should receive similar pay; allocation of outcomes should not be based on differences such as gender, race, or religion.

> **justice rule** An ethical decision distributes benefits and harms among people and groups in a fair, equitable, or impartial way.

The ethical dilemma for managers is to determine the fair rules and procedures for distributing outcomes to stakeholders. Managers must not give people they like bigger raises than they give to people they do not like, for example, or bend the rules to help their favorites. On the other hand, if employees want managers to act fairly toward them, then employees need to act fairly toward their companies by working hard and being loyal. Similarly, customers need to act fairly toward a company if they expect it to be fair to them.

PRACTICAL RULE Each of these rules offers a different and complementary way of determining whether a decision or behavior is ethical, and all three rules should be used to sort out the ethics of a particular course of action. Ethical issues, as we just discussed, are seldom clear-cut, however, because the rights, interests, goals, and incentives of different stakeholders often conflict. For this reason many experts on ethics add a fourth rule to determine whether a business decision is ethical: The practical rule is that an ethical decision is one that a manager has no hesitation or reluctance about communicating to people outside the company because

> **practical rule** An ethical decision is one that a manager has no reluctance about communicating to people outside the company because the typical person in a society would think it is acceptable.

the typical person in a society would think it is acceptable. A business decision is probably acceptable on ethical grounds if a manager can answer yes to each of these questions:

1. Does my decision fall within the accepted values or standards that typically apply in business activity today?
2. Am I willing to see the decision communicated to all people and groups affected by it—for example, by having it reported on TV or via social media?
3. Would the people with whom I have a significant personal relationship, such as family members, friends, or even managers in other organizations, approve of the decision?

Applying the practical rule to analyze a business decision ensures that managers are taking into account the interests of all stakeholders.[26]

Why Should Managers Behave Ethically?

LO 3-2
Explain why managers should behave ethically and strive to create ethical organizational cultures.

Why is it so important that managers, and people in general, act ethically and temper their pursuit of self-interest by considering the effects of their actions on others? The answer is that the relentless pursuit of self-interest can lead to a collective disaster when one or more people start to profit from being unethical, because this encourages other people to act in the same way.[27] More and more people jump onto the bandwagon, and soon everybody is trying to manipulate the situation to serve their personal ends with no regard for the effects of their action on others. This is called the "tragedy of the commons."

Suppose that in an agricultural community there is common land that everybody has an equal right to use. Pursuing self-interest, each farmer acts to make the maximum use of the free resource by grazing his or her own cattle and sheep. Collectively, all the farmers overgraze the land, which quickly becomes worn out. Then a strong wind blows away the exposed topsoil, so the common land is destroyed. The pursuit of individual self-interest with no consideration of societal interests leads to disaster for each individual and for the whole society because scarce resources are destroyed.[28] Consider digital piracy: The tragedy that would result if all people were to steal digital media would be the disappearance of music, movie, and book companies as creative people decided there was no point in working hard to produce original songs, stories, and so on.

We can look at the effects of unethical behavior on business activity in another way. Suppose companies and their managers operate in an unethical society, meaning one in which stakeholders routinely try to cheat and defraud one another. If stakeholders expect each other to cheat, how long will it take them to negotiate the purchase and shipment of products? When they do not trust each other, stakeholders will probably spend hours bargaining over fair prices, and this is a largely unproductive activity that reduces efficiency and effectiveness.[29] The time and effort that could be spent improving product quality or customer service are lost to negotiating and bargaining. Thus, unethical behavior ruins business commerce, and society has a lower standard of living because fewer goods and services are produced, as Figure 3.3 illustrates.

On the other hand, suppose companies and their managers operate in an ethical society, meaning stakeholders believe they are dealing with others who are basically moral and honest. In this society stakeholders have a greater reason to trust

Figure 3.3

Some Effects of
Ethical and Unethical
Behavior

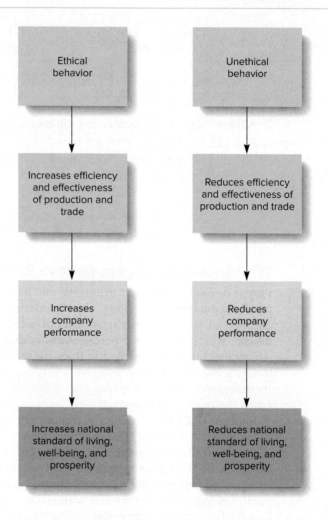

trust The willingness
of one person or
group to have faith
or confidence in the
goodwill of another
person, even though
this puts them at risk.

others. Trust is the willingness of one person or group to have faith or confidence in the goodwill of another person, even though this puts them at risk (because the other might act in a deceitful way). When trust exists, stakeholders are likely to signal their good intentions by cooperating and providing information that makes it easier to exchange and price goods and services. When one person acts in a trustworthy way, this encourages others to act in the same way. Over time, as greater trust between stakeholders develops, they can work together more efficiently and effectively, which raises company performance (see Figure 3.3). As people see the positive results of acting in an honest way, ethical behavior becomes a valued social norm, and society in general becomes increasingly ethical.

As noted in Chapter 1, a major responsibility of managers is to protect and nurture the resources under their control. Any organizational stakeholders—managers, workers, stockholders, suppliers—who advance their own interests by behaving unethically toward other stakeholders, either by taking resources or by denying resources to others, waste collective resources. If other individuals or groups copy the behavior of the unethical stakeholder, the rate at which collective resources are misused increases, and eventually few resources are available to produce goods and services. Unethical behavior that goes unpunished creates incentives for people to put their unbridled self-interests above the rights of others.[30] When this happens, the benefits that people reap from joining together in organizations disappear quickly.

An important safeguard against unethical behavior is the potential for loss of reputation.[31] Reputation, the esteem or high repute that people or organizations gain when they behave ethically, is an important asset. Stakeholders have valuable reputations, which they must protect because their ability to earn a living and obtain resources in the long run depends on how they behave.

reputation The esteem or high repute that individuals or organizations gain when they behave ethically.

If a manager misuses resources and other parties regard that behavior as being at odds with acceptable standards, the manager's reputation will suffer. Behaving unethically in the short run can have serious long-term consequences. A manager who has a poor reputation will have difficulty finding employment with other companies. Stockholders who see managers behaving unethically may refuse to invest in their companies, and this will decrease the stock price, undermine the companies' reputations, and ultimately put the managers' jobs at risk.[32]

All stakeholders have reputations to lose. Suppliers who provide shoddy inputs find that organizations learn over time not to deal with them, and eventually they go out of business. Powerful customers who demand ridiculously low prices find that their suppliers become less willing to deal with them, and resources ultimately become harder for them to obtain. Workers who shirk responsibilities on the job find it hard to get new jobs when they are fired. In general, if a manager or company is known for being unethical, other stakeholders are likely to view that individual or organization with suspicion and hostility, creating a poor reputation. But a manager or company known for ethical business practices will develop a good reputation.[33]

In summary, in a complex, diverse society, stakeholders, and people in general, need to recognize they are part of a larger social group. How they make decisions and act not only affects them personally but also affects the lives of many other people. Unfortunately, for some people, the daily struggle to survive and succeed or their total disregard for others' rights can lead them to lose that bigger connection to other people. We can see our relationships to our families and friends, school, church, and so on. But we must go further and keep in mind the effects of our actions on other people—people who will be judging our actions and whom we might harm by acting unethically. Our moral scruples are like those "other people" but are inside our heads.

Sources of an Organization's Code of Ethics

Codes of ethics are formal standards and rules, based on beliefs about right or wrong, that managers can use to help themselves make appropriate decisions with regard to the interests of their stakeholders.[34] Ethical standards embody views about abstractions such as justice, freedom, equity, and equality. An organization's code of ethics derives from three principal sources in the organizational environment: *societal* ethics, *professional* ethics, and the *individual* ethics of the organization's managers and employees (see Figure 3.4).

societal ethics Standards that govern how members of a society should deal with one another in matters such as fairness, justice, poverty, and the rights of the individual.

SOCIETAL ETHICS Societal ethics are standards that govern how members of a society deal with each other in matters involving issues such as fairness, justice, poverty, and the rights of the individual. Societal ethics emanate from a society's laws, customs, and practices and from the unwritten attitudes, values, and norms that influence how people interact with each other. People in a particular country

Figure 3.4

Sources of an
Organization's Code

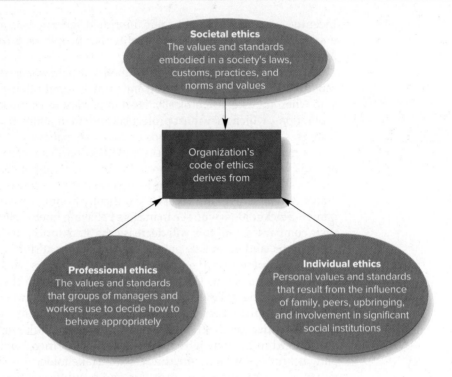

Societal ethics
The values and standards
embodied in a society's laws,
customs, practices, and
norms and values

Organization's
code of ethics
derives from

Professional ethics
The values and standards
that groups of managers and
workers use to decide how to
behave appropriately

Individual ethics
Personal values and standards
that result from the influence
of family, peers, upbringing,
and involvement in significant
social institutions

may automatically behave ethically because they have internalized values and norms that specify how they should behave in certain situations. Not all values and norms are internalized, however. The typical ways of doing business in a society and laws governing the use of bribery and corruption are the result of decisions made and enforced by people with the power to determine what is appropriate.

Societal ethics vary among societies. For example, ethical standards accepted in the United States are not accepted in all other countries. In many economically poor countries, bribery is standard practice to get things done, such as getting a telephone installed or a contract awarded. In the United States and many other Western countries, bribery is considered unethical and often illegal.

Societal ethics control self-interested behavior by individuals and organizations—behavior threatening to society's collective interests. Laws spelling out what is good or appropriate business practice provide benefits to everybody. Free and fair competition among organizations is possible only when laws and rules level the playing field and define what behavior is acceptable or unacceptable in certain situations. For example, it is ethical for a manager to compete with managers in other companies by producing a higher-quality or lower-priced product, but it is not ethical (or legal) to do so by spreading false claims about competitors' products, bribing stores to exclude competitors' products, or blowing up competitors' factories.

professional ethics Standards that govern how members of a profession are to make decisions when the way they should behave is not clear-cut.

PROFESSIONAL ETHICS Professional ethics are standards that govern how members of a profession, managers or workers, make decisions when the way in which they should behave is not clear-cut.[35] Medical ethics govern the way doctors and nurses are to treat patients. Doctors are expected to perform only necessary medical procedures and to act in the patient's interest and not in their own. The ethics of scientific research require scientists to conduct their experiments and present their findings in ways that ensure the validity of their conclusions. Like society at large, most professional groups can impose punishments for violations of ethical standards. Doctors and lawyers can be prevented from practicing their professions if they disregard professional ethics and put their own interests first.

Within an organization, professional rules and norms often govern how employees such as lawyers, researchers, and accountants make decisions and act in certain situations, and these rules and norms may become part of the organization's code of ethics. When they do, workers internalize the rules and norms of their profession (just as they do those of society) and often follow them automatically when deciding how to behave.[36] Because most people follow established rules of behavior, people often take ethics for granted. However, when professional ethics are violated, such as when scientists fabricate data to disguise the harmful effects of products, ethical issues rise to the forefront of attention.

individual ethics Personal values and attitudes that govern how individuals interact with other people.

INDIVIDUAL ETHICS Individual ethics are personal values (both terminal and instrumental) and attitudes that govern how individuals interact with other people.[37] Sources of individual ethics include the influence of one's family, peers, and upbringing in general, and an individual's personality and experience. The experiences gained over a lifetime—through membership in significant social institutions such as schools and religions, for example—also contribute to the development of the personal standards and values that a person applies to decide what is right or wrong and whether to perform certain actions or make certain decisions. Many decisions or behaviors that one person finds unethical, such as using animals for cosmetics testing, may be acceptable to another person because of differences in their personalities, values, and attitudes (see Chapter 2).

Ethical Organizational Cultures

Managers can emphasize the importance of ethical behavior and social responsibility by ensuring that ethical values and norms are central components of organizational culture. An organization's code of ethics guides decision making when ethical questions arise, but managers can go one step farther by ensuring that important ethical values and norms are key features of an organization's culture. For example, the organizational culture at Southwest Airlines values employee well-being; this emphasis translates into norms dictating that layoffs should be avoided.[38] Ethical values and norms such as these that are part of an organization's culture help organizational members resist self-interested action and recognize that they are part of something bigger than themselves.[39]

Managers' roles in developing ethical values and standards in other employees is very important. Employees naturally look to those in authority to provide leadership, and managers become ethical role models whose behavior is scrutinized by their employees. If top managers are not ethical, their employees are not likely to behave in an ethical manner. Employees may think that if it's all right for a top manager to engage in dubious behavior, it's all right for them, too. Managers should model the behavior expected from their employees, as well as educate employees in the ethical behavior the organization expects. The "Ethics in Action" feature describes how management consulting firm Accenture helps employees apply its code of ethical conduct.

Ethics in Action

Chatbot Provides Ethical Guidance

Ethical, responsible employee conduct is a critical objective for Accenture, because a consulting firm relies on its reputation to open clients' doors. Furthermore, with 425,000 employees in more than 120 countries, Accenture must guide employees representing diverse cultures and languages.[40] The firm posted its code of ethics online and provided training programs. But the code runs to more than 50 pages addressing values (respect, professionalism, nondiscrimination, and integrity), the importance of clients' best interests, social responsibility, and more.[41] Accenture's managers realized that asking employees to search through this document was no longer meeting the standards of how people get information today. As the firm is advising clients to do in other areas of business, Accenture wanted to create a way to interact with the information easily and naturally on computers and mobile devices. So Accenture developed a chatbot.

A chatbot combines a database with natural-language processing and artificial intelligence (AI).[42] Users text their questions, and the natural-language processing interprets the question to deliver a relevant answer from the database. The AI component helps the system improve the answers through experience with users. The use of chatbots is increasing as organizations realize that today's customers and employees prefer to share information by texting. With Accenture's chatbot, called COBE (for code of business ethics), the database is the code of conduct, and employees text questions about applying its contents.

To develop the COBE chatbot, Accenture turned to its digital marketing services group, which had been developing chatbots for clients to use in improving customer service.[43] The team applied the technology to Accenture's own employees, treating them as the customers. They created a chatbot for employees only, keeping queries anonymous and offering options to converse in several languages and with accommodations for visual impairments. The effort was part of a larger overhaul of the code of business ethics, modernizing the content to address issues such as the use of social media and artificial intelligence.

The introduction of COBE has increased employees' use of the company's code of conduct. According to Chad Jerdee, Accenture's chief compliance officer, each week, 20 times as many employees look up information on the website now that they can text a question rather than clicking through a lengthy document.[44] Jerdee considers this visible commitment to ethical, responsible conduct particularly appealing to the kinds of people Accenture recruits as employees. ●

ethics officer A senior manager who monitors an organization's practices and procedures to be sure they are ethical.

Managers can also provide a visible means of support to develop an ethical culture. Increasingly, organizations are creating the role of ethics officer to monitor their ethical practices and procedures. The ethics officer is responsible for communicating ethical standards to all employees, for designing systems to monitor employees' conformity to those standards, and for teaching managers and nonmanagerial employees at all levels of the organization how to respond to ethical dilemmas appropriately.[45] Because the ethics officer has organizationwide authority, organizational members in any department can communicate instances of unethical behavior by their managers or coworkers without fear of retribution. This arrangement makes it easier for everyone to behave ethically. In addition, ethics officers can provide guidance when organizational members are uncertain about whether an action is ethical. Some organizations have an organizationwide ethics committee to provide guidance on ethical issues and help write and update the company code of ethics.

The Increasing Diversity of the Workforce and the Environment

diversity
Dissimilarities or differences among people due to age, gender, race, ethnicity, religion, sexual orientation, socioeconomic background, education, experience, physical appearance, capabilities/disabilities, and any other characteristic that is used to distinguish among people.

One of the most important management issues to emerge over the last 40 years has been the increasing diversity of the workforce. Diversity is dissimilarities—differences—among people due to age, gender, race, ethnicity, religion, sexual orientation, socioeconomic background, education, experience, physical appearance, capabilities/disabilities, and any other characteristic that is used to distinguish among people (see Figure 3.5).

Diversity raises important ethical issues and social responsibility issues. It is also a critical issue for organizations—one that if not handled well can bring an organization to its knees, especially in our increasingly global environment. There are several reasons that diversity continues to be such a pressing concern and an issue, both in the popular press and for managers and organizations:

- There is a strong ethical imperative in many societies that diverse people must receive equal opportunities and be treated fairly and justly. Unfair treatment is also illegal.

- Effectively managing diversity can improve organizational effectiveness. When managers effectively manage diversity, they not only encourage other managers to treat diverse members of an organization fairly and justly but also realize that diversity is an important organizational resource that can help an organization gain a competitive advantage.[46] Current research suggests, however, that there are specific situations in which diversity can enhance performance; simply having a diverse workforce may not guarantee higher performance.[47] This last point is important as managers continue to explore the impact of diversity on the workplace and the challenges of moving employees and organizations forward in an effective manner.

- There is substantial evidence that diverse individuals continue to experience unfair treatment in the workplace as a result of biases, stereotypes, and overt discrimination. In a recent review of multiple studies, evidence suggests that hiring discrimination against African Americans has not changed significantly over the past 25 years in the United States, and Latinos have experienced only a moderate drop in discrimination.[48] In addition, a recent survey of U.S. workers suggests that "pay secrecy" within companies in the private sector may contribute to reducing women's bargaining power when it comes to salaries and may also be a factor in the ongoing gender wage gap.[49]

glass ceiling A metaphor alluding to the invisible barriers that prevent women and minorities from being promoted to top corporate positions.

- Finally, the glass ceiling—the invisible barrier that prevents women and minorities from being promoted to top corporate positions—is beginning to crack, though much work still needs to be done. For example, in December 2018, only 24 leaders of *Fortune* 500 companies were women (4.8%) and only 3 were African American men (0.6%). With the retirement of Xerox's Ursula Burns in 2016, there currently are no African American women running these top organizations.[50]

Figure 3.5

Sources of Diversity in
the Workplace

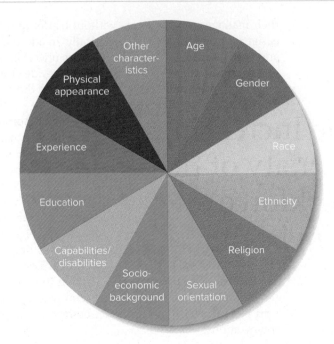

Before we can discuss the multitude of issues surrounding the effective management of diversity, we must document just how diverse the U.S. workforce is becoming.

Age

According to data from the U.S. Census Bureau, the median age of a person in the United States is the highest it has ever been, at 37.9 years. In addition, it is projected that by 2060, close to 24% of the U.S. population will be 65 or older. The Age Discrimination in Employment Act of 1967 prohibits age discrimination.[51] Major equal employment opportunity legislation that prohibits discrimination among diverse groups is summarized in Table 3.1.

The aging of the population suggests that managers need to be vigilant to ensure that employees are not discriminated against because of age. Moreover, managers need to ensure that the policies and procedures they have in place treat all workers fairly, regardless of their ages. Additionally, effectively managing diversity means employees of diverse ages are able to learn from each other, work well together, and take advantage of the unique perspective each has to offer.

Gender

Women and men both have substantial participation rates in the U.S. workforce (approximately 44.6% women and 55.3% men), yet women's median weekly earnings are estimated to be $801 compared to $979 for men.[52] Although the gender wage gap has narrowed in recent years, it continues to be as an issue, just like the glass ceiling. According to Catalyst, a nonprofit organization that studies women in business, while women compose about 44.7% of employees in managerial and professional positions, only around 26.5% of executive officers in Standard & Poor's (S&P's) 500 companies are women, and only 11% of the top earners in these companies are women.[53] These women, such as Mary Barra of GM, Ginni

Table 3.1

Major Equal Employment Opportunity Laws Affecting Human Resource Management

Year	Law	Description
1963	Equal Pay Act	Requires that men and women be paid equally if they are performing equal work.
1964	Title VII of the Civil Rights Act	Prohibits discrimination in employment decisions on the basis of race, religion, sex, color, or national origin; covers a wide range of employment decisions, including hiring, firing, pay, promotion, and working conditions.
1967	Age Discrimination in Employment Act	Prohibits discrimination against workers over the age of 40 and restricts mandatory retirement.
1978	Pregnancy Discrimination Act	Prohibits discrimination against women in employment decisions on the basis of pregnancy, childbirth, and related medical decisions.
1990	Americans with Disabilities Act	Prohibits discrimination against individuals with disabilities in employment decisions and requires that employers make accommodations for these workers to enable them to perform their jobs.
1991	Civil Rights Act	Prohibits discrimination (as does Title VII) and allows for the awarding of punitive and compensatory damages, in addition to back pay, in cases of intentional discrimination.
1993	Family and Medical Leave Act	Requires that employers provide 12 weeks of unpaid leave for medical and family reasons, including paternity and illness of a family member.
1994	Uniformed Services Employment and Reemployment Rights Act	Protects the civilian employment of active and reserve military personnel called to active duty; prohibits discrimination on the basis of military status and military service obligations; provides certain reemployment rights following military service.

Rometty of IBM, and Michele Buck of Hershey, stand out among their male peers and often receive a disparate amount of attention in the media. Women are also underrepresented on companies' boards of directors—they currently hold roughly 21% of the board seats on S&P 500 companies.[54]

A female executive enjoying the company plane is not as rare a sight today as it used to to be. Nevertheless, the glass ceiling remains a real barrier to women and minorities in the business workforce.
ColorBlind Images/Blend Images LLC RF

Additionally, research conducted by consulting firms suggests that female executives outperform their male colleagues in skills such as motivating others, promoting good communication, turning out high-quality work, and being good listeners. For example, the Hagberg Group performed in-depth evaluations of 425 top executives in a variety of industries, with each executive rated by approximately 25 people. Of the 52 skills assessed, women received higher ratings than men on 42 skills, although at times the differences were small.[55] Results of a study conducted by Catalyst found that organizations with higher proportions of women in top management positions had significantly better financial performance than organizations with lower proportions of female top managers.[56] Another study conducted by

Credit Suisse found that companies with one or more women on their boards of directors performed better in terms of returns on equity, sales, and invested capital than companies with fewer or no women on their boards.[57] Studies such as these make one wonder why the glass ceiling continues to hamper the progress of women in business.

Race and Ethnicity

The U.S. Census Bureau distinguished among the following races in the 2010 census: American Indian or Alaska Native; Asian Indian; black or African American; Chinese; Filipino; Japanese; Korean; Vietnamese; other Asian; Native Hawaiian; Guamanian or Chamorro; Samoan; other Pacific Islander; white; and other races. Although *ethnicity* refers to a grouping of people based on some shared characteristic such as national origin, language, or culture, the U.S. Census Bureau treats ethnicity in terms of whether a person is Hispanic, Latino, or of Spanish origin or not.[58] For the 2020 Census, the government has conducted extensive research to fine-tune the various ethnic groups that will be tracked in the upcoming national census survey. More than ever before, many individuals see themselves as multiracial with various ethnicities.[59]

The racial and ethnic diversity of the U.S. population continues to change, as does the diversity of the workforce. According to the U.S. Census Bureau, approximately one of every three U.S. residents belongs to a minority group (is not a non-Hispanic white). More specifically, 17.8% of the population is Hispanic or Latino, 82.2% is not Hispanic or Latino, and 61.3% of the population is white alone (that is, white and not Hispanic or Latino).[60] For those individuals self-identifying one race in the 2010 census, approximately 76.9% are white, 13.3% are black or African American, 1.3% are American Indian or Alaska Native, 5.7% are Asian, 0.2% are Native Hawaiian and other Pacific Islander alone, and 2.6% of the population self-identifies as two or more races.[61] According to projections released by the U.S. Census Bureau, the composition of the U.S. population in 2060 will be quite different from its composition today: In 2060 the U.S. population is projected to be close to 56% minority.[62] And while this discussion focuses on diversity in the United States, managers anywhere in the world need to be aware of their region's pattern of ethnic diversity. The "Focus on Diversity" feature describes a company based in Israel that works diligently to address diversity.

The increasing racial and ethnic diversity of the workforce and the population as a whole underscores the importance of effectively managing diversity. Statistics compiled by the Bureau of Labor Statistics suggest that much needs to be done in terms of ensuring that diverse employees have equal opportunities. For example, median weekly earnings for black men are approximately 72.3% of median earnings for white men; median weekly earnings for black women are approximately 76.6% of median earnings for white women.[63] In the remainder of this chapter, we focus on the fair treatment of diverse employees and explore why this is such an important challenge and what managers can do to meet it. We begin by taking a broader perspective and considering how increasing racial and ethnic diversity in an organization's environment (such as customers and suppliers) affects decision making and organizational effectiveness.

At a general level, managers and organizations are increasingly being reminded that stakeholders are diverse and expect organizational decisions and actions to reflect this diversity. For example, many advocacy groups continue to lobby the

Focus on Diversity

SodaStream's Oasis of Diversity

Daniel Birnbaum is CEO of SodaStream International, which makes countertop devices that inject carbon dioxide into liquids to add bubbles. A reusable bottle offers an alternative to buying soda in disposable bottles. Birnbaum took the position so he could stay in Israel.[64] Born in New York, he grew up in Israel and left to earn an MBA at Harvard. After returning to Israel, he worked for Pillsbury and Nike until his next career move would involve relocating. The job offer from SodaStream came in 2007, when the company was struggling financially. Birnbaum revitalized the company by repositioning the product as eco-friendly.

SodaStream employs over 2,000 people of 30 different nationalities at its headquarters and manufacturing facilities in five countries.[65] Its main production facility is in Rahat, a city in the Negev, the desert region in southern Israel. Rahat's dominant ethnic group is Bedouin, desert dwellers of the region, traditionally nomads. The SodaStream workers include Bedouins, Palestinians, Druze (a religious sect living mainly in Syria, Lebanon, and Israel), and Jews whose families came to Israel from Russia and Ethiopia.[66]

Building this diverse workforce was not originally Birnbaum's vision; rather, it met business needs.[67] Rising demand required more workers at the SodaStream factory, then located in the Palestinian-governed West Bank. Israeli workers weren't interested, so he recruited Palestinians. He admits to being surprised at how productive they were and how well the Palestinians and Israelis got along. Later, however, political pressures forced him to close the West Bank facility and relocate. Working in the Negev location requires Palestinians to get permits and spend hours commuting through Israeli checkpoints. But for those who meet the requirements, a job at SodaStream can be worthwhile.

In the larger political sphere, the ethnic groups represented at the Rahat factory feel mistrust, even hostility. Birnbaum unifies the workforce by focusing everyone on the business and treating workers justly and respectfully.[68] In contrast to other Israeli companies, SodaStream pays equally regardless of workers' ethnicity. Working together teaches employees to see one another's shared humanity. SodaStream, recognizing that inclusiveness enhances its reputation as an employer, recently posted a recruiting video aimed at creative, socially conscious workers.

Under Birnbaum, SodaStream's diverse workforce has delivered results. As consumers learn they can make fizzy drinks with healthful ingredients and low impact on the environment, sales have been rising briskly. SodaStream's market capitalization (total value of stock shares) is 250 times greater than when Birnbaum took the helm. In late 2018, PepsiCo purchased SodaStream for $3.2 billion and Birnbaum will stay on with the company.[69] ●

entertainment industry to increase the diversity in TV programming, acting, writing, and producing.[70] The need for such increased diversity is more than apparent. For example, while Hispanics make up more than 17% of the U.S. population (more than 57 million potential TV viewers), less than 6% of the characters in prime-time

TV shows are Hispanics, according to a study conducted by USC's Annenberg School for Communication and Journalism.[71] Pressure continues to mount on networks and the media in general to increase diversity within their ranks to reflect the diversity of the population as a whole.[72]

Religion

Title VII of the Civil Rights Act prohibits discrimination based on religion (as well as based on race/ethnicity, country of origin, and sex; see Table 3.1). In addition to enacting Title VII, in 1997 the federal government issued "The White House Guidelines on Religious Exercise and Expression in the Federal Workplace."[73] These guidelines, while technically applicable only in federal offices, also are frequently relied on by large corporations. The guidelines require that employers make reasonable accommodations for religious practices, such as observances of holidays, as long as doing so does not entail major costs or hardships.[74]

A key issue for managers in religious diversity is recognizing and being aware of different religions and their beliefs, with particular attention being paid to when religious holidays fall. For example, critical meetings should not be scheduled during a holy day for members of a certain faith, and managers should be flexible in allowing people to have time off for religious observances. According to Lobna Ismail, director of a diversity training company in Silver Spring, Maryland, when managers acknowledge, respect, and make even small accommodations for religious diversity, employee loyalty is often enhanced. For example, allowing employees to leave work early on certain days instead of taking a lunch break or posting holidays for different religions on the company calendar can go a long way toward making individuals of diverse religions feel respected and valued as well as enabling them to practice their faith.[75] According to research conducted by the Tanenbaum Center for Interreligious Understanding in New York, while only about 23% of employees who feel they are victims of religious discrimination actually file complaints, about 45% of these employees start looking for other jobs.[76]

Capabilities/Disabilities

The Americans with Disabilities Act (ADA) of 1990 prohibits discrimination against persons with disabilities and requires that employers make reasonable accommodations to enable these people to effectively perform their jobs. On the surface, few would argue with the intent of this legislation. However, as managers attempt to implement policies and procedures to comply with the ADA, they face a number of interpretation and fairness challenges.

On one hand, some people with real disabilities warranting workplace accommodations are hesitant to reveal their disabilities to their employers and claim the accommodations they deserve.[77] On the other hand, some employees abuse the ADA by seeking unnecessary accommodations for disabilities that may or may not exist.[78] Thus, it is perhaps not surprising that the passage of the ADA does not appear to have increased employment rates significantly for those with disabilities.[79] A key challenge for managers is to promote an environment in which employees needing accommodations feel comfortable disclosing their need while ensuring that the accommodations not only enable those with disabilities to effectively perform their jobs but also are perceived to be fair by those who do not have a disability.[80]

In addressing this challenge, often managers must educate both themselves and their employees about the disabilities, as well as the real capabilities, of those who have disabilities. According to recent statistics, the unemployment rate for workers with disabilities is twice that of workers without disabilities. However, many companies are committed to hiring workers with disabilities and recognize that diversity and inclusion are two strategies vital to their overall business success. In 2018, the American Association of People with Disabilities recognized more than 90 U.S. companies with their "best places to work for people with disabilities" award, including Facebook, Boeing, 3M, Microsoft, and Walmart. These companies scored 100% on the Disability Equality Index, a benchmarking tool that provides organizations with an objective score on their disability and inclusion policies and practices.[81]

Socioeconomic Background

The term *socioeconomic background* typically refers to a combination of social class and income-related factors. From a management perspective, socioeconomic diversity (and, in particular, diversity in income levels) requires that managers be sensitive and responsive to the needs and concerns of individuals who might not be as well off as others. U.S. welfare reform in the middle to late 1990s emphasized the need for single mothers and others receiving public assistance to join or return to the workforce. In conjunction with a strong economy, this led to record declines in the number of families, households, and children living below the poverty level, according to the 2000 U.S. census.[82] However, the economic downturns in the early and late 2000s suggest that some past gains that lifted families out of poverty have been reversed. In a strong economy, it is much easier for poor people with few skills to find jobs; in a weak economy, when companies lay off employees in hard times, people who need their incomes the most are unfortunately often the first to lose their jobs.[83] And in recessionary times, it is difficult for laid-off employees to find new positions.

According to statistics released by the U.S. Census Bureau, the official poverty rate in the United States in 2017 was 12.3%, or 39.7 million people; in 2012 the poverty rate was 15.0%, or 46.5 million people.[84] The Census Bureau relies on predetermined threshold income figures, based on family size and composition, adjusted annually for inflation, to determine the poverty level. Families whose income falls below the threshold level are considered poor. For example, in 2017 a family of four was considered poor if their annual income fell below $24,858.[85] When workers earn less than $15 per hour, it is often difficult, if not impossible, for them to meet their families' needs.[86] Moreover, increasing numbers of families are facing the challenge of finding suitable child care arrangements that enable the adults to work long hours and/or through the night to maintain an adequate income level. New information technology has led to more businesses operating 24 hours a day, creating challenges for workers on the night shift, especially those with children.[87]

Hundreds of thousands of parents across the country are scrambling to find someone to care for their children while they are working the night shift, commuting several hours a day, working weekends and holidays, or putting in long hours on one or more jobs. This has led to the opening of day-care facilities that operate around the clock as well as to managers seeking ways to provide such care for children of their employees. For example, Yessika Magdaleno, an experienced state-licensed child care provider in Garden Grove, California, offers early morning, evening, and overnight day-care services for parents with irregular work hours.[88]

Socioeconomic diversity suggests that managers need to be sensitive and responsive to the needs and concerns of workers who may be less fortunate than themselves in terms of income and financial resources, child care and elder care options, housing opportunities, and the existence of sources of social and family support. Moreover—and equally important—managers should try to give such individuals opportunities to learn, advance, and make meaningful contributions to their organizations while improving their economic well-being.

Sexual Orientation

According to research conducted by Gary Gates of the Williams Institute at the UCLA School of Law, approximately 4.5% of adults in the United States, or more than 10 million U.S. residents, self-identify as lesbian, gay, bisexual, or transgender (LGBT).[89] In 2015 the Equal Employment Opportunity Commission (EEOC) pronounced that workplace discrimination on the grounds of sexual orientation is illegal, according to federal law. In that same year, the U.S. Supreme Court declared same-sex marriage was legal in all 50 states.[90] More and more companies are recognizing the inclusion of LGBT employees, affirming their rights to fair and equal treatment, and providing benefits to their partners and/or spouses. Recently, The Walt Disney Company was recognized with a Diversity & Inclusion Award from the *Profiles in Diversity Journal* for its innovative solutions in the area of workforce diversity and inclusion. From providing benefits for same-sex partners to supporting community organizations and working to ensure a safe and welcoming environment for LGBT employees, the company has a long-standing and ongoing commitment to equality.[91]

Other Kinds of Diversity

Other kinds of diversity are important in organizations, are critical for managers to deal with effectively, and are potential sources of unfair treatment. For example, organizations and teams need members with diverse backgrounds and experiences. This is clearly illustrated by the prevalence of cross-functional teams in organizations whose members might come from various departments such as marketing, production, finance, and sales (teams are covered in depth in Chapter 11). A team responsible for developing and introducing a new product, for example, often needs the expertise of employees not only from research and design and engineering but also from marketing, sales, production, and finance.

Macy's employees raise awareness about diversity and equality at Miami's annual Pride Parade. Corporate support can go a long way toward making sure the workplace environment is safe, inclusive, and respectful for everyone. Jeff Greenburg/Getty Images

Other types of diversity can affect how employees are treated in the workplace. For example, employees differ from each other in how attractive they are (based on the standards of the cultures in which an organization operates) and in body weight. Whether individuals are attractive, unattractive, thin, or overweight in most cases has no bearing on their job performance unless they have jobs in which physical appearance plays a role, such as modeling. Yet sometimes these physical sources of diversity affect advancement rates and salaries. According to a recent Vanderbilt University study, overweight women are more likely to work in lower-paying and more physically demanding jobs; they are less likely to get higher-wage jobs that include interacting with the public; and they tend to make less money than do average-size women and all men.[92] Clearly, managers need to ensure that all employees are treated fairly, regardless of their physical appearance.

Managers and the Effective Management of Diversity

LO 3-4
Explain the central role that managers play in the effective management of diversity.

The increasing diversity—of the environment—which, in turn, increases the diversity of an organization's workforce—increases the challenges managers face in effectively managing diversity. Each of the kinds of diversity just discussed presents a particular set of issues managers need to appreciate before they can respond to them effectively. Understanding these issues is not always a simple matter, as many informed managers have discovered. Research on how different groups are currently treated and the unconscious biases that might adversely affect them is vital because it helps managers become aware of the many subtle and unobtrusive ways in which diverse employee groups can come to be treated unfairly over time. Managers can take many more steps to become sensitive to the ongoing effects of diversity in their organizations, take advantage of all the contributions diverse employees can make, and prevent employees from being unfairly treated.

Critical Managerial Roles

In each of their managerial roles (see Chapter 1), managers can either promote the effective management of diversity or derail such efforts; thus, they are critical to this process. For example, in their interpersonal roles, managers can convey that the effective management of diversity is a valued goal and objective (figurehead role), can serve as a role model and institute policies and procedures to ensure that all organizational members are treated fairly (leader role), and can enable diverse individuals and groups to coordinate their efforts and cooperate with each other both inside the organization and at the organization's boundaries (liaison role). Table 3.2 summarizes ways in which managers can ensure that diversity is effectively managed as they perform their different roles.

Given the formal authority that managers have in organizations, they typically have more influence than rank-and-file employees. When managers commit to supporting diversity, as is the case at Intel as described in "Management Snapshot," their authority and positions of power and status influence other members of an organization to make a similar commitment. Research on social influence supports such a link: People are likely to be influenced and persuaded by others who have high status.[93]

LO 3-5
Understand why effective management of diversity is both an ethical and a business imperative.

When managers commit to diversity, their commitment legitimizes the diversity management efforts of others.[94] In addition, resources are devoted to such efforts, and all members of an organization believe that their diversity-related efforts are supported and valued. Consistent with this reasoning, top management commitment and rewards for the support of diversity are often cited as critical ingredients in the success of diversity management initiatives.[95] Additionally, seeing managers express confidence in the abilities and talents of diverse employees causes other organizational members to be similarly confident and helps reduce any prejudice they have as a result of ignorance or stereotypes.[96]

Table 3.2

Managerial Roles and the Effective Management of Diversity

Type of Role	Specific Role	Example
Interpersonal	Figurehead	Conveys that the effective management of diversity is a valued goal and objective.
	Leader	Serves as a role model and institutes policies and procedures to ensure that diverse members are treated fairly.
	Liaison	Enables diverse individuals to coordinate their efforts and cooperate with one another.
Informational	Monitor	Evaluates the extent to which all employees are treated fairly.
	Disseminator	Informs employees about diversity policies and initiatives and the intolerance of discrimination.
	Spokesperson	Supports diversity initiatives in the wider community and speaks to diverse groups to interest them in career opportunities.
Decisional	Entrepreneur	Commits resources to develop new ways to effectively manage diversity and eliminate biases and discrimination.
	Disturbance handler	Takes quick action to correct inequalities and curtail discriminatory behavior.
	Resource allocator	Allocates resources to support and encourage the effective management of diversity.
	Negotiator	Works with organizations (e.g., suppliers) and groups (e.g., labor unions) to support and encourage the effective management of diversity.

Two other important factors emphasize why managers are so central to the effective management of diversity. The first factor is that women, African Americans, Hispanics, and other minorities often start out at a slight disadvantage due to how they are perceived by others in organizations, particularly in work settings where they are a numerical minority. As Virginia Valian, a psychologist at Hunter College who studies gender, indicates, "In most organizations women begin at a slight disadvantage. A woman does not walk into the room with the same status as an equivalent man, because she is less likely than a man to be viewed as a serious professional."[97]

The second factor is that research suggests that slight differences in treatment can accumulate and result in major disparities over time. Even small differences—such as a small favorable bias toward men for promotions—can lead to major differences in the number of male and female managers over time.[98] Thus, while women and other minorities are sometimes advised not to make "a mountain out of a molehill" when they perceive they have been unfairly treated, research conducted by Valian and others suggests that molehills (slight differences in treatment based on irrelevant distinctions such as race, gender, or ethnicity) can turn into mountains over time (major disparities in important outcomes such as promotions) if they are ignored.[99] Once again, managers have the obligation, from both an ethical and a business perspective, to prevent any disparities in treatment and outcomes due to irrelevant distinctions such as race or ethnicity.

Effectively Managing Diversity Makes Good Business Sense

Diverse organizational members can be a source of competitive advantage, helping an organization provide customers with better goods and services.[100] The variety of points of view and approaches to problems and opportunities that diverse employees provide can improve managerial decision making. Suppose a frozen food company is trying to come up with creative ideas for new frozen meals that will appeal to health-conscious, time-conscious customers tired of the same old frozen fare. Which group do you think is likely to come up with the most creative ideas: a group of white women with marketing degrees from Yale University who grew up in upper-middle-class families in the Northeast or a racially mixed group of men and women who grew up in families with varying income levels in different parts of the country and attended a variety of geographically dispersed business schools? Most people would agree that the diverse group is likely to have a wider range of creative ideas. Although this example is simplistic, it underscores one way in which diversity can lead to a competitive advantage.

Just as the workforce is becoming increasingly diverse, so are the customers who buy an organization's goods or services. In an attempt to suit local customers' needs and tastes, organizations like Target often vary the selection of products available in stores in different cities and regions.[101]

Diverse members of an organization are likely to be attuned to what goods and services diverse segments of the market want and do not want. Automakers, for example, are increasingly assigning women to their design teams to ensure that the needs and desires of female customers are taken into account in new car design.

Another way that effective management of diversity can improve profitability is by increasing retention of valued employees, which decreases the costs of hiring replacements for those who quit as well as ensures that all employees are highly motivated. In terms of retention, given the current legal environment, more and more organizations are attuned to the need to emphasize the importance of diversity in hiring. Once hired, if diverse employees think they are being unfairly treated, however, they will be likely to seek opportunities elsewhere. Thus, recruiting diverse employees has to be followed with ongoing effective management of diversity to retain valued organizational members.

If diversity is not effectively managed and turnover rates are higher for members of groups who are not treated fairly, profitability will suffer on several counts. Not only are the future contributions of diverse employees lost when they quit, but the organization also has to bear the costs of hiring replacement workers. According to a recent report, it costs employers an average of 33% of a worker's annual salary to hire a replacement if that employee leaves the organization. In addition, the company experiences substantial indirect costs associated with the new hire, which can include knowledge lost when an experienced worker leaves, time spent finding a replacement, and time the new employee needs to get up to speed in the new job.[102]

Effectively managing diversity makes good business sense for another reason. More and more, managers and organizations concerned about diversity are insisting that their suppliers also support diversity.[103]

Finally, from both business and ethical perspectives, effective management of diversity is necessary to avoid costly lawsuits. More than a decade ago, The Coca-Cola Company settled a class action suit brought by African American employees at a cost of $192 million. The damage such lawsuits cause goes beyond the monetary awards to the injured parties; it can tarnish a company's image. One positive outcome of Coca-Cola's settlement is the company's recognition of the need to commit additional resources to diversity management initiatives. Coca-Cola is increasing its use of minority suppliers, instituting a formal mentoring program, and instituting days to celebrate diversity with its workforce.[104] These efforts have paid off, and Coca-Cola has appeared on *DiversityInc.*'s list of the "Top 50 Companies for Diversity."

Sexual Harassment

Sexual harassment seriously damages both the people who are harassed and the reputation of the organization in which it occurs. It also can cost organizations billions. In late 2017, a new social movement called the #MeToo campaign began after Hollywood entertainment mogul Harvey Weinstein was accused of sexual harassment and assault by many women in the film industry over the last three decades.[105] Women were encouraged to tweet about their harassment experiences, and within the first 24 hours of the movement, the #MeToo hashtag was used more than 12 million times.[106] Other famous men accused of sexual harassment included Charlie Rose, Bill O'Reilly, Matt Lauer, Louis C.K., and Kevin Spacey.

But sexual harassment is not limited to the entertainment industry. According to a recent MSN poll, one in three (33%) people in the United States admits to being sexually harassed at work, with nearly 45% of women polled saying they have been sexually harassed in the workplace—this amounts to more than 33 million women.[107] In 2018, for example, Google fired 48 employees, including 13 senior managers, after a company investigation into sexual harassment claims and workplace culture.[108] And over the past seven years, women at Microsoft filed more than 238 complaints with the company's HR department for sexual harassment and gender discrimination.[109]

Unfortunately, these are not isolated incidents. Sexual harassment victims can be women or men, and their harassers do not necessarily have to be of the opposite sex.[110] However, women are the most frequent victims of sexual harassment, particularly those in male-dominated occupations or those who occupy positions stereotypically associated with certain gender relationships, such as a female administrative assistant reporting to a male boss. Sexual harassment is not only unethical but also illegal. Managers have an ethical obligation to ensure that they, their coworkers, and their employees never engage in sexual harassment—even unintentionally.

The #MeToo movement continues to bring the issue of sexual harassment out of the shadows and into the mainstream, increasing public awareness about this serious issue.
Sundry Photography/Shutterstock

Forms of Sexual Harassment

There are two basic forms of sexual harassment: quid pro quo sexual harassment and hostile work environment sexual harassment. Quid pro quo sexual harassment occurs when a harasser asks or forces an employee to perform sexual favors to keep a job, receive a promotion, receive a raise, obtain some other work-related opportunity, or avoid receiving negative consequences such as demotion or dismissal.[111] This "Sleep with me, honey, or you're fired" form of harassment is the more extreme type and leaves no doubt in anyone's mind that sexual harassment has taken place.[112]

quid pro quo sexual harassment Asking or forcing an employee to perform sexual favors in exchange for receiving some reward or avoiding negative consequences.

hostile work environment sexual harassment Telling lewd jokes, displaying pornography, making sexually oriented remarks about someone's personal appearance, and other sex-related actions that make the work environment unpleasant.

Hostile work environment sexual harassment is more subtle. It occurs when organizational members face an intimidating, hostile, or offensive work environment because of their sex.[113] Lewd jokes, sexually oriented comments or innuendos, vulgar language, displays of pornography, displays or distribution of sexually oriented objects, and sexually oriented remarks about one's physical appearance are examples of hostile work environment sexual harassment.[114] A hostile work environment interferes with organizational members' ability to perform their jobs effectively and has been deemed illegal by the courts. Managers who engage in hostile work environment harassment or allow others to do so risk costly lawsuits for their organizations. For example, a federal jury awarded Marion Schwab $3.24 million after deliberating on her sexual harassment case against FedEx. Schwab was the only female tractor-trailer driver at the FedEx facility serving the Harrisburg International Airport vicinity in Middletown, Pennsylvania, from 1997 to 2000. During that period she was the target of sexual innuendos, was given inferior work assignments, and was the brunt of derogatory comments about her appearance and the role of women in society. On five occasions the brakes on her truck were tampered with. The federal EEOC sued FedEx, and Schwab was part of the suit.[115]

The courts have also recognized other forms of hostile work environment harassment in addition to sexual harassment. For example, a California jury awarded $61 million in punitive and compensatory damages to two FedEx Ground drivers. The drivers, of Lebanese descent, indicated that they had faced a hostile work environment and high levels of stress because a manager had harassed them with racial slurs for two years.[116]

Steps Managers Can Take to Eradicate Sexual Harassment

Managers have an ethical obligation to eradicate sexual harassment in their organizations. There are many ways to accomplish this objective. Here are four steps managers can take to deal with the problem:[117]

- *Develop and clearly communicate a sexual harassment policy endorsed by top management.* This policy should include prohibitions against both quid pro quo and hostile work environment sexual harassment. It should contain (1) examples of types of behavior that are unacceptable, (2) a procedure for employees to use to report instances of harassment, (3) a discussion of the disciplinary actions that will be taken when harassment has taken place, and (4) a commitment to educate and train organizational members about sexual harassment.

- *Use a fair complaint procedure to investigate charges of sexual harassment.* Such a procedure should (1) be managed by a neutral third party, (2) ensure that complaints are dealt with promptly and thoroughly, (3) protect and fairly treat victims, and (4) ensure that alleged harassers are fairly treated.

- *When it has been determined that sexual harassment has taken place, take corrective actions as soon as possible.* These actions can vary depending on the severity of the harassment. When harassment is extensive, prolonged, of a quid pro quo nature, or severely objectionable in some other manner, corrective action may include firing the harasser.

- *Provide sexual harassment education and training to all organizational members, including managers.* The majority of *Fortune* 500 firms currently provide this education and training for their employees. Managers at DuPont, for example, developed DuPont's "A Matter of Respect" program to help educate employees about sexual harassment and eliminate its occurrence. The program includes a four-hour workshop in which participants are given information that defines sexual harassment, sets forth the company's policy against it, and explains how to report complaints and access a 24-hour hotline. Participants watch video clips showing actual instances of harassment. One clip shows a saleswoman having dinner with a male client who, after much negotiating, seems about to give her company his business when he suddenly suggests that they continue their conversation in his hotel room. The saleswoman is confused about what to do. Will she be reprimanded if she says no and the deal is lost? After watching a video, participants discuss what they have seen, why the behavior is inappropriate, and what organizations can do to alleviate the problem.[118] Throughout the program, managers stress to employees that they do not have to tolerate sexual harassment or get involved in situations in which harassment is likely to occur. The "Management Insight" feature provides tips for ensuring that the training is effective.

Management Insight

Providing Effective Anti-Harassment Training

A swirl of sexual harassment charges in workplaces has made preventing such behavior a hot topic. The sight of prominent women speaking up about their experiences and of perpetrators being held accountable has given more employees hope that if they speak up, they may be taken seriously. The Equal Employment Opportunity Commission indicated that in the months after the Harvey Weinstein scandal, its website began receiving four times as many visits.[119] Companies including Fox News, NBC, and Uber announced new training in harassment prevention.

The problem, however, is that there is little evidence to support the effectiveness of anti-harassment training programs.[120] Typical programs were designed mainly to tell people what sexual harassment is and that it is illegal. Often, it involves a set of videos to watch and identify bad behavior. Few companies follow up to find out if attitudes or behavior have changed. When they do, they sometimes discover that knowledge is unchanged or they have simply reinforced stereotypes.

But the evidence does suggest some ideas for effective training to prevent sexual harassment. One helpful tactic is to set up training in small groups.[121] Face-to-face conversations and job-related examples are more powerful than generic presentations. Further, having everyone, especially leaders, participate in the training signals that respectful behavior is valued and necessary at all levels of the organization. Another promising method is to focus the training on civil behavior.[122] Employees know they shouldn't grab a coworker, but some worry about what they can do. Civility training can promote behavior like respectful listening and affirmation of others' contributions, especially with regard to those who may feel marginalized. Managers can be trained in how to mentor employees in ways that empower rather than harass. Another good practice is to recognize that harassment is more about exerting power than about expressing sexuality.[123] Therefore, one way to stop it is to equip bystanders to intervene. Training can offer options: A bystander can point out the behavior's inappropriateness, provide a disruption, or find an occasion to talk to the target so he or she isn't isolated.

Finally, training should be embedded in an ethical culture of respect and inclusion.[124] Organizations that are inclusive in hiring, training, and promotions will place more women and people of color in positions of power. This restrains the power dynamic that supports harassment. And as with any other kind of behavior, the behavior of the organization's leaders sets the tone for everyone else. ●

Barry S. Roberts and Richard A. Mann, experts on business law and authors of several books on the topic, suggest a number of additional factors that managers and all members of an organization need to keep in mind about sexual harassment:[125]

- Every sexual harassment charge should be taken seriously.
- Employees who go along with unwanted sexual attention in the workplace can be sexual harassment victims.
- Employees sometimes wait before they file complaints of sexual harassment.
- An organization's sexual harassment policy should be communicated to each new employee and reviewed with current employees periodically.
- Suppliers and customers need to be familiar with an organization's sexual harassment policy.
- Managers should give employees alternative ways to report incidents of sexual harassment.
- Employees who report sexual harassment must have their rights protected; this includes being protected from any potential retaliation.
- Allegations of sexual harassment should be kept confidential; those accused of harassment should have their rights protected.
- Investigations of harassment charges and any resultant disciplinary actions need to proceed in a timely manner.
- Managers must protect employees from sexual harassment from third parties they may interact with while performing their jobs, such as suppliers or customers.

Summary and Review

ETHICS AND STAKEHOLDERS Ethics are moral principles or beliefs about what is right or wrong. These beliefs guide people in their dealings with other individuals and groups (stakeholders) and provide a basis for deciding whether behavior is right and proper. Many organizations have a formal code of ethics derived primarily from societal ethics, professional ethics, and the individual ethics of the organization's top managers. Managers can apply ethical standards to help themselves decide on the proper way to behave toward organizational stakeholders. Ethical organizational cultures are those in which ethical values and norms are emphasized. Ethical organizational cultures can help organizations and their members behave in a socially responsible manner. [LO 3-1, 3-2]

INCREASING DIVERSITY OF WORKFORCE AND ORGANIZATIONAL ENVIRONMENT Diversity is differences among people due to age, gender, race, ethnicity, religion, sexual orientation, socioeconomic background, and capabilities/disabilities. The workforce and the organizational environment have become increasingly diverse. Effectively managing diversity is an ethical imperative and can improve organizational effectiveness. [LO 3-3, 3-5]

MANAGING DIVERSITY The effective management of diversity is not only an essential responsibility of managers but an ethical and a business imperative. In each of their managerial roles, managers can encourage organizationwide acceptance and valuing of diversity. [LO 3-4, 3-5]

SEXUAL HARASSMENT Two forms of sexual harassment are quid pro quo sexual harassment and hostile work environment sexual harassment. Steps that managers can take to eradicate sexual harassment include development, communication, and enforcement of a sexual harassment policy, use of fair complaint procedures, prompt corrective action when harassment occurs, and sexual harassment training and education. [LO 3-6]

Management *in Action*

Topics for Discussion and Action

Discussion

1. When are ethics and ethical standards especially important in organizations? [LO 3-1]

2. Why might managers do things that conflict with their own ethical values? [LO 3-1]

3. How can managers ensure that they create ethical organizational cultures? [LO 3-2]

4. Sometimes LGBT employees experience discrimination in the workplace. As a manager, what steps would you take to ensure such discrimination is eliminated? [LO 3-3]

5. Some workers might resent accommodations made for employees with disabilities. As a manager, what could you do to ensure all employees are treated fairly? [LO 3-3]

Action

6. Choose a *Fortune* 500 company not mentioned in the chapter. Conduct research to determine what steps this organization has taken to effectively manage diversity and eliminate sexual harassment. [LO 3-4, 3-5, 3-6]

Building Management Skills

Solving Diversity-Related Problems [LO 3-3, 3-4, 3-5, 3-6]

Think about the last time that you (1) were treated unfairly because you differed from a decision maker on a particular dimension of diversity or (2) observed someone else being treated unfairly because that person differed from a decision maker on a particular dimension of diversity. Then answer these questions:

1. Why do you think the decision maker acted unfairly in this situation?

2. In what ways, if any, were biases, stereotypes, or overt discrimination involved in this situation?

3. Was the decision maker aware that he or she was acting unfairly?

4. What could you or the person who was treated unfairly have done to improve matters and rectify the injustice on the spot?

5. Was any sexual harassment involved in this situation? If so, what kind was it?

6. If you had authority over the decision maker (e.g., if you were his or her manager or supervisor), what steps would you take to ensure that the decision maker no longer treated diverse individuals unfairly?

Managing Ethically [LO 3-1]

Some companies require that their employees work very long hours and travel extensively. Employees with young children, employees taking care of elderly relatives, and employees who have interests outside the workplace sometimes find that their careers are jeopardized if they try to work more reasonable hours or limit their work-related travel. Some of these employees feel that it is unethical for their manager to expect so much of them in the workplace and not understand their needs as parents and caregivers.

Questions

1. Either individually or in a group, think about the ethical implications of requiring long hours and extensive amounts of travel for some jobs.

2. What obligations do you think managers and companies have to enable employees to have a balanced life and meet nonwork needs and demands?

Small Group Breakout Exercise [LO 3-3, 3-4, 3-5]

Determining If a Problem Exists

Form groups of three or four people, and appoint one member as the spokesperson who will communicate your findings to the whole class when called on by the instructor. Then discuss the following scenario:

You and your partners own and manage a local chain of restaurants, with moderate to expensive prices, that are open for lunch and dinner during the week and for dinner on weekends. Your staff is diverse, and you believe that you are effectively managing diversity. Yet on visits to the different restaurants you have noticed that your African American employees tend to congregate together and communicate mainly with each other. The same is true for your Hispanic employees and your white employees. You are meeting with your partners today to discuss this observation.

1. Discuss why the patterns of communication that you observed might be occurring in your restaurants.

2. Discuss whether your observation reflects an underlying problem. If so, why? If not, why not?

3. Discuss whether you should address this issue with your staff and in your restaurants. If so, how and why? If not, why not?

Be the Manager [LO 3-3, 3-4, 3-5, 3-6]

You are Maria Herrera and have been recently promoted to the position of director of financial analysis for a medium-size consumer goods firm. During your first few weeks on the job, you took the time to have lunch with each of your employees to try to get to know them better. You have 12 direct reports who are junior and senior financial analysts who support different product lines. Susan Epstein, one of the female financial analysts you had lunch with, made the following statement: "I'm so glad we finally have a woman in charge. Now, hopefully things will get better around here." You pressed Epstein to elaborate, but she clammed up. She indicated that she didn't want to unnecessarily bias you and that the problems were pretty self-evident. In fact, Epstein was surprised that you didn't know what she was talking about and jokingly mentioned that perhaps you should spend some time undercover, observing her group and their interactions with others.

You spoke with your supervisor and the former director who had been promoted and had volunteered to be on call if you had any questions. Neither man knew of any diversity-related issues in your group. In fact, your supervisor's response was, "We've got a lot of problems, but fortunately that's not one of them."

Question

1. What are you going to do to address this issue?

Case in the News [LO 3-1, 3-2]

Chevron Tries to Stay on the High Road in Venezuela

Oil companies have to operate where there is oil to pump, and that can lead them into places where ethical standards are difficult to uphold. Take Venezuela, for instance. It has important oil reserves but also a government widely viewed as corrupt and an economy in a downward spiral. Chevron has been the only major U.S. oil company to stay in Venezuela in recent years, and its recent experiences raise questions about its future there.

Chevron first got involved in Venezuela in the 1920s, with exploration there leading to the discovery of a major oil field. Doing business in Venezuela became more difficult following the election of governments that nationalized businesses, taking over their assets. But Chevron persevered and made arrangements to provide services to the government-owned oil operations. Working with the government was profitable during the decade beginning in 2004. Then oil prices fell, and so did profits. Other companies left, but as of 2018, Chevron was still involved in five projects in the country and offshore.

In Venezuela, Chevron sponsors social programs to promote the development of local communities, investing millions of dollars. It supports economic development through microloans to small businesses, coupled with a training program so that individuals can learn finance, marketing, and other business skills. Another economic development program teaches sewing skills to women enduring violence or extreme poverty, so they can become more independent. Chevron seeks to improve education by funding teacher training, school construction, and university education in energy-related fields. And it promotes better health care by supporting programs aimed at treating specific diseases and birth defects.

Under the socialist government of Nicolás Maduro, Chevron's business interests in Venezuela are all in the form of joint ventures, where it shares ownership with the state oil company, Petróleos de Venezuela SA (PdVSA). In each of these, Chevron holds a minority interest, between 25% and 40% of the company's shares. Being a minority owner limits Chevron's ability to guide day-to-day decisions. It can, of course, look for ways to be influential, even if PdVSA ultimately calls the shots.

Nevertheless, conditions in Venezuela are becoming increasingly difficult. Since 2014, when the price of oil tumbled, the government has been dealing with a financial crisis and pays late, fails to maintain equipment, and requires that employees take time off for political rallies. During the past few years, Chevron has been losing money on its Venezuelan operations, though it maintains hope that a new administration will take power and turn the situation around. So far, the economy remains in a crisis state, with prices skyrocketing, store shelves empty, and violence out of control. Despite all this, PdVSA executives and other government leaders seem to be prospering, raising questions about corruption in high places. Pointing to the appearance of corruption as well as the takeover of businesses in the nationalization program, the U.S. government imposed sanctions on Venezuela that limit how much businesses can be involved with the Maduro regime.

In recent incidents, the crisis has hit very close to home for Chevron managers. The government arrested two Chevron employees after they refused to sign a contract for equipment to be purchased at what they insist were above-market prices. According to reports, the Venezuelan employees were to be charged with treason. Two months later, they were released, but while they were imprisoned, Chevron evacuated other employees. Also, workers went on strike to protest a new minimum wage announced by the government. Amazingly, the 3,000% increase to 1,800 bolivars a month amounts to only about the equivalent of $15 a month and does not come near to keeping up with inflation, which at the time was raging at a rate of 111,000%.

As Chevron weighs what to do next, it has appointed a new chief of its Venezuelan operations. Javier La Rosa had been running Chevron Brazil and previously held an executive position at Chevron Venezuela.

Chevron has established criteria to apply to difficult decisions. Of course, as a business, it is concerned with choosing profitable alternatives. But it also has a code of conduct to guide decision making based on ethical principles. These include obeying not only the laws of Venezuela, but also those of the United States, including laws against bribery and other forms of corruption. Other requirements include abiding by values such as respect for diversity, commitment to high performance, and insistence on integrity and ethical behavior. The statement also expresses a commitment to human rights, such as respect and dignity.

Questions for Discussion

1. Do you think a business can maintain high ethical standards if it is operating where the government is corrupt and the economy is collapsing? Based on your opinion, what advice would you give Chevron's managers about operating in Venezuela?

2. What evidence do you see of a commitment to social responsibility at Chevron? If Chevron were to leave Venezuela, what do you think would be the impact on its employees and the communities where it operates?

3. If Chevron continues to be unprofitable in Venezuela, should it leave? What if it finds a way to become more profitable again? How, if at all, does profitability change your answer?

Sources: K. Crowley, "Chevron CEO Vows to Work with U.S. to Remain in Venezuela," *Yahoo Finance,* https://finance.yahoo.com, February 12, 2019; K. Vyas and B. Olson, "Chevron Stayed in Venezuela Long after Rivals Quit; It's Having Second Thoughts," *The Wall Street Journal,* www.wsj.com, November 8, 2018; Chevron, "Venezuela," www.chevron.com, accessed November 8, 2018; Chevron, *Business Conduct and Ethics Code,* www.chevron.com, accessed November 8, 2018; F. Zerpa, "Oil Workers Protest Pay in Venezuela," *Bloomberg,* www.bloomberg.com, October 1, 2018; A. Alper and M. Parraga, "Chevron Names Brazil Chief to Lead Venezuela Operations after Arrests," Reuters, www.reuters.com, June 8, 2018; C. Pons and M. Parraga, "Venezuela Frees Chevron Executives Held Since April," Reuters, www.reuters.com, June 6, 2018.

Endnotes

1. B. Ortutay, "Diversity in Tech: Lots of Attention, Little Progress," Associated Press, https://apnews.com, accessed November 20, 2018; L. Winning, "It's Time to Prioritize Diversity across Tech," *Forbes,* www.forbes.com, March 13, 2018.

2. M. R. Dickey, "Intel's Diversity Efforts Are Somewhat Paying Off," *TechCrunch,* https://techcrunch.com, accessed November 20, 2018; Erin Carson, "Intel Diversity Report Shows Progress Is Tough to Measure," *CNET,* www.cnet.com, August 15, 2017; Grace Donnelly, "Intel CEO in New Diversity Report: 'Let's Turn This Tragedy into Action,'" *Fortune,* http://fortune.com, August 15, 2017.

3. S. G. Carmichael, "Making Intel More Diverse," interview of Danielle Brown, *Harvard Business Review,* https://hbr.org, March 10, 2017; Carson, "Intel Diversity Report Shows Progress Is Tough to Measure."

4. Carmichael, "Making Intel More Diverse"; Donnelly, "Intel CEO in New Diversity Report."

5. S. Lynn, "Meet Intel's Newest Executive, Barbara Whye," *Black Enterprise,* www.blackenterprise.com, April 13, 2017.

6. Carmichael, "Making Intel More Diverse"; Dickey, "Intel's Diversity Efforts Are Somewhat Paying Off"; Carson, "Intel Diversity Report Shows Progress Is Tough to Measure."

7. Y. Koh, "Intel Hits an Internal Goal for Workforce Diversity," *The Wall Street Journal,* www.wsj.com, October 29, 2018.

8. Carmichael, "Making Intel More Diverse"; Dickey, "Intel's Diversity Efforts."

9. Intel, "2018 Annual Diversity and Inclusion Data Addendum," www.intel.com, accessed November 20, 2018.

10. R. Mayhew, "How to Handle Ethical Issues in the Workplace," *Houston Chronicle,* https://smallbusiness.chron.com, June 30, 2018.

11. J. Berke and S. Gould, "Michigan Is the 10th State to Legalize Recreational Marijuana," *Business Insider,* www.businessinsider.com, November 7, 2018.

12. "A Step Forward in the Fight against Gun Violence," *Bloomberg Opinion,* www.bloomberg.com, November 9, 2018; E. Levenson and J. Sterling, "These Are the Victims of the Florida School Shooting," *CNN,* www.cnn.com, February 21, 2018.

13. March for Our Lives, "Mission Statement," https://marchforourlives.com, accessed November 20, 2018; A. Held, "One by One, Companies Cut Ties with the NRA," *NPR,* www.npr.org, accessed November 20, 2018.

14. R. E. Freeman, *Strategic Management: A Stakeholder Approach* (Marshfield, MA: Pitman, 1984).

15. B. Gates and M. Gates, "Annual Letter 2018: The 10 Toughest Questions We Get," www.gatesnotes.com, accessed November 20, 2018; N. Kirsch, "Philanthropy King: Bill Gates Gives Away $4.6 Billion, Unveils New Campaign to Fight Malaria," *Forbes,* www.forbes.com, August 15, 2017.

16. Z. Mejia, "How the March for Our Lives Gen Z Organizers Changed the Gun Control Conversation When No One Else Could," *CNBC,* www.cnbc.com, accessed November 20, 2018; C. Ingraham, "Nobody Knows How Many Members the NRA Has, but Its Tax Returns Offer Some Clues," *The Washington Post,* www.washingtonpost.com, February 26, 2018.

17. Freeman, *Strategic Management.*

18. R. Ferris, "GM to Halt Production at Several Plants, Cut More Than 14,000 Jobs," *CNBC,* www.cnbc.com, November 26, 2018.

19. B. Bain, "Volcker Rule Changes Move Forward after SEC Votes on Overhaul," *Bloomberg,* www.bloomberg.com, accessed November 27, 2018.

20. D. Rushe, "US Bosses Now Earn 312 Times the Average Worker's Wage, Figures Show," *The Guardian,* www.theguardian.com, August 16, 2018.

21. W. G. Sanders and D. C. Hambrick, "Swinging for the Fences: The Effects of CEO Stock Options on Company Risk Taking and Performance," *Academy of Management Journal* 53, no. 5 (2007), 1055–78.

22. T. L. Beauchamp and N. E. Bowie, eds., *Ethical Theory and Business* (Engle-wood Cliffs, NJ: Prentice-Hall, 1929); A. MacIntyre, *After Virtue* (South Bend, IN: University of Notre Dame Press, 1981).

23. R. E. Goodin, "How to Determine Who Should Get What," *Ethics,* July 1975, 310–21.

24. T. M. Jones, "Ethical Decision Making by Individuals in Organization: An Issue Contingent Model," *Academy of Management Journal* 16 (1991), 366–95; G. F. Cavanaugh, D. J. Moberg, and M. Velasquez, "The Ethics of Organizational Politics," *Academy of Management Review* 6 (1981), 363–74.

25. T. M. Jones, "Instrumental Stakeholder Theory: A Synthesis of Ethics and Economics," *Academy of Management Review* 20 (1995), 404–37.

26. B. Victor and J. B. Cullen, "The Organizational Bases of Ethical Work Climates," *Administrative Science Quarterly* 33 (1988), 101–25.

27. D. Collins, "Organizational Harm, Legal Consequences and Stakeholder Retaliation," *Journal of Business Ethics* 8 (1988), 1–13.

28. R. C. Solomon, *Ethics and Excellence* (New York: Oxford University Press, 1992).

29. T. E. Becker, "Integrity in Organizations: Beyond Honesty and Conscientiousness," *Academy of Management Review* 23 (January 1998), 154–62.

30. S. W. Gellerman, "Why Good Managers Make Bad Decisions," in K. R. Andrews, ed., *Ethics in Practice: Managing the Moral Corporation* (Boston: Harvard Business School Press, 1989).

31. J. Dobson, "Corporate Reputation: A Free Market Solution to Unethical Behavior," *Business and Society* 28 (1989), 1–5.

32. M. S. Baucus and J. P. Near, "Can Illegal Corporate Behavior Be Predicted? An Event History Analysis," *Academy of Management Journal* 34 (1991), 9–36.

33. L. K. Trevino, "Ethical Decision Making in Organizations: A Person-Interactionist Model," *Academy of Management Review* 11 (1986), 601–17.

34. A. S. Waterman, "On the Uses of Psychological Theory and Research in the Process of Ethical Inquiry," *Psychological Bulletin* 103, no. 3 (1988), 283–98.

35. M. S. Frankel, "Professional Codes: Why, How, and with What Impact? *Ethics* 8 (1989): 283–98.

36. J. Van Maanen and S. R. Barley, "Occupational Communities: Culture and Control in Organizations," in B. Staw and L. Cummings, eds., *Research in Organizational Behavior,* vol. 6 (Greenwich, CT: JAI Press, 1984), 287–365.

37. Jones, "Ethical Decision Making by Individuals in Organizations."

38. M. Conlin, "Where Layoffs Are a Last Resort," *BusinessWeek,* October 8, 2001, *BusinessWeek* Archives; *Southwest Airlines Fact Sheet,* June 19, 2001, www.swabiz.com.

39. G. R. Jones, *Organizational Theory: Text and Cases* (Reading, MA: Addison-Wesley, 1997).

40. "Accenture Reimagines Its Code of Business Ethics through Intelligent Technology," news release, https://newsroom.accenture.com, accessed November 27, 2018.

41. *Welcome to the Code of Business Ethics: Your Guide to Responsible Behavior, Every Day,* www.accenture.com, accessed November 27, 2018.

42. "Accenture Reimagines Is Code of Business Ethics"; "Embracing the Disruptive Power of Chatbots," www.accenture.com, accessed November 27, 2018; A. Kramer, "Intelligent Technology Can Give Ethical Guidance," *Technology, Telecom and Internet Blog* (Bloomberg Law), www.bna.com, accessed November 27, 2018.

43. S. Rubenfeld, "Accenture Tries Chatbot for Code of Conduct," *The Wall Street Journal,* https://blogs.wsj.com, January 24, 2018; Kramer, "Intelligent Technology Can Give Ethical Guidance."

44. Rubenfeld, "Accenture Tries Chatbot."

45. P. E. Murphy, "Creating Ethical Structure," *Sloan Management Review* (Winter 1989), 81–87.

46. W. B. Swann, Jr., J. T. Polzer, D. C. Seyle and S. J. Ko, "Finding Value in Diversity: Verification of Personal and Social Self-Views in Diverse Groups," *Academy of Management Review* 29, no. 1 (2004), 9–27.

47. S. Tasheva and A. Hillman, "Integrating Diversity at Different Levels: Multi-Level Human Capital, Social Capital, and Demographic Diversity and Their Implications for Team Effectiveness," *Academy of Management Review,* January 19, 2018.

48. E. Sherman, "Hiring Bias Blacks and Latinos Face Hasn't Improved in 25 Years," *Forbes,* www.forbes.com, September 16, 2017.

49. "Private Sector Workers Lack Transparency," *Institute for Women's Policy Research,* https://iwpr.org, December 2017.

50. V. Zarya, "The Share of Female CEOs in the Fortune 500 Dropped by 25% in 2018," *Fortune,* http://fortune.com, May 21, 2018; J. Berman, "When a Woman or Person of Color Becomes CEO, White Men Have a Strange Reaction," *MarketWatch,* www.marketwatch.com, March 3, 2018.

51. "Fact Sheet: Aging in the United States," *Population Reference Bureau,* www.prb.org, accessed November 28, 2018; "Age Discrimination," www.eeoc.gov, accessed November 28, 2018; U.S. Census Bureau, "2030 Marks Important Demographic Milestone for U.S. Population," www.census.gov, September 6, 2018.

52. Bureau of Labor Statistics, "Usual Weekly Earnings of Wage and Salary Workers, Q3 2018," www.bls.gov, October 16, 2018.

53. Catalyst, "Pyramid: Women in S&P 500 Companies," www.catalyst.org, October 3, 2018.

54. Catalyst, "Women CEOs of the S&P 500," www.catalyst.org, October 3, 2018.

55. R. Sharpe, "As Leaders, Women Rule," *BusinessWeek,* November 20, 2000, 75–84.

56. "New Catalyst Study Reveals Financial Performance Is Higher for Companies with More Women at the Top," www.catalyst.org, accessed December 1, 2018.

57. "100 Women: Do Women on Boards Increase Company Profits?" *BBC,* www.bbc.com, accessed December 1, 2018.

58. "Race Data," www.census.org, accessed November 28, 2018.

59. U.S. Census Bureau, "Director's Blog: 2015 National Content Test Results Released This Week," www.census.gov, accessed November 28, 2018.

60. U.S. Census Bureau, "Civilian Labor Force by Age, Sex, Race, and Ethnicity," www.census.gov, accessed November 28, 2018.

61. U.S. Census Bureau, "Quick Facts," www.census.gov, accessed November 28, 2018.

62. U.S. Census Bureau, "Table 11: Percent Distribution of the Projected Population by Hispanic Origin and Race for the United States, 2015 to 2060," www.census.gov, accessed November 28, 2018.

63. Bureau of Labor Statistics, "Table 3. Median Usual Weekly Earnings of Full-Time Wage and Salary Workers by Age, Race, Hispanic or Latino Ethnicity, and Sex, Q3 2018 Averages," www.bls.gov, accessed November 28, 2018.

64. "About SodaStream," www.sodastream.com, accessed March 17, 2018; D. Leonard and Y. Benmeleh, "How SodaStream Makes—and Markets—Peace," *Bloomberg Businessweek,* December 25, 2017, 60–65.

65. "About SodaStream."

66. Leonard and Benmeleh, "How SodaStream Makes—and Markets—Peace."

67. Ibid.

68. J. O'Brien, "SodaStream Reveals Why 'Disruptive' Influencers Campaigns Are Vital to Reaching New Audiences," *CMO,* www.cmo.com.au, February 9, 2018; J. Rooney, "The Future of Recruiting Talent? SodaStream Launches Commercial to Find 'Rainmakers,'" *Forbes,* www.forbes.com, February 2, 2018; Leonard and Benmeleh, "How SodaStream Makes—and Markets—Peace."

69. G. Hoffman, "'Exodus' Survivor Inspires Son Who Sold SodaStream for $3.2 Billion," *The Jerusalem Post,* www.jpost.com, August 24, 2018; S. Eisen, "PepsiCo to Buy SodaStream for $3.2 Billion," *CNBC,* www.cnbc.com, August 20, 2018.

70. K. Shattuck, "Alan Cumming Helps CBS Unfurl Its Rainbow Flag with 'Instinct,'" *The New York Times,* www.nytimes.com, accessed November 28, 2018; M. Berg, Note to Networks: Diversity on TV Pays Off," *Forbes,* www.forbes.com, February 22, 2017.

71. B. Latimer, "Latinos in Hollywood: Few Roles, Frequent Stereotypes, New Study Finds," *NBC,* www.nbcnews.com, February 22, 2016.

72. T. Abbady, "The Modern Newsroom Is Stuck behind the Gender and Color Line," *NPR,* www.npr.org, May 1, 2017.

73. J. H. Conlan, "Putting a Little Faith in Diversity," *BusinessWeek Online,* December 21, 2000.

74. K. Klenner, "Religious Expression in Today's Workplace Is a Thorny Issue," *Labor and Employment Blog,* www.bna.com, accessed November 28, 2018.

75. Conlan, "Putting a Little Faith in Diversity."

76. K. Holland, "When Religious Needs Test Company Policy," *The New York Times,* www.nytimes.com, accessed March 17, 2018; K. K. Chang, "What Companies Can Do When Work and Religion Conflict," *Harvard Business Review,* https://hbr.org, March 15, 2016.

77. J. N. Cleveland, J. Barnes-Farrell, and J .M. Ratz, "Accommodation in the Workplace," *Human Resource Management Review* 7 (1997), 77–108; A. Colella, "Coworker Distributive Fairness Judgments of the Workplace Accommodations of Employees with Disabilities," *Academy of Management Review* 26 (2001), 100–16.

78. Colella, "Coworker Distributive Fairness Judgments of the

Workplace Accommodations of Employees with Disabilities"; M. S. West and R. L. Cardy, "Accommodating Claims of Disability: The Potential Impact of Abuses," *Human Resource Management Review* 7 (1997), 223–46.

79. A. Bhattacharya and H. Long, "America Still Leaves the Disabled Behind," *CNNMoney,* http://money.cnn.com, July 26, 2015.

80. Colella, "Coworker Distributive Fairness Judgments of the Workplace Accommodations of Employees with Disabilities."

81. "The Disability Equality Index: 2018 Best Places to Work," www.disabilityequalityindex.org, accessed November 28, 2018; S. Blahovec, "Why Hire Disabled Workers? 4 Powerful (and Inclusive) Companies Answer," *The Huffington Post,* www.huffingtonpost.com, February 24, 2017.

82. R. Brownstein, "Honoring Work Is Key to Ending Poverty," *Detroit News,* October 2, 2001, 9; G. Koretz, "How Welfare to Work Worked," *BusinessWeek,* September 24, 2001 (*BusinessWeek* Archives).

83. "As Ex-Welfare Recipients Lose Jobs, Offer Safety Net," *Atlanta Constitution,* October 10, 2001, A18.

84. K. Fontenot, J. Semega, and M. Kollar, "Income and Poverty in the United States: 2017," www.census.gov, accessed December 1, 2018.

85. "Poverty Thresholds for 2017 by Size of Family and Number of Related Children under 18 Years," www.census.gov, accessed December 1, 2018.

86. G. Thompson, "This Is What $15 an Hour Looks Like," *The Nation,* www.thenation.com, January 7, 2016.

87. N. Scheiber, "The Perils of Ever-Changing Work Schedules Extend to Children's Well-Being," *The New York Times,* www.nytimes.com, accessed December 1, 2018.

88. A. Chan, "Overnight Childcare Fills the Void in 24/7 Economy," *Los Angeles Times,* www.latimes.com, April 20, 2017.

89. F. Newport, "In U.S., Estimate of LGBT Population Rises to 4.5%," https://news.gallup.com, May 22, 2018; G. J. Gates, "In U.S., More Adults Identifying as LGBT," http://news.gallup.com, January 11, 2018.

90. D. Wiessner, "U.S. Appeals Court Says Title VII Covers Discrimination Based on Sexual Orientation," Reuters, www.reuters.com, February 26, 2018; B. Chappell, "Supreme Court Declares Same-Sex Marriage Legal in All 50 States," *NPR,* www.npr.org, June 26, 2015.

91. "Disney Recognized for Innovation on Workplace Equality," https://thewaltdisneycompany.com, October 16, 2017.

92. J. B. Shinall, "Occupational Characteristics and the Obesity Wage Penalty," Vanderbilt University Law School, Public Law & Legal Theory Working Paper 16-23, accessed at http://ssrn.com, March 16, 2018; A. Wolf, "Overweight Women Lose in the Job Market: Vanderbilt Study," https://news.vanderbilt.edu, October 21, 2014.

93. V. Valian, *Why So Slow? The Advancement of Women* (Cambridge, MA: MIT Press, 2000); S. T. Fiske and S. E. Taylor, *Social Cognition,* 2nd ed. (New York: McGraw-Hill, 1991).

94. Valian, *Why So Slow?*

95. S. Rynes and B. Rosen, "A Field Survey of Factors Affecting the Adoption and Perceived Success of Diversity Training," *Personnel Psychology* 48 (1995), 247–70; Valian, *Why So Slow?*

96. V. Brown and F. L. Geis, "Turning Lead into Gold: Leadership by Men and Women and the Alchemy of Social Consensus," *Journal of Personality and Social Psychology* 46 (1984), 811–24; Valian, *Why So Slow?*

97. Valian, *Why So Slow?*

98. J. Cole and B. Singer, "A Theory of Limited Differences: Explaining the Productivity Puzzle in Science," in H. Zuckerman, J. R. Cole, and J. T. Bruer, eds., *The Outer Circle: Women in the Scientific Community* (New York: Norton, 1991), 277–310; M. F. Fox, "Sex, Salary, and Achievement: Reward Dualism in Academia," *Sociology of Education* 54 (1981), 71–84; J. S. Long, "The Origins of Sex Differences in Science," *Social Forces* 68 (1990), 1297–315; R. F. Martell, D. M. Lane, and C. Emrich, "Male–Female Differences: A Computer Simulation," *American Psychologist* 51 (1996), 157–58; Valian, *Why So Slow?*

99. Ibid.

100. G. Robinson and K. Dechant, "Building a Case for Business Diversity," *Academy of Management Executive* 3 (1997), 32–47.

101. D. Keyes, "Target Opens New Small-Format Stores," *Business Insider,* www.businessinsider.com, accessed December 1, 2018.

102. V. Bolden-Barrett, "Study: Turnover Costs Employers $15,000 per Worker," *HR Dive,* www.hrdive.com, accessed December 1, 2018.

103. "Walmart Increases Support of Diverse Suppliers with Launch of Dedicated Online Showcase," https://news.walmart.com, accessed December 1, 2018.

104. J. Kahn, "Diversity Trumps the Downturn," *Fortune,* July 9, 2001, 114–116.

105. J. Kantor and M. Twohey, "Harvey Weinstein Paid Off Sexual Harassment Accusers for Decades," *The New York Times,* www.nytimes.com, accessed December 1, 2018.

106. N. Smartt, "Sexual Harassment in the Workplace in a #MeToo World," *Forbes,* www.forbes.com, accessed December 1, 2018.

107. R. Gillett, "Sexual Harassment Isn't a Hollywood, Tech, or Media Issue—It Affects Everyone," *Business Insider,* www.businessinsider.com, accessed December 1, 2018.

108. G. Fleishmann, "Google Fired 48 Employees for Sexual Harassment in Last 2 Years, Its CEO Says in Internal Email," *Fortune,* http://fortune.com, October 25, 2018.

109. S. Fiegerman, "Microsoft Received 238 Gender Discrimination and Harassment Complaints," *CNNMoney,* http://money.cnn.com, March 13, 2018.

110. R. DiGiacomo, "More Men Report Sexual Harassment at Work," *Monster,* www.monster.com, accessed December 1, 2018.

111. R. L. Paetzold and A. M. O'Leary-Kelly, "Organizational Communication and the Legal Dimensions of Hostile Work Environment Sexual Harassment,"

in G. L. Kreps, ed., *Sexual Harassment: Communication Implications* (Cresskill, NJ: Hampton Press, 1993).

112. M. Galen, J. Weber, and A. Z. Cuneo, "Sexual Harassment: Out of the Shadows," *Fortune,* October 28, 1991, 30–31.

113. A. M. O'Leary-Kelly, R. L. Paetzold, and R. W. Griffin, "Sexual Harassment as Aggressive Action: A Framework for Understanding Sexual Harassment," paper presented at the annual meeting of the Academy of Management, Vancouver, August 1995.

114. B. S. Roberts and R. A. Mann, "Sexual Harassment in the Workplace: A Primer," www3.uakron.edu/lawrev/robert1.html, May 1, 2004.

115. "Former FedEx Driver Wins EEOC Lawsuit," *Houston Chronicle,* February 26, 2004, 9B.

116. J. Robertson, "California Jury Awards $61M for Harassment," http://news.Yahoo.com, June 4, 2006.

117. S. J. Bresler and R. Thacker, "Four-Point Plan Helps Solve Harassment Problems," *HR Magazine,* May 1993, 117–24.

118. "Du Pont's Solution," *Training,* March 1992, 29.

119. R. Natour, "Does Sexual Harassment Training Work?," *PBS NewsHour,* www.pbs.org, January 8, 2018.

120. Natour, "Does Sexual Harassment Training Work?"; C. C. Miller, "Sexual Harassment Training Doesn't Work, but Some Things Do," *The New York Times,* www.nytimes.com, December 11, 2017; V. J. Magley and J. L. Grossman, "Do Sexual Harassment Prevention Trainings Really Work?," *Scientific American,* https://blogs.scientificamerican.com, November 10, 2017; M. Rhodan, "Does Sexual Harassment Training Work? Here's What the Research Shows," *Time,* http://time.com, November 21, 2017.

121. Natour, "Does Sexual Harassment Training Work?"; Rhodan, "Does Sexual Harassment Training Work?"

122. Natour, "Does Sexual Harassment Training Work?"

123. Ibid,; Miller, "Sexual Harassment Training Doesn't Work."

124. Natour, "Does Sexual Harassment Training Work?"; Rhodan, "Does Sexual Harassment Training Work?"

125. "Du Pont's Solution."

Polka Dot Images/Jupiterimages

4

Managing in the Global Environment

Learning Objectives

After studying this chapter, you should be able to:

LO 4-1 Explain why the ability to perceive, interpret, and respond appropriately to the global environment is crucial for managerial success.

LO 4-2 Differentiate between the global task and global general environments.

LO 4-3 Identify the main forces in the global task and general environments, and describe the challenges that each force presents to managers.

LO 4-4 Explain why the global environment is becoming more open and competitive, and identify the forces behind the process of globalization that increase the opportunities, complexities, challenges, and threats that managers face.

LO 4-5 Discuss why national cultures differ and why it is important that managers be sensitive to the effects of falling trade barriers and regional trade associations on the political and social systems of nations around the world.

Management Snapshot

Walmart Takes on Amazon in India

Which Factors Should Managers Consider When Going Global?

Walmart has played a dominant role in retailing, with $500 billion in annual sales. Although more than half of Walmart's 12,000 stores are located in 27 other countries, two-thirds of the company's revenues are still generated in the United States. Managers see potential for significant future growth if they can operate more successfully in foreign markets.[1]

Retailing is a turbulent industry, where yesterday's winners quickly become the has-beens of the future. To enjoy long-term success, retailers must continually anticipate the next growth markets and craft new strategies. Walmart executives are trying to keep pace with changing technology and identifying where consumer demand will most likely increase. India, for example, has a huge population, and as its economy moves more Indians into the middle class, they are increasingly gaining access to the Internet for shopping as well as other activities.[2]

As Walmart monitors the retail environment, it is shifting its focus away from some regions and toward others. The company recently announced sales of majority stakes in the 600-store Asda grocery chain in the United Kingdom and in a Brazilian supermarket group whose stores have posted disappointing sales growth, with some operating at a loss. In India, Walmart is looking for new pathways to growth in a country where retail sales are expected to top $1 trillion in the near future. Walmart entered the Indian market in 2009 but faced legal restrictions. Foreign-owned stores may not sell other companies' brands directly to consumers, so Walmart opened Best Price wholesale outlets serving business customers. The restriction to business customers limits sales, but the low-price strategy is effective enough that Walmart plans to add more outlets.[3]

Walmart is increasing its online presence in India with its largest acquisition so far: a 75% stake in an Indian retail site called Flipkart for $16 billion. Flipkart was started in India in 2007 by two former Amazon engineers, and under their leadership, it launched an innovative payment model (cash on delivery) in a country where few people have credit cards. Flipkart has grown into India's largest e-commerce site, with a market share of more than 30%. Walmart's majority ownership puts it in control of the company so that it is able to get around the restrictions placed on foreign-owned retail stores. It also positions Walmart to compete online with Amazon, the second-largest e-commerce site in India. Both companies are trying to enter on the ground floor of online

Walmart CEO Doug McMillon (right) and Flipkart CEO Binny Sansal (left) join forces in Bangalore, India, to announce Walmart's $16 billion stake in the Indian e-commerce giant. AFP/Getty Images

selling to consumers in India, where online shopping is still in its early stages. Just 15% of Indians shop online, but online sales have more than tripled since 2015 and are forecast to grow at 28% per year. Both sites have the potential to become the main destination for e-tailing in India, as Amazon is in the United States.[4]

Walmart hopes the Flipkart deal will rev up its growth in India, which has been slow. Besides the restrictions on store retailing, India's traditional mom-and-pop stores, called *kiranas,* are formidable competition. The costs for renting a tiny space and hiring workers in India are so low that the stores make a good profit selling to their neighborhoods. The owners know the names and needs of their local clientele and can offer swift delivery by store employees. The personal touch creates strong customer loyalty. So far, Walmart has been able to carve out a niche with its Best Price outlets selling to the kiranas. To serve consumers directly in this difficult environment, Walmart believes the combination of its expertise in store retail and Flipkart's local market knowledge and expertise in online selling will make the combined businesses unbeatable.[5]

Overview

Top managers of a global company like Walmart operate in an environment where they compete with other companies for scarce and valuable resources. Managers of companies large and small have found that to survive and prosper in the 21st century, most companies must become global organizations, which operate and compete not only domestically, at home, but also globally, in countries around the world. Operating in the global environment is uncertain and unpredictable because it is complex and changes constantly.

global organization
An organization that operates and competes in more than one country.

LO 4-1
Explain why the ability to perceive, interpret, and respond appropriately to the global environment is crucial for managerial success.

If organizations are to adapt successfully to this changing environment, their managers must learn to understand the forces that operate in it and how these forces give rise to opportunities and threats. In this chapter we examine why the environment, both domestically and globally, has become more open, vibrant, and competitive. We examine how forces in the task and general environments affect global organizations and their managers. By the end of this chapter, you will appreciate the changes that are taking place in the environment and understand why it is important for managers to develop a global perspective as they strive to increase organizational efficiency and effectiveness.

What Is the Global Environment?

The global environment is a set of forces and conditions in the world outside an organization's boundary that affect how it operates and shape its behavior.[6] These forces change over time and thus present managers with *opportunities* and *threats.* Some changes in the global environment, such as the development of efficient new production technology, the availability of lower-cost components, or the opening of new global markets, create opportunities for managers to make and sell more products, obtain more resources and capital, and thereby strengthen their organization. In contrast, the rise of new global competitors, a global economic recession, or an oil shortage poses threats that can devastate an organization if managers are unable to sell its products. The quality of managers' understanding of forces in the global environment and their ability to

LO 4-2
Differentiate between the global task and global general environments.

respond appropriately to those forces are critical factors affecting organizational performance.

In this chapter we explore the nature of these forces and consider how managers can respond to them. To identify opportunities and threats caused by forces in the global environment, it is helpful for managers to distinguish between the *task environment* and the more encompassing *general environment* (see Figure 4.1).

The task environment is the set of forces and conditions that originate with global suppliers, distributors, customers, and competitors; these forces and conditions affect an organization's ability to obtain inputs used to manufacture and sell its products or services. The task environment contains the forces that have the most *immediate* and *direct* effect on managers because they pressure and influence managers daily. When managers turn on the radio or television, arrive at their offices in the morning, check their emails, or look at their computers or mobile devices, they are likely to learn about problems facing them because of changing conditions in their organization's task environment.

The general environment includes the wide-ranging global, economic, technological, sociocultural, demographic, political, and legal forces that affect the organization and its task environment. For the individual manager, opportunities and threats resulting from changes in the general environment are often more difficult to identify and respond to than are events in the task environment. However, changes in these forces can have major impacts on managers and their organizations.

global environment The set of global forces and conditions that operate beyond an organization's boundaries but affect a manager's ability to acquire and utilize resources.

task environment The set of forces and conditions that originate with suppliers, distributors, customers, and competitors and affect an organization's ability to obtain inputs used to manufacture and sell its products or services because they influence managers daily.

The Task Environment

Forces in the task environment result from the actions of suppliers, distributors, customers, and competitors both at home and abroad (see Figure 4.1). These four groups affect a manager's ability to obtain resources and dispose of outputs daily, weekly, and monthly and thus have a significant impact on short-term decision making.

general environment The wide-ranging global, economic, technological, sociocultural, demographic, political, and legal forces that affect an organization and its task environment.

Suppliers

Suppliers are the individuals and organizations that provide an organization with the input resources (such as raw materials, component parts, or employees) it needs to produce goods and services. In return, the suppliers receive payment for those goods and services. An important aspect of a manager's job is to ensure a reliable supply of input resources.

Consider Dell Technologies—a leading PC and information technology company—as an example. Dell has many suppliers of component parts such as microprocessors (Intel) and disk drives (Nvidia and Intel). It also has suppliers of preinstalled software, including the operating systems and specific application software (Microsoft, Chrome, and Adobe). Dell's providers of capital, such as banks and other financial institutions, are also key suppliers.

Dell has several suppliers of labor. One source is the educational institutions that train future Dell employees and therefore provide the company with skilled workers. Another is trade unions, organizations that represent employee interests and can control the supply of labor by exercising the right of unionized workers to strike. Unions also can influence the terms and conditions under which labor is employed. In organizations and industries where unions are strong, an important

LO 4-3

Identify the main forces in the global task and general environments, and describe the challenges that each force presents to managers.

Figure 4.1

Forces in the Global Environment

suppliers Individuals and organizations that provide an organization with the input resources it needs to produce goods and services.

part of a manager's job is negotiating and administering agreements with unions and their representatives.

Changes in the nature, number, or type of suppliers produce opportunities and threats to which managers must respond if their organizations are to prosper. For example, a major supplier-related threat that confronts managers arises when suppliers' bargaining position is so strong that they can raise the prices of the inputs they supply to the organization. A supplier's bargaining position is especially strong when (1) the supplier is the sole source of an input and (2) the input is vital to the organization.[7] For example, for many years G. D. Searle was the sole supplier of NutraSweet, the artificial sweetener used in most diet soft drinks. Not only was NutraSweet an important ingredient in diet soft drinks, but it also was one for which there was no acceptable substitute (saccharin and other artificial sweeteners raised health concerns). Searle earned its privileged position because it invented and held the patent for NutraSweet, and patents prohibit other organizations from introducing competing products for 17 years. As a result Searle was able to demand a high price for NutraSweet, charging twice the price of an equivalent amount of sugar; and paying that price raised the costs of soft drink manufacturers such as Coca-Cola and PepsiCo. When Searle's patent expired many other companies introduced products similar to NutraSweet, and prices fell.[8] In the 2000s Splenda, which was made by McNeil Nutritionals, replaced NutraSweet as the artificial sweetener of choice, and NutraSweet's price fell further; Splenda began to command a high price from soft drink companies.[9] However, a natural sweetener introduced less than a decade ago has gained market share on Splenda and other sweeteners. A zero-calorie sweetener extracted from the stevia plant is expected to have a global market of more than $720 million by 2022, according to recent research, replacing many artificial sweeteners in soft drinks, other beverages, and food products.[10]

In contrast, when an organization has many suppliers for a particular input, it is in a relatively strong bargaining position with those suppliers and can demand low-cost, high-quality inputs from them. Often an organization can use its power with suppliers to force them to reduce their prices, as Dell frequently does. Dell, for example, is constantly searching for low-cost suppliers abroad to keep its PC prices competitive. At a global level, organizations can buy products from suppliers overseas or become their own suppliers by manufacturing their products abroad.

It is important that managers recognize the opportunities and threats associated with managing the global supply chain. On one hand, gaining access to low-cost products made abroad represents an opportunity for U.S. companies to lower their input costs. On the other hand, they have less control over production processes carried out by suppliers located far away. This poses a threat to the brand if the suppliers deliver poor quality. Buying from low-wage countries also involves a threat related to social responsibility: If stakeholders determine that suppliers aren't meeting minimum standards for ethical treatment of their workers, the company's reputation may be damaged. To see how Levi Strauss addressed this issue, read the "Ethics in Action" feature.

Ethics in Action

Levi Strauss Motivates Global Suppliers to Treat Workers Well

When Levi Strauss & Company began sourcing work from low-wage countries in the 1990s, it was concerned about poor working conditions. In response, the global retailer prepared a code of conduct—its Terms of Engagement, requiring measures to meet workers' basic needs and protect their rights and the environment.[11] A supplier wanting to sell to Levi's had to meet those terms. Eventually, this innovation became the norm in the clothing industry. But despite efforts to enforce the terms with suppliers, violations continued. CEO Chip Bergh decided that lasting change required a shift in managers' attitudes.

Levi's launched an initiative it calls Worker Well-Being.[12] Its goal is to improve the experience of workers at Levi's suppliers, leading to greater efficiency and reliability, thereby creating a stronger supply network. Caring for workers' interests thus generates a win for all. Levi's provides funds and guidance, but each supplier plans how to achieve worker well-being. The basic approach is to survey workers; learn what they need to be healthy, productive, and engaged at work; identify the company's labor-related areas of improvement; and work with nonprofit partners to meet those needs. Because "well-being" is a broad objective, Levi's partnered with Harvard's Center for Health and the Global Environment to develop success measures that connect worker well-being with business performance.[13] Ultimately, the measures should demonstrate to factory managers why worker well-being matters to the company.

Early participants in the well-being initiative included the 1,200-worker Apparel International factory in Nazareno, Mexico.[14] AI's president, Oscar González Franch, and CEO Tomas Bello Garza were uncertain how to start, but they already had a track record of innovating to improve the factory's environmental impact. After a company-provided survey didn't illuminate worker needs, they partnered with a nongovernmental organization, which created tools more appropriate for the community. They learned that the key issues were lack of access to health care and poor communication between managers and workers. AI trained its supervisors in communicating respectfully and creating a healthier work environment. As attitudes and productivity improved, González Franch and Bello Garza began using company resources to improve health conditions in the community.

In the first five years, Levi's rolled out the program to facilities in 12 countries with 100,000 workers.[15] In Egypt, health education reduced absenteeism and turnover among female employees, and in Turkey, changes to the work schedule did the same. Levi's set a timetable for the program to cover the factories producing 80% of its products by 2020 and to cover all suppliers' workers by 2025. ●

A common problem facing managers of large global companies such as Ford, Unilever, and Intel is managing the development of a global supplier network that will allow their companies to keep costs down and quality high. For example, Boeing's 777 jet was originally built using many components from more than 500 global suppliers; eight made parts for the 777 fuselage, doors, and wings. Boeing chose these suppliers because they were the best in the world at performing their particular activities, and Boeing's goal was to produce a high-quality final product.[16] Pleased with the outcome, Boeing decided to outsource a greater percentage of components to global suppliers when it designed the 787 Dreamliner; however, many serious problems delayed the introduction of the aircraft for several years.[17]

The purchasing activities of global companies have become increasingly complicated as a result of the development of a whole range of skills and competencies in different countries around the world. It is clearly in companies' interests to search out the lowest-cost, best-quality suppliers. Advances in technology and the global reach of the Internet continue to make it easier for companies to coordinate complicated, long-distance exchanges involving the purchasing of inputs and the disposal of outputs—something many global companies have taken advantage of as they consolidate the number of suppliers to reduce costs.

Global outsourcing occurs when a company contracts with suppliers in other countries to make the various inputs or components that go into its products or to assemble the final products to reduce costs. For example, Apple contracts with companies in Taiwan and China to make inputs such as the chips, batteries, and LCD displays that power its digital devices; then it contracts with outsourcers such as Foxconn to assemble its final products—such as iPhones and iPads. Apple also outsources the distribution of its products around the world by contracting with companies such as FedEx or UPS.

Global outsourcing has grown enormously to take advantage of national differences in the cost and quality of resources such as labor or raw materials that can significantly reduce manufacturing costs or increase product quality or reliability. Today such global exchanges are becoming so complex that some companies specialize in managing other companies' global supply chains. Global companies use the services of overseas intermediaries or brokers, which are located close to potential suppliers, to find the suppliers that can best meet the needs of a particular company. They can design

global outsourcing
The purchase or production of inputs or final products from overseas suppliers to lower costs and improve product quality or design.

The purchasing activities of global companies have become increasingly complicated in recent years. Hundreds of suppliers around the world produce parts for Boeing's 787 Dreamliner.
Thor Jorgen Udvang/Shutterstock.com RF

the most efficient supply chain for a company to outsource the component and assembly operations required to produce its final products. Because these suppliers are located in thousands of cities in many countries, finding them is difficult. Li & Fung, based in Hong Kong, is one broker that has helped hundreds of major U.S. companies outsource their component or assembly operations to suitable overseas suppliers, especially suppliers in mainland China.[18]

Although outsourcing to take advantage of low labor costs has helped many companies perform better, in the 2010s its risks have also become apparent, especially when issues such as reliability, quality, and speed are important. Consequently, some companies have decided to bring jobs back to the United States. For example, Trans-Lux, a New York–based manufacturer of LCD and LED displays including the large digital screens (i.e., the "Big Board") that run the tickers at the New York Stock Exchange, recently announced plans to bring back the remaining 40% of its production from China over the next year. Company officials explain that increasing labor and shipping costs in China have accelerated their decision to move jobs back home.[19]

On the other hand, some companies do not outsource manufacturing; they prefer to establish their own assembly operations and factories around the world to protect their proprietary technology. For example, most global automakers own their production operations in China and Mexico to retain control over global decision making and to keep their operations secret.

Distributors

distributors
Organizations that help other organizations sell their goods or services to customers.

Distributors are organizations that help other organizations sell their goods or services to customers. The decisions managers make about how to distribute products to customers can have important effects on organizational performance. For example, package delivery companies such as FedEx, UPS, and the U.S. Postal Service have become vital distributors for the millions of items bought online and shipped to customers by online companies both at home and abroad.

The changing nature of distributors and distribution methods can bring opportunities and threats for managers. If distributors become so large and powerful that they can control customers' access to a particular organization's goods and services, they can threaten the organization by demanding that it reduce the prices of its goods and services.[20] For example, the huge retail distributor Walmart controls its suppliers' access to millions of customers and thus can demand that its suppliers reduce their prices to keep its business. If an organization such as Procter & Gamble refuses to reduce its prices, Walmart might respond by buying products only from Procter & Gamble's competitors—companies such as Unilever and Colgate. Walmart recently asked its suppliers to deliver more goods to company warehouses on time or face a fine of 3% on the cost of the delayed goods. This strategy by the retail giant is an effort to keep inventory low and shelves stocked as it competes head-on with Amazon.[21]

Customers

customers
Individuals and groups that buy the goods and services an organization produces.

Customers are the individuals and groups that buy the goods and services an organization produces. For example, Dell's customers can be segmented into several distinct groups: (1) individuals who purchase PCs for home and mobile use, (2) small companies, (3) large companies, and (4) government agencies and educational institutions. Changes in the number and types of customers or in customers' tastes and needs create opportunities and threats. An organization's success depends on its responsiveness to customers—whether it can satisfy their needs. In the PC industry, customers are demanding smaller computers with faster speeds, increased mobility, new apps, and lower prices—and PC makers must respond to the changing types and needs of customers, such as by introducing tablets and other mobile devices. A school, too, must adapt to the changing needs of its customers. For example, if more Spanish-speaking students enroll, additional classes in English as a second language may need to be scheduled. A manager's ability to identify an organization's main customer groups, and make the products that best satisfy their particular needs, is a crucial factor affecting organizational and managerial success.

The most obvious opportunity associated with expanding into the global environment is the prospect of selling goods and services to millions or billions of new customers, as Walmart discovered when it expanded company operations to many other countries. Similarly, Accenture and Capgemini, two large consulting companies, established regional operating centers around the globe, and they recruit and train thousands of overseas consultants to serve the needs of customers in their respective world regions.

Today many products have gained global customer acceptance. This consolidation is occurring both for consumer goods and for business products and has created enormous opportunities for managers. The worldwide acceptance of Coca-Cola beverages, Apple iPads, McDonald's hamburgers, and Samsung smartphones is a sign that the tastes and preferences of customers in different countries may not be so different after all. Likewise, large global markets exist for business products such as telecommunications equipment, electronic components, and computer and financial services. Thus Cisco and Siemens sell their telecommunications equipment; Intel, its microprocessors; and Oracle and SAP, their business systems management software, to customers all over the world.

Competitors

competitors
Organizations that produce goods and services that are similar to a particular organization's goods and services.

One of the most important forces an organization confronts in its task environment is competitors. Competitors are organizations that produce goods and services that are similar and comparable to a particular organization's goods and services. In other words, competitors are organizations trying to attract the same customers. Dell's competitors include other domestic PC makers (such as Apple and HP) as well as overseas competitors (such as Sony and Toshiba in Japan; Lenovo in China; and Acer in Taiwan). Similarly, online stockbroker E*Trade has other competitors such as TD Ameritrade and Charles Schwab.

Rivalry between competitors is potentially the most threatening force managers must deal with. A high level of rivalry typically results in price competition, and falling prices reduce customer revenues and profits. In the early 2000s competition in the PC industry became intense because Dell was aggressively cutting costs and prices to increase its global market share. IBM had to exit the PC business after it lost billions in its battle against low-cost rivals, and HP also suffered losses while Dell's profits soared. By 2006, however, HP's fortunes had recovered because it had found ways to lower its costs and offer stylish new PCs, and Apple was growing rapidly, so Dell's profit margins shrank. In 2009, HP overtook Dell to become the largest global PC maker, and by 2010 Apple's and Acer's sales were also expanding rapidly. Dell's managers had failed to appreciate how fast its global competitors were catching up

Competition among PC makers continues to be strong as consumers look for the best prices and features, whether in retail stores or online. 97/Getty Images

potential competitors
Organizations that presently are not in a task environment but could enter if they so choose.

barriers to entry
Factors that make it difficult and costly for an organization to enter a particular task environment or industry.

economies of scale Cost advantages associated with large operations.

brand loyalty
Customers' preference for the products of organizations currently existing in the task environment.

and had not developed the right strategies to keep the company at the top. In 2014, after a long and harsh battle with investors over the future of the company, Michael Dell took the company private and shifted the company's focus to becoming more of an all-around technology company with less reliance on PC sales. In 2018, Lenovo continued to hold the title of the world's largest PC maker, followed by HP and Dell, although the overall PC market continues to shrink worldwide.[22]

Although extensive rivalry between existing competitors is a major threat to profitability, so is the potential for new competitors to enter the task environment. Potential competitors are organizations that are not currently in a task environment but have the resources to enter if they so choose. In 2010, Amazon, for example, was not in the furniture or large appliance business, but it could enter these businesses if its managers decided it could profitably sell such products online—and today it sells furniture and large appliances. When new competitors enter an industry, competition increases and prices and profits decrease—as furniture and electronic stores such as Best Buy have discovered as they battle Amazon.

BARRIERS TO ENTRY In general, the potential for new competitors to enter a task environment (and thus increase competition) is a function of barriers to entry. Barriers to entry are factors that make it difficult and costly for a company to enter a particular task environment or industry.[23] In other words, the more difficult and costly it is to enter the task environment, the higher are the barriers to entry. The higher the barriers to entry, the fewer the competitors in an organization's task environment and thus the lower the threat of competition. With fewer competitors, it is easier to obtain customers and keep prices high.

Barriers to entry result from three main sources: economies of scale, brand loyalty, and government regulations that impede entry (see Figure 4.2). Economies of scale are the cost advantages associated with large operations. Economies of scale result from factors such as manufacturing products in very large quantities, buying inputs in bulk, or making more effective use of organizational resources than do competitors by fully utilizing employees' skills and knowledge. If organizations already in the task environment are large and enjoy significant economies of scale, their costs are lower than the costs that potential entrants will face, and newcomers will find it expensive to enter the industry. Amazon, for example, enjoys significant economies of scale relative to most other online companies because of its highly efficient and expansive distribution system.[24]

Brand loyalty is customers' preference for the products of organizations currently in the task environment. If established organizations enjoy significant brand loyalty, a new entrant will find it difficult and costly to obtain a share of the market. Newcomers must bear huge advertising costs to build customer awareness of the goods or services they intend to provide. Today Google, Amazon, Samsung, and Apple enjoy a high level of brand loyalty and have some of the highest website hit rates, which allows them to increase their marketing revenues.

Figure 4.2
Barriers to Entry and
Competition

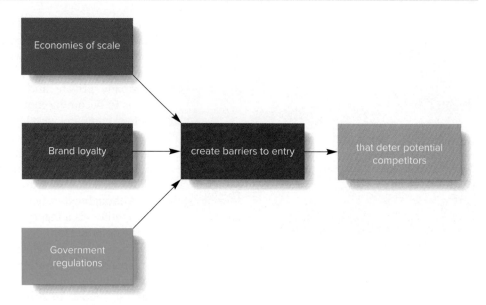

In some cases, *government regulations* function as a barrier to entry at both the industry and the country levels. Many industries that were deregulated, such as air transport, trucking, utilities, and telecommunications, experienced a high level of new entry after deregulation; this forced existing companies in those industries to operate more efficiently or risk being put out of business. At the national and global levels, administrative barriers are government policies that create barriers to entry and limit imports of goods by overseas companies. Japan is well known for the many ways in which it attempts to restrict the entry of overseas competitors or lessen their impact on Japanese firms. Japan has come under intense pressure to relax and abolish regulations such as those governing the import of rice, for example.

The Japanese rice market, like many other Japanese markets, was closed to overseas competitors until 1993 to protect Japan's thousands of high-cost, low-output rice farmers. Rice cultivation is expensive in Japan because of the country's mountainous terrain, and Japanese consumers have always paid high prices for rice. Under overseas pressure, the Japanese government opened the market; but overseas competitors were allowed to export to Japan only 8% of its annual rice consumption to protect its farmers.

In the 2000s, however, an alliance between organic rice grower Lundberg Family Farms of California and the Nippon Restaurant Enterprise Co. found a new way to break into the Japanese rice market. Because there is no tariff on rice used in processed foods, Nippon converts the U.S. organic rice into "O-bento," an organic hot boxed lunch packed with rice, vegetables, chicken, beef, and salmon, all imported from the United States. The lunches, which cost about $4 compared to a Japanese rice bento that costs about $9, are sold at railway stations and other outlets throughout Japan and have become very popular. A storm of protest from

Now that Japan imports rice from the United States, Japanese rice farmers, who cannot compete against lower-priced imports, have been forced to leave fields idle or grow less profitable crops. Mahathir Mohd Yasin/Shutterstock

Japanese rice farmers arose because the entry of U.S. rice growers forced them to leave their rice fields idle or grow less profitable crops. Recently Japan experienced a serious shortage of reasonably priced rice for its food service sector due to the country's strict policy on growing rice for animal feed. This resulted in a higher demand for U.S. rice, which accounted for roughly 49% of Japan's rice imports in 2018.[25]

In summary, intense rivalry among competitors creates a task environment that is highly threatening and makes it increasingly difficult for managers to gain access to the resources an organization needs to make goods and services. Conversely, low rivalry results in a task environment where competitive pressures are more moderate and managers have greater opportunities to acquire the resources they need to make their organizations effective.

The General Environment

Economic, technological, sociocultural, demographic, political, and legal forces in the general environment often have important effects on forces in the task environment that determine an organization's ability to obtain resources—effects that managers may not be aware of. For example, the sudden, dramatic upheavals in the mortgage and banking industry that started in 2007 were brought about by a combination of complex new financial lending instruments called derivatives; a speculative boom in commodities and housing prices; and lax government regulation that allowed unethical bankers and financial managers to exploit the derivatives to make immense short-term profits. These events triggered the economic crisis beginning in 2008 that caused stock markets around the world to plummet, devastating the retirement savings of hundreds of millions of ordinary people, and caused layoffs of millions of employees as companies slashed their workforces because customers reduced their spending. Fortunately, sound economic policies put in place during the recession have helped the economy rebound strongly over the past few years.

The implication is clear: Managers must continuously analyze forces in the general environment because these forces affect ongoing decision making and planning. How well managers can perform this task determines how quickly an organization can respond to the changes taking place. Next we discuss the major forces in the general environment and examine their impact on an organization's task environment.

Economic Forces

economic forces
Interest rates, inflation, unemployment, economic growth, and other factors that affect the general health and well-being of a nation or the regional economy of an organization.

Economic forces affect the general health and well-being of a country or world region. They include interest rates, inflation, unemployment, and economic growth. Economic forces produce many opportunities and threats for managers. Low levels of unemployment and falling interest rates give people more money to spend, and as a result organizations can sell more goods and services. Good economic times affect the supply of resources that become easier or more inexpensive to acquire, and organizations have an opportunity to flourish. High-tech companies enjoyed this throughout the 1990s when computer and electronics companies like Sony made record profits as the global economy boomed because of advances in technology and growing global trade.

In contrast, worsening macroeconomic conditions, like those in the early 2010s, posed a major threat because they reduced managers' ability to gain access to the resources their organizations needed to survive and prosper. Profit-seeking organizations such as hotels and retail stores have fewer customers during economic downturns; hotel rates dropped by 14% in 2009 compared to 2008, for example, just as retail sales plunged. Nonprofits such as charities and colleges also saw donations decline by more than 20% because of the economic downturn.

Poor economic conditions make the environment more complex and managers' jobs more difficult and demanding. Companies often need to reduce the number of their managers and employees, streamline their operations, and identify ways to acquire and use resources more efficiently and effectively. Successful managers realize the important effects that economic forces have on their organizations, and they pay close attention to what is occurring in the economy at the national and regional levels to respond appropriately.

Technological Forces

technology The combination of skills and equipment that managers use in designing, producing, and distributing goods and services.

Technology is the combination of tools, machines, computers, skills, information, and knowledge that managers use to design, produce, and distribute goods and services; technological forces are outcomes of changes in that technology. The overall pace of technological change has accelerated greatly in the last decades because technological advances in microprocessors and computer hardware and software have spurred technological advances in most businesses and industries. The effects of changing technological forces are still increasing in magnitude.

technological forces Outcomes of changes in the technology managers use to design, produce, or distribute goods and services.

Technological forces can have profound implications for managers and organizations. Technological change can make established products obsolete—for example, cathode-ray tube (CRT) computer monitors and televisions, printed sets of encyclopedias, and newspapers and magazines—forcing managers to find new ways to satisfy customer needs. Although technological change can threaten an organization, it also can create a host of new opportunities for designing, making, or distributing new and better kinds of goods and services. For example, AMD recently launched a second generation of Ryzen desktop processors with more speed, built-in graphics, and processing power. Innovations like these continue to push technology boundaries and spur demand for all kinds of new digital computing devices and services, which can affect the competitive position of technology companies.[26]

Changes in technology are altering the nature of work itself within organizations, including that of the manager's job. Today telecommuting, videoconferencing, and collaborative software programs are everyday activities that let managers supervise and coordinate geographically dispersed employees. Salespeople in many companies work from home offices and commute electronically to work. They communicate with other employees through companywide electronic communication networks using smartphones and other mobile devices to orchestrate "face-to-face" meetings with coworkers across the country or globe.

Sociocultural Forces

sociocultural forces Pressures emanating from the social structure of a country or society or from the national culture.

Sociocultural forces are pressures emanating from the social structure of a country or society or from the national culture, such as the concern for diversity, discussed in the previous chapter. Pressures from both sources can either constrain or facilitate the way organizations operate and managers behave. Social structure is the traditional system of relationships established between people and groups in a society. Societies differ substantially in social structure. In societies that have a high

social structure The traditional system of relationships established between people and groups in a society.

degree of social stratification, there are many distinctions among individuals and groups. Caste systems in India and Tibet and the recognition of numerous social classes in Great Britain and France produce a multilayered social structure in each of those countries. In contrast, social stratification is lower in relatively egalitarian New Zealand and in the United States, where the social structure reveals few distinctions among people. Most top managers in France come from the upper classes of French society, but top managers in the United States come from all strata of American society.

Societies also differ in the extent to which they emphasize the individual over the group. Such differences may dictate how managers need to motivate and lead employees.

national culture
The set of values that a society considers important and the norms of behavior that are approved or sanctioned in that society.

National culture is the set of values that a society considers important and the norms of behavior that are approved or sanctioned in that society. Societies differ substantially in the values and norms they emphasize. For example, in the United States individualism is highly valued, but in Korea and Japan individuals are expected to conform to group expectations.[27] National culture, discussed at length later in this chapter, also affects how managers motivate and coordinate employees and how organizations do business. Ethics, an important aspect of national culture, were discussed in detail in Chapter 3.

Social structure and national culture not only differ across societies but also change within societies over time. In the United States, attitudes toward the roles of women, sex, marriage, and the LGBT community changed in each past decade. Many people in Asian countries such as Hong Kong, Singapore, Korea, and even China think the younger generation is far more individualistic and "American-like" than previous generations. Currently, throughout much of eastern Europe, new values that emphasize individualism and entrepreneurship are replacing communist values based on collectivism and obedience to the state. The pace of change continues to accelerate.

Individual managers and organizations must be responsive to changes in, and differences among, the social structures and national cultures of all the countries in which they operate. In today's increasingly integrated global economy, managers are likely to interact with people from several countries, and many managers live and work abroad. Effective managers are sensitive to differences between societies and adjust their behavior accordingly.

Managers and organizations also must respond to social changes within a society. In the last decade, for example, Americans have become increasingly interested in their personal health and fitness. Managers who recognized this trend early and took advantage of the opportunities that resulted from it were able to reap significant gains for their organizations, such as chains of health clubs. PepsiCo used the opportunity presented by the fitness trend to take market share from archrival Coca-Cola by being the first to introduce diet colas, fruit-based soft drinks, and flavored waters. Then Quaker Oats made Gatorade the most popular energy drink, and now others like Red Bull, Monster, and Rockstar are increasing in

The organic produce industry has taken advantage of U.S. consumers' push for chemical-free food by offering home delivery of organic fruits, vegetables, and other products. kritchanut/123RF

popularity. The health trend, however, did not offer opportunities to all companies; to some it posed a threat. Tobacco companies came under intense pressure due to consumers' greater awareness of negative health impacts from smoking. The rage for "low-carb" foods in the 2000s increased demand for meat and protein, and bread and doughnut companies such as Kraft and Krispy Kreme suffered. Today consumers are looking for healthier, "cleaner" foods, which are being promoted by grocery chains, fast-casual restaurants, and home delivery of organic produce and other products.[28]

Demographic Forces

demographic forces
Outcomes of changes in, or changing attitudes toward, the characteristics of a population, such as age, gender, ethnic origin, race, sexual orientation, and social class.

Demographic forces are outcomes of changes in, or changing attitudes toward, the characteristics of a population, such as age, gender, ethnic origin, race, sexual orientation, and social class. Like the other forces in the general environment, demographic forces present managers with opportunities and threats and can have major implications for organizations. We examine the nature of these challenges throughout this book.

Today most industrialized nations are experiencing the aging of their populations as a consequence of falling birth and death rates and the aging of the baby boom generation. Consequently, the absolute number of older people has increased substantially, generating opportunities for organizations that cater to older people, such as the home health care, recreation, and medical industries, which have seen an upswing in demand for their services. The aging of the population also has several implications for the workplace. Most significant are a relative decline in the number of young people joining the workforce and an increase in the number of active employees who are postponing retirement beyond the traditional age of 65. Indeed, the global financial crisis in the late 2000s made it impossible for millions of older people to retire because their savings were decimated. These changes suggest that organizations need to find ways to motivate older employees and use their skills and knowledge—an issue that many Western societies continue to tackle.

Political and Legal Forces

political and legal forces Outcomes of changes in laws and regulations, such as deregulation of industries, privatization of organizations, and increased emphasis on environmental protection.

Political and legal forces are outcomes of changes in laws and regulations. They result from political and legal developments that take place within a nation, within a world region, or across the world, and significantly affect managers and organizations everywhere. Political processes shape a nation's laws and the international laws that govern the relationships between nations. Laws constrain the operations of organizations and managers and thus create both opportunities and threats.[29] For example, throughout much of the industrialized world there has been a strong trend toward deregulation of industries previously controlled by the state and privatization of organizations once owned by the state such as airlines, railways, and utility companies.

Another important political and legal force affecting managers and organizations is the political integration of countries that has been taking place during the last several decades. Increasingly, nations are forming political unions that allow free exchange of resources and capital. The growth of the European Union (EU) is one example: Common laws govern trade and commerce between EU member countries, and the European Court has the right to examine the business of any global organization and to approve any proposed mergers between overseas companies that operate inside the EU. For example, in April 2018, Apple's proposed acquisition of Shazam, a UK-based app, was delayed more than six months as the European Commission insisted on reviewing the sale because of its potential threat to competition among music-sharing platforms in Europe. The Shazam app uses the microphone on a smartphone or computer to identify almost any song playing nearby and then directs users to places where they can listen to the music, such as Apple Music or Spotify. Critics suggested that acquiring Shazam would help Apple embed that capability deeper into its music offerings, which might push more consumers to sign on with Apple Music. The commission took up the review at the request of several EU members, including Austria, Italy, and Sweden, and eventually allowed the acquisition to proceed in late 2018.[30]

In addition, the departure of the United Kingdom from the EU will have a significant impact on political and legal forces worldwide. The start of "Brexit" was scheduled for March 2019, after many months of contentious negotiations between the UK and the European Commission. As of this writing, however, the final deal between the UK and the EU has yet to be approved by EU member-states and the UK parliament, and UK Prime Minister Theresa May announced her resignation.[31]

Indeed, international agreements to abolish laws and regulations that restrict and reduce trade between countries have been having profound effects on global organizations. The falling legal trade barriers create enormous opportunities for companies to sell goods and services internationally. But by allowing overseas companies to compete in a nation's domestic market for customers, falling trade barriers also pose a serious threat because they increase competition in the task environment. For example, the Obama administration negotiated for several years for the United States to join the Trans-Pacific Partnership (TPP), a trade agreement between the United States and 11 other countries. In 2017, in the early days of his presidency, Donald Trump issued an executive order pulling the United States out of the TPP, taking a stand against foreign competitors as part of his "America First" strategy.[32]

Deregulation, privatization, and the removal of legal barriers to trade are just a few of the many ways in which changing political and legal forces can challenge organizations and managers. Others include increased emphasis on environmental protection and the preservation of endangered species, increased emphasis on workplace safety, and legal constraints against discrimination on the basis of race, gender, or age. Managers face major challenges when they seek to take advantage of the opportunities created by changing political, legal, and economic forces.

LO 4-4

Explain why the global environment is becoming more open and competitive, and identify the forces behind the process of globalization that increase the opportunities, complexities, challenges, and threats that managers face.

The Changing Global Environment

The 21st century has banished the idea that the world is composed of distinct national countries and markets that are separated physically, economically, and culturally. Managers need to recognize that companies compete in a truly global marketplace, which is the source of the opportunities and threats they must respond to. Managers continually confront the challenges of global competition such as establishing operations in a country abroad, obtaining inputs from suppliers abroad, or managing in a different national culture.[33]

In essence, as a result of falling trade barriers, managers view the global environment as open—that is, as an environment in which companies are free to buy goods and services from, and sell goods and services to, whichever companies and countries they choose. They also are free to compete against each other to attract customers around the world. All large companies must establish an international network of operations and subsidiaries to build global competitive advantage.

Despite recent economic challenges, Africa's economy continues to be on a positive track, with an overall estimated growth forecasted at close to 4% in the coming year. African countries continue to face economic, political, and environmental challenges as globalization continues to accelerate changes to business and everyday life in cities such as Lagos, Nigeria, pictured here. Pius Utomi Ekpei/AFP/ Getty Images

Coca-Cola and PepsiCo, for example, have competed aggressively for decades to develop the strongest global soft drink empire, just as Toyota and Honda have built hundreds of car plants around the world to provide the vehicles that global customers like.

In this section we first explain how this open global environment is the result of globalization and the flow of capital around the world. Next we examine how specific economic, political, and legal changes, such as the lowering of barriers to trade and investment, have increased globalization and led to greater interaction and exchanges between organizations and countries. Then we discuss how declining barriers of distance and culture have also increased the pace of globalization, and we consider the specific implications of these changes for managers and organizations. Finally we note that nations still differ widely from each other because they have distinct cultural values and norms and that managers must appreciate these differences to compete successfully across countries.

The Process of Globalization

globalization The set of specific and general forces that work together to integrate and connect economic, political, and social systems *across* countries, cultures, or geographic regions.

Perhaps the most important reason why the global environment has become more open and competitive is the increase in globalization. Globalization is the set of specific and general forces that work together to integrate and connect economic, political, and social systems *across* countries, cultures, or geographic regions. The result of globalization is that nations and peoples become increasingly *interdependent* because the same forces affect them in similar ways. The fates of peoples in different countries become interlinked as the world's markets and businesses become increasingly interconnected. And as nations become more interdependent, they become more similar to one another in the sense that people develop a similar liking for products as diverse as mobile phones, iPads, jeans, soft drinks, sports teams, hybrid cars, and foods such as curry, green tea, and Colombian coffee.

But what drives or spurs globalization? What makes companies like IKEA, Toyota, or Microsoft want to venture into an uncertain global environment? The answer is that the path of globalization is shaped by the ebb and flow of *capital*—valuable wealth-generating assets or resources that people move through companies, countries, and world regions to seek their greatest returns or profits. Managers, employees, and companies like Microsoft and IKEA are motivated to try to profit or benefit by using their skills to make products customers around the world want to buy. The four principal forms of capital that flow between countries are these:

- *Human capital:* the flow of people around the world through immigration, migration, and emigration.

- *Financial capital:* the flow of money capital across world markets through overseas investment, credit, lending, and aid.

- *Resource capital:* the flow of natural resources, parts, and components between companies and countries, such as metals, minerals, lumber, energy, food products, microprocessors, and auto parts.

- *Political capital:* the flow of power and influence around the world using diplomacy, persuasion, aggression, and force of arms to protect the right or access of a country, world region, or political bloc to the other forms of capital.

Most of the economic advances associated with globalization are the result of these four capital flows and the interactions between them, as nations compete on the world stage to protect and increase their standards of living and to further the political goals and social causes that are espoused by their societies' cultures. The next sections look at the factors that have increased the rate at which capital flows between companies and countries. In a positive sense, the faster the flow, the more capital is being utilized where it can create the most value, such as people moving to where their skills earn them more money, or investors switching to the stocks or bonds that give them higher dividends or interest, or companies finding lower-cost sources of inputs. In a negative sense, however, a fast flow of capital also means that individual countries or world regions can find themselves in trouble when companies and investors move their capital to invest it in more productive ways in other countries or world regions—often those with lower labor costs or rapidly expanding markets. When capital leaves a country, the results are higher unemployment, recession, and a lower standard of living for its people.

Declining Barriers to Trade and Investment

tariff A tax that a government imposes on imported or, occasionally, exported goods.

One of the main factors that has accelerated globalization by freeing the movement of capital has been the decline in barriers to trade and investment, discussed earlier. During the 1920s and 1930s many countries erected formidable barriers to international trade and investment in the belief that this was the best way to promote their economic well-being. Many of these barriers were high tariffs on imports of manufactured goods. A tariff is a tax that a government imposes on goods imported into one country from another. The aim of import tariffs is to protect domestic industries and jobs, such as those in the auto or steel industry, from overseas competition by raising the price of these products from abroad. For example, in early 2018 President Trump announced a 10% tariff on certain Chinese imports including steel and aluminum, which caused a global outcry from other countries and received mixed reviews from U.S. business leaders. Later that year, China retaliated with tariffs on U.S. exports, which also caused concerns. As of this writing, the United States has increased tariffs on $200 billion worth of Chinese goods, which may have a serious impact on trade relations as well as U.S. jobs, as the two countries reach a stalemate in trade talks.[34]

The reason for removing tariffs is that, very often, when one country imposes an import tariff, others follow suit and the result is a series of retaliatory moves as countries progressively raise tariff barriers against each other. In the 1920s this behavior depressed world demand and helped usher in the Great Depression of the 1930s and massive unemployment. Beginning with the 2009 economic crisis, the governments of most countries have worked hard in the 2010s not to fall into the trap of raising tariffs to protect jobs and industries in the short run because they know the long-term consequences of this would be the loss of even more jobs. Governments of countries that resort to raising tariff barriers ultimately reduce employment and undermine the economic growth of their countries because capital and resources will always move to their most highly valued use—wherever that is in the world.

GATT AND THE RISE OF FREE TRADE After World War II, advanced Western industrial countries, having learned from the Great Depression, committed themselves to the goal of removing barriers to the free flow of resources and capital between countries. This commitment was reinforced by acceptance of the principle that free trade, rather than tariff barriers, was the best way to foster a healthy domestic economy and low unemployment.[35]

free-trade doctrine
The idea that if each country specializes in the production of the goods and services that it can produce most efficiently, this will make the best use of global resources.

The free-trade doctrine predicts that if each country agrees to specialize in the production of the goods and services that it can produce most efficiently, this will make the best use of global capital resources and will result in lower prices.[36] For example, if Indian companies are highly efficient in the production of textiles and U.S. companies are highly efficient in the production of computer software, then, under a free-trade agreement, capital would move to India and be invested there to produce textiles, while capital from around the world would flow to the United States and be invested in its innovative computer software companies. Consequently, prices of both textiles and software should fall because each product is being produced where it can be made at the lowest cost, benefiting consumers and making the best use of scarce capital. This doctrine is also responsible for the increase in global outsourcing and the loss of millions of U.S. jobs in textiles and manufacturing as capital has been invested in factories in Asian countries such as China and Malaysia. However, millions of U.S. jobs have also been created because of new capital investments in the technology and service sectors, which in theory should offset manufacturing job losses in the long run.

Historically, countries that accepted this free-trade doctrine set as their goal the removal of barriers to the free flow of goods, services, and capital between countries. They attempted to achieve this through an international treaty known as the General Agreement on Tariffs and Trade (GATT). In the nearly 75 years since World War II, there have been multiple rounds of GATT negotiations aimed at lowering tariff barriers. For example, the Uruguay Round involved 117 countries and succeeded in lowering tariffs by more than 30% from the previous level. It also led to the dissolution of GATT and its replacement by the World Trade Organization (WTO), which continues the struggle to reduce tariffs and has more power to sanction countries that break global agreements. The latest round of negotiations, called the Doha Round, effectively ended in 2015, when trade ministers failed to agree to keep the negotiations and discussions alive. It seems that many of the key countries (United States, China, India, and EU members) were unwilling or unable to make fundamental concessions.[37]

Even as free trade has become the norm, it is under pressure from its opponents and skeptics, including governments with nationalist policies. An example is the "America First" perspective of the Trump administration in the United States, which has led to greater tariffs. The "Management Insight" box describes some of the impact on the global auto industry.

Management Insight

Tariffs Are Tangling Auto Supply Chains

After decades of free-trade policies, the United States has shifted focus under the Trump administration, targeting the impact of trade agreements on U.S. jobs. To gain the upper hand in trade negotiations, the government has imposed tariffs. Most notable for the auto industry are tariffs of 25% on steel and 10% on aluminum, as well as tariffs of 10% to 25% on auto parts from China.[38]

For auto companies and their suppliers, the tariffs pose significant challenges. Vehicle production involves complex supply chains in which hundreds of companies turn raw materials into 30,000 parts, shipped to producers of components, who ship the components to assembly plants. Parts and components often move back and forth across national borders before reaching assembly plants. For each model, supply chain members engage in years of planning, negotiation, and testing to develop products that meet quality and safety requirements, as well as terms for schedule and price. Even the Ford F-150 pickup, with more U.S. parts than most vehicles, includes 15% of parts from Canada and Mexico plus 15% from outside North America. In addition, producers improve quality and efficiency by using tools specifically designed for making a particular model; thus, toolmakers are links in the supply chains.[39]

The announcement of a tariff creates unplanned-for change in supply chains. Prices suddenly jump significantly. Who will pay for the increase? Since major tariffs only recently displaced free trade, few existing contracts have terms for this situation. Domestic steelmakers have raised prices in line with price increases for imported steel, and parts makers have told their customers they won't ship imported parts unless they can pass on the cost of tariffs. Some buyers are small businesses with little leverage to negotiate. They must pay the higher prices and cut spending elsewhere, including investments in growth.[40]

Auto companies are big customers, which gives them power in supply chains. Some have informed suppliers not to expect to renegotiate existing agreements. When negotiating new agreements, they seek provisions that protect them from future tariffs. Still, they face challenges as they purchase steel and decide where to locate facilities years down the road. They report that tariff-related costs are eating into profits; Ford alone forecast a billion-dollar hit to its profits in 2018. In late 2018, automakers were particularly concerned that a cycle of strong vehicle sales was winding down—bad timing for vehicle price increases to discourage consumers.[41] ●

Declining Barriers of Distance and Culture

Historically, barriers of distance and culture also closed the global environment and kept managers focused on their domestic market. The management problems Unilever, the huge British-based soap and detergent maker, experienced at the turn of the 20th century illustrate the effect of these barriers.

Founded in London during the 1880s by William Lever, a Quaker, Unilever had a worldwide reach by the early 1900s and operated subsidiaries in most major countries of the British Empire, including India, Canada, and Australia. Lever had a very hands-on, autocratic management style and found his far-flung business empire difficult to control. The reason for Lever's control problems was that communication over great distances was difficult. It took six weeks to reach India by ship from England, and international telephone and telegraph services were unreliable.

Another problem Unilever encountered was the difficulty of doing business in societies that were separated from Britain by barriers of language and culture. Different countries have different sets of national beliefs, values, and norms, and Lever found that a management approach that worked in Britain did not necessarily work in India or Persia (now Iran). As a result, management practices had to be tailored to suit each unique national culture. After Lever's death in 1925, top management at Unilever lowered or *decentralized* (see Chapter 7) decision-making authority to the managers of the various national subsidiaries so they could develop a management approach that suited the country in which they were operating. One result of this strategy was that the subsidiaries grew distant and remote from one another, which reduced Unilever's performance.[42]

Since the end of World War II, a continuing stream of advances in communications and transportation technology has worked to reduce the barriers of distance and culture that affected Unilever and all global organizations. Over the last decades, global communication has been revolutionized by developments in satellites, digital technology, the Internet and global computer networks, and video teleconferencing that allow transmission of vast amounts of information and make reliable, secure, and instantaneous communication possible between people and companies anywhere in the world. This revolution has made it possible for a global organization—a tiny garment factory in Li & Fung's network or a huge company such as IKEA or Unilever—to do business anywhere, anytime, and to search for customers and suppliers around the world.

One of the most important innovations in transportation technology that has opened the global environment has been the growth of commercial jet travel. New York is now closer in travel time to Tokyo than it was to Philadelphia in the days of the 13 colonies—a fact that makes control of far-flung international businesses much easier today than in William Lever's era. In addition to speeding travel, modern communications and transportation technologies have also helped reduce the cultural distance between countries. The Internet and its millions of websites facilitate the development of global communications networks and media that are helping to create a worldwide culture above and beyond unique national cultures. Moreover, television networks such as CNN, MTV, ESPN, BBC, and HBO can now be transmitted to many countries, and Hollywood films and other original content are streamed via the Internet across the globe.

Effects of Free Trade on Managers

The lowering of barriers to trade and investment and the decline of distance and culture barriers have created enormous opportunities for companies to expand the market for their goods and services through exports and investments in overseas countries. The shift toward a more open global economy has created not only more opportunities to sell goods and services in markets abroad but also the opportunity to buy more from other countries. A manager's job is more challenging in a dynamic global environment because of the increased intensity of competition that goes hand in hand with the lowering of barriers to trade and investment.

REGIONAL TRADE AGREEMENTS The growth of regional trade agreements—such as the North American Free Trade Agreement (NAFTA), and more recently the Central American Free Trade Agreement (CAFTA)—also presents opportunities and threats for managers and their organizations. In North America, NAFTA, which became effective in 1994, aimed to abolish the tariffs on 99% of the goods traded between Mexico, Canada, and the United States by 2004. Although it did not achieve this lofty goal, NAFTA has removed most barriers on the cross-border flow of resources, giving, for example, financial institutions and retail businesses in Canada and the United States unrestricted access to the Mexican marketplace. After NAFTA was signed, there was a flood of investment into Mexico from the United States, as well as many other countries such as Germany and Japan. Walmart, Costco, Ford, and many major U.S. companies expanded their operations in Mexico; Walmart, for example, is stocking many more products from Mexico in its U.S. stores, and its Mexican store chain is also expanding rapidly.

After almost a year of negotiations, at the insistence of President Trump, the NAFTA agreement has been modified and agreed to by the leaders of Mexico and Canada. The revised plan will now be known as the U.S.–Mexico–Canada Agreement (USMCA) and will need to be approved by Congress and the legislatures of the other two countries before it can go into effect and replace NAFTA. Although the new agreement retains a substantial amount of the NAFTA framework, the plan calls for notable changes with regard to auto manufacturing, agricultural products, and labor protections among the three nations.[43]

The establishment of free-trade areas creates an opportunity for manufacturing organizations because it lets them reduce their costs. They can do this either by shifting production to the lowest-cost location within the free-trade area (e.g., U.S. auto and textile companies shifting production to Mexico) or by serving the whole region from one location rather than establishing separate operations in each country. Some managers, however, view regional free-trade agreements as a threat because they expose a company based in one member country to increased competition from companies based in the other member countries. NAFTA has had this effect; today Mexican managers in some industries face the threat of head-to-head competition against efficient U.S. and Canadian companies. But the opposite is true as well: U.S. and Canadian managers are experiencing threats in labor-intensive industries, such as the flooring tile, roofing, and textile industries, where Mexican businesses have a cost advantage.

There are many regional trade agreements around the world. For example, founded in 1999, the African Union's purpose is both political and economic. Its goals include removing any remnants of colonization and apartheid, as well as creating cooperation for development. Complementing the role of the African Union is the Southern African Development Community, a 15-country group whose goals include socioeconomic development and poverty eradication. Another trade agreement is the Cooperation Council for the Arab States of the Gulf, which is made up of several countries, including Qatar, Oman, Bahrain, the United Arab Emirates, Kuwait, and Saudi Arabia. As part of the agreement, countries work on regional cooperation and economic relations.[44] All these trade agreements are designed to allow managers to take advantage of opportunities that other members of the agreements can provide.

The Role of National Culture

Despite evidence that countries are becoming more similar because of globalization, and that the world may become "a global village," the cultures of different countries still vary widely because of vital differences in their values, norms, and attitudes. As noted earlier, national culture includes the values, norms, knowledge, beliefs, moral principles, laws, customs, and other practices that unite the citizens of a country. National culture shapes individual behavior by specifying appropriate and inappropriate behavior and interaction with others. People learn national culture in their everyday lives by interacting with those around them. This learning starts at an early age and continues throughout their lives.

Cultural Values and Norms

values Ideas about what a society believes to be good, right, desirable, or beautiful.

The basic building blocks of national culture are values and norms. Values are beliefs about what a society considers to be good, right, desirable, or beautiful—or their opposites. They provide the basic underpinnings for notions of individual freedom, democracy, truth, justice, honesty, loyalty, social obligation, collective responsibility, the appropriate roles for men and women, love, sex, marriage, and so on. Values are more than merely abstract concepts; they are invested with considerable emotional significance. People argue, fight, and even die over values such as freedom or dignity.

Although deeply embedded in society, values are not static; they change over time, but change is often the result of a slow and painful process. For example, the value systems of many formerly communist states such as Georgia, Hungary, and Romania have undergone significant changes as those countries move away from values that emphasize state control toward values that emphasize individual freedom. Social turmoil often results when countries undergo major changes in their values, as is happening today in Asia, South America, and the Middle East.

norms Unwritten, informal codes of conduct that prescribe how people should act in particular situations and that are considered important by most members of a group or an organization.

Norms are unwritten, informal codes of conduct that prescribe appropriate behavior in particular situations and are considered important by most members of a group or organization. They shape the behavior of people toward one another. Two types of norms play a major role in national culture: mores and folkways. Mores are norms that are considered to be of central importance to the functioning of society and to social life. Accordingly, the violation of mores brings serious retribution. Mores include proscriptions against murder, theft, adultery, and incest. In many societies mores have been enacted into law. Thus, all advanced societies have laws against murder and theft. However, there are many differences in mores from one society to another. In the United States, for example, drinking alcohol is widely accepted; but in Saudi Arabia consumption of alcohol is viewed as a serious violation of social mores and is punishable by imprisonment or even death.

mores Norms that are considered to be central to the functioning of society and to social life.

folkways The routine social conventions of everyday life.

Folkways are the routine social conventions of everyday life. They concern customs and practices such as dressing appropriately for particular situations, using good social manners, eating with the correct utensils, and displaying neighborly behavior. Although folkways define how people are expected to behave, violation of folkways is not a serious or moral matter. People who violate folkways are often thought to be eccentric or ill-mannered, but they are not usually considered immoral or wicked. In many countries, strangers are usually excused for violating folkways because they are unaccustomed to local behavior; but if they repeat the violation, they are censured because they are expected to learn appropriate behavior. Hence the importance for managers working in countries abroad to gain wide experience.

LO 4-5
Discuss why national cultures differ and why it is important that managers be sensitive to the effects of falling trade barriers and regional trade associations on the political and social systems of nations around the world.

Hofstede's Model of National Culture

individualism A world-view that values individual freedom and self-expression and adherence to the principle that people should be judged by their individual achievements rather than by their social background.

Researchers have spent considerable time and effort identifying similarities and differences in the values and norms of different countries. One model of national culture was developed by Geert Hofstede.[45] As a psychologist for IBM, Hofstede collected data on employee values and norms from more than 100,000 IBM employees in 64 countries. Based on his research, Hofstede developed five dimensions along which national cultures can be placed: individualism versus collectivism; power distance; achievement versus nurturing orientation; uncertainty avoidance; and long-term versus short-term orientation.[46]

collectivism A world-view that values subordination of the individual to the goals of the group and adherence to the principle that people should be judged by their contribution to the group.

INDIVIDUALISM VERSUS COLLECTIVISM The first dimension, which Hofstede labeled "individualism versus collectivism," has a long history in human thought.

In Asian countries such as Japan where collectivism is highly valued, coworkers identify strongly with being part of a group, rather than being recognized as an individual. Imagemore Co., Ltd./ Corbis RF

power distance The degree to which societies accept the idea that inequalities in the power and well-being of their citizens are due to differences in individuals' physical and intellectual capabilities and heritage.

achievement orientation A worldview that values assertiveness, performance, success, and competition.

nurturing orientation A worldview that values the quality of life, warm personal friendships, and services and care for the weak.

uncertainty avoidance The degree to which societies are willing to tolerate uncertainty and risk.

Individualism is a worldview that values individual freedom and self-expression and adherence to the principle that people should be judged by their individual achievements rather than by their social background. In Western countries, individualism usually includes admiration for personal success, a strong belief in individual rights, and high regard for individual entrepreneurs.[47]

In contrast, collectivism is a worldview that values subordination of the individual to the goals of the group and adherence to the principle that people should be judged by their contribution to the group. Collectivism was widespread in communist countries but has become less prevalent since the collapse of communism in most of those countries. Japan is a noncommunist country where collectivism is highly valued.

Managers must realize that organizations and organizational members reflect their national culture's emphasis on individualism or collectivism. Indeed, one of the major reasons why Japanese and American management practices differ is that Japanese culture values collectivism and U.S. culture values individualism.

POWER DISTANCE By power distance Hofstede meant the degree to which societies accept the idea that inequalities in the power and well-being of their citizens are due to differences in individuals' physical and intellectual capabilities and heritage. This concept also encompasses the degree to which societies accept the economic and social differences in wealth, status, and well-being that result from differences in individual capabilities.

Societies in which inequalities are allowed to persist or grow over time have *high power distance.* In high-power-distance societies, workers who are professionally successful amass wealth and pass it on to their children, and, as a result, inequalities may grow over time. In such societies, the gap between rich and poor, with all the attendant political and social consequences, grows very large. In contrast, in societies with *low power distance,* large inequalities between citizens are not allowed to develop. In low-power-distance countries, the government uses taxation and social welfare programs to reduce inequality and improve the welfare of the least fortunate. These societies are more attuned to preventing a large gap between rich and poor and minimizing discord between different classes of citizens.

Advanced Western countries such as the United States, Germany, the Netherlands, and the United Kingdom have relatively low power distance and high individualism. Economically poor Latin American countries such as Guatemala and Panama, and Asian countries such as Malaysia and the Philippines, have high power distance and low individualism.[48] These findings suggest that the cultural values of richer countries emphasize protecting the rights of individuals and, at the same time, provide a fair chance of success to every member of society.

ACHIEVEMENT VERSUS NURTURING ORIENTATION Societies that have an achievement orientation value assertiveness, performance, success, competition, and results. Societies that have a nurturing orientation value the quality of life, warm personal relationships, and services and care for the weak. Japan and the United States tend to be achievement-oriented; the Netherlands, Sweden, and Denmark are more nurturing-oriented.

UNCERTAINTY AVOIDANCE Societies as well as individuals differ in their tolerance for uncertainty and risk. Societies low on uncertainty avoidance (such as the United

States and Hong Kong) are easygoing, value diversity, and tolerate differences in personal beliefs and actions. Societies high on uncertainty avoidance (such as Japan and France) are more rigid and skeptical about people whose behaviors or beliefs differ from the norm. In these societies, conformity to the values of the social and work groups to which a person belongs is the norm, and structured situations are preferred because they provide a sense of security.

LONG-TERM VERSUS SHORT-TERM ORIENTATION The last dimension that Hofstede described is orientation toward life and work.[49] A national culture with a long-term orientation rests on values such as thrift (saving) and persistence in achieving goals. A national culture with a short-term orientation is concerned with maintaining personal stability or happiness and living for the present. Societies with a long-term orientation include Taiwan and Hong Kong, well known for their high rate of per capita savings. The United States and France have a short-term orientation, and their citizens tend to spend more and save less.

> **long-term orientation** A worldview that values thrift and persistence in achieving goals.

> **short-term orientation** A worldview that values personal stability or happiness and living for the present.

The GLOBE Project

Hofstede's research has inspired other major international research projects, including the GLOBE Project, which extends Hofstede's work by looking at additional cultural dimensions. Conceived in the early 1990s by Professor Robert J. House of the University of Pennsylvania, the GLOBE (Global Leadership and Organizational Behavior Effectiveness) Project is an ongoing international research endeavor involving more than 200 researchers who have collected data from more than 17,000 managers in 62 countries.[50] The GLOBE Project looks at nine cultural dimensions:

- *Performance Orientation:* the degree to which individuals in a society are rewarded for performance improvement and excellence.
- *Assertiveness:* the degree to which members of organizations are confrontational and aggressive in their relationships with others.
- *Future Orientation:* the extent to which individuals engage in behaviors such as planning, investing in the future, and delaying gratification.
- *Humane Orientation:* the degree to which an organization encourages and rewards individuals for being fair, altruistic, generous, caring, and kind to others.
- *Institutional Collectivism:* the degree to which organizational and societal practices encourage and reward collective distribution of resources and collective action.
- *In-Group Collectivism:* the degree to which individuals express pride, loyalty, and cohesiveness in their organizations or families.
- *Gender Egalitarianism:* the degree to which an organization minimizes gender inequality.
- *Power Distance:* the extent to which the community accepts and endorses authority, unequal distribution of power, and status privileges.
- *Uncertainty Avoidance:* the extent to which a society or organization uses rules, regulations, and procedures to alleviate the unpredictability of future events.[51]

Based on the data, countries receive an average score on the nine cultural dimensions. For example, Russia scored high on power distance, Singapore scored low on humane orientation, and China scored high on gender differentiation. Managers can also use GLOBE data to cluster countries based on similar cultural values, which would give people working in foreign countries a research-based "starting point" on how individuals from these cultural clusters are likely to behave.[52]

National Culture and Global Management

Differences among national cultures have important implications for managers. First, because of cultural differences, management practices that are effective in one country might be troublesome in another. General Electric's managers learned this while trying to manage Tungsram, a Hungarian lighting products company GE acquired for $150 million. GE was attracted to Tungsram, widely regarded as one of Hungary's best companies, because of Hungary's low wage rates and the possibility of using the company as a base from which to export lighting products to western Europe. GE transferred some of its best managers to Tungsram and hoped it would soon become a leader in Europe. Unfortunately many problems arose.

One problem resulted from major misunderstandings between the American managers and the Hungarian workers. The Americans complained that the Hungarians were lazy; the Hungarians thought the Americans were pushy. The Americans wanted strong sales and marketing functions that would pamper customers. In the prior Hungarian economy, sales and marketing activities were unnecessary. In addition, Hungarians expected GE to deliver Western-style wages, but GE came to Hungary to take advantage of the country's low-wage structure. As Tungsram's losses mounted, GE managers had to admit that, because of differences in basic attitudes between countries, they had underestimated the difficulties they would face in turning Tungsram around. Nevertheless, these problems were eventually solved, and the increased efficiency of GE's Hungarian operations made General Electric a major player in the European lighting market for more than a decade. Recently GE sold its lighting operations in Europe, the Middle East, Africa, and Turkey to a company now headed by the former president of GE Hungary.[53]

Often, management practices must be tailored to suit the cultural contexts within which an organization operates. An approach effective in the United States might not work in Japan, Hungary, or Mexico because of differences in national culture. For example, U.S.-style pay-for-performance systems that emphasize the performance of individuals might not work well in Japan, where individual performance in pursuit of group goals is the value that receives emphasis.

Managers doing business with individuals from another country must be sensitive to the value systems and norms of that country and behave accordingly. For example, Friday is the Islamic Sabbath. Thus it would be impolite and inappropriate for a U.S. manager to schedule a busy day of activities for Saudi Arabian managers on a Friday.

A culturally diverse management team can be a source of strength for an organization participating in the global marketplace. Compared to organizations with culturally homogeneous management teams, organizations that employ managers from a variety of cultures have a better appreciation of how national cultures differ, and they tailor their management systems and behaviors to the differences.[54] Indeed, one advantage that many Western companies have over their Japanese competitors is greater willingness to create global teams composed of employees from different countries around the world who can draw on and share their different cultural experiences and knowledge to provide service that is customized to the needs of companies in different countries. For example, because technology services account for more than half of IBM's annual revenues, it has been searching for ways to better use its talented workforce to both lower costs and offer customers unique,

IBM's competency centers customize teams of workers who have just the right mix of skills to address a specific client's business needs. ColorBlind Images/Blend Images LLC RF

specialized kinds of services that its competitors cannot. IBM has developed several kinds of techniques to accomplish this.[55]

In the 2000s, IBM created "competency centers" around the world staffed by employees who share the same specific skill. Most of IBM's employees are concentrated in competency centers located in the countries in which IBM has the most clients and does the most business. These employees have a wide variety of skills, developed from their previous work experience, and the challenge facing IBM is to use these experts efficiently. To accomplish this, IBM used its own technology expertise to develop sophisticated software that allows it to create self-managed teams composed of IBM experts who have the optimum mix of skills to solve a client's particular problems. First, IBM programmers analyze the skills and experience of its global employees and enter the results into the software program. Then they analyze and code the nature of a client's specific problem and input that information. IBM's program matches each specific client problem to the skills of IBM's experts and identifies a list of "best fit" employees. One of IBM's senior managers narrows this list and decides on the actual composition of the self-managed team. Once selected, team members, from wherever they happen to be in the world, assemble as quickly as possible and go to work analyzing the client's problem. Together, team members use their authority. This lets IBM create an ever-changing set of global self-managed teams that form to develop the software and service package necessary to solve the problems of IBM's global clients. At the same time, IBM's technology expertise also optimizes the use of its entire talented workforce because each employee is placed in his or her "most highly valued use"— that is, in the team where the employee's skills can best increase efficiency and effectiveness.

There are many factors involved in working for a global organization, including the opportunity to work for the company overseas as an *expatriate*—an employee who lives and works in a foreign country. The accompanying "Manager as a Person" feature describes some of factors that may impact individuals working in a foreign country.

Manager as a Person

Ready to Work in a Foreign Country?

Where in the world would you like to work? The annual Expat Explorer Survey by HSBC Bank International could help you decide. The survey ranks the best (and worst) places in the world to work as an expat. The results are available on the company's website (https://expatexplorer.hsbc.com) and can help managers understand what it takes to be an expatriate in different countries.[56]

According to responses from the more than 100,000 expats who have completed the survey over the past decade, they seem to echo some of the same advice regardless of where they live in a foreign land:

- Learn to work with the local culture and people rather than try to get them to do things your way.
- Join group activities that interest you (fitness classes, cooking classes, cycling clubs, etc.), so you can meet and make friends.
- Make an effort to learn the local language and take an interest in local customs.
- Don't "hide" in the local expat community—go out and meet other people.[57]

The HSBC survey ranks countries based on economics, experience, and family. The economic factors include disposable income and host economic satisfaction. The experience factor includes a long list of issues from entertainment, to work–life balance, local culture, friendships, and learning of the local language. The family factors include such issues as the quality and cost of child care, access to good schools, and learning of a new language.

Some of the key findings from the 2018 survey include the following: Switzerland, Norway, Germany, and Singapore top the list for earning the best level of disposable income (economics); New Zealand, Spain, and Portugal are the best three destinations for lifestyle and quality of life (experience); and the Netherlands, Sweden, and Singapore are top contenders when it comes to children's education and the positive impact of raising children abroad (family).[58]

While the factors can be selected to tailor a list of the best countries for an individual deciding whether he or she wants to work in a foreign country, the survey does rank the countries overall from best to worst. Singapore, Norway, and New Zealand were the "best" places to live for expats, and Argentina, Peru, and Egypt were the "worst" destinations for foreign workers. The United States ranked 27 out of 46 countries overall due to average scores in experience and family factors. Some of the top reasons individuals choose an expatriate experience include looking for a new challenge, improving the quality of life, hoping to improve job prospects, trying to improve earnings, and finding purpose in a career.[59]

Despite some of the challenges encountered in foreign countries, most expats believe their work and life experiences overseas allow them to broaden their horizons, pursue new opportunities, and embrace different cultures.[60] ●

Summary and Review

WHAT IS THE GLOBAL ENVIRONMENT? The global environment is the set of forces and conditions that operate beyond an organization's boundaries but affect a manager's ability to acquire and use resources. The global environment has two components: the task environment and the general environment. [LO 4-1]

THE TASK ENVIRONMENT The task environment is the set of forces and conditions that originate with global suppliers, distributors, customers, and competitors and influence managers daily. The opportunities and threats associated with forces in the task environment become more complex as a company expands globally. [LO 4-2, 4-3]

THE GENERAL ENVIRONMENT The general environment consists of wide-ranging global economic, technological, sociocultural, demographic, political, and legal forces that affect an organization and its task environment. [LO 4-2, 4-3]

THE CHANGING GLOBAL ENVIRONMENT In recent years there has been a marked shift toward a more open global environment in which capital flows more freely as people and companies search for new opportunities to create profit and wealth. This has hastened the process of globalization. Globalization is the set of specific and general forces that work together to integrate and connect economic, political, and social systems across countries, cultures, or geographic regions so that nations become increasingly interdependent and similar. The process of globalization has been furthered by declining barriers to international trade and investment and declining barriers of distance and culture. [LO 4-4, 4-5]

Management *in Action*

Topics for Discussion and Action

Discussion

1. Why is it important for managers to understand the forces in the global environment that are affecting them and their organizations? [LO 4-1]

2. Which organization is likely to face the most complex task environment—a biotechnology company trying to develop a cure for cancer or a large retailer like The Gap or Macy's? Why? [LO 4-2, 4-3]

3. The population is aging because of declining birth rates, declining death rates, and the aging of the baby boomer generation. What might some of the implications of this demographic trend be for (a) a pharmaceutical company and (b) the home construction industry? [LO 4-1, 4-2, 4-3]

4. How do political, legal, and economic forces shape national culture? What characteristics of national culture do you think have the most important effect on how successful a country is in doing business abroad? [LO 4-3, 4-5]

5. After the passage of NAFTA, many companies shifted production operations to Mexico to take advantage of lower labor costs and lower standards for environmental and worker protection. As a result, they cut their costs and were better able to survive in an increasingly competitive global environment. Was their behavior ethical—that is, did the ends justify the means? [LO 4-4]

Action

6. Choose an organization and ask a manager in that organization to list the number and strengths of forces in the organization's task environment. Ask the manager to pay particular attention to identifying opportunities and threats that result from pressures and changes in customers, competitors, and suppliers. [LO 4-1, 4-2, 4-3]

Building Management Skills

Analyzing an Organization's Environment [LO 4-1, 4-2, 4-3]

Pick an organization with which you are familiar. It can be an organization in which you have worked or currently work or one that you interact with regularly as a customer (such as the college you are attending). For this organization do the following:

1. Describe the main forces in the global task environment that are affecting the organization.

2. Describe the main forces in the global general environment that are affecting the organization.

3. Explain how environmental forces affect the job of an individual manager within this organization. How do they determine the opportunities and threats that its managers must confront?

Managing Ethically [LO 4-4, 4-5]

Home Depot misjudged the market in China. The world's largest home improvement chain entered the Chinese market and decided to leave it six years later. The company was unable to sell its do-it-yourself brand to Chinese consumers. Cheap labor in China means many people can hire someone else to do home improvement work for them. In addition, apartment--based living in China meant there was not much demand for products such as lumber.[61]

Questions

1. What could Home Depot have done to avoid its mistake in China?

2. In what cultures might Home Depot find better success?

Small Group Breakout Exercise [LO 4-1, 4-2]

How to Enter the Copying Business

Form groups of three to five people, and appoint one group member as the spokesperson who will communicate your findings to the whole class when called on by the instructor. Then discuss the following scenario:

You and your partners have decided to open a small printing and copying business in a college town of 100,000 people. Your business will compete with companies like FedEx Office. You know that over 50% of small businesses fail in their first year, so to increase your chances of success, you have decided to perform a detailed analysis of the task environment of the copying business to discover what opportunities and threats you will encounter.

1. Decide what you must know about (a) your future customers, (b) your future competitors, and (c) other critical forces in the task environment if you are to be successful.

2. Evaluate the main barriers to entry into the copying business.

3. Based on this analysis, list some steps you would take to help your new copying business succeed.

Be the Manager [LO 4-1, 4-2]

The Changing Environment of Retailing

You are the new manager of a major clothing store that is facing a crisis. This clothing store has been the leader in its market for the last 15 years. In the last 3 years, however, two other major clothing store chains have opened, and they have steadily been attracting customers away from your store—your sales are down 30%. To find out why, your store surveyed former customers and learned that they perceive your store as not keeping up with changing fashion trends and online shopping options. In examining how the store operates, you found out that the purchasing managers who buy the clothing and accessories for the store have been buying from the same clothing suppliers and have become reluctant to try new ones. Moreover, salespeople rarely, if ever, make suggestions for changing how the store operates, and they don't respond to customer requests; the culture of the store has become conservative and risk-averse.

Questions

1. Analyze the major forces in the task environment of a retail clothing store.

2. Devise a program that will help other managers and employees better understand and respond to their store's task environment.

Case in the News [LO 4-1, 4-2, 4-3, 4-4]

Foxconn Takes a Chance on Wisconsin

Foxconn Technology Group is best known for its Chinese factories that make components for iPhones. In the electronics industry, it is the world's largest contract manufacturer (making parts for and assembling customers' branded products), employing about a million people in China. Its biggest manufacturing facility is in the Pearl River Delta, an area that is China's manufacturing powerhouse. There it makes products for Apple, the Taiwan-based company's biggest customer.

While many U.S. companies have found low-cost labor in China, Foxconn has recently reversed that story by announcing plans to build a factory in southeastern Wisconsin, in the town of Mount Pleasant. The state government offered $3 billion in financial incentives if the company meets targets for workers hired, wages paid, and dollars invested in the state. Foxconn said it expects to invest $10 billion and hire about 13,000 employees, including factory workers, engineers, and support staff. It aims to have the plant up and running by 2020. The original announcement was that it would make large liquid crystal displays (LCDs), but the company later amended the plan to produce smaller displays instead, thus requiring a smaller facility, a smaller investment, and fewer workers.

The political context for Foxconn's move has made the decision attractive in several ways. One is that Wisconsin's then governor, Scott Walker, was enthusiastic about bringing jobs to the state. He pushed for the incentive deal, which critics have described as overly optimistic and expensive (he later lost a bid for reelection). Still, Foxconn's promises to support education and help build a technology hub in the Midwest—including funds for "innovation centers," R&D facilities in the Wisconsin cities of Eau Claire, Green Bay, and Racine—gave a shine to the company's reputation and won the company support for the deal.

Another political factor has been the Trump administration's concern about Chinese imports. Opening a facility in the United States helps Foxconn limit the amount of product subject to tariffs on goods made in China. Of course, China's government, too, is a part of the political environment, and it is pursuing ambitious plans for moving its industries away from low-priced items to high-technology, high-value goods. The Chinese government is not reluctant to spend money to make the country a leader in robots, electric vehicles, and other products of the future. As companies shift their low-end work to lower-wage countries such as Vietnam, government subsidies are helping them develop their manufacturing of higher-end products to sell locally or export—to Europe, if not the United States.

Ironically, a booming economy could pose an economic threat to Foxconn's plans for operating in Mount Pleasant. The unemployment rate in the United States is low overall, and it is even lower in Wisconsin (just 3% in a recent month). This is making it difficult to find enough qualified workers, even without the Foxconn factory in the area. Foxconn began interviewing U.S. workers in Wisconsin, but talk eventually spread that the company was having trouble finding enough interested engineers and might need to persuade some of its Chinese employees to transfer to the U.S. factory—rumors that management downplayed. Looking at long-term demand for labor, Foxconn has been working with local educational institutions to prepare students for careers in high-tech manufacturing.

Threats also exist in Foxconn's task environment. Even as managers were planning the company's expansion in Wisconsin, they were looking to what they viewed as a challenging year ahead. Among those challenges is less robust demand for new iPhones, suggesting that Foxconn's biggest customer might not buy as many components in the future. Foxconn reportedly set out to engage in cost cutting and downsizing in order to weather the slowdown, but publicly, Foxconn's position is that it is moving ahead with its plans for Wisconsin.

A less-noticed aspect of Foxconn's move into Wisconsin involves a personal connection related to a crop that is mostly exported. Paul Hsu is a farmer who grows ginseng in Wisconsin, which has excellent climate and soil conditions for the root crop that people, especially in Asia, value for medicinal qualities. Most U.S. ginseng is grown in Wisconsin and sold in Asia, so Chinese consumers of herbal remedies associate Wisconsin with ginseng. While Hsu was traveling in China, he met Foxconn CEO Terry Gou. That meeting provided the seed for another Foxconn investment: modernizing the ginseng business in Wisconsin with crop and processing technologies. Why ginseng? One possibility is that making this cross-cultural link to Wisconsin agriculture will bolster Foxconn's reputation as a company that plays a valued role in the communities where it operates—even communities halfway around the world from its headquarters.

Questions for Discussion

1. What forces does this case describe operating in Foxconn's global environment?

2. In light of the threats and opportunities described in this case, do you think Foxconn's plans to open a facility in Wisconsin will help it compete? Why or why not?

3. The trend toward globalization gave Foxconn a major business opportunity to be a supplier of technology, especially to Apple. To the extent that political forces have recently led to tariffs and other barriers to trade, what impact on Foxconn would you expect to see (or have you seen)?

Sources: A. Carr, "Another Glorious Day in Trump's Manufacturing Paradise," *Bloomberg Businessweek,* February 11, 2019, 56–61; Y. Jie, "Foxconn Considers Bringing Chinese Workers to Wisconsin as U.S. Labor Market Tightens," *The Wall Street Journal,* www.wsj.com, November 6, 2018; Jeff Bollier, "Foxconn's Green Bay Innovation Center Plans Not Impacted by Evers Election," *Green Bay* (WI) *Press Gazette,* www.greenbaypressgazette.com, November 21, 2018; R. Romell and P. Marley, "Foxconn Looks to Slash Corporate Expenses and Cut Jobs in 2019, Bloomberg Reports," *Milwaukee Journal Sentinel,* www.jsonline.com, November 21, 2018; Nathan Phelps, "Foxconn Seeks Employees at 5 Wisconsin Hiring Events," *Green Bay Press Gazette,* www.greenbaypressgazette.com, October 8, 2018; L. Lin and D. Strumpf, "A Twist in the U.S. Tariff Battle: 'It's Helping China Be More Competitive,'" *The Wall Street Journal,* www.wsj.com, September 17, 2018; L. Wei and Y. Kubota, "China Warns U.S. Firms as Trade War Brews: Buckle Up," *The Wall Street Journal,* June 15, 2018; M. Silver, "Taiwan's Foxconn and Wisconsin Farmers Bond over Ginseng," *Morning Edition,* www.npr.org, October 22, 2018.

Endnotes

1. S. Nassauer, L. Magalhães, and N. Purnell, "Walmart Looks to Scale Back in U.K. and Brazil, with an Eye on India," *The Wall Street Journal,* www.wsj.com, April 29, 2018; C. Abrams, S. Nassauer, and D. MacMillan, "Walmart Takes on Amazon with $15 Billion Bid for Stake in India's Flipkart," *The Wall Street Journal,* www.wsj.com, May 4, 2018; S. Dhume, "Walmart's Big Bet Could Pay Off for India," *The Wall Street Journal,* www.wsj.com, May 17, 2018.

2. Nassauer et al., "Walmart Looks to Scale Back."

3. C. R. Sukumar, "Flipkart Acquisition Won't Hit Walmart India Plans," *Economic Times,* https://economictimes.indiatimes.com, November 1, 2018.

4. Abrams et al., "Walmart Takes on Amazon"; K. Hu, "Walmart's Missteps in China Could Provide

a Crucial Lesson for Its India Expansion," *Yahoo Finance,* https://finance.yahoo.com, October 16, 2018.

5. Abrams et al., "Walmart Takes on Amazon"; E. Bellman and V. Agarwal, "India's Biggest Competitors to Walmart and Amazon? Mom and Pop," *The Wall Street Journal,* www.wsj.com, May 28, 2018.

6. L. J. Bourgeois, "Strategy and Environment: A Conceptual Integration," *Academy of Management Review* 5 (1985), 25–39.

7. M. E. Porter, *Competitive Strategy* (New York: Free Press, 1980).

8. "Coca-Cola versus Pepsi-Cola and the Soft Drink Industry," Harvard Business School Case 9-391–179.

9. www.splenda.com, 2017.

10. "Stevia Use in Beverages and Foods Continue to Increase. Launches with Stevia Leaf Sweetener Up +10% in 2017," https://purecircle.com, March 22, 2018; J. Gelski, "Stevia Use to Grow Fastest in Beverages," *Food Business News,* www.foodbusinessnews.net, September 15, 2016.

11. Levi Strauss & Co., "Sustainability: People," www.levistrauss.com, accessed December 1, 2018; Erika Fry, "The Ties That Bind at Levi's," *Fortune,* September 15, 2017, 104–10; Adele Peters, "How Levi's Is Building Well-Being Programs Where They Matter Most: In Its Factories," *Fast Company,* www.fastcompany.com, October 13, 2016.

12. Ibid.

13. Harvard School of Public Health, Center for Health and the Global Environment, "Worker Health and Well-Being in the Supply Chain," https://chge.hsph.harvard.edu, accessed December 1, 2018.

14. Fry, "The Ties That Bind at Levi's."

15. Levi Strauss & Co., "Sustainability: People"; Peters, "How Levi's Is Building."

16. "Boeing's Worldwide Supplier Network," *Seattle Post-Intelligencer,* April 9, 1994, 13; I. Metthee, "Playing a Larger Part," *Seattle Post-Intelligencer,* April 1994, 13.

17. J. Bogaisky, "Boeing's Vertical Leap: Where Will It Squeeze Suppliers Next?," *Forbes,* www.forbes.com, June 6, 2018.

18. "What We Do," www.lifung.com, accessed December 1, 2018.

19. J. Thornton-O'Connell, "7 Companies That Have Reinvested in America Following Trump's Election," *Go Banking Rates,* www.gobankingrates.com, September 6, 2018.

20. M. E. Porter, *Competitive Advantage* (New York: Free Press, 1985).

21. S. Nassauer and J. Smith, "Wal-Mart Tightens Delivery Windows for Suppliers," *The Wall Street Journal,* www.wsj.com, accessed December 1, 2018.

22. "Gartner Says Worldwide PC Shipments Experienced Flat Growth in the Third Quarter of 2018," www.gartner.com, accessed December 1, 2018.

23. For views on barriers to entry from an economics perspective, see Porter, *Competitive Advantage.* For the sociological perspective, see J. Pfeffer and G. R. Salancik, *The External Control of Organization: A Resource Dependence Perspective* (New York: Harper & Row, 1978).

24. P. Sisson, "9 Facts about Amazon's Unprecedented Warehouse Empire," *Curbed,* www.curbed.com, accessed December 1, 2018.

25. T. Simmons, "U.S. Exports to Japan Fall Short; Implications for TPP Unsettles Industry," *Ag Watch Network,* https://agwatchnetwork.com, accessed December 1, 2018.

26. K. Lee, "Best Processors 2018: Top CPUs for Your PC," *Tech Radar,* www.techradar.com, November 26, 2018; "AMD Launches World's Most Powerful Desktop Processor," www.amd.com, August 31, 2018.

27. N. Goodman, *An Introduction to Sociology* (New York: HarperCollins, 1991); C. Nakane, *Japanese Society* (Berkeley: University of California Press, 1970).

28. A. Smith, "Walmart Is Bringing Meal Kits to Thousands of Stores," *CNNMoney,* http://money.cnn.com, accessed December 1, 2018; C. Siegner, "6 Major Food Trends to Watch in 2018," *Food Dive,* www.fooddive.com, January 23, 2018.

29. For a detailed discussion of the importance of the structure of law as a factor explaining economic change and growth, see D. C. North, *Institutions, Institutional Change, and Economic Performance* (Cambridge: Cambridge University Press, 1990).

30. S. Salinas, "Apple Is Cleared to Buy Shazam in Boost for Apple Music and Siri," *CNBC,* www.cnbc.com, September 6, 2018; D. Meyer, "Why the EU Is Holding Up Apple's Shazam Takeover," *Fortune,* http://fortune.com, February 7, 2018; A. White, "Apple-Shazam Deal May Hurt Competition in Europe, EU Says," *Bloomberg Technology,* www.bloomberg.com, February 6, 2018.

31. R. Picheta, "Theresa May to Resign as UK Prime Minister," *CNN,* www.cnn.com, May 25, 2019; J. Henley, "'Soft' Brexit Agreement Not a Done Deal, Warn EU Leaders," *The Guardian,* www.theguardian.com, November 15, 2018.

32. F. Ungku and C. Greenfield, "Trump Says U.S. Could Rejoin TPP If Deal Is Improved. How Hard Would That Be?" Reuters, www.reuters.com, April 24, 2018; P. Baker, "Trump Abandons Trans-Pacific Partnership, Obama's Signature Trade Deal," *The New York Times,* www.nytimes.com, January 23, 2017.

33. M. A. Carpenter and J. W. Frederickson, "Top Management Teams, Global Strategic Posture, and the Moderating Role of Uncertainty," *Academy of Management Journal* 44 (June 2001), 533–46.

34. A. Swanson and A. Rappeport, "Trump Increases China Tariffs as Trade Deal Hangs in the Balance," *The New York Times,* www.nytimes.com, May 9, 2019.

35. For a summary of these theories, see P. Krugman and M. Obstfeld, *International Economics: Theory and Policy* (New York: HarperCollins, 1991). Also see C. W. L. Hill, *International Business* (New York: McGraw-Hill, 1997), Chapter 4.

36. A. M. Rugman, "The Quest for Global Dominance," *Academy of Management Executive* 16 (August 2002), 157–60.

37. "The Doha Round," www.wto.org, accessed December 2, 2018; "Opinion: Global Trade after the Failure of the Doha Round," *The*

New York Times, www.nytimes.com, January 1, 2016.

38. C. Dawson and M. Colias, "Trump Tariffs Pit Auto Companies against Each Other," *The Wall Street Journal,* www.wsj.com, November 9, 2018; S. Garnsey, "Tariffs Disrupting US Car Industry, Lawmakers Told," *Automotive Logistics,* https://automotivelogistics.media, October 3, 2018; P. Wall Howard, "Buying a Car before December 31 Will Save You Money," *Detroit Free Press,* www.freep.com, September 18, 2018.

39. "How America's Car Industry Is Coping with Trade Disputes," *The Economist,* www.economist.com, August 23, 2018; L. Chappell, "Toolmakers Caught in Tariff Crossfire," *Automotive News,* http://canada.autonews.com, August 18, 2018.

40. Dawson and Colias, "Trump Tariffs."

41. Ibid.; Howard, "Buying a Car before December 31."

42. C. A. Bartlett and S. Ghoshal, *Managing across Borders* (Boston: Harvard Business School Press, 1989).

43. B. Bryan, "Trump Just Sealed the Landmark Trade Deal with Mexico and Canada, but There's Still a Long Road toward Victory," *Business Insider,* www.businessinsider.com, November 30, 2018.

44. Organization website, "AU in a Nutshell," www.au.int, accessed December 2, 2018; organization website, www.sadc.int, accessed December 2, 2018; organization website, "Areas of Cooperation Achievements," www.gcc-sg.org, accessed December 2, 2018.

45. G. Hofstede, B. Neuijen, D. D. Ohayv, and G. Sanders, "Measuring Organizational Cultures: A Qualitative and Quantitative Study across Twenty Cases," *Administrative Science Quarterly* 35 (1990), 286–316.

46. G. Hofstede, G. J. Hofstede, and M. Minkov, *Cultures and Organizations: Software of the Mind,* Revised and Expanded 3rd Edition (New York: McGraw-Hill, 2010).

47. R. Bellah, *Habits of the Heart: Individualism and Commitment in American Life* (Berkeley: University of California Press, 1985).

48. G. Hofstede, "The Cultural Relativity of Organizational Practices and Theories," *Journal of International Business Studies,* Fall 1983, 75–89.

49. Hofstede et al., "Measuring Organizational Cultures."

50. R. House, M. Javidan, P. Hanges, and P. Dorfman, "Understanding Cultures and Implicit Leadership Theories across the Globe: An Introduction to Project GLOBE," *Journal of World Business,* no. 37 (2002), 3–10.

51. R. J. House et al., *Culture, Leadership, and Organizations: The GLOBE Studies of 62 Societies* (Los Angeles: Sage, 2004).

52. M. Javidan and A. Dastmalchian, "Managerial Implications of the GLOBE Project: A Study of 62 Societies," *Asia Pacific Journal of Human Resources* 47, no. 1 (2009), 41–58.

53. T. Gryta, "GE Begins to Sell Off One of Its Oldest Businesses: Lights," *The Wall Street Journal,* www.wsj.com, accessed December 2, 2018.

54. J. P. Fernandez and M. Barr, *The Diversity Advantage* (New York: Lexington Books, 1994).

55. "Center of Competency," www.ibm.com, accessed December 2, 2018.

56. "How Countries & Territories Compare," https://expatexplorer.com, accessed December 2, 2018.

57. "Expat Hints & Tips," https://expatexplorer.hsbc.com, accessed March 18, 2018.

58. "Expat Explorer: Broadening Perspectives," https://expatexplorer.com, accessed December 2, 2018.

59. Ibid.

60. R. McMunn, "Taking a Job Overseas Is Challenging, but So Rewarding," *Entrepreneur,* www.entrepreneur.com, accessed December 2, 2018; "What's an Expat Anyway?," *InterNations,* www.internations.org, accessed December 2, 2018.

61. L. Burkitt, "Home Depot Learns Chinese Prefer 'Do-It-for-Me,'" *The Wall Street Journal,* www.wsj.com, accessed December 2, 2018; "University Study Concludes Why Home Depot Failed in China: It Ignored Women," *Fierce Retail,* www.fierceretail.com, April 29, 2013.

PART 3

Robert Nicholas/Ojo Images/age fotostock

5 Decision Making, Learning, and Creativity

Learning Objectives

After studying this chapter, you should be able to:

LO 5-1 Understand the nature of managerial decision making, differentiate between programmed and nonprogrammed decisions, and explain why nonprogrammed decision making is a complex, uncertain process.

LO 5-2 Describe the six steps managers should take to make the best decisions.

LO 5-3 Identify the advantages and disadvantages of group decision making, and describe techniques that can improve it.

LO 5-4 Explain the role that organizational learning and creativity play in helping managers improve their decisions.

Management Snapshot

Creativity and Ability to Learn Keep 23andMe Strong

How Do Managers Make Decisions That Add Value?

Anne Wojcicki, cofounder and CEO of 23andMe, applies a creative mind-set with adaptability in the face of change. These qualities propelled decisions to launch the company she helped start in 2006 and to identify ways forward when the company ran into trouble.

Wojcicki's business idea would have been unimaginable 15 years ago. Scientists were developing ways to interpret human DNA, and as techniques advanced, their cost was falling. Wojcicki, who studied biology in college and worked in the financial industry as a biotech analyst, saw an opportunity to put health information into the hands of individuals. The product would be a test kit: a tube in which a person spits some saliva to mail in for a genetic analysis.[1] Wojcicki developed a business plan that was cautious on spending for office supplies but ambitious in terms of the product. Her company, 23andMe, was the first to offer genetic screening to the general public. Besides selling a technologically advanced product, 23andMe overturned a business model by competing with the medical facilities that had provided this service to patients. Within a few years, 23andMe offered customers more than 250 possible reports.[2]

In 2013, however, 23andMe hit a roadblock. The Food and Drug Administration determined that its test kit was a medical device, because it provided information patients would use for making medical decisions.[3] The company had not sought the required FDA approval to sell such a device. Managers had assumed the test kit was a diagnostic test carried out in a single lab, and that is what they obtained approval to sell it to consumers. The FDA investigated when doctors and geneticists expressed concern that the test provided insufficient information for making informed decisions. The agency ruled that 23andMe could continue selling the test kit if the results addressed customers' ancestry only, not their health risks. This restriction destroyed the company's fundamental business model, but Wojcicki decided it was a challenge that perseverance could solve, not a death blow to 23andMe.[4]

Wojcicki and her staff began working with the FDA to address its concerns.[5] They began meeting with FDA staff every couple of months and sending frequent messages as they prepared an application for approval. After rejecting the first application, the FDA considered a second. Wojcicki saw the situation as a learning opportunity. She identified a key problem: 23andMe had originally lacked the right people for navigating the complex process of meeting regulatory requirements. She hired an expert in regulatory affairs, and they divided the desired tests into chunks, focusing first on tests they thought would most easily win approval. Finally, four years later, the FDA began allowing 23andMe to report results indicating risk factors for certain diseases, including Parkinson's and Alzheimer's.

23andMe CEO Anne Wojcicki learned a valuable lesson about decision making and flexibility when it came to a viable business model for the company. Kimberly White/Getty Images

In the meantime, Wojcicki had recognized an even more significant way forward. Consumers—more than a million—kept buying tests, even just to learn about their ancestry, and most agreed to allow their data to be used in scientific research.[6] These customers filled out surveys, creating a massive and growing database about their health, genetics, and behaviors. Managers at 23andMe realized they were building a product more valuable than the test kits: the data. They decided to identify ethical ways to use the data as an asset. They began selling data sets (without patients' names) to drug companies and makers of health-related products. For Wojcicki, the process was like starting up a company all over again.[7] And this time, she already had the added advantage of experience.

Overview

The "Management Snapshot" illustrates how decision making can have a profound influence on organizational effectiveness. The decisions managers make at all levels in companies large and small can change the growth and prosperity of these companies and the well-being of their employees, customers, and other stakeholders. Yet such decisions can be difficult to make because they are fraught with uncertainty.

In this chapter we examine how managers make decisions, and we explore how individual, group, and organizational factors affect the quality of the decisions they make and ultimately determine organizational performance. We discuss the nature of managerial decision making and examine some models of the decision-making process that help reveal the complexities of successful decision making. Then we outline the main steps of the decision-making process. Next we examine how managers can promote organizational learning and creativity and improve the quality of decision making throughout an organization. Finally, we discuss the important role of intrapreneurship in promoting organizational learning and innovation. By the end of this chapter you will appreciate the critical role of management decision making in creating a high-performing organization.

The Nature of Managerial Decision Making

Every time managers plan, organize, direct, or control organizational activities, they make a stream of decisions. In opening a new restaurant, for example, managers have to decide where to locate it, what kinds of food to provide, which people to employ, and so on. Decision making is a basic part of every task managers perform.

As we discussed in the previous chapter, one of the main tasks facing a manager is to manage the organizational environment. Forces in the external environment give rise to many opportunities and threats for managers and their organizations. In addition, inside an organization, managers must address many opportunities and threats that may arise as organizational resources are used. To deal with these opportunities and threats, managers must make decisions—that is, they must select one solution from a set of alternatives. Decision making is the process by which managers respond to opportunities and threats by analyzing the options and making determinations, or *decisions*, about specific organizational goals and courses of action. Good decisions result in the selection of appropriate goals and courses of action that increase organizational performance; bad decisions lower performance.

Decision making in response to opportunities occurs when managers search for ways to improve organizational performance to benefit customers, employees, and other stakeholder groups. As described in the "Management Snapshot," Anne Wojcicki seized the opportunity to develop new products that capitalize on 23andMe's strengths. *Decision making in response to threats* occurs when events inside or outside the organization adversely affect organizational performance, and managers search for ways to increase performance.[8] Wojcicki responded to the FDA's complaint that the 23andMe product was actually a medical device by hiring experts experienced in navigating the maze of regulatory requirements and by working closely with FDA staff every step of the way during the approval process. Decision making is central to being a manager, and whenever managers engage in planning, organizing, leading, and controlling—their four principal tasks—they are constantly making decisions.

Managers are always searching for ways to make better decisions to improve organizational performance. At the same time, they do their best to avoid costly mistakes that will hurt organizational performance. Examples of spectacularly good decisions include Martin Cooper's decision to develop the first cell phone at Motorola and Apple's decision to develop the iPod.[9] Examples of spectacularly bad decisions include the decision by managers at NASA and Morton Thiokol to launch the *Challenger* space shuttle—a decision that killed seven astronauts in 1986—and the decision by NASA to launch the *Columbia* space shuttle in 2003, which also killed seven astronauts.

Programmed and Nonprogrammed Decision Making

Regardless of the specific decisions a manager makes, the decision-making process is either programmed or nonprogrammed.[10]

programmed decision making
Routine, virtually automatic decision making that follows established rules or guidelines.

PROGRAMMED DECISION MAKING Programmed decision making is a *routine*, virtually automatic process. Programmed decisions are decisions that have been made so many times in the past that managers have developed rules or guidelines to be applied when certain situations inevitably occur. Programmed decision making takes place when a school principal asks the school board to hire a new teacher whenever student enrollment increases by 40 students; when a manufacturing supervisor hires new workers whenever existing workers' overtime increases by more than 10%; and when an office manager orders basic office supplies, such as paper and pens, whenever the inventory of supplies drops below a certain level. Furthermore, in the last example, the office manager probably orders the same amount of supplies each time.

This decision making is called *programmed* because office managers, for example, do not need to repeatedly make new judgments about what should be done. They can rely on long-established decision rules such as these:

- *Rule 1:* When the storage shelves are three-quarters empty, order more copy paper.
- *Rule 2:* When ordering paper, order enough to fill the shelves.

Managers can develop rules and guidelines to regulate all routine organizational activities. For example, rules can specify how a worker should perform a certain task, and rules can specify the quality standards that raw materials must meet to be acceptable. Most decision making that relates to the day-to-day running of an organization is programmed decision making. Examples include deciding how much inventory to hold, when to pay bills, when to bill customers, and when to order materials and supplies. Programmed decision making occurs when managers have the information they need to create rules that will guide decision making. There is little ambiguity involved in assessing when the stockroom is empty or counting the number of new students in class.

NONPROGRAMMED DECISION MAKING Suppose, however, that managers are not certain that a course of action will lead to a desired outcome. Or in even more ambiguous terms, suppose managers are not even sure what they are trying to achieve. Obviously, rules cannot be developed to predict uncertain events.

nonprogrammed decision making Nonroutine decision making that occurs in response to unusual, unpredictable opportunities and threats.

Nonprogrammed decision making is required for these *nonroutine* decisions. Nonprogrammed decisions are made in response to unusual or novel opportunities and threats. Nonprogrammed decision making occurs when there are no ready-made decision rules that managers can apply to a situation. Rules do not exist because the situation is unexpected or uncertain and managers lack the information they would need to develop rules to cover it. Examples of nonprogrammed decision making include decisions to invest in a new technology, develop a new kind of product, launch a new promotional campaign, enter a new market, expand internationally, start a new business, or invest in research and development like Anne Wojcicki and 23andMe did, as discussed in the chapter's opening story.

intuition Feelings, beliefs, and hunches that come readily to mind, require little effort and information gathering, and result in on-the-spot decisions.

How do managers make decisions in the absence of decision rules? They may rely on their intuition—feelings, beliefs, and hunches that come readily to mind, require little effort and information gathering, and result in on-the-spot decisions.[11] Or they may make reasoned judgments—decisions that require time and effort and result from careful information gathering, generation of alternatives, and evaluation of alternatives. "Exercising" one's judgment is a more rational process than "going with" one's intuition. For reasons that we examine later in this chapter, both intuition and judgment often are flawed and can result in poor decision making. Thus, the likelihood of error is much greater in nonprogrammed decision making than in programmed decision making.[12] In the remainder of this chapter, when we talk about decision making, we are referring to *nonprogrammed* decision making because it causes the most problems for managers and is inherently challenging.

reasoned judgment A decision that requires time and effort and results from careful information gathering, generation of alternatives, and evaluation of alternatives.

Sometimes managers have to make rapid decisions and don't have time to carefully consider the issues involved. They must rely on their intuition to respond quickly to a pressing concern. For example, when fire chiefs, captains, and lieutenants manage firefighters battling dangerous, out-of-control fires, they often need to rely on their expert intuition to make on-the-spot decisions that will protect the lives of the firefighters and save the lives of others, contain the fires, and preserve property—decisions made in emergency situations entailing high uncertainty, high risk, and rapidly changing conditions.[13] In other cases managers do have time to make reasoned judgments, but there are no established rules to guide their decisions, such as when deciding whether to proceed with a proposed merger or how to take a start-up business to a new level, as described in the "Manager as a Person" feature.

Manager as a Person

Glossier Shines Because Founder Seeks Advice

Emily Weiss's success as a business founder comes from following her passions and working hard. As a teen attracted to fashion, she worked as a model and talked her way into an internship with Ralph Lauren.[14] Impressed with her dedication and enthusiasm, a design director introduced her to the editor in chief of *Teen Vogue*, resulting in a part-time internship while she attended college. After graduating, Weiss returned to the fashion business as an assistant at *W* and *Vogue*.

For her next step, starting a business, Weiss applied her people skills and industry knowledge.[15] Working around fashion designers and models at *Vogue*, she demonstrated interest, asking about beauty regimens and listening attentively to hear their insecurities and needs as well as their best ideas. She then applied her knowledge about magazine design and content to publish her own blog, *Into the Gloss*. Tapping her network of contacts, she interviewed industry insiders and landed advertisers for the blog. As the blog began getting 10 million page views per month, she realized that in today's beauty industry, opinions about products are shared and formed through social media. Weiss decided to use this insight as the basis for a bigger business, called Glossier (pronounced GLOSS-ee-ay). To achieve her goal of building a beauty company focused on positive body messages and social media, she began seeking investors.

Seasoned investors immediately saw the limits of Weiss's decision making.[16] She listened and communicated effectively; she knew about skin care and makeup, but she lacked training in how to run a business. She didn't know how to write a business plan or even formulate products. Even after 11 rejections for financing, Weiss never gave up. She met venture capitalist Kirsten Green, who was impressed not only with Weiss's ability to turn an idea into a successful blogging venture but also with her broad vision of the industry's potential. Green invested enough for Weiss to build a team of decision makers, including a creative director and a chief operating officer to organize her vision into projects. They started with four products, priced affordably. Within a few years, they built a $34 million company selling two dozen beauty products and posting an annual sales increase of 600 percent.[17]

Weiss's team continues to build on her responsiveness to consumers' needs. As Glossier grew, the team invested early in collecting data from social media to identify what customers loved and hated about the products.[18] When customers offer feedback, Weiss or other employees reply, and when customers have ideas, Glossier quickly adapts. Every few weeks, another product launches. As Weiss learned quickly, making any type of business decision may require more than intuition; it may require investors and sound advice from others. ●

Glossier CEO Emily Weiss learned the importance of enlisting others to help make effective decisions about her e-commerce beauty business. Vivien Killilea/Getty Images

Figure 5.1

The Classical Model of Decision Making

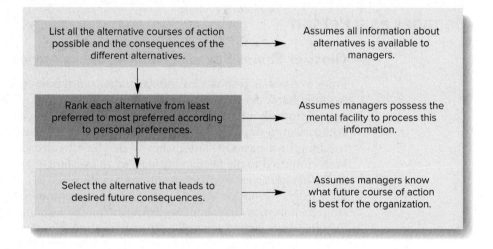

The classical and administrative decision-making models reveal many of the assumptions, complexities, and pitfalls that affect decision making. These models help reveal the factors that managers and other decision makers must be aware of to improve the quality of their decision making. Keep in mind, however, that the classical and administrative models are just guides that can help managers understand the decision-making process. In real life the process is typically not cut and dried, but these models can help guide a manager through it.

The Classical Model

classical model A prescriptive approach to decision making based on the assumption that the decision maker can identify and evaluate all possible alternatives and their consequences and rationally choose the most appropriate course of action.

One of the earliest models of decision making, the classical model, is *prescriptive*, which means it specifies how decisions *should* be made. Managers using the classical model make a series of simplifying assumptions about the nature of the decision-making process (see Figure 5.1). The premise of the classical model is that once managers recognize the need to make a decision, they should be able to generate a complete list of *all* alternatives and consequences and make the best choice. In other words, the classical model assumes managers have access to *all* the information they need to make the optimum decision, which is the most appropriate decision possible in light of what they believe to be the most desirable consequences for the organization. Furthermore, the classical model assumes managers can easily list their own preferences for each alternative and rank them from least to most preferred to make the optimum decision.

The Administrative Model

optimum decision The most appropriate decision in light of what managers believe to be the most desirable consequences for the organization.

James March and Herbert Simon disagreed with the underlying assumptions of the classical model of decision making. In contrast, they proposed that managers in the real world do *not* have access to all the information they need to make a decision. Moreover, they pointed out that even if all information were readily available, many managers would lack the mental or psychological ability to absorb and evaluate it correctly. As a result, March and Simon developed the administrative model of decision making to explain why decision making is always an inherently uncertain and risky process—and why managers can rarely make decisions in the

Figure 5.2

Why Information Is Incomplete

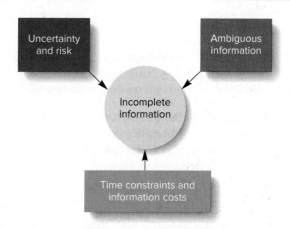

administrative model An approach to decision making that explains why decision making is inherently uncertain and risky and why managers usually make satisfactory rather than optimum decisions.

manner prescribed by the classical model. The administrative model is based on three important concepts: *bounded rationality, incomplete information,* and *satisficing.*

BOUNDED RATIONALITY March and Simon pointed out that human decision-making capabilities are bounded by people's cognitive limitations—that is, limitations in their ability to interpret, process, and act on information.[19] They argued that the limitations of human intelligence constrain the ability of decision makers to determine the optimum decision. March and Simon coined the term bounded rationality to describe the situation in which the number of alternatives a manager must identify is so great and the amount of information so vast that it is difficult for the manager to even come close to evaluating it all before making a decision.[20]

bounded rationality Cognitive limitations that constrain one's ability to interpret, process, and act on information.

INCOMPLETE INFORMATION Even if managers had unlimited ability to evaluate information, they still would not be able to arrive at the optimum decision because they would have incomplete information. Information is incomplete because the full range of decision-making alternatives is unknowable in most situations, and the consequences associated with known alternatives are uncertain.[21] In other words, information is incomplete because of risk and uncertainty, ambiguity, and time constraints (see Figure 5.2).

risk The degree of probability that the possible outcomes of a particular course of action will occur.

RISK AND UNCERTAINTY As we saw in Chapter 4, forces in the organizational environment are constantly changing. Risk is present when managers know the possible outcomes of a particular course of action and can assign probabilities to them. For example, managers in the biotechnology industry know that new drugs have a 10% probability of successfully passing advanced clinical trials and a 90% probability of failing. These probabilities reflect the experiences of thousands of drugs that have gone through advanced clinical trials. Thus, when managers in the biotechnology industry decide to submit a drug for testing, they know that there is only a 10% chance that the drug will succeed, but at least they have some information on which to base their decision.

uncertainty Unpredictability.

When uncertainty exists, the probabilities of alternative outcomes *cannot* be determined and future outcomes are *unknown.* Managers are working blind. Because the probability of a given outcome occurring is not known, managers have little information to use in making a decision. For example, in 1993, when Apple Computer introduced the Newton, its personal digital assistant (PDA), managers had no idea what the probability of a successful product launch for a PDA might be.

Because Apple was the first to market this totally new product, there was no body of well-known data that Apple's managers could draw on to calculate the probability of a successful launch. Uncertainty plagues most managerial decision making. Although Apple's initial launch of its PDA was a disaster due to technical problems, an improved version was more successful.[22]

AMBIGUOUS INFORMATION A second reason information is incomplete is that much of the information managers have at their disposal is ambiguous information. Its meaning is not clear—it can be interpreted in multiple and often conflicting ways.[23] Take a look at Figure 5.3. Do you see a young woman or an old woman? In a similar fashion, managers often interpret the same piece of information differently and make decisions based on their own interpretations.

ambiguous information Information that can be interpreted in multiple and often conflicting ways.

TIME CONSTRAINTS AND INFORMATION COSTS The third reason information is incomplete is that managers have neither the time nor the money to search for all possible alternative solutions and evaluate all the potential consequences of those alternatives. Consider the situation confronting a Ford Motor Company purchasing manager who has one month to choose a supplier for a small engine part. There are 20,000 potential suppliers for this part in the United States alone. Given the time available, the purchasing manager cannot contact all potential suppliers and ask each for its terms (price, delivery schedules, and so on). Moreover, even if the time were available, the costs of obtaining the information, including the manager's own time, would be prohibitive.

SATISFICING March and Simon argued that managers do not attempt to discover every alternative when faced with bounded rationality, an uncertain future, unquantifiable risks, considerable ambiguity, time constraints, and high information costs. Rather, they use a strategy known as satisficing, which is exploring a limited sample of all potential alternatives.[24] When managers satisfice, they search for and choose acceptable, or satisfactory, ways to respond to problems and opportunities rather than trying to make the optimum decision.[25] In the case of the Ford purchasing manager's search, for example, satisficing may involve asking a limited number of

satisficing Searching for and choosing an acceptable, or satisfactory, response to problems and opportunities, rather than trying to make the best decision.

Figure 5.3
Ambiguous Information: Young Woman or Old Woman?

Chronicle of World History/Alamy Stock Photo

suppliers for their terms, trusting that they are representative of suppliers in general, and making a choice from that set. Although this course of action is reasonable from the perspective of the purchasing manager, it may mean that a potentially superior supplier is overlooked.

March and Simon pointed out that managerial decision making is often more art than science. In the real world, managers must rely on their intuition and judgment to make what seems to them to be the best decision in the face of uncertainty and ambiguity.[26] Moreover, managerial decision making is often fast-paced; managers use their experience and judgment to make crucial decisions under conditions of incomplete information. Although there is nothing wrong with this approach, decision makers should be aware that human judgment is often flawed. As a result, even the best managers sometimes make poor decisions.[27]

Steps in the Decision-Making Process

Using the work of March and Simon as a basis, researchers have developed a step-by-step model of the decision-making process and the issues and problems that managers confront at each step. Perhaps the best way to introduce this model is to examine the real-world nonprogrammed decision making of Scott McNealy at a crucial point in Sun Microsystems's history. McNealy was a founder of Sun Microsystems and was the chair of the board of directors until Sun was acquired by Oracle in 2010.[28]

LO 5-2
Describe the six steps managers should take to make the best decisions.

In early August 1985, Scott McNealy, then CEO of Sun Microsystems[29] (a hardware and software computer workstation manufacturer focused on network solutions), had to decide whether to go ahead with the launch of the new Carrera workstation computer, scheduled for September 10. Sun's managers had chosen the date nine months earlier when the development plan for the Carrera was first proposed. McNealy knew it would take at least a month to prepare for the September 10 launch, and the decision could not be put off.

Customers were waiting for the new machine, and McNealy wanted to be the first to provide a workstation that took advantage of Motorola's powerful 16-megahertz 68020 microprocessor. Capitalizing on this opportunity would give Sun a significant edge over Apollo, its main competitor in the workstation market. McNealy knew, however, that committing to the September 10 launch date was risky. Motorola was having production problems with the 16-megahertz 68020 microprocessor and could not guarantee Sun a steady supply of these chips. Moreover, the operating system software was not completely free of bugs.

If Sun launched the Carrera on September 10, the company might have to ship some machines with software that was not fully operational, was likely to crash the system, and utilized Motorola's less powerful 12-megahertz 68020 microprocessor instead of the 16-megahertz version.[30] Of course, Sun could later upgrade the microprocessor and operating system software in any machines purchased by early customers, but the company's reputation would suffer. If Sun did not go ahead with the September launch, the company would miss an important opportunity.[31] Rumors were circulating in the industry that Apollo would be launching a new machine of its own in December.

McNealy clearly had a difficult decision to make. He had to decide quickly whether to launch the Carrera, but he did not have all the facts. He did not know, for example, whether the microprocessor or operating system problems could be resolved by September 10; nor did he know whether Apollo was going to launch a competing machine in December. But he could not wait to find these things out—he had to make a decision. We'll see what he decided later in the chapter.

Many managers who must make important decisions with incomplete information face dilemmas similar to McNealy's. Managers should consciously follow six steps to make a good decision (see Figure 5.4).[32] We review these steps in the remainder of this section.

Recognize the Need for a Decision

The first step in the decision-making process is to recognize the need for a decision. Scott McNealy recognized this need, and he realized a decision had to be made quickly.

Some stimuli usually spark the realization that a decision must be made. These stimuli often become apparent because changes in the organizational environment result in new kinds of opportunities and threats. This happened at Sun Microsystems. The September 10 launch date had been set when it seemed that Motorola chips would be readily available. Later, with the supply of chips in doubt and bugs remaining in the system software, Sun was in danger of failing to meet its launch date.

The stimuli that spark decision making are as likely to result from the actions of managers inside an organization as they are from changes in the external environment. An organization possesses a set of skills, competencies, and resources in its employees and in departments such as marketing, manufacturing, and research and development. Managers who actively pursue opportunities to use these competencies create the need to make decisions. Managers thus can be proactive or reactive in recognizing the need to make a decision, but the important issue is that they must recognize this need and respond in a timely and appropriate way.[33]

Generate Alternatives

Having recognized the need to make a decision, a manager must generate a set of feasible alternative courses of action to take in response to the opportunity or threat.

Figure 5.4

Six Steps in Decision Making

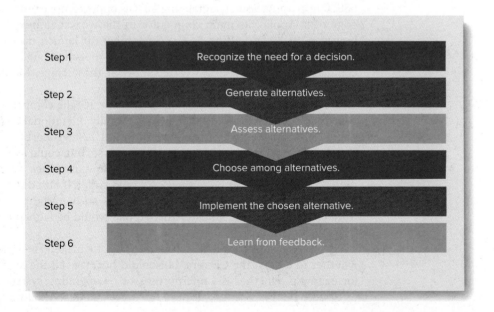

Step 1 — Recognize the need for a decision.

Step 2 — Generate alternatives.

Step 3 — Assess alternatives.

Step 4 — Choose among alternatives.

Step 5 — Implement the chosen alternative.

Step 6 — Learn from feedback.

Management experts cite failure to properly generate and consider different alternatives as one reason that managers sometimes make bad decisions.[34] In the Sun Microsystems decision, the alternatives seemed clear: go ahead with the September 10 launch or delay the launch until the Carrera was 100% ready for market introduction. Often, however, the alternatives are not so obvious or so clearly specified.

One major problem is that managers may find it difficult to come up with creative alternative solutions to specific problems. Perhaps some of them are used to seeing the world from a single perspective—they have a certain "managerial mindset." Many managers find it difficult to view problems from a fresh perspective. According to best-selling management author Peter Senge, we all are trapped within our personal mental models of the world—our ideas about what is important and how the world works.[35] Generating creative alternatives to solve problems and take advantage of opportunities may require that we abandon our existing mind-sets and develop new ones—something that usually is difficult to do.

The importance of getting managers to set aside their mental models of the world and generate creative alternatives is reflected in the growth of interest in the work of authors such as Peter Senge and Edward de Bono, who have popularized techniques for stimulating problem solving and creative thinking among managers.[36] Later in this chapter, we discuss the important issues of organizational learning and creativity in detail.

Assess Alternatives

Once managers have generated a set of alternatives, they must evaluate the advantages and disadvantages of each one.[37] The key to a good assessment of the alternatives is to define the opportunity or threat exactly and then specify the criteria that *should* influence the selection of alternatives for responding to the problem or opportunity. One reason for bad decisions is that managers often fail to specify the criteria that are important in reaching a decision.[38] In general, successful managers use four criteria to evaluate the pros and cons of alternative courses of action (see Figure 5.5):

1. *Legality:* Managers must ensure that a possible course of action will not violate any domestic or international laws or government regulations.

2. *Ethicalness:* Managers must ensure that a possible course of action is ethical and will not unnecessarily harm any stakeholder group. Many decisions managers make may help some organizational stakeholders and harm others (see Chapter 3). When examining alternative courses of action, managers need to be clear about the potential effects of their decisions.

3. *Economic feasibility:* Managers must decide whether the alternatives are economically feasible—that is, whether they can be accomplished, given the organization's performance goals. Typically, managers perform a cost–benefit analysis of the various alternatives to determine which one will have the best net financial payoff.

4. *Practicality:* Managers must decide whether they have the capabilities and resources required to implement the alternative, and they must be sure the alternative will not threaten the attainment of other organizational goals. At first glance an alternative might seem economically superior to other alternatives, but if managers realize it is likely to threaten other important projects, they might decide it is not practical after all.

Figure 5.5

General Criteria for
Evaluating Possible
Courses of Action

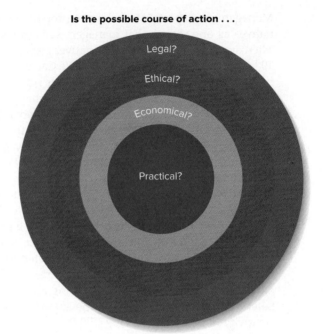

Is the possible course of action . . .

Legal?

Ethical?

Economical?

Practical?

Often a manager must consider these four criteria simultaneously. Scott McNealy framed the problem at hand at Sun Microsystems quite well. The key question was whether to go ahead with the September 10 launch date. Two main criteria were influencing McNealy's choice: the need to ship a machine that was as "complete" as possible (the *practicality* criterion) and the need to beat Apollo to market with a new workstation (the *economic feasibility* criterion). These two criteria conflicted. The first suggested that the launch should be delayed; the second, that the launch should go ahead. McNealy's actual choice was based on the relative importance that he assigned to these two criteria. In fact, Sun Microsystems went ahead with the September 10 launch, which suggests that McNealy thought the need to beat Apollo to market was the more important criterion.

Some of the worst managerial decisions can be traced to poor assessment of the alternatives, such as the decision to launch the *Challenger* space shuttle, mentioned earlier. In that case, the desire of NASA and Morton Thiokol managers to demonstrate to the public the success of the U.S. space program in order to ensure future funding (*economic feasibility*) conflicted with the need to ensure the safety of the astronauts (*ethicalness*). Managers deemed the economic criterion more important and decided to launch the space shuttle even though there were unanswered questions about safety. Tragically, some of the same decision-making problems that resulted in the *Challenger* tragedy led to the demise of the *Columbia* space shuttle 17 years later, killing all seven astronauts on board.[39] In both the *Challenger* and the *Columbia* disasters, safety questions were raised before the shuttles were launched; safety concerns took second place to budgets, economic feasibility, and schedules; top decision makers seemed to ignore or downplay the inputs of those with relevant technical expertise; and speaking up was discouraged.[40] Rather than making safety a top priority, decision makers seemed overly concerned with keeping on schedule and within budget.[41]

Choose among Alternatives

Once the set of alternative solutions has been carefully evaluated, the next task is to rank the various alternatives (using the criteria discussed in the previous section) and make a decision. When ranking alternatives, managers must be sure *all* the information available is brought to bear on the problem or issue at hand. As the Sun Microsystems case indicates, however, identifying all *relevant* information for a decision does not mean the manager has *complete* information; in most instances, information is incomplete.

Perhaps more serious than the existence of incomplete information is the often documented tendency of managers to ignore critical information, even when it is available. We discuss this tendency in detail later when we examine the operation of cognitive biases and groupthink.

Implement the Chosen Alternative

Once a decision has been made and an alternative has been selected, it must be implemented, and many subsequent and related decisions must be made. After a course of action has been decided—say, to develop a new line of women's clothing—thousands of subsequent decisions are necessary to implement it. These decisions would involve recruiting dress designers, obtaining fabrics, finding high-quality manufacturers, and signing contracts with clothing stores and websites to sell the new line.

Although the need to make subsequent decisions to implement the chosen course of action may seem obvious, many managers make a decision and then fail to act on it. This is the same as not making a decision at all. To ensure that a decision is implemented, top managers must assign to middle managers the responsibility for making the follow-up decisions necessary to achieve the goal. They must give middle managers sufficient resources to achieve the goal, and they must hold the middle managers accountable for their performance. If the middle managers succeed in implementing the decision, they should be rewarded; if they fail, they should be subject to sanctions.

Learn from Feedback

The final step in the decision-making process is learning from feedback. Effective managers always conduct a retrospective analysis to see what they can learn from past successes or failures. Managers who do not evaluate the results of their decisions do not learn from experience; instead they stagnate and are likely to make the same mistakes again and again.[42] To avoid this problem, managers must establish a formal procedure with which they can learn from the results of past decisions. The procedure should include these steps:

1. Compare what actually happened to what was expected to happen as a result of the decision.
2. Explore why any expectations for the decision were not met.
3. Derive guidelines that will help in future decision making.

Managers who always strive to learn from past mistakes and successes are likely to continuously improve the decisions they make. A significant amount of learning can take place when the outcomes of decisions are evaluated, and this assessment can produce enormous benefits.

Group Decision Making

Many (or perhaps most) important organizational decisions are made by groups or teams of managers rather than by individuals. Group decision making is superior to individual decision making in several respects. When managers work as a team to make decisions and solve problems, they are able to draw on the combined skills, competencies, and accumulated knowledge of group members and thereby improve their ability to generate feasible alternatives and make good decisions. Group decision making also allows managers to process more information and to correct one another's errors. And in the implementation phase, all managers affected by the decisions agree to cooperate. When a group of managers makes a decision (as opposed to one top manager making a decision and imposing it on subordinate managers), the probability that the decision will be implemented successfully increases.

LO 5-3
Identify the advantages and disadvantages of group decision making, and describe techniques that can improve it.

Some potential disadvantages are associated with group decision making. Groups often take much longer than individuals to make decisions. Getting two or more managers to agree to the same solution can be difficult because managers' interests and preferences are often different. In addition, just like decision making by individual managers, group decision making can be undermined by biases. A major source of group bias is *groupthink.*

The Perils of Groupthink

groupthink A pattern of faulty and biased decision making that occurs in groups whose members strive for agreement among themselves at the expense of accurately assessing information relevant to a decision.

Groupthink is a pattern of faulty and biased decision making that occurs in groups whose members strive for agreement among themselves at the expense of accurately assessing information relevant to a decision.[43] When managers are subject to groupthink, they collectively embark on a course of action without developing appropriate criteria to evaluate alternatives. Typically, a group rallies around one central manager, such as the CEO, and the course of action that manager supports. Group members become blindly committed to that course of action without evaluating its merits. Commitment is often based on an emotional, rather than an objective, assessment of the optimal course of action.

The decision President Kennedy and his advisers made to launch the unfortunate Bay of Pigs invasion in Cuba in 1962, the decisions made by President Johnson and his advisers from 1964 to 1967 to escalate the war in Vietnam, the decision made by President Nixon and his advisers in 1972 to cover up the Watergate break-in, and the decision made by NASA and Morton Thiokol in 1986 to launch the ill-fated *Challenger* shuttle—all were likely influenced by groupthink. After the fact, decision makers such as these who may fall victim to groupthink are often surprised that their decision-making process and outcomes were so flawed.

When groupthink occurs, pressures for agreement and harmony within a group have the unintended effect of discouraging individuals from raising issues that run counter to majority opinion. For example, when managers at NASA and Morton Thiokol fell victim to groupthink, they convinced each other that all was well and that there was no need to delay the launch of the *Challenger* space shuttle.

Devil's Advocacy

The existence of groupthink raises questions of how to improve the quality of group and individual decision making so managers make decisions that are realistic and are based on thorough evaluation of alternatives. One technique known to counteract groupthink is devil's advocacy.[44]

devil's advocacy
Critical analysis of a preferred alternative, made in response to challenges raised by a group member who, playing the role of devil's advocate, defends unpopular or opposing alternatives for the sake of argument.

Devil's advocacy is a critical analysis of a preferred alternative to ascertain its strengths and weaknesses before it is implemented.[45] Typically, one member of the decision-making group plays the role of devil's advocate. The devil's advocate critiques and challenges the way the group evaluated alternatives and chose one over the others. The purpose of devil's advocacy is to identify all the reasons that might make the preferred alternative unacceptable. In this way, decision makers can be made aware of the possible perils of recommended courses of action.

Diversity among Decision Makers

Another way to improve group decision making is to promote diversity in decision-making groups (see Chapter 3).[46] Bringing together managers of both genders from various ethnic, national, and functional backgrounds broadens the range of life experiences and opinions that group members can draw on as they generate, assess, and choose among alternatives. Moreover, diverse groups are sometimes less prone to groupthink because group members already differ from each other and thus are less subject to pressures for uniformity.

Organizational Learning and Creativity

LO 5-4
Explain the role that organizational learning and creativity play in helping managers improve their decisions.

organizational learning
The process through which managers seek to improve employees' desire and ability to understand and manage the organization and its task environment.

learning organization
An organization in which managers try to maximize the ability of individuals and groups to think and behave creatively and thus maximize the potential for organizational learning to take place.

The quality of managerial decision making ultimately depends on innovative responses to opportunities and threats. How can managers increase their ability to make nonprogrammed decisions that will allow them to adapt to, modify, and even drastically alter their task environments so they can continually increase organizational performance? The answer is by encouraging organizational learning.[47]

Organizational learning is the process through which managers seek to improve employees' desire and ability to understand and manage the organization and its task environment so employees can make decisions that continuously increase organizational effectiveness.[48] A learning organization is one in which managers do everything possible to maximize the ability of individuals and groups to think and behave creatively and thus maximize the potential for organizational learning to take place. At the heart of organizational learning is creativity, which is the ability of a decision maker to discover original and novel ideas that lead to feasible alternative courses of action. Encouraging creativity among managers is such a pressing organizational concern that many organizations hire outside experts to help them develop programs to train their managers in the art of creative thinking and problem solving.

Creating a Learning Organization

How can managers foster a learning organization? Learning theorist Peter Senge identified five principles for creating a learning organization (see Figure 5.6).[49]

1. For organizational learning to occur, top managers must allow every person in the organization to develop a sense of personal mastery, which is the process by which an individual develops the desire for personal learning that will continue throughout the person's life. Managers must understand this process and empower each employee to experiment, create, and explore his or her own ideas of personal learning, which can have a positive impact on the overall organization.[50]

Figure 5.6

Senge's Principles for Creating a Learning Organization

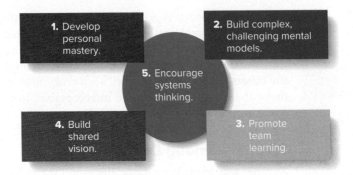

1. Develop personal mastery.

2. Build complex, challenging mental models.

5. Encourage systems thinking.

4. Build shared vision.

3. Promote team learning.

creativity A decision maker's ability to discover original and novel ideas that lead to feasible alternative courses of action.

personal mastery Process by which individuals develop a desire for personal learning that may continue indefinitely in the person's daily life, including work activities.

Get off email and lose the desk! Giving yourself and your employees the time and space to know that contributions off the beaten track are valued increases the ability to think outside the box.

D. Hurst/Alamy Stock Photo

2. As part of attaining personal mastery, individuals should think about some of the assumptions they have about how the world works and develop ideas about these so-called *mental models.* Often, however, individuals are unaware of the mental models or assumptions they hold and must look within to understand how they see the world. Once individuals gain perspective on how they view the world, they can use this information to expand their way of thinking not only on a personal level but also at work. Developing complex mental models—sophisticated ways of thinking that challenge them to find new or better ways of performing a task—can assist individuals and managers in expanding the way an organization thinks about how they perform work. To expand thinking in this way requires experimenting, taking risks, and thinking outside the lines, which can help reshape how an organization performs—at all levels.[51]

3. Managers must do everything they can to promote creativity within groups. Team members must be encouraged to learn together through exchanging ideas, listening to one another, and working together to solve problems. Ongoing dialog among group members is very important. Senge thought that *team learning* is more important than individual learning as a way to increase organizational learning. He pointed out that most important decisions are made within organization subunits such as groups, functions, and divisions.

4. Managers must emphasize the importance of building a shared vision—meaning that employees share their ideas for the future of the organization. Once this shared vision is identified, members of the organization can frame problems and opportunities with the shared vision in mind and work together to achieve common goals that correspond to the vision.

5. Managers must encourage *systems thinking.* This concept is a way of seeing the whole picture. It is a framework for seeing interrelationships and patterns rather than static "snapshots" within an organization. Systems thinking can be thought of as a "conceptual cornerstone" that pulls together the other four principles for creating a learning organization.[52]

Building a learning organization requires that managers change their management assumptions radically. Developing a learning organization is neither a quick nor an easy process. Senge worked with Ford Motor Company to help managers make Ford a learning organization. Why would Ford want this? Top management believed that to compete successfully Ford must improve its members' ability to be creative and make the right decisions.

Increasingly, managers are being called on to promote global organizational learning. The "Managing Globally" feature provides one example of such an effort. Likewise, managers at Walmart have used the lessons derived from its failures and successes in one country to promote global organizational learning across the many countries in which it now operates. When Walmart entered Malaysia, it was convinced customers there would respond to its one-stop shopping format. It found, however, that Malaysians enjoy the social experience of shopping in a lively market or bazaar and thus did not like the impersonal efficiency of the typical Walmart store. As a result, Walmart learned the importance of designing store layouts to appeal specifically to the customers of each country in which it operates. Clearly, global organizational learning is essential for companies such as Walmart that have significant business operations in multiple countries.

Managing Globally

Constant Learning Keeps Western Union Relevant

Western Union (WU) offers a financial lifeline worldwide, sending 130 currencies to recipients in 200-plus countries.[53] When a customer pays, a code is sent to the recipient, who presents it to an agent, who hands over cash minus a processing fee. WU later reimburses the agent. Currency transfers could include support from emigrants to family members back home, help to a stranded traveler overseas, or tuition payments for a student studying abroad.

WU outlasted competitors by learning to embrace industry transformations.[54] The company started as a telegraph operator, transmitting information to newspapers, banks, brokerages, and even betting parlors. After stumbling by turning down a chance to buy the patent for the telephone, WU learned it must commit to technological advances. It kept communication services up to date with teleprinters, faxes, and satellites until anyone could deliver messages from home or work. By then, however, the company had built its money transfer business. Profits accelerated along with immigration into the United States.

WU's CEO is Hikmet Ersek, son of a Turkish father and Austrian mother, who was raised in Istanbul, studied economics in Vienna, and worked in Europe.[55] Hired by WU to run its southeastern European operations, Ersek noticed rising international migration there as in the United States, and he expanded operations. Ersek maintains that a multicultural mind-set is a competitive strength. Every international transaction requires knowledge of customer needs and legal requirements in the sending and receiving countries. Learning these facts is easier with local experience and open-mindedness. Thus, when WU launched a project to create a mobile app, Ersek chose a leader with a multicultural-customer focus: the head of WU's Africa business.

Western Union's culture of continuous learning has helped the company and its employees outlast competitors in the global marketplace. Alexander Podshivalov/123RF

The next front for learning will be technological. Digital and mobile devices enable easy, low-cost methods of money transfer for Western Union—and new competitors.[56] WU's size is an advantage, because millions of daily digital transactions provide valuable data. WU monitors patterns in money flows to quickly identify changing needs. In mid-2014, managers saw a spike in money transfers from North America and northern Europe to the Mediterranean region. Soon the Greek government was calling, asking for locations of WU's facilities. Such data showed WU knew before others about the flood of refugees into Europe. Monitoring patterns of increased traffic, managers opened additional facilities accordingly.

As Western Union continues to navigate global trends, it has adopted WU Way, a program in which everyone learns to provide better service more efficiently.[57] Top leaders assigned to champion the change meet with managers for informal learning. As employees make processes more efficient and as more consumers use WU's app to make transfers themselves, the company can maintain its strength with competitive fees. ●

Promoting Individual Creativity

Research suggests that when certain conditions are met, managers are more likely to be creative. People must be given the opportunity and freedom to generate new ideas.[58] Creativity declines when managers look over the shoulders of talented employees and try to "hurry up" a creative solution. How would you feel if your boss said you had one week to come up with a new product idea to beat the competition? Creativity results when employees have an opportunity to experiment, to take risks, and to make mistakes and learn from them. And employees must not fear that they will be looked down on or penalized for ideas that might at first seem outlandish; sometimes those ideas yield truly innovative products and services.[59] Highly innovative companies such as Amazon, Netflix, and Facebook are well known for the wide degree of freedom they give their managers and employees to experiment and develop innovative goods and services.[60]

Once managers have generated alternatives, creativity can be fostered by giving them constructive feedback so they know how well they are doing. Ideas that seem to be going nowhere can be eliminated and creative energies refocused in other directions. Ideas that seem promising can be promoted, and help from other managers can be obtained.[61]

Top managers must stress the importance of looking for alternative solutions and should visibly reward employees who come up with creative ideas. Being creative can be demanding and stressful. Employees who believe they are working on important, vital issues are motivated to put forth the high levels of effort that creativity demands. Creative people like to receive the acclaim of others, and innovative organizations have many kinds of ceremonies and rewards to recognize creative employees.

Employees on the front line are often in a good position to come up with creative ideas for improvements but may be reluctant to speak up or share their ideas. To encourage frontline employees to come up with creative ideas and share them, some managers have used contests and rewards.[62] Contests and rewards signal the importance of coming up with creative ideas and encourage employees to share them.

Promoting Group Creativity

Brainstorming is one example of a group problem-solving technique that helps promote creative ideas and innovative solutions within an organization Jacob Lund/Shutterstock

To encourage creativity at the group level, organizations can use group problem-solving techniques that promote creative ideas and innovative solutions. These techniques can also prevent groupthink and help managers uncover biases. Here we look at three group decision-making techniques: *brainstorming,* the *nominal group technique,* and the *Delphi technique.*

BRAINSTORMING *Brainstorming* is a group problem-solving technique in which managers meet face-to-face to generate and debate a wide variety of alternatives from which to make a decision.[63] Generally, from 5 to 15 managers meet in a closed-door session and proceed like this:

- One manager describes in broad outline the problem the group is to address.

- Group members share their ideas and generate alternative courses of action.

- As each alternative is described, group members are not allowed to criticize it; everyone withholds judgment until all alternatives have been heard. One member of the group records the alternatives on a flip chart.

- Group members are encouraged to be as innovative and radical as possible. Anything goes; and the greater the number of ideas put forth, the better. Moreover, group members are encouraged to "piggyback," or build on, each other's suggestions.

- When all alternatives have been generated, group members debate the pros and cons of each and develop a short list of the best alternatives.

production blocking A loss of productivity in brainstorming sessions due to the unstructured nature of brainstorming.

Brainstorming is useful in some problem-solving situations—for example, when managers are trying to find a name for a new perfume or car model. But sometimes individuals working alone can generate more alternatives. The main reason for the loss of productivity in brainstorming appears to be production blocking, which occurs because group members cannot always simultaneously make sense of all the alternatives being generated, think up additional alternatives, and remember what they were thinking.[64]

nominal group technique A decision-making technique in which group members write down ideas and solutions, read their suggestions to the whole group, and discuss and then rank the alternatives.

NOMINAL GROUP TECHNIQUE To avoid production blocking, the nominal group technique is often used. It provides a more structured way of generating alternatives in writing and gives each manager more time and opportunity to come up with potential solutions. The nominal group technique is especially useful when an issue is controversial and when different managers might be expected to champion different courses of action. Generally, a small group of managers meets in a closed-door session and adopts the following procedures:

- One manager outlines the problem to be addressed, and 30 or 40 minutes are allocated for group members, working individually, to write down their ideas and solutions. Group members are encouraged to be innovative.

- Managers take turns reading their suggestions to the group. One manager writes all the alternatives on a flip chart. No criticism or evaluation of alternatives is allowed until all alternatives have been read.

- The alternatives are then discussed, one by one, in the sequence in which they were proposed. Group members can ask for clarifying information and critique each alternative to identify its pros and cons.

- When all alternatives have been discussed, each group member ranks all the alternatives from most preferred to least preferred, and the alternative that receives the highest ranking is chosen.[65]

DELPHI TECHNIQUE Both the nominal group technique and brainstorming require that managers meet to generate creative ideas and engage in joint problem solving. What happens if managers are in different cities or in different parts of the world and cannot meet face to face? Videoconferencing is one way to bring distant managers together to brainstorm. Another way is to use the Delphi technique, which is a written approach to creative problem solving.[66] The Delphi technique works like this:

Delphi technique
A decision-making technique in which group members do not meet face-to-face but respond in writing to questions posed by the group leader.

- The group leader writes a statement of the problem and a series of questions to which participating managers are to respond.

- The questionnaire is sent to the managers and departmental experts who are most knowledgeable about the problem. They are asked to generate solutions and mail the questionnaire back to the group leader.

- A team of top managers records and summarizes the responses. The results are then sent back to the participants, with additional questions to be answered before a decision can be made.

- The process is repeated until a consensus is reached and the most suitable course of action is apparent.

Promoting Intrapreneurship and Learning

The intensity of competition today, particularly from agile, small companies, has made it increasingly important for large, established organizations to promote and encourage intrapreneurship to raise their level of innovation and organizational learning. As we discussed in Chapter 1, intrapreneurs are people who work inside an organization and have the ability to seize on opportunities to develop new or improved products and services that can provide competitive advantages to their companies. A successful learning organization encourages all employees to identify opportunities and solve problems, thus enabling the organization to continuously experiment, improve, and increase its ability to provide customers with new and improved goods and services. The higher the level of intrapreneurship, the higher will be the level of learning and innovation. How can organizations promote organizational learning and intrapreneurship?

PRODUCT CHAMPIONS One way to promote intrapreneurship is to encourage individuals to assume the role of product champion, a manager who takes "ownership" of a project and provides the leadership and vision that take a product from the idea stage to the final customer. 3M, a company well known for its attempts to promote intrapreneurship, encourages all its managers to become product champions and identify new product ideas. A product champion becomes responsible for developing a business plan for the product. Armed with this business plan, the champion appears before 3M's product development committee, a team of senior 3M managers who probe the strengths and weaknesses of the plan to decide whether it should be funded. If the plan is accepted, the product champion assumes responsibility for product development.

product champion
A manager who takes "ownership" of a project and provides the leadership and vision that take a product from the idea stage to the final customer.

SKUNKWORKS The idea behind the product champion role is that employees who feel ownership for a project are inclined to act as outside entrepreneurs and go to great lengths to make the project succeed. Using skunkworks and new venture divisions can also strengthen this feeling of ownership. A skunkworks is a group of intrapreneurs who are deliberately separated from the normal operation of an organization—for example, from the normal chain of command—to encourage them to devote all their attention to developing new products. The idea is that if these people are isolated, they will become so intensely involved in a project that development time will be relatively brief and the quality of the final product will be enhanced. The term *skunkworks* was coined at the Lockheed Corporation, which formed a team of design engineers to develop special aircraft such as the U2 spy plane. The secrecy with which this unit functioned and speculation about its goals led others to refer to it as "the skunkworks."

skunkworks
A group of intrapreneurs who are deliberately separated from the normal operation of an organization to encourage them to devote all their attention to developing new products.

REWARDS FOR INNOVATION To encourage managers to bear the uncertainty and risk associated with the hard work of intrapreneurship, it is necessary to link performance to rewards. Increasingly companies are rewarding intrapreneurs on the basis of the outcome of the product development process. Intrapreneurs are paid large bonuses if their projects succeed, or they are granted stock options that can make them millionaires if their products sell well. Both Microsoft and Google, for example, have made hundreds of their employees multimillionaires as a result of the stock options they were granted as part of their reward packages. In addition to receiving money, successful intrapreneurs can expect to receive promotion to the ranks of top management. Most of 3M's top managers, for example, reached the executive suite because they had a track record of successful intrapreneurship. Organizations must reward intrapreneurs equitably if they wish to prevent them from leaving and becoming outside entrepreneurs who might form a competitive new venture. Nevertheless, intrapreneurs frequently do so.

Summary and Review

THE NATURE OF MANAGERIAL DECISION MAKING Programmed decisions are routine decisions made so often that managers have developed decision rules to be followed automatically. Nonprogrammed decisions are made in response to situations that are unusual or novel; they are nonroutine decisions. The classical model of decision making assumes that decision makers have complete information; are able to process that information in an objective, rational manner; and make optimum decisions. March and Simon argued that managers exhibit bounded rationality, rarely have access to all the information they need to make optimum decisions, and consequently satisfice and rely on their intuition and judgment when making decisions. [LO 5-1]

STEPS IN THE DECISION-MAKING PROCESS When making decisions, managers should take these six steps: recognize the need for a decision, generate alternatives, assess alternatives, choose among alternatives, implement the chosen alternative, and learn from feedback. [LO 5-2]

GROUP DECISION MAKING Many advantages are associated with group decision making, but there are also several disadvantages. One major source of poor decision making is groupthink. Afflicted decision makers collectively embark on a dubious course of action without questioning the assumptions that underlie their decision. Managers can improve the quality of group decision making by using techniques such as devil's advocacy and dialectical inquiry and by increasing diversity in the decision-making group. [LO 5-3]

ORGANIZATIONAL LEARNING AND CREATIVITY Organizational learning is the process through which managers seek to improve employees' desire and ability to understand and manage the organization and its task environment so employees can make decisions that continuously raise organizational effectiveness. Managers must take steps to promote organizational learning and creativity at the individual and group levels to improve the quality of decision making. In addition, organizations need to encourage intrapreneurship because it leads to organizational learning and innovation. [LO 5-4]

Management *in Action*

Topics for Discussion and Action

Discussion

1. What are the main differences between programmed decision making and nonprogrammed decision making? [LO 5-1]

2. In what ways do the classical and administrative models of decision making help managers appreciate the complexities of real-world decision making? [LO 5-1]

3. Why do capable managers sometimes make bad decisions? What can individual managers do to improve their decision-making skills? [LO 5-1, 5-2]

4. In what kinds of groups is groupthink most likely to be a problem? When is it least likely to be a problem? What steps can group members take to ward off groupthink? [LO 5-3]

5. What is organizational learning, and how can managers promote it? [LO 5-4]

Action

6. Ask a manager to recall the best and the worst decisions he or she ever made. Try to determine why these decisions were so good or so bad. [LO 5-1, 5-2, 5-3]

7. Think about an organization in your local community or your university, or an organization that you are familiar with, that is doing poorly. Now think of questions managers in the organization should ask stakeholders to elicit creative ideas for turning around the organization's fortunes. [LO 5-4]

Building Management Skills

How Do You Make Decisions? [LO 5-1, 5-2, 5-4]

Pick a decision you made recently that has had important consequences for you. It may be your decision about which college to attend, which major to select, whether to take a part-time job, or which part-time job to take. Using the material in this chapter, analyze how you made the decision:

1. Identify the criteria you used, either consciously or unconsciously, to guide your decision making.

2. List the alternatives you considered. Were they all possible alternatives? Did you unconsciously (or consciously) ignore some important alternatives?

3. How much information did you have about each alternative? Were you making the decision on the basis of complete or incomplete information?

4. Try to remember how you reached the decision. Did you sit down and consciously think through the implications of each alternative, or did you make the decision on the basis of intuition? Did you use any rules of thumb to help you make the decision?

5. Having answered the previous questions, do you think in retrospect that you made a reasonable decision? What, if anything, might you do to improve your ability to make good decisions in the future?

Managing Ethically [LO 5-3]

Sometimes groups make extreme decisions—decisions that are either more risky or more conservative than they would have been if individuals acting alone had made them. One explanation for the tendency of groups to make extreme decisions is diffusion of responsibility. In a group, responsibility for the outcomes of a decision is spread among group members, so each person feels less than fully accountable. The group's decision is extreme because no individual has taken full responsibility for it.

Questions

1. Either alone or in a group, think about the ethical implications of extreme decision making by groups.

2. When group decision making takes place, should each member of a group feel fully accountable for the outcomes of the decision? Why or why not?

Small Group Breakout Exercise [LO 5-3, 5-4]

Brainstorming

Form groups of three or four people, and appoint one member as the spokesperson who will communicate your findings to the class when called on by the instructor. Then discuss the following scenario:

You and your partners are trying to decide which kind of restaurant to open in a centrally located shopping center that has just been built in your city. The problem confronting you is that the city already has many restaurants that provide different kinds of food at all price ranges. You have the resources to open any type of restaurant. Your challenge is to decide which type is most likely to succeed.

Use brainstorming to decide which type of restaurant to open. Follow these steps:

1. As a group, spend 5–10 minutes generating ideas about the alternative restaurants that the members think will be most likely to succeed. Each group member should be as innovative and creative as possible, and no suggestions should be criticized.

2. Appoint one group member to write down the alternatives as they are identified.

3. Spend the next 10–15 minutes debating the pros and cons of the alternatives. As a group, try to reach a consensus on which alternative is most likely to succeed.

After making your decision, discuss the pros and cons of the brainstorming method, and decide whether any production blocking occurred.

When called on by the instructor, the spokesperson should be prepared to share your group's decision with the class, as well as the reasons for the group's decision.

Be the Manager [LO 5-1, 5-2, 5-3, 5-4]

You are a top manager who was recently hired by an oil field services company in Oklahoma to help it respond more quickly and proactively to potential opportunities in its market. You report to the chief operating officer (COO), who reports to the CEO, and you have been on the job for eight months. Thus far, you have come up with three initiatives you carefully studied, thought were noteworthy, and proposed and justified to the COO. The COO seemed cautiously interested when you presented the proposals, and each time he indicated he would think about them and discuss them with the CEO because considerable resources were involved. Each time you never heard back from the COO, and after a few weeks elapsed, you casually asked the COO if there was any news on the proposal in question. For the first proposal, the COO said, "We think it's a good idea, but the timing is off. Let's shelve it for the time being and reconsider it next year." For the second proposal, the COO said, "Mike [the CEO] reminded me that we tried that two years ago and it wasn't well received in the market. I am surprised I didn't remember it myself when you first described the proposal, but it came right back to me once Mike mentioned it." For the third proposal, the COO simply said, "We're not convinced it will work."

You believe your three proposed initiatives are viable ways to seize opportunities in the marketplace, yet you cannot proceed with any of them. Moreover, for each proposal, you invested considerable time and even worked to bring others on board to support the proposal, only to have it shot down by the CEO. When you interviewed for the position, both the COO and the CEO claimed they wanted "an outsider to help them step out of the box and innovate." However, your experience to date has been just the opposite. What are you going to do?

Case in the News [LO 5-1, 5-2, 5-4]

Marine Makers Are Building an Agile Future for Military Logistics

The Internet revolution has transformed war as well as business. Soldiers often fight insurgents, rather than national armed forces with all their systems and weaponry. The enemy seeks its advantage from being agile and making do with what information and materials it can get its hands on. An insurgent needing to repair guns or vehicles or even build drones might literally place an order for parts from an online retailer and have them shipped by express delivery. Insurgents can build drones and fly a swarm into an airbase to damage expensive aircraft. U.S. troops on the ground can expect that the next landmine they encounter will look nothing like the last one; they have to expect that innovation is taking place all around them, carried out by desperate freedom fighters.

The U.S. Marine Corps has been seeking greater agility in an environment of constant change. Its Next Generation Logistics (NexLog) group, charged with applying technology to logistics, embraced the so-called maker movement, in which individuals apply the power of computer-aided technologies to create and build devices whose manufacture once required a fully equipped factory. Technologies central to the maker movement include computer-aided design (CAD), 3D printing, microcontrollers, and laser cutting. A person equipped with a laptop can quickly make precision parts to build robots, drones, and other devices. Examples include 3D-printing replacement tools, truck parts, and gun sights, as well as quickly making plastic "rocks" or other camouflage for hiding sensors. Laser-cut pieces can fit together so well that no glue is needed to secure them.

NexLog set up a program called Marine Maker to prepare soldiers to use these skills and technologies on the battlefield. Essentially, it is creating hackers, in the sense of people who craft solutions from whatever is at hand. Those selected to participate in the Marine Maker training, or Innovation Boot Camp, are chosen for their technical ability—for example, excellence in jobs such as electronics technicians, radio repair technicians, and vehicle mechanics. Infantry and other front-line fighters also may be selected if they show aptitude. Only a few enter the program with high-tech and engineering backgrounds.

The goal is to teach them enough about the basics of soldering, 3D printing, circuit board assembly, and the use of sensors and other electronics that they can solve problems fast and with limited resources. In one exercise, trainees get a supply of wood and basic electronics to build a fighting robot; in another, they have to construct a small human-powered "canoe" out of a collection of metal parts. Innovation Boot Camp ends with an exercise in which trainees prepare for a simulated attack by crafting their own surveillance devices and a simulated counterattack, all within hours. All the challenges proceed on a tight schedule, to prepare trainees to innovate under time pressure.

Innovations crafted by program participants can make a significant difference on the battlefield. In just the first day of their Innovation Boot Camp, Marines in Kuwait figured out how to build a solar-powered surveillance system, which they installed at ammunition supply points. Another group 3D-printed a metal rotor for a tank motor, and it survived hours of testing. This kind of solution could keep a valuable piece of machinery operating until the next delivery of supplies arrives.

The key advantage of this approach is that it spurs creative thinking. People with advanced training in a particular technology are more likely to think only in terms of what they already know. In contrast, the Marines who complete Marine Maker training have practiced how to come up with ideas to try quickly, under pressure. They don't assume the usual methods are necessary, and they aren't afraid to fail. The Marine Corps is known for a culture of resourcefulness and adaptability—achieving missions in any way possible; thus, being creative under stress is already part of the organization's values.

In NexLog rollout of Marine Maker training, hundreds of Marines have completed Innovation Boot Camp at maker labs in California, North Carolina, Virginia, and Washington, DC, as well as on the ground in Kuwait. Trainers are looking at expanding into programs focused on specific kinds of capabilities, such as anti-drone warfare and explosive ordnance disposal. One NexLog leader envisions a future in which agile-thinking Marines can develop customized drones on demand for a given mission—say, in a city or in cold weather—and deploy them as needed. NexLog's mission is to prepare for the logistics needs of the next decade. Marine Maker is already helping to create that future.

Questions for Discussion

1. Which type of decision making are Marines being taught in the Marine Maker training: programmed or nonprogrammed decisions? Explain.

2. Does the classical model or the administrative model of decision making better fit the decision process of the Marine Maker program? Why?

3. Which of the chapter's ideas for creating a learning organization and promoting individual creativity support creative thinking by the Marines?

Sources: Captain A. Morrow, "The Corps Challenges Marines to Make Their Future," www.secnav.navy.mil, accessed January 3, 2019; Josh Dean, "An Army of MacGyvers," *Bloomberg Businessweek,* September 24, 2018, 50–55; "Marine Maker, Innovation Labs," 1st Marine Logistics Group, www.1stmlg.marines.mil, March 19, 2018; Randy Rieland, "Giving Marines the Tools to Build Drones on the Battlefield," *Smithsonian,* www.smithsonianmag.com, May 19, 2017.

Endnotes

1. A. Regalado, "23andMe," *MIT Technology Review,* July–August 2016, 68–69; J. Bercovici, "The DNA Whisperer," *Inc.,* October 2015, 62–64, 148.

2. A. Bluestein, "After a Comeback, 23andMe Faces Its Next Test," *Fast Company,* www.fastcompany.com, August 9, 2017.

3. Bluestein, "After a Comeback"; Regalado, "23andMe."

4. C. Clifford, "How Anne and Susan Wojcicki's Parents Raised the Founder of 23andMe and the CEO of YouTube," *CNBC,* www.cnbc.com, accessed January 3, 2019.

5. Bluestein, "After a Comeback"; Bercovici, "The DNA Whisperer."

6. Bercovici, "The DNA Whisperer"; K. Ryssdal and R. Garrova, "Why 23andMe Wants Your Genetic Data" (interview with Anne Wojcicki), *Marketplace,* www.marketplace.org, April 19, 2017.

7. Ryssdal and Garrova, "Why 23andMe Wants Your Genetic Data."

8. G. P. Huber, *Managerial Decision Making* (Glenview, IL: Scott, Foresman, 1993).

9. "Martin Cooper: American Engineer," *Encyclopaedia Britannica,* www.britannica.com, accessed January 3, 2019; G. Blazeski, "Martin Cooper Invented the Mobile Phone in 1973; Was Inspired by Star Trek," *The Vintage News,* www.thevintagenews.com, accessed January 3, 2019.

10. H. A. Simon, *The New Science of Management* (Englewood Cliffs, NJ: Prentice-Hall, 1977).

11. D. Kahneman, "Maps of Bounded Rationality: A Perspective on Intuitive Judgment and Choice," *Prize Lecture,* December 8, 2002; E. Jaffe, "What Was I Thinking? Kahneman Explains How Intuition Leads Us Astray," *American Psychological Society* 17, no. 5 (May 2004), 23–26; E. Dane and M. Pratt, "Exploring Intuition and Its Role in Managerial Decision Making," *Academy of Management Review* 32 (2007), 33–54.

12. One should be careful not to generalize too much here, however, for as Peter Senge has shown, programmed decisions rely on the implicit assumption that the environment is in a steady state. If environmental conditions change, sticking to a routine decision rule can produce disastrous results. See P. Senge, *The Fifth Discipline: The Art and Practice of the Learning Organization* (New York: Doubleday, 1990).

13. Kahneman, "Maps of Bounded Rationality"; Jaffe, "What Was I Thinking?"

14. A. Larocca, "The Magic Skin of Glossier's Emily Weiss," *New York,* www.thecut.com, January 9, 2018; A. Giacobbe, "The People's Gloss," *Entrepreneur,* September 2017, 36–42.

15. Larocca, "The Magic Skin of Glossier's Emily Weiss"; E. Canal, "How This Beauty Blogger Created a Cult Brand (and Raised $34 Million)," *Inc.,* www.inc.com, December 5, 2017.

16. Giacobbe, "The People's Gloss"; Larocca, "The Magic Skin of Glossier's Emily Weiss"; L. Fessler, "Glossier CEO Emily Weiss Doesn't Have Time for Excuses: 'Just Do Your Job,'" *Quartz,* https://work.qz.com, February 6, 2018.

17. P. N. Danziger, "5 Reasons That Glossier Is So Successful," *Forbes,* www.forbes.com, accessed January 3, 2019.

18. J. Wolf and K. Bhasin, "Inside Glossier's Plans to Shake Up Your Makeup Routine," *Bloomberg,* www.bloomberg.com, August 30, 2018.

19. H. A. Simon, *Administrative Behavior* (New York: Macmillan, 1947), 79.

20. H. A. Simon, *Models of Man* (New York: Wiley, 1957).

21. K. J. Arrow, *Aspects of the Theory of Risk Bearing* (Helsinki: Yrjo Johnssonis Saatio, 1965).

22. T. Huddleston Jr., "Remember These Failed Apple Products? They Were Some of the Tech Giant's Biggest Flops," *CNBC,* www.cnbc.com, September 1, 2018; Arrow, *Aspects of the Theory of Risk Bearing.*

23. R. L. Daft and R. H. Lengel, "Organizational Information Requirements, Media Richness and Structural Design," *Management Science* 32 (1986), 554–71.

24. R. Cyert and J. March, *Behavioral Theory of the Firm* (Englewood Cliffs, NJ: Prentice-Hall, 1963).

25. J. G. March and H. A. Simon, *Organizations* (New York: Wiley, 1958).

26. H. A. Simon, "Making Management Decisions: The Role of Intuition and Emotion," *Academy of Management Executive* 1 (1987), 57–64.

27. M. H. Bazerman, *Judgment in Managerial Decision Making* (New York: Wiley, 1986). Also see Simon, *Administrative Behavior.*

28. "Scott G. McNealy Profile," Forbes.com, http://people.forbes.com/profile/scott-g-mcnealy/75347, February 16, 2010; Sun Oracle, "Overview and Frequently Asked Questions," www.oracle.com, February 16, 2010.

29. "Sun Microsystems—Investor Relations: Officers and Directors," www.sun.com/aboutsun/investor/sun_facts/officers_directors.html, June 1, 2004; "How Sun Delivers Value to Customers," *Sun Microsystems—Investor Relations: Support & Training,* www.sun.com/aboutsun/investor/sun_facts/core_strategies.html, June 1, 2004; "Sun at a Glance," *Sun Microsystems—Investor Relations: Sun Facts,* www.sun.com/aboutsun/investor/sun_facts/index.html, June 1, 2004; "Plug In the System, and Everything Just Works," *Sun Microsystems—Investor Relations: Product Portfolio,* www.sun.com/aboutsun/investor/sun_facts/portfolio/html, June 1, 2004.

30. N. J. Langowitz and S. C. Wheelright, "Sun Microsystems, Inc. (A)," Harvard Business School Case, 686–133.

31. R. D. Hof, "How to Kick the Mainframe Habit," *BusinessWeek,* June 26, 1995, 102–4.

32. Bazerman, *Judgment in Managerial Decision Making;* Huber, *Managerial*

Decision Making; J. E. Russo and P. J. Schoemaker, *Decision Traps* (New York: Simon & Schuster, 1989).

33. M. D. Cohen, J. G. March, and J. P. Olsen, "A Garbage Can Model of Organizational Choice," *Administrative Science Quarterly* 17 (1972), 1–25.

34. Bazerman, *Judgment in Managerial Decision Making.*

35. Senge, *The Fifth Discipline.*

36. E. de Bono, *Lateral Thinking* (London: Penguin, 1968); Senge, *The Fifth Discipline.*

37. Russo and Schoemaker, *Decision Traps.*

38. Bazerman, *Judgment in Managerial Decision Making.*

39. E. Howell, "Columbia Disaster: What Happened, What NASA Learned," www.space.com, November 14, 2017.

40. J. Glanz and J. Schwartz, "Dogged Engineer's Effort to Assess Shuttle Damage," *The New York Times,* September 26, 2003, A1.

41. M. L. Wald and J. Schwartz, "NASA Chief Promises a Shift in Attitude," *The New York Times,* August 28, 2003, A23.

42. Russo and Schoemaker, *Decision Traps.*

43. I. L. Janis, *Groupthink: Psychological Studies of Policy Decisions and Disasters,* 2nd ed. (Boston: Houghton Mifflin, 1982).

44. C. R. Schwenk, *The Essence of Strategic Decision Making* (Lexington, MA: Lexington Books, 1988).

45. See R. O. Mason, "A Dialectic Approach to Strategic Planning," *Management Science* 13 (1969), 403–14; R. A. Cosier and J. C. Aplin, "A Critical View of Dialectic Inquiry in Strategic Planning," *Strategic Management Journal* 1 (1980), 343–56; I. I. Mitroff and R. O. Mason, "Structuring III—Structured Policy Issues: Further Explorations in a Methodology for Messy Problems," *Strategic Management Journal* 1 (1980), 331–42.

46. M. C. Gentile, *Differences That Work: Organizational Excellence through Diversity* (Boston: Harvard Business School Press, 1994); F. Rice, "How to Make Diversity Pay," *Fortune,* August 8, 1994, 78–86.

47. B. Hedberg, "How Organizations Learn and Unlearn," in W. H. Starbuck and P. C. Nystrom, eds., *Handbook of Organizational Design,* vol. 1 (New York: Oxford University Press, 1981), 1–27.

48. Senge, *The Fifth Discipline.*

49. Ibid.

50. P. M. Senge, "The Leader's New Work: Building Learning Organizations," *Sloan Management Review,* Fall 1990, 7–23.

51. Ibid.

52. Senge, "The Leader's New Work," 12, 23.

53. "What We Do," https://corporate. westernunion.com, accessed January 4, 2019.

54. L. Davison and K. Rajgopal, "Working across Many Cultures at Western Union" (interview with Hikmet Ersek), *McKinsey Quarterly,* www.mckinsey.com, January 2018; D. Bennett and L. Etter, "Give Us Your Tired, Your Poor, Your Huddled Masses Yearning to Send Cash," *Bloomberg Businessweek,* https:// bloomberg.com, June 16, 2017.

55. Bennett and Etter, "Give Us Your Tired."

56. Ibid.

57. "Western Union Digital Expands in Asia: Mobile App Now Live in Singapore," http://ir.westernunion. com, December 18, 2018; P. Harris, "The Relentless Pursuit of Better," *TD,* October 2017, 28–30.

58. J. M. George, "Creativity in Organizations," in J. P. Walsh and A. P. Brief, eds., *The Academy of Management Annals,* vol. 1 (New York: Erlbaum, 2008), 439–77.

59. George, "Creativity in Organizations."

60. "The World's Most Innovative Companies 2018," *Forbes,* www .forbes.com, accessed January 3, 2019.

61. R. W. Woodman, J. E. Sawyer, and R. W. Griffin, "Towards a Theory of Organizational Creativity," *Academy of Management Review* 18 (1993), 293–321.

62. J. Haden, "25 Rewards That Great Employees Actually Love to Receive," *Inc.,* www.inc.com, accessed January 3, 2019.

63. T. J. Bouchard Jr., J. Barsaloux, and G. Drauden, "Brainstorming Procedure, Group Size, and Sex as Determinants of Problem Solving Effectiveness of Individuals and Groups," *Journal of Applied Psychology* 59 (1974), 135–38.

64. M. Diehl and W. Stroebe, "Productivity Loss in Brainstorming Groups: Towards the Solution of a Riddle," *Journal of Personality and Social Psychology* 53 (1987), 497–509.

65. D. H. Gustafson, R. K. Shulka, A. Delbecq, and W. G. Walster, "A Comparative Study of Differences in Subjective Likelihood Estimates Made by Individuals, Interacting Groups, Delphi Groups, and Nominal Groups," *Organizational Behavior and Human Performance* 9 (1973), 280–91.

66. N. Dalkey, *The Delphi Method: An Experimental Study of Group Decision Making* (Santa Monica, CA: Rand Corp., 1989).

6 Planning, Strategy, and Competitive Advantage

Learning Objectives

After studying this chapter, you should be able to:

LO 6-1 Identify the three main steps of the planning process, and explain the relationship between planning and strategy.

LO 6-2 Differentiate between the main types of business-level strategies, and explain how they give an organization a competitive advantage that may lead to superior performance.

LO 6-3 Differentiate between the main types of corporate-level strategies, and explain how they are used to strengthen a company's business-level strategy and competitive advantage.

LO 6-4 Describe the vital role managers play in implementing strategies to achieve an organization's mission and goals.

Management Snapshot

Sorenson Plans for Continued Growth at Marriott

What Do Successful Managers Consider When They Plan a Way Forward?

Marriott's CEO is a good example. Marriott International is the world's largest hotel chain, with 226,500 employees at over 6,700 properties and the company's headquarters in Bethesda, Maryland.[1] Its recent acquisition of Starwood Hotels & Resorts gave it a huge lead over its next-largest competitor, Hilton. That deal closed under the leadership of Arne Sorenson, the company's third CEO. Before joining Marriott, he was a lawyer handling cases related to mergers and acquisitions. Sorenson loves exploring the world; he grew up in Japan as the child of missionaries and continues to enjoy travels with his wife and children.

Sorenson intends for Marriott to accelerate its growth. His three-year plan is to add about 100,000 rooms per year, up from 76,000 added in 2017.[2] He is optimistic but grounds his plans in observations about the environment for the travel business. A key opportunity is growing demand for travel-related services; more than a billion people travel internationally, a number expected to grow 50% by 2030.[3] The major threat Sorenson identifies is online travel agencies (OTAs). Travelers, especially tourists, increasingly seek low-priced flights and hotel stays on websites like Expedia, Priceline, and Travelocity. Given their price-consciousness, OTAs pressure the hotels they represent to offer discounts. A second challenge is home-sharing businesses, especially Airbnb, which is offering new competition, especially at the low end of the price range. Finally, in the United States, businesses have recently reported a decline in tourism from overseas, despite the growth worldwide. On this last problem, competitors have a common interest, so industry organizations are trying to present a more favorable face of the United States to the world.[4]

In facing these challenges, Marriott benefits from its size and international presence.[5] Controlling a major share of the hotel rooms in the United States and a growing share abroad gives Marriott greater clout when negotiating with OTAs. The acquisition of Starwood brought Marriott Starwood's very successful customer-loyalty rewards program. Despite a recently reported hack of the Starwood reservation system that exposed personal data for more than 500 million guests, customers who belong to a rewards program are likelier to book directly with a hotel rather than through an OTA, which takes a share of the price as its fee.[6] Starwood also had more experience with distinctive hotel properties that draw customers looking for a fun experience. Marriott has a further advantage in its business model. Rather than focusing on building and owning hotel properties, it staffs and manages hotels that others own. This

According to Marriott CEO Arne Sorenson, the company's growth strategies include international expansion, particularly in China, as more and more Chinese consumers want to travel abroad. Bloomberg/Getty Images

has allowed Marriott to focus on delivering a great experience to guests without the expense, risk, and time of construction and other real-estate projects.

Marriott's growth strategy includes adding distinctive properties to its chain, which includes hotel brands Aloft, Courtyard, Fairfield Inn, Ritz-Carlton, and more.[7] Sorenson sees features such as entertainment lounges and comfortable lobbies as a way to lure travelers away from Airbnb. Even a low-priced hotel can offer fun amenities that a traveler is unlikely to find in a spare bedroom or apartment for rent. At the new Moxy Times Square in New York, for example, guests can play miniature golf at a rooftop bar.

A key part of Marriott's growth plan involves international expansion, particularly in China. In the United States, years of business expansion have pushed the supply of hotel rooms ahead of demand. China, in contrast, is a dramatic growth story: The population is huge, accelerating numbers are moving up into the middle class, and many want to travel. Serving the Chinese domestically develops brand loyalty these travelers pack with them when they go abroad.[8]

Overview

In a fast-changing, competitive environment, managers must continually evaluate how well products are meeting customer needs, and they must engage in thorough, systematic planning to find new strategies to better meet those needs. This chapter explores the manager's role both as planner and as strategist. First, we discuss the nature and importance of planning, the kinds of plans managers develop, and the levels at which planning takes place. Second, we discuss the three major steps in the planning process: (1) determining an organization's mission and major goals, (2) choosing or formulating strategies to realize the mission and goals, and (3) selecting the most effective ways to implement and put these strategies into action. We also examine techniques such as SWOT analysis that can help managers improve the quality of their planning; and we discuss a range of strategies managers can use to give their companies a competitive advantage over their rivals. By the end of this chapter, you will understand the vital role managers carry out when they plan, develop, and implement strategies to create a high-performing organization.

Planning and Strategy

Planning, as we noted in Chapter 1, is a process managers use to identify and select appropriate goals and courses of action for an organization.[9] The organizational plan that results from the planning process details the goals of the organization and the specific strategies managers will implement to attain those goals. Recall from Chapter 1 that a strategy is a cluster of related managerial decisions and actions to help an organization attain one of its goals. Thus planning is both a goal-making and a strategy-making process.

In most organizations, planning is a three-step activity (see Figure 6.1). The first step is determining the organization's mission and goals. A mission statement is a broad declaration of an organization's overriding purpose, what it is seeking to achieve from its activities; this statement also identifies what is *unique or important*

Figure 6.1

Three Steps in
Organizational
Planning

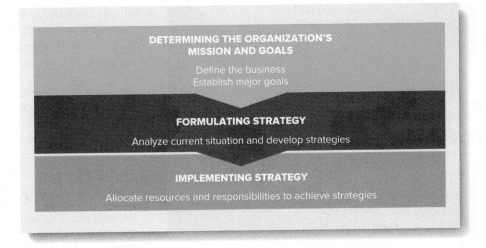

DETERMINING THE ORGANIZATION'S MISSION AND GOALS

Define the business
Establish major goals

FORMULATING STRATEGY

Analyze current situation and develop strategies

IMPLEMENTING STRATEGY

Allocate resources and responsibilities to achieve strategies

mission statement
A broad declaration
of an organization's
purpose that identifies
the organization's
products and
customers and
distinguishes the
organization from its
competitors.

about its products to its employees and customers; finally it *distinguishes or differentiates* the organization in some ways from its competitors. (Three examples of mission statements, those created by Google, Twitter, and Facebook, are illustrated later in Figure 6.4.)

The second step is formulating strategy. Managers analyze the organization's current situation and then conceive and develop the strategies necessary to attain the organization's mission and goals. The third step is implementing strategy. Managers decide how to allocate the resources and responsibilities required to implement the strategies among people and groups within the organization.[10] In subsequent sections of this chapter we look in detail at the specifics of these steps. But first we examine the general nature and purpose of planning.

The Nature of the Planning Process

Essentially, to perform the planning task, managers (1) establish and discover where an organization is at the *present time;* (2) determine where it should be in the future, its *desired future state;* and (3) decide how to *move it forward* to reach that future state. When managers plan, they must forecast what may happen in the future to decide what to do in the present. The better their predictions, the more effective will be the strategies they formulate to take advantage of future opportunities and counter emerging competitive threats in the environment. As previous chapters noted, however, the external environment is uncertain and complex, and managers typically must deal with incomplete information, scores of technical data, and inevitable time constraints. This is why planning and strategy making are so difficult and risky; and if managers' predictions are wrong and strategies fail, organizational performance falls.

Why Planning Is Important

Almost all managers participate in some kind of planning because they must try to predict future opportunities and threats and develop a plan and strategies that will result in a high-performing organization. Moreover, the absence of a plan often

A group of managers meet to plot their company's strategy. Their ability to assess opportunities and challenges and to forecast the future doesn't just depend on intelligence. Such tools as SWOT analysis can significantly bolster the accuracy of their predictions.
Ryan McVay/Getty Images

results in hesitations, false steps, and mistaken changes of direction that can hurt an organization or even lead to disaster. Planning is important for four main reasons:

1. *Planning is necessary to give the organization a sense of direction and purpose.*[11] A plan states what goals an organization is trying to achieve and what strategies it intends to use to achieve them. Without the sense of direction and purpose that a formal plan provides, managers may interpret their own specific tasks and jobs in ways that best suit themselves. The result will be an organization that is pursuing multiple and often conflicting goals and a set of managers who do not cooperate and work well together. By stating which organizational goals and strategies are important, a plan keeps managers on track so they use the resources under their control efficiently and effectively.

2. *Planning is a useful way of getting managers to participate in decision making about the appropriate goals and strategies for an organization.* Effective planning gives all managers the opportunity to participate in decision making. At Intel, for example, top managers, as part of their annual planning process, regularly request input from lower-level managers to determine what the organization's goals and strategies should be.

3. *A plan helps coordinate managers of the different functions and divisions of an organization to ensure that they all pull in the same direction and work to achieve its desired future state.* Without a well-thought-out plan, for example, it is possible that the manufacturing function will make more products than the sales function can sell, resulting in a mass of unsold inventory. In fact, this happened on the East Coast recently when harsh winter weather slowed car sales and left automakers with unsold inventory. To sell the inventory, many car dealers had to offer deep discounts to sell off their excess stock.

4. *A plan can be used as a device for controlling managers within an organization.* A good plan specifies not only which goals and strategies the organization is committed to but also *who* bears the responsibility for putting the strategies into action to attain the goals. When managers know they will be held accountable for attaining a goal, they are motivated to do their best to make sure the goal is achieved.

Henri Fayol, the originator of the model of management we discussed in Chapter 1, said that effective plans should have four qualities: unity, continuity, accuracy, and flexibility.[12] *Unity* means that at any time only one central, guiding plan is put into operation to achieve an organizational goal; more than one plan to achieve a goal would cause confusion and disorder. *Continuity* means that planning is an ongoing process in which managers build and refine previous plans and continually modify plans at all levels—corporate, business, and functional—so they fit together into one broad framework. *Accuracy* means that managers need to make every attempt to collect and use all available information in the planning process. Of course managers must recognize that uncertainty exists and that information is almost always incomplete (for reasons we discussed in Chapter 5). Despite the need for continuity and accuracy, however, Fayol emphasized that the planning process should be *flexible* enough so plans can be altered and changed if the situation changes; managers must not be bound to a static plan.

Levels of Planning

In large organizations, planning usually takes place at three levels of management: corporate, business or division, and department or functional. Consider how General Mills operates. The Minneapolis-based global consumer food company has been in business for more than 150 years and has experienced both growth and headwinds over the past several years. Its current CEO, Jeff Harmening, is a company veteran with nearly 25 years of experience who took over the top job in 2017.[13] Like many large organizations, General Mills has three main levels of management: corporate level, business or divisional level, and functional level (see Figure 6.2). At the corporate level are CEO Harmening, his top management team, and their corporate support staff. Together they are responsible for planning and strategy making for the organization as a whole.

Figure 6.2

Levels of Planning at General Mills

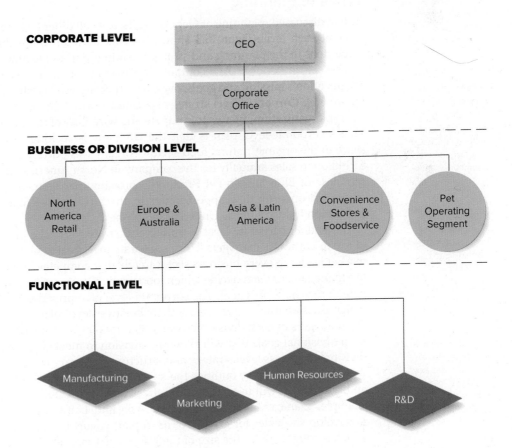

Below the corporate level is the business level. At the business level are the different *divisions* or *business units* of the company. Each division or business unit has its own set of *divisional managers* who control planning and strategy for their division or unit. For example, the managers in General Mills's North America Retail division plan how to operate efficiently and keep costs in check while still meeting the shifting tastes of consumers in the United States and Canada. In 2017, General Mills revised its organizational structure in an effort to increase operational agility and scale global operations efficiently. Each of the four business units includes five global platforms: cereal, snacks, yogurts, convenient meals, and super-premium ice cream. More than 75% of the company's global sales are concentrated in these five areas. In 2018, the company added a fifth business unit to address its growing natural pet food business, which now includes Blue Buffalo Pet Products, acquired recently for $8 billion.[14]

Going down one more level of the organizational structure, each division has its own set of *functions* or *departments,* such as manufacturing, marketing, human resources, and research and development (R&D). Each division's *functional managers* are responsible for the planning and strategy making necessary to increase the efficiency and effectiveness of their particular function. For example, the sales managers in General Mills's Convenience Stores & Foodservice division would be responsible for working with marketing colleagues to ensure various advertising and sales campaigns targeted potential customers in supermarket bakeries.

Types of Planning

As just discussed, planning at General Mills, as at all other large organizations, takes place at each level. Figure 6.3 shows the link between these three levels and the three steps in the planning and strategy-making process illustrated in Figure 6.1.

The corporate-level plan contains top management's decisions concerning the organization's mission and goals, overall (corporate-level) strategy, and structure (see Figure 6.3). Corporate-level strategy specifies in which industries and national markets an organization intends to compete and why. One of the goals stated in General Mills's corporate-level plan is that the company is seeking to increase its market share in the organic/natural food sector. Already this portfolio generates more than $1 billion in sales annually for the company in North America alone. With its recent purchase of Blue Buffalo Pet Products, company management believes this acquisition will open up new opportunities in the lucrative pet food sector, which is a $30 billion industry in the United States alone.[15]

In general, corporate-level planning and strategy are the primary responsibility of top or corporate managers.[16] The corporate-level goal of General Mills is to be the market leader in every business sector in which it competes. Jeff Harmening and his top management team decide which food product sectors General Mills should compete in to achieve this goal. The corporate-level plan provides the framework within which divisional managers create their business-level plans. At the business level, the managers of each division create a business-level plan that details (1) the long-term divisional goals that will allow the division to meet corporate goals and (2) the division's business-level strategy and structure necessary to achieve divisional goals. Business-level strategy outlines the specific methods a division, a business unit, or an organization will use to compete effectively against its rivals in an industry. For example, managers in General Mills's Asia and Latin America division continue to develop strategies for growth of its Yoplait yogurt brand to the Chinese market, which is roughly twice the size of the U.S. yogurt market.[17]

corporate-level plan Top management's decisions pertaining to the organization's mission, overall strategy, and structure.

corporate-level strategy A plan that indicates in which industries and national markets an organization intends to compete.

business-level plan Divisional managers' decisions pertaining to divisions' long-term goals, overall strategy, and structure.

business-level strategy A plan that indicates how a division intends to compete against its rivals in an industry.

Figure 6.3 Levels and Types of Planning

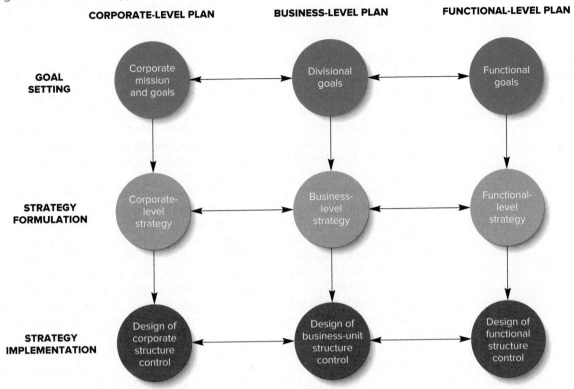

CORPORATE-LEVEL PLAN BUSINESS-LEVEL PLAN FUNCTIONAL-LEVEL PLAN

GOAL SETTING

- Corporate mission and goals
- Divisional goals
- Functional goals

STRATEGY FORMULATION

- Corporate-level strategy
- Business-level strategy
- Functional-level strategy

STRATEGY IMPLEMENTATION

- Design of corporate structure control
- Design of business-unit structure control
- Design of functional structure control

functional-level plan Functional managers' decisions pertaining to the goals that they propose to pursue to help the division attain its business-level goals.

functional-level strategy A plan of action to improve the ability of each of an organization's functions to perform its task-specific activities in ways that add value to an organization's goods and services.

At the functional level, the business-level plan provides the framework within which functional managers devise their plans. A functional-level plan states the goals that the managers of each function will pursue to help their division attain its business-level goals, which, in turn, will allow the entire company to achieve its corporate goals. Functional-level strategy is a plan of action that managers of individual functions (such as manufacturing or marketing) can follow to improve the ability of each function to perform its task-specific activities in ways that add value to an organization's goods and services and thereby increase the value customers receive. Thus, for example, consistent with the strategy of increasing Yoplait sales in China, General Mills might adopt the goal "To increase production by 20% over the next three years," and functional strategies to achieve this goal might include (1) investing in state-of-the-art manufacturing facilities and (2) developing a global supply chain that will increase efficiencies and reduce shipping/transportation costs.

In the planning process, it is important to ensure that planning across the three different levels is *consistent*—functional goals and strategies should be consistent with divisional goals and strategies, which, in turn, should be consistent with corporate goals and strategies, and vice versa. When consistency is achieved, the whole company operates in harmony; activities at one level reinforce and strengthen those at the other levels, increasing efficiency and effectiveness. To help accomplish this, each function's plan is linked to its division's business-level plan, which, in turn, is linked to the corporate plan. With a renewed vigor and detailed business strategies in place at each level of the organization, General Mills continues to review and revise its plans to ensure they are an effective guide to managerial decision making.[18]

Time Horizons of Plans

time horizon The intended duration of a plan.

Plans differ in their time horizons, the periods of time over which they are intended to apply or endure. Managers usually distinguish among *long-term plans,* with a time horizon of five years or more; *intermediate-term plans,* with a horizon between one and five years; and *short-term plans,* with a horizon of one year or less. Typically corporate- and business-level goals and strategies require long- and intermediate-term plans, and functional-level goals and strategies require intermediate- and short-term plans.

Although most companies operate with planning horizons of five years or more, this does not mean that managers undertake major planning exercises only once every five years and then "lock in" a specific set of goals and strategies for that period. Most organizations have an annual planning cycle that is usually linked to the annual financial budget (although a major planning effort may be undertaken only every few years). So a corporate- or business-level plan that extends over several years is typically treated as a *rolling plan*—a plan that is updated and amended every year to take account of changing conditions in the external environment. Thus the time horizon for an organization's 2020 corporate-level plan might be 2025; for the 2021 plan it might be 2026, and so on. The use of rolling plans is essential because of the high rate of change in the environment and the difficulty of predicting competitive conditions five years in the future. Rolling plans enable managers to make midcourse corrections if environmental changes warrant or to change the thrust of the plan altogether if it no longer seems appropriate. The use of rolling plans allows managers to plan flexibly without losing sight of the need to plan for the long term.

Standing Plans and Single-Use Plans

Another distinction often made between plans is whether they are standing plans or single-use plans. Managers create standing and single-use plans to help achieve an organization's specific goals. *Standing plans* are used in situations in which programmed decision making is appropriate. When the same situations occur repeatedly, managers develop policies, rules, and standard operating procedures (SOPs) to control the way employees perform their tasks. A policy is a general guide to action; a rule is a formal, written guide to action; and a standing operating procedure is a written instruction describing the exact series of actions that should be followed in a specific situation. For example, an organization may have a standing plan about ethical behavior by employees. This plan might include a policy that all employees are expected to behave ethically in their dealings with suppliers and customers; a rule that requires any employee who receives from a supplier or customer a gift worth more than $50 to report the gift; and an SOP that obliges the recipient of the gift to make the disclosure in writing within 30 days.

In contrast, *single-use plans* are developed to handle nonprogrammed decision making in unusual or one-of-a-kind situations. Examples of single-use plans include *programs,* which are integrated sets of plans for achieving certain goals, and *projects,* which are specific action plans created to complete various aspects of a program. For instance, NASA is working on a major program to launch a rover in 2020 to investigate a specific environment on the surface of Mars. One project in this program is to develop the scientific instruments to bring samples back from Mars.[19] To learn more about the role of projects in planning at Los Angeles World Airports, read the "Manager as a Person" feature.

Manager as a Person

With CEO's Guidance, LAX Projects Take Off

As CEO of Los Angeles World Airports, Deborah Ale Flint is responsible for running Los Angeles International (LAX), Van Nuys, and Ontario International Airports.[20] It's a job she prepared for as director of aviation for the Port of Oakland, in Northern California. Flint is enthusiastic about airports. She relishes mingling with travelers in the terminals, because it's "where the magic happens for the passenger."[21]

Flint knew projects would be a major part of her work in Los Angeles. LAX, the nation's second-busiest airport and the world's fourth-busiest, is her biggest responsibility. When she arrived, LAX was already undergoing a multibillion-dollar renovation.[22] The terminals are being upgraded to prepare for technological advances and the expected further growth in passenger traffic. The entire effort consists of dozens of projects that must be planned, funded, and implemented. Flint arrived after completion of the international terminal and in time to lead work on additional terminals and connecting spaces. The plans aim to reduce congestion, lower energy consumption, and update technology with, for example, flight information displays that travelers can scan with a smartphone to get personalized maps.

A key project under Flint's guidance is the Landside Access Modernization Program (LAMP).[23] Besides lounges, baggage claim areas, and walkways between terminals, LAMP includes a consolidated facility for car rental agencies and a people-mover system to transport travelers swiftly from terminals to garages and public transit. Funding for LAMP was recently authorized by the airport commissioners, triggering the start of the design process. The plan calls for completion in three years.

As CEO of Los Angeles World Airports, Deborah Flint manages many critical projects that impact both business and leisure travelers. Earl Gibson III/Getty Images

Running an airport poses special planning challenges because U.S. airports are managed by the cities they serve. Unlike a business selling tickets or charging admission, LAX assesses fees from the airlines using terminals and collects passenger facility charges from passengers when they pay for flights.[24] The city also can borrow for projects by issuing bonds. Therefore, to get the go-ahead for projects, Flint has to win the backing of the local community, including the government. Her enthusiasm for her city surely helps. Flint's vision for LAX is that it represents a vibrant, creative city to local and world travelers, so it should be as creative and forward-thinking as the city. As Flint describes the renovation, it's not merely a construction project, but a means of "creating an experience" for travelers, giving them a "great first and last impression of Los Angeles."[25]

Determining the Organization's Mission and Goals

As we discussed earlier, determining the organization's mission and goals is the first step of the planning process. Once the mission and goals are agreed upon and formally stated in the corporate plan, they guide the next steps by defining which strategies are appropriate.[26] Figure 6.4 presents the mission statements for three Internet companies: Google, Twitter, and Facebook.

Defining the Business

To determine an organization's *mission*—the overriding reason it exists to provide customers with goods or services they value—managers must first *define its business* so they can identify what kind of value customers are receiving. To define the business, managers must ask three related questions about a company's products: (1) *Who* are our customers? (2) *What* customer needs are being satisfied? (3) *How* are we satisfying customer needs?[27] Managers ask these questions to identify the customer needs that the organization satisfies and how the organization satisfies those needs. Answering these questions helps managers identify not only the customer needs they are satisfying now but also the needs they should try to satisfy in the future and who their true competitors are. All this information helps managers plan and establish appropriate goals.

Establishing Major Goals

Once the business is defined, managers must establish a set of primary goals to which the organization is committed. Developing these goals gives the organization a sense of direction or purpose. In most organizations, articulating major goals is the job of the CEO, although other managers have input into the process. Thus, at General Mills, the CEO's primary goal is still to be one of the two best performers in every industry in which the company competes, even though this is highly challenging. However, the best statements of organizational goals are ambitious—that is, they *stretch* the organization and require that each of its members work to improve company performance.[28] The role of strategic leadership, the ability of the CEO and top managers to convey a compelling vision of what they want to achieve to their employees, is important here. If employees buy into the vision and model

strategic leadership The ability of the CEO and top managers to convey a compelling vision of what they want the organization to achieve to their employees.

Figure 6.4

Mission Statements for Three Internet Companies

COMPANY	MISSION STATEMENT
Google	"To organize the world's information and make it universally accessible and useful."
Twitter	"To give everyone the power to create and share ideas and information instantly, without barriers."
Facebook	"To give people the power to build community and bring the world closer together."

Sources: Google's mission statement: https://google.com; Twitter's mission statement: https://abouttwitter.com; Facebook's mission statement: https://newsroom.fb.com; all accessed January 3, 2019.

their behaviors on their leaders', they develop a willingness to undertake the hard, stressful work that is necessary for creative, risk-taking strategy making.[29]

Although goals should be challenging, they should also be realistic. Challenging goals give managers at all levels an incentive to look for ways to improve organizational performance, but a goal that is clearly unrealistic and impossible to attain may prompt managers to give up.[30] For example, General Mills's CEO has to be careful not to set unrealistic sales targets for the company's business units that might discourage their top managers.

Finally, the time period in which a goal is expected to be achieved should be stated. Time constraints are important because they emphasize that a goal must be attained within a reasonable period; they inject a sense of urgency into goal attainment and act as a motivator. For example, General Mills recently announced its global sustainability goals that include reducing greenhouse gas emissions across the entire value chain by 28% from 2010 levels by 2025; developing water stewardship plans for the most at-risk watersheds in its global supply chain by 2025; and sustainably sourcing 100% of its 10 priority ingredients by 2020—which represents more than 40% of its annual raw material purchases on a global basis.[31]

Formulating Strategy

In strategy formulation managers work to develop the set of strategies (corporate, divisional, and functional) that will allow an organization to accomplish its mission and achieve its goals. Strategy formulation begins with managers systematically analyzing the factors or forces inside an organization and outside in the global environment that affect the organization's ability to meet its goals now and in the future. SWOT analysis and the five forces model are two handy techniques managers can use to analyze these factors.

strategy formulation The development of a set of corporate, business, and functional strategies that allow an organization to accomplish its mission and achieve its goals.

SWOT Analysis

SWOT analysis is a planning exercise in which managers identify *internal* organizational strengths (S) and weaknesses (W) and *external* environmental opportunities (O) and threats (T). Based on a SWOT analysis, managers at different levels of the organization select the corporate, business, and functional strategies to best position the organization to achieve its mission and goals (see Figure 6.5). In Chapter 4 we discussed forces in the task and general environments that have the potential to affect an organization. We noted that changes in these forces can produce opportunities that an organization might take advantage of and threats that may harm its current situation.

SWOT analysis A planning exercise in which managers identify organizational strengths (S) and weaknesses (W) and environmental opportunities (O) and threats (T).

The first step in SWOT analysis is to identify an organization's strengths and weaknesses. Table 6.1 lists many important strengths (such as high-quality skills in marketing and in research and development) and weaknesses (such as rising manufacturing costs and outdated technology). The task facing managers is to identify the strengths and weaknesses that characterize the present state of their organization.

The second step in SWOT analysis begins when managers embark on a full-scale SWOT planning exercise to identify potential opportunities and threats in the environment that affect the organization now or may affect it in the future. Examples of possible opportunities and threats that must be anticipated (many of which were discussed in Chapter 4) are listed in Table 6.1.

Figure 6.5

Planning and Strategy
Formulation

Table 6.1

Questions for SWOT Analysis

Potential Strengths	Potential Opportunities	Potential Weaknesses	Potential Threats
Well-developed strategy?	Expand core business(es)?	Poorly developed strategy?	Attacks on core business(es)?
Strong product lines?	Exploit new market segments?	Obsolete product lines?	Increase in domestic competition?
Broad market coverage?	Widen product range?	Rising manufacturing costs?	Increase in foreign competition?
Manufacturing competence?	Extend cost or differentiation advantage?	Decline in R&D innovations?	Outdated technology?
Good marketing skills?	Diversify into new growth businesses?	Poor marketing plan?	Change in consumer tastes?
Good materials management systems?	Expand into foreign markets?	Poor materials management systems?	Fall in barriers to entry?
R&D skills and leadership?	Apply R&D skills in new areas?	Loss of customer goodwill?	Rise in new or substitute products?
Human resource competencies?	Enter new related businesses?	Inadequate human resources?	Increase in industry rivalry?
Brand-name reputation?	Vertically integrate forward?	Loss of brand name?	New forms of competition?
Cost of differentiation advantage?	Vertically integrate backward?	Growth without direction?	Potential for takeover?
Appropriate management style?	Overcome barriers to entry?	Loss of corporate direction?	Changes in demographic factors?
Appropriate organizational structure?	Reduce rivalry among competitors?	Infighting among divisions?	Changes in economic factors?
Appropriate control systems?	Apply brand-name capital in new areas?	Loss of corporate control?	Downturn in economy?
Ability to manage strategic change?	Seek fast market growth?	Inappropriate organizational structure and control systems?	Rising labor costs?
Other strengths?	Other opportunities?	High conflict and politics?	Slower market growth?
		Other weaknesses?	Other threats?

With the SWOT analysis completed, and strengths, weaknesses, opportunities, and threats identified, managers can continue the planning process and determine specific strategies for achieving the organization's mission and goals. The resulting strategies should enable the organization to attain its goals by taking advantage of opportunities, countering threats, building strengths, and correcting organizational weaknesses. To appreciate how managers use SWOT analysis to formulate strategy, consider a recent comparison between e-tailer Amazon.com and clicks-and-mortar retailer Walmart. Although each company has differing strengths and weaknesses, they both face similar threats and opportunities in the expanding e-commerce sector.[32] For example, Walmart's recent acquisition of several e-commerce companies, including Jet.com, Mod Cloth, ShoeBuy, Bonobos, Bare Necessities, and India's Flipkart, provides some interesting opportunities for the world's largest retailer to gain market share in the online retail space—as well as some threats to Amazon's position as a top online apparel retailer. In addition, Amazon's recent acquisition of Whole Food Markets specialty grocery chain provides some interesting opportunities for Amazon in the home meal-kit delivery market sector as it provides a viable threat to Walmart and other food retailers that sell grocery items such as organic fruits and vegetables.[33]

Using information from a SWOT analysis helps managers identify weaknesses that can be turned into competitive advantages. As described in the "Management Insight" feature, cable and entertainment giant Comcast took a hard look at the customer experience and turned it into a win for both consumers and the company.

Management Insight

Comcast Rethinks the Customer Experience

Cable companies know they can gain a competitive advantage by delivering a great customer experience, but getting there isn't easy. Comcast found in its product development group someone who could lead such an effort: Charlie Herrin, one of the executives who led the development of the Xfinity X1 entertainment platform.[34] Comcast made him executive vice president and chief customer experience officer of its cable division.

A basic question facing Herrin and his team was *how* to improve performance. In today's fast-paced business environment, Herrin knew he needed a broader view of systems and processes that would take into account technology, workflow, and the needs of employees as well as customers. Efficiency and worker empowerment would be part of the plan. Herrin's key insight was that product design and customer service are inseparable. With Internet-connected systems such as X1, the potential for product design to ease service problems is especially great. Herrin focuses on giving customers useful information. Ideally, that would be a message that Comcast is already working on the problem or, second best, a menu customers step through to correct the problem or schedule a service call.

Herrin worked with his team to methodically redesign the experiences of starting up service and getting help with problems. They mapped out customers' points of interaction with the company and identified those seen as difficult or unpleasant in order to redesign them. A major frustration is waiting for service technicians, so Comcast upgraded its technology to send customers updates about when help will arrive. Messaging tools include follow-up texts to make sure the customer knows what to expect and is satisfied.[35]

Charlie Herrin, Comcast's chief customer experience officer, leads the company's efforts to make sure customers are a key component of Comcast's business strategies. Tribune Content Agency LLC/Alamy Stock Photo

Comcast has made customer experience a companywide focus. Customer experience is now a component of all executives' budgets and project reviews. One of Herrin's early successes was witnessing that teams throughout the company were talking about customer experience. Throughout these changes, Herrin continues to address the impact on employees. He includes an HR staff member on his customer experience team. Together they ensure that all employees have training in what customer experience is and why it matters.[36]

The customer experience team is delivering results, according to Comcast. Even as more consumers are moving from cable to Internet-based entertainment, plugging in more devices, Comcast officials see complaints declining by some measures.[37] The customer satisfaction ratings collected for the American Customer Satisfaction Index show a marked improvement. And Herrin says the investment has begun showing a positive return.[38] Recognizing the positive impact of Herrin's systemwide approach, Comcast restructured its departments to make customer service and customer experience part of its technology and products division, rather than independent functions.[39] ●

The Five Forces Model

A well-known model that helps managers focus on the five most important competitive forces, or potential threats, in the external environment is Michael Porter's five forces model. We discussed the first four forces in the following list in Chapter 4. Porter identified these five factors as major threats because they affect how much profit organizations competing within the same industry can expect to make:

- *The level of rivalry among organizations in an industry:* The more that companies compete against one another for customers—for example, by lowering the prices of their products or by increasing advertising—the lower is the level of industry profits (low prices mean less profit).

- *The potential for entry into an industry:* The easier it is for companies to enter an industry—because, for example, barriers to entry, such as brand loyalty, are low—the more likely it is for industry prices and therefore industry profits to be low.

- *The power of large suppliers:* If there are only a few large suppliers of an important input, then suppliers can drive up the price of that input, and expensive inputs result in lower profits for companies in an industry.

- *The power of large customers:* If only a few large customers are available to buy an industry's output, they can bargain to drive down the price of that output. As a result, industry producers make lower profits.

- *The threat of substitute products:* Often the output of one industry is a substitute for the output of another industry (plastic may be a substitute for steel in some applications, for example; similarly, bottled water is a substitute for cola). When a substitute for their product exists, companies cannot demand high prices for it or customers will switch to the substitute, and this constraint keeps their profits low.

Porter argued that when managers analyze opportunities and threats, they should pay particular attention to these five forces because they are the major threats an organization will encounter. It is the job of managers at the corporate, business, and functional levels to formulate strategies to counter these threats so an organization can manage its task and general environments, perform at a high level, and generate high profits. Sometimes, however, management's review of competitive forces or potential threats cannot keep a company from filing bankruptcy or liquidating its stores. Consider the case of toy retailer Toys "R" Us (TRU). The past decade or so has been quite challenging for the retailer—with holiday sales unable to provide the turnaround the company needed to regain profitability. Looking at Porter's framework, TRU experienced a high level of rivalry from other retailers selling the same toys, which pushed down prices when TRU could least likely afford to reduce its profit margins. By 1998, Walmart began selling more toys than TRU. The potential for entry into the retail toy industry was high and devastating for TRU because there were few barriers to entry—very little brand loyalty for TRU itself from consumers who could buy toys and other items cheaper and more conveniently from discount retailers and e-commerce websites.

With regard to the power of large suppliers and customers, economies of scale could have played to TRU's advantage; however, the company had been highly leveraged with almost insurmountable debt, and many of its suppliers refused to give the company additional financing or extended credit to purchase the inventory it desperately needed for the all-important holiday season.[40] Last, the threat of substitute products was high in the case of TRU, especially if one considers alternative forms of entertainment (such as video games and streaming content) that met the same consumer needs as toys. Analyzing TRU's plight using the five forces model shows the company was vulnerable in several areas, which caused it to reduce its prices to attract shoppers while trying to pay back enormous amounts of debt. TRU first filed for bankruptcy protection from creditors, and then, in March 2018, started liquidating and closing stores in the United States and abroad, leaving more than 33,000 employees without jobs.[41] Seven months later, in October 2018, TRU's controlling lenders canceled a bankruptcy auction amid speculation that they would attempt to revive the TRU brand in the near future.[42]

hypercompetition
Permanent, ongoing, intense competition brought about in an industry by advancing technology or changing customer tastes.

Today competition is tough in most industries, whether companies make cars, soup, computers, or dolls. The term hypercompetition applies to industries that are characterized by permanent, ongoing, intense competition brought about by advancing technology or changing customer tastes and fads and fashions.[43] Clearly, planning and strategy formulation are much more difficult and risky when hypercompetition prevails in an industry.

Formulating Business-Level Strategies

Michael Porter, the researcher who developed the five forces model, also developed a theory of how managers can select a business-level strategy—a plan to gain a competitive advantage in a particular market or industry.[44] Porter argued that business-level strategy creates a competitive advantage because it allows an organization (or a division of a company) to *counter and reduce* the threat of the five

LO 6-2

Differentiate between the main types of business-level strategies, and explain how they give an organization a competitive advantage that may lead to superior performance.

industry forces. That is, successful business-level strategy reduces rivalry, prevents new competitors from entering the industry, reduces the power of suppliers or buyers, and lowers the threat of substitutes—and this raises prices and profits.

According to Porter, to obtain these higher profits managers must choose between two basic ways of increasing the value of an organization's products: *differentiating the product* to increase its value to customers or *lowering the costs* of making the product. Porter also argues that managers must choose between serving the whole market or serving just one segment or part of a market. Based on those choices, managers choose to pursue one of four business-level strategies: low cost, differentiation, focused low cost, or focused differentiation (see Table 6.2).

Low-Cost Strategy

low-cost strategy
Driving the organization's costs down below the costs of its rivals.

With a low-cost strategy, managers try to gain a competitive advantage by focusing the energy of all the organization's departments or functions on driving the company's costs down below the costs of its industry rivals. This strategy, for example, would require that manufacturing managers search for new ways to reduce production costs, R&D managers focus on developing new products that can be manufactured more cheaply, and marketing managers find ways to lower the costs of attracting customers. According to Porter, companies pursuing a low-cost strategy can sell a product for less than their rivals sell it and yet still make a good profit because of their lower costs. Thus such organizations enjoy a competitive advantage based on their low prices. For example, BIC pursues a low-cost strategy: It offers customers razor blades priced lower than Gillette's and ballpoint pens less expensive than those offered by Cross or Waterman. Also, when existing companies have low costs and can charge low prices, it is difficult for new companies to enter the industry because entering is always an expensive process.

Differentiation Strategy

differentiation strategy
Distinguishing an organization's products from the products of competitors on dimensions such as product design, quality, or after-sales service.

With a differentiation strategy, managers try to gain a competitive advantage by focusing all the energies of the organization's departments or functions on *distinguishing* the organization's products from those of competitors on one or more important dimensions, such as product design, quality, or after-sales service and support. Often the process of making products unique and different is expensive. This strategy, for example, frequently requires that managers increase spending on product design or R&D to differentiate products, and costs rise as a result. Organizations that successfully pursue a differentiation strategy may be able to charge a

Table 6.2

Porter's Business-Level Strategies

Strategy	Number of Market Segments Served	
	Many	Few
Low cost	✓	
Focused low cost		✓
Differentiation	✓	
Focused differentiation		✓

premium price for their products; the premium price lets organizations pursuing a differentiation strategy recoup their higher costs. Coca-Cola, PepsiCo, and Procter & Gamble are some of the many well-known companies that pursue a strategy of differentiation. They spend enormous amounts of money on advertising to differentiate and create a unique image for their products. Also, differentiation makes industry entry difficult because new companies have no brand name to help them compete and customers don't perceive other products to be close substitutes, so this also allows premium pricing and results in high profits.

According to Porter's theory, managers cannot simultaneously pursue both a low-cost strategy and a differentiation strategy. Porter identified a simple correlation: Differentiation raises costs and thus necessitates premium pricing to recoup those high costs. For example, if BIC suddenly began to advertise heavily to try to build a strong global brand image for its products, BIC's costs would rise. BIC then could no longer make a profit simply by pricing its blades or pens lower than Gillette or Cross. According to Porter, managers must choose between a low-cost strategy and a differentiation strategy.

More and more, however, exceptions to Porter's ideas about the "either/or" approach to gaining competitive advantage by low cost or differentiation can be found in today's business environment. For example, Southwest Airlines has written its mission statement to say "dedication to the highest quality of customer service delivered with a sense of warmth, friendliness, individual pride, and company spirit."[45] Based on this statement, the company seems to be pursuing a differentiation strategy based on customer service. Yet the average price of a one-way ticket on a Southwest flight continues to be among the lowest, which suggests a cost leadership strategy. Likewise, Apple has a story that mixes cost leadership with differentiation. Apple CEO Tim Cook emphasizes that Apple's strategy is to focus on making great products that customers love—a differentiation strategy. He said the company never had the goal of selling a low-cost phone.[46] However, he said, the company did find a way to reach its goal of providing a great experience with a phone while reducing its cost. Cook emphasizes that differentiation was the goal, but low cost also became possible. These examples suggest that although Porter's ideas may be valid in most cases, well-managed companies such as Southwest Airlines and Apple may pursue both low costs and differentiated products.

Focused Low-Cost and Focused Differentiation Strategies

focused low-cost strategy Serving only one segment of the overall market and trying to be the lowest-cost organization serving that segment.

Both the differentiation strategy and the low-cost strategy are aimed at serving many or most segments of a particular market, such as for cars, toys, foods, or computers. Porter identified two other business-level strategies that aim to serve the needs of customers in only one or a few market segments.[47] Managers pursuing a focused low-cost strategy serve one or a few segments of the overall market and aim to make their organization the lowest-cost company serving that segment. By contrast, managers pursuing a focused differentiation strategy serve just one or a few segments of the market and aim to make their organization the most differentiated company serving that segment.

focused differentiation strategy Serving only one segment of the overall market and trying to be the most differentiated organization serving that segment.

Companies pursuing either of these strategies have chosen to *specialize* in some way by directing their efforts at a particular kind of customer (such as serving the needs of babies or affluent customers) or even the needs of customers in a specific geographic region (customers on the East or West Coast). BMW, for example, pursues a focused differentiation strategy, producing cars exclusively for higher-income

Zara's ongoing retail success is based on a focused strategy that identifies fashion trends quickly and turns out new products in record time. Markel Redondo/Bloomberg via Getty Images

customers. By contrast, Toyota pursues a differentiation strategy and produces cars that appeal to consumers in almost all segments of the car market, from basic transportation (Toyota Corolla) through the middle of the market (Toyota Camry) to the high-income end of the market (Lexus).

Increasingly, smaller companies are finding it easier to pursue a focused strategy and compete successfully against large, powerful, low-cost and differentiated companies because of advances in technology that lower costs and enable them to reach and attract customers. By establishing a storefront on the web, thousands of small, specialized companies have been able to carve out a profitable niche against large bricks-and-mortar competitors.

Zara is a flagship brand for Spanish global retailer Inditex, whose sales have soared in recent years, and who provides an excellent example of the way even a bricks-and-mortar company can use technology to pursue a focused strategy and compete globally.[48] Zara has managed to position itself as the low-price, low-cost leader in the fashion segment of the clothing market, against differentiators such as Gucci and H&M, because it has applied technology to its specific needs. Zara manages its design and manufacturing process in a way that minimizes the inventory it has to carry—the major cost borne by a clothing retailer. However, technological advances also give its designers instantaneous feedback on which clothes are selling well and in which countries, and this gives Zara a competitive advantage from differentiation. Specifically, Zara can manufacture more of a particular kind of dress or coat to meet high customer demand, decide which clothing should be sold in its rapidly expanding network of global stores, and constantly change the mix of clothes it offers customers to keep up with fashion—at low cost.

Zara's approach to technology also lets it efficiently manage the interface between its design and manufacturing operations, which work side by side in its corporate headquarters in Arteixo, Spain. Zara sometimes takes only two weeks to design, manufacturer, and ship new clothing items to stores across the globe. By contrast, H&M, the trendy Swedish retailer, takes several months to get its advanced orders into the hands of customers.[49] This short time to market gives Zara great flexibility and allows the company to respond quickly to the rapidly changing fashion market, in which fashions can change several times a year. Because of the quick manufacturing-to-sales cycle and just-in-time fashion, Zara offers its clothes collections at relatively low prices and still makes profits that are the envy of the fashion clothing industry.

Zara has been able to pursue a focused strategy that is simultaneously low-cost and differentiated because it has developed many strengths in functions such as clothing design, marketing, and technology that have given it a competitive advantage. Developing functional-level strategies that strengthen business-level strategy and increase competitive advantage is a vital managerial task. Discussion of this important issue is left until the next chapter. First, we need to go up one planning level and examine how corporate strategy helps an organization achieve its mission and goals.

Formulating Corporate-Level Strategies

Once managers have formulated the business-level strategies that will best position a company, or a division of a company, to compete in an industry and outperform its rivals, they must look to the future. If their planning has been successful the company will be generating high profits, and their task now is to plan how to invest these profits to increase performance over time.

Recall that *corporate-level strategy* is a plan of action that involves choosing in which industries and countries a company should invest its resources to achieve its mission and goals. In choosing a corporate-level strategy, managers ask, How should the growth and development of our company be managed to increase its ability to create value for customers (and thus increase its performance) over the long run? Managers of effective organizations actively seek new opportunities to use a company's resources to create new and improved goods and services for customers. Examples of organizations whose product lines are growing rapidly are Google, Intel, and Toyota, whose managers pursue any feasible opportunity to use their companies' skills to provide customers with new products.

In addition, some managers must help their organizations respond to threats due to changing forces in the task or general environment that have made their business-level strategies less effective and reduced profits. For example, customers may no longer be buying the kinds of goods and services a company is producing (high-salt soup, bulky televisions, or gas-guzzling cars), or other organizations may have entered the market and attracted away customers (this happened to Sony in the 2000s after Apple and Samsung began to produce better MP3 players, laptops, and flat-screen televisions). Top managers aim to find corporate strategies that can help the organization strengthen its business-level strategies and thus respond to these changes and improve performance.

The principal corporate-level strategies that managers use to help a company grow and keep it at the top of its industry, or to help it retrench and reorganize to stop its decline, are (1) concentration on a single industry, (2) vertical integration, (3) diversification, and (4) international expansion. An organization will benefit from pursuing any of these strategies only when the strategy helps further increase the value of the organization's goods and services so more customers buy them. Specifically, to increase the value of goods and services, a corporate-level strategy must help a company, or one of its divisions, either (1) lower the costs of developing and making products or (2) increase product differentiation so more customers want to buy the products even at high or premium prices. Both of these outcomes strengthen a company's competitive advantage and increase its performance.

LO 6-3
Differentiate between the main types of corporate-level strategies, and explain how they are used to strengthen a company's business-level strategy and competitive advantage.

Concentration on a Single Industry

Most growing companies reinvest their profits to strengthen their competitive position in the industry in which they are currently operating; in doing so, they pursue the corporate-level strategy of concentration on a single industry. Most commonly, an organization uses its functional skills to develop new kinds of products, or it expands the number of locations in which it uses those skills. For example, Apple continuously introduces improved mobile wireless digital devices such as the iPhone and iPad, whereas McDonald's, which began as one restaurant in California, focused all its efforts on using its resources to quickly expand across the globe to become the biggest and most profitable U.S. fast-food company.

concentration on a single industry Reinvesting a company's profits to strengthen its competitive position in its current industry.

On the other hand, when organizations are performing effectively, they often decide to enter *new industries* in which they can use their growing profits to establish new operating divisions to create and make a wider range of more valuable products. Thus they begin to pursue vertical integration or diversification—such as Coca-Cola, PepsiCo, and Campbell's Soup.

Vertical Integration

vertical integration
Expanding a company's operations either backward into an industry that produces inputs for its products or forward into an industry that uses, distributes, or sells its products.

When an organization is performing well in its industry, managers often see new opportunities to create additional value either by producing the inputs it uses to make products or by distributing and selling its products to customers. This process is called vertical integration. Vertical integration is a corporate-level strategy in which a company expands it business operations either backward into a new industry that produces inputs for the company's products (*backward vertical integration*) or forward into a new industry that uses, distributes, or sells the company's products (*forward vertical integration*).[50] For example, as Tesla Motors worked toward its goal of mass-producing an electric car that will sell for close to $35,000, it recognized it would need batteries for the vehicles. To meet that need, Tesla became its own battery supplier, building the $5 billion Gigafactory outside Sparks, Nevada, which went on line a few years ago. This backward vertical integration not only supplies Tesla's need for inputs to make the new electric car model, it is also expected to help lower the cost of the car's batteries.[51]

Figure 6.6 illustrates the four main stages in a typical raw material to customer value chain; value is added to the product at each stage by the activities involved in each industry. For a company based in the assembly stage, backward integration would involve establishing a new division in the intermediate manufacturing or raw material production industries; and forward integration would involve establishing a new division to distribute its products to wholesalers or a retail division to sell directly to customers. A division at one stage or one industry receives the product produced by the division in the previous stage or industry, transforms it in some way—adding value—and then transfers the output at a higher price to the division at the next stage in the chain.

As an example of how this industry value chain works, consider the soft drink industry. In the raw materials industry, suppliers include sugar companies and manufacturers of artificial sweeteners such as NutraSweet and Splenda, which are used

Figure 6.6

Stages in a Vertical Value Chain

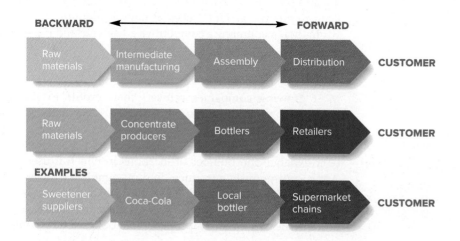

in diet drinks. These companies sell their products to companies in the soft drink industry that make concentrate—such as Coca-Cola and PepsiCo, which mix these inputs with others to produce the concentrate. In the process, they add value to these inputs. The concentrate producers then sell the concentrate to companies in the bottling and distribution industry, which add carbonated water to the concentrate and package the resulting drinks—again adding value to the concentrate. Next the bottlers distribute and sell the soft drinks to retailers, including stores such as Costco and Walmart and fast-food chains such as McDonald's. Companies in the retail industry add value by making the product accessible to customers, and they profit from direct sales to customers. Thus value is added by companies at each stage in the raw materials to consumer chain.

The reason managers pursue vertical integration is that it allows them either to add value to their products by making them special or unique or to lower the costs of making and selling them. An example of using forward vertical integration to increase differentiation is Apple's decision to open its own stores to make its unique products more accessible to customers who could try them out before they bought them. So too is PepsiCo's decision to buy its bottlers so they can better differentiate their products and lower costs in the future.

Although vertical integration can strengthen an organization's competitive advantage and increase its performance, it also reduce an organization's flexibility to respond to changing environmental conditions and create threats that must be countered by changing the organization's strategy. For example, when Procter & Gamble acquired the Gillette Company in 2005, Duracell batteries, a vertical integration for Gillette, came with it. However, Duracell stood out as an oddball among the other products in P&G's portfolio, and some analysts suggested that P&G sell off Duracell, which it did in 2016 to Warren Buffett's Berkshire Hathaway.[52]

Thus, when considering vertical integration as a strategy to add value, managers must be careful because sometimes it may *reduce* a company's ability to create value when the environment changes. This is why so many companies have divested themselves of units that draw attention and resources away from an organization's primary purpose.

Diversification

Diversification is the corporate-level strategy of expanding a company's business operations into a new industry in order to produce new kinds of valuable goods or services.[53] Examples include PepsiCo's diversification into the snack food business with the purchase of Frito-Lay, and Cisco's diversification into consumer electronics when it purchased Linksys. There are two main kinds of diversification: related and unrelated.

RELATED DIVERSIFICATION Related diversification is the strategy of entering a new business or industry to create a competitive advantage in one or more of an organization's existing divisions or businesses. Related diversification can add value to an organization's products if managers can find ways for its various divisions or business units to share their valuable skills or resources so that synergy is created.[54] Synergy is obtained when the value created by two divisions cooperating is greater than the value that would be created if the two divisions operated separately and independently. For example, suppose two or more divisions of a diversified company can use the same manufacturing facilities, distribution channels, or advertising

diversification
Expanding a company's business operations into a new industry in order to produce new kinds of valuable goods or services.

related diversification
Entering a new business or industry to create a competitive advantage in one or more of an organization's existing divisions or businesses.

synergy Performance gains that result when individuals and departments coordinate their actions.

campaigns—that is, share functional activities. Each division has to invest fewer resources in a shared functional activity than it would have to invest if it performed the functional activity by itself. Related diversification can be a major source of cost savings when divisions share the costs of performing a functional activity.[55] Similarly, if one division's R&D skills can improve another division's products and increase their differentiated appeal, this synergy can give the second division an important competitive advantage over its industry rivals—so the company as a whole benefits from diversification.

The way Procter & Gamble's disposable diaper and paper towel divisions cooperate is a good example of the successful production of synergies. These divisions share the costs of procuring inputs such as paper and packaging; a joint sales force sells both products to retail outlets; and both products are shipped using the same distribution system. This resource sharing has enabled both divisions to reduce their costs, and as a result, they can charge lower prices than their competitors and so attract more customers.[56] In addition, the divisions can share the research costs of developing new and improved products, such as finding more absorbent material, that increase both products' differentiated appeal. This is something that is also at the heart of 3M's corporate strategy. From the beginning, 3M has pursued related diversification and created new businesses by leveraging its skills in research and development. Today the company has five business groups that share resources such as technology and marketing. The five groups are industrial, consumer, safety and graphics, health care, and electronics and energy. The company spends about 6% of its annual sales on research and development, which helps produce more than 3,000 new patents each year and a steady stream of unique products for consumers and businesses alike.[57]

How does 3M do it? First, the company is a science-based enterprise with a strong tradition of innovation and risk taking. Risk taking is encouraged and failure is not punished but is seen as a natural part of the process of creating new products and business. Second, 3M's management is relentlessly focused on the company's customers and the problems they face. Many of 3M's products have come from helping customers solve difficult problems. Third, managers set stretch goals that require the company to create new products and businesses at a rapid rate. Fourth, employees are given considerable autonomy to pursue their own ideas; indeed, 15% of employees' time can be spent working on projects of their own choosing without management approval. Many products have resulted from this autonomy, including the ubiquitous Post-it Notes. Fifth, while products belong to business units and business units are responsible for generating profits, the technologies belong to every unit within the company. Anyone at 3M is free to try to develop new applications for a technology developed by its business units. Finally, 3M organizes many company-wide meetings where researchers from its different divisions are brought together to share the results of their work.[58]

In sum, to pursue related diversification successfully, managers search for new businesses where they can use the existing skills

How did we ever survive without Post-it Notes? 3M's intense focus on solving customer problems results in new products that sell well, including countless variations of the original sticky note. Kuznetsov Alexey/Shutterstock

and resources in their departments and divisions to create synergies, add value to new products and businesses, and improve their competitive position and that of the entire company. In addition, managers may try to acquire a company in a new industry because they believe it possesses skills and resources that will improve the performance of one or more of their existing divisions. If successful, such skill transfers can help an organization lower its costs or better differentiate its products because they create synergies between divisions.

UNRELATED DIVERSIFICATION Managers pursue unrelated diversification when they establish divisions or buy companies in new industries that are *not* linked in any way to their current businesses or industries. One main reason for pursuing unrelated diversification is that sometimes managers can buy a poorly performing company, transfer their management skills to that company, turn around its business, and increase its performance—all of which create value.

unrelated diversification
Entering a new industry or buying a company in a new industry that is not related in any way to an organization's current businesses or industries.

Another reason for pursuing unrelated diversification is that purchasing businesses in different industries lets managers engage in *portfolio strategy,* which is apportioning financial resources among divisions to increase financial returns or spread risks among different businesses, much as individual investors do with their own portfolios. For example, managers may transfer funds from a rich division (a "cash cow") to a new and promising division (a "star") and, by appropriately allocating money between divisions, create value. Though used as a popular explanation in the 1980s for unrelated diversification, portfolio strategy ran into increasing criticism in the 1990s because it simply does not work.[59] Why? As managers expand the scope of their organization's operations and enter more and more industries, it becomes increasingly difficult for top managers to be knowledgeable about all of the organization's diverse businesses. Managers do not have the time to process all of the information required to adequately assess the strategy and performance of each division, and so the performance of the entire company often falls.

Thus, although unrelated diversification can potentially create value for a company, research evidence suggests that *too much* diversification can cause managers to lose control of their organization's core business. As a result, diversification can reduce value rather than create it.[60] Because of this, during the last decade there has been an increasing trend for diversified companies to divest many of their unrelated, and sometimes related, divisions. Managers in companies such as Novartis, Nestlé, and General Electric have sold off numerous divisions and focused on increasing the performance of the businesses that remained—in other words, they went back to a strategy of concentrating on a limited number of industries. For example, in 2018 General Electric began selling off several divisions in an effort to simplify its business strategies, raise cash to pay down debt, and cut costs. The company has sold off its century-old locomotive division, spun off GE Healthcare (which makes medical equipment such as MRI machines), and sold off its power business to private equity firms.[61]

International Expansion

As if planning whether to vertically integrate, diversify, or concentrate on the core business were not a difficult enough task, corporate-level managers also must decide on the appropriate way to compete internationally. A basic question confronts the managers of any organization that needs to sell its products abroad and compete in more than one national market: To what extent should the organization customize features of its products and marketing campaign to different national conditions?

global strategy
Selling the same standardized product and using the same basic marketing approach in each national market.

If managers decide that their organization should sell the same standardized product in each national market in which it competes, and use the same basic marketing approach, they adopt a global strategy. Such companies undertake little, if any, customization to suit the specific needs of customers in different countries. But if managers decide to customize products and marketing strategies to specific national conditions, they adopt a multidomestic strategy. Panasonic has traditionally pursued a global strategy, selling the same basic TVs, camcorders, and DVD and MP3 players in every country in which it does business and often using the same basic marketing approach. Unilever, the European food and household products company, has pursued a multidomestic strategy. Thus, to appeal to German customers, for example, Unilever's German division sells a different range of food products and uses a different marketing approach than its North American division.

multidomestic strategy Customizing products and marketing strategies to specific national conditions.

Both global and multidomestic strategies have advantages and disadvantages. The major advantage of a global strategy is the significant cost savings associated with not having to customize products and marketing approaches to different national conditions. For example, Rolex watches, Ralph Lauren or Tommy Hilfiger clothing, Chanel or Armani clothing or accessories or perfume, Microsoft tablets, Chinese-made plastic toys, and U.S.-grown rice and wheat are all products that can be sold using the same marketing across many countries by simply changing the language. Thus, companies can save a significant amount of money. Organizations that serve business customers often adopt a global strategy because customer needs such as improving quality and lowering costs are consistent from place to place. For an example of such a company, see the "Managing Globally" feature.

Managing Globally

Early U.S. Wins Help FourKites Fly Overseas

The founders of FourKites met in engineering school in Chennai, India, and then embarked on careers with U.S.-based companies.[62] Arun Chandrasekaran worked for Cognizant, Microsoft, and Groupon. Mathew Elenjickal continued his studies in engineering and management at Northwestern University before taking jobs at Oracle and i2 Technologies/JDA. The two friends encountered a widespread business problem: When will deliveries arrive? Having kept in touch, they decided to form a company that would provide reliable answers.

FourKites gathers data from trucks' onboard computers, along with weather and traffic updates, to recalculate each truck's expected arrival time at a given location.[63] Even without FourKites, an individual driver can use a smartphone app or global positioning system (GPS) to get an arrival estimate. But big companies await deliveries from thousands of trucks run by independent contractors using different devices. FourKites combines data from all those sources and provides updates for any truck in the fleet. Further, the analytical software identifies information changes that will affect arrival time, so the system sends only relevant notifications. For example, a storm or traffic jam likely to delay delivery would trigger an alert. Since launching, FourKites has added tracking of ships and trains, as well as tracking of temperature in refrigerated trucks, which is essential for transporting perishable foods.

FourKites delivers alerts in real time, as problems arise. When customers recognize problems right away, they often can make corrections. FourKites's customers

FourKites provides real-time tracking data for the transportation industry that helps clients improve on-time deliveries. Aleksandr Medvedkov/123RF

report measurable improvements in the percentage of on-time deliveries. For example, Smithfield Foods says on-time deliveries rose from 87% to 94%, and Kraft Heinz improved on-time deliveries from around 50% to better than 75%.[64]

On-time deliveries translate into efficient operations and satisfied customers. The salespeople at FourKites say business clients are eager to discuss this solution to a vexing problem.[65] Those who signed a deal include Best Buy, Kraft Heinz, Nokia, AB InBev, Cargill, and Unilever.[66] They report less time wasted waiting for deliveries at warehouses and declines in stock shortages.

FourKites started with two headquarters, in Chicago and Chennai. The Chennai office focuses on developing new software, while the Chicago office started by building sales in the United States, later signing up a trucking firm that also operates in Mexico. As FourKites grows, it has raised $35 million for global expansion and recently began operations in the United Kingdom.[67] ●

The major disadvantage of pursuing a global strategy is that by ignoring national differences, managers may leave themselves vulnerable to local competitors that differentiate their products to suit local tastes. Global food makers Kellogg's and Nestlé learned this when they entered the Indian processed food market, which is worth more than $100 billion a year. These companies did not understand how to customize their products to the tastes of the Indian market and initially suffered large losses. When Kellogg's launched its breakfast cereals in India, for example, it failed to understand that most Indians eat cooked breakfasts because milk is normally not pasteurized. Today, with the growing availability of pasteurized or canned milk, Kellogg's offers exotic cereals made from basmati rice and flavored with mango to appeal to customers. Similarly, Nestlé's Maggi noodles failed to please Indian customers until it gave them a "marsala" or mixed curry spice flavor; today its noodles have become a staple in Indian diets.[68]

The advantages and disadvantages of a multidomestic strategy are the opposite of those of a global strategy. The major advantage of a multidomestic strategy is that by customizing product offerings and marketing approaches to local conditions, managers may be able to gain market share or charge higher prices for their products. The major disadvantage is that customization raises production costs and puts the multidomestic company at a price disadvantage because it often has to charge prices higher than the prices charged by competitors pursuing a global strategy. Obviously the choice between these two strategies calls for trade-offs.

CHOOSING A WAY TO EXPAND INTERNATIONALLY As we have discussed, a more competitive global environment has proved to be both an opportunity and a threat for organizations and managers. The opportunity is that organizations that expand globally can open new markets, reach more customers, and gain access to new sources of raw materials and to low-cost suppliers of inputs. The threat is that organizations that expand globally are likely to encounter new competitors in the foreign countries they enter and must respond to new political, economic, and cultural conditions.

Before setting up foreign operations, managers of companies such as Amazon, Lands' End, P&G, and Boeing needed to analyze the forces in the environment of a particular country (such as Korea or Brazil) to choose the right method to expand and respond to those forces in the most appropriate way. In general, four basic ways to operate in the global environment are importing and exporting, licensing and franchising, strategic alliances, and wholly owned foreign subsidiaries. We briefly discuss each one, moving from the lowest level of foreign involvement and investment required of a global organization and its managers, and the least amount of risk, to the high end of the spectrum (see Figure 6.7).

Importing and Exporting   The least complex global operations are exporting and importing. A company engaged in exporting makes products at home and sells them abroad. An organization might sell its own products abroad or allow a local organization in the foreign country to distribute its products. Few risks are associated with exporting, because a company does not have to invest in developing manufacturing facilities abroad. It can further reduce its investment abroad if it allows a local company to distribute its products.

A company engaged in importing sells products at home that are made abroad (products it makes itself or buys from other companies). For example, most of the products that Pier 1 Imports and Marshalls sell to their customers are made abroad. In many cases the appeal of a product—Irish crystal, French wine, Italian furniture, or Indian silk—is that it is made abroad. The Internet has made it much easier for companies to tell potential foreign buyers about their products; detailed product specifications and features are available online 24/7, and informed buyers can communicate easily with prospective sellers.

Licensing and Franchising   In licensing, a company (the licenser) allows a foreign organization (the licensee) to take charge of both manufacturing and distributing one or more of its products in the licensee's country or world region in return for a negotiated fee. Chemical maker DuPont, for example, might license a local factory in India to produce nylon or Teflon. The advantage of licensing is that the licenser does not have to bear the development costs associated with opening up in a foreign country; the licensee bears the costs. The risks associated with this strategy are that the company granting the license has to give its foreign partner access to its technological know-how and so risks losing control of its secrets.

Whereas licensing is pursued primarily by manufacturing companies, franchising is pursued primarily by service organizations. In franchising, a company

exporting Making products at home and selling them abroad.

importing Selling products at home that are made abroad.

licensing Allowing a foreign organization to take charge of manufacturing and distributing a product in its country or world region in return for a negotiated fee.

Figure 6.7

Four Ways to Expand Internationally

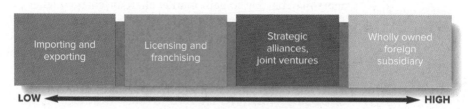

Level of foreign involvement and investment and degree of risk

franchising Selling to a foreign organization the rights to use a brand name and operating know-how in return for a lump-sum payment and a share of the profits.

(the franchiser) sells to a foreign organization (the franchisee) the rights to use its brand name and operating know-how in return for a lump-sum payment and share of the franchiser's profits. Hilton Hotels might sell a franchise to a local company in Chile to operate hotels under the Hilton name in return for a franchise payment. The advantage of franchising is that the franchiser does not have to bear the development costs of overseas expansion and avoids the many problems associated with setting up foreign operations. The downside is that the organization that grants the franchise may lose control over how the franchisee operates, and product quality may fall. In this way franchisers, such as Hilton, Avis, and McDonald's, risk losing their good names. American customers who buy McDonald's hamburgers in Korea may reasonably expect those burgers to be as good as the ones they get at home. If they are not, McDonald's reputation will suffer over time. Once again, the Internet facilitates communication between partners and allows them to better meet each other's expectations.

Strategic Alliances & Joint Ventures One way to overcome the loss-of-control problems associated with exporting, licensing, and franchising is to expand globally by means of a strategic alliance. In a strategic alliance, managers pool or share their organization's resources and know-how with those of a foreign company, and the two organizations share the rewards or risks of starting a new venture in a foreign country. Sharing resources allows a U.S. company, for example, to take advantage of the high-quality skills of foreign manufacturers and the specialized knowledge of foreign managers about the needs of local customers and to reduce the risks involved in a venture. At the same time, the terms of the alliance give the U.S. company more control over how the good or service is produced or sold in the foreign country than it would have as a franchiser or licenser.

strategic alliance An agreement in which managers pool or share their organization's resources and know-how with a foreign company, and the two organizations share the rewards and risks of starting a new venture.

A strategic alliance can take the form of a written contract between two or more companies to exchange resources, or it can result in the creation of a new organization. A joint venture is a strategic alliance among two or more companies that agree to jointly establish and share the ownership of a new business.[69] An organization's level of involvement abroad increases in a joint venture because the alliance normally involves a capital investment in production facilities abroad in order to produce goods or services outside the home country. Risk, however, is reduced. The Internet and global teleconferencing provide the increased communication and coordination necessary for global partners to work together. For example, General Mills participates in two international joint ventures. Cereal Partners Worldwide (CPW) is a 50–50 joint venture between General Mills and Nestlé, which markets breakfast cereals in more than 130 countries. CPW combines the expertise of General Mills—the second-largest cereal manufacturer in North America—with the worldwide presence and distribution strength of global giant Nestlé. General Mills's other joint venture is Häagen-Dazs Japan—a partnership that operates an ice cream business in Japan, marketing premium ice cream to consumers at retail outlets and through a network of Häagen-Dazs shops. In 2018, these two joint ventures accounted for $1.1 billion of revenue for General Mills.[70]

joint venture A strategic alliance among two or more companies that agree to jointly establish and share the ownership of a new business.

wholly owned foreign subsidiary Production operations established in a foreign country independent of any local direct involvement.

Wholly Owned Foreign Subsidiaries When managers decide to establish a wholly owned foreign subsidiary, they invest in establishing production operations in a foreign country independent of any local direct involvement. Many Japanese car component companies, for example, have established their own operations in the United States to supply U.S.-based Japanese carmakers such as Toyota and Honda with high-quality car components.

Operating alone, without any direct involvement from foreign companies, an organization receives all of the rewards and bears all of the risks associated with operating abroad.[71] This method of international expansion is much more expensive than the others because it requires a higher level of foreign investment and presents managers with many more threats. However, investment in a foreign subsidiary or division offers significant advantages: It gives an organization high potential returns because the organization does not have to share its profits with a foreign organization, and it reduces the level of risk because the organization's managers have full control over all aspects of their foreign subsidiary's operations. Moreover, this type of investment allows managers to protect their technology and know-how from foreign organizations. Large well-known companies such as DuPont, GM, and P&G, which have plenty of resources, make extensive use of wholly owned subsidiaries.

Planning and Implementing Strategy

After identifying appropriate business and corporate strategies to attain an organization's mission and goals, managers confront the challenge of putting those strategies into action. Strategy implementation is a five-step process:

1. Allocating responsibility for implementation to the appropriate individuals or groups.
2. Drafting detailed action plans that specify how a strategy is to be implemented.
3. Establishing a timetable for implementation that includes precise, measurable goals linked to the attainment of the action plan.
4. Allocating appropriate resources to the responsible individuals or groups.
5. Holding specific individuals or groups responsible for the attainment of corporate, divisional, and functional goals.

LO 6-4
Describe the vital role managers play in implementing strategies to achieve an organization's mission and goals.

The planning process goes beyond just identifying effective strategies; it also includes plans to ensure that these strategies are put into action. Normally the plan for implementing a new strategy requires the development of new functional strategies, the redesign of an organization's structure, and the development of new control systems; it might also require a new program to change an organization's culture. These are issues we address in the next three chapters.

Summary and Review

PLANNING Planning is a three-step process: (1) determining an organization's mission and goals; (2) formulating strategy; and (3) implementing strategy. Managers use planning to identify and select appropriate goals and courses of action for an organization and to decide how to allocate the resources they need to attain those goals and carry out those actions. A good plan builds commitment for the organization's goals, gives the organization a sense of direction and purpose, coordinates the different functions and divisions of the organization, and controls managers by making them accountable for specific goals. In large organizations planning takes place at three levels: corporate, business or divisional, and functional or departmental. Long-term plans have a time horizon of five years or more; intermediate-term plans, between one and five years; and short-term plans, one year or less. **[LO 6-1]**

DETERMINING MISSION AND GOALS AND FORMULATING STRATEGY
Determining the organization's mission requires that managers define the business of the organization and establish major goals. Strategy formulation requires that managers

perform a SWOT analysis and then choose appropriate strategies at the corporate, business, and functional levels. At the business level, managers are responsible for developing a successful low-cost and/or differentiation strategy, either for the whole market or a particular segment of it. At the functional level, departmental managers develop strategies to help the organization either add value to its products by differentiating them or lower the costs of value creation. At the corporate level, organizations use strategies such as concentration on a single industry, vertical integration, related and unrelated diversification, and international expansion to strengthen their competitive advantage by increasing the value of the goods and services provided to customers. [LO 6-1, 6-2, 6-3]

IMPLEMENTING STRATEGY Strategy implementation requires that managers allocate responsibilities to appropriate individuals or groups; draft detailed action plans that specify how a strategy is to be implemented; establish a timetable for implementation that includes precise, measurable goals linked to the attainment of the action plan; allocate appropriate resources to the responsible individuals or groups; and hold individuals or groups accountable for the attainment of goals. [LO 6-4]

Management *in Action*

Topics for Discussion and Action

Discussion

1. Describe the three steps of planning. Explain how they are related. [LO 6-1]

2. What is the relationship among corporate-, business-, and functional-level strategies, and how do they create value for an organization? [LO 6-2, 6-3]

3. Pick an industry and identify four companies in the industry that pursue one of the four main business-level strategies (low-cost, focused low-cost, etc.). [LO 6-1, 6-2]

4. What is the difference between vertical integration and related diversification? [LO 6-3]

5. Describe the five-step process managers can use to implement organizational strategies. [LO 6-4]

Action

6. Ask a manager about the kinds of planning exercises he or she regularly uses. What are the purposes of these exercises, and what are their advantages or disadvantages? [LO 6-1]

7. Ask a manager to identify the corporate- and business-level strategies used by his or her organization. [LO 6-2, 6-3]

Building Management Skills

How to Analyze a Company's Strategy [LO 6-2, 6-3]

Pick a well-known business organization that has received recent media coverage and that provides its annual reports on its website. From the information in the media and annual reports, answer the following questions:

1. What is (are) the main industry(ies) in which the company competes?

2. What business-level strategy does the company seem to be pursuing in this industry? Why?

3. What corporate-level strategies is the company pursuing? Why?

4. Have there been any major changes in its strategy recently? Why?

Managing Ethically [LO 6-1, 6-4]

A few years ago, IBM announced that it had fired the three top managers of its Argentine division because of their involvement in a scheme to secure a $250 million contract for IBM to provide and service the computers of one of Argentina's largest state-owned banks. The three executives paid $14 million of the contract money to a third company, CCR, which paid nearly $6 million to phantom companies. This $6 million was then used to bribe the bank executives who agreed to give IBM the contract.

These bribes are not necessarily illegal under Argentine law. Moreover, the three managers argued that all companies have to pay bribes to get new business contracts and they were not doing anything that managers in other companies were not.

Questions

1. Either by yourself or in a group, decide if the business practice of paying bribes is ethical or unethical.
2. Should IBM allow its foreign divisions to pay bribes if all other companies are doing so?
3. If bribery is common in a particular country, what effect would this likely have on the nation's economy and culture?

Small Group Breakout Exercise [LO 6-1, 6-2]

Low Cost or Differentiation?

Form groups of three or four people, and appoint one member as the spokesperson who will communicate your findings to the class when called on by the instructor. Then discuss the following scenario:

You are a team of managers of a major national clothing chain, and you have been charged with finding a way to restore your organization's competitive advantage. Recently, your organization has been experiencing increasing competition from two sources. First, discount stores such as Walmart and Target have been undercutting your prices because they buy their clothes from low-cost foreign manufacturers while you buy most of yours from high-quality domestic suppliers.

Discount stores have been attracting your customers who buy at the low end of the price range. Second, online retailers provide trendy, high-price designer clothing and are attracting your customers at the high end of the market. Your company has become stuck in the middle, and you have to decide what to do: Should you start to buy abroad so that you can lower your prices and begin to pursue a low-cost strategy? Should you focus on the high end of the market and become more of a differentiator?

Or should you try to pursue both a low-cost strategy and a differentiation strategy?

1. Using SWOT analysis, analyze the pros and cons of each alternative.
2. Think about the various clothing retailers in your local area and the ones you shop regularly online. Analyze the choices they have made about how to compete with one another along the low-cost and differentiation dimensions.

Be the Manager [LO 6-1, 6-2]

A group of investors in your city are considering opening a new upscale supermarket to compete with the major supermarket chains currently dominating the city's marketplace. They have called you in to help them determine what kind of upscale supermarket they should open. In other words, how can they best develop a competitive advantage against existing supermarket chains?

Questions

1. List the supermarket chains in your city, and identify their strengths and weaknesses.

2. What business-level strategies are these supermarkets currently pursuing?

3. What kind of supermarket would do best against the competition? What kind of business-level strategy should it pursue?

Case in the News [LO 6-1, 6-2, 6-3, 6-4]

Best Buy Strategies Evolve with the Times

Best Buy operates more than 1,000 electronics stores and employs around 125,000 people. That the electronics retailer continues to exist at all at the time of this writing is a testimony to management's ability to reinvent the company for changing times. Best Buy launched when its founders accepted that their regional music store could not compete in the 1980s against the hot retail trend of "big-box" stores offering choice and convenience at low prices. Best Buy outperformed its preexisting competitor, Circuit City, in selecting locations and keeping pace with technology through the 1990s. As computer technology became more popular and complex, Best Buy began offering services through its Geek Squad, a start-up company that Best Buy acquired in 2002. When the Great Recession hit several years later, Circuit City went out of business, but Best Buy survived through aggressive cost cutting, including the closing of operations in Europe and China and downsizing at its U.S. corporate headquarters. It lived to face the new challenge: online retailing.

During the past decade, as Best Buy evaluated its opportunities and threats, it benefited from the loss of some key retail competition—not only Circuit City but also cutbacks at Sears and other department stores selling electronics. Meanwhile, Amazon transformed from a bookseller with a line of CDs into a major low-priced threat to almost every retailer. In 2010, Amazon introduced an app for comparing prices across retailers, and Best Buy suddenly found that it was losing comparisons despite its low-price strategy. On top of that, Amazon offered the convenience of shopping anywhere and anytime.

In the face of this major threat, Best Buy needed more than low prices. It invested in better distribution and inventory management to keep up with Amazon's superior customer fulfillment. Best Buy improved employee benefits and training, to provide better customer service in stores despite the stiff competition for talent in the labor market. Best Buy also wanted to give consumers something that Amazon didn't offer. An online retailer can offer low prices and fast delivery, but the human touch from an online company is rare. Best Buy's executives saw an opportunity to deliver that human touch.

Management opted for a differentiation strategy. Best Buy would offer more services; building on its experience with the Geek Squad, it began offering a service called In-Home Advisor. Best Buy had convinced consumers that calling Geek Squad was like having their own tech support team. In-Home Advisor added an experience like having a technology consultant to advise them in using electronics to improve their lifestyle. The service includes free home visits lasting 60 to 90 minutes. Best Buy is betting that building long-term relationships with households will be profitable in the long run.

Best Buy trains its advisers to fill the role of consultant by putting consumers at ease and quietly appraising what technologies are in use and what potential there is for modernizing. Rather than pitching ideas, consultants learn to ask about preferences and needs. In addition, the company pays advisers a salary, removing the pressure to close sales in order to earn commissions.

Best Buy also seeks distinctive products to sell. It was a leader in opening boutique-style store departments for Apple, Samsung, and Microsoft; those brands pay rent and use their own salespeople or train Best Buy associates. This way, Best Buy can improve customer service while increasing revenues. Another move was to form a joint venture with Amazon. The two rivals agreed to sell a line of smart televisions equipped with Amazon Fire TV and Alexa voice assistant, available only from Best Buy and Amazon. Best Buy also sells

213

service packages, including the Total Support Tech program, which costs $199 for a year of tech support from the Geek Squad for any electronics product purchased from any retailer. For elderly customers concerned about their health and safety, a program called Assured Living equips them with remote monitoring and communication.

Recent sales results suggest that Best Buy's strategy was smart, at least for the latest changes in retailing. Sales have risen significantly. Best Buy's chief executive, Hubert Joly, sees plenty of growth potential as he prepares to retire and turn over CEO duties to Corie Barry, a long-time company executive and one of the few women leading a Fortune 500 company. Joly notes that Best Buy customers typically direct only one-fourth of their spending on electronics to Best Buy, leaving the remainder as a potential source of growth from existing customers. Further, Best Buy and Amazon together hold about one-fourth of the U.S. consumer electronics market. The other three-fourths is a potential source of growth. Joly wants Best Buy to win more of those sales by continuing to differentiate itself from the competition.

Questions for Discussion

1. Review the details in this case and identify an example of (a) a corporate-level plan or strategy and (b) a functional-level plan or strategy.

2. Which of the changes in Best Buy's strategy do you see as being related to its rivalry with Amazon? Explain.

3. Best Buy has opted for a strategy of differentiation from online retailers. How do you expect the opportunities and threats associated with this strategy might change over the next few years?

Sources: N. Meyersohn, "How Best Buy's Outgoing CEO, Hubert Joly, Rescued the Company," *CNN Business*, www.cnn.com, April 16, 2019; E. Minaya and L. Cook, "These Old-Line Retailers Are among the Top-Managed Companies," *The Wall Street Journal*, www.wsj.com, November 30, 2018; T. Shumsky and M. Sun, "What Retail CFOs Are Watching as Holiday Shopping Season Kicks Off," *The Wall Street Journal*, https://blogs.wsj.com, November 23, 2018; S. Berfield and M. Boyle, "Best Buy Is Back!," *Bloomberg Businessweek*, July 23, 2018, 44–49; A. Wolf, "Get Him to the Geek," *TWICE*, June 4, 2018, 8; P. Wahba, "Best Buy Is Showing How Retailers Can Keep Amazon at Bay," *Fortune*, http://fortune.com, May 24, 2018.

Endnotes

1. Marriott International, "Marriott International Reports Third Quarter 2018 Results," news release, http://news.marriott.com November 5, 2018; K. Ryssdal and R. Garrova, "How the World's Largest Hotel Company Adapts to a Changing Economy," *Marketplace*, www.marketplace.org, October 4, 2017; S. Tully, "Marriott Goes All In," *Fortune*, June 15, 2017, 200–208.

2. Tully, "Marriott Goes All In."

3. Ryssdal and Garrova, "How the World's Largest Hotel Company Adapts."

4. J. T. Fox, "At Davos, U.S. Hospitality Industry Responds to International Visitor Downturn," *Hotel Management*, www.hotelmanagement.net, January 26, 2018; L. Gallagher, "Marriott's Latest New York Hotel Is for the Airbnb Generation," *Fortune*, http://fortune.com, November 11, 2017.

5. Ryssdal and Garrova, "How the World's Largest Hotel Company Adapts."

6. D. E. Sanger, N. Periroth, G. Thrush, and A. Rappeport, "Marriott Data Breach Is Traced to Chinese Hackers as U.S. Readies Crackdown on Beijing," *The New York Times*, www.nytimes.com, December 11, 2018.

7. Gallagher, "Marriott's Latest New York Hotel."

8. Tully, "Marriott Goes All In"; Fox, "At Davos, U.S. Hospitality Industry Responds."

9. A. Chandler, *Strategy and Structure: Chapters in the History of the American Enterprise* (Cambridge, MA: MIT Press, 1962).

10. Ibid.

11. H. Fayol, *General and Industrial Management* (1884; New York: IEEE Press, 1984).

12. Fayol, *General and Industrial Management*, 18.

13. K. Kuehner-Hebert, "General Mills CEO Succeeds with Adaptability, Efficiency," *Chief Executive*, https://chiefexecutive.net, accessed January 3, 2019.

14. *General Mills 2018 Annual Report*, https://investors.generalmills.com; "Businesses," www.generalmills.com, accessed January 3, 2019; "General Mills Announces New Organizational Structure to Maximize Global Scale," www.prnewswire.com, December 5, 2016.

15. J. Semple, "General Mills Completes Blue Buffalo Acquisition," *Food Business News*, www.foodbusinessnews.net, April 24, 2018.

16. L. Chevreux, J. Lopez, and X. Mesnard, "The Best Companies Know How to Balance Strategy and Purpose," *Harvard Business Review*, https://hbr.org, accessed January 3, 2019.

17. M. E. Shoup, "General Mills Optimistic on Yogurt Business as It Eyes More Markets," *Dairy Reporter*, www.dairyreporter.com, February 22, 2018.

18. *General Mills 2018 Annual Report*.

19. J. Bennett, "NASA's Next Great Mars Rover Will Search for Martians and Prepare for Humans to Follow," *Popular Mechanics*, www.popularmechanics.com, January 17, 2018.

20. K. Ryssdal and B. Bodnar, "CEO Deborah Flint Is at the Helm of LAX and Its Multibillion Dollar Makeover," *Marketplace,* www.marketplace.org, June 9, 2017; "Ale Flint Confirmed as New Head of Los Angeles Airports Authority," KPCC, www.scpr.org, June 23, 2015.

21. Ryssdal and Bodnar, "CEO Deborah Flint Is at the Helm."

22. J. Bates, "LA Story," *Airport World,* www.airport-world.com, May 11, 2017; "Here's a Look into LAX's $14 Billion Facelift," *CBS Los Angeles,* http://losangeles.cbslocal.com, November 15, 2017; J. Bates, "Airport Carbon Accreditation Success for LAX and Van Nuys," *Airport World,* www.airport-world.com, September 19, 2017.

23. Bates, "LA Story"; D. Symonds, "LAX Board Authorizes Contract for LAMP Infrastructure," *Passenger Terminal Today,* www.passengerterminaltoday.com, January 25, 2018.

24. S. M. Hoffman, "New $516.7 Million Terminal 1 at LAX Is Steeped in LA Imagery, Food and Retail," *Daily Breeze,* www.dailybreeze.com, November 30, 2018.

25. Ryssdal and Bodnar, "CEO Deborah Flint Is at the Helm."

26. J. A. Pearce, "The Company Mission as a Strategic Tool," *Sloan Management Review,* Spring 1992, 15–24.

27. D. F. Abell, *Defining the Business: The Starting Point of Strategic Planning* (Englewood Cliffs, NJ: Prentice-Hall, 1980).

28. G. Hamel and C. K. Prahalad, "Strategic Intent," *Harvard Business Review,* May–June 1989, 63–73.

29. J. Coleman, "The Best Strategic Leaders Balance Agility and Consistency," *Harvard Business Review,* https://hbr.org, January 4, 2017.

30. E. A. Locke, G. P. Latham, and M. Erez, "The Determinants of Goal Commitment," *Academy of Management Review* 13 (1988), 23–39.

31. "General Mills 2018 Global Responsibility Report," https://globalresponsibility.generalmills.com, accessed January 3, 2019.

32. S. Kumar, J. Eiden, and D. N. Perdomo, "Clash of the e-Commerce Titans: A New Paradigm for Consumer Purchase Process Improvement," *International Journal of Productivity and Performance Management* 61, no. 7 (2012), 805–30.

33. K. Clark, "Walmart Continues M&A Spree with Acquisition of Lingerie Retailer Bare Necessities," *TechCrunch,* https://techcrunch.com, accessed January 3, 2019; G. Petro, "Amazon's Acquisition of Whole Foods Is about Two Things: Data and Product," *Forbes,* www.forbes.com, accessed January 3, 2019.

34. Mike Farrell, "Customer Service Makeover Yields Results," *Multichannel News,* September 18–25, 2017, 12–15; Mike Farrell, "Comcast Names Herrin SVP Customer Experience," *Multichannel News,* www.multichannel.com, September 26, 2014.

35. Dan Gingiss, "How Comcast Customer Service Agents Are Following Issues All the Way to Resolution," *Forbes,* www.forbes.com, January 11, 2018.

36. D. Sills, "How Charlie Herrin Is Transforming Customer Experience at Comcast," *Brand Channel,* www.brandchannel.com, April 10, 2018; Jeanne Bliss, "Comcast Customer Experience Improvement Plan, with Charlie Herrin," *The Chief Customer Officer Human Duct Tape Show,* episode 73, www.customerbliss.com, October 17, 2017.

37. Bob Fernandez, "Comcast Customer Gripes about Internet Surpass Those for Cable TV," *Philadelphia Inquirer,* www.philly.com, August 3, 2017; Mike Rogoway, "Comcast Says Customer Service Overhaul Is Showing Results," *Oregonian,* www.oregonlive.com, April 23, 2017.

38. Bliss, "Comcast Customer Experience Improvement Plan."

39. Jeff Baumgartner, "Comcast Folds Customer Experience, Service Teams into Technology and Products Division," *Multichannel News,* www.multichannel.com, May 4, 2017.

40. M. Segarra, "Toys R Us and Why the Retail Downturn Is All about Debt," *Marketplace,* www.marketplace.org, March 14, 2018.

41. D. Green, "Toys R Us Is Closing or Selling All of Its US Stores—Here's Why the Company Couldn't Be Saved," *Business Insider,* www.businessinsider.com, March 15, 2018.

42. Associated Press, "Toys 'R' Us Plans a United States Comeback," *The New York Times,* www.nytimes.com, February 11, 2019.

43. R. D. Aveni, *Hypercompetition* (New York: Free Press, 1994).

44. M. E. Porter, *Competitive Strategy* (New York: Free Press, 1980).

45. "About Southwest," www.southwest.com, accessed January 3, 2019.

46. S. Grobart, "Tim Cook: The Complete Interview," *Bloomberg Businessweek,* www.bloomberg.com, accessed January 3, 2019; A. Stevenson, "Tim Cook: The Most Important Thing for Apple Long Term," *CNBC,* www.cnbc.com, May 2, 2016.

47. Porter, *Competitive Strategy.*

48. S. Chaudhuri and P. Kowsmann, "Zara Owner Inditex Stays Ahead of the Competition," *The Wall Street Journal,* www.wsj.com, accessed January 3, 2019.

49. P. Kowsmann, "Fast Fashion: How a Zara Coat Went from Design to Fifth Avenue in 25 Days," *The Wall Street Journal,* www.wsj.com, accessed January 3, 2019.

50. M. K. Perry, "Vertical Integration: Determinants and Effects," in R. Schmalensee and R. D. Willig, *Handbook of Industrial Organization,* vol. 1 (New York: Elsevier Science, 1989).

51. F. Lambert, "Tesla's Gigafactory 1 Battery Cells Have a 20% Cost Advantage over LG, New Report Says," *Electrek,* https://electrek.co, November 20, 2018; M. Holland, "Tesla Is 2 Years Ahead of Schedule on Gigafactory 1," *Clean Technica,* https://cleantechnica.com, October 1, 2018.

52. Zacks Equity Research, "P&G Completes Duracell Battery Sale to Buffett's Berkshire," *Nasdaq,* www.nasdaq.com, March 1, 2016.

53. E. Penrose, *The Theory of the Growth of the Firm* (Oxford: Oxford University Press, 1959).

54. M. E. Porter, "From Competitive Advantage to Corporate Strategy," *Harvard Business Review* 65 (1987), 43–59.

55. D. J. Teece, "Economies of Scope and the Scope of the Enterprise," *Journal of Economic Behavior and Organization* 3 (1980), 223–47.

56. M. E. Porter, *Competitive Advantage: Creating and Sustaining Superior Performance* (New York: Free Press, 1985).

57. 3M, "2017 Annual Report," https://investors.3m.com, accessed January 3, 2019.

58. D. Schiff, "How 3M Drives Innovation through Empathy and Collaboration," *Forbes*, www.forbes.com, accessed January 3, 2019.

59. For a review of the evidence, see C. W. L. Hill and G. R. Jones, *Strategic Management: An Integrated Approach*, 5th ed. (Boston: Houghton Mifflin, 2011), chap. 10.

60. "Global Corporate Divestment Study 2018," https://divest.ey.com, accessed January 3, 2019.

61. M. Egan, "The Dismantling of GE Continues: It Is Selling Yet Another Business," *CNN Business*, www.cnn.com, accessed January 3, 2019.

62. M. Siva, "A View from the Top on Supply Chain Process," *Hindu Business Line*, www.hindubusinessline.com, October 30, 2017.

63. J. Smith, "'Amazon Effect' Sparks Deals for Software-Tracking Firms," *The Wall Street Journal*, www.wsj.com, August 29, 2017; R. Starr, "Is FourKites Tracking Technology a Game Changer for Small Trucking Companies?," *Small Business Trends*, https://smallbiztrends.com, June 21, 2017; C. Loizos, "FourKites Raises $13 Million to Track Trucks on the Road for Customers Like Staples," *TechCrunch*, https://techcrunch.com, October 12, 2016.

64. J. Smith, "Startup FourKites Raises $35 Million to Expand Abroad, Improve Shipping-Time Prediction," *The Wall Street Journal*, www.wsj.com, February 20, 2018.

65. A. Rekdal, "'I've Got to Be Part of This': How This Sales Team Pitches Big Data to an Old-School Industry," *Built in Chicago*, www.builtinchicago.org, March 21, 2017; Loizos, "FourKites Raises $13 Million."

66. "Success Stories," www.fourkites.com, accessed January 3, 2019.

67. Smith, "Startup FourKites Raises $35 Million"; "FourKites Expands Global Presence into Europe," www.fourkites.com, accessed January 3, 2019.

68. E. Fry, "Is Nestlé's Maggi Noodle Crisis in India Finally Over?," *Fortune*, http://fortune.com, April 26, 2016.

69. B. Kogut, "Joint Ventures: Theoretical and Empirical Perspectives," *Strategic Management Journal* 9 (1988), 319–33.

70. *General Mills 2018 Annual Report.*

71. N. Hood and S. Young, *The Economics of the Multinational Enterprise* (London: Longman, 1979).

Designing Organizational Structure

Learning Objectives

After studying this chapter, you should be able to:

LO 7-1 Identify the factors that influence managers' choice of an organizational structure.

LO 7-2 Explain how managers group tasks into jobs that are motivating and satisfying for employees.

LO 7-3 Describe the types of organizational structures managers can design, and explain why they choose one structure over another.

LO 7-4 Explain why managers must coordinate jobs, functions, and divisions using the hierarchy of authority and integrating mechanisms.

LO 7-5 Describe how technology continues to help managers build strategic alliances and network structures to increase organizational efficiency and effectiveness.

Management Snapshot

Alaska Air Structures Work with Passengers in Mind

How Can an Effective Organizational Structure Increase Productivity?

Compared with other airlines, Alaska Airlines gives employees wide latitude to handle customer service. This approach goes back to the Seattle-based airline's roots as a small organization serving customers in the northwestern United States. With the slogan "Whatever it takes," employees were encouraged to maintain a friendly, informal environment and commitment to keeping passengers happy. Customer loyalty was supposed to result.[1]

This empowerment of customer-facing employees (pilots, cabin crew members, gate agents, mechanics, call center employees, and so on) let them go to extraordinary lengths, even delaying a departure or refunding a ticket. The practice served Alaska Air well for years—most notably, following a plane crash into the Pacific in 2000. Hundreds of employees dedicated themselves to arranging care for victims' family members. However, that incident also shifted strategy, elevating safety over service.[2]

Employee empowerment came into question following the terrorist attacks of September 11, 2001. First, planes were grounded; then passengers began avoiding air travel. Like other airlines, Alaska Air saw profits evaporate. Management concluded that spending cuts were essential—and presumably meant that employees could no longer be allowed to do "whatever it takes" to make passengers happy. Managers crafted detailed rules and policies for handling various situations. Costs did fall, and profits rose, but on measures of customer service, Alaska Air began to slip. Employees felt confused and frustrated, no longer sure of what was important. Alaska Air found a middle ground, defining four standards—safety, caring, delivery, and presentation, in that order of priority—and guidelines for what each would look like. The company trained employees in the four standards and trained managers in leading employees who have autonomy to make decisions and to learn from what does and does not work.[3]

This combination of broad guidance and freedom to make decisions has delivered results. Alaska Air has earned the J.D. Power award to the airline delivering the best customer satisfaction, and over the past few years, it has been rated the top or number-two U.S. airline on the *Wall Street Journal*'s performance scorecard. At the same time, it has excelled at efficiency measures such as fuel consumption. Fuel efficiency is a constant concern: When the cost of fuel spikes, as it did in 2017 and 2018, profits dive. The average airfare generates just $18 in profits for a U.S. air carrier, and a rise in fuel prices can erase it all. By this measure, Alaska Air is a high performer; in 2017, it reported average profits of $23 per passenger, through careful pricing and route selection.[4]

Management at Alaska Airlines regularly evaluates the company's organizational structure in an effort to increase productivity and customer satisfaction. John Gress Media Inc/Shutterstock

Under CEO Brad Tilden, with more than 25 years at the company, Alaska Air continues to make customer service a core value and organizing principle along with profitability. As part of its growth strategy to build a presence throughout the Northwest, Alaska Air acquired Virgin America in 2016. That airline, too, had loyal customers; it also had gates serving key markets such as Los Angeles and San Francisco. Tilden and other executives concluded that the acquisition could add $300 million a year to the bottom line from increased revenues plus the efficiency of combining back-office operations. More recently, management has begun the tough job of coordinating the work done by what were once two headquarters, aiming to improve efficiency. This involves eliminating redundant positions, so it requires layoffs. Alaska Air is focused on reducing management, rather than customer-facing, positions. Other cost cutting will target employees' health care benefits and the hotel expenses of pilots and flight crews. Focusing on these areas should make Alaska Airlines leaner with no impact on travelers' experiences.[5]

Overview

As the opening story suggests, organizational structure and culture are powerful influences on how employees work. The way an organization's structure is designed also affects employee behavior and how well the organization functions. In a quickly changing global environment, managers at all levels of an organization must identify the best way to organize people and resources to increase efficiency and effectiveness.

By the end of this chapter, you will be familiar with the main types of organizational structure as well as with the important factors that determine how managers design such structures. Then, in Chapter 8, we examine issues related to the design of an organization's control systems.

Designing Organizational Structure

Organizing is the process by which managers establish the structure of working relationships among employees to allow them to achieve organizational goals efficiently and effectively. Organizational structure is the formal system of task and job reporting relationships that determines how employees use resources to achieve organizational goals.[6] Organizational design is the process by which managers create a specific type of organizational structure and culture so a company can operate in the most efficient and effective way.[7]

According to *contingency theory,* managers design organizational structures to fit the factors or circumstances that are affecting the company the most and causing them the most uncertainty.[8] Thus, there is no one best way to design an organization: Design reflects each organization's specific situation, and researchers have argued that in some situations stable, mechanistic structures may be most appropriate while in others flexible, organic structures might be the most effective. Four factors are important determinants of the type of organizational structure or organizing method managers select: the nature of the organizational environment, the type of strategy the organization pursues, the technology (and particularly *information technology*) the organization uses, and the characteristics of the organization's human resources (see Figure 7.1).[9]

LO 7-1
Identify the factors that influence managers' choice of an organizational structure.

organizational structure A formal system of task and reporting relationships that coordinates and motivates organizational members so that they work together to achieve organizational goals.

The Organizational Environment

In general, the more quickly the external environment is changing and the greater the uncertainty within it, the greater are the problems facing managers in trying to

Figure 7.1

Factors Affecting
Organizational
Structure

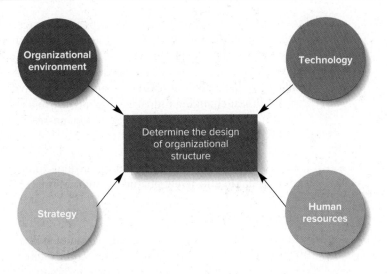

**organizational
design** The
process by which
managers make
specific organizing
choices that result
in a particular kind
of organizational
structure.

gain access to scarce resources. In this situation, to speed decision making and communication and make it easier to obtain resources, managers typically make organizing choices that result in more flexible structures and entrepreneurial cultures.[10] They are likely to decentralize authority, empower lower-level employees to make important operating decisions, and encourage values and norms that emphasize change and innovation—a more organic form of organizing.

In contrast, if the external environment is stable, resources are readily available, and uncertainty is low, then less coordination and communication among people and functions are needed to obtain resources. Managers can make organizing choices that bring more stability or formality to the organizational structure and can establish values and norms that emphasize obedience and being a team player. Managers in this situation prefer to make decisions within a clearly defined hierarchy of authority and to use detailed rules, standard operating procedures (SOPs), and restrictive norms to guide and govern employees' activities—a more mechanistic form of organizing.

Change is rapid in today's global marketplace, and increasing competition both at home and abroad is putting greater pressure on managers to attract customers and increase efficiency and effectiveness. Consequently, interest in finding ways to structure organizations—such as through empowerment and self-managed teams—to allow people and departments to behave flexibly has been increasing.

Strategy

Once managers decide on a strategy, they must choose the right means to implement it. Different strategies often call for the use of different organizational structures and cultures. For example, a differentiation strategy aimed at increasing the value customers perceive in an organization's goods and services usually succeeds best in a flexible structure with a culture that values innovation; flexibility facilitates a differentiation strategy because managers can develop new or innovative products quickly—an activity that requires extensive cooperation among functions or departments. In contrast, a low-cost strategy that is aimed at driving down costs in all functions usually fares best in a more formal structure with more conservative norms, which gives managers greater control over the activities of an organization's various departments.[11]

In addition, at the corporate level, when managers decide to expand the scope of organizational activities by vertical integration or diversification, for example, they need to design a flexible structure to provide sufficient coordination among the different business divisions.[12] Many companies have been divesting businesses because managers have been unable to create a competitive advantage to keep them up to speed in fast-changing industries. By moving to a more flexible structure, managers gain more control over their different businesses. Finally, expanding internationally and operating in many different countries challenges managers to create organizational structures that allow organizations to be flexible on a global level.[13] As we discuss later, managers can group their departments or divisions in several ways to allow them to effectively pursue an international strategy.

Technology

Recall that technology is the combination of skills, knowledge, machines, and computers that are used to design, make, and distribute goods and services. As a rule, the more complicated the technology an organization uses, the more difficult it is to regulate or control it because more unexpected events can occur. Thus, the more complicated the technology, the greater is the need for a flexible structure and progressive culture to enhance managers' ability to respond to unexpected situations—and give them the freedom and desire to work out new solutions to the problems they encounter. In contrast, the more routine the technology, the more appropriate is a formal structure, because tasks are simple and the steps needed to produce goods and services have been worked out in advance.

What makes a technology routine or complicated? One researcher who investigated this issue, Charles Perrow, argued that two factors determine how complicated or nonroutine technology is: task variety and task analyzability.[14] *Task variety* is the number of new or unexpected problems or situations that a person or function encounters in performing tasks or jobs. *Task analyzability* is the degree to which programmed solutions are available to people or functions to solve the problems they encounter. Nonroutine or complicated technologies are characterized by high task variety and low task analyzability; this means that many varied problems occur and that solving these problems requires significant nonprogrammed decision making. In contrast, routine technologies are characterized by low task variety and high task analyzability; this means that the problems encountered do not vary much and are easily resolved through programmed decision making.

Examples of nonroutine technology are found in the work of scientists in an R&D laboratory who develop new products or discover new drugs, and they are seen in the planning exercises an organization's top management team uses to chart the organization's future strategy. Examples of routine technology include typical mass-production or assembly operations, where workers perform the same task repeatedly and where managers have already identified the programmed solutions necessary to perform a task efficiently. Similarly, in service organizations such as fast-food restaurants, the tasks that crew members perform in making and serving fast food are routine.

Human Resources

A final important factor affecting an organization's choice of structure and culture is the characteristics of the human resources it employs. In general, the more highly skilled its workforce, and the greater the number of employees who work together in groups or teams, the more likely an organization is to use a flexible, decentralized structure and a professional culture based on values and norms that foster employee autonomy and self-control. Highly skilled employees, or employees who have internalized strong professional values and norms of behavior as part of their training, usually desire greater freedom and autonomy and dislike close supervision.

Flexible structures, characterized by decentralized authority and empowered employees, are well suited to the needs of highly skilled people. Similarly, when people work in teams, they must be allowed to interact freely and develop norms to guide their own work interactions, which also is possible in a flexible organizational structure. Thus, when designing organizational structure and culture, managers must pay close attention to the needs of the workforce and to the complexity and kind of work employees perform.

In summary, an organization's external environment, strategy, technology, and human resources are the factors to be considered by managers in seeking to design the best structure and culture for an organization. The greater the level of uncertainty in the organization's environment, the more complex its strategy and technologies, and the more highly qualified and skilled its workforce, the more likely managers are to design a structure and a culture that are flexible, can change quickly, and allow employees to be innovative in their responses to problems, customer needs, and so on. The more stable the organization's environment, the less complex and more well understood its strategy or technology, and the less skilled its workforce, the more likely managers are to design an organizational structure that is formal and controlling and a culture whose values and norms prescribe how employees should act in particular situations.

Later in the chapter we discuss how managers can create different kinds of organizational cultures. First, however, we discuss how managers can design flexible or formal organizational structures. The way an organization's structure works depends on the organizing choices managers make about three issues:

- How to group tasks into individual jobs.
- How to group jobs into functions and divisions.
- How to allocate authority and coordinate or integrate functions and divisions.

Grouping Tasks into Jobs: Job Design

LO 7-2
Explain how managers group tasks into jobs that are motivating and satisfying for employees.

job design The process by which managers decide how to divide tasks into specific jobs.

The first step in organizational design is **job design**, the process by which managers decide how to divide into specific jobs the tasks that have to be performed to provide customers with goods and services. Managers at McDonald's, for example, have decided how best to divide the tasks required to provide customers with fast, cheap food in each McDonald's restaurant. After experimenting with different job arrangements, McDonald's managers decided on a basic division of labor among chefs and food servers. Managers allocated all the tasks involved in actually cooking the food (putting oil in the fat fryers, opening packages of frozen french fries, putting beef patties on the grill, making salads, and so on) to the job of chef. They allocated all the tasks involved in giving the food to customers (such as greeting customers, taking orders, putting fries and burgers into bags, adding salt, pepper, and napkins, and taking money) to food servers. In addition, they created other jobs—the job of dealing with drive-through customers, the job of keeping the restaurant clean, and the job of overseeing employees and responding to unexpected events. The result of the job design process is a *division of labor* among employees, one that McDonald's managers have discovered through experience is most efficient.

Establishing an appropriate division of labor among employees is a critical part of the organizing process, one that is vital to increasing efficiency and effectiveness. At McDonald's, the tasks associated with chef and food server were split into different jobs because managers found that, for the kind of food McDonald's serves, this approach was most efficient. It is efficient because when each employee is given fewer tasks to perform (so that each job becomes more specialized), employees become more productive at performing the tasks that constitute each job.

At Subway sandwich shops, however, managers chose a different kind of job design. At Subway, there is no division of labor among the people who make the sandwiches, wrap the sandwiches, give them to customers, and take the money. The roles of chef and food server are combined into one. This different division of tasks and jobs is efficient for Subway and not for McDonald's because Subway serves a limited menu of mostly submarine-style sandwiches that are prepared to order. Subway's production system is far simpler than McDonald's, because McDonald's menu is much more varied and its chefs must cook many different kinds of foods.

Managers of every organization must analyze the range of tasks to be performed and then create jobs that best allow the organization to give customers the goods and services they want. In deciding how to assign tasks to individual jobs, however, managers must be careful not to take job simplification, the process of reducing the number of tasks that each worker performs, too far.[15] Too much job simplification may reduce efficiency rather than increase it if workers find their simplified jobs boring and monotonous, become demotivated and unhappy, and, as a result, perform at a low level.

job simplification
The process of reducing the number of tasks that each worker performs.

Job Enlargement and Job Enrichment

In an attempt to create a division of labor and design individual jobs to encourage workers to perform at a higher level and be more satisfied with their work, several researchers have proposed ways other than job simplification to group tasks into jobs: job enlargement and job enrichment.

Job enlargement is increasing the number of different tasks in a given job by changing the division of labor.[16] For example, because Subway food servers make the food as well as serve it, their jobs are "larger" than the jobs of McDonald's food servers. The idea behind job enlargement is that increasing the range of tasks performed by a worker will reduce boredom and fatigue and may increase motivation to perform at a high level—increasing both the quantity and the quality of goods and services provided.

job enlargement
Increasing the number of different tasks in a given job by changing the division of labor.

Job enrichment is increasing the degree of responsibility a worker has over a job by, for example, (1) empowering workers to experiment to find new or better ways of doing the job, (2) encouraging workers to develop new skills, (3) allowing workers to decide how to do the work and giving them the responsibility for deciding how to respond to unexpected situations, and (4) allowing workers to monitor and measure their own performance.[17] The idea behind job enrichment is that increasing workers' responsibility increases their involvement in their jobs and thus increases their interest in the quality of the goods they make or the services they provide.

job enrichment
Increasing the degree of responsibility a worker has over his or her job.

In general, managers who make design choices that increase job enrichment and job enlargement are likely to increase the degree to which people behave flexibly rather than rigidly or mechanically. Narrow, specialized jobs are likely to lead people to behave in predictable ways; workers who perform a variety of tasks and who are allowed and encouraged to discover new and better ways to perform their jobs are likely to act flexibly and creatively. Thus, managers who enlarge and enrich jobs create a flexible organizational structure, and those who simplify jobs create a more formal structure. If workers are grouped into self-managed work teams, the organization is likely to be flexible because team members provide support for each other and can learn from one another. To learn how these issues have affected work at IKEA, read the "Managing Globally" feature.

Managing Globally

IKEA Is Redesigning Itself for the Future

The world's top-selling furniture retailer is Sweden's IKEA, famous for kits packed in flat boxes with an Allen wrench. At 400 stores in four dozen countries, buyers stroll through displays and head to warehouse shelves to load up on assemble-it-yourself dressers and tables, getting Scandinavian design at low prices. Typical IKEA stores offer a sensory experience—model rooms, colorful displays, a supervised play area, and a restaurant featuring Swedish meatballs.[18]

This strategy built a multibillion-dollar business, but consumers are changing how they shop and live.[19] More live in big cities, away from IKEA's sprawling suburban stores. Fewer consumers care to drive miles to shop. Above all, online shopping is more convenient. Sales growth has stalled at IKEA's stores, so the company is changing.

In the United States, managers tried improving results with Organizing for Growth (O4G), their plan for restructuring. Instead of learning particular departments, store employees hold jobs that differ by function. Some are "active sellers," charged with looking for shoppers with questions and providing assistance; others handle "merchandising basics," earning less for focusing on keeping the shelves stocked. However, shoppers cannot distinguish the two sets of employees and have difficulty locating active sellers. The merchandising employees are aware of their lower pay grade and the time pressures of their jobs, so they may feel unmotivated to answer customer questions.[20]

Globally, IKEA has launched a more up-to-date strategy.[21] The company is expanding the availability of online shopping and is experimenting with various smaller-store formats—about one-fourth the size of a typical IKEA store—located in urban centers or inside shopping malls. Smaller displays satisfy consumers who shop after researching online. IKEA also announced plans to eliminate 7,500 jobs in the back office and create 11,500 new jobs—mainly in delivery, in-store services, and website design. In addition, IKEA

IKEA is rethinking its large, suburban retail stores, designing smaller, urban footprints that focus on a particular set of products such as kitchen items and cookware. Gail Mooney/Corbis/VCG/Getty Images

is expanding opportunities for contract workers: It acquired the TaskRabbit online labor marketplace, whose workers can bid on furniture assembly for consumers who prefer paying someone to assemble their new furniture purchases.

The U.S. experience can help IKEA's managers envision how jobs should change.[22] Some small-format stores focus on a particular set of products. In a store featuring kitchen items, consumers can cook in a test kitchen and use augmented-reality technology to view 3D images of how cabinets would look in their homes. A specialty store such as this will benefit from employees having in-depth product knowledge and a focus on service. Online selling depends more on highly efficient operations with most employees working behind the scenes. ●

The Job Characteristics Model

J. R. Hackman and G. R. Oldham's job characteristics model is an influential model of job design that explains in detail how managers can make jobs more interesting and motivating.[23] Hackman and Oldham's model also describes the likely personal and organizational outcomes that will result from enriched and enlarged jobs.

According to Hackman and Oldham, every job has five characteristics that determine how motivating the job is. These characteristics determine how employees react to their work and lead to outcomes such as high performance and satisfaction and low absenteeism and turnover:

- *Skill variety:* The extent to which a job requires that an employee use a wide range of different skills, abilities, or knowledge. Example: The skill variety required by the job of a research scientist is higher than that called for by the job of a Panera food server.

- *Task identity:* The extent to which a job requires that a worker perform all the tasks necessary to complete the job, from the beginning to the end of the production process. Example: A craftsworker who takes a piece of wood and transforms it into a custom-made desk has higher task identity than does a worker who performs only one of the numerous operations required to assemble a flat-screen TV.

- *Task significance:* The degree to which a worker feels his or her job is meaningful because of its effect on people inside the organization, such as coworkers, or on people outside the organization, such as customers. Example: A teacher who sees the effect of his or her efforts in a well-educated and well-adjusted student enjoys high task significance compared to a dishwasher who monotonously washes dishes as they come to the kitchen.

- *Autonomy:* The degree to which a job gives an employee the freedom and discretion needed to schedule different tasks and decide how to carry them out. Example: Salespeople who have to plan their schedules and decide how to allocate their time among different customers have relatively high autonomy compared to assembly-line workers, whose actions are determined by the speed of the production line.

- *Feedback:* The extent to which actually doing a job provides a worker with clear and direct information about how well he or she has performed the job. Example: An air traffic controller whose mistakes may result in a midair collision receives immediate feedback on job performance; a person who compiles statistics for a business magazine often has little idea of when he or she makes a mistake or does a particularly good job.

Hackman and Oldham argue that these five job characteristics affect an employee's motivation because they affect three critical psychological states. The more employees feel that their work is *meaningful* and that they are *responsible for work outcomes and responsible for knowing how those outcomes affect others,* the more motivating work becomes and the more likely employees are to be satisfied and to perform at a high level. Moreover, employees who have jobs that are highly motivating are called on to use their skills more and to perform more tasks, and they are given more responsibility for doing the job. All of the foregoing are characteristic of jobs and employees in flexible structures where authority is decentralized and where employees commonly work with others and must learn new skills to complete the range of tasks for which their group is responsible.

Grouping Jobs into Functions and Divisions: Designing Organizational Structure

Once managers have decided which tasks to allocate to which jobs, they face the next organizing decision: how to group jobs together to best match the needs of the organization's environment, strategy, technology, and human resources. Typically, managers first decide to group jobs into departments and they design a *functional structure* to use organizational resources effectively. As an organization grows and becomes more difficult to control, managers must choose a more complex organizational design, such as a divisional structure or a matrix or product team structure. The different ways in which managers can design organizational structure are discussed next. Selecting and designing an organizational structure to increase efficiency and effectiveness is a significant challenge. As noted in Chapter 6, managers reap the rewards of a well-thought-out strategy only if they choose the right type of structure to implement the strategy. The ability to make the right kinds of organizing choices is often what differentiates effective from ineffective managers and creates a high-performing organization.

Functional Structure

A *function* is a group of people, working together, who possess similar skills or use the same kind of knowledge, tools, or techniques to perform their jobs. Manufacturing, sales, and research and development are often organized into functional departments. A functional structure is an organizational structure composed of all the departments that an organization requires to produce its goods or services. Figure 7.2 shows the functional structure that Pier 1 Imports, the home furnishings company, uses to supply its customers with a range of goods from around the world to satisfy their desires for new and innovative products.[24]

Within Pier 1's organizational structure, the main functions include finance and administration, merchandising (developing products and purchasing goods), the global supply chain (managing the vendors who supply the goods), marketing and sales, planning and allocation (managing credit and product distribution), and human resources. Each job within a function exists because it helps the function perform the activities necessary for high organizational performance. Thus, within the marketing function are all the jobs necessary to efficiently advertise Pier 1's products to increase their appeal to customers, such as promotion, photography, visual communications, and social media.

Figure 7.2

The Functional
Structure of Pier 1
Imports

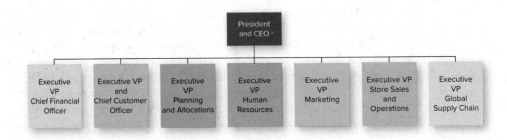

There are several advantages to grouping jobs according to function. First, when people who perform similar jobs are grouped together, they can learn from observing one another and thus become more specialized and can perform at a higher level. The tasks associated with one job often are related to the tasks associated with another job, which encourages cooperation within a function. In Pier 1's marketing department, for example, the person designing the photography program for an ad campaign or online catalog works closely with the person responsible for designing store layouts and with visual communication experts. As a result, Pier 1 can develop a strong, focused marketing campaign to differentiate its products from competitors'.

Second, when people who perform similar jobs are grouped together, it is easier for managers to monitor and evaluate their performance.[25] Imagine if marketing experts, purchasing experts, and real-estate experts were grouped together in one function and supervised by a manager from merchandising. Obviously, the merchandising manager would not have the expertise to evaluate all these different people appropriately. A functional structure allows workers to evaluate how well co-workers are performing their jobs, and if some workers are performing poorly, more experienced workers can help them develop new skills.

Finally, managers appreciate functional structure because it allows them to create the set of functions they need to scan and monitor the competitive environment and obtain information about the way it is changing.[26] With the right set of functions in place, managers are then in a good position to develop a strategy that allows the organization to respond to its changing situation. Employees in the marketing group can specialize in monitoring new marketing developments that will allow Pier 1 to better target its customers. Employees in merchandising can monitor all potential suppliers of home furnishings both at home and abroad to find the goods most likely to appeal to Pier 1's customers.

As an organization grows, and particularly as its task environment and strategy change because it is beginning to produce a wider range of goods and services for different kinds of customers, several problems can make a functional structure less efficient and effective.[27] First, managers in different functions may find it more difficult to communicate and coordinate with one another when they are responsible for several different kinds of products, especially as the organization grows both domestically and internationally. Second, functional managers may become so preoccupied with supervising their own specific departments and achieving their departmental goals that they lose sight of organizational goals. If that happens, organizational effectiveness will suffer because managers will be viewing issues and problems facing the organization only from their own, relatively narrow, departmental perspectives.[28] Both of these problems can reduce efficiency and effectiveness.

Pier 1 organizes its operations by function, which means that employees can more easily learn from one another and improve the service they provide to customers. Marlin Levison/ZUMAPRESS/Newscom

Divisional Structures: Product, Geographic, and Market

As the problems associated with growth and diversification increase over time, managers must search for new ways to organize their activities to overcome the problems associated with a functional structure. Most managers of large organizations choose a divisional structure and create a series of business units to produce a specific kind of product for a specific kind of customer. Each *division* is a collection of functions or departments that work together to produce the product. The goal behind the change to a divisional structure is to create smaller, more manageable units within the organization. There are three forms of divisional structure (see Figure 7.3).[29] When managers organize divisions according to the *type of good or service* they provide, they adopt a product structure. When managers organize divisions according to the *area of the country or world* they operate in, they adopt a geographic structure. When managers organize divisions according to *the type of customer* they focus on, they adopt a market structure.

divisional structure
An organizational structure composed of separate business units within which are the functions that work together to produce a specific product for a specific customer.

PRODUCT STRUCTURE Imagine the problems that managers at Pier 1 would encounter if they decided to diversify into producing and selling cars, fast food, and health insurance—in addition to home furnishings—and tried to use their existing set of functional managers to oversee the production of all four kinds of products. No manager would have the necessary skills or abilities to oversee those four products. No individual marketing manager, for example, could effectively market cars, fast food, health insurance, and home furnishings at the same time. To perform a functional activity successfully, managers must have experience in specific markets or industries. Consequently, if managers decide to diversify into new industries or to expand their range of products, they commonly design a product structure to organize their operations (see Figure 7.3a).

product structure
An organizational structure in which each product line or business is handled by a self-contained division.

Using a product structure, managers place each distinct product line or business in its own self-contained division and give divisional managers the responsibility for devising an appropriate business-level strategy to allow the division to compete effectively in its industry or market.[30] Each division is self-contained because it has a complete set of all the functions—marketing, R&D, finance, and so on—that it needs to produce or provide goods or services efficiently and effectively. Functional managers report to divisional managers, and divisional managers report to top or corporate managers.

Grouping functions into divisions focused on particular products has several advantages for managers at all levels in the organization. First, a product structure allows functional managers to specialize in only one product area, so they are able to build expertise and fine-tune their skills in this particular area. Second, each division's managers can become experts in their industry; this expertise helps them choose and develop a business-level strategy to differentiate their products or lower

Figure 7.3

Product, Geographic, and Market Structures

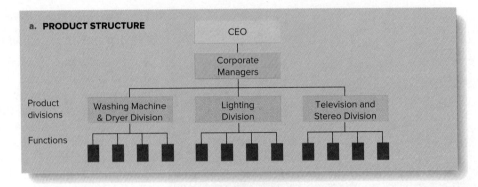

a. **PRODUCT STRUCTURE**

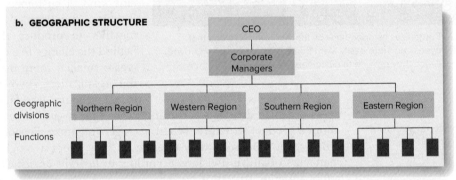

b. **GEOGRAPHIC STRUCTURE**

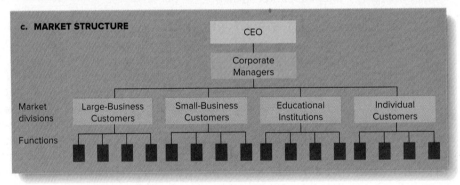

c. **MARKET STRUCTURE**

their costs while meeting the needs of customers. Third, a product structure frees corporate managers from the need to supervise directly each division's day-to-day operations; this latitude allows corporate managers to create the best corporate-level strategy to maximize the organization's future growth and ability to create value. Corporate managers are likely to make fewer mistakes about which businesses to diversify into or how to best expand internationally, for example, because they are able to take an organizationwide view.[31] Corporate managers also are likely to evaluate better how well divisional managers are doing, and they can intervene and take corrective action as needed. To learn how a company applied these advantages of a division structure in a difficult business environment, read the "Ethics in Action" feature.

Ethics in Action

Pfizer's Prescription for a Healthier Organizational Structure

Drugmakers operate in a tough environment. They must excel at innovation (or allow competition from generics to erase profits) and quality (lest defects harm patients). Their customer mix is complex, because sales are often not to patients, but to wholesalers, pharmacy benefits companies, and government payers.[32] And since pharmaceuticals restore health and save lives, society judges companies harshly for any action that limits access to their products. How to stay competitive and ethical?

Pfizer ran into trouble with its involvement in a patient-assistance program.[33] Such charities offer financial help to patients who cannot afford copayments for their medications. Under federal law, drug companies may donate to these programs but not specify how the programs use the money. The U.S. Attorney's Office investigated allegations that drug companies, including Pfizer, made contributions with an expectation that the money was for purchasing the donor company's drugs. Pfizer agreed to pay $24 million to settle the allegations without admitting to wrongdoing.

Pfizer also failed to prevent drug shortages. In 2017, U.S. hospitals could not buy basic but critical medicines such as local anesthetics or even saline solution to deliver IV medicines.[34] Part of the problem was Hurricane Maria's devastation of Puerto Rico, where many drugs are produced. But Pfizer already had been struggling since its 2015 purchase of Hospira, the biggest maker of generic sterile injectable drugs. Given slim profit margins on these products, Hospira and later Pfizer slashed costs. Underinvestment in quality and innovation resulted in defects and recalls, forcing production shutdowns. At one point, more than 300 products were on back order. Pfizer is the largest U.S. pharmaceutical company, so competitors lacked scale to meet the need.

Finally, drugmakers come under criticism for price increases, which they announce regularly. Patients see drug expenses as high and rising fast, seemingly without regard for their well-being. When Pfizer announced increases of around 9% in the summer of 2018, President Trump shamed the company, which then agreed to postpone the increase.[35]

To master these difficulties, pharma managers need deep understanding of markets and brands. This provides insight into Pfizer's recent decision to restructure. Pfizer planned three divisions: innovative medicines, consumer health care (for example, Advil and Centrum), and established medicines (drugs no longer protected by patent). The innovative-medicines division would be organized into units for particular kinds of treatment—say, oncology and inflammation. Its products include those from the Hospira deal; managers familiar with these will know to emphasize quality improvement. The established-medicines group has low margins but is designed to operate globally, so

Pharmaceutical giant Pfizer recently revised its organizational structure into three separate divisions in an effort to streamline its business operations. Stockbyte/Getty Images

it can seek growth in regions where people are entering the middle class and value established brands. Finally, keeping consumer health care separate lets its managers focus on the marketing challenges associated with serving consumers.[36] In late 2018, Pfizer and GSK (GlaxoSmithKline) announced they would spin off their consumer health care divisions into a new joint venture.[37] ●

The extra layer of management, the divisional management layer, can improve the use of organizational resources. Moreover, a product structure puts divisional managers close to their customers and lets them respond quickly and appropriately to the changing task environment. One pharmaceutical company that successfully adopted a product structure to better organize its activities with great success is GlaxoSmith-Kline (GSK). The need to innovate new kinds of prescription drugs to boost performance is a continual battle for pharmaceutical companies. Over the past decade, many of these companies have been merging to try to increase their research productivity, and one of them, GlaxoSmithKline, was created from the merger between Glaxo Wellcome and SmithKline Beecham. Prior to the merger, both companies experienced a steep decline in the number of new prescription drugs their scientists were able to invent. The problem facing the new company's top managers was how to best use and combine the talents of the scientists and researchers from both of the former companies to allow them to quickly innovate promising new drugs.

Top managers realized that after the merger there would be enormous problems associated with coordinating the activities of the thousands of research scientists who were working on hundreds of different kinds of drug research programs. Understanding the problems associated with large size, the top managers decided to group the researchers into eight smaller product divisions to allow them to focus on particular clusters of diseases such as heart disease or viral infections. The members of each product division were told that they would be rewarded based on the number of new prescription drugs they were able to invent and the speed with which they could bring these new drugs to the market. GlaxoSmithKline's new product structure worked well, its research productivity doubled after the reorganization, and a record number of new drugs moved into clinical trials. Recently GSK announced it would enter into a joint venture with Pfizer to spin off both companies' consumer health divisions into a new global company that potentially could be worth billions in annual sales. Both companies agreed that this new synergy and structure would allow them to concentrate their efforts in bolstering their drug-discovery pipelines while giving the over-the-counter consumer health care products a separate structure and business model.[38]

GEOGRAPHIC STRUCTURE When organizations expand rapidly both at home and abroad, functional structures can create special problems because managers in one central location may find it increasingly difficult to deal with the different problems and issues that may arise in each region of a country or area of the world. In these cases, a geographic structure, in which divisions are broken down by geographic location, is often chosen (see Figure 7.3b). To achieve the corporate mission of providing next-day mail service, Fred Smith, CEO of FedEx, chose a geographic structure and divided up operations by creating a division in each region. Large retailers such as Macy's, Neiman Marcus, and Brooks Brothers also use a geographic structure. Since the needs of retail customers differ by region—for example, shorts

geographic structure An organizational structure in which each region of a country or area of the world is served by a self-contained division.

in California and down parkas in the Midwest—a geographic structure gives retail regional managers the flexibility they need to choose the range of products that best meets the needs of regional customers.

In adopting a *global geographic structure,* such as shown in Figure 7.4a, managers locate different divisions in each of the world regions where the organization operates. Managers are most likely to do this when they pursue a multidomestic strategy because customer needs vary widely by country or world region. For example, if products that appeal to U.S. customers do not sell in Europe, the Pacific Rim, or South America, managers must customize the products to meet the needs of customers in those different world regions; a global geographic structure with global divisions may allow them to do this.

In contrast, to the degree that customers abroad are willing to buy the same kind of product or slight variations thereof, managers are more likely to pursue a global strategy. In this case they are more likely to use a global product structure. In a *global product structure,* each product division, not the country and regional managers, takes responsibility for deciding where to manufacture its products and how to market them in countries worldwide (see Figure 7.4b). Product division managers manage their own global value chains and decide where to establish foreign subsidiaries to distribute and sell their products to customers in foreign countries.

MARKET STRUCTURE Sometimes the pressing issue facing managers is to group functions according to the type of customer buying the product in order to tailor the

Figure 7.4

Global Geographic and Global Product Structures

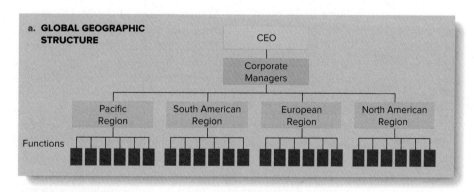

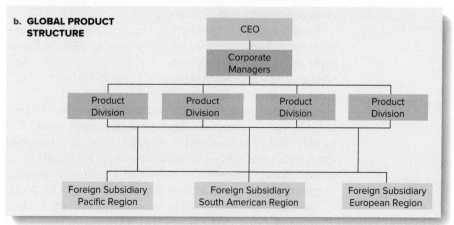

products the organization offers to each customer's unique demands. A PC maker, for example, has several kinds of customers, including large businesses (which might demand networks of computers linked to a mainframe computer), small companies (which may need just a few PCs linked together), educational users in schools and universities (which might want thousands of independent PCs for their students), and individual users (who may want a high-quality multimedia PC so they can play the latest video games).

To satisfy the needs of diverse customers, a company might adopt a market structure, which groups divisions according to the particular kinds of customers they serve (see Figure 7.3c). A market structure lets managers be responsive to the needs of their customers and allows them to act flexibly in making decisions in response to customers' changing needs.

Organizations and their managers need to continually evaluate hierarchy and culture to ensure that operations are working according to plan. The accompanying "Manager as a Person" feature provides an example of what can happen when a CEO drives both structural and cultural changes throughout an organization.

> **market structure** An organizational structure in which each kind of customer is served by a self-contained division; also called *customer structure.*

Manager as a Person

McDonald's CEO Continues to Change Things Up

Steve Easterbrook is a 25-year veteran of the McDonald's Corporation, serving in a variety of roles in Europe and the UK before becoming president and CEO in 2015. In his role as CEO, Easterbrook continues to make significant changes to the global organization in an effort to streamline company hierarchy, increase efficiencies and revenues, and provide owner-operators (McDonald's franchisees) with a clear line of communication and support from field consultants and corporate headquarters.[39]

Making drastic changes at a large organization is never easy. McDonald's has had a long tradition of successful employees coming up through the ranks of supervisors, managers, and senior executives. While this strategy proved successful from an HR standpoint, the company's financial picture seemed to remain flat. In addition, younger consumers (millennials and others) decided they were looking for healthier choices when it came to dining out.

Easterbrook decided the organization needed a reset—and significant changes continue to happen at the Golden Arches. In 2018, McDonald's returned to its urban roots by moving its corporate headquarters (and well-known Hamburger University) to a new location in the West Loop neighborhood of Chicago, down the street from the offices of Google, LinkedIn, and Glassdoor.[40] Moving to the city was only part of Easterbrook's strategy. At the same time the organization was moving downtown, several senior executives who had spent most of their professional careers at McDonald's announced their retirement, and hundreds of longtime corporate employees were offered voluntary buyouts. And contrary to McDonald's typical corporate moves, Easterbrook promoted a relative newcomer to the company, Chris Kempczinski, to become president of McDonald's USA division.[41]

Now that the company has relocated to the city, Easterbrook continues to make changes as the company faces stiff competition from other fast-casual chains such

McDonald's CEO Steve Easterbrook continues to transform the fast-food chain by streamlining company hierarchy, installing self-service kiosks in stores, and moving corporate headquarters to an urban setting. Tannen Maury/EPA-EFE/ Shutterstock

as Shake Shack and In-N-Out Burger. McDonald's recently announced changes to its signature Quarter Pounder at its 14,000 U.S. restaurants: The sandwich is now made with fresh—not frozen—beef patties, a move greeted enthusiastically by both consumers and Wall Street.[42]

In addition to installing digital self-service kiosks in many restaurants and launching a successful mobile app, McDonald's recently announced more changes, eliminating its region structure in favor of field offices, which removes several layers of management in the corporate structure. This move was made in an effort to work more closely with the company's all-important franchise operators around the country and to boost efficiency. The new structure provides a single point of contact for franchisees who will now work closely with company field consultants tasked with helping them improve their overall business strategies and operations.[43]

Millennials might want to take another look at the Golden Arches and its urban setting as a possible new workplace. As Easterbrook acknowledges, the 50+ years in a suburban setting are a proud part of McDonald's heritage, but he thinks it's time to drive change in the overall organization and bring in people with a fresh perspective. He hopes the changes will help McDonald's "get closer to customers, encourage innovation, and ensure great talent is excited about where they work."[44] ●

Matrix and Product Team Designs

Moving to a product, geographic, or market divisional structure allows managers to respond more quickly and flexibly to the particular circumstances they confront. However, when information technology or customer needs are changing rapidly and the environment is uncertain, even a divisional structure may not give managers enough flexibility to respond to the environment quickly. To operate effectively under these conditions, managers must design the most flexible kind of organizational structure available: a matrix structure or a product team structure (see Figure 7.5).

matrix structure An organizational structure that simultaneously groups people and resources by function and by product.

MATRIX STRUCTURE In a matrix structure, managers group people and resources in two ways simultaneously: by function and by product.[45] Employees are grouped by *functions* to allow them to learn from one another and become more skilled and productive. In addition, employees are grouped into *product teams* in which members of different functions work together to develop a specific product. The result is a complex network of reporting relationships among product teams and functions that makes the matrix structure very flexible (see Figure 7.5a). Each person in a product team reports to two managers: (1) a functional boss, who assigns individuals to a team and evaluates their performance from a functional perspective; and (2) the boss of the product team, who evaluates their performance on the team. Thus team members are known as *two-boss employees*. The functional employees assigned to product teams change over time as the specific skills that the team needs change. At the beginning of the product development process, for example, engineers and R&D specialists are assigned to a product team because their skills are needed to

Figure 7.5

Matrix and Product
Team Structures

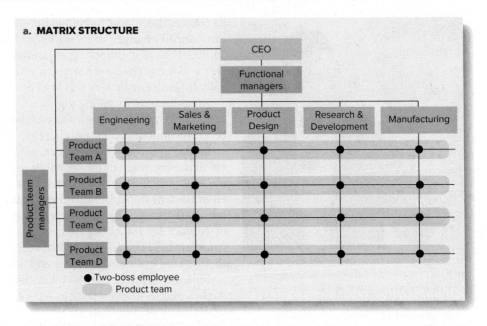

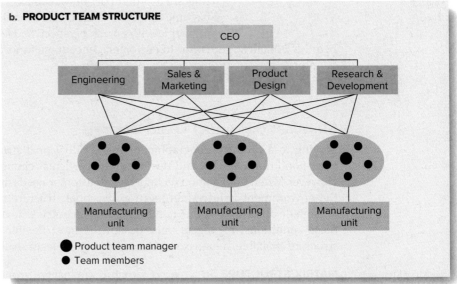

develop new products. When a provisional design has been established, marketing experts are assigned to the team to gauge how customers will respond to the new product. Manufacturing personnel join when it is time to find the most efficient way to produce the product. As their specific jobs are completed, team members leave and are reassigned to new teams. In this way the matrix structure makes the most use of human resources.

To keep the matrix structure flexible, product teams are empowered and team members are responsible for making most of the important decisions involved in product development.[46] The product team manager acts as a facilitator, controlling the financial resources and trying to keep the project on time and within budget. The functional managers try to ensure that the product is the best it can be to maximize its differentiated appeal.

High-tech companies that operate in environments where new product development takes place monthly or yearly have used matrix structures successfully for many years, and the need to innovate quickly is vital to the organization's survival. The flexibility afforded by a matrix structure lets managers keep pace with a changing and increasingly complex environment.[47]

PRODUCT TEAM STRUCTURE The dual reporting relationships that are at the heart of a matrix structure have always been difficult for managers and employees to deal with. Often the functional boss and the product boss make conflicting demands on team members, who do not know which boss to satisfy first. Also, functional and product team bosses may come into conflict over precisely who is in charge of which team members and for how long. To avoid these problems, managers have devised a way of organizing people and resources that still allows an organization to be flexible but makes its structure easier to operate: a product team structure.

The product team structure differs from a matrix structure in two ways: (1) It does away with dual reporting relationships and two-boss employees, and (2) functional employees are permanently assigned to a cross-functional team that is empowered to bring a new or redesigned product to market. A cross-functional team is a group of managers brought together from different departments to perform organizational tasks. When managers are grouped into cross-functional teams, the artificial boundaries between departments disappear, and a narrow focus on departmental goals is replaced with a general interest in working together to achieve organizational goals. For example, when mattress company Sealy saw its sales slipping, it pulled together a cross-functional team that was allowed to work outside the organization's hierarchy and quickly designed a new mattress. With everyone focused on the goal, team members created a mattress that broke previous sales records.[48]

Members of a cross-functional team report only to the product team manager or to one of his or her direct reports. The heads of the functions have only an informal, advisory relationship with members of the product teams—the role of functional managers is only to counsel and help team members, share knowledge among teams, and provide new technological developments that can help improve each team's performance (see Figure 7.5b).[49] Increasingly, organizations are making empowered cross-functional teams an essential part of their organizational architecture to help them gain a competitive advantage in fast-changing organizational environments.

product team structure An organizational structure in which employees are permanently assigned to a cross-functional team and report only to the product team manager or to one of his or her direct reports.

cross-functional team A group of managers brought together from different departments to perform organizational tasks.

Coordinating Functions and Divisions

The more complex the structure a company uses to group its activities, the greater are the problems of *linking and coordinating* its different functions and divisions. Coordination becomes a problem because each function or division develops a different orientation toward the other groups that affects how it interacts with them. Each function or division comes to view the problems facing the company from its own perspective; for example, they may develop different views about the major goals, problems, or issues facing a company.

At the functional level, the manufacturing function typically has a short-term view; its major goal is to keep costs under control and get the product out the factory door on time. By contrast, the product development function has a long-term viewpoint because developing a new product is a relatively slow process and high product quality is seen as more important than low costs. Such differences in viewpoint

LO 7-4
Explain why managers must coordinate jobs, functions, and divisions using the hierarchy of authority and integrating mechanisms.

may make manufacturing and product development managers reluctant to cooperate and coordinate their activities to meet company goals. At the divisional level, in a company with a product structure, employees may become concerned more with making *their* division's products a success than with the profitability of the entire company. They may refuse, or simply not see, the need to cooperate and share information or knowledge with other divisions.

The problem of linking and coordinating the activities of different functions and divisions becomes more acute as the number of functions and divisions increases. We look first at how managers design the hierarchy of authority to coordinate functions and divisions so they work together effectively. Then we focus on integration and examine the different integrating mechanisms managers can use to coordinate functions and divisions.

Allocating Authority

authority The power to hold people accountable for their actions and to make decisions concerning the use of organizational resources.

As organizations grow and produce a wider range of goods and services, the size and number of their functions and divisions increase. To coordinate the activities of people, functions, and divisions and to allow them to work together effectively, managers must develop a clear hierarchy of authority.[50] Authority is the power vested in a manager to make decisions and use resources to achieve organizational goals by virtue of his or her position in an organization. The hierarchy of authority is an organization's *chain of command*—the relative authority that each manager has—extending from the CEO at the top, down through the middle managers and first-line managers, to the nonmanagerial employees who actually make goods or provide services. Every manager, at every level of the hierarchy, supervises one or more individuals. The term span of control refers to the number of employees who report directly to a manager.

hierarchy of authority An organization's chain of command, specifying the relative authority of each manager.

span of control The number of employees who report directly to a manager.

Within an organization's structure, there are also line managers, individuals in the direct line or chain of command who have formal authority over people and resources at lower levels of the organization. In addition, staff managers are responsible for managing a specialist function, such as finance, marketing, human resources, or communications. For example, considered a staff manager, Robert Gibbs is McDonald's chief communications officer and reports directly to CEO Steve Easterbrook.[51]

line manager Someone in the direct line or chain of command who has formal authority over people and resources at lower levels.

Managers at each level of the hierarchy confer on managers at the next level down the authority to decide how to use organizational resources. Accepting this authority, those lower-level managers are accountable for how well they make those decisions. Managers who make the right decisions are typically promoted, and organizations motivate managers with the prospects of promotion and increased responsibility within the chain of command.

staff manager Someone responsible for managing a specialist function, such as finance or marketing.

TALL AND FLAT ORGANIZATIONS As an organization grows in size (normally measured by the number of its managers and employees), its hierarchy of authority normally lengthens, making the organizational structure taller. A *tall* organization has many levels of authority relative to company size; a *flat* organization has fewer levels relative to company size (see Figure 7.6).[52] As a hierarchy becomes taller, problems that make the organization's structure less flexible and slow managers' response to changes in the organizational environment may result.

Communication problems may arise when an organization has many levels in the hierarchy. It can take a long time for the decisions and orders of upper-level managers to reach managers further down in the hierarchy, and it can take a long time for

Figure 7.6

Flat and Tall
Organizations

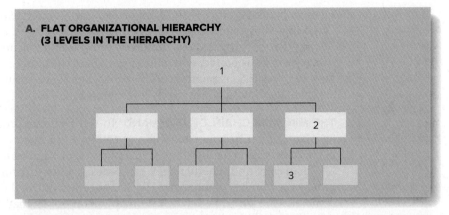

A. **FLAT ORGANIZATIONAL HIERARCHY**
   (3 LEVELS IN THE HIERARCHY)

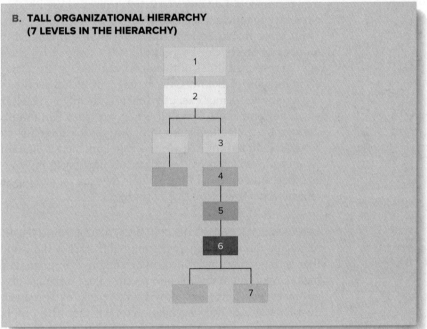

B. **TALL ORGANIZATIONAL HIERARCHY**
   (7 LEVELS IN THE HIERARCHY)

top managers to learn how well their decisions worked. Feeling out of touch, top managers may want to verify that lower-level managers are following orders and may require written confirmation from them. Middle managers, who know they will be held strictly accountable for their actions, start devoting too much time to the process of making decisions to improve their chances of being right. They might even try to avoid responsibility by making top managers decide what actions to take.

Another communication problem that can result is the distortion of commands and messages being transmitted up and down the hierarchy, which causes managers at different levels to interpret what is happening differently. Distortion of orders and messages can be accidental, occurring because different managers interpret messages from their own narrow, functional perspectives. Or distortion can be intentional, occurring because managers low in the hierarchy decide to interpret information in a way that increases their own personal advantage.

Another problem with tall hierarchies is that they usually indicate that an organization is employing many managers, and managers are expensive. Managerial salaries, benefits, offices, and support staff are a huge expense for organizations. Large companies such as IBM and GM pay their managers millions of dollars a year. During the global recession, hundreds of thousands of managers were laid off as companies restructured and downsized their workforces to reduce costs. Today, however, the U.S. economy continues to experience hiring gains among workers and managers, with a historically low jobless rate.[53]

THE MINIMUM CHAIN OF COMMAND To ward off the problems that result when an organization becomes too tall and employs too many managers, top managers need to ascertain whether they are employing the right number of middle and first-line managers and whether they can redesign their organizational architecture to reduce the number of managers. Top managers might well follow a basic organizing principle—the principle of the minimum chain of command—which states that top managers should always construct a hierarchy with the fewest levels of authority necessary to efficiently and effectively use organizational resources.

Effective managers constantly scrutinize their hierarchies to see whether the number of levels can be reduced—for example, by eliminating one level and giving the responsibilities of managers at that level to managers above and by empowering employees below. One manager who has worked to empower employees is David Novak, former executive chair and CEO of YUM! Brands. Instead of dictating what the company's Taco Bell, KFC, and Pizza Hut brands should do, Novak turned the corporate headquarters into a support center for worldwide operations. Also a best-selling author, Novak recently launched a digital leadership platform called "oGoLead," which provides online training programs in effective leadership, as well as other sources to help individuals develop leadership skills that can be important tools in today's workplace environment.[54]

decentralizing authority Giving lower-level managers and nonmanagerial employees the right to make important decisions about how to use organizational resources.

CENTRALIZATION AND DECENTRALIZATION OF AUTHORITY Another way in which managers can keep the organizational hierarchy flat is by decentralizing authority—that is, by giving lower-level managers and nonmanagerial employees the right to make important decisions about how to use organizational resources.[55] If managers at higher levels give lower-level employees the responsibility of making important decisions and only *manage by exception,* then the problems of slow and distorted communication noted previously are kept to a minimum. Moreover, fewer managers are needed because their role is not to make decisions but to act as coach and facilitator and to help other employees make the best decisions. In addition, when decision-making authority is low in the organization and near the customer, employees are better able to recognize and respond to customer needs.

Decentralizing authority allows an organization and its employees to behave in a flexible way even as the organization grows and becomes taller. This is why managers are so interested in empowering employees, creating self-managed work teams, establishing cross-functional teams, and even moving to a product team structure. These design innovations help keep the organizational architecture flexible and responsive to complex task and general environments, complex technologies, and complex strategies.

Although more and more organizations are taking steps to decentralize authority, *too much* decentralization has certain disadvantages. If divisions, functions, or teams are given too much decision-making authority, they may begin to pursue their own goals at the expense of organizational goals. Managers in engineering design or R&D, for example, may become so focused on making the best possible product they fail to realize that the best product may be so expensive few people are willing or able to buy it. Also, too much decentralization can cause lack of communication among functions or divisions; this prevents the synergies of cooperation from ever materializing, and organizational performance suffers.

Top managers must seek the balance between centralization and decentralization of authority that best meets the four major contingencies an organization faces (see Figure 7.1). If managers are in a stable environment, are using well-understood technology, and are producing stable kinds of products (such as cereal, canned soup, or books), there is no pressing need to decentralize authority, and managers at the top can maintain control of much of organizational decision making.[56] However, in uncertain, changing environments where high-tech companies are producing state-of-the-art products, top managers must often empower employees and allow teams to make important strategic decisions so the organization can keep up with the changes taking place. No matter what its environment, a company that fails to control the balance between centralization and decentralization of authority will find its performance suffering.

Integrating and Coordinating Mechanisms

Much coordination takes place through the hierarchy of authority. However, several problems are associated with establishing contact among managers in different functions or divisions. As discussed earlier, managers from different functions and divisions may have different views about what must be done to achieve organizational goals. But if the managers have equal authority (as functional managers typically do), the only manager who can tell them what to do is the CEO, who has the ultimate authority to resolve conflicts. The need to solve everyday conflicts, however, wastes top management time and slows strategic decision making; indeed, one sign of a poorly performing structure is the number of problems sent up the hierarchy for top managers to solve.

integrating mechanisms
Organizing tools that managers can use to increase communication and coordination among functions and divisions.

To increase communication and coordination among functions or between divisions and to prevent these problems from emerging, top managers incorporate various integrating mechanisms into their organizational architecture. The greater the complexity of an organization's structure, the greater is the need for coordination among people, functions, and divisions to make the organizational structure work efficiently and effectively. Thus when managers adopt a divisional, matrix, or product team structure, they must use complex integrating mechanisms to achieve organizational goals. Several integrating mechanisms are available to managers to increase communication and coordination.[57] Figure 7.7 lists these mechanisms, as well as examples of the individuals or groups who might use them.

LIAISON ROLES Managers can increase coordination among functions and divisions by establishing liaison roles. When the volume of contacts between two functions increases, one way to improve coordination is to give one manager in each function or division the responsibility for coordinating with the other. These managers may meet daily, weekly, monthly, or as needed. A liaison role is illustrated in Figure 7.7; the small dot represents the person within a function who has responsibility for coordinating with the other function. Coordinating is part of the liaison's full-time job, and usually an informal relationship develops among the people involved, greatly easing strains between functions. Furthermore, liaison roles provide a way of transmitting information across an organization, which is important in large organizations whose employees may know no one outside their immediate function or division.

Figure 7.7   Types and Examples of Integrating Mechanisms

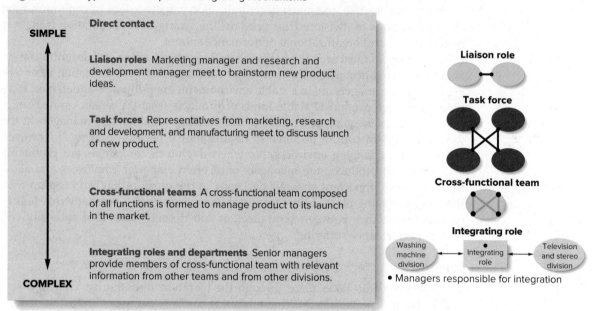

SIMPLE

Direct contact

Liaison roles Marketing manager and research and development manager meet to brainstorm new product ideas.

Task forces Representatives from marketing, research and development, and manufacturing meet to discuss launch of new product.

Cross-functional teams A cross-functional team composed of all functions is formed to manage product to its launch in the market.

Integrating roles and departments Senior managers provide members of cross-functional team with relevant information from other teams and from other divisions.

COMPLEX

Liaison role

Task force

Cross-functional team

Integrating role

Washing machine division — Integrating role — Television and stereo division

• Managers responsible for integration

---

task force A committee of managers from various functions or divisions who meet to solve a specific, mutual problem; also called *ad hoc committee.*

TASK FORCES When more than two functions or divisions share many common problems, direct contact and liaison roles may not provide sufficient coordination. In these cases, a more complex integrating mechanism, a task force, may be appropriate (see Figure 7.7). One manager from each relevant function or division is assigned to a task force that meets to solve a specific, mutual problem; members are responsible for reporting to their departments on the issues addressed and the solutions recommended. Task forces are often called *ad hoc committees* because they are temporary; they may meet on a regular basis or only a few times. When the problem or issue is solved, the task force is no longer needed; members return to their normal roles in their departments or are assigned to other task forces. Typically task force members also perform many of their normal duties while serving on the task force.

CROSS-FUNCTIONAL TEAMS In many cases the issues addressed by a task force are recurring problems, such as the need to develop new products or find new kinds of customers. To address recurring problems effectively, managers are increasingly using integrating mechanisms such as cross-functional teams. An example of a cross-functional team is a new product development committee that is responsible for the choice, design, manufacturing, and marketing of a new product. Such an activity obviously requires a great deal of integration among functions if new products are to be successfully introduced, and using a complex integrating mechanism such as a cross-functional team accomplishes this. As discussed earlier, in a product team structure people and resources are grouped into cross-functional teams to speed products to market. These teams assume long-term responsibility for all aspects of developing and making the product.

INTEGRATING ROLES An integrating role is a role whose only function is to increase coordination and integration among functions or divisions to achieve performance gains from synergies. Usually managers who perform integrating roles are experienced senior managers who can envision how to use the resources of the functions or divisions to obtain new synergies. At PepsiCo, Amy Chen, now a vice president in the snacks business unit, coordinated with several company divisions to create a program that would deliver meals during the summer months to children from low-income families. The resulting program, Food for Good, now makes healthy meals accessible year-round to low-income families. To date, Food for Good has delivered 80 million healthy servings to low-income families in need.[58] The more complex an organization and the greater the number of its divisions, the more important integrating roles are.

In summary, to keep an organization responsive to changes in its task and general environments as it grows and becomes more complex, managers must increase coordination among functions and divisions by using complex integrating mechanisms. Managers must decide on the best way to organize their structures—that is, choose the structure that allows them to make the best use of organizational resources.

Strategic Alliances, B2B Network Structures, and Technology

Increasing globalization and technological advances have brought about two innovations in organizational architecture used frequently by U.S. and other companies: strategic alliances and business-to-business (B2B) network structures. As mentioned in Chapter 6, a *strategic alliance* is a formal agreement that commits two or more companies to exchange or share their resources in order to produce and market a product. Strategic alliances are typically formed because companies share similar interests and believe they can benefit from cooperating with each other. For example, recently Disney entered into a strategic alliance with McDonald's that will bring Disney movie toys back to Happy Meals for the first time in more than a decade. This business move will give both global brands new ways to market their products to families over the next several years. More than a decade ago, Disney ended a pact with the fast-food giant to include movie toys in Happy Meals because the children's meals didn't meet Disney's nutritional guidelines.[59]

The growing sophistication of technology using global intranets, videoconferencing, and cloud computing makes it much easier to manage strategic alliances and encourage managers to share information and cooperate with each other across the globe. One outcome of this increased use of technology has been the growth of strategic alliances into a technology-based network structure for businesses. A B2B network structure is a formal series of global strategic alliances that one or several organizations create with suppliers, manufacturers, and distributors to product and market a product. Network structures allow an organization to manage its global value chain and to find new ways to reduce costs while increasing the quality of products—without incurring the high costs of operating a complex organizational structure (such as the costs of employing many managers). More and more companies rely on global network structures to gain access to low-cost foreign sources of inputs, including global retailer Nike.

Nike is the largest and most profitable athletic shoe manufacturer in the world. The key to Nike's success is the network structure that Nike founder Philip Knight created to allow his company to produce and market shoes. The most successful companies today are trying to pursue simultaneously a low-cost and a differentiation strategy. Knight decided early that to do this at Nike he needed organizational architecture that would allow his company to focus on some functions, such as design, and leave others, such as manufacturing, to other organizations.

By far the largest function at Nike's Oregon headquarters is the design function, composed of talented designers who pioneered innovations in sports shoe design such as the air pump and Air Jordans that Nike introduced so successfully. Designers use computer-aided design (CAD) to design Nike shoes, and they electronically store all new product information, including manufacturing instructions. When the designers have finished their work, they electronically transmit all the blueprints for the new products to a network of suppliers and manufacturers with which Nike has formed strategic alliances.[60] Instructions for the design of a new sole may be sent to a supplier in Taiwan; instructions for the leather uppers, to a supplier in Malaysia. The suppliers produce the shoe parts and send them for final assembly to a manufacturer in China with which Nike has established another strategic alliance. From China the shoes are shipped to distributors throughout the world. In a recent year, Nike moved more than 900 million pairs of shoes through its manufacturing network of nearly 600 factories in 41 countries.[61]

This network structure gives Nike two important advantages. First, Nike is able to respond to changes in athletic shoe fashion very quickly. Using its global technology system, Nike literally can change the instructions it gives each of its suppliers overnight, so that within a few weeks its foreign manufacturers are producing new kinds of shoes.[62] Any alliance partners that fail to perform up to Nike's standards are replaced with new partners through the regular B2B marketplace.

Second, Nike's costs are very low because wages in other countries are a fraction of what they are in the United States, and this difference gives Nike a low-cost advantage. Also, Nike's ability to outsource and use foreign manufacturers to produce all its shoes abroad allows Knight to keep the organization's U.S. structure flat and flexible. Nike is able to use a relatively inexpensive functional structure to organize its activities. Recently Nike announced a breakthrough in the materials it uses to create its global brand. With a nod toward innovation and sustainability, the retailer announced its scientists and engineers have developed a new "super material" made from recyclable natural leather fibers. The product, called Flyleather, will be used in some of Nike's best-selling shoes. The new material will ensure that Nike's products retain their style and comfort while also contributing to the global effort of conserving resources and protecting the environment.[63]

The use of network structures is increasing rapidly as companies recognize the many opportunities they offer to reduce costs and increase organizational flexibility. Supply chain spending by U.S. firms is expected to exceed $19 billion annually over the next few years.[64] The push to reduce costs has led to the development of B2B marketplaces in which most or all of the companies in a specific industry (e.g., automakers) use the same platform link to each other and establish industry specifications and standards. Then these companies jointly list the quantity and specifications of the inputs they require and solicit bids from thousands of potential suppliers from around the world. Suppliers also use the same software platform, so electronic bidding, auctions, and transactions are possible between buyers and sellers on a global basis. The idea is that high-volume, standardized transactions can help drive down costs at the industry level.

The ability of managers to develop a network structure to produce or provide the goods and services customers want, rather than create a complex organizational structure to do so, has led many researchers and consultants to popularize the idea of a **boundaryless organization**. Such an organization is composed of people linked by technology—computers, mobile and virtual technology, computer-aided design

outsource To use outside suppliers and manufacturers to produce goods and services.

boundaryless organization An organization whose members are linked by computers, mobile and virtual technology, computer-aided design systems, videoconferencing, and cloud computing, and who rarely, if ever, see one another face-to-face.

**knowledge
management system**
A company-specific
virtual information
system that systematizes
the knowledge of
its employees and
facilitates the sharing
and integration of their
expertise.

systems, videoconferencing, and cloud computing—who may rarely, if ever, see one another face-to-face. People are utilized when their services are needed, much as in a matrix structure, but they are not formal members of an organization; they are functional experts who form an alliance with an organization, fulfill their contractual obligations, and then move on to the next project.

Large consulting companies, such as Accenture, IBM, and McKinsey & Co., utilize their global consultants in this way. Consultants are connected by laptops to an organization's knowledge management system, its company-specific virtual information system that systematizes the knowledge of its employees and facilitates the sharing and integration of expertise within and between functions and divisions through real-time interconnected technology.

Summary and Review

DESIGNING ORGANIZATIONAL STRUCTURE The four main determinants of organizational structure are the external environment, strategy, technology, and human resources. In general, the higher the level of uncertainty associated with these factors, the more appropriate is a flexible, adaptable structure as opposed to a formal, rigid one. [LO 7-1]

GROUPING TASKS INTO JOBS Job design is the process by which managers group tasks into jobs. To create more interesting jobs, and to get workers to act flexibly, managers can enlarge and enrich jobs. The job characteristics model provides a tool managers can use to measure how motivating or satisfying a particular job is. [LO 7-2]

GROUPING JOBS INTO FUNCTIONS AND DIVISIONS Managers can choose from many kinds of organizational structures to make the best use of organizational resources. Depending on the specific organizing problems they face, managers can choose from functional, product, geographic, market, matrix, product team, and hybrid structures. [LO 7-3]

COORDINATING FUNCTIONS AND DIVISIONS No matter which structure managers choose, they must decide how to distribute authority in the organization, how many levels to have in the hierarchy of authority, and what balance to strike between centralization and decentralization to keep the number of levels in the hierarchy to a minimum. As organizations grow, managers must increase integration and coordination among functions and divisions. Six integrating mechanisms are available to facilitate this: direct contact, liaison roles, task forces, cross-functional teams, integrating roles, and the matrix structure. [LO 7-3, 7-4]

STRATEGIC ALLIANCES, B2B NETWORK STRUCTURES, AND TECHNOLOGY To avoid many of the communication and coordination problems that emerge as organizations grow, managers continue to use technology to develop new ways of organizing. In a strategic alliance, managers enter into an agreement with another organization to provide inputs or to perform a functional activity. If managers enter into a series of these agreements, they create a network structure. A network structure, most commonly based on some shared form of technology, can be formed around one company, or a number of companies can join together to create an industry B2B network. Increasingly, technology encourages more cross-functional communication among departments and with other organizations. As this continues, the concept of a *boundaryless*, or virtual, organization has become commonplace, in which employees and others are linked electronically and may not encounter each other in face-to-face work situations. [LO 7-5]

Management *in Action*

Topics for Discussion and Action

Discussion

1. Would a flexible or a more formal structure be appropriate for these organizations: (a) a large department store, (b) a Big Four accounting firm, (c) a biotechnology company? Explain your reasoning. [LO 7-1, 7-2]

2. Using the job characteristics model as a guide, discuss how a manager can enrich or enlarge employees' jobs. [LO 7-2]

3. How might a salesperson's job or an administrative assistant's job be enlarged or enriched to make it more motivating? [LO 7-2, 7-3]

4. When and under what conditions might managers change from a functional to (a) a product, (b) a geographic, or (c) a market structure? [LO 7-1, 7-3]

5. How do matrix structures and product team structures differ? Why is the product team structure more widely used? [LO 7-1, 7-3, 7-4]

6. As high-powered, low-cost wireless technologies continue to grow, many managers soon may not need to come to an office to do their jobs but may work at home. What are the pros and cons of such an arrangement? [LO 7-5]

Action

7. Find and interview a manager, and identify the kind of organizational structure that his or her organization uses to coordinate its people and resources. Why is the organization using that structure? Do you think a different structure would be more appropriate? If so which one? [LO 7-1, 7-3, 7-4]

8. With the same or another manager, discuss the distribution of authority in the organization. Does the manager think that decentralizing authority and empowering employees are appropriate? [LO 7-1, 7-3]

9. What are the advantages and disadvantages of business-to-business networks? [LO 7-5]

Building Management Skills

Understanding the Concept of Organizing [LO 7-1, 7-2, 7-3]

Think of an organization with which you are familiar, perhaps one you have worked for—such as a store, restaurant, office, church, or school. Then answer the following questions:

1. Referring to Figure 7.1, which factors are most important in explaining how the organization is organized? Do you think it is organized in the best way? Why or why not?

2. Using the job characteristics model, how motivating do you think the job of a typical employee is in this organization?

3. Provide examples of how a typical job in this organization could be enlarged or enriched.

4. What kind of organizational structure does the organization use? If it is part of a chain, what kind of structure does the entire organization use? What other structures discussed in the chapter might allow the organization to operate more effectively? For example, would the move to a product team structure lead to greater efficiency or effectiveness? Why or why not?

5. How many levels are there in the organization's hierarchy? Is authority centralized or decentralized? Describe the span of control of the top manager and of middle or first-line managers.

6. Is the distribution of authority appropriate for the organization and its activities? Would it be possible to flatten

the hierarchy by decentralizing authority and empowering employees?

7. What are the principal integrating mechanisms used in the organization? Do they provide sufficient coordination among individuals and functions? How might they be improved?

8. Now that you have analyzed the way this organization is structured, what advice would you give its managers to help them improve the way it operates?

Managing Ethically [LO 7-1, 7-3]

Suppose an organization is downsizing and laying off many of its middle managers. Some top managers charged with deciding whom to terminate might decide to keep the employees they like, and who are obedient to them, rather than the ones who are difficult but the best performers. They might also decide to lay off the most highly paid employees even if they are high performers. Think of the ethical issues involved in designing a hierarchy, and discuss the following issues.

Questions

1. What ethical rules (see Chapter 3) should managers use to decide which employees to terminate when redesigning their hierarchy?

2. Some people argue that employees who have worked for an organization for many years have a claim on the organization at least as strong as that of its shareholders. What do you think of the ethics of this position—can employees claim to "own" their jobs if they have contributed significantly to the organization's past success? How does a socially responsible organization behave in this situation?

Small Group Breakout Exercise [LO 7-1, 7-3]

Bob's Appliances

Form groups of three or four people, and appoint one member as the spokesperson who will communicate your findings to the class when called on by the instructor. Then discuss the following scenario:

Bob's Appliances sells and services household appliances such as washing machines, dishwashers, ranges, and refrigerators. Over the years, the company has developed a good reputation for the quality of its customer service, and many local builders patronize the store. Recently, other national retailers, including Best Buy, Walmart, and Costco, have begun to offer appliances for sale. To attract more customers, however, these stores also carry a complete range of consumer electronics products—televisions, computers, and digital devices. Bob Lange, the owner of Bob's Appliances, has decided that if he is to stay in business, he must widen his product range and compete directly with the chains.

Lange decides to build a 20,000-square-foot store and service center, and he is now hiring new employees to sell and service the new line of consumer electronics. Because of his company's increased size, Lange is not sure of the best way to organize the employees. Currently, he uses a functional structure; employees are divided into sales, purchasing and accounting, and repair. Bob is wondering whether selling and servicing consumer electronics is so different from selling and servicing appliances that he should move to a product structure (see the figure on the next page) and create separate sets of functions for each of his two lines of business.[65]

Questions

1. You are a team of local consultants whom Bob has called in to advise him as he makes this crucial choice. Which structure do you recommend? Why?

FUNCTIONAL STRUCTURE

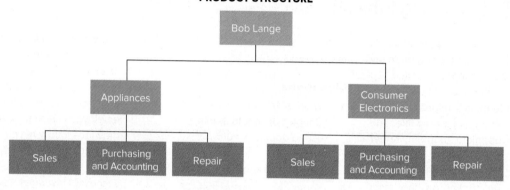

PRODUCT STRUCTURE

Be the Manager [LO 7-1, 7-3, 7-4]

Speeding Up Website Design

You have been hired by a website design, production, and hosting company whose new animated website designs are attracting a lot of attention and a lot of customers. Currently, employees are organized into different functions such as hardware, software design, graphic art, and website hosting, as well as functions such as marketing and human resources. Each function takes its turn to work on a new project from initial customer request to final online website hosting.

The problem the company is experiencing is that it typically takes one year from the initial idea stage to the time that the website is up and running; the company wants to shorten this time by half to protect and expand its market niche. In talking to other managers, you discover that they believe the company's current functional structure is the source of the problem—it is not allowing employees to develop websites fast enough to satisfy customers' demands. They want you to design a better structure.

Questions

1. Discuss ways in which you can improve how the current functional structure operates so that it speeds website development.

2. Discuss the pros and cons of moving to a (a) multidivisional, (b) matrix, or (c) product team structure to reduce website development time.

3. Which of these structures do you think is most appropriate, and why?

Case in the News [LO 7-1, 7-2, 7-3, 7-4, 7-5]

Restructuring and Rebranding Go Hand in Hand at Ogilvy

When John Seifert took over as CEO of the advertising agency Ogilvy & Mather in 2016, the company was a struggling success story. It was a success because turbulence in the ad industry had not prevented the company from growing into a global giant. Ogilvy & Mather had a well-respected name, more than 15,000 employees working in 450 offices in 120 countries, and a host of big clients buying a wide variety of services—advertising, public relations, direct marketing, program branding, and much more. The agency continues to be known for famous ad campaigns such as Dove's "Campaign for Real Beauty" and American Express's "Don't Leave Home without It." But much of its growth came from acquiring smaller agencies, and the result was a hodgepodge of independently operating entities whose work was poorly coordinated. A client might need several services and not know where to begin to find each one. Instead of seeing Ogilvy's extensive and modern capabilities, many clients just felt confused about what the company did. Thus, Ogilvy has struggled to maintain its growth.

Seifert was determined to simplify operations so that employees would better coordinate their work, and clients would understand how the company could serve them. The effort started with Ogilvy's U.S. operations. Lou Aversano, the CEO of U.S. operations, set up a USA Capabilities team, headed by a chief strategy officer and including members in charge of particular functions, such as data analysis and digital advertising. The new structure initially had nine such groups, later narrowed to seven. Management also shrank the size of the top leadership team and the number of advertising groups serving different customers out of separate offices.

As the Ogilvy USA project began to show results, Seifert announced a global rollout, which included rebranding the firm as Ogilvy Group. The new structure is built on what Ogilvy's strategists define as its six core capabilities. These might be thought of as product categories, because they are the areas of expertise in which Ogilvy offers services: brand strategy, advertising, customer engagement and commerce, public relations and influence, digital transformation, and partnerships.

Within the core capabilities, the company defines jobs in terms of "crafts"—essentially functions related to the advertising business. The categories of crafts are creative (developing ideas for advertisements), strategy, delivery, client service, data, finance, technology, talent (human resources), business development (identifying new markets and acquiring and building relationships with clients), marketing and communications, administration, and production. The orientation to "crafts" helps employees see that they all have something to contribute toward the broader objective of serving clients. Under the previous structure, it was easier for employees to think first of their alliance to, say, a PR agency or a media-buying agency operating independently of other parts of the firm. Under the new structure, it should be easier for employees to focus on the totality of a client's advertising and marketing needs. Furthermore, the term *crafts* suggests to employees that adding to their skill sets will make them more valuable.

An important objective of the restructuring was to promote coordination and efficiency—acting as a kind of global partnership, rather than a set of independent offices. Beginning with the Ogilvy USA strategy, management began to shift away from offices being financially independent of one another. Instead, groups measure their financial performance on a shared statement. Managers who had prided themselves on independence had to shift to seeing the offices united in serving clients and carrying out Ogilvy's mission of "making brands matter." That way, if clients in, say, the Chicago office need a service best provided by the Atlanta office, managers have an incentive to coordinate their work to meet the client's needs. To enable the coordination, Ogilvy added

information technology: the Connect software platform, which makes it easy for employees at any of its locations to share and look up knowledge online. With Connect, employees also can link to training modules and coworkers throughout the organization. Increased coordination is not just an end, but also a means to help the organization respond faster when a customer need arises.

The smoother operations should reduce expenses. But more than that, CEO Seifert hopes this reorganization will help existing and potential clients understand what Ogilvy is—a brand representing an agency that offers, above all, creativity.

Questions for Discussion

1. How well does Ogilvy's restructuring fit the principles of the contingency theory of organizational design? Explain.

2. Where do you see examples of a functional structure and a divisional structure in the redesigned version of Ogilvy?

3. What was Ogilvy's approach to coordinating functions and divisions in its restructured organization? What other methods of coordination might it use?

Sources: L. O'Reilly, "Ad Agency Ogilvy Rebrands and Restructures to Simplify Its Offering," *The Wall Street Journal,* www.wsj.com, June 5, 2018; J. Beer, "Ad Giant Ogilvy Unveils Global Company Rebrand and Reorganization," *Fast Company,* www.fastcompany.com, June 5, 2018; P. Coffee, "Ogilvy Rebrands Itself after 70 Years with New Visual Identity, Logo and Organizational Design," *Adweek,* www.adweek.com, June 5, 2018; C. Beale, "Ogilvy Unveils New Identity: CEO Seifert Explains Agency's New Structure and Purpose," *Campaign,* www.campaignlive.co.uk, June 5, 2018; P. Coffee, "Ogilvy Unveils 'USA 2.0' Restructuring Plan, Promises to Close Gender Pay Gap," *Adweek,* www.adweek.com, April 23, 2018; J. Beer, "Ogilvy CEO on How Restructuring One of the World's Largest Ad Agencies Is Going So Far," *Fast Company,* www.fastcompany.com, May 30, 2017.

Endnotes

1. R. Gulati, "Structure That's Not Stifling," *Harvard Business Review,* May–June 2018, 68–79; A. Karp, "Building from Strength," *Air Transport World,* May 2017, 16–20.

2. D. Gates, "Management Shake-Up at Alaska Air Will Bring Layoffs," *Seattle Times,* www.seattletimes.com, October 11, 2018.

3. Gulati, "Structure That's Not Stifling."

4. Karp, "Building from Strength"; A. Levine-Weinberg, "Path to Higher Profits," *Motley Fool,* www.fool.com, November 28, 2018; S. McCartney, "How Much of Your $355 Ticket Is Profit for Airlines?," *The Wall Street Journal,* www.wsj.com, February 14, 2018; S. McCartney, "The Best and Worst U.S. Airlines of 2017," *The Wall Street Journal,* www.wsj.com, January 10, 2018.

5. Gates, "Management Shake-Up at Alaska Air"; M. Goldstein, "Alaska Airlines–Virgin America Merger Still a Work in Progress," *Forbes,* www.forbes.com, June 13, 2018.

6. G. R. Jones, *Organizational Theory, Design and Change: Text and Cases* (Upper Saddle River: Prentice Hall, 2011).

7. J. Child, *Organization: A Guide for Managers and Administrators* (New York: Harper & Row, 1977).

8. P. R. Lawrence and J. W. Lorsch, *Organization and Environment* (Boston: Graduate School of Business Administration, Harvard University, 1967).

9. R. Duncan, "What Is the Right Organizational Design?," *Organizational Dynamics,* Winter 1979, 59–80.

10. T. Burns and G. R. Stalker, *The Management of Innovation* (London: Tavistock, 1966).

11. D. Miller, "Strategy Making and Structure: Analysis and Implications for Performance," *Academy of Management Journal* 30 (1987), 7–32.

12. A. D. Chandler, *Strategy and Structure* (Cambridge, MA: MIT Press, 1962).

13. J. Stopford and L. Wells, *Managing the Multinational Enterprise* (London: Longman, 1972).

14. C. Perrow, *Organizational Analysis: A Sociological View* (Belmont, CA: Wadsworth, 1970).

15. F. W. Taylor, *The Principles of Scientific Management* (New York: Harper, 1911).

16. R. W. Griffin, *Task Design: An Integrative Approach* (Glenview, IL: Scott, Foresman, 1982).

17. Ibid.

18. C. Matlack, "IKEA Tries Breaking Out of the Big Box," *Bloomberg Businessweek,* January 15, 2018, 20–21.

19. R. Milne, "Ikea Vows 'Transformation' as It Reshapes Business Model," *Financial Times,* www.ft.com, April 10, 2018.

20. Á. Cain, "Ikea Employees Say That Changes to the Stores Are Creating a Divisive Environment Where 'Nobody Is Willing to Help,'" *Business Insider,* www.businessinsider.com, November 28, 2018.

21. S. Chaudhuri, "IKEA to Slash Thousands of Jobs in Restructuring," *The Wall Street Journal,* www.wsj.com, November 21, 2018; B. Murphy Jr., "IKEA Just Announced Some Radical Changes That Will Change Everything You Think about IKEA (They Sure Hope So Anyway)," *Inc.,* www.inc.com, November 22, 2018.

22. Matlack, "IKEA Tries Breaking out of the Big Box."

23. J. R. Hackman and G. R. Oldham, *Work Redesign* (Reading, MA: Addison-Wesley, 1980).

24. "Executive Management," https://investors.pier1.com, accessed January 3, 2019.

25. J. R. Galbraith and R. K. Kazanjian, *Strategy Implementation: Structure, System, and Process,* 2nd ed. (St. Paul, MN: West, 1986).

26. Lawrence and Lorsch, *Organization and Environment.*

27. Jones, *Organizational Theory.*

28. Lawrence and Lorsch, *Organization and Environment.*

29. R. H. Hall, *Organizations: Structure and Process* (Englewood Cliffs, NJ: Prentice Hall, 1972); R. Miles, *Macro Organizational Behavior* (Santa Monica, CA: Goodyear, 1980).

30. Chandler, *Strategy and Structure.*

31. G. R. Jones and C. W. L. Hill, "Transaction Cost Analysis of Strategy-Structure Choice," *Strategic Management Journal* 9 (1988), 159–72.

32. E. Fry, "Critical Condition," *Fortune,* June 1, 2018, 134–144; Charley Grant, "Drug Supply Chain Feels the Trump Effect," *The Wall Street Journal,* www.wsj.com, July 11, 2018.

33. J. D. Rockoff, "Pfizer to Pay $24 Million to Settle Probe into Copay Assistance Charities," *The Wall Street Journal,* www.wsj.com, May 24, 2018.

34. Fry, "Critical Condition."

35. J. D. Rockoff, "Pfizer to Roll Back Price Increases after Trump Criticism," *The Wall Street Journal,* www.wsj.com, July 10, 2018; A. Gatlin, "Pfizer Opts to Defer Price Hikes amid Trump Scrutiny—So, Who's Next?," *Investor's Business Daily,* www.investors.com, July 11, 2018.

36. A. Prang, "Pfizer to Reorganize Business Units," *The Wall Street Journal,* www.wsj.com, July 11, 2018; K. Speights, "About Pfizer's Restructuring Plans," *Motley Fool,* www.fool.com, July 11, 2018.

37. "Pfizer and GlaxoSmithKline Announce Joint Venture to Create a Premier Global Consumer Healthcare Company," *BusinessWire,* www.businesswire.com, accessed January 4, 2019.

38. D. Roland and J. S. Hopkins, "Pfizer, Glaxo to Create Over-the-Counter Drug Giant," *The Wall Street Journal,* www.wsj.com, accessed January 4, 2019.

39. "Executive Team: Steve Easterbrook," https://news.mcdonalds.com, accessed January 4, 2019; J. Jargon, "McDonald's Promises Franchisees More

Support," *The Wall Street Journal,* www.wsj.com, June 11, 2018.

40. B. Mikel, "Want to Attract Top Talent? Follow the Lead of McDonald's and Do This," *Inc.,* www.inc.com, accessed January 4, 2019.

41. Reuters, "McDonald's Already Found Its Next U.S. President," *Forbes,* www.forbes.com, accessed January 4, 2019; P. Rosenthal, "Innovate or Not, McDonald's New President Will Find It's Harder to Hit a Home Run in the Hot Seat," *Chicago Tribune,* www.chicagotribune.com, August 31, 2016.

42. J. Ringen, "The Inside Story of How McDonald's Innovated the Quarter Pounder," *Fast Company,* www.fastcompany.com, accessed January 4, 2019.

43. D. Klein, "McDonald's Outlines U.S. Organizational Changes," *QSR Magazine,* www.qsrmagazine.com, accessed January 4, 2019; J. Jargon, "McDonald's Plans Corporate Job Cuts, 'Eliminating Layers,'" *The Wall Street Journal,* www.wsj.com, June 7, 2018.

44. R. K. Beals, "The Live-Work-Play HQs That Amazon—and Even McDonald's—Embrace Could Prove Pivotal to Their Growth," *MarketWatch,* www.marketwatch.com, accessed January 4, 2019.

45. S. M. Davis and P. R. Lawrence, *Matrix* (Reading, MA: Addison-Wesley, 1977); J. R. Galbraith,

"Matrix Organization Designs: How to Combine Functional and Project Forms," *Business Horizons* 14 (1971), 29–40.

46. L. R. Burns, "Matrix Management in Hospitals: Testing Theories of Matrix Structure and Development," *Administrative Science Quarterly* 34 (1989), 349–68.

47. C. W. L. Hill, *International Business* (Homewood, IL: Irwin, 2003).

48. D. Lock, "Using Cross-Functional Teams to Drive Innovation and Improvement," *Innovation Excellence Weekly,* www.innovationexcellence.com, accessed January 4, 2019.

49. Jones, *Organizational Theory.*

50. P. Blau, "A Formal Theory of Differentiation in Organizations," *American Sociological Review* 35 (1970), 684–95.

51. "Executive Team: Robert Gibbs," https://news.mcdonalds.com, accessed January 4, 2019.

52. Child, *Organization.*

53. S. Chandra, "U.S. Payrolls and Wages Cool While Jobless Rate Hits 48-Year Low," *Bloomberg,* www.bloomberg.com, October 5, 2018.

54. "Essential Leadership Traits," http://ogolead.com, accessed January 4, 2019; D. Novak, "Here's the Best Way to Cure Toxic Leadership, Says Former Yum Brands CEO," *CNBC,* www.cnbc.com, accessed January 4, 2019.

55. P. M. Blau and R. A. Schoenherr, *The Structure of Organizations* (New York: Basic Books, 1971).

56. Jones, *Organizational Theory.*

57. J. R. Galbraith, *Designing Complex Organizations* (Reading, MA: Addison-Wesley, 1977), chap. 1; Galbraith and Kazanjian, *Strategy Implementation,* chap. 7.

58. "Program Growth," www.pepsicofoodforgood.com, accessed January 4, 2019; "The Women Holding Up More Than Half the PepsiCo Sky," *Global Times,* www.globaltimes.cn, March 7, 2018.

59. S. Witten, "McDonald's Reunites with Disney on Happy Meals after More Than a Decade Apart," *CNBC,* www.cnbc.com, accessed January 4, 2019.

60. G. S. Capowski, "Designing a Corporate Identity," *Management Review,* June 1993, 37–38.

61. "Where Nike Products Are Made," http://manufacturingmap.nikeinc.com, accessed January 4, 2019.

62. J. Marcia, "Just Doing It," *Distribution,* January 1995, 36–40.

63. L. Jones, "There Is No Innovation without Sustainability, Says Nike's Chief Operating Officer," www.dezeen.com, accessed January 4, 2019.

64. "Gartner Says Supply Chain Management Will Exceed $13 Billion in 2017, Up 11 Percent from 2016," www.gartner.com, accessed January 4, 2019.

65. Copyright © 2006, Gareth R. Jones.

8 Organizational Control and Change

Learning Objectives

After studying this chapter, you should be able to:

LO 8-1 Define organizational control, and explain how it increases organizational effectiveness.

LO 8-2 Describe the four steps in the control process and the way it operates over time.

LO 8-3 Identify the main output controls, and discuss their advantages and disadvantages as means of coordinating and motivating employees.

LO 8-4 Identify the main behavior controls, and discuss their advantages and disadvantages as a means of managing and motivating employees.

LO 8-5 Explain how organizational culture or clan control creates an effective organizational architecture.

LO 8-6 Discuss the relationship between organizational control and change, and explain why managing change is a vital management task.

Management Snapshot

P&G Takes a Hard Look at Digital Ads

What Controls Can Managers Use to Ensure Organizational Success?

Procter & Gamble, the seller of dozens of major consumer brands, including Bounty, Crest, Pampers, and Tide, spends more on advertising than any other company in the world.[1] As a marketing leader, P&G was early to direct many of its billions of advertising dollars to the Internet. Eventually, online ad spending reached about one-third of its total advertising budget.

Advertising must fulfill a business purpose, of course. P&G, like other organizations, wants to know how many people are receiving its ad messages and whether the messages produce an increase in sales. Ineffective ads are a wasted expense, while effective ads increase sales. Furthermore, P&G wants to spend ad dollars efficiently, in order to increase profits along with sales. These are all considerations of Chief Brand Officer Marc Pritchard, while CEO David Taylor keeps an eye on the company's overall performance.

As Pritchard and Taylor reviewed the company's marketing performance, they became increasingly dissatisfied with what they were learning about the performance of digital media. More consumers have been installing ad blockers, a sign that they felt overwhelmed by ads. The more consumers who used ad blockers, the more P&G was paying for ads that would go unseen because they were blocked. In addition, ads sometimes appeared next to controversial content. A famous example occurred on YouTube, which for a time was running ads for Tide next to videos of the "Tide Pod challenge" in which people tried eating the laundry detergent. Even the number of clicks on an ad was becoming a questionable performance measure: Sites were counting clicks by software bots that had been created just to click on links in order to drive up results. Pritchard and Taylor expressed their concerns publicly, and media companies took note. If they didn't satisfy P&G's concerns, they risked losing a major source of revenue. In particular, Google and Facebook agreed to let the Media Rating Council audit their performance data.[2]

Over the months that followed, Pritchard and Taylor analyzed the audit results and other data. Much of what they learned was not favorable to digital media. For example, they learned that, on average, consumers looked at an online ad for just 17 seconds. P&G tried cutting digital marketing expenses by more than $100 million and saw little measurable impact on sales—suggesting that those ads had not delivered the most important kind of results.[3]

Pritchard responded to the information by making changes in P&G's advertising budgets. The company directed hundreds of millions of dollars away from digital, especially from sites that had not placed ads next to appropriate content or generated much response from

Evaluating poor digital media results caused Procter & Gamble's senior management (including Chief Brand Officer Marc Pritchard, pictured here) to redirect spending to other forms of advertising for P&G's products.
Neil Hall/Reuters

consumers. Of the money still spent on Internet media, more now goes to retail sites, such as Amazon and Walmart, where shoppers can see P&G's brands while looking for related products. Along with these changes, Pritchard continues to look for cost savings that keep the overall marketing program operating as efficiently as possible.[4]

One immediate outcome of P&G's pressure and changes in spending is that online media companies have scrambled to create a more favorable environment for P&G and other advertisers. These changes include rewriting algorithms for what content is featured and what ads are displayed. Furthermore, as P&G cut online ad spending, it posted stronger profits.[5]

Overview

As discussed in Chapter 7, the first task facing managers is to establish the structure of task- and job-reporting relationships that allows organizational members to use resources most efficiently and effectively. Structure alone, however, does not provide the incentive or motivation for people to behave in ways that help achieve organizational goals. The purpose of organizational control is to provide managers with a means of directing and motivating employees to work toward achieving organizational goals and to provide managers with specific feedback on how well an organization and its members are performing.

Organizational structure provides an organization with a skeleton, and control and culture give it the muscles, nerves, and sensations that allow managers to regulate and govern its activities. The managerial functions of organizing and controlling are inseparable, and effective managers must learn to make them work together in a harmonious way.

In this chapter, we look in detail at the nature of organizational control and describe the steps in the control process. We discuss three types of control available to managers to control and influence organizational members: output control, behavior control, and clan control (which operates through the values and norms of an organization's culture).[6] Then we discuss the important issue of organizational change, change that is possible only when managers have put in place a control system that allows them to alter the way people and groups behave. By the end of this chapter, you will appreciate the rich variety of control systems available to managers and understand why developing an appropriate control system is vital to increasing the performance of an organization and its members.

What Is Organizational Control?

As we noted in Chapter 1, *controlling* is the process whereby managers monitor and regulate how efficiently and effectively an organization and its members are performing the activities necessary to achieve organizational goals. As discussed in previous chapters, when planning and organizing, managers develop the organizational strategy and structure that they hope will allow the organization to use resources most effectively to create value for customers. In controlling, managers monitor and evaluate whether the organization's strategy and structure are working as intended, how they could be improved, and how they might be changed if they are not working.

LO 8-1
Define organizational control, and explain how it increases organizational effectiveness.

Control, however, does not mean just reacting to events after they have occurred. It also means keeping an organization on track, anticipating events that might occur, and then changing the organization to respond to whatever opportunities or threats have been identified. Control is concerned with keeping employees motivated, focused on the important problems confronting the organization, and working together to make the changes that will help an organization perform better over time.

The Importance of Organizational Control

To understand the importance of organizational control, consider how it helps managers obtain superior efficiency, quality, responsiveness to customers, and innovation—the four building blocks of competitive advantage.

To determine how efficiently they are using their resources, managers must be able to accurately measure how many units of inputs (raw materials, human resources, and so on) are being used to produce a unit of output, such as a Ford or Toyota vehicle. Managers also must be able to measure how many units of outputs (goods and services) are being produced. A control system contains the measures or yardsticks that let managers assess how efficiently the organization is producing goods and services. Moreover, if managers experiment with changing how the organization produces goods and services to find a more efficient way of producing them, these measures tell managers how successful they have been. Without a control system in place, managers have no idea how well their organization is performing and how its performance can be improved—information that is becoming increasingly important in today's highly competitive environment.

Today much of the competition among organizations centers on increasing the quality of goods and services. In the car industry, for example, cars within each price range compete in features, design, and reliability. Thus whether a customer will buy a Ford Focus, Toyota Camry, or Honda Accord depends significantly on the quality of each product. Organizational control is important in determining the quality of goods and services because it gives managers feedback on product quality. If the managers of carmakers consistently measure the number of customer complaints and the number of new cars returned for repairs, or if school principals measure how many students drop out of school or how achievement scores on nationally based tests vary over time, they have a good indication of how much quality they have built into their product—be it an educated student or a car that does not break down. Effective managers create a control system that consistently monitors the quality of goods and services so they can continuously improve quality—an approach to change that gives them a competitive advantage.

Managers can help make their organizations more responsive to customers if they develop a control system that allows them to evaluate how well customer-contact employees perform their jobs. Monitoring employee behavior can help managers find ways to increase employees'

From whom would you rather buy a new car? A company that reinforces and rewards employee responsiveness, consistency, and know-how in customer care, or a company that doesn't? Toyota bets you'll pick the former. Hongqi Zhang/Alamy Stock Photo

performance levels, perhaps by revealing areas in which skill training can help employees or in which new procedures can allow employees to perform their jobs better. Also, when employees know their behaviors are being monitored, they have more incentive to be helpful and consistent in how they act toward customers. To improve customer service, for example, Toyota regularly surveys customers about their experiences with particular Toyota dealers. If a dealership receives too many customer complaints, Toyota's managers investigate the dealership to uncover the sources of the problems and suggest solutions; if necessary, they might even threaten to reduce the number of cars a dealership receives to force the dealer to improve the quality of its customer service.

Finally, controlling can raise the level of innovation in an organization. Successful innovation takes place when managers create an organizational setting in which employees feel empowered to be creative and in which authority is decentralized to employees so they feel free to experiment and take control of their work activities. Deciding on the appropriate control systems to encourage risk taking is an important management challenge; organizational culture is vital in this regard. To encourage work teams at Toyota to perform at a high level, for example, top managers monitored the performance of each team by examining how each team reduced costs or increased quality—and used a bonus system related to performance to reward each team. The team manager then evaluated each team member's individual performance, and the most innovative employees received promotions and rewards based on their superior performance. Sometimes, however, organizational control systems, including the use of email, can lead to challenges, frustrations, and lost productivity. As the accompanying "Management Insight" suggests, implementing email policies to help control the overload of information may help employee productivity and morale.

Management Insight

Controlling Your Office Inbox

In terms of challenges in the modern workplace, email may be at the top of the list. Overuse of this communication method and problems surrounding it continue to hinder employee effectiveness and efficiency.[7] Research suggests that the average worker spends more than 13 hours a week on email—and those hours are not limited to time spent in the office.[8] In this 24/7 world, with people connected to multiple devices simultaneously, how can managers implement controls that help employees handle email so that the quality of their work and work–life balance don't suffer? Philadelphia-based Vynamic may have the answer: a Zmail policy.

Vynamic is a health care consulting firm that prides itself on a strong organizational culture. Several years ago, employees started to complain about the stress of constant email contact at all hours. Founder Dan Calista describes a common scenario that many professionals experience in this digital world. An employee checks email before going to sleep. Next thing the person knows, he or she is now thinking about the email instead of getting a restful stretch of "ZZZs." Thus, the Zmail policy was born. Vynamic employees (including managers) are requested not to send

Implementing company controls such as email policies may help improve employee productivity and morale. Rawpixel.com/Shutterstock

emails between 10 p.m. and 6 a.m. during the week and all day Saturday and Sunday.[9]

The company recognizes that some employees like to spend a few hours over the weekend reviewing pertinent emails and sending communications to clients and colleagues when no one is distracting them. For some people, there are benefits to this type of work habit. However, Calista recommends saving the email as a draft and sending it off first thing Monday morning. He asks, "Why is it so important to you that the other person join your weekend time?"[10]

Despite Vynamic's ban on late night and weekend emails, employees are expected to communicate with clients and colleagues as needed to keep business moving forward.[11] Calista says that unplugging from email and mentally disconnecting from work is not only liberating, it might also help employees become more productive after a good night's sleep. Vynamic employees see the Zmail policy as an important company benefit: The company is routinely rated as a top place to work among consulting firms in the country.[12]

Not all companies have the tools or the time to implement organizational controls like the one initiated by Vynamic. However, there are ways that managers and employees alike can get a handle on managing the email challenge. The following tips can be useful to professionals at all levels of an organization:

- Turn off notifications so you're not distracted by every message received in your inbox.
- Don't check email more than three times a day, and select specific times in the work day to check for messages.
- If you need information from a colleague in less than three hours, use a mode of communication other than email—how about picking up the phone and asking for the information? This allows coworkers to work on other tasks without dreading one more email notification.
- Respond to simple and urgent messages, file those that do not require a reply, and flag any that require more thought and follow-up before sending a response.
- Empty the email trash at the end of the day. Sometimes you will need to retrieve an email that you mistakenly trashed, so make this the last thing you do at the end of the workday.[13] ●

Control Systems and Technology

Control systems are formal target-setting, monitoring, evaluation, and feedback systems that provide managers with information about whether the organization's strategy and structure are working efficiently and effectively.[14] Effective control systems alert managers when something is going wrong and give them time to respond

control systems
Formal target-setting, monitoring, evaluation, and feedback systems that provide managers with information about how well the organization's strategy and structure are working.

to opportunities and threats. An effective control system has three characteristics: It is flexible enough to allow managers to respond as necessary to unexpected events; it provides accurate information about organizational performance; and it gives managers information in a timely manner because making decisions on the basis of outdated information is a recipe for failure.

Technology has revolutionized control systems because they facilitate the flow of accurate and timely information up and down the organizational hierarchy and between functions and divisions. Today employees at all levels of the organization routinely feed information into a company's information system or network and start the chain of events that affect decision making in some other part of the organization. This could be the retail clerk who scans a tag on a purchased piece of sportswear that tells merchandise managers what items need to be reordered, or the salesperson in the field who inputs data into a mobile device to alert the marketing department about customers' changing wants or needs.

Control and information systems are developed to measure performance at each stage in the process of transforming inputs into finished goods and services (see Figure 8.1). At the input stage, managers use feedforward control to anticipate problems before they arise so problems do not occur later during the conversion process.[15] For example, by giving strict product specifications to suppliers in advance (a form of performance target), an organization can control the quality of the inputs it receives from its suppliers and thus avoid potential problems during the conversion process. Also, technology can be used to keep in contact with suppliers and to monitor their progress. Similarly, by screening job applicants, often by viewing their résumés electronically and using several interviews to select the most highly skilled people, managers can lessen the chance that they will hire people who lack the necessary skills or experience to perform effectively. In general, the development of management information systems promotes feedforward control that gives managers timely information about changes in the task and general environments that may impact their organization later on. Effective managers always monitor trends and changes in the external environment to try to anticipate problems.

feedforward control Control that allows managers to anticipate problems before they arise.

At the conversion stage, concurrent control gives managers immediate feedback on how efficiently inputs are being transformed into outputs so managers can correct problems as they arise. Concurrent control through the use of technology alerts managers to the need to react quickly to whatever is the source of the problem, be it a defective batch of inputs, a machine that is out of alignment, or a worker who lacks the skills necessary to perform a task efficiently. Concurrent control is at the heart of programs to increase quality, in which workers are expected to constantly monitor the quality of

concurrent control
Control that gives managers immediate feedback on how efficiently inputs are being transformed into outputs so managers can correct problems as they arise.

Figure 8.1
Three Types of Control

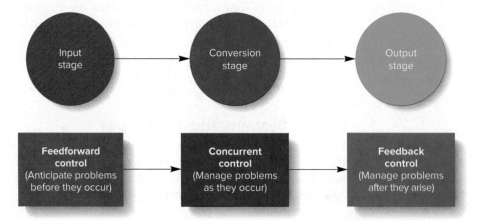

the goods or services they provide at every step of the production process and inform managers as soon as they discover problems. One of the strengths of Toyota's production system, for example, is that individual workers have the authority to push a button to stop the assembly line whenever they discover a quality problem. When all problems are corrected, the result is a finished product that is much more reliable.

At the output stage, managers use feedback control to provide information about customers' reactions to goods and services so corrective action can be taken if necessary. For example, a feedback control system that monitors the number of customer returns alerts managers when defective products are being produced, and a management information system (MIS) that measures increases or decreases in relative sales of different products alerts managers to changes in customer tastes so they can increase or reduce the production of specific products.

feedback control
Control that gives managers information about customers' reactions to goods and services so corrective action can be taken if necessary.

The Control Process

LO 8-2
Describe the four steps in the control process and the way it operates over time.

The control process, whether at the input, conversion, or output stage, can be broken down into four steps: establishing standards of performance, and then measuring, comparing, and evaluating actual performance (see Figure 8.2).[16]

- Step 1: *Establish the standards of performance, goals, or targets against which performance is to be evaluated.*

At step 1 in the control process managers decide on the standards of performance, goals, or targets that they will use in the future to evaluate the performance of the entire organization or part of it (such as a division, a function, or an individual). The standards of performance that managers select measure efficiency, quality, responsiveness to customers, and innovation.[17] If managers decide to pursue a low-cost strategy, for example, they need to measure efficiency at all levels in the organization.

At the corporate level, a standard of performance that measures efficiency is operating costs, the actual costs associated with producing goods and services, including all employee-related costs. Top managers might set a corporate goal of "reducing operating costs by 10% for the next three years" to increase efficiency. Corporate managers might then evaluate divisional managers for their ability to reduce operating costs within their respective divisions, and divisional managers might set cost-saving targets for functional managers. Thus performance standards selected at one level affect those at the other levels, and ultimately the performance of individual managers is evaluated in terms of their ability to reduce costs.

Figure 8.2

Four Steps in the Organizational Control Process

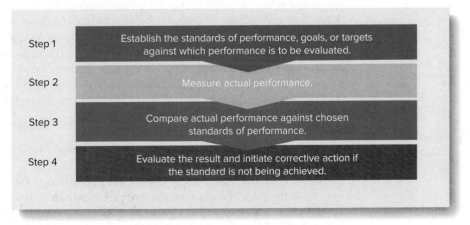

Step 1 Establish the standards of performance, goals, or targets against which performance is to be evaluated.

Step 2 Measure actual performance.

Step 3 Compare actual performance against chosen standards of performance.

Step 4 Evaluate the result and initiate corrective action if the standard is not being achieved.

The number of standards or indicators of performance that an organization's managers use to evaluate efficiency, quality, and so on can run into the thousands or hundreds of thousands. Managers at each level are responsible for selecting standards that will best allow them to evaluate how well the part of the organization they are responsible for is performing.[18] Managers must be careful to choose standards of performance that let them assess how well they are doing with all four building blocks of competitive advantage. If managers focus on just one standard (such as efficiency), and ignore others (such as determining what customers really want and innovating a new line of products to satisfy them), managers may end up hurting their organization's performance.

- Step 2: *Measure actual performance.*

Once managers have decided which standards or targets they will use to evaluate performance, the next step in the control process is to measure actual performance. In practice, managers can measure or evaluate two things: (1) the actual *outputs* that result from the behavior of their members and (2) the *behaviors* themselves (hence the terms *output control* and *behavior control* used in this chapter).[19]

Sometimes both outputs and behaviors can be easily measured. Measuring outputs and evaluating behavior are relatively easy in a fast-food restaurant, for example, because employees are performing routine tasks. Managers at Home Depot are rigorous in using output control to measure how fast inventory flows through stores. Similarly, managers of a fast-food restaurant can easily measure outputs by counting how many customers their employees serve, the time each transaction takes, and how much money each customer spends. Managers can easily observe each employee's behavior and quickly take action to solve any problems that may arise.

When an organization and its members perform complex, nonroutine activities that are intrinsically hard to measure, it is more challenging for managers to measure outputs or behavior. It is difficult, for example, for managers in charge of R&D departments at Intel or Apple to measure performance or to evaluate the performance of individual members because it can take several years to determine whether the new products that engineers and scientists are developing will be profitable. Moreover, it is impossible for a manager to measure how creative an engineer or scientist is by watching his or her actions.

In general, the more nonroutine or complex organizational activities are, the harder it is for managers to measure outputs or behaviors.[20] Outputs, however, are usually easier to measure than behaviors because they are more tangible and objective. Therefore, the first kind of performance measures that managers tend to use are those that measure outputs. Then managers develop performance measures or standards that allow them to evaluate behaviors to determine whether employees at all levels are working toward organizational goals. Some simple behavior measures are (1) whether employees come to work on time and (2) whether employees consistently follow the established rules for greeting and serving customers. The various types of output and behavior control and how they are used at the different organizational levels—corporate, divisional, functional, and individual—are discussed in detail later.

- Step 3: *Compare actual performance against chosen standards of performance.*

During step 3, managers evaluate whether—and to what extent—performance deviates from the standards of performance chosen in step 1. If performance is higher than expected, managers might decide they set performance standards too low and may raise them for the next period to challenge their employees.[21] Managers at successful companies are well known for the way they try to improve performance in manufacturing settings by constantly raising performance standards to motivate managers and workers to find new ways to reduce costs or increase quality.

However, if performance is too low and standards were not reached, or if standards were set so high that employees could not achieve them, managers must decide whether to take corrective action.[22] It is easy to take corrective action when the reasons for poor performance can be identified—for instance, high labor costs. To reduce costs, managers can search for low-cost overseas suppliers, invest more in technology, or implement cross-functional teams. More often, however, the reasons for poor performance are hard to identify. Changes in the environment, such as the emergence of a new global competitor, a recession, or an increase in interest rates, might be the source of the problem. Within an organization, perhaps the R&D function underestimated the problems it would encounter in developing a new product or the extra costs of doing unforeseen research. If managers are to take any form of corrective action, step 4 is necessary.

- Step 4: *Evaluate the result and initiate corrective action (that is, make changes) if the standard is not being achieved.*

The final step in the control process is to evaluate the results and implement change as appropriate. Whether or not performance standards have been met, managers can learn a great deal during this step. If managers decide the level of performance is unacceptable, they must try to change how work activities are performed to solve the problem. Sometimes performance problems occur because the work standard was too high—for example, a sales target was too optimistic and impossible to achieve. In this case, adopting more realistic standards can reduce the gap between actual performance and desired performance.

However, if managers determine that something in the situation is causing the problem, then to raise performance they will need to change how resources are utilized or shared.[23] Perhaps the latest technology is not being used; perhaps workers lack the advanced training needed to perform at a higher level; perhaps the organization needs to buy its inputs or assemble its products abroad to compete against low-cost rivals; perhaps it needs to restructure itself or reengineer its work processes to increase efficiency.

The simplest example of a control system is the thermostat in a home. By setting the thermostat, you establish the standard of performance with which actual temperature is to be compared. The thermostat contains a sensing or monitoring device, which measures the actual temperature against the desired temperature. Whenever there is a difference between them, the furnace or air-conditioning unit is activated to bring the temperature back to the standard. In other words, corrective action is initiated. This is a simple control system: It is entirely self-contained, and the target (temperature) is easy to measure.

Establishing targets and designing measurement systems are much more difficult for managers because the high level of uncertainty in the organizational environment means managers rarely know what might happen in the future. Thus it is vital for managers to design control systems to alert them to problems quickly so they can be dealt with before they become threatening. Another issue is that managers are not just concerned about bringing the organization's performance up to some predetermined standard; they want to push that standard forward to encourage employees at all levels to find new ways to raise performance.

In the following sections, we consider three important types of control systems that managers use to coordinate and motivate employees to ensure that they pursue superior efficiency, quality, innovation, and responsiveness to customers: output control, behavior control, and clan control (see Figure 8.3). Managers use all three to shape, regulate, and govern organizational activities, no matter what specific organizational structure is in place.

Figure 8.3

Three Organizational
Control Systems

Type of control	Mechanisms of control
Output control	Financial measures of performance Organizational goals Operating budgets
Behavior control	Direct supervision MBO/Balanced scorecard Rules and standard operating procedures
Organizational culture/clan control	Values Norms Socialization

Output Control

All managers develop a system of output control for their organizations. First they choose the goals or output performance standards or targets that they think will best measure efficiency, quality, innovation, and responsiveness to customers. Then they measure to see whether the performance goals and standards are being achieved at the corporate, divisional, functional, and individual employee levels of the organization. The three main mechanisms that managers use to assess output or performance are financial measures, organizational goals, and operating budgets.

LO 8-3
Identify the main output controls, and discuss their advantages and disadvantages as means of coordinating and motivating employees.

Financial Measures of Performance

Top managers are most concerned with overall organizational performance and use various financial measures to evaluate it. The most common are profit ratios, liquidity ratios, leverage ratios, and activity ratios. They are discussed here and summarized in Table 8.1.[24]

- *Profit ratios* measure how efficiently managers are using the organization's resources to generate profits. *Return on investment (ROI),* an organization's net income before taxes divided by its total assets, is the most commonly used financial performance measure because it allows managers of one organization to compare performance with that of other organizations. ROI lets managers assess an organization's competitive advantage. *Operating margin* is calculated by dividing a company's operating profit (the amount it has left after all the costs of making the product and running the business have been deducted) by sales revenues. This measure tells managers how efficiently an organization is using its resources; every successful attempt to reduce costs will be reflected in increased operating profit, for example. Also, operating margin is a means of comparing one year's performance to another; for example, if managers discover operating margin has improved by 5% from one year to the next, they know their organization is building a competitive advantage.

- *Liquidity ratios* measure how well managers have protected organizational resources to be able to meet short-term obligations. The *current ratio* (current assets divided by current liabilities) tells managers whether they have the resources available to meet the claims of short-term creditors. The *quick ratio* shows whether they can pay these claims without selling inventory.

- *Leverage ratios,* such as the *debt-to-assets ratio* and the *times-covered ratio,* measure the degree to which managers use debt (borrow money) or equity (issue new

Table 8.1

Four Measures of Financial Performance

Profit Ratios		
Return on investment	$= \dfrac{\text{Net profit before taxes}}{\text{Total assets}}$	Measures how well managers are using the organization's resources to generate profits.
Operating margin	$= \dfrac{\text{Total operating profit}}{\text{Sales revenues}}$	Measures how much percentage of profit a company is earning on sales; the higher the percentage, the better a company is using its resources to make and sell the product.
Liquidity Ratios		
Current ratio	$= \dfrac{\text{Current assets}}{\text{Current liabilities}}$	Measures the availability of resources to meet claims of short-term creditors.
Quick ratio	$= \dfrac{\text{Current assets} - \text{Inventory}}{\text{Current liabilities}}$	Measures the ability to pay off claims of short-term creditors without selling inventory.
Leverage Ratios		
Debt-to-assets ratio	$= \dfrac{\text{Total debt}}{\text{Total assets}}$	Measures the extent to which managers have used borrowed funds to finance investments.
Times-covered ratio	$= \dfrac{\text{Profit before interest and taxes}}{\text{Total interest charges}}$	Measures how far profits can decline before managers cannot meet interest charges. If this ratio declines to less than 1, the organization is technically insolvent.
Activity Ratios		
Inventory turnover	$= \dfrac{\text{Cost of goods sold}}{\text{Inventory}}$	Measures how efficiently managers are turning over inventory so that excess inventory is not carried.
Days sales outstanding	$= \dfrac{\text{Current accounts receivable}}{\text{Sales for period divided by days in period}}$	Measures how efficiently managers are collecting revenues from customers to pay expenses.

shares) to finance ongoing operations. An organization is highly leveraged if it uses more debt than equity. Debt can be risky when net income or profit fails to cover the interest on the debt—as some people learn too late when their paychecks do not allow them to pay off their credit cards.

- *Activity ratios* show how well managers are creating value from organizational assets. *Inventory turnover* measures how efficiently managers are turning over inventory so excess inventory is not carried. *Days sales outstanding* reveals how efficiently managers are collecting revenue from customers to pay expenses.

The objectivity of financial measures of performance is the reason why so many managers use them to assess the efficiency and effectiveness of their organizations. When an organization fails to meet performance standards such as ROI, revenue, or stock price targets, managers know they must take corrective action. Thus financial controls tell managers when a corporate reorganization might be necessary, when they should sell off divisions and exit businesses, or when they should rethink their corporate-level strategies. In addition to quantitative skills, job candidates need strong written communication and problem-solving skills in today's workplace, as described in the accompanying "Management Insight" feature.

Management Insight

Wanted: Strong Writing and Problem-Solving Skills

Looking to land your first real job? Research suggests that work experience as an intern gets high marks from company recruiters looking to hire recent grads. Click_and_Photo/Getty Images

In today's highly competitive job market, strong writing and problem-solving skills are the top attributes employers are looking for on a college grad's résumé. According to the *Job Outlook 2019 Survey* by the National Association of Colleges and Employers (NACE), close to 82% of respondents cite strong written communication and problem-solving skills as the most important attributes for job candidates. In addition to a strong GPA, other desirable attributes include the ability to work on a team, show initiative, and possess analytical/quantitative skills.[25]

While past NACE research found a student's major the deciding factor between two otherwise qualified candidates, the 2019 survey results suggest that the most influential factor is whether the candidate has internship experience either within the hiring organization or within the organization's industry. On a scale of 1 to 5, with 1 being no influence at all and 5 being extreme influence, completing an internship with the hiring organization or within the same industry rated scores of 4.6 and 4.5, respectively.[26] This finding underscores employer sentiment that internships provide students with professional experience and opportunities to fine tune communication and problem-solving skills, as well as learn basic office etiquette, which will help them hit the ground running on the first day of their new job.[27]

The good news for 2019 college grads? NACE estimates that employers plan to hire nearly 17% more new graduates for their U.S. operations than they did in 2018. This comes as welcomed news and marks the best initial hiring outlook for college grads since 2007. Among employers planning to increase their new hires, an improved economy, company growth, anticipated retirements, and a focus on early talent/succession planning were cited as primary reasons behind the hiring plans. In addition, most employers surveyed said their major recruiting push would happen in the fall semester (and not the spring) of students' final year.[28] Some of the top companies looking to hire interns or recent grads include Citi, Nasdaq, Northern Trust, Under Armour, and Verizon.[29] ●

Although financial information is an important output control, financial information by itself does not tell managers all they need to know about the four building blocks of competitive advantage. Financial results inform managers about the results of decisions they have already made; they do not tell managers how to find new opportunities to build competitive advantage in the future. To encourage a future-oriented approach, top managers must establish organizational goals that encourage middle and first-line managers to achieve superior efficiency, quality, innovation, and responsiveness to customers.

Organizational Goals

Once top managers consult with lower-level managers and set the organization's overall goals, they establish performance standards for the divisions and functions.

Figure 8.4

Organizationwide
Goal Setting

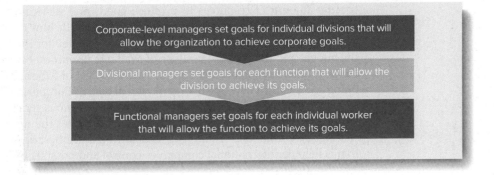

Corporate-level managers set goals for individual divisions that will allow the organization to achieve corporate goals.

Divisional managers set goals for each function that will allow the division to achieve its goals.

Functional managers set goals for each individual worker that will allow the function to achieve its goals.

These standards specify for divisional and functional managers the level at which their units must perform if the organization is to achieve its overall goals.[30] Each division is given a set of specific goals to achieve (see Figure 8.4). We saw in Chapter 6, for example, that General Mills has established the goal of having each business unit be a market leader in its industry in terms of profits. Divisional managers then develop a business-level strategy (based on achieving superior efficiency or innovation) that they hope will allow them to achieve that goal.[31] In consultation with functional managers, they specify the functional goals that the managers of different functions need to achieve to allow the division to achieve its goals. For example, sales managers might be evaluated for their ability to increase sales; materials management managers for their ability to increase the quality of inputs or lower their costs; R&D managers for the number of products they innovate or the number of patents they receive. In turn, functional managers establish goals that first-line managers and nonmanagerial employees need to achieve to allow the function to achieve its goals.

Output control is used at every level of the organization, and it is vital that the goals set at each level align with the goals set at other levels so managers and other employees throughout the organization work together to attain the corporate goals that top managers have set.[32] It is also important that goals be set appropriately so managers are motivated to accomplish them. If goals are set at an impossibly high level, managers might work only half-heartedly to achieve them because they are certain they will fail. In contrast, if goals are set so low that they are too easy to achieve, managers will not be motivated to use all their resources as efficiently and effectively as possible. Research suggests that the best goals are specific, difficult goals that challenge and stretch managers' abilities but are not out of reach and do not require an impossibly high expenditure of managerial time and energy. Such goals are often called *stretch goals*.

Deciding what is a specific, difficult goal and what is a goal that is too difficult or too easy is a skill that managers must develop. Based on their own judgment and work experience, managers at all levels must assess how difficult a certain task is, and they must assess the ability of a particular subordinate manager to achieve the goal. If they do so successfully, challenging, interrelated goals—goals that reinforce one another and focus on achieving overall corporate objectives—will energize the organization.

Operating Budgets

operating budget
A budget that states how managers intend to use organizational resources to achieve organizational goals.

Once managers at each level have been given a goal or target to achieve, the next step in developing an output control system is to establish operating budgets that regulate how managers and workers attain their goals. An operating budget is a blueprint that states how managers intend to use organizational resources to achieve organizational goals efficiently. Typically managers at one level allocate to subordinate managers a specific amount of resources to produce goods and services. Once they have been given a budget, these lower-level managers must decide how to allocate money for different organizational activities. They are then evaluated for their ability to stay within the budget and to make the best use of available resources. For example, managers in General Mills's cereal business might have a budget of $25 million to spend on developing and selling a new line of organic cereal bars in Europe and Southeast Asia. They must decide how much money to allocate to the various functions, such as finance, R&D, production, and sales, so the business generates the most revenue and makes the biggest profit. The "Managing Globally" feature describes a budgeting method that is helping international companies control and possibly reduce their expenses.

Managing Globally

Zero-Based Budgeting Helps Control Expenses

More and more global businesses are telling investors or researchers that they have adopted a budgeting practice called zero-based budgeting (ZBB). With ZBB, the manager of each group or business division creates each year's budget from a blank worksheet. Every amount for every line item is established based on what is necessary for carrying out the year's work to accomplish the year's goals. This may sound basic, but in practice, most managers have saved both time and effort by starting with the previous year's budget and adjusting it upward (or downward) to reflect any changes in goals or circumstances. This tends to leave in place spending done out of habit or provided as a cushion for managers confronting unexpected needs. Creating a budget from scratch is harder, but today's information systems are making the use of ZBB more practical because they can quickly deliver detailed data about spending almost in real time.[33]

A study by Accenture of large global companies found that the percentage of companies using ZBB has been rising 57% per year during this decade. Among the organizations adopting the method are the Anglo-Dutch company Unilever, the United Kingdom's Tesco supermarket chain, and the U.S.-based food giants Kraft Heinz and Mondelez International.[34]

A chief reason for using ZBB is to cut unnecessary spending in the face of international competition for resources and customers. Unilever, for example, announced expected savings greater than $6 billion in marketing and logistics expenses. In the Accenture survey, the companies using ZBB saved an average of $280 million per year, representing reductions of 15% on average. To be effective, cost cutting should be linked to organizational strategy. Most companies in the Accenture study did this by using savings from ZBB to increase profitability; about half used the savings to free up funds for growth. At Kraft Heinz, the chief information officer used ZBB strategically by emphasizing robotics and artificial-intelligence projects, because they could help the company the most in its cost-reduction efforts. The annual routine of ZBB also helps embed cost consciousness into an organization's culture.[35]

Consultants at Accenture see a bigger future for the principles of ZBB. They believe that the annual process—ground-up planning followed by performance measurement and control—applies to more than budgets. With this mind-set, organizations can look anew at all their processes to see where performance data can help them create a system that does the essentials and does them well.[36] ●

Large organizations often treat each division as a singular or stand-alone responsibility center. Corporate managers then evaluate each division's contribution to corporate performance. Managers of a division may be given a fixed budget for resources and be evaluated on the amount of goods or services they can produce using those resources (this is a cost or expense budget approach). Alternatively, managers may be asked to maximize the revenues from the sales of goods and services produced (a revenue budget approach). Or managers may be evaluated on the difference between the revenues generated by the sales of goods and services and the budgeted cost of making those goods and services (a profit budget approach). Japanese companies' use of operating budgets and challenging goals to increase efficiency is instructive in this context.

In summary, three components—objective financial measures, challenging goals and performance standards, and appropriate operating budgets—are the essence of effective output control. Most organizations develop sophisticated output control systems to allow managers at all levels to keep accurate account of the organization so they can move quickly to take corrective action as needed.[37] Output control is an essential part of management.

Problems with Output Control

When designing an output control system, managers must be careful to avoid some pitfalls. For example, they must be sure the output standards they create motivate managers at all levels and do not cause managers to behave in inappropriate ways to achieve organizational goals.

Suppose top managers give divisional managers the goal of doubling profits over a three-year period. This goal seems challenging and reachable when it is jointly agreed upon, and in the first two years profits go up by 70%. In the third year, however, an economic recession hits and sales plummet. Divisional managers think it is increasingly unlikely that they will meet their profit goal. Failure will mean losing the substantial monetary bonus tied to achieving the goal. How might managers behave to try to preserve their bonuses?

Perhaps they might find ways to reduce costs because profit can be increased either by raising sales revenues or reducing costs. Thus divisional managers might cut back on expensive research activities, delay machinery maintenance, reduce marketing expenditures, and lay off middle managers and workers to reduce costs so that at the end of the year they will make their target of doubling profits and receive their bonuses. This tactic might help them achieve a short-run goal—doubling profits—but such actions could hurt long-term profitability or ROI (because a cutback in R&D can reduce the rate of product innovation, a cutback in marketing will lead to the loss of customers, and so on).

The message is clear: Although output control is a useful tool for keeping managers and employees at all levels motivated and the organization on track, it is only a guide to appropriate action. Managers must be sensitive in how they use output control and must constantly monitor its effects at all levels in the organization—and on customers and other stakeholders.

Behavior Control

Organizational structure by itself does not provide any mechanism that motivates managers and nonmanagerial employees to behave in ways that make the structure work—or even improve how it works: hence the need for control. Put another way, managers can develop an organizational structure that has the right grouping of divisions and functions and an effective chain of command, but it will work as designed *only* if managers also establish control systems that motivate and shape employee behavior in ways that *match* this structure.[38] Output control is one method of motivating employees; behavior control is another method. This section examines three mechanisms of behavior control that managers can use to keep employees on track and make organizational structures work as they are designed to work: direct supervision, management by objectives, and rules and standard operating procedures.

Direct Supervision

The most immediate and potent form of behavior control is direct supervision by managers who actively monitor and observe the behavior of their employees, teach them the behaviors that are appropriate and inappropriate, and intervene to take corrective action as needed. Moreover, when managers personally supervise employees, they lead by example and in this way can help employees develop and increase their own skill levels.

Direct supervision allows managers at all levels to become personally involved with their employees and allows them to mentor employees and develop their management skills. Thus control through personal supervision can be an effective way of motivating employees and promoting behaviors that increase efficiency and effectiveness.[39]

Nevertheless, certain problems are associated with direct supervision. First, it is expensive because a manager can personally manage only a relatively small number of employees effectively. Therefore, if direct supervision is the main kind of control being used in an organization, a lot of managers will be needed and costs will increase. For this reason, output control is usually preferred to behavior control; indeed, output control tends to be the first type of control that managers at all levels use to evaluate performance. Second, direct supervision can *demotivate* employees. This occurs if employees feel they are under such close scrutiny that they are not free to make their own decisions or if they feel they are not being evaluated in an accurate and impartial way. Team members and other employees may start to pass the buck, avoid responsibility, and cease to cooperate with other team members if they feel their manager is not accurately evaluating their performance and is favoring some people over others.

Third, as noted previously, for many jobs personal control through direct supervision is simply not feasible. The more complex a job is, the more difficult it is for a manager to evaluate how well an employee is performing. The performance of divisional and functional managers, for example, can be evaluated only over relatively long periods (which is why an output control system is developed), so it makes little sense for top managers to continually monitor their performance. However, managers can still communicate the organization's mission and goals to their employees and reinforce the values and norms in the organization's culture through their own personal style.

Management by Objectives

To provide a framework within which to evaluate employees' behavior and, in particular, to allow managers to monitor progress toward achieving goals, many organizations implement some version of management by objectives. **Management by objectives (MBO)** is a formal system of evaluating employees on their ability to achieve specific organizational goals or performance standards and to meet operating budgets.[40] Most organizations use some form of MBO system because it is pointless to establish goals and then fail to evaluate whether they are being achieved. Management by objectives involves three specific steps:

- Step 1: *Specific goals and objectives are established at each level of the organization.*

MBO starts when top managers establish overall organizational objectives, such as specific financial performance goals or targets. Then objective setting cascades down throughout the organization as managers at the divisional and functional levels set their goals to achieve corporate objectives. Finally first-level managers and employees jointly set goals that will contribute to achieving functional objectives.

- Step 2: *Managers and their employees together determine the employees' goals.*

An important characteristic of management by objectives is its participatory nature. Managers at every level sit down with each of the subordinate managers who report directly to them, and together they determine appropriate and feasible goals for the subordinate and bargain over the budget that the subordinate will need to achieve his or her goals. The participation of employees in the objective-setting process is a way of strengthening their commitment to achieving their goals and meeting their budgets.[41] Another reason why it is so important for employees (both individuals and teams) to participate in goal setting is that doing so enables them to tell managers what they think they can realistically achieve.[42]

- Step 3: *Managers and their employees periodically review the employees' progress toward meeting goals.*

Once specific objectives have been agreed on for managers at each level, managers are accountable for meeting those objectives. Periodically they sit down with their employees to evaluate their progress. Normally salary raises and promotions are linked to the goal-setting process, and managers who achieve their goals receive greater rewards than those who fall short.

In the companies that have decentralized responsibility for the production of goods and services to empowered teams and cross-functional teams, management by objectives works somewhat differently. Managers ask each team to develop a set of goals and performance targets that the team hopes to achieve—goals that are consistent with organizational objectives. Managers then negotiate with each team to establish its final goals and the budget the team will need to achieve them. The reward system is linked to team performance, not to the performance of any one team member.

MBO does not always work out as planned, however. Managers and their employees at all levels must believe that performance evaluations are accurate and fair. Any suggestion that personal biases and political objectives play a part in the evaluation process can lower or even destroy MBO's effectiveness as a control system. This is why many organizations work so hard to protect the integrity of their systems.

Similarly, when people work in teams, each member's contribution to the team, and each team's contribution to the goals of the organization, must be fairly evaluated. This is no easy thing to do. It depends on managers' ability to create an organizational control system that measures performance accurately and fairly and links performance evaluations to rewards so employees stay motivated and coordinate their activities to achieve the organization's mission and goals.

THE BALANCED SCORECARD In recent years, an extension of the MBO approach to organizational control has become popular, which provides a more balanced view of a company's performance. Developed by Robert Kaplan and David Norton in the early 1990s, the balanced scorecard addresses financial measures as well as three other operational components: customer service, internal business processes, and an organization's potential for learning and growth.[43]

balanced scorecard
A management control system that takes a comprehensive look at an organization's overall performance using four measures: financial, customer service, internal business processes, and the organization's capability for strategic learning and growth.

The *financial* component of the scorecard pertains to how well company actions contribute to the organization's overall financial condition; it typically includes measurements such as return on investment and net income. The *customer service* perspective concentrates on how well an organization provides service to its customers; it typically includes a variety of information on customer satisfaction and retention, which can be obtained in several ways including online surveys. The *internal business processes* component addresses whether the organization's processes and workflow add value to customers and shareholders; it typically includes production and other operational statistics. Finally, the *learning and growth* component focuses on how well company resources, including the workforce, are being managed to ensure a successful future for the company. This effective management tool is used by both large and small businesses as a way to achieve company objectives. Some of the companies that use the balanced scorecard approach include Citibank, Philips Electronics, Thomas Reuters, Mobil, Apple, Verizon, and AT&T.[44]

Bureaucratic Control

When direct supervision is too expensive and management by objectives is inappropriate, managers might turn to another mechanism to shape and motivate employee behavior: bureaucratic control. Bureaucratic control is control by means of a comprehensive system of rules and standard operating procedures (SOPs) that shapes and regulates the behavior of divisions, functions, and individuals. In the appendix to Chapter 1, we discussed Weber's theory of bureaucracy and noted that all organizations use bureaucratic rules and procedures, but some use them more than others.

bureaucratic control
Control of behavior by means of a comprehensive system of rules and standard operating procedures.

Rules and SOPs guide behavior and specify what employees are to do when they confront a problem that needs a solution. It is the responsibility of a manager to develop rules that allow employees to perform their activities efficiently and effectively. When employees follow the rules that managers have developed, their behavior is standardized—actions are performed the same way time and time again—and the outcomes of their work are predictable. And, to the degree that managers can make employees' behavior predictable, there is no need to monitor the outputs of behavior because standardized behavior leads to standardized outputs.

Suppose a worker at Honda comes up with a way to attach exhaust pipes that reduces the number of steps in the assembly process and increases efficiency. Always on the lookout for ways to standardize procedures, managers make this idea the basis of a new rule that says, "From now on, the procedure for attaching the exhaust pipe to the car is as follows." If all workers followed the rule to the letter, every car would come off the assembly line with its exhaust pipe attached in the new way and there would be no need to check exhaust pipes at the end of the line. In practice, mistakes and lapses of attention do happen, so output control is used at the end of the line, and each car's exhaust system is given a routine inspection. However, the number of quality problems with the exhaust system is minimized because the rule (bureaucratic control) is being followed.

Service organizations such as retail stores, fast-food restaurants, and home-improvement stores attempt to standardize the behavior of employees by instructing them on the correct way to greet customers or the appropriate way to serve and bag food. Employees are trained to follow the rules that have proved to be most effective in a particular situation, and the better trained the employees are, the more standardized is their behavior and the more trust managers can have that outputs (such as food quality) will be consistent.

Problems with Bureaucratic Control

All organizations make extensive use of bureaucratic control because rules and SOPs effectively control routine organizational activities. With a bureaucratic control system in place, managers can manage by exception and intervene and take corrective action only when necessary. However, managers need to be aware of a number of problems associated with bureaucratic control, because such problems can reduce organizational effectiveness.

First, establishing rules is always easier than discarding them. Organizations tend to become overly bureaucratic over time as managers do everything according to the rule book. If the amount of red tape becomes too great, decision making slows and managers react slowly to changing conditions. This sluggishness can imperil an organization's survival if agile new competitors emerge.

Second, because rules constrain and standardize behavior and lead people to behave in predictable ways, there is a danger that people become so used to automatically following rules that they stop thinking for themselves. Thus, too much standardization can actually reduce the level of learning taking place in an organization and get the organization off track if managers and workers focus on the wrong issues. An organization thrives when its members are constantly thinking of new ways to increase efficiency, quality, and customer responsiveness. By definition, new ideas do not come from blindly following standardized procedures. Similarly, the pursuit of innovation implies a commitment by managers to discover new ways of doing things; innovation, however, is incompatible with the use of extensive bureaucratic control.

Consider, for example, what happened at the Walt Disney Company when Bob Iger became CEO of the then-troubled company. Iger had been Disney's chief operating officer under CEO Michael Eisner, and he noticed that Disney was plagued by slow decision making that had led to many mistakes in putting new corporate strategies into action. Its Disney retail stores were losing money; its Internet properties were flops; and even its theme parks seemed to have lost their luster, as few new attractions were being introduced. Iger believed one of the main reasons for Disney's declining performance was that the company had become too tall and bureaucratic and its top managers were following financial rules that did not lead to innovation.

In an effort to turn around the company's performance, Iger's first move as CEO was to dismantle Disney's central strategic planning office. In this office, several levels of managers were responsible for sifting through all the

Employees demonstrate standardized behavior when they follow the rules that management has developed, actions performed the same way time and time again, such as tasks performed on an auto manufacturing assembly line. This type of bureaucratic control helps maintain quality and increase efficiency. Monty Rakusen/Getty Images

Eliminating unnecessary layers in Disney's organizational hierarchy has helped CEO Bob Iger foster an environment of innovation and creativity. VCG/VCG/Getty Images

new ideas and innovations sent up by Disney's different business units, such as theme parks, movies, and gaming, and then deciding which ones to present to the CEO. Iger saw the strategic planning office as a bureaucratic bottleneck that reduced the number of ideas coming from lower levels of the organization's hierarchy. So he dissolved the office and reassigned its managers back to various business units.[45]

The result of cutting this unnecessary layer in Disney's hierarchy has been that various business units within the company generate more ideas. The level of innovation has increased because managers are more willing to speak out and champion their ideas when they know they are dealing directly with the CEO and a top management team searching for creative ways to improve performance—and not with a layer of strategic planning bureaucrats concerned only with the bottom line.[46] In 2018, the company announced a strategic reorganization including a new business unit that will focus on Disney's direct-to-consumer streaming platforms (including ESPN+ and a Disney-branded streaming service), as well as its international offerings. The company also said its consumer products and interactive media business would now become part of the parks and resort division. CEO Iger said the recent changes would better position the company for future success and suggested the new streaming platforms would provide strong competition for Netflix and other streaming services, as many consumers continue to cut the cord on traditional cable and TV offerings.[47]

Managers must be sensitive about the way they use bureaucratic control. It is most useful when organizational activities are routine and well understood and when employees are making programmed decisions—for example, in mass-production settings such as Ford or in routine service settings such as stores like Target or Starbucks. Bureaucratic control is much less useful in situations where nonprogrammed decisions have to be made and managers have to react quickly to changes in the organizational environment.

To use output control and behavior control, managers must be able to identify the outcomes they want to achieve and the behaviors they want employees to perform to achieve those outcomes. For many of the most important and significant organizational activities, however, output control and behavior control are inappropriate for several reasons:

- A manager cannot evaluate the performance of workers such as doctors, research scientists, or engineers by observing their behavior on a day-to-day basis.

- Rules and SOPs are of little use in telling a doctor how to respond to an emergency situation or a scientist how to discover something new.

- Output controls such as the amount of time a surgeon takes for each operation or the costs of making a discovery are very crude measures of the quality of performance.

How can managers attempt to control and regulate the behavior of their employees when personal supervision is of little use, when rules cannot be developed to tell employees what to do, and when outputs and goals cannot be measured at all or can be measured usefully only over long periods? One source of control increasingly being used by organizations is a strong organizational culture.

Organizational Culture and Clan Control

organizational culture The set of values, norms, and standards of behavior that control the way individuals and groups interact and work together to achieve organizational goals.

clan control The control exerted on individuals and groups by shared organizational values, norms, and standards of behavior.

Organizational culture is another important control system that regulates and governs employee attitudes and behavior. As we discussed in Chapter 2, organizational culture is the shared set of beliefs, expectations, values, norms, and work routines that influences how members of an organization relate to one another and work together to achieve organizational goals. Clan control is the control exerted on individuals and groups in an organization by shared values, norms, standards of behavior, and expectations. Organizational culture is not an externally imposed system of constraints, such as direct supervision or rules and procedures. Rather, employees internalize organizational values and norms and then let these values and norms guide their decisions and actions. Just as people in society at large generally behave in accordance with socially acceptable values and norms—such as the norm that people should line up at the checkout counters in supermarkets—so are individuals in an organizational setting mindful of the force of organizational values and norms.

Organizational culture functions as a kind of control system because managers can deliberately try to influence the kind of values and norms that develop in an organization—values and norms that specify appropriate and inappropriate behaviors and so determine the way its members behave.

Adaptive Cultures versus Inert Cultures

Many researchers and managers believe that employees of some organizations go out of their way to help the organization because it has a strong and cohesive organizational culture—an *adaptive culture* that controls employee attitudes and behaviors. Adaptive cultures are ones whose values and norms help an organization build momentum and grow and change as needed to achieve its goals and be effective. By contrast, *inert cultures* are those that lead to values and norms that fail to motivate or inspire employees; they lead to stagnation and often failure over time. What leads to an adaptive or inert culture?

Researchers have found that organizations with strong adaptive cultures, like 3M, UPS, Microsoft, and Southwest Airlines, invest in their employees. They demonstrate their commitment to their members by, for example, emphasizing the long-term nature of the employment relationship and trying to avoid layoffs. These companies develop long-term career paths for their employees and invest heavily in training and development to increase employees' value to the organization. In these ways, terminal and instrumental values pertaining to the worth of human resources encourage the development of supportive work attitudes and behaviors.

In adaptive cultures employees often receive rewards linked directly to their performance and to the performance of the company as a whole. Sometimes, employee stock ownership plans (ESOPs) are developed in which workers as a group are allowed to buy a significant percentage of their company's stock. Workers who are owners of the company have additional incentive to develop skills that allow them to perform highly and search actively for ways to improve quality, efficiency, and performance. Publix Super Markets, headquartered in Lakeland, Florida, recently ranked as America's largest majority employee-owned company.[48]

Some organizations, however, develop cultures with values that do not include protecting and increasing the worth of their human resources as a major goal. Their employment practices are based on short-term employment according to the needs of the organization and on minimal investment in employees who perform simple, routine tasks. Moreover, employees are not often rewarded based on their performance and thus have little incentive to improve their skills or otherwise invest in the organization to help it achieve goals. If a company has an inert culture, poor working relationships frequently develop between the organization and its employees, and instrumental values of noncooperation, laziness, and loafing and work norms of output restriction are common.

Moreover, an adaptive culture develops an emphasis on entrepreneurship and respect for the employee and allows the use of organizational structures, such as the cross-functional team structure, that empower employees to make decisions and motivate them to succeed. By contrast, in an inert culture, employees are content to be told what to do and have little incentive or motivation to perform beyond minimum work requirements. As you might expect, the emphasis is on close supervision and hierarchical authority, which result in a culture that makes it difficult to adapt to a changing environment.

Organizational Change

As we have discussed, many problems can arise if an organization's control systems are not designed correctly. One of these problems is that an organization cannot change or adapt in response to a changing environment unless it has effective control over its activities. Companies can lose this control over time, or they can change in ways that make them more effective. Organizational change is the movement of an organization away from its present state toward some preferred future state to increase its efficiency and effectiveness.

organizational change The movement of an organization away from its present state and toward some desired future state to increase its efficiency and effectiveness.

Interestingly enough, there is a fundamental tension or need to balance two opposing forces in the control process that influences the way organizations change. As just noted, organizations and their managers need to be able to control their activities and make their operations routine and predictable. At the same time, however, organizations have to be responsive to the need to change, and managers and employees have to "think on their feet" and realize when they need to depart from routines to be responsive to unpredictable events. In other words, even though adopting the right set of output and behavior controls is essential for improving efficiency, because the environment is dynamic and uncertain, employees also need to feel that they have the autonomy to depart from routines as necessary to increase effectiveness. (See Figure 8.5.)

Figure 8.5
Organizational Control and Change

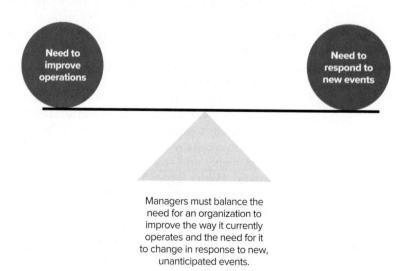

Need to improve operations

Need to respond to new events

Managers must balance the need for an organization to improve the way it currently operates and the need for it to change in response to new, unanticipated events.

For this reason many researchers believe that the highest-performing organizations are those that are constantly changing—and thus become experienced at doing so—in their search to become more efficient and effective. Companies like UPS, Toyota, and Walmart are constantly changing the mix of their activities to move forward even as they seek to make their existing operations more efficient. For example, UPS entered the air express package market, bought a chain of mailbox stores, and began offering consulting services. At the same time, the company's ORION on-board technology system, which has increased the efficiency of UPS's delivery process in the United States, is projected to save the company between $300 and $400 million annually while cutting annual fuel usage by 10 million gallons every year.[49]

The need to constantly search for ways to improve efficiency and effectiveness makes it vital that managers develop the skills necessary to manage change effectively. Several experts have proposed a model that managers can follow to implement change successfully.[50] Figure 8.6 outlines the steps that managers must take to manage change effectively. In the rest of this section we examine each one.

Assessing the Need for Change

Organizational change can affect practically all aspects of organizational functioning, including organizational structure, culture, strategies, control systems, and groups and teams, as well as the human resource management system and critical organizational processes such as communication, motivation, and leadership. Organizational change can bring alterations in the ways managers carry out the critical tasks of planning, organizing, leading, and controlling and the ways they perform their managerial roles.

Deciding how to change an organization is a complex matter because change disrupts the status quo and poses a threat, prompting employees to resist attempts to alter work relationships and procedures. *Organizational learning,* the process through which managers try to increase organizational members' abilities to understand and appropriately respond to changing conditions, can be an important impetus for change and can help all members of an organization, including managers, effectively make decisions about needed changes.

Assessing the need for change calls for two important activities: recognizing that there is a problem and identifying its source. Sometimes the need for change is obvious, such as when an organization's performance is suffering. Often, however, managers have trouble determining that something is going wrong because problems develop gradually; organizational performance may slip for a number of years before a problem becomes obvious. Thus, during the first step in the change process, managers need to recognize that there is a problem that requires change.

Figure 8.6   Four Steps in the Organizational Change Process

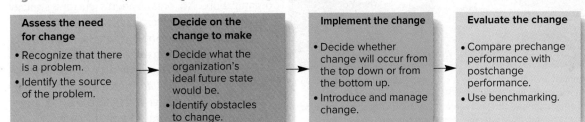

Often the problems that managers detect have produced a gap between desired performance and actual performance. To detect such a gap, managers need to look at performance measures—such as falling market share or profits, rising costs, or employees' failure to meet their established goals or stay within budgets—which indicate whether change is needed. These measures are provided by organizational control systems, discussed earlier in the chapter.

To discover the source of the problem, managers need to look both inside and outside the organization. Outside the organization, they must examine how changes in environmental forces may be creating opportunities and threats that are affecting internal work relationships. Perhaps the emergence of low-cost competitors abroad has led to conflict among different departments that are trying to find new ways to gain a competitive advantage. Managers also need to look within the organization to see whether its structure is causing problems between departments. Perhaps a company does not have integrating mechanisms in place to allow different departments to respond to low-cost competition.

Deciding on the Change to Make

Once managers have identified the source of the problem, they must decide what they think the organization's ideal future state would be. In other words, they must decide where they would like their organization to be in the future—what kinds of goods and services it should be making, what its business-level strategy should be, how the organizational structure should be changed, and so on. During this step, managers also must engage in planning how they are going to attain the organization's ideal future state.

This step in the change process also includes identifying obstacles or sources of resistance to change. Managers must analyze the factors that may prevent the company from reaching its ideal future state. Obstacles to change are found at the corporate, divisional, departmental, and individual levels of the organization.

Corporate-level changes in an organization's strategy or structure, even seemingly trivial changes, may significantly affect how divisional and departmental managers behave. Suppose that to compete with low-cost foreign competitors, top managers decide to increase the resources spent on state-of-the-art machinery and reduce the resources spent on marketing or R&D. The power of manufacturing managers would increase, and the power of marketing and R&D managers would fall. This decision would alter the balance of power among departments and might lead to increased conflict as departments start fighting to retain their status in the organization. An organization's current strategy and structure are powerful obstacles to change.[51]

Whether a company's culture is adaptive or inert facilitates or obstructs change. Organizations with entrepreneurial, flexible cultures, such as high-tech companies, are much easier to change than are organizations with more rigid cultures, such as those sometimes found in large, bureaucratic organizations like the military or GM.

Organizational change can be a slow and painful process for both managers and employees. Resistance to new processes and other changes can be overcome by improving communication from leadership as to why and how such changes need to be made. fizkes/Shutterstock

The same obstacles to change exist at the divisional and departmental levels as well. Division managers may differ in their attitudes toward the changes that top managers propose and, if their interests and power seem threatened, will resist those changes. Managers at all levels usually fight to protect their power and control over resources.[52] Given that departments have different goals and time horizons, they may also react differently to the changes that other managers propose. When top managers are trying to reduce costs, for example, sales managers may resist attempts to cut back on sales expenditures if they believe that problems stem from manufacturing managers' inefficiencies.

At the individual level, too, people are often resistant to change because change brings uncertainty and uncertainty brings stress. For example, individuals may resist the introduction of a new technology because they are uncertain about their abilities to learn it and effectively use it. Or, by their very nature, other individuals may take comfort in the status quo and believe any type of change will require more work on their part, so they resist.[53]

All of these obstacles make organizational change a slow and sometimes painful process. Managers at all levels of the organization must recognize the potential obstacles to change and take them into consideration. Some obstacles can be overcome by improving communication from leadership, so all organizational members are aware of the need for change and the nature of the changes being implemented. Empowering employees and inviting them to participate in planning for change may overcome some resistance and allay employees' fears. However, it is also important for managers to listen to employees' sentiment about possible changes, especially when the employees believe they have rational reasons why the change could prove detrimental to the organization. Considering this alternate view of resistance allows organizations to engage in better decision making regarding which changes to undertake.[54]

Implementing the Change

top-down change
A fast, revolutionary approach to change in which top managers identify what needs to be changed and then move quickly to implement the changes throughout the organization.

Generally, managers implement—that is, introduce and manage—change from the top down or from the bottom up.[55] Top-down change is implemented quickly: Top managers identify the need for change, decide what to do, and then move quickly to implement the changes throughout the organization. For example, top managers may decide to restructure and downsize the organization and then give divisional and departmental managers specific goals to achieve. With top-down change, the emphasis is on making the changes quickly and dealing with problems as they arise; it is revolutionary in nature. For an example of a company implementing top-down change, see the "Ethics in Action" feature.

Ethics in Action

Volkswagen Sets Off on a Long Road to Redemption

By number of vehicles sold, Volkswagen is the world's largest automaker, with 600,000 workers in more than 100 factories producing 12 brands including Audi, Bentley, and Porsche. Just a few years ago, however, some observers expected the company to fail as a result of a scandal involving its "clean diesel" cars. Volkswagen said those cars used technology to reduce emissions of nitrogen oxide, which causes smog. But university students conducting research found that the levels were up to 40 times the legal limit. The students tipped off state and local officials, who launched investigations tracing the problem to software that engineers had written to disguise the actual emissions during testing of millions of vehicles. Besides damaging the company's reputation, the scandal rocked its financial position, with legal settlements at $30 billion and rising. Lawsuits by customers and investors are expected to continue for years.[56]

Volkswagen's response to the emissions scandal was awkward at first.[57] CEO Martin Winterkorn issued a stiff apology, blaming the "few" who had erred. However, authorities in Canada, France, Germany, South Korea, and the United States launched criminal investigations that implicated management. As the board of directors saw the company's situation unraveling, they replaced Winterkorn with Matthias Müller, who had been running the Porsche division. Even after Müller's appointment, the scandal spread as the software turned up in more models.

Müller reviewed all the company's models and committed Volkswagen to change. Under his plan, the company would develop all-electric or hybrid versions of every model by 2030.[58] Three years after Müller took over, the board replaced him with Herbert Diess, who has continued the commitment to electric vehicles and intensified the commitment to changing the company's culture. The diesel scandal occurred in a rigid culture where people were afraid to question decisions made at higher levels; Diess is seeking to push decision making down to lower levels and build a culture in which employees speak up about problems.

As Volkswagen's leaders reflect on the changes that have followed the emissions scandal, some are saying the crisis actually helped the company by making the need for change obvious.[59] One of them is CEO Diess, who said technology had already made change necessary, but the scandal pushed the company to move faster. The approach seems to have Volkswagen on the road to recovery; so far, it is posting record levels of revenues and vehicles sold. ●

bottom-up change
A gradual or evolutionary approach to change in which managers at all levels work together to develop a detailed plan for change.

Bottom-up change is typically more gradual or evolutionary. Top managers consult with middle and first-line managers about the need for change. Then, over time, managers at all levels work to develop a detailed plan for change. A major advantage of bottom-up change is that it can co-opt resistance to change from employees. Because the emphasis in bottom-up change is on participation and on keeping people informed about what is going on, uncertainty and resistance are minimized.

Evaluating the Change

The last step in the change process is to evaluate how successful the change effort has been in improving organizational performance.[60] Using measures such as changes in market share, in profits, or in the ability of managers to meet their goals, managers compare how well an organization is performing after the change with how well it was performing before. Managers also can use benchmarking, comparing their performance on specific dimensions with the performance of high-performing organizations, to decide how successful a change effort has been. For example, when Xerox was doing poorly in the 1980s, it benchmarked the efficiency of its distribution operations against that of L.L.Bean, the efficiency of its central computer operations against that of John Deere, and the efficiency of its marketing abilities against that of Procter & Gamble. Those three companies are renowned for their skills in these different areas, and by studying how they performed, Xerox was able to dramatically increase its own performance. Benchmarking is a key tool in total quality management, an important change program discussed in Chapter 14.

benchmarking The process of comparing one company's performance on specific dimensions with the performance of other, high-performing organizations.

In summary, organizational control and change are closely linked because organizations operate in environments that are constantly changing and so managers must be alert to the need to change their strategies and structures. High-performing organizations are those whose managers are attuned to the need to continually modify the way they operate and adopt techniques like empowered work groups and teams, benchmarking, and global outsourcing to remain competitive in a global world.

Summary and Review

WHAT IS ORGANIZATIONAL CONTROL? Controlling is the process whereby managers monitor and regulate how efficiently and effectively an organization and its members are performing the activities necessary to achieve organizational goals. Controlling is a four-step process: (1) establishing performance standards, (2) measuring actual performance, (3) comparing actual performance against performance standards, and (4) evaluating the results and initiating corrective action if needed. [LO 8-1, 8-2]

OUTPUT CONTROL To monitor output or performance, managers choose goals or performance standards that they think will best measure efficiency, quality, innovation, and responsiveness to customers at the corporate, divisional, departmental or functional, and individual levels. The main mechanisms that managers use to monitor output are financial measures of performance, organizational goals, and operating budgets. [LO 8-3]

BEHAVIOR CONTROL In an attempt to shape behavior and influence employees to work toward achieving organizational goals, managers utilize direct supervision, management by objectives, and bureaucratic control by means of rules and standard operating procedures. Direct supervision allows managers to actively monitor and observe the behavior of their employees. Management by objectives (MBO) is a goal-process setting typically accomplished by a manager and each of his or her employees, which provides a framework to evaluate employee performance. An extension of the MBO approach, the balanced scorecard takes a comprehensive look at an organization's overall performance using four measures: financial, customer service, internal business processes, and the organization's capability for strategic learning and growth. Bureaucratic control is a mechanism that shapes and regulates the behavior of divisions, functions, and individuals within an organization. [LO 8-4]

ORGANIZATIONAL CULTURE AND CLAN CONTROL Organizational culture is the set of values, norms, standards of behavior, and common expectations that control the ways individuals and groups in an organization interact with one another and work to achieve organizational goals. Clan control is the control exerted on individuals and groups by shared values, norms, standards of behavior, and expectations. Organizational culture is transmitted to employees through the values of the founder, the process of socialization, organizational ceremonies and rites, and stories and language. The way managers perform their management functions influences the kind of culture that develops in an organization. [LO 8-5]

ORGANIZATIONAL CONTROL AND CHANGE There is a need to balance two opposing forces in the control process that influences the way organizations change. On the one hand, managers need to be able to control organizational activities and make their operations routine and predictable. On the other hand, organizations have to be responsive to the need to change, and managers must understand when they need to depart from routines to be responsive to unpredictable events. The four steps in managing change are (1) assessing the need for change, (2) deciding on the changes to make, (3) implementing change, and (4) evaluating the results of change. [LO 8-6]

Management *in Action*

Topics for Discussion and Action

Discussion

1. What is the relationship between organizing and controlling? [LO 8-1]

2. How do output control and behavior control differ? [LO 8-1, 8-2, 8-3, 8-4]

3. Why is it important for managers to involve employees in the control process? [LO 8-3, 8-5]

4. What kind of controls would you expect to find most used in (a) a hospital, (b) the Navy, (c) a city police force? Why? [LO 8-1, 8-2, 8-3]

5. What is organizational culture, and how does it affect the way employees behave? [LO 8-5]

Action

6. Ask a manager to list the main performance measures that he or she uses to evaluate how well the organization is achieving its goals. [LO 8-1, 8-3, 8-5]

7. Ask the same or a different manager to list the main forms of output control and behavior control that he or she uses to monitor and evaluate employee behavior. [LO 8-3, 8-4]

Building Management Skills

Understanding Controlling [LO 8-1, 8-3, 8-4, 8-5]

For this exercise you will analyze the control systems used by a real organization such as a department store, restaurant, hospital, police department, or small business. Your objective is to uncover all the different ways in which managers monitor and evaluate the performance of the organization and employees.

1. At what levels does control take place in this organization?

2. Which output performance standards (such as financial measures and organizational goals) do managers use most often to evaluate performance at each level?

3. Does the organization have a management-by-objectives system in place? If it does, describe it. If it does not, speculate about why not.

4. How important is behavior control in this organization? For example, how much of managers' time is spent directly supervising employees? How formalized is the organization? Do employees receive a book of rules to instruct them about how to perform their jobs?

5. What kind of culture does the organization have? What are the values and norms? What effect does the organizational culture have on the way employees behave or treat customers?

6. Based on this analysis, do you think there is a fit between the organization's control systems and its culture? What is the nature of this fit? How could it be improved?

Managing Ethically [LO 8-4, 8-5]

Some managers and organizations go to great lengths to monitor their employees' behavior, and they keep extensive records about employees' behavior and performance. Some organizations also seem to possess norms and values that cause their employees to behave in certain ways.

Questions

1. Either by yourself or in a group, think about the ethical implications of

organizations' monitoring and collecting information about their employees. What kind of information is it ethical or unethical to collect? Why? Should managers and organizations inform employees they are collecting such information? Explain your reasoning.

2. Similarly, some organizations' cultures seem to develop norms and values that cause their members to behave in unethical ways. When and why does a strong norm that encourages high performance become one that can cause people to act unethically? How can organizations keep their values and norms from becoming "too strong"?

Small Group Breakout Exercise [LO 8-3, 8-4, 8-5]

How Best to Control the Sales Force?

Form groups of three or four people, and appoint one member as the spokesperson who will communicate your findings to the whole class when called on by the instructor. Then discuss the following scenario:

You are the regional sales managers of an organization that supplies high-quality windows and doors to building supply centers nationwide. Over the last three years, the rate of sales growth has declined. There is increasing evidence that, to make their jobs easier, salespeople are primarily servicing large customer accounts and ignoring small accounts. In addition, the salespeople are not dealing promptly with customer questions and complaints, and this inattention has resulted in a drop in after-sales service. You have talked about these problems, and you are meeting to design a control system to increase both the amount of sales and the quality of customer service.

1. Design a control system that you think will best motivate salespeople to achieve these goals.

2. What relative importance do you put on (a) output control, (b) behavior control, and (c) organizational culture in this design?

Be the Manager [LO 8-1, 8-6]

You have been asked by your company's CEO to find a way to improve the performance of its teams of web-design and web-hosting specialists and programmers. Each team works on a different aspect of website production, and while each is responsible for the quality of its own performance, its performance also depends on how well the other teams perform. Your task is to create a control system that will help increase the performance of each team separately and facilitate cooperation among the teams. This is necessary because the various projects are interlinked and affect one another just as the different parts of a car must fit together. Since competition in the website production market is intense, it is imperative that each website be up and running as quickly as possible and incorporate all the latest advances in website software technology.

Questions

1. What kind of output controls will best facilitate positive interactions both within the teams and among the teams?

2. What kind of behavior controls will best facilitate positive interactions both within the teams and among the teams?

3. How would you go about helping managers develop a culture to promote high team performance?

Case in the News [LO 8-1, 8-2, 8-3, 8-5, 8-6]

How Stitch Fix Controls Inventory and Customer Experience

San Francisco–based Stitch Fix embodies what founder and CEO Katrina Lake envisions as the future of apparel retailing. Lake observed retailers seeking organizational change only after an innovator entered the market, and she was determined to get ahead of the curve. In the Internet age, what would be the alternative to buying clothes in a store or from a catalog? Most retailers offer online shopping at a website that functions as a catalog. But information technology offers more than order taking; it also can gather and analyze massive quantities of data, so managers can use the analysis to improve decisions.

Lake decided to apply these capabilities to make retailing more like a personal shopping assistant. She created Stitch Fix as a retailer grounded in data science. The focus on data is apparent in its hiring of more than 80 data scientists, who work in a group reporting directly to the CEO. Typically, data analytics is a support function reporting to a technology or other support executive, but this organizational structure keeps the company's leaders focused on data as a driver of success.

Data collection begins when consumers sign up to receive Stitch Fix boxes. They complete a questionnaire about their size, tastes, desired price ranges, and clothing needs. Periodically, according to the schedule selected by the consumer, Stitch Fix sends out a box containing several items compatible with the consumer's questionnaire responses. Clothing purchases have an emotional component, so human stylists make the final selections in each box based on the data-driven recommendations, personal information that shoppers choose to share, and their own sense of style. For each box, the company charges a $20 styling fee, which is applied to reduce the price of any items purchased. The consumer decides which items to keep and returns the others along with feedback. The choices and feedback shape the next round of selections.

Stitch Fix also compiles data across millions of shoppers to find patterns. For example, men tend to overstate their height, so the software adjusts inseam lengths when selecting pants for male shoppers, and women over 40 often request sleeves, so Stitch Fix added more sleeved shirts to its inventory. While some adjustments involve human decision making, Stitch Fix also applies machine learning, in which software applies the results of past decisions—say, that a client tends to select certain colors of shirts or that a particular ratio of specific measurements will make a shirt appealing to men with large chest sizes—to adjust its recommendations.

This business model involves significant risks. The company must acquire a wide variety of inventory and then hope that consumers who receive selections they didn't make themselves will want to pay for those items. If consumers return most of them, the company has to pay for buying, storing, and shipping clothes without earning much from the expense. The primary quality control Stitch Fix uses is the application of data analytics to ensure that the choices the company makes are likely to appeal to its customers. When this works, Stitch Fix sells items fast enough that it can pay vendors with earnings from sales.

In addition, data analytics helps the company control costs. Having employed highly educated scientists to solve problems with data, Stitch Fix gives them latitude to apply their skills throughout the organization. Their initial charge was to write software for selecting clothes, but the group has also created programs for timing reorders of inventory, telling which warehouses will fill particular orders, and arranging work flow in warehouses.

As of 2018, Stitch Fix had 2.7 million active clients (customers who received a shipment during the previous 12 months), revenues exceeding $1 billion, and an inventory drawn from hundreds of brands. It has expanded from women's apparel to include offerings for men and children. However, growth in the number of active clients has slowed, and other retailers have observed Stitch Fix's initial success and are preparing to compete. The company has planned an entry into the United Kingdom, where it will hire local stylists who can recommend brands familiar to local consumers. Managers at Stitch Fix also have to figure out how to stay ahead of the curve in anticipating consumers' wishes. The better the company predicts what shoppers will order, the less it will spend on shipping and inventory of unwanted items. Even more important, it will retain more loyal customers to fuel future growth.

Questions for Discussion

1. In general terms, according to the information provided, what measures of efficiency and effectiveness are important for controlling Stitch Fix's corporate performance?

2. How can Stitch Fix's organizational culture support the achievement of its goals?

3. How do you think the establishment of Stitch Fix might have created a need for organizational change at other clothing retailers? How might their responses create a need for organizational change at Stitch Fix?

Sources: Stitch Fix, "What Is Stitch Fix and How Does It Work?," https://support.stitchfix.com, accessed January 6, 2019; S. Halzack, "Stitch Fix's Success Story Is Underappreciated," *Bloomberg*, www.bloomberg.com, January 3, 2019; E. Winkler, "Tall Tales Won't Fool This Clothier," *The Wall Street Journal*, www.wsj.com, November 15, 2018; L. Galligan, "Stitch Fix Shares Lose Almost a Third of Value on Disappointing User Growth," *CNBC*, www.cnbc.com, October 2, 2018; M. Armental, "Stitch Fix Looks to U.K. as Active Client Growth Stalls," *The Wall Street Journal*, www.wsj.com, October 1, 2018; E. Winkler, "Fashion Emergency at Stitch Fix," *The Wall Street Journal*, www.wsj.com, October 1, 2018; K. Lake, "Stitch Fix's CEO on Selling Personal Style to the Mass Market," *Harvard Business Review*, May–June 2018, 35–40; B. Marr, "Stitch Fix: The Amazing Use Case of Using Artificial Intelligence in Fashion Retail," *Forbes*, www.forbes.com, May 25, 2018.

Endnotes

1. S. Vranica, "P&G Contends Too Much Digital Ad Spending Is a Waste," *The Wall Street Journal*, www.wsj.com, accessed January 5, 2019; J. Neff, "Procter & Gamble Gets Smarter at Ad Tech," *Advertising Age*, http://adage.com, accessed January 5, 2019; A. Bruell, "P&G's Marc Pritchard Doubles Down on Demands of Digital Ad Giants," *The Wall Street Journal*, www.wsj.com, accessed January 5, 2019.

2. Vranica, "P&G Contends"; Bruell, "P&G's Marc Pritchard Doubles Down."

3. A. Bruell and S. Terlep, "P&G Cuts More than $100 Million in 'Largely Ineffective' Digital Ads," *The Wall Street Journal*, www.wsj.com, July 27, 2017.

4. J. Neff, "P&G Will Cut Another $400 Million in Agency, Production Costs," *Advertising Age*, http://adage.com, February 22, 2018.

5. R. Stewart, "Marc Pritchard Says P&G Will Soon Have Slashed 'Wasted' Digital Media Spend by 50%," *The Drum*, www.thedrum.com, March 6, 2018.

6. W. G. Ouchi, "Markets, Bureaucracies, and Clans," *Administrative Science Quarterly* 25 (1980), 129–41.

7. A. LaFrance, "Is Email Evil?," *The Atlantic*, www.theatlantic.com, November 12, 2015.

8. D. Bates, "You've Got (More) Mail: The Average Office Worker Spends over a Quarter of Their Day Dealing with Email," *Daily Mail*, www.dailymail.co.uk, accessed January 7, 2019.

9. A. Peters, "One Trick to Make Employees Happy: Ban Emails on Nights and Weekends," *Fast Company*, www.fastcoexist.com, June 1, 2016.

10. L. Vanderkam, "Should Your Company Use 'Zmail'? The Case for Inbox Curfews," *Fast Company*, www.fastcompany.com, accessed January 7, 2019.

11. D. Calista, "CEO's Goal: Build the Happiest, Healthiest Company in Philly," *BizPhilly*, www.phillymag.com, October 28, 2015.

12. S. McLaren, "These 6 Companies Make Work–Life Balance a Buzzword," *LinkedIn Talent Blog*, https://business.linkedin.com, November 19, 2018; E. Kewsin, "Prioritizing Employee Well-Being Helps This Consultancy Improve Its Bottom Line," *Fast Company*, www.fastcompany.com, September 25, 2018.

13. C. Chua, "11 Simple Tips to Effective Email Management," *Lifehack*, www.lifehack.org, accessed January 6, 2019; J. Whitmore, "4 Tips to Better Manage Your Inbox," *Entrepreneur*, www.entrepreneur.com, accessed January 6, 2019.

14. P. Lorange, M. Morton, and S. Ghoshal, *Strategic Control* (St. Paul, MN: West, 1986).

15. H. Koontz and R. W. Bradspies, "Managing through Feedforward Control," *Business Horizons*, June 1972, 25–36.

16. E. E. Lawler III and J. G. Rhode, *Information and Control in Organizations* (Pacific Palisades, CA: Goodyear, 1976).

17. C. W. L. Hill and G. R. Jones, *Strategic Management: An Integrated Approach*, 10th ed. (Mason, OH: Cengage Learning, 2012).

18. E. Flamholtz, "Organizational Control Systems as a Management Tool," *California Management Review*, Winter 1979, 50–58.

19. W. G. Ouchi, "The Transmission of Control through Organizational Hierarchy," *Academy of Management Journal* 21 (1978), 173–92.

20. Ouchi, "Markets, Bureaucracies, and Clans."

21. W. H. Newman, *Constructive Control* (Englewood Cliffs, NJ: Prentice-Hall, 1975).

22. J. D. Thompson, *Organizations in Action* (New York: McGraw-Hill, 1967).

23. R. N. Anthony, *The Management Control Function* (Boston: Harvard Business School Press, 1988).

24. Ouchi, "Markets, Bureaucracies, and Clans."

25. National Association of Colleges and Employers (NACE), *Job Outlook 2019,* www.naceweb.org, accessed January 6, 2019.

26. Ibid.

27. P. Loretto, "Importance of Internships for Your Professional Career," *The Balance,* www.thebalancecareers.com, accessed January 6, 2019.

28. "U.S. College Hiring to Increase by Almost 17 Percent," and "Fall vs. Spring Recruiting," *Job Outlook 2019.*

29. J. Chavez, "Recruiters: Job Prospects Look Bright for 2019 College Grads," *The Toledo Blade,* www.toledoblade.com, November 10, 2018; "33 Companies Hiring Interns and Recent Grads for Full-Time Jobs This Month," www.wayup.com, October 3, 2018.

30. R. Simons, "Strategic Orientation and Top Management Attention to Control Systems," *Strategic Management Journal* 12 (1991), 49–62.

31. G. Schreyogg and H. Steinmann, "Strategic Control: A New Perspective," *Academy of Management Review* 12 (1987), 91–103.

32. B. Woolridge and S. W. Floyd, "The Strategy Process, Middle Management Involvement, and Organizational Performance," *Strategic Management Journal* 11 (1990), 231–41.

33. S. Fritzen, M. Jochim, C. Mgnerey, and M. Sen, "Zero-Based Productivity: The Power of Informed Choices," www.mckinsey.com, July 2018; N. Trentmann, "Global Companies Extend Use of Zero-Based Budgeting to Slash Costs," *The Wall Street Journal,* https://blogs.wsj.com, February 27, 2018; K. Timmermans and R. Abdalla, *Beyond the ZBB Buzz,* Accenture, 2018, www.accenture.com; N. Trentmann, "European Companies Use Old-School Budget Tactic to Cut Costs," *The Wall Street Journal,* www.wsj.com, April 7, 2017; A. Loten, "Kraft Heinz CIO Spends on AI, Robots to Cut Costs," *The Wall Street Journal,* https://blogs.wsj.com, October 3, 2017.

34. Trentmann, "Global Companies Extend Use"; Timmermans and Abdalla, *Beyond the ZBB Buzz;* Trentmann, "European Companies Use Old-School Budget Tactic."

35. Trentmann, "Global Companies Extend Use"; Timmermans and Abdalla, *Beyond the ZBB Buzz;* Trentmann, "European Companies Use Old-School Budget Tactic."

36. Timmermans and Abdalla, *Beyond the ZBB Buzz.*

37. J. A. Alexander, "Adaptive Changes in Corporate Control Practices," *Academy of Management Journal* 34 (1991), 162–93.

38. Hill and Jones, *Strategic Management.*

39. G. H. B. Ross, "Revolution in Management Control," *Management Accounting* 72 (1992), 23–27.

40. P. F. Drucker, *The Practice of Management* (New York: Harper & Row, 1954).

41. R. Rodgers and J. E. Hunter, "Impact of Management by Objectives on Organizational Productivity," *Journal of Applied Psychology* 76 (1991), 322–26.

42. M. B. Gavin, S. G. Green, and G. T. Fairhurst, "Managerial Control—Strategies for Poor Performance over Time and the Impact on Subordinate Reactions," *Organizational Behavior and Human Decision Processes* 63 (1995), 207–21.

43. T. Jackson, "A Brief History of the Balanced Scorecard—and 4 Critical Takeaways," www.clearpointstrategy.com, accessed January 5, 2019; R. S. Kaplan and D. P. Norton, "The Balanced Scorecard—Measures That Drive Performance," *Harvard Business Review,* January–February 1992, accessed at https://hbr.org.

44. T. Jackson, "20 Companies Using the Balanced Scorecard (and Why)," www.clearpointstrategy.com, accessed January 5, 2019; R. S. Kaplan and D. P. Norton, "Using the Balanced Scorecard as a Strategic Management System," *Harvard Business Review,* July–August 2007, accessed at https://hbr.org.

45. J. McGregor, "The World's Most Innovative Companies," www.businessweek.com, May 4, 2007.

46. www.waltdisney.com, 2010, 2012.

47. C. Wang, "Disney Announces Strategic Reorganization, Effective Immediately," *CNBC,* www.cnbc.com, March 14, 2018.

48. "3 Examples of Great Organizational Culture You Can Learn From," http://blog.indeed.com, accessed January 7, 2019; National Center for Employee Ownership, "The Employee Ownership 100: America's Largest Majority Employee-Owned Companies," www.nceo.org, July 2018.

49. E. Woyke, "How UPS Delivers Faster Using $8 Headphones and Code That Decides When Dirty Trucks Get Cleaned," *MIT Technology Review,* www.technologyreview.com, February 16, 2018; T. Kilgore, "UPS's ORION on Pace for Up to $350 Million in Savings," *MarketWatch,* www.marketwatch.com, October 27, 2016.

50. N. Margulies and A. P. Raia, eds., *Conceptual Foundations of Organizational Development* (New York: McGraw-Hill, 1978); L. Brown, "Research Action: Organizational Feedback, Understanding and Change," *Journal of Applied Behavioral Research* 8 (1972), 697–711; P. A. Clark, *Action Research and Organizational Change* (New York: Harper & Row, 1972).

51. M. Choi and W. E. A. Ruona, "Individual Readiness for Organizational Change and Its Implications for Human Resource and Organization Development," *Human Resource Development Review* 10, no. 1 (2011), 46–73.

52. M. Peiperl, "Resistance to Change," in N. Nicholson, P. G. Audia, and M. M. Pillutla, eds., *The Blackwell Encyclopedia of Management,* vol. 11: *Organizational Behavior,* 2nd ed. (New York: Wiley, 2005), 348.

53. Choi and Ruona, "Individual Readiness for Organizational Change."

54. K. Piderit, "Rethinking Resistance and Recognizing Ambivalence: A Multidimensional View of Attitudes toward an Organizational Change," *Academy of Management Review* 25, no. 4 (2000), 783–94.

55. W. L. French and C. H. Bell, *Organizational Development* (Englewood Cliffs, NJ: Prentice-Hall, 1990).

56. M. Campbell, C. Rauwald, and C. Reiter, "Volkswagen's Peace Offering," *Bloomberg Businessweek,* April 2, 2018, 50–55; V. Walt, "Inside VW's Big Fix-It Job," *Fortune,* August 1, 2018, 104–11.

57. Campbell at al., "Volkswagen's Peace Offering"; C. Atiyeh, "Volkswagen CEO Matthias Müller Resigns [Update]," *Car and Driver,* www.caranddriver.com, April 12, 2018.

58. Walt, "Inside VW's Big Fix-It Job"; W. Boston, "Volkswagen to Pour Billions into Electric Cars," *The Wall Street Journal,* www.wsj.com, November 16, 2018.

59. W. Boston, "Volkswagen Profit Rises Despite Emissions Headwinds," *The Wall Street Journal,* www.wsj.com, October 30, 2018.

60. W. L. French, "A Checklist for Organizing and Implementing an OD Effort," in W. L. French, C. H. Bell, and R. A. Zawacki, eds., *Organizational Development and Transformation* (Homewood, IL: Irwin, 1994), 484–95.

Yuri Arcurs/Cutcaster

9 Motivation

Learning Objectives

After studying this chapter, you should be able to:

LO 9-1 Explain what motivation is and why managers need to be concerned about it.

LO 9-2 Describe from the perspectives of expectancy theory and equity theory what managers should do to have a highly motivated workforce.

LO 9-3 Explain how goals and needs motivate people and what kinds of goals are especially likely to result in high performance.

LO 9-4 Identify the motivation lessons that managers can learn from operant conditioning theory and social learning theory.

LO 9-5 Explain why and how managers can use pay as a major motivation tool.

PART 5

Management Snapshot

Martha Firestone Ford Is a Motivating Force for Her Detroit Lions

How to Get a Losing Team to Aim Higher and Win

After years of humiliation, Detroit Lions fans are pinning their hopes on a tiny woman in her 90s—Martha Firestone Ford, the team's owner. Since its 1957 championship, the team has won just a single playoff game, and it has never played in a Super Bowl. Furthermore, frustrated fans have been less likely to attend games. The team's future looked bleak until control shifted to Ford, who has deep roots in the Detroit area. The granddaughter of the founder of Firestone Tire and Rubber, she married the grandson of Henry Ford and moved to Detroit, where she was active in the community. When her husband, the Lions's owner, died in 2014, Ford surprised observers by stepping up boldly to take an active role in team operations.[1]

What gives hope to fans and players alike is Ford's commitment to high performance. The team started the first season under Ford with a 1–7 record, and she swiftly decided that leadership changes were overdue. She fired the team's president, Tom Lewand, and its general manager, Martin Mayhew. Before long, other executives also were on their way out. She hired the well-respected Bob Quinn to be the new general manager. On the business side, she brought in the family's longtime financial adviser Rod Wood to serve as president. Wood has focused on listening to fans about their experience at games in order to address day-to-day issues with stadium cleanliness, safety, and lines at concession stands. Every aspect of the franchise needs to excel, not just play on the field.[2]

Ford quickly signaled that the Lions would be driven by loftier goals, and everyone would be held accountable for achieving those goals. Immediately after the firings, she held a news conference to explain her goals and then met with team players to explain her actions. She answered their questions and emphasized the need to make changes in order to build a team that wins—which is, after all, exactly what players hope to do when they sign with a professional sports franchise. She wrote to season ticket holders telling them, "You deserve better."[3] Further demonstrating that she cares, she attends every game and greets all the players by name.[4]

The impact on the players—after surprise—was to rekindle their enthusiasm. For example, kicker Matt Prater concluded that Ford was demonstrating that "she's willing to do whatever it takes to win, which is what you want from your owner."[5]

The more motivated players haven't yet won a championship as of this writing, but the team's record has improved. Out of six seasons, they have played in the postseason three times. With more wins to see, fans are returning to the games, with every game sold out since October 2010.[6] And still the pressure to do better

Detroit Lions's owner Martha Firestone Ford, pictured here with team executives, is not afraid to make organizational changes to help motivate employees as well as the NFL players who work for her.
Paul Sancya/AP Images

continues. After a 9–7 record in 2017, the Lions fired coach Jim Caldwell and replaced him with someone Bob Quinn said could "take the team to the next level": Matt Patricia, who had been defensive coordinator with the New England Patriots through that franchise's participation in the 2018 Super Bowl.[7] Despite a shaky first season, Patricia and team executives continue to make changes to improve the storied franchise; for example, not renewing the contract of the team's offensive coordinator for the upcoming NFL season.[8] Perhaps some of that Super Bowl glory will yet rub off on the Lions and their highly motivated owner.

Overview

Even with the best strategy in place and an appropriate organizational architecture, an organization will be effective only if its members are motivated to perform at a high level. For example, Martha Firestone Ford and her Detroit Lions's management team, described in "Management Snapshot," clearly realize this. One reason that leading is such an important managerial activity is that it entails ensuring that each member of an organization is motivated to perform highly and help the organization achieve its goals. When managers are effective, the outcome of the leading process is a highly motivated workforce. A key challenge for managers of organizations both large and small is to encourage employees to perform at a high level.

In this chapter we describe what motivation is, where it comes from, and why managers need to promote high levels of it for an organization to be effective and achieve its goals. We examine important theories of motivation: expectancy theory, need theories, equity theory, goal-setting theory, and learning theories. Each gives managers important insights into how to motivate organizational members. The theories are complementary in that each focuses on a different aspect of motivation. Considering all the theories together helps managers gain a rich understanding of the many issues and problems involved in encouraging high levels of motivation throughout an organization. Last, we consider the use of pay as a motivation tool. By the end of this chapter you will understand what it takes to have a highly motivated workforce.

LO 9-1
Explain what motivation is and why managers need to be concerned about it.

The Nature of Motivation

Motivation may be defined as psychological forces that determine the direction of a person's behavior in an organization, a person's level of effort, and a person's level of persistence in the face of obstacles.[9] The *direction of a person's behavior* refers to the many possible behaviors a person can engage in. For example, employees of the Detroit Lions know they should do whatever it takes to provide high-quality customer service, such as providing top-notch food items at stadium concession stands or clean and safe restroom facilities at each home game. *Effort* refers to how hard people work. Detroit Lions's employees—players as well as managers—exert high levels of effort to make sure they continue their winning ways and provide an exceptional experience for their fans. *Persistence* refers to whether, when faced with roadblocks or other obstacles, people keep trying or give up. Managers with the Detroit Lions continually seek to improve the profitability of the team's operations while maintaining high levels of customer service.

motivation
Psychological forces that determine the direction of a person's behavior in an organization, a person's level of effort, and a person's level of persistence.

288

Motivation is central to management because it explains *why* people behave the way they do in organizations.[10] Motivation also explains why a server is polite or rude and why a kindergarten teacher really tries to get children to enjoy learning or just goes through the motions. It explains why some managers truly put their organizations' best interests first, whereas others are more concerned with maximizing their salaries and why—more generally—some workers put forth twice as much effort as others.

Motivation can come from either *intrinsic* or *extrinsic* sources. Intrinsically motivated behavior is behavior that is performed for its own sake; the source of motivation is actually performing the behavior, and motivation comes from doing the work itself. Many managers are intrinsically motivated; they derive a sense of accomplishment and achievement from helping the organization achieve its goals and gain competitive advantages. Jobs that are interesting and challenging are more likely to lead to intrinsic motivation than are jobs that are boring or do not use a person's skills and abilities. An elementary school teacher who really enjoys teaching children, a software engineer who loves solving programming problems, and a commercial photographer who relishes taking creative photographs are all intrinsically motivated. For these individuals, motivation comes from performing their jobs—teaching children, finding bugs in computer programs, and taking pictures.

Extrinsically motivated behavior is behavior that is performed to acquire material or social rewards or to avoid punishment; the source of motivation is the consequences of the behavior, not the behavior itself. A car salesperson who is motivated by receiving a commission on all cars sold, a lawyer who is motivated by the high salary and status that go along with the job, and a factory worker who is motivated by the opportunity to earn a secure income are all extrinsically motivated. Their motivation comes from the consequences they receive as a result of their work behaviors.

People can be intrinsically motivated, extrinsically motivated, or both intrinsically and extrinsically motivated.[11] A top manager who derives a sense of accomplishment and achievement from managing a large corporation and strives to reach year-end targets to obtain a hefty bonus is both intrinsically and extrinsically motivated. Similarly, a nurse who enjoys helping and taking care of patients and is motivated by having a secure job with good benefits is both intrinsically and extrinsically motivated. Within the Detroit Lions organization, employees are both extrinsically motivated because of opportunities for promotions and having their pay linked to the team's overall performance, and intrinsically motivated because they get a sense of satisfaction from serving customers (Lions fans) and learning new things.

Whether workers are intrinsically motivated, extrinsically motivated, or both depends on a wide variety of factors: (1) workers' own personal characteristics (such as their personalities, abilities, values, attitudes, and needs), (2) the nature of their jobs (such as whether they have been enriched or where they are on the five core characteristics of the job characteristics model), and (3) the nature of the organization (such as its structure, its culture, its control systems, its human resource management system, and the ways in which rewards such as pay are distributed to employees).

In addition to being intrinsically or extrinsically motivated, some people are prosocially motivated by their work.[12] Prosocially motivated behavior is behavior that is performed to benefit or help others.[13] Behavior can be prosocially motivated in addition to being extrinsically and/or intrinsically motivated. An elementary

intrinsically motivated behavior Behavior that is performed for its own sake.

extrinsically motivated behavior Behavior that is performed to acquire material or social rewards or to avoid punishment.

prosocially motivated behavior Behavior that is performed to benefit or help others.

Where are you more likely to find prosocial motivation? Here in the classroom as a teacher walks her student through that tricky math problem. Getting companies to foster this type of motivation is a bit trickier! LWA/Dann Tardif/Blend Images LLC

school teacher who not only enjoys the process of teaching young children (has high intrinsic motivation) but also has a strong desire to give children the best learning experience possible and help those with learning disabilities overcome their challenges, and who keeps up with the latest research on child development and teaching methods in an effort to continually improve the effectiveness of her teaching, has high prosocial motivation in addition to high intrinsic motivation. Recent preliminary research suggests that when workers have high prosocial motivation, also having high intrinsic motivation can be especially beneficial for job performance.[14]

Regardless of whether people are intrinsically, extrinsically, or prosocially motivated, they join and are motivated to work in organizations to obtain certain outcomes. An **outcome** is anything a person gets from a job or an organization. Some outcomes, such as autonomy, responsibility, a feeling of accomplishment, and the pleasure of doing interesting or enjoyable work, result in intrinsically motivated behavior. Outcomes such as improving the lives or well-being of other people and doing good by helping others result in prosocially motivated behavior. Other outcomes, such as pay, job security, benefits, and vacation time, result in extrinsically motivated behavior.

outcome Anything a person gets from a job or an organization.

input Anything a person contributes to his or her job or organization.

Organizations hire people to obtain important inputs. An **input** is anything a person contributes to the job or organization, such as time, effort, education, experience, skills, knowledge, and actual work behaviors. Inputs such as these are necessary for an organization to achieve its goals. Managers strive to motivate members of an organization to contribute inputs—through their behavior, effort, and persistence—that help the organization achieve its goals. How do managers do this? They ensure that members of an organization obtain the outcomes they desire when they make valuable contributions to the organization. Managers use outcomes to motivate people to contribute their inputs to the organization. Giving people outcomes when they contribute inputs and perform well aligns the interests of employees with the goals of the organization as a whole because when employees do what is good for the organization, they personally benefit.

This alignment between employees and organizational goals as a whole can be described by the motivation equation depicted in Figure 9.1. Managers seek to ensure that people are motivated to contribute important inputs to the organization, that these inputs are put to good use or focused in the direction of high performance, and that high performance results in workers' obtaining the outcomes they desire.

Each of the theories of motivation discussed in this chapter focuses on one or more aspects of this equation. Each theory focuses on a different set of issues that managers need to address to have a highly motivated workforce. Together the theories provide a comprehensive set of guidelines for managers to follow to promote high levels of employee motivation. Effective managers tend to follow many of these guidelines, whereas ineffective managers often fail to follow them and seem to have trouble motivating organizational members.

Figure 9.1

The Motivation Equation

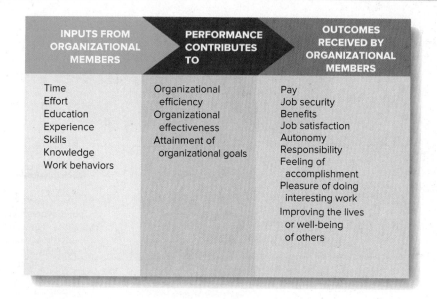

INPUTS FROM ORGANIZATIONAL MEMBERS	PERFORMANCE CONTRIBUTES TO	OUTCOMES RECEIVED BY ORGANIZATIONAL MEMBERS
Time Effort Education Experience Skills Knowledge Work behaviors	Organizational efficiency Organizational effectiveness Attainment of organizational goals	Pay Job security Benefits Job satisfaction Autonomy Responsibility Feeling of accomplishment Pleasure of doing interesting work Improving the lives or well-being of others

Expectancy Theory

Expectancy theory, formulated by Victor H. Vroom in the 1960s, posits that motivation is high when workers believe that high levels of effort lead to high performance and high performance leads to the attainment of desired outcomes. Expectancy theory is one of the most popular theories of work motivation because it focuses on all three parts of the motivation equation: inputs, performance, and outcomes. Expectancy theory identifies three major factors that determine a person's motivation: *expectancy, instrumentality,* and *valence* (see Figure 9.2).[15]

LO 9-2
Describe from the perspectives of expectancy theory and equity theory what managers should do to have a highly motivated workforce.

expectancy theory The theory that motivation will be high when workers believe that high levels of effort lead to high performance and high performance leads to the attainment of desired outcomes.

expectancy In expectancy theory, a perception about the extent to which effort results in a certain level of performance.

Expectancy

Expectancy is a person's perception about the extent to which effort (an input) results in a certain level of performance. A person's level of expectancy determines whether he or she believes that a high level of effort results in a high level of performance. People are motivated to put forth a lot of effort on their jobs only if they think that their effort will pay off in high performance—that is, if they have high expectancy. Think about how motivated you would be to study for a test if you thought that no matter how hard you tried, you would get a D. Think about how motivated a marketing manager would be who thought that no matter how hard he or she worked, there was no way to increase sales of an unpopular product. In these cases, expectancy is low, so overall motivation is also low.

Members of an organization are motivated to put forth a high level of effort only if they think that doing so leads to high performance.[16] In other words, in order for people's motivation to be high, expectancy must be high. Thus, in attempting to influence motivation, managers need to make sure their employees believe that if they do try hard, they can actually succeed. One way managers can boost expectancies is through expressing confidence in their employees' capabilities. Managers at The Container Store, for example, express high levels of confidence in their employees. As Container Store cofounder Garrett Boone put it, "Everybody we hire, we hire

Figure 9.2
Expectancy,
Instrumentality, and
Valence

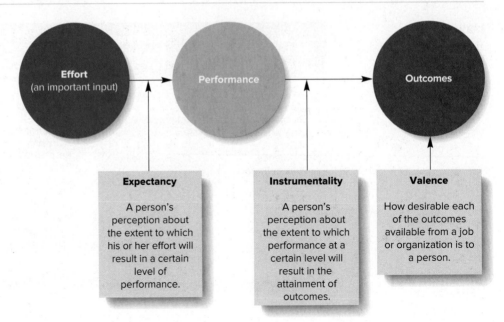

as a leader. Anybody in our store can take an action that you might think of typically being a manager's action."[17]

In addition to expressing confidence in employees, other ways for managers to boost employees' expectancy levels and motivation are by providing training so people have the expertise needed for high performance and increasing their levels of autonomy and responsibility as they gain experience so they have the freedom to do what it takes to perform at a high level. For example, the Best Buy chain of stores, selling electronics, computers, music and movies, and gadgets of all sorts, boosts salespeople's expectancies by giving them extensive training in on-site meetings and online. Salespeople also receive extensive training in how to determine customers' needs.[18]

Instrumentality

instrumentality In expectancy theory, a perception about the extent to which performance results in the attainment of outcomes.

Expectancy captures a person's perceptions about the relationship between effort and performance. Instrumentality, the second major concept in expectancy theory, is a person's perception about the extent to which performance at a certain level results in the attainment of outcomes (see Figure 9.2). According to expectancy theory, employees are motivated to perform at a high level only if they think high performance will lead to (or is *instrumental* in attaining) outcomes such as pay, job security, interesting job assignments, bonuses, or a feeling of accomplishment. In other words, instrumentalities must be high for motivation to be high—people must perceive that because of their high performance they will receive outcomes.[19]

Managers promote high levels of instrumentality when they link performance to desired outcomes. In addition, managers must clearly communicate this linkage to employees. By making sure that outcomes available in an organization are distributed to organizational members on the basis of their performance, managers promote high instrumentality and motivation. When outcomes are linked to performance in this way, high performers receive more outcomes than low performers.

In the "Management Snapshot," managers in the Detroit Lions' organization raise levels of instrumentality and motivation for employees by linking opportunities for promotion and pay to performance.

Valence

Although all members of an organization must have high expectancies and instrumentalities, expectancy theory acknowledges that people differ in their preferences for outcomes. For many people, pay is the most important outcome of working. For others, a feeling of accomplishment or enjoying one's work is more important than pay. The term valence refers to how desirable each of the outcomes available from a job or an organization is to a person. To motivate organizational members, managers need to determine which outcomes have high valence for them—are highly desired—and make sure that those outcomes are provided when members perform at a high level. For example, at Enterprise Holdings, the largest car rental company in the world, autonomy, responsibility, and opportunities for promotion are highly valent outcomes for many employees. The company's management training program is touted not only for promoting a strong "promote-from-within" culture but also for developing new hires into the next generation of business leaders. According to Enterprise, more than 16,000 employees were promoted in a recent year.[20]

Bringing It All Together

According to expectancy theory, high motivation results from high levels of expectancy, instrumentality, and valence (see Figure 9.3). If any one of these factors is low, motivation is likely to be low. No matter how tightly desired outcomes are linked to performance, if a person thinks it is practically impossible to perform at a high level, motivation to perform at a high level will be low. Similarly, if a person does not

Almost all entry-level employees participate in Enterprise's management training program, which allows new hires to learn all aspects of the company business, including how to provide excellent customer service and prepare for possible promotion opportunities. This strategy has helped Enterprise cultivate a highly motivated workforce. Carlos Osorio/AP Images

Figure 9.3
Expectancy Theory

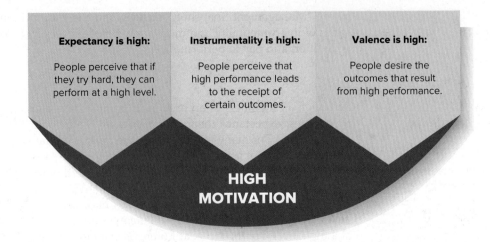

Expectancy is high:

People perceive that if they try hard, they can perform at a high level.

Instrumentality is high:

People perceive that high performance leads to the receipt of certain outcomes.

Valence is high:

People desire the outcomes that result from high performance.

HIGH MOTIVATION

think outcomes are linked to high performance, or if a person does not desire the outcomes that are linked to high performance, motivation to perform at a high level will be low. Effective managers realize the importance of high levels of expectancy, instrumentality, and valence and take concrete steps to ensure that their employees are highly motivated.

Need Theories

A **need** is a requirement or necessity for survival and well-being. The basic premise of **need theories** is that people are motivated to obtain outcomes at work that will satisfy their needs. Need theory complements expectancy theory by exploring in depth which outcomes motivate people to perform at a high level. Need theories suggest that to motivate a person to contribute valuable inputs to a job and perform at a high level, a manager must determine what needs the person is trying to satisfy at work and ensure that the person receives outcomes that help satisfy those needs when the person performs at a high level and helps the organization achieve its goals.

There are several need theories. Here we discuss Abraham Maslow's hierarchy of needs, Frederick Herzberg's motivator-hygiene theory, and David McClelland's needs for achievement, affiliation, and power. These theories describe needs that people try to satisfy at work. In doing so, they give managers insights into what outcomes motivate members of an organization to perform at a high level and contribute inputs to help the organization achieve its goals.

Maslow's Hierarchy of Needs

Psychologist Abraham Maslow proposed that all people seek to satisfy five basic kinds of needs: physiological needs, safety needs, belongingness needs, esteem needs, and self-actualization needs (see Table 9.1).[21] He suggested that these needs constitute a **hierarchy of needs**, with the most basic or compelling needs—physiological and safety needs—at the bottom. Maslow argued that these lowest-level needs must be met before a person strives to satisfy needs higher up in the hierarchy, such as self-esteem needs. Once a need is satisfied, Maslow proposed, it ceases to operate as a source of motivation. The lowest level of *unmet* needs in

LO 9-3
Explain how goals and needs motivate people and what kinds of goals are especially likely to result in high performance.

need A requirement or necessity for survival and well-being.

need theories Theories of motivation that focus on what needs people are trying to satisfy at work and what outcomes will satisfy those needs.

Table 9.1

Maslow's Hierarchy of Needs

	Needs	Description	Examples of How Managers Can Help People Satisfy These Needs at Work
Highest-Level Needs	**Self-actualization needs**	The needs to realize one's full potential as a human being.	Giving people the opportunity to use their skills and abilities to the fullest extent possible.
	Esteem needs	The needs to feel good about oneself and one's capabilities, to be respected by others, and to receive recognition and appreciation.	Granting promotions and recognizing accomplishments.
	Belongingness needs	Needs for social interaction, friendship, affection, and love.	Promoting good interpersonal relations and organizing social functions such as company picnics and holiday parties.
	Safety needs	Needs for security, stability, and a safe environment.	Providing job security, adequate health care benefits, and safe working conditions.
Lowest-Level Needs (Most Basic or Compelling)	**Physiological needs**	Basic needs for things such as food, water, and shelter that must be met in order for a person to survive.	Providing a level of pay that enables a person to buy food and clothing and have adequate housing.
	The lowest level of unsatisfied needs motivates behavior; once this level of needs is satisfied, a person tries to satisfy the needs at the next level.		

Maslow's hierarchy of needs An arrangement of five basic needs that, according to Maslow, motivate behavior. Maslow proposed that the lowest level of unmet needs is the prime motivator and that only one level of needs is motivational at a time.

the hierarchy is the prime motivator of behavior; if and when this level is satisfied, needs at the next highest level in the hierarchy motivate behavior.

Although this theory identifies needs that are likely to be important sources of motivation for many people, research does not support Maslow's contention that there is a need hierarchy or his notion that only one level of needs is motivational at a time.[22] Nevertheless, a key conclusion can be drawn from Maslow's theory: People try to satisfy different needs at work. To have a motivated workforce, managers must determine which needs employees are trying to satisfy in organizations and then make sure that individuals receive outcomes that satisfy their needs when they perform at a high level and contribute to organizational effectiveness. By doing this, managers align the interests of individual members with the interests of the organization as a whole. By doing what is good for the organization (that is, performing at a high level), employees receive outcomes that satisfy their needs.

In our increasingly global economy, managers must realize that citizens of different countries might differ in the needs they seek to satisfy through work.[23] Some research suggests, for example, that people in Greece and Japan are especially motivated by safety needs and that people in Sweden, Norway, and Denmark are motivated by belongingness needs.[24] In less-developed countries with low standards of living, physiological and safety needs are likely to be the prime motivators of behavior. As countries become wealthier and have higher standards of living, needs related to personal growth and accomplishment (such as esteem and self-actualization) become important motivators of behavior.

No one pumps their fist over their laptop unless it's for a good reason! Clearly, whipping an obnoxious spreadsheet into shape and sending out a calmly worded press release makes for satisfied self-actualization needs. Jim Esposito/Getty Images

Herzberg's Motivator-Hygiene Theory

Adopting an approach different from Maslow's, Frederick Herzberg focused on two factors: (1) outcomes that can lead to high levels of motivation and job satisfaction and (2) outcomes that can prevent people from being dissatisfied. According to Herzberg's motivator-hygiene theory, people have two sets of needs or requirements: motivator needs and hygiene needs.[25] *Motivator needs* are related to the nature of the work itself and how challenging it is. Outcomes such as interesting work, autonomy, responsibility, the ability to grow and develop on the job, and a sense of accomplishment and achievement help to satisfy motivator needs. To have a highly motivated and satisfied workforce, Herzberg suggested, managers should take steps to ensure that employees' motivator needs are being met.

Hygiene needs are related to the physical and psychological context in which the work is performed. Hygiene needs are satisfied by outcomes such as pleasant and comfortable working conditions, pay, job security, good relationships with coworkers, and effective supervision. According to Herzberg, when hygiene needs are not met, workers are dissatisfied, and when hygiene needs are met, workers are not dissatisfied. Satisfying hygiene needs, however, does not result in high levels of motivation or even high levels of job satisfaction. For motivation and job satisfaction to be high, motivator needs must be met. Many research studies have tested Herzberg's propositions, and, by and large, the theory fails to receive support.[26] Nevertheless, Herzberg's formulations have contributed to our understanding of motivation in at least two ways. First, Herzberg helped focus researchers' and managers' attention on the important distinction between intrinsic motivation (related to motivator needs) and extrinsic motivation (related to hygiene needs), covered earlier in the chapter. Second, his theory prompted researchers and managers to study how jobs could be designed or redesigned to be intrinsically motivating.

Herzberg's motivator-hygiene theory A need theory that distinguishes between motivator needs (related to the nature of the work itself) and hygiene needs (related to the physical and psychological context in which the work is performed) and proposes that motivator needs must be met for motivation and job satisfaction to be high.

McClelland's Needs for Achievement, Affiliation, and Power

Psychologist David McClelland extensively researched the needs for achievement, affiliation, and power.[27] The need for achievement is the extent to which an individual has a strong desire to perform challenging tasks well and to meet personal standards for excellence. People with a high need for achievement often set clear goals for themselves and like to receive performance feedback. The need for affiliation is the extent to which an individual is concerned about establishing and maintaining good interpersonal relations, being liked, and having the people around him or her get along with each other. The need for power is the extent to which an individual desires to control or influence others.[28]

Although each of these needs is present in each of us to some degree, their importance in the workplace depends on the position one occupies. For example, research suggests that high needs for achievement and for power are assets for first-line and middle managers and that a high need for power is especially important for upper managers.[29] One study found that U.S. presidents with a relatively high need for

need for achievement The extent to which an individual has a strong desire to perform challenging tasks well and to meet personal standards for excellence.

power tended to be especially effective during their terms of office.[30] A high need for affiliation may not always be desirable in managers and other leaders because it might lead them to try too hard to be liked by others (including their employees) rather than doing all they can to ensure that performance is as high as it can and should be. Although most research on these needs has been done in the United States, some studies suggest that the findings may be applicable to people in other countries as well, such as India and New Zealand.[31]

Other Needs

Clearly, more needs motivate workers than the needs described by these three theories. For example, more and more workers are feeling the need for work–life balance and time to take care of their loved ones while being highly motivated at work. Interestingly enough, recent research suggests that being exposed to nature (even just being able to see some trees from an office window) has many valuable effects, and a lack of such exposure can impair well-being and performance.[32] Thus, having some time during the day when one can at least see nature may be another important need.

need for affiliation The extent to which an individual is concerned about establishing and maintaining good interpersonal relations, being liked, and having the people around him or her get along with each other.

need for power The extent to which an individual desires to control or influence others.

Equity Theory

Equity theory is a theory of motivation that concentrates on people's perceptions of the fairness of their work *outcomes* relative to, or in proportion to, their work *inputs*. Equity theory complements expectancy and need theories by focusing on how people perceive the relationship between the outcomes they receive from their jobs and organizations and the inputs they contribute. Equity theory was formulated in the 1960s by J. Stacy Adams, who stressed that what is important in determining motivation is the *relative* rather than the *absolute* levels of outcomes a person receives and inputs a person contributes. Specifically, motivation is influenced by the comparison of one's own outcome–input ratio with the outcome–input ratio of a referent.[33] The *referent* might be another person or a group of people who are perceived to be similar to oneself; the referent also might be oneself in a previous job or one's expectations about what outcome–input ratios should be. In a comparison of one's own outcome–input ratio to a referent's ratio, one's *perceptions* of outcomes and inputs (not any objective indicator of them) are key.

LO 9-2
Describe from the perspectives of expectancy theory and equity theory what managers should do to have a highly motivated workforce.

equity theory A theory of motivation that focuses on people's perceptions of the fairness of their work outcomes relative to their work inputs.

Equity

Equity exists when a person perceives his or her own outcome–input ratio to be equal to a referent's outcome–input ratio. Under conditions of equity (see Table 9.2), if a referent receives more outcomes than you receive, the referent contributes proportionally more inputs to the organization, so his or her outcome–input ratio still equals your ratio. Maria Sanchez and Claudia King, for example, both work in a shoe store in a large mall. Sanchez is paid more per hour than King but also contributes more inputs, including being responsible for some of the store's bookkeeping, closing the store, and periodically depositing cash in the bank. When King compares her outcome–input ratio to Sanchez's (her referent's), she perceives the ratios to be equitable because Sanchez's higher level of pay (an outcome) is proportional to her higher level of inputs (bookkeeping, closing the store, and going to the bank).

Similarly, under conditions of equity, if you receive more outcomes than a referent, your inputs are perceived to be proportionally higher. Continuing with our example, when Sanchez compares her outcome–input ratio to King's (her referent's)

equity The justice, impartiality, and fairness to which all organizational members are entitled.

Table 9.2

Equity Theory

Condition	Person		Referent	Example
Equity	$\dfrac{\text{Outcomes}}{\text{Inputs}}$	$=$	$\dfrac{\text{Outcomes}}{\text{Inputs}}$	An engineer perceives that he contributes more inputs (time and effort) and receives proportionally more outcomes (a higher salary and choice job assignments) than his referent.
Underpayment inequity	$\dfrac{\text{Outcomes}}{\text{Inputs}}$	$<$ (less than)	$\dfrac{\text{Outcomes}}{\text{Inputs}}$	An engineer perceives that he contributes more inputs but receives the same outcomes as his referent.
Overpayment inequity	$\dfrac{\text{Outcomes}}{\text{Inputs}}$	$>$ (greater than)	$\dfrac{\text{Outcomes}}{\text{Inputs}}$	An engineer perceives that he contributes the same inputs but receives more outcomes than his referent.

ratio, she perceives them to be equitable because her higher level of pay is proportional to her higher level of inputs. When equity exists, people are motivated to continue contributing their current levels of inputs to their organizations to receive their current levels of outcomes. If people wish to increase their outcomes under conditions of equity, they are motivated to increase their inputs.

Inequity

inequity Lack of fairness.

Inequity, or lack of fairness, exists when a person's outcome–input ratio is not perceived to be equal to a referent's. Inequity creates pressure or tension inside people and motivates them to restore equity by bringing the two ratios back into balance.

There are two types of inequity: underpayment inequity and overpayment inequity (see Table 9.2). **Underpayment inequity** exists when a person's own outcome–input ratio is perceived to be *less* than that of a referent. In comparing yourself to a referent, you think you are *not* receiving the outcomes you should be, given your inputs. **Overpayment inequity** exists when a person perceives that his or her own outcome–input ratio is *greater* than that of a referent. In comparing yourself to a referent, you think you are receiving *more* outcomes than you should be, given your inputs.

underpayment inequity The inequity that exists when a person perceives that his or her own outcome–input ratio is less than the ratio of a referent.

Ways to Restore Equity

overpayment inequity The inequity that exists when a person perceives that his or her own outcome–input ratio is greater than the ratio of a referent.

According to equity theory, both underpayment inequity and overpayment inequity create tension that motivates most people to restore equity by bringing the ratios back into balance.[34] When people experience *underpayment* inequity, they may be motivated to lower their inputs by reducing their working hours, putting forth less effort on the job, or being absent; or they may be motivated to increase their outcomes by asking for a raise or a promotion. Susan Richie, a financial analyst at a large corporation, noticed that she was working longer hours and getting more work accomplished than a coworker who had the same position, yet they both received exactly the same pay and other outcomes. To restore equity, Richie decided to stop going in early and staying late. Alternatively, she could have tried to restore equity by trying to increase her outcomes, perhaps by asking her boss for a raise.

When people experience underpayment inequity and other means of equity restoration fail, they can change their perceptions of their own or the referent's inputs or outcomes. For example, they may realize that their referent is really working on more difficult projects than they are or that they really take more time off from work than their referent does. Alternatively, if people who feel they are underpaid have other employment options, they may leave the organization. As an example, John Steinberg, an assistant principal in a high school, experienced underpayment inequity when he realized all the other assistant principals of high schools in his school district had received promotions to the position of principal even though they had been in their jobs for a shorter time than he had. Steinberg's performance had always been appraised as being high, so after his repeated requests for a promotion went unheeded, he found a job as a principal in a different school district.

When people experience *overpayment* inequity, they may try to restore equity by changing their perceptions of their own or their referent's inputs or outcomes. Equity can be restored when people realize they are contributing more inputs than they originally thought. Equity also can be restored by perceiving the referent's inputs to be lower or the referent's outcomes to be higher than one originally thought. When equity is restored in this way, actual inputs and outcomes are unchanged, and the person being overpaid takes no real action. What is changed is how people think about or view their or the referent's inputs and outcomes. For instance, Mary McMann experienced overpayment inequity when she realized she was being paid $2 an hour more than a coworker who had the same job as she did in a health food store and who contributed the same amount of inputs. McMann restored equity by changing her perceptions of her inputs. She realized she worked harder than her coworker and solved more problems that came up in the store.

Experiencing either overpayment or underpayment inequity, you might decide that your referent is not appropriate because, for example, the referent is too different from yourself. Choosing a more appropriate referent may bring the ratios back into balance. Angela Martinez, a middle manager in the engineering department of a chemical company, experienced overpayment inequity when she realized she was being paid quite a bit more than her friend, who was a middle manager in the marketing department of the same company. After thinking about the discrepancy for a while, Martinez decided that engineering and marketing were so different that she should not be comparing her job to her friend's job even though they were both middle managers. Martinez restored equity by changing her referent; she picked a middle manager in the engineering department as a new referent.

Motivation is highest when as many people as possible in an organization perceive that they are being equitably treated—their outcomes and inputs are in balance. Top contributors and performers are motivated to continue contributing a high level of inputs because they are receiving the outcomes they deserve. Mediocre contributors and performers realize that if they want to increase their outcomes, they have to increase their inputs. Managers of effective organizations realize the importance of equity for motivation and performance and continually strive to ensure that employees believe they are being equitably treated. For another example of an issue related to equity, see the following "Focus on Diversity" feature.

Equity and Justice in Organizations

distributive justice A person's perception of the fairness of the distribution of outcomes in an organization.

Equity theory, given its focus on the fair distribution of outcomes in organizations to foster high motivation, is often labeled a theory of distributive justice.[35] Distributive justice refers to an employee's perception of the fairness of the distribution of outcomes (such as promotions, pay, job assignments, and working conditions) in an organization.[36] Employees are more likely to be highly motivated when they perceive distributive justice to be high rather than low.

Focus on Diversity

For Diversity to Motivate, It Must Come with Equity

Many organizations have sought to hire a diverse workforce in order to bring more points of view to their decision making and build stronger relationships with their different customers. Some are then surprised when people who differ from the majority group—say, women in a male-dominated workplace or blacks in a white-dominated workplace—are quick to leave. One cause of the turnover may be that these employees are experiencing inequity. Quitting is one way to restore the equity balance.

This is a widely reported problem in the high-tech industry. Although some observers assume that women aren't particularly interested in programming and would prefer jobs that are more "social," the women themselves are more apt to report that they felt uncomfortable at work and were often overlooked when they offered ideas or sought mentors. In fact, some have left their employer and started their own technology companies.[37]

Microsoft, for example, has made efforts to hire women and track their pay to make sure it is equitable. Even so, women there have reported pressure to act more like stereotypical college men in order to fit in with the culture. Aggression and criticism characterized the communication style, some have said. When everyone is expected to adopt a similar tone, the benefits of diversity get lost in the efforts at sameness, and some people are unable to contribute fully and receive the intrinsic and extrinsic rewards associated with valuable contributions.[38]

Like Microsoft, other companies also have focused on pay when considering their treatment of a diverse workforce. Starbucks, for example, spent 10 years adjusting pay to reach the point where pay for equal work in the United States is equal regardless of an employee's race or gender. The company continues to pursue pay equity for employees outside the United States. Intel measured its own achievement of pay equity one year earlier. The microchip maker also seeks to ensure equity in promoting and retaining workers. Lyft recently started annual audits of employee compensation, aiming to ensure that pay is equitable across race and gender. The ride-sharing company also hired a vice president of talent and inclusion, charged with ensuring the company welcomes diverse employees, so they can contribute fully.[39] Equitable treatment, because it empowers and retains an organization's workforce, is not only ethical, but also good for business. ●

Equitable treatment of all employees helps empower individuals and retain top talent, which is a good business strategy. Rawpixel.com/Shutterstock

procedural justice A person's perception of the fairness of the procedures that are used to determine how to distribute outcomes in an organization.

interpersonal justice A person's perception of the fairness of the interpersonal treatment he or she receives from whoever distributes outcomes to him or her.

Three other forms of justice are important for high motivation. Procedural justice refers to an employee's perception of the fairness of the procedures used to determine how to distribute outcomes in an organization.[40] For example, if important outcomes such as pay and promotions are distributed based on performance appraisals (see Chapter 12) and an employee perceives that the procedure that is used (i.e., the performance appraisal system) is unfair, then procedural justice is low and motivation is likely to suffer. More generally, motivation is higher when procedural justice is high rather than low.[41] Interpersonal justice refers to an employee's perception of the fairness of the interpersonal treatment he or she receives from whoever distributes outcomes to him or her (typically his or her manager).[42] Interpersonal justice is high when managers treat employees with dignity and respect and are polite and courteous.[43] Motivation is higher when interpersonal justice is high rather than low. Informational justice refers to an employee's perception of the extent to which his or her manager provides explanations for decisions and the procedures used to arrive at them.[44] For example, if a manager explains how performance is appraised and how decisions about the distribution of outcomes are made, informational justice (and motivation) are more likely to be high than if the manager does not do this.[45] All in all, it is most advantageous for distributive, procedural, interpersonal, and informational justice all to be high.

Goal-Setting Theory

Goal-setting theory focuses on motivating workers to contribute their inputs to their jobs and organizations; in this way it is similar to expectancy theory and equity theory. But goal-setting theory takes this focus a step further by considering as well how managers can ensure that organizational members focus their inputs in the direction of high performance and the achievement of organizational goals.

LO 9-3
Explain how goals and needs motivate people and what kinds of goals are especially likely to result in high performance.

informational justice A person's perception of the extent to which his or her manager provides explanations for decisions and the procedures used to arrive at them.

Ed Locke and Gary Latham, the leading researchers for goal-setting theory, suggested that the goals organizational members strive to attain are prime determinants of their motivation and subsequent performance. A *goal* is what a person is trying to accomplish through his or her efforts and behaviors.[46] Just as you may have a goal to get a good grade in this course, so do members of an organization have goals they strive to meet. For example, salespeople at Nordstrom strive to meet sales goals, while top managers pursue market share and profitability goals.

Goal-setting theory suggests that to stimulate high motivation and performance, goals must be *specific* and *difficult*.[47] Specific goals are often quantitative—a salesperson's goal to sell $500 worth of merchandise per day, a scientist's goal to finish a project in one year, a CEO's goal to reduce debt by 40% and increase revenues by 20%, a restaurant manager's goal to serve 150 customers per evening. In contrast to specific goals, vague goals such as "doing your best" or "selling as much as you can" do not have much motivational impact.

goal-setting theory A theory that focuses on identifying the types of goals that are most effective in producing high levels of motivation and performance and explaining why goals have these effects.

Difficult goals are hard but not impossible to attain. In contrast to difficult goals, easy goals are those that practically everyone can attain, and moderate goals are goals that about one-half of the people can attain. Both easy and moderate goals have less motivational power than difficult goals.

Regardless of whether specific, difficult goals are set by managers, workers, or teams of managers and workers, they lead to high levels of motivation and performance. When managers set goals for their employees, the employees must accept the goals or agree to work toward them; also, they should be committed to them or really want to attain them. Some managers find that having employees participate in the actual

Specific, difficult goals can encourage people to exert high levels of effort and to focus efforts in the right direction.

Stockbyte/Punchstock Images

setting of goals boosts their acceptance of and commitment to the goals. In addition, organizational members need to receive *feedback* about how they are doing; feedback can often be provided by the performance appraisal and feedback component of an organization's human resource management system as discussed in Chapter 12.

Specific, difficult goals affect motivation in two ways. First, they motivate people to contribute more inputs to their jobs. Specific, difficult goals cause people to put forth high levels of effort, for example. Just as you would study harder if you were trying to get an A in a course instead of a C, so will a salesperson work harder to reach a $500 sales goal instead of a $200 sales goal. Specific, difficult goals also cause people to be more persistent when they run into difficulties than do easy, moderate, or vague goals. Salespeople who are told to sell as much as possible might stop trying on a slow day, whereas having a specific, difficult goal to reach motivates them to keep trying.

A second way in which specific, difficult goals affect motivation is by helping people focus their inputs in the right direction. These goals let people know what they should be focusing their attention on, whether it is increasing the quality of customer service or sales or lowering new product development times. The fact that the goals are specific and difficult also frequently causes people to develop *action plans* for reaching them.[48] Action plans can include the strategies needed to attain the goals and timetables or schedules for the completion of different activities crucial to goal attainment. Like the goals themselves, action plans also help ensure that efforts are focused in the right direction and that people do not get sidetracked along the way.

Although specific, difficult goals have been found to increase motivation and performance in a wide variety of jobs and organizations both in the United States and abroad, recent research suggests that they may detract from performance under certain conditions. When people are performing complicated and challenging tasks that require them to focus on a considerable amount of learning, specific, difficult goals may actually impair performance.[49] Striving to reach such goals may direct some of a person's attention away from learning about the task and toward trying to figure out how to achieve the goal. Once a person has learned the task and it no longer seems complicated or difficult, then the assignment of specific, difficult goals is likely to have its usual effects. Additionally, for work that is very creative and uncertain, specific, difficult goals may be detrimental.

Learning Theories

The basic premise of learning theories as applied to organizations is that managers can increase employee motivation and performance by how they link the outcomes that employees receive to the performance of desired behaviors and the attainment of goals. Thus, learning theory focuses on the linkage between performance and outcomes in the motivation equation (see Figure 9.1).

Learning can be defined as a relatively permanent change in a person's knowledge or behavior that results from practice or experience.[50] Learning takes place in organizations when people learn to perform certain behaviors to receive certain

LO 9-4

Identify the motivation lessons that managers can learn from operant conditioning theory and social learning theory.

outcomes. For example, a person learns to perform at a higher level than in the past or to come to work earlier because he or she is motivated to obtain the outcomes that result from these behaviors, such as a pay raise or praise from a supervisor. As mentioned earlier, Enterprise's emphasis on training ensures that new hires learn how to provide excellent customer service and perform all the activities necessary for successful branch operations.

Of the different learning theories, operant conditioning theory and social learning theory provide the most guidance to managers in their efforts to have a highly motivated workforce.

Operant Conditioning Theory

According to operant conditioning theory, developed by psychologist B. F. Skinner, people learn to perform behaviors that lead to desired consequences and learn not to perform behaviors that lead to undesired consequences.[51] Translated into motivation terms, Skinner's theory means that people will be motivated to perform at a high level and attain their work goals to the extent that high performance and goal attainment allow them to obtain outcomes they desire. Similarly, people avoid performing behaviors that lead to outcomes they do not desire. By linking the performance of *specific behaviors* to the attainment of *specific outcomes*, managers can motivate organizational members to perform in ways that help an organization achieve its goals.

Operant conditioning theory provides four tools that managers can use to motivate high performance and prevent workers from engaging in absenteeism and other behaviors that detract from organizational effectiveness. These tools are positive reinforcement, negative reinforcement, extinction, and punishment.[52]

POSITIVE REINFORCEMENT Positive reinforcement gives people outcomes they desire when they perform organizationally functional behaviors. These desired outcomes, called *positive reinforcers,* include any outcomes that a person desires, such as pay, praise, or a promotion. Organizationally functional behaviors are behaviors that contribute to organizational effectiveness; they can include producing high-quality goods and services, providing high-quality customer service, and meeting deadlines. By linking positive reinforcers to the performance of functional behaviors, managers motivate people to perform the desired behaviors.

NEGATIVE REINFORCEMENT Negative reinforcement also can encourage members of an organization to perform desired or organizationally functional behaviors. Managers using negative reinforcement actually eliminate or remove undesired outcomes once the functional behavior is performed. These undesired outcomes, called *negative reinforcers,* can range from a manager's constant criticism, unpleasant assignments, or the threat of losing one's job. When negative reinforcement is used, people are motivated to perform behaviors because they want to stop receiving or want to avoid undesired outcomes. Managers who try to encourage salespeople to sell more by threatening them with monthly all-day sales meetings are using negative reinforcement. In this case, the negative reinforcer is the threat of being stuck in an all-day meeting, which is removed once the functional behavior is performed.

Whenever possible, managers should try to use positive reinforcement. Negative reinforcement can create a very unpleasant work environment and even a negative culture in an organization. No one likes to be nagged or exposed to other kinds of negative outcomes. The use of negative reinforcement sometimes causes employees to resent managers and sends them looking for new jobs.

learning theories Theories that focus on increasing employee motivation and performance by linking the outcomes that employees receive to the performance of desired behaviors and the attainment of goals.

learning A relatively permanent change in knowledge or behavior that results from practice or experience.

operant conditioning theory The theory that people learn to perform behaviors that lead to desired consequences and learn not to perform behaviors that lead to undesired consequences.

positive reinforcement Giving people outcomes they desire when they perform organizationally functional behaviors.

negative reinforcement Eliminating or removing undesired outcomes when people perform organizationally functional behaviors.

IDENTIFYING THE RIGHT BEHAVIORS FOR REINFORCEMENT Even managers who use positive reinforcement (and refrain from using negative reinforcement) can get into trouble if they are not careful to identify the right behaviors to reinforce—behaviors that are truly functional for the organization. Doing this is not always as straightforward as it might seem. First, it is crucial for managers to choose behaviors over which employees have control; in other words, they must have the freedom and opportunity to perform the behaviors that are being reinforced. Second, it is crucial that these behaviors contribute to organizational effectiveness.

EXTINCTION Sometimes members of an organization are motivated to perform behaviors that detract from organizational effectiveness. According to operant conditioning theory, all behavior is controlled or determined by its consequences; one way for managers to curtail the performance of dysfunctional behaviors is to eliminate whatever is reinforcing the behaviors. This process is called extinction.

extinction Curtailing the performance of dysfunctional behaviors by eliminating whatever is reinforcing them.

Suppose a manager has an employee who frequently stops by his office to chat—sometimes about work-related matters but at other times about various topics ranging from politics to last night's football game. The manager and the employee share certain interests and views, so these conversations can get quite involved, and both seem to enjoy them. The manager, however, realizes that these frequent and sometimes lengthy conversations are causing him to stay at work later in the evenings to make up for the time he loses during the day. The manager also realizes that he is reinforcing his employee's behavior by acting interested in the topics the employee brings up and responding at length to them. To extinguish this behavior, the manager stops acting interested in these non-work-related conversations and keeps his responses polite and friendly but brief. No longer being reinforced with a pleasurable conversation, the employee eventually ceases to be motivated to interrupt the manager during working hours to discuss non-work-related issues.

PUNISHMENT Sometimes managers cannot rely on extinction to eliminate dysfunctional behaviors because they do not have control over whatever is reinforcing the behavior or because they cannot afford the time needed for extinction to work. When employees are performing dangerous behaviors or behaviors that are illegal or unethical, the behaviors need to be eliminated immediately. Sexual harassment, for example, is an organizationally dysfunctional behavior that cannot be tolerated. In such cases managers often rely on punishment, which is administering an undesired or negative consequence to individuals when they perform the dysfunctional behavior. Punishments used by organizations include verbal reprimands, pay cuts, temporary suspensions, demotions, and firings. Punishment, however, can have some unintended side effects—resentment, loss of self-respect, a desire for retaliation—and should be used only when necessary.

punishment Administering an undesired or negative consequence when dysfunctional behavior occurs.

To avoid the unintended side effects of punishment, managers should keep in mind these guidelines:

- Downplay the emotional element involved in punishment. Make it clear that you are punishing a person's performance of a dysfunctional behavior, not the person himself or herself.

- Try to punish dysfunctional behaviors as soon as possible after they occur, and make sure the negative consequence is a source of punishment for the individuals involved. Be certain that organizational members know exactly why they are being punished.

- Try to avoid punishing someone in front of others because this can hurt a person's self-respect and lower esteem in the eyes of coworkers, as well as make coworkers feel uncomfortable.[53] Even so, making organizational members aware that an individual who has committed a serious infraction has been punished can sometimes be effective in preventing future infractions and in teaching all members of the organization that certain behaviors are unacceptable. For example, when organizational members are informed that a manager who has sexually harassed others has been punished, they learn or are reminded of the fact that sexual harassment is not tolerated in the organization.

Managers and students alike often confuse negative reinforcement and punishment. To avoid such confusion, keep in mind the two major differences between them. First, negative reinforcement is used to promote the performance of functional behaviors in organizations; punishment is used to stop the performance of dysfunctional behaviors. Second, negative reinforcement entails the *removal* of a negative consequence when functional behaviors are performed; punishment entails the *administration* of negative consequences when dysfunctional behaviors are performed.

Social Learning Theory

social learning theory A theory that takes into account how learning and motivation are influenced by people's thoughts and beliefs and their observations of other people's behavior.

Social learning theory proposes that motivation results not only from direct experience of rewards and punishments but also from a person's thoughts and beliefs. Social learning theory extends operant conditioning's contribution to managers' understanding of motivation by explaining (1) how people can be motivated by observing other people performing a behavior and being reinforced for doing so (*vicarious learning*), (2) how people can be motivated to control their behavior themselves (*self-reinforcement*), and (3) how people's beliefs about their ability to successfully perform a behavior affect motivation (*self-efficacy*).[54] We look briefly at each of these motivators.

vicarious learning Learning that occurs when the learner becomes motivated to perform a behavior by watching another person performing it and being reinforced for doing so; also called observational learning.

VICARIOUS LEARNING Vicarious learning, often called *observational learning,* occurs when a person (the learner) becomes motivated to perform a behavior by watching another person (the model) performing the behavior and being positively reinforced for doing so. Vicarious learning is a powerful source of motivation on many jobs in which people learn to perform functional behaviors by watching others. Salespeople learn how to help customers, medical school students learn how to treat patients, law clerks learn how to practice law, and nonmanagers learn how to be managers, in part, by observing experienced members of an organization perform these behaviors properly and be reinforced for them. In general, people are more likely to be motivated to imitate the behavior of models who are highly competent, are (to some extent) experts in the behavior, have high status, receive attractive reinforcers, and are friendly or approachable.[55]

To promote vicarious learning, managers should strive to have the learner meet the following conditions:

- The learner observes the model performing the behavior.
- The learner accurately perceives the model's behavior.
- The learner remembers the behavior.
- The learner has the skills and abilities needed to perform the behavior.
- The learner sees or knows that the model is positively reinforced for the behavior.[56]

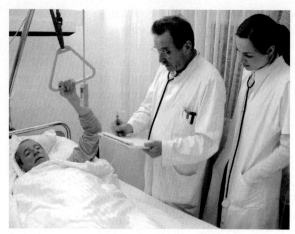

How do you treat that? When medical students enter residency, they learn vicariously by shadowing a full physician on his or her rounds. vario images GmbH & Co.KG/Alamy

self-reinforcer Any desired or attractive outcome or reward that a person gives to himself or herself for good performance.

self-efficacy A person's belief about his or her ability to perform a behavior successfully.

SELF-REINFORCEMENT Although managers are often the providers of reinforcement in organizations, sometimes people motivate themselves through self-reinforcement. People can control their own behavior by setting goals for themselves and then reinforcing themselves when they achieve the goals.[57] Self-reinforcers are any desired or attractive outcomes or rewards that people can give to themselves for good performance, such as a feeling of accomplishment, going to a movie, having dinner out, or taking time out for a golf game. When members of an organization control their own behavior through self-reinforcement, managers do not need to spend as much time as they ordinarily would trying to motivate and control behavior through the administration of consequences because employees are controlling and motivating themselves. In fact, this self-control is often referred to as the *self-management of behavior.*

When employees are highly skilled and are responsible for creating new goods and services, managers typically rely on self-control and self-management of behavior, as is the case at Google. Employees at Google are given the flexibility and autonomy to experiment, take risks, and sometimes fail as they work on new projects. They are encouraged to learn from their failures and apply what they learn to subsequent projects.[58]

SELF-EFFICACY Self-efficacy is a person's belief about his or her ability to perform a behavior successfully.[59] Even with all the most attractive consequences or reinforcers hinging on high performance, people are not going to be motivated if they do not think they can actually perform at a high level. Similarly, when people control their own behavior, they are likely to set for themselves difficult goals that will lead to outstanding accomplishments only if they think they can reach those goals. Thus, self-efficacy influences motivation both when managers provide reinforcement and when workers themselves provide it.[60] The greater the self-efficacy, the greater the motivation and performance.

Pay and Motivation

In Chapter 12 we discuss how managers establish a pay level and structure for an organization as a whole. Here we focus on how, once a pay level and structure are in place, managers can use pay to motivate employees to perform at a high level and attain their work goals. Pay is used to motivate entry-level workers, first-line and middle managers, and even top managers such as CEOs. Pay can motivate people to perform behaviors that help an organization achieve its goals, and it can motivate people to join and remain with an organization.

LO 9-5
Explain why and how managers can use pay as a major motivation tool.

Each of the theories described in this chapter alludes to the importance of pay and suggests that pay should be based on performance:

- *Expectancy theory:* Instrumentality, the association between performance and outcomes such as pay, must be high for motivation to be high. In addition, pay is an outcome that has high valence for many people.

- *Need theories:* People should be able to satisfy their needs by performing at a high level; pay can be used to satisfy several kinds of needs.
- *Equity theory:* Outcomes such as pay should be distributed in proportion to inputs (including performance levels).
- *Goal-setting theory:* Outcomes such as pay should be linked to the attainment of goals.
- *Learning theories:* The distribution of outcomes, such as pay, should be contingent on the performance of organizationally functional behaviors.

As these theories suggest, to promote high motivation, managers should base the distribution of pay to organizational members on performance levels so that high performers receive more pay than low performers (other things being equal).[61] A compensation plan basing pay on performance is often called a merit pay plan. This approach also addresses ethical issues related to motivation, as discussed earlier in the chapter in the context of equity theory and in the following "Ethics in Action" feature.

merit pay plan A compensation plan that bases pay on performance.

Ethics in Action

The Fairness of Merit Pay

A recent attempt by United Airlines to make merit pay more motivating backfired. The company had been setting quarterly goals and paying a bonus of up to $300 per employee if the company met the goals. Managers thought the bonuses were too small to have much impact on employees' total pay and therefore not significant enough as a motivator. (In terms of expectancy theory, they saw the quarterly bonuses as having a low valence.) They decided to roll out a system they believed employees would consider exciting: Bonus spending by the company would be pooled to create major prizes, from $2,000 cash to vacations and fancy cars. Each quarter, there would be a lottery in which several employees would receive one of these prizes, and one employee would receive the grand prize of $100,000.[62]

To the planners' surprise, the employees were not motivated, but upset. They saw the new plan as inequitable. Most employees would work hard to meet the quarterly goals yet receive no bonus (underpayment inequity). A few employees would receive big prizes regardless of how much they did to help the company achieve its goals (possible overpayment inequity). Employees began gathering signatures on a public petition, and management, realizing its mistake, discontinued the planned change.[63]

A more widespread, if less dramatic, example of employees perceiving merit pay as unfair and therefore unmotivating is pay that differs according to the employee's sex, race, or other personal characteristic, rather than his or her contribution to the company. In Britain, employers have been reporting their gender pay gaps to meet government regulations. In comparing salaries, the telecommunications company Sky reported pay gaps between about 5% and 11%, but the difference was more dramatic for merit pay: the gender gap for bonuses was 40%.[64] This identifies an area where the company, to be equitable, will need to investigate its process of setting goals and pay systems to reward performance. For example, are women at Sky being assigned to high-value projects at the same rate as their male counterparts?

In general, an employer should consider basic motivational issues to make merit pay equitable.[65] At a minimum, fairness requires defining the performance measures and goals ahead of time, so employees know what their incentive pay depends on. Also, employees need to see a link between what they do and what they can earn—the problem area with United's bonus lottery. ●

In tough economic times, when organizations lay off employees and pay levels and benefits of those who are at least able to keep their jobs may be cut while their responsibilities are often increased,[66] managers are often limited in the extent to which they can use merit pay, if at all. Nonetheless, in such times, managers can still try to recognize top performers. Jenny Miller, manager of 170 engineers in the commercial systems engineering department at Rockwell Collins, an aerospace electronics company in Cedar Rapids, Iowa, experienced firsthand the challenge of not being able to recognize top performers with merit pay during tough economic times. Rockwell Collins laid off 8% of its workforce, and the workloads for the engineers Miller managed increased by about 15%. The engineers were working longer hours without receiving any additional pay; there was a salary freeze, so they knew raises were not in store. With a deadline approaching for flight deck software for a customer, she needed some engineers to work over the Thanksgiving holiday and so sent out an email request for volunteers. Approximately 20 employees volunteered. In recognition of their contributions, Miller gave them each a $100 gift card.[67]

A $100 gift card might not seem like much for an employee who is already working long hours to work over the Thanksgiving holiday for no additional pay or time off. However, Steve Nieuwsma, division vice president at Rockwell Collins, indicates that the gift cards at least signaled that managers recognized and appreciated employees' efforts and sought to thank them for it. Not being able to give his employees raises at that time, Nieuwsma also gave gift cards to recognize contributions and top performers in amounts varying between $25 and $500.[68]

Once managers have decided to use a merit pay plan, they face two important choices: whether to base pay on individual, group, or organizational performance and whether to use salary increases or bonuses.

Basing Merit Pay on Individual, Group, or Organizational Performance

Managers can base merit pay on individual, group, or organizational performance. When individual performance (such as the dollar value of merchandise a salesperson sells, the number of loudspeakers a factory worker assembles, or a lawyer's billable hours) can be accurately determined, individual motivation is likely to be highest when pay is based on individual performance.[69] When members of an organization work closely together and individual performance cannot be accurately determined (as in a team of computer programmers developing a single software package), pay cannot be based on individual performance, and a group- or organization-based plan must be used. When the attainment of organizational goals hinges on members' working closely together and cooperating with each other (as in a small construction company that builds custom homes), group- or organization-based plans may be more appropriate than individual-based plans.[70]

It is possible to combine elements of an individual-based plan with a group- or organization-based plan to motivate each individual to perform highly and, at the same time, motivate all individuals to work well together, cooperate with one another, and help one another as needed. Lincoln Electric, a very successful company and a leading manufacturer of welding equipment, uses a combination individual- and organization-based plan.[71] Pay is based on individual performance. In addition, each year the size of a bonus fund depends on organizational performance. Money from the bonus fund is distributed to people on the basis of their contributions to the organization, attendance, levels of cooperation, and other indications of performance. Employees of Lincoln Electric are motivated to cooperate and help one another because when the firm as a whole performs well, everybody benefits by having a larger bonus fund. Employees also are motivated to contribute their inputs to the organization because their contributions determine their share of the bonus fund.

Salary Increase or Bonus?

Managers can distribute merit pay to people in the form of a salary increase or a bonus on top of regular salaries. Although the dollar amounts of a salary increase and of a bonus might be identical, bonuses tend to have more motivational impact for at least three reasons. First, salary levels are typically based on performance levels, cost-of-living increases, and so forth from the day people start working in an organization, which means the absolute level of the salary is based largely on factors unrelated to *current* performance. A 5% merit increase in salary, for example, may seem relatively small in comparison to one's total salary. Second, a current salary increase may be affected by other factors in addition to performance, such as cost-of-living increases or across-the-board market adjustments. Third, because organizations rarely reduce salaries, salary levels tend to vary less than performance levels do. Related to this point is the fact that bonuses give managers more flexibility in distributing outcomes. If an organization is doing well, bonuses can be relatively high to reward employees for their contributions. However, unlike salary increases, bonus levels can be reduced when an organization's performance lags. All in all, bonus plans have more motivational impact than salary increases because the amount of the bonus can be directly and exclusively based on performance.[72]

Consistent with the lessons from motivation theories, bonuses can be linked directly to performance and vary from year to year and employee to employee, as at Gradient Corporation, a Cambridge, Massachusetts, environmental consulting firm.[73] Another organization that successfully uses bonuses is Nucor Corporation. Steelworkers at Nucor tend to be much more productive than steelworkers in other companies—probably because they can receive bonuses tied to performance and quality that can range from 130% to 150% of their regular base pay.[74] During the economic recession in 2007–2009, Nucor struggled, as did many other companies, and bonus pay for steelworkers dropped considerably. However, managers at Nucor avoided having to lay off employees by finding ways to cut costs and having employees work on maintenance activities and safety manuals, along with taking on tasks that used to be performed by independent contractors, such as producing specialty parts and mowing the grass.[75]

employee stock option A financial instrument that entitles the bearer to buy shares of an organization's stock at a certain price during a certain period or under certain conditions.

In addition to receiving pay raises and bonuses, high-level managers and executives are sometimes granted employee stock options. Employee stock options are financial instruments that entitle the bearer to buy shares of an organization's stock at a certain price during a certain period or under certain conditions.[76] For example, in addition to salaries, stock options are sometimes used to attract high-level managers. The exercise price is the stock price at which the bearer can buy the stock, and the vesting conditions specify when the bearer can actually buy the stock at the exercise price. The option's exercise price is generally set equal to the market price of the stock on the date it is granted, and the vesting conditions might specify that the manager has to have worked at the organization for 12 months or perhaps met some performance target (perhaps an increase in profits) before being able to exercise the option. In technology firms and start-ups, options are sometimes used in a similar fashion for employees at various levels in the organization.[77]

From a motivation standpoint, stock options are used not so much to reward past individual performance but, rather, to motivate employees to work in the future for the good of the company as a whole. This is true because stock options issued at current stock prices have value in the future only if an organization does well and its stock price appreciates; thus, giving employees stock options should encourage them to help the organization improve its performance over time.[78] At technology start-ups, stock options have often motivated potential employees to leave promising jobs in larger companies and work for the start-ups. In the late 1990s and early 2000s, many tech workers were devastated to learn not only that their stock options were worthless, because their companies went out of business or were doing poorly, but also that they were unemployed. Unfortunately, stock options have also led to unethical behavior; for example, sometimes individuals seek to artificially inflate the value of a company's stock to increase the value of stock options.

Examples of Merit Pay Plans

Managers can choose among several merit pay plans, depending on the work that employees perform and other considerations. Using *piece-rate pay,* an individual-based merit plan, managers base employees' pay on the number of units each employee produces, whether televisions, computer components, or welded auto parts. Managers at Lincoln Electric use piece-rate pay to determine individual pay levels. Advances in information technology have dramatically simplified the administration of piece-rate pay in a variety of industries.

Using *commission pay,* another individual-based merit pay plan, managers base pay on a percentage of sales. Managers at the successful real-estate company RE/MAX International Inc. use commission pay for their agents, who are paid a percentage of their sales. Some department stores, such as Nordstrom, use commission pay for their salespeople.

Examples of organizational-based merit pay plans include the Scanlon plan and profit sharing. The *Scanlon plan* (developed by Joseph Scanlon, a union leader in a steel and tin plant in the 1920s) focuses on reducing expenses or cutting costs; members of an organization are motivated to propose and implement cost-cutting strategies because a percentage of the cost savings achieved during a specified time is distributed to the employees.[79] Under *profit sharing,* employees receive a share of an organization's profits. Regardless of the specific kind of plan that is used, managers should always strive to link pay to the performance of behaviors that help an organization achieve its goals.

Japanese managers in large corporations have long shunned merit pay plans in favor of plans that reward seniority. However, more and more Japanese companies are adopting merit-based pay due to its motivational benefits; among such companies are Toyota, Hitachi, Panasonic, and Nomura Securities.[80]

Summary and Review

THE NATURE OF MOTIVATION Motivation encompasses the psychological forces within a person that determine the direction of the person's behavior in an organization, the person's level of effort, and the person's level of persistence in the face of obstacles. Managers strive to motivate people to contribute their inputs to an organization, to focus these inputs in the direction of high performance, and to ensure that people receive the outcomes they desire when they perform at a high level. [LO 9-1]

EXPECTANCY THEORY According to expectancy theory, managers can promote high levels of motivation in their organizations by taking steps to ensure that expectancy is high (people think that if they try, they can perform at a high level), instrumentality is high (people think that if they perform at a high level, they will receive certain outcomes), and valence is high (people desire these outcomes). [LO 9-2]

NEED THEORIES Need theories suggest that to motivate their workforces, managers should determine what needs people are trying to satisfy in organizations and then ensure that people receive outcomes that satisfy these needs when they perform at a high level and contribute to organizational effectiveness. [LO 9-3]

EQUITY THEORY According to equity theory, managers can promote high levels of motivation by ensuring that people perceive that there is equity in the organization or that outcomes are distributed in proportion to inputs. Equity exists when a person perceives that his or her own outcome–input ratio equals the outcome–input ratio of a referent. Inequity motivates people to try to restore equity. Equity theory is a theory of distributive justice. It is most advantageous for distributive, procedural, interpersonal, and informational justice all to be high. [LO 9-2]

GOAL-SETTING THEORY Goal-setting theory suggests that managers can promote high motivation and performance by ensuring that people are striving to achieve specific, difficult goals. It is important for people to accept the goals, be committed to them, and receive feedback about how they are doing. [LO 9-3]

LEARNING THEORIES Operant conditioning theory suggests that managers can motivate people to perform highly by using positive reinforcement or negative reinforcement (positive reinforcement being the preferred strategy). Managers can motivate people to avoid performing dysfunctional behaviors by using extinction or punishment. Social learning theory suggests that people can also be motivated by observing how others perform behaviors and receive rewards, by engaging in self-reinforcement, and by having high levels of self-efficacy. [LO 9-4]

PAY AND MOTIVATION Each of the motivation theories discussed in this chapter alludes to the importance of pay and suggests that pay should be based on performance. Merit pay plans can be individual-, group-, or organization-based and can entail the use of salary increases or bonuses. [LO 9-5]

Management *in Action*

Topics for Discussion and Action

Discussion

1. Discuss why two people with similar abilities may have very different expectancies for performing at a high level. [LO 9-2]

2. Describe why some people have low instrumentalities even when their managers distribute outcomes based on performance. [LO 9-2]

3. Analyze how professors try to promote equity to motivate students. [LO 9-2]

4. Describe three techniques or procedures that managers can use to determine whether a goal is difficult. [LO 9-3]

5. Discuss why managers should always try to use positive reinforcement instead of negative reinforcement. [LO 9-4]

Action

6. Interview three people who have the same kind of job (such as salesperson, server, or teacher), and determine what kinds of needs each is trying to satisfy at work. [LO 9-3]

7. Interview a manager in an organization in your community to determine the extent to which the manager takes advantage of vicarious learning to promote high motivation among employees. [LO 9-3]

Building Management Skills

Diagnosing Motivation [LO 9-1, 9-2, 9-3, 9-4]

Think about the ideal job that you would like to obtain after graduation. Describe this job, the kind of manager you would like to report to, and the kind of organization you would be working in. Then answer the following questions:

1. What would be your levels of expectancy and instrumentality on this job? Which outcomes would have high valence for you on this job? What steps would your manager take to influence your levels of expectancy, instrumentality, and valence?

2. Whom would you choose as a referent on this job? What steps would your manager take to make you feel that you were being equitably treated? What would you do if, after a year on the job, you experienced underpayment inequity?

3. What goals would you strive to achieve on this job? Why? What role would your manager play in determining your goals?

4. What needs would you strive to satisfy on this job? Why? What role would your manager play in helping you satisfy these needs?

5. What behaviors would your manager positively reinforce on this job? Why? What positive reinforcers would your manager use?

6. Would there be any vicarious learning on this job? Why or why not?

7. To what extent would you be motivated by self-control on this job? Why?

8. What would be your level of self-efficacy on this job? Why would your self-efficacy be at this level? Should your manager take steps to boost your self-efficacy? If not, why not? If so, what would these steps be?

Managing Ethically [LO 9-5]

Sometimes pay is so contingent upon performance that it creates stress for employees. Imagine a salesperson who knows that if sales targets are not met, he or she will not be able to make a house mortgage payment or pay the rent.

Questions

1. Either individually or in a group, think about the ethical implications of closely linking pay to performance.

2. Under what conditions might contingent pay be most stressful, and what steps can managers take to try to help their employees perform effectively and not experience excessive amounts of stress?

Small Group Breakout Exercise [LO 9-1, 9-2, 9-3, 9-4, 9-5]

Increasing Motivation

Form groups of three or four people, and appoint one member as the spokesperson who will communicate your findings to the class when called on by the instructor. Then discuss the following scenario:

You and your partners own a chain of 15 dry-cleaning stores in a medium-size town. All of you are concerned about a problem in customer service that has surfaced recently. When any one of you spends the day, or even part of the day, in a particular store, clerks seem to provide excellent customer service, spotters make sure all stains are removed from garments, and pressers do a good job of pressing difficult items such as silk blouses. Yet during those same visits, customers complain to you about such things as stains not being removed and items being poorly pressed in some of their previous orders; indeed, several customers have brought garments in to be redone. Customers also sometimes comment on having waited too long for service on previous visits. You and your partners are meeting today to address this problem.

1. Discuss the extent to which you believe that you have a motivation problem in your stores.

2. Given what you have learned in this chapter, design a plan to increase the motivation of clerks to provide prompt service to customers even when they are not being watched by one of the business owners.

3. Design a plan to increase the motivation of spotters to remove as many stains as possible even when they are not being watched by one of the business owners.

4. Design a plan to increase the motivation of pressers to do a top-notch job on all clothes they press, no matter how difficult.

Be the Manager [LO 9-1, 9-2, 9-3, 9-4, 9-5]

You supervise a team of marketing analysts who work on different snack products in a large food products company. The marketing analysts have recently received undergraduate degrees in business or liberal arts and have been on the job between one and three years. Their responsibilities include analyzing the market for their respective products, including competitors; tracking current marketing initiatives; and planning future marketing campaigns. They also need to prepare quarterly sales and expense reports for their products and estimated budgets for the next three quarters; to prepare these reports, they need to obtain data from financial and accounting analysts assigned to their products.

When they first started on the job, you took each marketing analyst through the reporting cycle, explaining what needs to be done and how to accomplish it and emphasizing the need for timely reports. Although preparing the reports can be tedious, you think the task is pretty straightforward and easily accomplished if the analysts plan ahead and allocate sufficient time for it. When reporting time approaches, you remind the analysts through email messages and emphasize the need for accurate and timely reports in team meetings.

You believe this element of the analysts' jobs couldn't be more straightforward. However, at the end of each quarter, the majority of the analysts submit their reports a day or two late, and, worse yet, your own supervisor (to whom the reports are eventually given) has indicated that information is often missing and sometimes the reports contain errors. Once you started getting flak from your supervisor about this problem, you decide you

had better fix things quickly. You met with the marketing analysts, explained the problem, told them to submit the reports to you a day or two early so you could look them over, and more generally emphasized that they really need to get their act together. Unfortunately, things have not improved much and you are spending more and more of your own time doing the reports. What are you going to do?

Case in the News [LO 9-1, 9-2, 9-3, 9-4]

DTE Energy Ignites Employees with a Shared Sense of Purpose

As an energy utility, Detroit-based DTE Energy serves more than 2 million electricity customers and more than 1 million natural-gas customers in southeastern Michigan. It also owns business units that operate power projects, ship natural gas through pipelines, engage in energy trading, and more. It employs more than 10,000 workers in Michigan and other states.

When Gerry Anderson became president of DTE in 2004, its performance was mediocre: costs exceeded goals, stock value was underperforming, customers were dissatisfied, and employees were disengaged from their work. Attempts to improve performance with new training programs, compensation plans, and greater supervision had little impact. On that unsteady foundation, DTE was unprepared to weather the shock of the Great Recession beginning in 2008. The auto companies that had once brought prosperity to Michigan, along with their suppliers,

found themselves teetering on the edge of bankruptcy, closing plants, and laying off employees. That would bring a tremendous drop in the demand for energy. The company estimated it would lose $200 million in revenue.

Anderson could keep DTE afloat with drastic layoffs, but he wanted to do something different. He announced that the company was sticking to its value of continuous improvement, including the principle that layoffs are a last resort. He challenged managers to find ways to cut costs by $200 million so they could avoid layoffs altogether. Then he shared with all employees a video in which he presented his challenge and commitment. As the months passed, DTE's executives were astonished to see costs falling below budgeted levels. Newly energized employees were finding one way after another to operate more efficiently so they could keep everyone employed. By the following year, with zero layoffs, the company had to revise its projected

profits upward to reflect the performance improvement.

From this experience, Anderson concluded that a shared sense of purpose has a practical value to a company: It energizes employees at all levels to give of themselves because they care. At that point, as CEO as well as president, he set about making purposefulness part of DTE's culture. He portrayed the company as a necessary part of the community. As Michigan's people struggled through the recession, Anderson and the other managers communicated that making energy available to Michigan's residents was a way to empower their communities to get stronger. The more efficiently DTE operated, the better off its customers and its community would be. The company expressed this vision in a video that showed workers on the job at all levels of the organization, along with a message that the energy they provided is the "lifeblood of communities and the engine of progress." DTE incorporated the message into its training programs and meetings. According to DTE's surveys of employee engagement, employees have become more committed to their work and more satisfied with their jobs.

Several years into the purpose-driven culture, however, Anderson realized that union employees were not on board as managers and salaried workers were. In a meeting between company executives and union leaders, a safety report detailed exceptional performance, yet the tone of the meeting was mostly critical. So Anderson spoke from the heart and asked how they could work together on addressing the engagement of the union members, who were also Anderson's employees. The union leaders replied that engagement was poor because supervision was poor. Rather than defending the company's first-line management, Anderson agreed to address the issue. This provided a favorable context for management and union to define a shared purpose: engaging unionized employees and achieving continuous improvement.

In the years that followed, Anderson further engaged employees by broadening his message of purpose. The idea of the company being a force for growth and prosperity in its community now extends to community service and greater use of renewable energy sources. Employees serve hundreds of community nonprofits each year, including the establishment of new schools in Detroit. DTE has committed to reducing its carbon emissions by more than 80% by 2050, including the replacement of all its coal-burning power plants by 2040.

Since DTE has begun motivating employees with a shared purpose, its business performance has improved significantly. Between 2008 and 2017, its stock price more than tripled. It also has become a desirable place to work, landing on Indeed's list of the 50 Best Places to Work, based on employees' reviews of their experiences with the company. This is a practical advantage in a tight labor market, especially because DTE expects about half its workforce to reach retirement age over the next decade.

Questions for Discussion

1. How could expectancy theory explain the success of DTE Energy's approach to motivating employees during the Great Recession?

2. How well do need theories support Anderson's approach to motivating employees?

Would these models alone have prepared him to solve this challenge? Why or why not?

3. In DTE's effort to motivate its employees, what were the goals? What kinds of reinforcement existed? Would you have expected these to be effective? Why or why not?

Sources: DTE Energy, "About DTE," www.newlook.dteenergy.com, accessed January 25, 2019; S. Welch, "Crain's Newsmaker: Gerry Anderson, Chairman and CEO, DTE Energy Co.," *Crain's Detroit Business*, www.crainsdetroit.com, accessed January 8, 2019; J. Clifton, "Culture Is Personal to DTE Energy CEO Gerry Anderson," *Gallup*, www.gallup.com, accessed January 8, 2019; L. D. Green, "Want Your Business to Do Well? Do Some Good," *Crain's Detroit Business*, www.crainsdetroit.com, October 29, 2018; R. E. Quinn and A. V. Thakor, "Creating a Purpose-Driven Organization," *Harvard Business Review*, July–August 2018, 78–85; J. Oostin, "DTE, Consumers Boost Renewable Energy Goals," *Detroit News*, www.detroitnews.com, May 18, 2018; C. Livengood, "DTE, Consumers Agree to 25 Percent Renewable Energy Goal," *Crain's Detroit Business*, www.crainsdetroit.com, May 18, 2018; J. Clifton, "How DTE Energy Emerged Stronger after the Great Recession," *Gallup*, https://news.gallup.com, December 13, 2017; J. Clifton, "How to Engage a Union Workforce: One CEO's Lessons," *Gallup*, https://news.gallup.com, December 14, 2017; A. Dixon, "DTE Energy Ranks High in '50 Best Places to Work,'" *Michigan Chronicle*, https://michronicle.com, July 25, 2017.

Endnotes

1. B. Shea, "How to Change a Culture, Detroit Lions Edition," *Crain's Detroit Business*, www.crainsdetroitbusiness.com, November 12, 2017; T. Foster, "Martha Ford Attempts to Tame the Detroit Lions," *Detroit Metro Times*, www.metrotimes.com, September 6, 2017; Johnette Howard, "Why Martha Ford, 90, Has Been Exactly the Owner the Lions Need," *ESPN*, www.espn.com, December 30, 2015; J. Vrentas, "Martha Firestone Ford's Patience Has Run Out," *Sports Illustrated*, www.si.com, December 2, 2015.

2. Shea, "How to Change a Culture"; Howard, "Why Martha Ford, 90, Has Been Exactly the Owner the Lions Need"; Vrentas, "Martha Firestone Ford's Patience."

3. Howard, "Why Martha Ford, 90, Has Been Exactly the Owner the Lions Need."

4. Shea, "How to Change a Culture; Vrentas, "Martha Firestone Ford's Patience"; Howard, "Why Martha

Ford, 90, Has Been Exactly the Owner the Lions Need."

5. Howard, "Why Martha Ford, 90, Has Been Exactly the Owner the Lions Need"; Shea, "How to Change a Culture."

6. Shea, "How to Change a Culture."

7. J. Rogers, "Lions' Owner Ford: We Finished in a Good Way," *The Detroit News,* www.detroitnews.com, accessed January 18, 2019; M.Rothstein, "Lions Officially Name Matt Patricia as Head Coach," *ESPN,* www.espn.com, February 5, 2018.

8. K. Haddad, "Detroit Lions Offensive Coordinator Jim Bob Cooter Won't Return in 2019," www.clickondetroit.com, accessed January 18, 2019.

9. R. Kanfer, "Motivation Theory and Industrial and Organizational Psychology," in M. D. Dunnette and L. M. Hough, eds., *Handbook of Industrial and Organizational Psychology,* 2nd ed., vol. 1 (Palo Alto, CA: Consulting Psychologists Press, 1990), 75–170.

10. G. P. Latham and M. H. Budworth, "The Study of Work Motivation in the 20th Century," in L. L. Koppes, ed., *Historical Perspectives in Industrial and Organizational Psychology* (Hillsdale, NJ: Erlbaum, 2006).

11. N. Nicholson, "How to Motivate Your Problem People," *Harvard Business Review,* January 2003, 57–65.

12. A. M. Grant, "Does Intrinsic Motivation Fuel the Prosocial Fire? Motivational Synergy in Predicting Persistence, Performance, and Productivity," *Journal of Applied Psychology* 93, no. 1 (2008), 48–58.

13. Grant, "Does Intrinsic Motivation Fuel the Prosocial Fire?"; C. D. Batson, "Prosocial Motivation: Is It Ever Truly Altruistic?" in L. Berkowitz, ed., *Advances in Experimental Social Psychology,* vol. 20 (New York: Academic Press, 1987), 65–122.

14. Grant, "Does Intrinsic Motivation Fuel the Prosocial Fire?"; Batson, "Prosocial Motivation."

15. J. P. Campbell and R. D. Pritchard, "Motivation Theory in Industrial and Organizational Psychology," in M. D. Dunnette, ed., *Handbook*

of Industrial and Organizational Psychology (Chicago: Rand McNally, 1976), 63–130; T. R. Mitchell, "Expectancy Value Models in Organizational Psychology," in N. T. Feather, ed., *Expectations and Actions: Expectancy Value Models in Psychology* (Hillsdale, NJ: Erlbaum, 1982), 293–312; V. H. Vroom, *Work and Motivation* (New York: Wiley, 1964).

16. N. Shope Griffin, "Personalize Your Management Development," *Harvard Business Review* 8, no. 10 (2003), 113–19.

17. T. A. Stewart, "Just Think: No Permission Needed," *Fortune,* www.fortune.com, January 8, 2001, accessed June 26, 2001.

18. C. Ruff, "Why Best Buy Is Investing in Employees," *Retail Dive,* www.retaildive.com, February 7, 2018.

19. T. J. Maurer, E. M. Weiss, and F. G. Barbeite, "A Model of Involvement in Work-Related Learning and Development Activity: The Effects of Individual, Situational, Motivational, and Age Variables," *Journal of Applied Psychology* 88, no. 4 (2003), 707–24.

20. "From a 'No Black Hole' Candidate Experience to Supporting Veterans: Lessons from Enterprise," *Indeed Blog,* http://blog.indeed.com, accessed January 19, 2019.

21. A. H. Maslow, *Motivation and Personality* (New York: Harper & Row, 1954); Campbell and Pritchard, "Motivation Theory in Industrial and Organizational Psychology."

22. Kanfer, "Motivation Theory and Industrial and Organizational Psychology."

23. S. Ronen, "An Underlying Structure of Motivational Need Taxonomies: A Cross-Cultural Confirmation," in H. C. Triandis, M. D. Dunnette, and L. M. Hough, eds., *Handbook of Industrial and Organizational Psychology,* vol. 4 (Palo Alto, CA: Consulting Psychologists Press, 1994), 241–69.

24. N. J. Adler, *International Dimensions of Organizational Behavior,* 2nd ed. (Boston: P.W.S. Kent, 1991); G. Hofstede, "Motivation, Leadership, and Organization: Do American Theories Apply Abroad?,"

Organizational Dynamics, Summer 1980, 42–63.

25. F. Herzberg, *Work and the Nature of Man* (Cleveland: World, 1966).

26. N. King, "Clarification and Evaluation of the Two-Factor Theory of Job Satisfaction," *Psychological Bulletin* 74 (1970), 18–31; E. A. Locke, "The Nature and Causes of Job Satisfaction," in M. D. Dunnette, ed., *Handbook of Industrial and Organizational Psychology* (Cleveland: Rand McNally, 1976), 1297–349.

27. D. C. McClelland, *Human Motivation* (Glenview, IL: Scott, Foresman, 1985); D. C. McClelland, "How Motives, Skills, and Values Determine What People Do," *American Psychologist* 40 (1985), 812–25; D. C. McClelland, "Managing Motivation to Expand Human Freedom," *American Psychologist* 33 (1978), 201–10.

28. D. G. Winter, *The Power Motive* (New York: Free Press, 1973).

29. M. J. Stahl, "Achievement, Power, and Managerial Motivation: Selecting Managerial Talent with the Job Choice Exercise," *Personnel Psychology* 36 (1983), 775–89; D. C. McClelland and D. H. Burnham, "Power Is the Great Motivator," *Harvard Business Review* 54 (1976), 100–10.

30. R. J. House, W. D. Spangler, and J. Woycke, "Personality and Charisma in the U.S. Presidency: A Psychological Theory of Leader Effectiveness," *Administrative Science Quarterly* 36 (1991), 364–96.

31. G. H. Hines, "Achievement, Motivation, Occupations, and Labor Turnover in New Zealand," *Journal of Applied Psychology* 58 (1973), 313–17; P. S. Hundal, "A Study of Entrepreneurial Motivation: Comparison of Fast- and Slow-Progressing Small Scale Industrial Entrepreneurs in Punjab, India," *Journal of Applied Psychology* 55 (1971), 317–23.

32. R. A. Clay, "Green Is Good for You," *Monitor on Psychology,* April 2001, 40–42.

33. J. S. Adams, "Toward an Understanding of Inequity," *Journal of Abnormal and Social Psychology* 67 (1963), 422–36.

34. Adams, "Toward an Understanding of Inequity"; J. Greenberg, "Approaching Equity and Avoiding Inequity in Groups and Organizations," in J. Greenberg and R. L. Cohen, eds., *Equity and Justice in Social Behavior* (New York: Academic Press, 1982), 389–435; J. Greenberg, "Equity and Workplace Status: A Field Experiment," *Journal of Applied Psychology* 73 (1988), 606–13; R. T. Mowday, "Equity Theory Predictions of Behavior in Organizations," in R. M. Steers and L. W. Porter, eds., *Motivation and Work Behavior* (New York: McGraw-Hill, 1987), 89–110.

35. L. J. Skitka and F. J. Crosby, "Trends in the Social Psychological Study of Justice," *Personality and Social Psychology Review* 7 (April 2003), 282–85.

36. J. A. Colquitt, J. Greenbery, and C. P. Zapata-Phelan, "What Is Organizational Justice? A Historical Overview," in J. Greenberg and J. A. Colquitt, eds., *Handbook of Organizational Justice* (Mahwah, NJ: Erlbaum, 2005), 12–45; J. A. Colquitt, "On the Dimensionality of Organizational Justice: A Construct Validation of a Measure," *Journal of Applied Psychology* 86 (March 2001), 386–400.

37. Matt Day, "'I Felt So Alone': What Women at Microsoft Face, and Why Many Leave," *Seattle Times,* www.seattletimes.com, April 12, 2018; P. B. Salgado, "Reframing Diversity to Achieve Equity in the Tech Industry," *Phys.org*, https://phys.org, March 15, 2018.

38. Day, "'I Felt So Alone'"; B. Davis, "Gender Equality: A Trend the Tech Sector Needs to Get Behind," *Forbes*, www.forbes.com, June 27, 2018.

39. D. Kerr, "Lyft Pledges Equal Pay for Women, Men, People of Color," *CNET*, www.cnet.com, March 27, 2018; C. Connley, "Starbucks Has Closed Its Pay Gap in the US; Here Are 4 Other Companies That Have Done the Same," *CNBC*, www.cnbc.com, March 23, 2018.

40. R. Folger and M. A. Konovsky, "Effects of Procedural and Distributive Justice on Reactions to Pay Raise Decisions," *Academy of Management Journal* 32 (1989), 115–30; J. Greenberg, "Organizational Justice: Yesterday, Today, and Tomorrow," *Journal of Management* 16 (1990), 339–432; M. L. Ambrose and A. Arnaud, "Are Procedural Justice and Distributive Justice Conceptually Distinct?" in J. Greenberg and J. A. Colquitt, eds., *Handbook of Organizational Justice* (Mahwah, NJ: Erlbaum, 2005), 60–78.

41. M. L. Ambrose and M. Schminke, "Organization Structure as a Moderator of the Relationship between Procedural Justice, Interactional Justice, Perceived Organizational Support, and Supervisory Trust," *Journal of Applied Psychology* 88 (February 2003), 295–305.

42. J. A. Colquitt, "On the Dimensionality of Organizational Justice: A Construct Validation of a Measure," *Journal of Applied Psychology* 86 (March 2001), 386–400.

43. Greenberg, "Organizational Justice"; E. A. Lind and T. Tyler, *The Social Psychology of Procedural Justice* (New York: Plenum, 1988).

44. R. J. Bies, "The Predicament of Injustice: The Management of Moral Outrage," in L. L. Cummings and B. M. Staw, eds., *Research in Organizational Behavior,* vol. 9 (Greenwich, CT: JAI Press, 1987), 289–319; R. J. Bies and D. L. Shapiro, "Interactional Fairness Judgments: The Influence of Casual Accounts," *Social Justice Research* 1 (1987), 199–218; J. Greenberg, "Looking Fair vs. Being Fair: Managing Impression of Organizational Justice," in B. M. Staw and L. L. Cummings, eds., *Research in Organizational Behavior,* vol. 12 (Greenwich, CT: JAI Press, 1990), 111–57; T. R. Tyler and R. J. Bies, "Beyond Formal Procedures: The Interpersonal Context of Procedural Justice," in J. Carroll, ed., *Advances in Applied Social Psychology: Business Settings* (Hillsdale, NJ: Erlbaum, 1989), 77–98; Colquitt, "On the Dimensionality of Organizational Justice."

45. Colquitt, "On the Dimensionality of Organizational Justice"; J. A. Colquitt and J. C. Shaw, "How Should Organizational Justice Be Measured?" in J. Greenberg and J. A. Colquitt, eds., *Handbook of Organizational Justice* (Mahwah, NJ: Erlbaum, 2005), 115–41.

46. E. A. Locke and G. P. Latham, *A Theory of Goal Setting and Task Performance* (Englewood Cliffs, NJ: Prentice-Hall, 1990).

47. Ibid., J. J. Donovan and D. J. Radosevich, "The Moderating Role of Goal Commitment on the Goal Difficulty–Performance Relationship: A Meta-Analytic Review and Critical Analysis," *Journal of Applied Psychology* 83 (1998), 308–15; M. E. Tubbs, "Goal Setting: A Meta Analytic Examination of the Empirical Evidence," *Journal of Applied Psychology* 71 (1986), 474–83.

48. E. A. Locke, K. N. Shaw, L. M. Saari, and G.P. Latham, "Goal Setting and Task Performance: 1969–1980," *Psychological Bulletin* 90 (1981), 125–52.

49. P. C. Earley, T. Connolly, and G. Ekegren, "Goals, Strategy Development, and Task Performance: Some Limits on the Efficacy of Goal Setting," *Journal of Applied Psychology* 74 (1989), 24–33; R. Kanfer and P. L. Ackerman, "Motivation and Cognitive Abilities: An Integrative/Aptitude–Treatment Interaction Approach to Skill Acquisition," *Journal of Applied Psychology* 74 (1989), 657–90.

50. W. C. Hamner, "Reinforcement Theory and Contingency Management in Organizational Settings," in H. Tosi and W. C. Hamner, eds., *Organizational Behavior and Management: A Contingency Approach* (Chicago: St. Clair Press, 1974).

51. B. F. Skinner, *Contingencies of Reinforcement* (New York: Appleton-Century-Crofts, 1969).

52. H. W. Weiss, "Learning Theory and Industrial and Organizational Psychology," in M. D. Dunnette and L. M. Hough, eds., *Handbook of Industrial and Organizational Psychology* (Palo Alto, CA: Consulting Psychologists Press, 1991), 171–221.

53. Hamner, "Reinforcement Theory and Contingency Management."

54. A. Bandura, *Principles of Behavior Modification* (New York: Holt, Rinehart and Winston, 1969); A.

Bandura, *Social Learning Theory* (Englewood Cliffs, NJ: Prentice-Hall, 1977); T. R. V. Davis and F. Luthans, "A Social Learning Approach to Organizational Behavior," *Academy of Management Review* 5 (1980), 281–90.

55. A. P. Goldstein and M. Sorcher, *Changing Supervisor Behaviors* (New York: Pergamon Press, 1974); F. Luthans and R. Kreitner, *Organizational Behavior Modification and Beyond* (Glenview, IL: Scott, Foresman, 1985);

56. Bandura, *Social Learning Theory;* Luthans and Kreitner, *Organizational Behavior Modification and Beyond.* Davis and Luthans, "A Social Learning Approach to Organizational Behavior."

57. A. Bandura, "Self-Reinforcement: Theoretical and Methodological Considerations," *Behaviorism* 4 (1976), 135–55.

58. S. Vozza, "Why Employees at Apple and Google Are More Productive," *Fast Company,* www.fastcompany.com, March 13, 2017.

59. A. Bandura, *Self-Efficacy: The Exercise of Control* (New York: W.H. Freeman, 1997); J. B. Vancouver, K. M. More, and R. J. Yoder, "Self-Efficacy and Resource Allocation: Support for a Nonmonotonic, Discontinuous Model," *Journal of Applied Psychology* 93, no. 1 (2008), 35–47.

60. A. Bandura, "Self-Efficacy Mechanism in Human Agency," *American Psychologist* 37 (1982), 122–27; M. E. Gist and T. R. Mitchell, "Self-Efficacy: A Theoretical Analysis of Its Determinants and Malleability," *Academy of Management Review* 17 (1992), 183–211.

61. E. E. Lawler III, *Pay and Organization Development* (Reading, MA: Addison-Wesley, 1981).

62. S. Bomkamp and L. Zumbach, "United Walks Back New Bonus Lottery System That Angered Employees," *Chicago Tribune,* www.chicagotribune.com, March 5, 2018.

63. C. Cancialosi, "Why United's Bonus Lottery Was Doomed from the Start," *Forbes,* www.forbes.com, March 12, 2018.

64. C. Tobitt, "Sky Reports Overall Gender Pay Gap of 11.5 Percent but Figure Much Lower among Broadcasters," *Press Gazette* (London), http://pressgazette.co.uk, March 21, 2018.

65. S. Waters, "Questioning the Power of Money," *HR Magazine,* November 2017, 58.

66. P. Dvorak and S. Thurm, "Slump Prods Firms to Seek New Compact with Workers," *The Wall Street Journal,* October 19, 2009, A1, A18.

67. D. Mattioli, "Rewards for Extra Work Come Cheap in Lean Times," *The Wall Street Journal,* January 4, 2010, B7.

68. Ibid.

69. Lawler, *Pay and Organization Development.*

70. Ibid.

71. "Greater as One: 2018 Proxy Statement," http://ir.lincolnelectric.com, accessed January 19, 2019; J. F. Lincoln, *Incentive Management* (Cleveland: Lincoln Electric Company, 1951); R. Zager, "Managing Guaranteed Employment," *Harvard Business Review* 56 (1978), 103–15.

72. Lawler, *Pay and Organization Development.*

73. "Benefits," https://gradientcorp.com, accessed January 19, 2019; M. Gendron, "Gradient Named 'Small Business of Year,'" *Boston Herald,* May 11, 1994, 35.

74. "Our Story," www.nucor.com, accessed January 19, 2019; W. Zeller, R. D. Hof, R. Brandt, S. Baker, and D. Greising, "Go-Go Goliaths," *BusinessWeek,* February 13, 1995, 64–70.

75. R. G. Brewer, "7 Fascinating Things You Probably Don't Know about Nucor Corp.," *Motley Fool,* www.fool.com, August 20, 2017; M. Byrnes, "A Steely Resolve," *BusinessWeek,* April 6, 2009, 54.

76. T. Stobierski, "Employee Stock Options, Explained," *LearnVest,* https://learnvest.com, accessed January 19, 2019; personal interview with Professor Bala Dharan, Jones Graduate School of Business, Rice University, June 28, 2001.

77. Personal interview with Professor Bala Dharan.

78. Ibid.

79. C. D. Fisher, L. F. Schoenfeldt, and J.B. Shaw, *Human Resource Management* (Boston: Houghton Mifflin, 1990); B. E. Graham-Moore and T. L. Ross, *Productivity Gainsharing* (Englewood Cliffs, NJ: Prentice-Hall, 1983); A. J. Geare, "Productivity from Scanlon Type Plans," *Academy of Management Review* 1 (1976), 99–108.

80. T. Nakamichi, "Nomura to Switch to Merit-Based Pay for Japan-Based Brokers," *Bloomberg,* www.bloomberg.com, January 8, 2019; K. Inagaki, "Japan Inc Shuns Seniority in Favour of Merit-Based Pay," *Financial Times,* www.ft.com, January 27, 2015.

10 Leaders and Leadership

Learning Objectives

After studying this chapter, you should be able to:

LO 10-1 Explain what leadership is, when leaders are effective and ineffective, and the sources of power that enable managers to be effective leaders.

LO 10-2 Identify the traits that show the strongest relationship to leadership, the behaviors leaders engage in, and the limitations of the trait and behavior models of leadership.

LO 10-3 Explain how contingency models of leadership enhance our understanding of effective leadership and management in organizations.

LO 10-4 Describe what transformational leadership is, and explain how managers can engage in it.

LO 10-5 Characterize the relationship between gender and leadership, and explain how emotional intelligence may contribute to leadership effectiveness.

Management Snapshot

Leaders Point Cancer Institute in the Right Direction

What Does Effective Leadership Look Like?

The answer depends partly on the situation. The two most recent CEOs of the Dana-Farber Cancer Institute provide an example of leadership that matches the organization's needs.

Based in Boston, the Dana-Farber Cancer Institute is affiliated with Harvard Medical School. It offers cancer treatment to adults and children and has research facilities for advancing knowledge of cancer and the best ways to treat it. The organization's vision is "the eradication of cancer, AIDS, and related diseases and the fear that they engender."[1]

When Edward Benz was CEO, he observed that Dana-Farber was excellent at doing research in the usual way, but he also envisioned a new way that would lead to even better results. The usual practice for a research institution is to bring in top scientists and let them pursue their passions. As long as they can win grants and get results published in prestigious journals, their research advances knowledge and makes the institute a desirable place for scientists to work. This approach was generating a lot of good research at Dana-Farber, but the research was not always related to the institution's mission. Also, new knowledge about cancer was showing that cancer is not a single illness but takes many forms, and finding the best treatments increasingly requires a multidisciplinary approach. Consequently, the practice of funding research by individual scientists with narrow specialties was creating a competition for resources when the organization would benefit more from collaboration across different medical fields.[2]

Benz worked with the institute's chief scientific officer to transform Dana-Farber into an organization built on collaboration. They knew they would need the support of the top scientists, whose knowledge and reputation gave them significant power. Scientists would be reluctant to give that up. Benz brought them together to develop a research strategy for the institution as a whole. The scientists reviewed cancer research to identify 10 areas with the most potential to advance cancer treatment. Then the institute began creating what it calls Integrative Research Centers to oversee research in these areas. While individual labs would continue their work, scientists could take positions running the research centers, which would receive significant additional funding. In exchange, the centers required a business plan with financial as well as scientific objectives. The job of managing a center offers great visibility and potential to contribute important scientific advances, but the business aspects of the job were unfamiliar to most of the scientists. Benz and his executive team held frequent one-on-one meetings to help scientists learn their new roles.[3]

Laurie Glimcher, current CEO of the Dana-Farber Cancer Institute, is an effective leader who empowers employees to do their best while making sure the organization stays at the forefront of innovation in cancer research. ©Michael Blanchard/Metro Corp

As the collaborative programs began delivering breakthroughs, they increasingly attracted new talent and more funding. The projects hired scientists drawn to the interdisciplinary work. The organization's culture began shifting to one that highly values collaboration.[4]

Following this organizational transformation, Benz retired as chief executive, and the institution brought in a respected researcher and medical school dean, Laurie Glimcher, to serve as CEO. By hiring a noted physician and immunologist, Dana-Farber made the leader someone who understands and is respected by the professionals who work there. She does not need to transform the organization, as Benz did, but she must keep it moving forward. Glimcher has empowered employees and maintained the drive for innovation and collaboration. She does not hesitate to hire enough staff to enable researchers to balance work and family needs, and she is assertive about ensuring that women are represented. One of her female appointees is the institute's first chief innovation officer, who brings together scientists, clinicians, and hospital administrators to apply information technology to improving patient care.[5]

Overview

Laurie Glimcher and Edward Benz exemplify the many facets of effective leadership. In Chapter 1 we explained that one of the four primary tasks of managers is leading. Thus, it should come as no surprise that leadership is a key ingredient in effective management. When leaders are effective, their followers are highly motivated, committed, and high-performing. When leaders are ineffective, chances are good that their followers do not perform up to their capabilities, are demotivated, and may be dissatisfied as well. Laurie Glimcher is a leader at the top of an organization, but leadership is an important ingredient for managerial success at all levels of organizations: top management, middle management, and first-line management. Moreover, leadership is a key ingredient of managerial success for organizations large and small.

In this chapter we describe what leadership is and examine the major leadership models that shed light on the factors that contribute to a manager being an effective leader. We look at trait and behavior models, which focus on what leaders are like and what they do, and contingency models—Fiedler's contingency model, path–goal theory, and the leader substitutes model—each of which takes into account the complexity surrounding leadership and the role of the situation in leader effectiveness. We also describe how managers can use transformational leadership to dramatically affect their organizations. By the end of this chapter, you will appreciate the many factors and issues that managers face in their quest to be effective leaders.

LO 10-1
Explain what leadership is, when leaders are effective and ineffective, and the sources of power that enable managers to be effective leaders.

The Nature of Leadership

Leadership is the process by which a person exerts influence over other people and inspires, motivates, and directs their activities to help achieve group or organizational goals.[6] The person who exerts such influence is a leader. When leaders are effective, the influence they exert over others helps a group or an organization achieve its performance goals. When leaders are ineffective, their influence does not contribute to, and often detracts from, goal attainment. As the "Management Snapshot" makes clear, both recent Dana-Farber CEOs took multiple steps to inspire and motivate employees at all levels of the medical facility so they can help the organization achieve its goals.

leadership The process by which an individual exerts influence over other people and inspires, motivates, and directs their activities to help achieve group or organizational goals.

Beyond facilitating the attainment of performance goals, effective leadership increases an organization's ability to meet all the contemporary challenges discussed throughout this book, including the need to obtain a competitive advantage, the need to foster ethical behavior, and the need to manage a diverse workforce fairly and equitably. Leaders who exert influence over organizational members to help meet these goals increase their organizations' chances of success.

In considering the nature of leadership, we first look at leadership styles and how they affect managerial tasks; we then look at the influence of culture on leadership styles. We then focus on the key to leadership, *power,* which can come from a variety of sources. Finally, we consider the contemporary dynamic of empowerment and how it relates to effective leadership.

Personal Leadership Style and Managerial Tasks

leader An individual who is able to exert influence over other people to help achieve group or organizational goals.

A manager's *personal leadership style*—that is, the specific ways in which a manager chooses to influence other people—shapes how that manager approaches planning, organizing, and controlling (the other principal tasks of managing). Consider Laurie Glimcher's personal leadership style described in "Management Snapshot": She empowers employees, emphasizes doing what's best for patients, and fosters an environment for collaboration among the organization's various medical specialties.

Managers at all levels and in all kinds of organizations have their own personal leadership styles, which determine not only how they lead their employees but also how they perform the other management tasks. Michael Kraus, owner and manager of a dry cleaning store in the northeastern United States, for example, takes a hands-on approach to leadership. He has the sole authority for determining work schedules and job assignments for the 15 employees in his store (an organizing task), makes all important decisions by himself (a planning task), and closely monitors his employees' performance and rewards top performers with pay increases (a control task). Kraus's personal leadership style is effective in his organization. His employees generally are motivated, perform highly, and are satisfied; and his store is highly profitable.

Developing an effective personal leadership style often is a challenge for managers at all levels in an organization. This challenge is often exacerbated when times are tough; due, for example, to an economic downturn or a decline in customer demand. The recession in the late 2000s provided many managers with just such a challenge.

Although leading is one of the four principal tasks of managing, a distinction is often made between managers and leaders. When this distinction is made, managers are thought of as those organizational members who establish and implement procedures and processes to ensure smooth functioning and are accountable for goal accomplishment.[7] Leaders look to the future, chart the course for the organization, and attract, retain, motivate, inspire, and develop relationships with employees based on trust and mutual respect. They also provide meaning and purpose, seek innovation rather than stability, and impassion employees to work together to achieve the leaders' vision.[8]

Servant Leadership

As part of their personal leadership style, some leaders strive to serve others. Robert Greenleaf, who was director of management research at AT&T and upon his retirement embarked on a second career focused on writing, speaking, and consulting,

servant leader A leader who has a strong desire to serve and work for the benefit of others.

came up with the term *servant leadership* to describe these leaders.[9] Servant leaders, above all else, have a strong desire to work for the benefit of others. Servant leaders share power with followers and strive to ensure that followers' most important needs are met, that they are able to develop as individuals, that their well-being is enhanced, and that attention is paid to those who are least well-off in a society.[10] Servant leadership is unique as a leadership approach because the leader views his or her role more as a motivator and listener, someone who empowers followers to act as collaborators and innovators within the organization.[11] Greenleaf founded a nonprofit organization called the Greenleaf Center for Servant Leadership (formerly called the Center for Applied Ethics) to foster leadership focused on service to others, power sharing, and a sense of community between organizations and their multiple stakeholders.[12] Some entrepreneurs strive to incorporate servant leadership into their personal leadership styles, as profiled in the accompanying "Ethics in Action" feature.

Ethics in Action

Servant Leadership at Zingerman's

Ari Weinzweig and Paul Saginaw founded Zingerman's Delicatessen in Ann Arbor, Michigan, in 1982.[13] Food lovers at heart, Weinzweig and Saginaw delighted in finding both traditional and exotic foods from around the world, making delicious sandwiches to order, and having extensive selections of food items ranging from olives, oils, and vinegars to cheeses, smoked fish, and salami. As their business grew, and to maintain an intimate atmosphere with excellent customer service, Weinzweig and Saginaw expanded from their original deli into a community of related businesses called Zingerman's Community of Businesses. In addition to the original deli, Zingerman's Community of Businesses includes a mail-order business, a bakery, a catering business, a creamery, a restaurant, a wholesale coffee business, and a training business and has combined annual sales of around $62 million.[14] From the start, Weinzweig and Saginaw have been devoted to excellent customer service, great food, and a commitment to people and community.[15]

As part of their commitment to people and community, Weinzweig and Saginaw have incorporated servant leadership into their personal leadership styles. As their business has grown and prospered, they have realized that increasing success means greater responsibility to serve others. They strive to treat their employees as well as they treat their customers and give their employees opportunities for growth and development on the job. They have also realized that when their own needs or desires differ from what is best for their company, they should do what is best for the company.[16]

To this day, the cofounders encourage their employees to let them know how they can help them and what they can do for them. And given Zingerman's culture of mutual respect and trust, employees do not hesitate to communicate how their leaders can serve them in many and varied ways. For example, when Weinzweig visits the Zingerman's Roadhouse restaurant and the staff is very busy, they may ask him to help out by serving customers or cleaning off tables. As he indicated, "People give me assignments all the time. Sometimes I'm the note-taker. Sometimes I'm the cleaner-upper. . . . Sometimes I'm on my hands and knees wiping up what people spilled."[17]

Paul Saginaw (left) and Ari Weinzweig have incorporated servant leadership into their personal leadership styles at Zingerman's. Courtesy of Zingerman's Community of Businesses

Weinzweig and Saginaw also have a strong sense of commitment to serving the local community; Zingerman's founded the nonprofit organization Food Gatherers to eliminate hunger and distribute food to the needy, and Food Gatherers is now an independent nonprofit responsible for the Washtenaw County Food Bank, with over 7,000 volunteers and a 30-member staff.[18] On Zingerman's 20th anniversary, 13 nonprofit community organizations in Ann Arbor erected a plaque next to Zingerman's Delicatessen with a dedication that read "Thank you for feeding, sheltering, educating, uplifting, and inspiring an entire community."[19] Clearly, for Weinzweig and Saginaw, leadership entails being of service to others.[20] ●

Leadership Styles across Cultures

Some evidence suggests that leadership styles vary not only among individuals but also among countries or cultures. Some research indicates that European managers tend to be more humanistic, or people-oriented, than both Japanese and American managers. The collectivistic culture in Japan places prime emphasis on the group rather than the individual, so the importance of individuals' own personalities, needs, and desires is minimized. Organizations in the United States tend to be very profit-oriented and thus tend to downplay the importance of individual employees' needs and desires. Many countries in Europe have a more individualistic perspective than Japan and a more humanistic perspective than the United States, and this may result in some European managers' being more people-oriented than their Japanese or American counterparts. European managers, for example, tend to be reluctant to lay off employees, and when a layoff is absolutely necessary, they take careful steps to make it as painless as possible.[21]

Another cross-cultural difference occurs in time horizons. While managers in any one country often differ in their time horizons, there are also national differences. For example, U.S. organizations tend to have a short-term profit orientation; thus, U.S. managers' personal leadership styles emphasize short-term performance. Japanese organizations tend to have a long-term growth orientation, so Japanese managers' personal leadership styles emphasize long-term performance. Justus Mische, a personnel manager at the European organization Hoechst, suggested that "Europe, at least the big international firms in Europe, has a philosophy between the Japanese, long term, and the United States, short term."[22] Research on these and other global aspects of leadership is ongoing; as it continues, more cultural differences in managers' personal leadership styles may be discovered.

Power: The Key to Leadership

No matter what one's leadership style is, a key component of effective leadership is found in the *power* the leader has to affect other people's behavior and to get them to act in certain ways.[23] There are several types of power: legitimate, reward, coercive, expert, and referent power (see Figure 10.1).[24] Effective leaders take steps to ensure that they have sufficient levels of each type and that they use their power in beneficial ways.

legitimate power The authority that a manager has by virtue of his or her position in an organization's hierarchy.

LEGITIMATE POWER Legitimate power is the authority a manager has by virtue of his or her position in an organization's hierarchy. Personal leadership style often influences how a manager exercises legitimate power. Take the case of Carol Loray, who is a first-line manager in a greeting card company and leads a group of 15 artists and designers. Loray has the legitimate power to hire new employees, assign projects to the artists and designers, monitor their work, and appraise their performance. She uses this power effectively. She always makes sure her project assignments match the interests of her employees as much as possible so they will enjoy

Figure 10.1

Types of Managerial Power

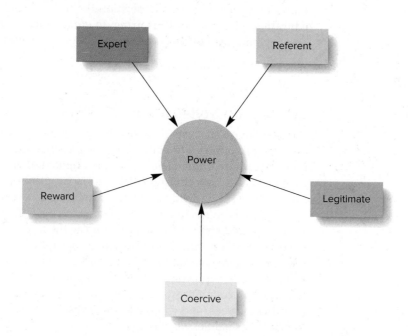

their work. She monitors their work to make sure they are on track but does not engage in close supervision, which can hamper creativity. She makes sure her performance appraisals are developmental, providing concrete advice for areas where improvements could be made. Recently, Loray negotiated with her manager to increase her legitimate power so she can now initiate and develop proposals for new card lines.

reward power The ability of a manager to give or withhold tangible and intangible rewards.

REWARD POWER Reward power is the ability of a manager to give or withhold tangible rewards (pay raises, bonuses, choice job assignments) and intangible rewards (verbal praise, a pat on the back, respect). As you learned in Chapter 9, members of an organization are motivated to perform at a high level by a variety of rewards. Being able to give or withhold rewards based on performance is a major source of power, which allows managers to have a highly motivated workforce. Managers of salespeople in retail organizations, like Neiman Marcus, Nordstrom, and Macy's,[25] and in car dealerships such as Mazda, Ford, and Volvo, often use their reward power to motivate their employees. Employees in organizations such as these often receive commissions on whatever they sell and rewards for the quality of their customer service, which motivate them to do the best they can.

Effective managers use their reward power to show appreciation for employees' good work and efforts. Ineffective managers use rewards in a more controlling manner that signals to employees that the manager has the upper hand. Managers also can take steps to increase their reward power.

coercive power The ability of a manager to punish others.

COERCIVE POWER Coercive power is the ability of a manager to punish others. Punishment can range from verbal reprimands to reductions in pay or working hours to actual dismissal. In the previous chapter we discussed how punishment can have negative side effects, such as resentment and retaliation, and should be used only when necessary (e.g., to curtail a dangerous behavior). Managers who rely heavily on coercive power tend to be ineffective as leaders and sometimes even get fired themselves. William J. Fife is one example; he was fired from his position as CEO of Giddings and Lewis Inc., a manufacturer of factory equipment, because of his overreliance on coercive power. In meetings, Fife often verbally criticized, attacked, and embarrassed top managers. Realizing how destructive Fife's use of punishment was for them and the company, these managers complained to the board of directors, who, after careful consideration of the issues, asked Fife to resign.[26]

Excessive use of coercive power seldom produces high performance and is questionable ethically. Sometimes it amounts to a form of mental abuse, robbing workers of their dignity and causing excessive levels of stress. Overuse of coercive power can even result in dangerous working conditions. Better results and, importantly, an ethical workplace that respects employee dignity can be obtained by using reward power.

expert power Power that is based on the special knowledge, skills, and expertise that a leader possesses.

EXPERT POWER Expert power is based on the special knowledge, skills, and expertise that a leader possesses. The nature of expert power varies, depending on the leader's level in the hierarchy. First-level and middle managers often have technical expertise relevant to the tasks their employees perform. Their expert power gives them considerable influence over employees. The Dana-Farber CEOs highlighted in "Management Snapshot" have expert power from their knowledge and expertise in the health care industry, acquired over many years.

The Chrysler Jefferson North Assembly plant in Detroit. Empowered employees make some decisions that managers or other leaders used to make. Paul Sancya/AP Images

Some top managers derive expert power from their technical expertise. Other top-level managers lack technical expertise and derive their expert power from their abilities as decision makers, planners, and strategists. Jack Welch, the former leader and CEO of General Electric, summed it up this way: "The basic thing that we at the top of the company know is that we don't know the business. What we have, I hope, is the ability to allocate resources, people, and dollars."[27]

Effective leaders take steps to ensure that they have an adequate amount of expert power to perform their leadership roles. They may obtain additional training or education in their fields, make sure they keep up with the latest developments and changes in technology, stay abreast of changes in their fields through involvement in professional associations, and read widely to be aware of momentous changes in the organization's task and general environments. Expert power tends to be best used in a guiding or coaching manner rather than in an arrogant, high-handed way.

referent power Power that comes from employees' and coworkers' respect, admiration, and loyalty.

REFERENT POWER Referent power is more informal than the other kinds of power. Referent power is a function of the personal characteristics of a leader; it is the power that comes from employees' and coworkers' respect, admiration, and loyalty. Leaders who are likable and whom employees wish to use as role models are especially likely to possess referent power, such as Tesla's Elon Musk and Apple's Tim Cook.

In addition to being a valuable asset for top managers, referent power can help first-line and middle managers be effective leaders as well. Sally Carruthers, for example, is the first-level manager of a group of administrative assistants in the finance department of a large state university. Carruthers's employees are known to be among the best in the university. Much of their willingness to go above and beyond the call of duty has been attributed to Carruthers's warm and caring nature, which makes each of them feel important and valued. Managers can take steps to increase their referent power, such as taking time to get to know their employees and showing interest in and concern for them.

Empowerment: An Ingredient in Modern Management

More and more managers today are incorporating into their personal leadership styles an aspect that at first glance seems to be the opposite of being a leader. Empowerment is the process of giving employees at all levels the authority to make decisions, be responsible for their outcomes, improve quality, and cut costs, and this managerial strategy has become increasingly popular in organizations. When leaders empower their employees, the employees typically take over some responsibilities and authority that used to reside with the leader or manager, such as the right to reject parts that do not meet quality standards, the right to check one's own work, and the right to schedule work activities. Empowered employees are given the power to make some decisions that their leaders or supervisors used to make.

empowerment The expansion of employees' knowledge, tasks, and decision-making responsibilities.

Empowerment might seem to be the opposite of effective leadership, because managers are allowing employees to take a more active role in leading themselves. In actuality, however, empowerment can contribute to effective leadership for several reasons:

- Empowerment increases a manager's ability to get things done, because the manager has the support and help of employees who may have special knowledge of work tasks.
- Empowerment often increases workers' involvement, motivation, and commitment; this helps ensure that they are working toward organizational goals.
- Empowerment gives managers more time to concentrate on their pressing concerns because they spend less time on day-to-day supervision.

Effective managers, like Laurie Glimcher, realize the benefits of empowerment. The personal leadership style of managers who empower employees often entails developing their ability to make good decisions as well as being their guide, coach, and source of inspiration. Empowerment is a popular trend in the United States and is a part of servant leadership. Empowerment is also taking off around the world.[28] For instance, companies in South Korea (such as Samsung and Hyundai), in which decision making typically was centralized with the founding families, are now empowering managers at lower levels to make decisions.[29]

Trait and Behavior Models of Leadership

Leading is such an important process in all organizations—nonprofit organizations, government agencies, and schools, as well as for-profit corporations—that it has been researched for decades. Early approaches to leadership, called the *trait model* and the *behavior model,* sought to determine what effective leaders are like as people and what they do that makes them so effective.

LO 10-2
Identify the traits that show the strongest relationship to leadership, the behaviors leaders engage in, and the limitations of the trait and behavior models of leadership.

The Trait Model

The trait model of leadership focused on identifying the personal characteristics that cause effective leadership. Researchers thought effective leaders must have certain personal qualities that set them apart from ineffective leaders and from people who never become leaders. Decades of research (beginning in the 1930s) and hundreds of studies indicate that certain personal characteristics do appear to be associated with effective leadership. (See Table 10.1 for a list of these.[30]) Notice that although this model is called the "trait" model, some of the personal characteristics that it identifies are not personality traits per se but, rather, are concerned with a leader's skills, abilities, knowledge, and expertise. As the "Management Snapshot" shows, Dana-Farber's Laurie Glimcher certainly appears to possess many of these characteristics (such as intelligence, knowledge and expertise, self-confidence, high energy, and integrity and honesty). Leaders who do not possess these traits may be ineffective.

Traits alone are not the key to understanding leader effectiveness, however. Some effective leaders do not possess all these traits, and some leaders who possess them are not effective in their leadership roles. This lack of a consistent relationship between leader traits and leader effectiveness led researchers to shift their attention away from traits and to search for new explanations for effective leadership. Rather than focusing on what leaders are like (the traits they possess), researchers began

Table 10.1

Traits Related to Effective Leadership

Trait	Description
Intelligence	Helps managers understand complex issues and solve problems.
Knowledge and expertise	Help managers make good decisions and discover ways to increase efficiency and effectiveness.
Dominance	Helps managers influence their employees to achieve organizational goals.
Self-confidence	Contributes to managers' effectively influencing employees and persisting when faced with obstacles or difficulties.
High energy	Helps managers deal with the many demands they face.
Tolerance for stress	Helps managers deal with uncertainty and make difficult decisions.
Integrity and honesty	Help managers behave ethically and earn their employees' trust and confidence.
Maturity	Helps managers avoid acting selfishly, control their feelings, and admit when they have made a mistake.

looking at what effective leaders actually do—in other words, at the behaviors that allow effective leaders to influence their employees to achieve group and organizational goals.

The Behavior Model

After extensive study in the 1940s and 1950s, researchers at The Ohio State University identified two basic kinds of behaviors that many leaders in the United States, Germany, and other countries engaged in to influence their employees: *consideration* and *initiating structure.*[31]

consideration
Behavior indicating that a manager trusts, respects, and cares about employees.

CONSIDERATION Leaders engage in consideration when they show their employees that they trust, respect, and care about them. Managers who truly look out for the well-being of their employees, and do what they can to help employees feel good and enjoy their work, perform consideration behaviors.

initiating structure
Behavior that managers engage in to ensure that work gets done, employees perform their jobs acceptably, and the organization is efficient and effective.

INITIATING STRUCTURE Leaders engage in initiating structure when they take steps to make sure that work gets done, employees perform their jobs acceptably, and the organization is efficient and effective. Assigning tasks to individuals or work groups, letting employees know what is expected of them, deciding how work should be done, making schedules, encouraging adherence to rules and regulations, and motivating employees to do a good job are all examples of initiating structure.[32]

Michael Teckel, the manager of an upscale store selling imported men's and women's shoes in a midwestern city, engages in initiating structure when he establishes weekly work, lunch, and break schedules to ensure that the store has enough salespeople on the floor. Teckel also initiates structure when he discusses the latest shoe designs with his employees so they are knowledgeable with customers, when he encourages adherence to the store's refund and exchange policies, and when he encourages his staff to provide high-quality customer service and to avoid a hard-sell approach.

Initiating structure and consideration are independent leader behaviors. Leaders can be high on both, low on both, or high on one and low on the other. Many effective leaders, like Laurie Glimcher of Dana-Farber Cancer Institute, engage in both of these behaviors.

You might expect that effective leaders and managers would perform both kinds of behaviors, but research has found that this is not necessarily the case. The relationship between performance of consideration and initiating-structure behaviors and leader effectiveness is not clear-cut. Some leaders are effective even when they do not perform consideration or initiating-structure behaviors, and some leaders are ineffective even when they perform both kinds of behaviors. Like the trait model of leadership, the behavior model alone cannot explain leader effectiveness. Realizing this, researchers began building more complicated models of leadership, focused not only on the leader and what he or she does but also on the situation or context in which leadership occurs.

Contingency Models of Leadership

Simply possessing certain traits or performing certain behaviors does not ensure that a manager will be an effective leader in all situations calling for leadership. Some managers who seem to possess the right traits and perform the right behaviors turn out to be ineffective leaders. Managers lead in a wide variety of situations and organizations and have various kinds of employees performing diverse tasks in a multiplicity of environmental contexts. Given the wide variety of situations in which leadership occurs, what makes a manager an effective leader in one situation (such as certain traits or behaviors) is not necessarily what that manager needs to be equally effective in a different situation. An effective army general might not be an effective university president; an effective restaurant manager might not be an effective clothing store manager; an effective football team coach might not be an effective fitness center manager; and an effective first-line manager in a manufacturing company might not be an effective middle manager. The traits or behaviors that may contribute to a manager's being an effective leader in one situation might actually result in the same manager being an ineffective leader in another situation.

Contingency models of leadership take into account the situation, or context, within which leadership occurs. According to contingency models, whether or not a manager is an effective leader is the result of the interplay among what the manager is like, what he or she does, and the situation in which leadership takes place. Contingency models propose that whether a leader who possesses certain traits or performs certain behaviors is effective depends on, or is contingent on, the situation, or context. In this section we discuss three prominent contingency models developed to shed light on what makes managers effective leaders: Fred Fiedler's contingency model, Robert House's path–goal theory, and the leader substitutes model. As you will see, these leadership models are complementary; each focuses on a somewhat different aspect of effective leadership in organizations.

LO 10-3
Explain how contingency models of leadership enhance our understanding of effective leadership and management in organizations.

Fiedler's Contingency Model

Fred E. Fiedler was among the first leadership researchers to acknowledge that effective leadership is contingent on, or depends on, the characteristics of the leader *and* the situation. Fiedler's contingency model helps explain why a manager may be an effective leader in one situation and ineffective in another; it also suggests which kinds of managers are likely to be most effective in which situations.[33]

relationship-oriented leaders Leaders whose primary concern is to develop good relationships with their employees and to be liked by them.

LEADER STYLE As with the trait approach, Fiedler hypothesized that personal characteristics can influence leader effectiveness. He used the term *leader style* to refer to a manager's characteristic approach to leadership and identified two basic leader styles: *relationship-oriented* and *task-oriented*. All managers can be described as having one of these styles.

Relationship-oriented leaders are primarily concerned with developing good relationships with their employees and being liked by them. Relationship-oriented managers focus on having high-quality interpersonal relationships with employees. This does not mean, however, that the job does not get done when such leaders are at the helm. But it does mean that the quality of interpersonal relationships with employees is a prime concern for relationship-oriented leaders.

task-oriented leaders Leaders whose primary concern is to ensure that employees perform at a high level.

Task-oriented leaders are primarily concerned with ensuring that employees perform at a high level and focus on task accomplishment. While task-oriented leaders also may be concerned about having good interpersonal relationships with their employees, task accomplishment is their prime concern.

SITUATIONAL CHARACTERISTICS According to Fiedler, leadership style is an enduring characteristic; managers cannot change their style, nor can they adopt different styles in different kinds of situations. With this in mind, Fiedler identified three situational characteristics that are important determinants of how favorable a situation is for leading: leader–member relations, task structure, and position power. When a situation is favorable for leading, it is relatively easy for a manager to influence employees so they perform at a high level and contribute to organizational efficiency and effectiveness. In a situation unfavorable for leading, it is much more difficult for a manager to exert influence.

leader–member relations The extent to which followers like, trust, and are loyal to their leader; a determinant of how favorable a situation is for leading.

Leader–Member Relations   The first situational characteristic Fiedler described, leader–member relations, is the extent to which followers like, trust, and are loyal to their leader. Situations are more favorable for leading when leader–member relations are good.

task structure The extent to which the work to be performed is clear-cut so that a leader's employees know what needs to be accomplished and how to go about doing it; a determinant of how favorable a situation is for leading.

Task Structure   The second situational characteristic Fiedler described, task structure, is the extent to which the work to be performed is clear-cut so that a leader's employees know what needs to be accomplished and how to go about doing it. When task structure is high, the situation is favorable for leading. When task structure is low, goals may be vague, employees may be unsure of what they should be doing or how they should do it, and the situation is unfavorable for leading.

Task structure was low for Geraldine Laybourne when she was a top manager at Nickelodeon, the children's television network. It was never precisely clear what would appeal to her young viewers, whose tastes can change dramatically, or how to motivate her employees to come up with creative and novel ideas.[34] In contrast, Herman Mashaba, founder of Black Like Me, a hair care products company based in South Africa, seemed to have relatively high task structure when he started his company. His company's goals were to produce and sell inexpensive hair care products to native Africans, and managers accomplished these goals by using simple yet appealing packaging and distributing the products through neighborhood beauty salons.[35]

position power The amount of legitimate, reward, and coercive power that a leader has by virtue of his or her position in an organization; a determinant of how favorable a situation is for leading.

Position Power   The third situational characteristic Fiedler described, position power, is the amount of legitimate, reward, and coercive power a leader has by virtue of his or her position in an organization. Leadership situations are more favorable for leading when position power is strong.

Figure 10.2   Fielder's Contingency Theory of Leadership

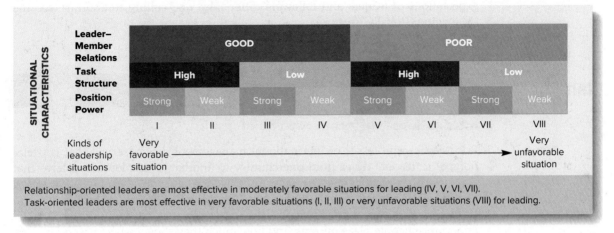

Relationship-oriented leaders are most effective in moderately favorable situations for leading (IV, V, VI, VII).
Task-oriented leaders are most effective in very favorable situations (I, II, III) or very unfavorable situations (VIII) for leading.

COMBINING LEADER STYLE AND THE SITUATION By considering all possible combinations of good and poor leader–member relations, high and low task structure, and strong and weak position power, Fiedler identified eight leadership situations, which vary in their favorability for leading (see Figure 10.2). After extensive research, he determined that relationship-oriented leaders are most effective in moderately favorable situations (IV, V, VI, and VII in Figure 10.2), and task-oriented leaders are most effective in situations that are either very favorable (I, II, and III) or very unfavorable (VIII).

PUTTING THE CONTINGENCY MODEL INTO PRACTICE Recall that according to Fiedler, leader style is an enduring characteristic that managers cannot change. This suggests that for managers to be effective, either managers need to be placed in leadership situations that fit their style or situations need to be changed to suit the managers. Situations can be changed, for example, by giving a manager more position power or by taking steps to increase task structure, such as by clarifying goals.

Take the case of Mark Compton, a relationship-oriented leader employed by a small construction company. Compton was in a very unfavorable situation and was having a rough time leading his construction crew. His employees did not trust him to look out for their well-being (poor leader–member relations); the construction jobs he supervised tended to be novel and complex (low task structure); and he had no control over the rewards and disciplinary actions his employees received (weak position power). Recognizing the need to improve matters, Compton's supervisor gave him the power to reward crew members with bonuses and overtime work as he saw fit and to discipline crew members for poor-quality work and unsafe on-the-job behavior. As his leadership situation improved to moderately favorable, so did Compton's effectiveness as a leader and the performance of his crew.

Research studies tend to support some aspects of Fiedler's model but also suggest that, like most theories, it needs some modifications.[36] Some researchers have questioned what the scale described in Figure 10.2 really measures. Others find fault with the model's premise that leaders cannot alter their styles. That is, it is likely that at least some leaders can diagnose the situation they are in and, when their style is inappropriate for the situation, modify their style so that it is more in line with what the leadership situation calls for. The ability to modify one's leadership style is especially important in today's global business environment, because the expectations of leaders and followers differ from one culture to another (see the "Managing Globally" feature).

Managing Globally

International Differences in Leadership

Erin Meyer, a professor of international management, has observed that expectations of a "leader" differ from one country to another. If employees perceive that a manager is not acting like their idea of a leader, they may feel confused or upset. Meyer has seen misunderstandings related to cultural ideas of authority, decision making, and the interactions between them. Authority has to do with how much importance people place on rank and how much they show respect based on rank. Decision making refers to whether leaders issue decisions or the group arrives at a consensus.[37]

These differences become more complex when combined. For example, in China and Indonesia, hierarchy is important, and leaders make top-down decisions. The Scandinavian countries downplay hierarchy, and decisions are reached through consensus. But in the United States and Great Britain, which also are egalitarian, a leader is typically expected to listen to views and then decide. And in Japan, although hierarchy is important, employees at lower levels of the organization confer, reach a consensus, and present their proposal to the next level up. The process can be slow, but once an idea has worked its way up through the hierarchy, it already has buy-in, the decision is firm, and the people are committed to implementing it.[38]

How can leaders navigate these differences? An important start is to learn about the cultures of followers' countries. A culturally agile leader can recognize and name those differences in order to identify which cultural style will be effective for particular decisions. Then the leader should clarify expectations—for example, by saying, "I want to hear three ideas from the team before I express my views" or "Here's our decision, but it's not firm until we get approval from the finance department." In addition to learning general cultural patterns, leaders should gather information from the group being led, according to Jo Owen, who has led international business and nonprofit groups. Owen advises that the best way to observe cultural norms and personal differences is to engage with people face to face. Like Meyer, Owen advises talking about norms, so people understand their group's dynamics. Leadership coach Amir Ghannad takes Owen's thinking one step further, urging leaders to see their followers first as unique individuals, rather than generic members of a culture. This prepares leaders to expect differences while seeing the other person's shared humanity.[39] ●

House's Path–Goal Theory

In what he called path–goal theory, leadership researcher Robert House focused on what leaders can do to motivate their employees to achieve group and organizational goals.[40] The premise of path–goal theory is that effective leaders motivate employees to achieve goals by (1) clearly identifying the outcomes that employees are trying to obtain from the workplace, (2) rewarding employees with these outcomes for high performance and the attainment of work goals, and (3) clarifying for employees the *paths* leading to the attainment of work *goals*. Path–goal theory is a contingency model because it proposes that the steps managers should take to motivate employees depend on both the nature of the employees and the type of work they do.

Path–goal theory identifies four kinds of leadership behaviors that motivate employees:

- *Directive behaviors* are similar to initiating structure and include setting goals, assigning tasks, showing employees how to complete tasks, and taking concrete steps to improve performance.
- *Supportive behaviors* are similar to consideration and include expressing concern for employees and looking out for their best interests.
- *Participative behaviors* give employees a say in matters and decisions that affect them.
- *Achievement-oriented behaviors* motivate employees to perform at the highest level possible by, for example, setting challenging goals, expecting that they be met, and believing in employees capabilities.

Which of these behaviors should managers use to lead effectively? The answer to this question depends, or is contingent, on the nature of the employees and the kind of work they do.

Directive behaviors may be beneficial when employees are having difficulty completing assigned tasks, but they might be detrimental when employees are independent thinkers who work best when left alone. *Supportive* behaviors are often advisable when employees are experiencing high levels of stress. *Participative* behaviors can be particularly effective when employees support of a decision is required. *Achievement-oriented* behaviors may increase motivation levels of highly capable employees who are bored from having too few challenges, but they might backfire if used with employees who are already pushed to their limit.

The Leader Substitutes Model

The leader substitutes model suggests that leadership is sometimes unnecessary because substitutes for leadership are present. A leadership substitute is something that acts in place of the influence of a leader and makes leadership unnecessary. This model suggests that under certain conditions managers do not have to play a leadership role—members of an organization sometimes can perform at a high level without a manager exerting influence over them.[41] The leader substitutes model is a contingency model because it suggests that in some situations leadership is unnecessary.

Take the case of David Cotsonas, who teaches English at a foreign language school in Cyprus, an island in the Mediterranean Sea. Cotsonas is fluent in Greek, English, and French; is an excellent teacher; and is highly motivated. Many of his students are businesspeople who have some rudimentary English skills and wish to increase their fluency to be able to conduct more of their business in English. He enjoys not only teaching them English but also learning about the work they do, and he often keeps in touch with his students after they finish his classes. Cotsonas meets with the director of the school twice a year to discuss semiannual class schedules and enrollments.

You could stand over your employee and berate him or you could empower him to find the solution by working to see where the issue developed. Supportive managers make a world of difference in retaining and motivating employees. Stockbyte/Getty Images

With practically no influence from a leader, Cotsonas is a highly motivated top performer at the school. In his situation, leadership is unnecessary because substitutes for leadership are present. Cotsonas's teaching expertise, his motivation, and his enjoyment of his work are substitutes for the influence of a leader—in this case, the school's director. If the school's director were to try to influence how Cotsonas performs his job, Cotsonas would probably resent this infringement on his autonomy, and it is unlikely that his performance would improve, because he is already one of the school's best teachers.

As in Cotsonas's case, *characteristics of employees*—such as their skills, abilities, experience, knowledge, and motivation—can be substitutes for leadership.[42] *Characteristics of the situation, or context*—such as the extent to which the work is interesting and enjoyable—also can be substitutes. When work is interesting and enjoyable, as it is for Cotsonas, job-holders do not need to be coaxed into performing because performing is rewarding in its own right. Similarly, when managers *empower* their employees or use *self-managed work teams* (discussed in detail in Chapter 11), the need for leadership influence from a manager is decreased because team members manage themselves.

The concept of shared leadership is another effective example of a leadership substitute. In this situation, leadership is distributed among team members rather than being exhibited by one leader. Research suggests teams that successfully share the leadership role among members may provide higher-quality outcomes to their customers.[43] Substitutes for leadership can increase organizational efficiency and effectiveness because they free up some of managers' valuable time and allow managers to focus their efforts on discovering new ways to improve organizational effectiveness. The director of the language school, for example, was able to spend much of his time making arrangements to open a second school in Rhodes, an island in the Aegean Sea, because of the presence of leadership substitutes, not only for Cotsonas but for most other teachers at the school as well.

Bringing It All Together

Effective leadership in organizations occurs when managers take steps to lead in a way that is appropriate for the situation, or context, in which leadership occurs and for the employees who are being led. The three contingency models of leadership just discussed help managers focus on the necessary ingredients for effective leadership. They are complementary in that each one looks at the leadership question from a different angle. Fiedler's contingency model explores how a manager's leadership style needs to be matched to that person's leadership situation for maximum effectiveness. House's path–goal theory focuses on how managers should motivate employees and describes the specific kinds of behaviors managers can engage in to have a highly motivated workforce. The leadership substitutes model alerts managers to the fact that sometimes they do not need to exert influence over employees and thus can free up their time for other important activities. Table 10.2 recaps these three contingency models of leadership.

Table 10.2

Contingency Models of Leadership

Model	Focus	Key Contingencies
Fiedler's contingency model	Describes two leader styles, relationship-oriented and task-oriented, and the kinds of situations in which each kind of leader will be most effective.	Whether a relationship-oriented or a task-oriented leader is effective is contingent on the situation.
House's path–goal theory	Describes how effective leaders motivate their followers.	The behaviors that managers should engage in to be effective leaders are contingent on the nature of the employees and the work they do.
Leader substitutes model	Describes when leadership is unnecessary.	Whether leadership is necessary for employees to perform highly is contingent on characteristics of the employees and the situation.

Transformational Leadership

LO 10-4
Describe what transformational leadership is, and explain how managers can engage in it.

transformational leadership
Leadership that makes employees aware of the importance of their jobs and performance to the organization and aware of their own needs for personal growth and that motivates employees to work for the good of the organization.

Time and time again, throughout business history, certain leaders seem to transform their organizations, making sweeping changes to revitalize and renew operations. For example, when Sue Nokes became senior vice president of sales and customer service at T-Mobile USA in 2002, the quality of T-Mobile's customer service was lower than that of its major competitors; on average, 12% of employees were absent on any day; and annual employee turnover was over 100%.[44] When Nokes arrived at T-Mobile, valuable employees were quitting their jobs and customers weren't receiving high-quality service; neither employees nor customers were satisfied with their experience with the company.[45] However, by the late 2000s T-Mobile was regularly receiving highest rankings for customer care and satisfaction in the wireless category by J. D. Power and Associates, absence and turnover rates substantially declined, and around 80% of employees indicated that they were satisfied with their jobs.[46] In fact, when Nokes visited call centers, it was not uncommon for employees to greet her with cheers and accolades.[47]

Nokes transformed T-Mobile into a company in which satisfied employees provide excellent service to customers. When managers have such dramatic effects on their employees and on an organization as a whole, they are engaging in transformational leadership. Transformational leadership occurs when managers change (or transform) their employees in three important ways:[48]

1. *Transformational managers make employees aware of how important their jobs are for the organization and how necessary it is for them to perform those jobs as best they can so the organization can attain its goals.* At T-Mobile, Nokes visited call centers, conducted focus groups, and had town hall meetings to find out what employees and customers were unhappy with and what steps she could take to improve matters. Her philosophy was that when employees are satisfied with their jobs and view their work as important, they are much more likely to provide high-quality customer service. She made employees aware of how important their jobs were by the many steps she took to improve their working conditions, ranging from providing them with their own workspaces to substantially raising their salaries. She emphasized the importance of providing excellent customer service

Sue Nokes exhibited transformational leadership at T-Mobile. IPON-BONESS/SIPA/Newscom

by periodically asking employees what was working well and what was not working well, asking them what steps could be taken to improve problem areas, and taking actions to ensure that employees were able to provide excellent customer service. Nokes also instituted a performance measurement system to track performance in key areas such as quality of service and speed of problem resolution. She sincerely told employees, "You are No. 1, and the customer is why."[49]

2. *Transformational managers make their employees aware of their own needs for personal growth, development, and accomplishment.* Nokes made T-Mobile's employees aware of their own needs in this regard by transforming training and development at T-Mobile and increasing opportunities for promotions to more responsible positions. Employees now spend over 130 hours per year in training and development programs and team meetings. Nokes also instituted a promote-from-within policy, and around 80% of promotions are given to current employees.

3. *Transformational managers motivate their employees to work for the good of the organization as a whole, not just for their own personal gain or benefit.* Nokes emphasized that employees should focus on what matters to customers, coworkers, and T-Mobile as a whole. She let employees know that when they were unnecessarily absent from their jobs, they were not doing right by their coworkers. And she emphasized the need to try to resolve customer problems in a single phone call so customers can get on with their busy lives.[50]

When managers transform their employees in these three ways, employees trust the managers, are highly motivated, and help the organization achieve its goals. How do managers such as Nokes transform employees and produce dramatic effects in their organizations? There are at least three ways in which transformational leaders can influence their followers: by being a charismatic leader, by intellectually stimulating employees, and by engaging in developmental consideration (see Table 10.3).

charismatic leader
An enthusiastic, self-confident leader who is able to clearly communicate his or her vision of how good things could be.

Being a Charismatic Leader

Transformational managers such as Nokes are charismatic leaders. They have a vision of how good things could be in their work groups and organizations, which is in contrast to the status quo. Their vision usually entails dramatic improvements in

Table 10.3

Transformational Leadership

Transformational managers:

- Are charismatic.

- Stimulate employees intellectually.

- Engage in developmental consideration.

Employees of transformational managers:

- Have increased awareness of the importance of their jobs and high performance.

- Recognize their own needs for growth, development, and accomplishment.

- Work for the good of the organization and not just their own personal benefit.

group and organizational performance as a result of changes in the organization's structure, culture, strategy, decision making, and other critical processes and factors. This vision paves the way for gaining a competitive advantage.

Charismatic leaders are excited and enthusiastic about their vision and clearly communicate it to their employees. The creativity, enthusiasm, and self-confidence of a charismatic leader contribute to the leader's being able to inspire followers to enthusiastically support his or her vision.[51] People often think of charismatic leaders or managers as being "larger than life." The essence of charisma, however, is having a vision and enthusiastically communicating it to others. Thus, managers who appear to be quiet and earnest can also be charismatic.

Stimulating Employees Intellectually

intellectual stimulation Behavior a leader engages in to make followers aware of problems and view these problems in new ways, consistent with the leader's vision.

Transformational managers openly share information with their employees, so everyone is aware of existing problems and the need for change. This open communication strategy causes employees to view problems in their department and throughout the organization from a different perspective, consistent with the manager's vision for change. Previously, employees may not have been aware of some problems, may have viewed them as a "management issue" beyond their concern or pay grade, or may have viewed problems as insurmountable. The transformational manager's intellectual stimulation may lead employees to view problems as challenges that can be met and conquered. In addition, the manager engages and empowers employees to take personal responsibility for helping solve problems, as Nokes was able to do successfully at T-Mobile.[52]

Engaging in Developmental Consideration

developmental consideration Behavior a leader engages in to support and encourage followers and help them develop and grow on the job.

When managers engage in developmental consideration, they not only perform the consideration behaviors described earlier, such as demonstrating true concern for the well-being of employees, but also go one step further. The manager goes out of his or her way to support and encourage employees, giving them opportunities to enhance their skills and capabilities and to grow and excel on the job.[53] As mentioned earlier, Nokes did this in numerous ways. In fact, after she first met with employees in a call center in Albuquerque, New Mexico, the manager of the call center said, "Everyone came out crying. The people said that they had never felt so inspired in their lives, and that they had never met with any leader at that level who [they felt] cared."[54]

All organizations, no matter how large or small, successful or unsuccessful, can benefit when their managers engage in transformational leadership. Moreover, while the benefits of transformational leadership are often most apparent when an organization is in trouble, transformational leadership can be an enduring approach to leadership, leading to long-term organizational effectiveness.

The Distinction between Transformational and Transactional Leadership

transactional leadership Leadership that motivates employees by rewarding them for high performance and reprimanding them for low performance.

Transformational leadership is often contrasted with transactional leadership. In transactional leadership, managers use their reward and coercive powers to encourage high performance. When managers reward high performers, reprimand or otherwise punish low performers, and motivate employees by reinforcing desired behaviors and extinguishing or punishing undesired ones, they are engaging in transactional leadership.[55] Managers who effectively influence their employees to achieve goals, yet do not seem to be making the kind of dramatic changes that are part of transformational leadership, are engaging in transactional leadership.

Many transformational leaders engage in transactional leadership. They reward employees for a job well done and notice and respond to substandard performance. But they also have their eyes on the bigger picture of how much better things could be in their organizations, how much more their employees are capable of achieving, and how important it is to treat them with respect and help them reach their full potential.

Research has found that when leaders engage in transformational leadership, their employees tend to have higher levels of job satisfaction and performance.[56] Additionally, employees of transformational leaders may be more likely to trust their leaders and their organizations and feel that they are being fairly treated, and this in turn may positively influence their work motivation (see Chapter 9).[57]

Gender and Leadership

The increasing number of women entering the ranks of management, as well as the problems some women face in their efforts to be hired as managers or promoted into management positions, has prompted researchers to explore the relationship between gender and leadership. Although there are relatively more women in management positions today than there were 10 years ago, there are still relatively few women in top management and, in some organizations, even in middle management.

LO 10-5
Characterize the relationship between gender and leadership, and explain how emotional intelligence may contribute to leadership effectiveness.

When women do advance to top management positions, special attention often is focused on them and the fact that they are women. For example, women CEOs of large companies are still rare; those who make it to the top post, such as Mary Barra of General Motors and Michele Buck of The Hershey Company, are scarce.[58] Although women have made inroads into senior positions in many organizations, they continue to be underrepresented in top leadership posts. For example, while almost 45% of the employees in managerial and professional jobs are women, only about 26% of corporate officers in the *Fortune* 500 are women, and only 11% of the top earners are women.[59]

A widespread stereotype of women is that they are nurturing, supportive, and concerned with interpersonal relations. Men are stereotypically viewed as being directive and focused on task accomplishment. Such stereotypes suggest that women tend to be more relationship-oriented as managers and engage in more consideration behaviors, whereas men are more task-oriented and engage in more initiating-structure behaviors. Does the behavior of actual male and female managers bear out these stereotypes? Do women managers lead in different ways than men do? Are male or female managers more effective as leaders?

Research suggests that male and female managers who have leadership positions in organizations behave in similar ways.[60] Women do not engage in more consideration than men, and men do not engage in more initiating structure than women. Research does suggest, however, that leadership style may vary between women and men. Women tend to

Research suggests that women tend to be more participative as leaders than men, involving employees in decision making and seeking their input. nd3000/Shutterstock

be somewhat more participative as leaders than are men, involving employees in decision making and seeking their input.[61] Male managers tend to be less participative than are female managers, making more decisions on their own and wanting to do things their own way.

There are at least two reasons that female managers may be more participative as leaders than are male managers.[62] First, employees may try to resist the influence of female managers more than they do the influence of male managers. Some employees may never have reported to a woman before, some may incorrectly see a management role as being more appropriate for a man than for a woman, and some may just resist being led by a woman. To overcome this resistance and encourage employees' trust and respect, women managers may adopt a participative approach.

A second reason that female managers may be more participative is that they sometimes have better interpersonal skills than male managers.[63] A participative approach to leadership requires high levels of interaction and involvement between a manager and his or her employees, sensitivity to their feelings, and the ability to make decisions that may be unpopular with employees but necessary for goal attainment. Good interpersonal skills may help female managers have the effective interactions with their employees that are crucial to a participative approach.[64] To the extent that male managers have more difficulty managing interpersonal relationships, they may shy away from the high levels of interaction with employees necessary for true participation.

The key finding from research on leader behaviors, however, is that male and female managers do *not* differ significantly in their propensities to perform different leader behaviors. Even though they may be more participative, female managers do not engage in more consideration or less initiating structure than male managers.

Perhaps a question even more important than whether male and female managers differ in the leadership behaviors they perform is whether they differ in effectiveness. Consistent with the findings for leader behaviors, research suggests that across different kinds of organizational settings, male and female managers tend to be *equally effective* as leaders.[65] Thus, there is no logical basis for stereotypes favoring male managers and leaders or for the existence of the "glass ceiling" (an invisible barrier that seems to prevent women from advancing as far as they should in some organizations). Because women and men are equally effective as leaders, the increasing number of women in the workforce should result in a larger pool of highly qualified candidates for management positions in organizations, ultimately enhancing organizational effectiveness.[66]

Emotional Intelligence and Leadership

Do the moods and emotions leaders experience on the job influence their behavior and effectiveness as leaders? Research suggests this is likely to be the case. For example, one study found that when store managers experienced positive moods at work, salespeople in their stores provided high-quality customer service and were less likely to quit.[67] Another study found that groups whose leaders experienced positive moods had better coordination, whereas groups whose leaders experienced negative moods exerted more effort; members of groups with leaders in positive moods also tended to experience more positive moods themselves; and members of groups with leaders in negative moods tended to experience more negative moods.[68]

A leader's level of emotional intelligence (see Chapter 2) may play a particularly important role in leadership effectiveness.[69] For example, emotional intelligence may help leaders develop a vision for their organizations, motivate their employees to commit to this vision, and energize them to enthusiastically work to achieve this vision. Moreover, emotional intelligence may enable leaders to develop a significant identity for their organization and instill high levels of trust and cooperation throughout the organization while maintaining the flexibility needed to respond to changing conditions.[70]

Emotional intelligence also plays a crucial role in how leaders relate to and deal with their followers, particularly when it comes to encouraging followers to be creative.[71] Creativity in organizations is an emotion-laden process; it often entails challenging the status quo, being willing to take risks and accept and learn from failures, and doing much hard work to bring creative ideas to fruition in terms of new products, services, or procedures and processes when uncertainty is bound to be high.[72] Leaders who are high on emotional intelligence are more likely to understand all the emotions surrounding creative endeavors, to be able to awaken and support the creative pursuits of their followers, and to provide the kind of support that enables creativity to flourish in organizations.[73]

The "Management Insight" feature provides some guidelines for applying the concept of emotional intelligence to the practice of leadership.

Management Insight

Becoming a High-EQ Leader

What behaviors should a manager practice in order to lead with emotional intelligence (EQ)? A good starting point is to become aware of one's emotions. When someone puts forth an idea different from what you were advocating, what do you feel? Are you curious to learn more or defensive of an idea you were proud of? Or when you hear a critical remark, do you feel hurt, angry, or interested you might have information that will help you do better in the future? Defining these feelings can help you evaluate your options for possible actions more accurately and fully.[74]

Another essential behavior to practice is empathy. The objective is to understand how people feel, not to encourage negative behavior or even necessarily to agree. To practice empathy, when you observe others, try to imagine yourself in their place. If you aren't sure how another person feels, ask and try to understand the answer. Even when you cannot—or do not think it is appropriate to—solve another person's problem, you demonstrate respect when you try to understand how he or she is feeling about a situation.[75]

Empathy increases when you practice listening. Communication skills are a mark of a high-EQ leader, and listening is among the most important of those skills. While listening, practice focusing on understanding rather than judging what the person says. Jumping to a judgment makes it harder to get the full message. Listening to learn about others, in contrast, is motivational as well as informative. When Tom Gartland became president of Avis Budget Group, he spent weeks on a bus tour to meet the company's employees face to face. Focusing on others and learning how he could help them resulted in the employees being highly committed to the company.[76]

Finally, emotionally intelligent leaders manage their emotions. The other practices can help with this. For example, anger at an employee is easier to manage if you have listened and practiced empathy, so that you have some understanding of what behavior to expect and why it is occurring. Learning to recognize your emotions alerts you to situations in which self-control will help you. For example, if conflict erupts during a meeting, awareness of your own and others' feelings can put you on guard to keep your own anger or dismay under control. Then you can explore the ideas in play and perhaps even steer the group to a creative solution built on a variety of perspectives.[77] ●

Summary and Review

THE NATURE OF LEADERSHIP Leadership is the process by which a person exerts influence over other people and inspires, motivates, and directs their activities to help achieve group or organizational goals. Leaders can influence others because they possess power. The five types of power available to managers are legitimate power, reward power, coercive power, expert power, and referent power. Many managers are using empowerment as a tool to increase their effectiveness as leaders. [LO 10-1]

TRAIT AND BEHAVIOR MODELS OF LEADERSHIP The trait model of leadership describes personal characteristics, or traits, that contribute to effective leadership. However, some managers who possess these traits are not effective leaders, and some managers who do not possess all the traits are nevertheless effective leaders. The behavior model of leadership describes two kinds of behavior that most leaders engage in: consideration and initiating structure. [LO 10-2]

CONTINGENCY MODELS OF LEADERSHIP Contingency models take into account the complexity surrounding leadership and the role of the situation in determining whether a manager is an effective leader. Fiedler's contingency model explains why managers may be effective leaders in one situation and ineffective in another. According to Fiedler's model, relationship-oriented leaders are most effective in situations that are moderately favorable for leading, and task-oriented leaders are most effective in situations that are very favorable or very unfavorable for leading. House's path–goal theory describes how effective managers motivate their employees by determining what outcomes their employees want, rewarding them with these outcomes when they achieve their goals and perform at a high level, and clarifying the paths to goal attainment. Managers can engage in four kinds of behaviors to motivate employees: directive, supportive, participative, and achievement-oriented behaviors. The leader substitutes model suggests that sometimes managers do not have to play a leadership role because their employees perform at a high level without the manager's having to exert influence over them. [LO 10-3]

TRANSFORMATIONAL LEADERSHIP Transformational leadership occurs when managers have dramatic effects on their employees and on the organization as a whole and they inspire and energize employees to solve problems and improve performance. These effects include making employees aware of the importance of their own jobs and high performance; making employees aware of their own needs for personal growth, development, and accomplishment; and motivating employees to work for the good of the organization and not just their own personal gain. Managers can engage in transformational leadership by being charismatic leaders, by intellectually stimulating employees, and by engaging in developmental consideration. Transformational managers also often engage in transactional leadership by using their reward and coercive powers to encourage high performance. [LO 10-4]

GENDER AND LEADERSHIP Female and male managers do not differ in the leadership behaviors they perform, contrary to stereotypes suggesting that women are more relationship-oriented and men more task-oriented. Female managers sometimes are more participative than male managers, however. Research has found that women and men are equally effective as managers and leaders. [LO 10-5]

EMOTIONAL INTELLIGENCE AND LEADERSHIP The moods and emotions leaders experience on the job, and their ability to effectively manage these feelings, can influence their effectiveness as leaders. Moreover, emotional intelligence can contribute to leadership effectiveness in multiple ways, including encouraging and supporting creativity among followers. [LO 10-5]

Management *in Action*

Topics for Discussion and Action

Discussion

1. Describe the steps managers can take to increase their power and ability to be effective leaders. [LO 10-1]

2. Think of specific situations in which it might be especially important for a manager to engage in consideration and in initiating structure. [LO 10-2]

3. Discuss why managers might want to change the behaviors they engage in, given their situation, their employees, and the nature of the work being done. Do you think managers can readily change their leadership behaviors? Why or why not? [LO 10-3]

4. Discuss why substitutes for leadership can contribute to organizational effectiveness. [LO 10-3]

5. Describe what transformational leadership is, and explain how managers can engage in it. [LO 10-4]

6. Imagine that you are working in an organization in an entry-level position after graduation and have come up with what you think is a great idea for improving a critical process in the organization that relates to your job. In what ways might your supervisor encourage you to implement your idea? How might your supervisor

discourage you from even sharing your idea with others? [LO 10-4, 10-5]

Action

7. Interview a manager to find out how the three situational characteristics that Fiedler identified affect his or her ability to provide leadership. [LO 10-3]

8. Find a company that has dramatically turned around its fortunes and improved its performance. Determine whether a transformational manager was behind the turnaround and, if one was, what this manager did. [LO 10-4]

Building Management Skills

Analyzing Failures of Leadership [LO 10-1, 10-2, 10-3, 10-4]

Think about a situation you are familiar with in which a leader was very ineffective. Then answer the following questions:

1. What sources of power did this leader have? Did the leader have enough power to influence his or her followers?

2. What kinds of behaviors did this leader engage in? Were they appropriate for the situation? Why or why not?

3. From what you know, do you think this leader was a task-oriented leader or a relationship-oriented leader? How favorable was this leader's situation for leading?

4. What steps did this leader take to motivate his or her followers? Were these steps appropriate or inappropriate? Why?

5. What signs, if any, did this leader show of being a transformational leader?

Managing Ethically [LO 10-1]

Managers who verbally criticize their employees, put them down in front of their coworkers, or use the threat of job loss to influence behavior are exercising coercive power. Some employees subject to coercive power believe that using it is unethical.

Questions

1. Either alone or in a group, think about the ethical implications of the use of coercive power.

2. To what extent do managers and organizations have an ethical obligation to put limits on the amount of coercive power that is exercised?

Small Group Breakout Exercise [LO 10-1, 10-2, 10-3, 10-4]

Improving Leadership Effectiveness

Form groups of three to five people, and appoint one member as the spokesperson who will communicate your findings and conclusions to the class when called on by the instructor. Then discuss the following scenario:

You are a team of human resource consultants who have been hired by Carla Caruso, an entrepreneur who has started her own interior design business. A highly competent and creative interior designer, Caruso has established a working relationship with most of the major home builders in her community. At first she worked on her own as an independent contractor. Then because of a dramatic increase in the number of new homes being built, she became swamped with requests for her services and decided to start her own company.

She hired an assistant/bookkeeper and four interior designers, all of whom are highly competent. Caruso still does decorating jobs herself and has adopted a hands-off approach to leading the four interior designers who report to her, because she feels that interior design is a very personal, creative endeavor. Rather than pay the designers on some kind of commission basis (such as a percentage of their customers' total billings), she pays them a premium salary, higher than average, so they are motivated to do what's best for a customer's needs and not what will result in higher billings and commissions.

Caruso thought everything was going smoothly until customer complaints started coming in. The complaints ranged from the designers being hard to reach, promising unrealistic delivery times, and being late for or failing to keep appointments to their being impatient and rude when customers had trouble making up their minds. Caruso knows her designers are competent and is concerned that she is not effectively leading and managing them. She wonders, in particular, if her hands-off approach is to blame and if she should change the manner in which she rewards or pays her designers. She has asked for your advice.

1. Analyze the sources of power that Caruso has available to her to influence the designers. What advice can you give her to either increase her power base or use her existing power more effectively?

2. Given what you have learned in this chapter (for example, from the behavior model and path–goal theory), does Caruso seem to be performing appropriate leader behaviors in this situation? What advice can you give her about the kinds of behaviors she should perform?

3. What steps would you advise Caruso to take to increase the designers' motivation to deliver high-quality customer service?

4. Would you advise Caruso to try to engage in transformational leadership in this situation? If not, why not? If so, what steps would you advise her to take?

Be the Manager [LO 10-1, 10-2, 10-3, 10-4, 10-5]

You are the CEO of a medium-size company that makes window coverings such as blinds and shutters. Your company has a cost advantage in terms of being able to make custom window coverings at costs that are relatively low in the industry. However, the performance of your company has been lackluster. To make needed changes and improve performance, you met with the eight other top managers in your company and charged them with identifying problems and missed opportunities in each of their areas and coming up with action plans to address the problems and take advantage of opportunities.

Once you gave the managers the okay, they were charged with implementing their action plans in a timely fashion and monitoring the effects of their initiatives monthly for the next 8 to 12 months.

You approved each of the managers' action plans, and a year later most of the managers were reporting that their initiatives had been successful in addressing the problems and opportunities they had identified a year ago. However, overall company performance continues to be lackluster and shows no signs of improvement. You are confused and starting to question your leadership capabilities and approach to change. What are you going to do to improve the performance and effectiveness of your company?

Case in the News [LO 10-1, 10-2, 10-4]

CEO's Leadership Helps Levi Strauss Succeed

When Chip Bergh became CEO of Levi Strauss in 2011, he soon discovered that the company's financial condition was unexpected. After almost three decades of managing brands for Procter & Gamble, Bergh expected that an icon like Levi's would have greater financial strength. Levi's proudly notes that its work pants became the first blue jeans in 1873, when the company and its partner, Nevada tailor Jacob Davis, received a patent for Davis's idea to secure denim with rivets so the clothing would hold together under stress. Like the sturdy apparel itself, the brand has weathered the decades and developed a worldwide image associated with the freedom, hard work, and wide-open spaces of the American West. But sales at the privately held company, which had climbed to a peak of $7 billion in

1997, fell to $4.1 billion in 2002, after which they bumped along below $4.5 billion annually. Consumers respected the brand, but when shopping, they chose up-market brands or even yoga pants. Worse, when Bergh asked the company's top executives about their vision for the future, he found little evidence of a clear strategy or sense of urgency.

Bergh had joined Levi's to make a lasting difference, so he set about his work in earnest. First, he focused on listening, so he could identify what needed to change. He met one-on-one with the top 60 executives, which is how he discovered they had difficulty linking their areas of responsibility to the company's overall business strategy. He held a town hall meeting, where he learned that employees generally thought the company was doing fine, despite its mediocre results. And he traveled to meet customers, learning that despite management flaws, they still loved the jeans.

Bergh started replacing his executive team and working with the finance department to craft a growth strategy. Within six months, they had developed a four-part strategy. First, Levi's would maintain profitable operations of its core products: men's jeans and Dockers apparel, which brought in 80% percent of company profits, primarily from sales in the United States, France, Germany, Mexico, and the United Kingdom. Second, it would seek expansion where it had low market share—including women's clothing, especially tops—and sales in developing markets. Third, it would become a leader in "omnichannel" retailing—that is, selling on the company website and in its stores as well as through retailers. Finally, it would improve efficiency, which would help the company pay down its substantial debt. Early successes freed up enough money to open the Eureka Innovation Lab near Levi's San Francisco headquarters.

The Eureka Lab then contributed to the company's growth and efficiency objectives. Its people started by redesigning Levi's women's denim to make it more appealing in today's market, where casual clothing is more focused on comfort. Greater stretch and softness have boosted the sales of Levi's for women, yielding quarter after quarter of sales growth. More recently, the lab created Project FLX to automate the production of distressed jeans. The process consists of fully digital design combined with the programming of lasers to etch the design into each pair of jeans (rather than workers in factories using scraping and chemicals). This high-speed process lets the company get specific designs to market as fast as they are introduced and consumers make purchases.

As Bergh led the implementation of these changes, he was also changing himself—in particular, learning to manage the fast-paced product cycles of the fashion business and to understand the requirements of serving customers directly. At the same time, he found the biggest challenge was changing the organizational culture.

Levi Strauss's financial performance suggests the company is on a better course. Revenues have grown in each of Bergh's first five years, nearing $5 billion in 2017 and placing Levi's in the top slot for sales of jeans. Its market share in women's apparel is increasing, and international sales have surpassed domestic sales. On the omnichannel objective, the company has posted greater than 50% growth in sales via its website and company-owned stores, which offer better profit margins than do sales through retail chains. Efficiency has improved with the automation of production and other functions, even finance. The company has paid down debt to the point where it finally owns more than it owes. The National Retail Federation named Bergh the winner of its Visionary Award for 2019, signaling that his peers see him as a leader in creating positive change. Bergh's vision is now for Levi Strauss to increase revenues to $10 billion—the level he had expected when he signed on.

Questions for Discussion

1. What traits and behaviors do you think have helped Chip Bergh succeed as a leader at Levi Strauss?

2. When Bergh arrived at Levi Strauss, he identified a need for the organization to be transformed. Consider the kinds of changes transformational leadership brings about in a leader's employees. What are some challenges that Bergh faced in bringing about these changes?

3. If you had been coaching Bergh in how to be a transformational leader, what would you have suggested he do to bring about change in the organization's people and culture?

Sources: Levi Strauss, "Our Story," www.levistrauss.com, accessed January 25, 2019; D. Crouch, "Levi Strauss & Co. President and CEO Chip Bergh Named The Visionary 2019 by NRF," *Apparel News,* www.apparelnews.net, September 26, 2018; C. Bergh, "The CEO of Levi Strauss on Leading an Iconic Brand Back to Growth," *Harvard Business Review,* July–August 2018, 33–39; M. Bain, "The Simple Mantra That Helped Levi's Turn Its Business Around," *Quartz,* https://qz.com, May 1, 2018; E. Minaya, "Levi's CFO Turns to Robots to Help Keep the Books," *The Wall Street Journal,* https://blogs.wsj.com, April 11, 2018; A. Nusca, "Tablets, Lasers, and Time to Market: How Levi Strauss Reinvented the Way It Makes Jeans," *Fortune,* https://fortune.com, February 27, 2018; S. Kapner, "Levi's Wants Lasers, Not People, to Rip Your Jeans," *The Wall Street Journal,* www.wsj.com, February 27, 2018; S. Halzack, "How Levi's Thrives Despite the 'Death of Denim,'" *Bloomberg Businessweek,* www.bloomberg.com, February 8, 2018.

Endnotes

1. Dana-Farber Cancer Institute, "About Us," www.dana-farber.org, accessed January 19, 2019.

2. H. K. Gardner, "Getting Your Stars to Collaborate," *Harvard Business Review,* January–February 2017, 100–108.

3. Gardner, "Getting Your Stars to Collaborate."

4. Ibid.

5. J. Zehel, "Leaders of Innovation: Lesley Solomon of Dana-Farber Cancer Institute," *Redox,* www.redoxengine.com, accessed January 19, 2019; P. D. McCluskey, "Five Things You Should Know about Laurie Glimcher," *Boston Globe,* www.bostonglobe.com, April 28, 2017; M. Bailey, "Recruited to Lead Harvard Med, 'Fearless' Scientist Chose Dana-Farber," *Stat,* www.statnews.com, March 1, 2016.

6. G. Yukl, *Leadership in Organizations,* 2nd ed. (New York: Academic Press, 1989); R. M. Stogdill, *Handbook of Leadership: A Survey of the Literature* (New York: Free Press, 1974).

7. W. D. Spangler, R. J. House, and R. Palrecha, "Personality and Leadership," in B. Schneider and D. B. Smith, eds., *Personality and Organizations* (Mahwah, NJ: Erlbaum, 2004), 251–90.

8. Spangler, et al., "Personality and Leadership"; L. Ryan, "Management vs. Leadership: Five Ways They Are Different," *Forbes,* www.forbes.com, March 27, 2016; V. Nayar, "Three Differences between Managers and Leaders," *Harvard Business Review,* https://hbr.org, August 2, 2013.

9. Greenleaf Center for Servant Leadership, "Our History," www.greenleaf.org, accessed January 20, 2019.

10. Greenleaf Center for Servant Leadership, "What Is Servant Leadership?," www.greenleaf.org, accessed January 20, 2019; Review by F. Hamilton of L. Spears and M. Lawrence, *Practicing Servant Leadership: Succeeding through Trust, Bravery, and Forgiveness* (San Francisco: Jossey-Bass, 2004), in *Academy of Management Review* 30 (October 2005), 875–87; R. R. Washington, "Empirical Relationships between Theories of Servant, Transformational, and Transactional Leadership," *Academy of Management,* Best Paper Proceedings, 2007, 1–6.

11. M. Schwantes, "To Inspire and Influence Others, Make Sure to Do These 3 Things in 2018," *Inc.,* www.inc.com, January 3, 2018; J. E. Hoch, W. H. Bommer, J. H. Dulebohn, and D. Wu, "Do Ethical, Authentic, and Servant Leadership Explain Variance Above and Beyond Transformational Leadership? A Meta-Analysis," *Journal of Management,* http://journals.sagepub.com, August 31, 2016.

12. Greenleaf Center for Servant Leadership, "What Is Servant Leadership?"

13. B. Burlingham, "The Coolest Company in America," *Inc.,* www.inc.com, accessed January 20, 2019; "Zingerman's Community—Frequently Asked Questions," www.zingermanscommunity.com, accessed January 20, 2019; A. Weinzweig, "Step into the Future," *Inc.,* February 2011, 85–91.

14. D. Blitchok, "The Tao of Zingerman's, the Deli That Grew into a $62 Million Business: 'We Exist to Give People Better Lives,' " *Benzinga,* www.benzinga.com, July 17, 2017.

15. Burlingham, "The Coolest Small Company in America"; Zingerman's Community of Businesses"; L. Buchanan, "In Praise of Selflessness," *Inc.,* May 2007, 33–35.

16. Buchanan, "In Praise of Selflessness."

17. Ibid.

18. Burlingham, "The Coolest Small Company in America"; Food Gatherers, "Mission & History," www.foodgatherers.org, accessed January 20, 2019.

19. Ibid. Burlingham, "The Coolest Small Company in America."

20. Buchanan, "In Praise of Selflessness."

21. R. Calori and B. Dufour, "Management European Style," *Academy of Management Executive* 9, no. 3 (1995), 61–70.

22. Ibid.

23. H. Mintzberg, *Power in and around Organizations* (Englewood Cliffs, NJ: Prentice-Hall, 1983); J. Pfeffer, *Power in Organizations* (Marshfield, MA: Pitman, 1981).

24. R. P. French Jr., and B. Raven, "The Bases of Social Power," in D. Cartwright and A. F. Zander, eds., *Group Dynamics* (Evanston, IL: Row, Peterson, 1960), 607–23.

25. D. J. Chung, "How to Really Motivate Salespeople," *Harvard Business Review,* https://hbr.org, April 2015.

26. R. L. Rose, "After Turning Around Giddings and Lewis, Fife Is Turned Out Himself," *The Wall Street Journal,* June 22, 1993, A1.

27. M. Loeb, "Jack Welch Lets Fly on Budgets, Bonuses, and Buddy Boards," *Fortune,* May 29, 1995, 146.

28. A. Lee, S. Willis, and A. W. Tian, "When Empowering Employees Works, and When It Doesn't," *Harvard Business Review,* https://hbr.org, March 2, 2018.

29. L. Nakarmi, "A Flying Leap toward the 21st Century? Pressure from Competitors and Seoul May Transform the Chaebol," *BusinessWeek,* March 20, 1995, 78–80.

30. B. M. Bass, *Bass and Stogdill's Handbook of Leadership: Theory, Research, and Managerial Applications,* 3rd ed. (New York: Free Press, 1990); R. J. House and M. L. Baetz, "Leadership: Some Empirical Generalizations and New Research Directions," in B. M. Staw and L. L. Cummings, eds., *Research in Organizational Behavior,* vol. 1 (Greenwich, CT: JAI Press, 1979), 341–423; S. A. Kirpatrick and E. A. Locke, "Leadership: Do Traits Matter?," *Academy of Management Executive* 5, no. 2 (1991), 48–60; Yukl, *Leadership in Organizations;* G. Yukl and D. D. Van Fleet, "Theory and Research on Leadership in Organizations," in M. D. Dunnette and L. M. Hough,

eds., *Handbook of Industrial and Organizational Psychology,* 2nd ed., vol. 3 (Palo Alto, CA: Consulting Psychologists Press, 1992), 147–97.

31. E. A. Fleishman, "Performance Assessment Based on an Empirically Derived Task Taxonomy," *Human Factors* 9 (1967), 349–66; E. A. Fleishman, "The Description of Supervisory Behavior," *Personnel Psychology* 37 (1953), 1–6; A. W. Halpin and B. J. Winer, "A Factorial Study of the Leader Behavior Descriptions," in R. M. Stogdill and A. I. Coons, eds., *Leader Behavior: Its Description and Measurement* (Columbus Bureau of Business Research, Ohio State University, 1957); D. Tscheulin, "Leader Behavior Measurement in German Industry," *Journal of Applied Psychology* 56 (1971), 28–31.

32. E. A. Fleishman and E. F. Harris, "Patterns of Leadership Behavior Related to Employee Grievances and Turnover," *Personnel Psychology* 15 (1962), 43–56.

33. F. E. Fiedler, *A Theory of Leadership Effectiveness* (New York: McGraw-Hill, 1967); F. E. Fiedler, "The Contingency Model and the Dynamics of the Leadership Process," in L. Berkowitz, ed., *Advances in Experimental Social Psychology* (New York: Academic Press, 1978).

34. "Geraldine Laybourne," https://allwomeninmedia.org, accessed January 19, 2019; J. Fierman, "Winning Ideas from Maverick Managers," *Fortune,* February 6, 1995, 66–80.

35. "Who Is Herman Mashaba?," www.enca.com, accessed January 19, 2019; M. Schuman, "Free to Be," *Forbes,* May 8, 1995, 78–80.

36. House and Baetz, "Leadership"; L. H. Peters, D. D. Hartke, and J. T. Pohlmann, "Fiedler's Contingency Theory of Leadership: An Application of the Meta-Analysis Procedures of Schmidt and Hunter," *Psychological Bulletin* 97 (1985), 274–85; C. A. Schriesheim, B. J. Tepper, and L. A. Tetrault, "Least Preferred Co-Worker Score, Situational Control, and Leadership Effectiveness: A Meta-Analysis of Contingency Model

Performance Predictions," *Journal of Applied Psychology* 79 (1994), 561–73.

37. E. Meyer, "Being the Boss in Brussels, Boston, and Beijing," *Harvard Business Review,* July–August 2017, 70–77.

38. Ibid., 75–77.

39. A. Ghannad, "The Simple Key to Cross-Cultural Leadership," Association for Talent Development blog, www.td.org, February 5, 2018; J. Owen, "How to Be a Global Leader," *Director,* November 2017, 56–57.

40. M. G. Evans, "The Effects of Supervisory Behavior on the Path–Goal Relationship," *Organizational Behavior and Human Performance* 5 (1970), 277–98; R. J. House, "A Path–Goal Theory of Leader Effectiveness," *Administrative Science Quarterly* 16 (1971), 321–38; J. C. Wofford and L. Z. Liska, "Path–Goal Theories of Leadership: A Meta-Analysis," *Journal of Management* 19 (1993), 857–76.

41. S. Kerr and J. M. Jermier, "Substitutes for Leadership: Their Meaning and Measurement," *Organizational Behavior and Human Performance* 22 (1978), 375–403; P. M. Podsakoff, B. P. Niehoff, S. B. MacKenzie, and M. L. Williams, "Do Substitutes for Leadership Really Substitute for Leadership? An Empirical Examination of Kerr and Jermier's Situational Leadership Model," *Organizational Behavior and Human Decision Processes* 54 (1993), 1–44.

42. Kerr and Jermier, "Substitutes for Leadership"; Podsakoff et al., "Do Substitutes for Leadership Really Substitute for Leadership?"

43. J. B. Carson, P. E. Tesluk, and J. A. Marrone, "Shared Leadership in Teams: An Investigation of Antecedent Conditions and Performance," *Academy of Management Journal* 50, no. 5 (2007), 1217–34.

44. J. Luce, "Lessons Learned by Customer Service Expert Sue Nokes," http://medium.com, November 20, 2017; J. Reingold, "You Got Served," *Fortune,* October 1, 2007, 55–58.

45. Reingold, "You Got Served."

46. Ibid.; "Company Information"; "Highest Customer Satisfaction & Wireless Call Quality—J.D. Power Awards," http://www.t-mobile.com/Company/CompanyInfo.aspx?tp5Abt_Tab_Awards, April 8, 2008.

47. Reingold, "You Got Served."

48. B. M. Bass, *Leadership and Performance beyond Expectations* (New York: Free Press, 1985); Bass, *Bass and Stogdill's Handbook of Leadership;* Yukl and Van Fleet, "Theory and Research on Leadership."

49. Reingold, "You Got Served."

50. Ibid.

51. S. Patel, "The 5 Characteristics That Make a Charismatic Leader," *Entrepreneur,* www.entrepreneur.com, accessed January 20, 2019.

52. Bass, *Leadership and Performance beyond Expectations;* Bass, *Bass and Stogdill's Handbook of Leadership;* Yukl and Van Fleet, "Theory and Research on Leadership"; Reingold, "You Got Served."

53. Ibid.

54. Reingold, "You Got Served."

55. Bass, *Leadership and Performance beyond Expectations.*

56. Bass, *Bass and Stogdill's Handbook of Leadership;* B. M. Bass and B. J. Avolio, "Transformational Leadership: A Response to Critiques," in M. M. Chemers and R. Ayman, eds., *Leadership Theory and Research: Perspectives and Directions* (San Diego: Academic Press, 1993), 49–80; B. M. Bass, B. J. Avolio, and L. Goodheim, "Biography and the Assessment of Transformational Leadership at the World Class Level," *Journal of Management* 13 (1987), 7–20; J. J. Hater and B. M. Bass, "Supervisors' Evaluations and Subordinates' Perceptions of Transformational and Transactional Leadership," *Journal of Applied Psychology* 73 (1988), 695–702; R. Pillai, "Crisis and Emergence of Charismatic Leadership in Groups: An Experimental Investigation," *Journal of Applied Psychology* 26 (1996), 543–62; J. Seltzer and B. M. Bass, "Transformational Leadership: Beyond Initiation

and Consideration," *Journal of Management* 16 (1990), 693–703; D. A. Waldman, B. M. Bass, and W. O. Einstein, "Effort, Performance, Transformational Leadership in Industrial and Military Service," *Journal of Occupation Psychology* 60 (1987), 1–10.

57. R. Pillai, C. A. Schriesheim, and E. S. Williams, "Fairness Perceptions and Trust as Mediators of Transformational and Transactional Leadership: A Two-Sample Study," *Journal of Management* 25 (1999), 897–933; "About Us," HP, http://www8. hp.com/us/en/hp-information/ about-hp/index.html, May 14, 2012.

58. S. Gharib, "Hershey's CEO on Professional Growth and Women in Business," *Fortune,* http://fortune. com, accessed January 20, 2019; J. Carpenter, "This Is What Women Have to Do to Become CEO," *CNNMoney,* http://money.cnn.com, February 1, 2018.

59. Catalyst, "Pyramid: Women in S&P 500 Companies," www.catalyst.org, accessed January 20, 2019.

60. A. H. Eagly and B. T. Johnson, "Gender and Leadership Style: A Meta-Analysis," *Psychological Bulletin* 108 (1990), 233–56.

61. Ibid.

62. V. Lipman, "Are Women Better Managers Than Men?," *Psychology Today,* www.psychologytoday.com, April 23, 2015.

63. J. Baldoni, "Few Executives Are Self-Aware, but Women Have the Edge," *Harvard Business Review,* https://hbr.org, May 9, 2013.

64. Ibid.

65. A. H. Eagly, S. J. Karau, and M. G. Makhijani, "Gender and the Effectiveness of Leaders: A Meta-Analysis," *Psychological Bulletin* 117 (1995), 125–45.

66. Ibid.

67. J. M. George and K. Bettenhausen, "Understanding Prosocial Behavior, Sales Performance, and Turnover: A Group-Level Analysis in a Service Context," *Journal of Applied Psychology* 75 (1990), 698–709.

68. T. Sy, S. Cote, and R. Saavedra, "The Contagious Leader: Impact of the Leader's Mood on the Mood of Group Members, Group Affective Tone, and Group Processes," *Journal of Applied Psychology* 90, no. 2, (2005), 295–305.

69. J. M. George, "Emotions and Leadership: The Role of Emotional Intelligence," *Human Relations* 53 (2000), 1027–55.

70. Ibid.

71. J. Zhou and J. M. George, "Awakening Employee Creativity: The Role of Leader Emotional Intelligence," *The Leadership Quarterly* 14, no. 45 (August–October 2003), 545–68.

72. Ibid.

73. Ibid.

74. J. Garfinkle, "Five Qualities of Emotionally Intelligent Leaders," *Smart Brief,* www.smartbrief. com, January 15, 2018; B. Tracy, "Why Emotional Intelligence Is Indispensable for Leaders," *Forbes,* October 30, 2017, www.forbes.com; S. T. A. Phipps, "Why Emotional Intelligence Is Necessary for Effective Leadership," *Leadership Excellence Essentials,* June 2017, 56–57.

75. Garfinkle, "Five Qualities"; S. Bawany, "The Art and Practice of Servant Leadership," *Leadership Excellence Essentials,* November 2017, 34–35.

76. M. Prokopeak, "Building the Leader of the Future," *Chief Learning Officer,* www.clomedia. com, March 22, 2018.

77. S. Goldstein, "EQ Is Massively More Important Than IQ for Leaders. Here's Why," *Inc.,* www .inc.com, September 26, 2017.

El Nariz/Shutterstock

11 Effective Team Management

Learning Objectives

After studying this chapter, you should be able to:

LO 11-1 Explain why groups and teams are key contributors to organizational effectiveness.

LO 11-2 Identify the different types of groups and teams that help managers and organizations achieve their goals.

LO 11-3 Explain how different elements of group dynamics influence the functioning and effectiveness of groups and teams.

LO 11-4 Explain why it is important for groups and teams to have a balance of conformity and deviance and a moderate level of cohesiveness.

LO 11-5 Describe how managers can motivate group members to achieve organizational goals and reduce social loafing in groups and teams.

Management Snapshot

Leading the Army's Battle against Red Tape

How Can Managers Use Teams to Enhance Performance?

When it comes to technology and the development of new weapons, the worst enemy of the U.S. Army is its slow-moving layers of bureaucracy. When the army identifies a need, the process of creating specifications and designing a new product can take several years—so long, that by the time the product is available, it is no longer considered advanced technology. The edge the army wants to maintain over any adversaries is all but wiped out.[1]

The army's leadership identified a solution involving teamwork. Specifically, it set up a Futures Command that identified eight areas in which development is crucial: long-range precision fires; a next-generation combat vehicle; improvement in lift capacity for aircraft; a data and communications network; air and missile defenses; and advances in soldier performance. For each, the command set up a team bringing together members from different functions, including planning, science and technology, finance, program management, testing, and materials. Each team is led by a one- or two-star officer with combat experience. The teams collectively report to Under Secretary of the Army Ryan D. McCarthy and Army Vice Chief of Staff Gen. James C. McConville,

whose positions give them authority to allocate major resources.[2]

The team process benefits from accelerated learning from experimentation, prototyping, and adaptation. Instead of trying to design a perfect project with requirements for all possible features, the team develops an idea, perhaps using off-the-shelf systems, and goes straight to the prototype stage. This involves bringing in soldiers to test the prototype, which increases their support and gives them an opportunity to deliver feedback from a user's perspective. Through all of this, the team is learning and adapting the idea, based on test results and the soldiers' feedback. In some cases, it might begin producing a less-than-full-featured product as a best option while it continues the development process to improve requirements for the final version.[3]

For example, the cross-functional team responsible for tactical networks is working to bring out a system that will survive modern-day threats like cyberattacks. The team is pressing for faster purchases of prototypes and more frequent feedback from soldiers, so the system design can be improved faster. This enables the team to create better requirements than if designers worked on their own. Another team, charged with updating the system for position, navigation, and timing, is working on several areas for improvement. It is rolling out upgrades to solve urgent needs as the system

Under Secretary of the U.S. Army, Ryan D. McCarthy, believes effective teamwork within the military spurs innovation and reduces bureaucracy.
Source: United States Army

moves forward, rather than waiting to deploy a system that would theoretically be perfect.[4]

Early results suggest that teamwork is a success. Among the most dramatic results is acceleration of the pace of work. McCarthy sees evidence that the kinds of decisions that used to wend their way up and down the hierarchy over a period of months now get done in a few days. In addition, he notes, years are being shaved off the

overall process, which in the past could take a decade to complete. New night-vision goggles are ready for distribution just one year after being proposed. Development of a long-range precision artillery missile is advancing at a pace that could lead to completion five years ahead of schedule. Further, McCarthy notes that the more extensive prototyping and testing are yielding better decisions about where to spend money and how to improve products.[5]

Overview

The U.S. Army is not alone in using groups and teams to innovate and improve organizational effectiveness. Managers in companies large and small are using groups and teams to enhance performance, increase responsiveness to customers, spur innovation, and motivate employees. In this chapter we look in detail at how groups and teams can contribute to organizational effectiveness and the types of groups and teams used in organizations. We discuss how different elements of group dynamics influence the functioning and effectiveness of groups, and we describe how managers can motivate group members to achieve organizational goals and reduce social loafing in groups and teams. By the end of this chapter you will appreciate why the effective management of groups and teams is a key ingredient in organizational performance and effectiveness.

Groups, Teams, and Organizational Effectiveness

A **group** may be defined as two or more people who interact with each other to accomplish certain goals or meet certain needs.[6] A **team** is a group whose members work *intensely* with one another to achieve a specific common goal or objective. As these definitions imply, all teams are groups, but not all groups are teams. The two characteristics that distinguish teams from groups are the *intensity* with which team members work together and the presence of a *specific, overriding team goal or objective.*

LO 11-1
Explain why groups and teams are key contributors to organizational effectiveness.

Recall some of the goals of the army's teams highlighted in the "Management Snapshot." In contrast, the accountants who work in a small CPA firm are a group: They may interact with one another to achieve goals such as keeping up to date on the latest changes in accounting rules and regulations, maintaining a smoothly functioning office, satisfying clients, and attracting new clients, but they are not a team because they do not work intensely with one another. Each accountant concentrates on serving the needs of his or her own clients.

group Two or more people who interact with each other to accomplish certain goals or meet certain needs.

Because all teams are also groups, whenever we use the term *group* in this chapter, we are referring to both groups *and* teams. As you might imagine, because members of teams work intensely together, teams can sometimes be difficult to form, and it may take time for members to learn how to work effectively together. Under these conditions, for team development and performance to succeed, team members need to develop "soft" skills, as described in the "Management Insight" feature.

Management Insight

Team Members Need Soft Skills

Teams are often formed for challenging activities: developing products, rolling out software systems, or planning a marketing campaign. These require the expertise of engineers, software developers, marketing researchers, finance professionals, and others. In addition to this technical expertise, all teams require "soft" skills. These are the people-related skills that get team members connected with each other and aligned on carrying out a shared purpose. Soft skills include organizing, collaborating, solving interpersonal problems, and communicating (speaking, writing, and above all, listening).[7]

On teams with soft skills, members share ideas, pool their knowledge to solve problems, and keep each other updated on their progress. People are unafraid to make mistakes, are open to learning from one another, and listen to one another's ideas. Team members with soft skills benefit the team by connecting with the rest of the organization to gather information and other resources. These individuals bring out other members' ideas and get them motivated.[8]

However, soft skills are hard to measure, so it is difficult to select job candidates with soft skills. Furthermore, employers struggle to teach these skills. A recruiting manager for the Motley Fool, a media company focused on investing, recalls interviewing a candidate whose technical skills were so impressive that she did not fully explore the candidate's soft skills. The company made the hire but has since needed to intervene a great deal to make up for the person's lack of focus on teamwork.[9]

The first and most important way to form teams with soft skills is to hire people who have those skills or at least have shown potential to develop them. This requires identifying which soft skills will contribute to the team's success and developing questions that ask job candidates to describe situations in which they have used or would use the particular skills. Commercially available tests can screen for particular qualities such as empathy or emotional intelligence. Other tests measure individual differences such as problem-solving styles. Team leaders can be taught to use information from these tests to ensure that each person is contributing effectively according to his or her style.[10]

In addition, training should address development of soft skills. It should extend beyond classroom or coaching sessions by assigning behaviors to practice and situations in which to practice them. Along with training, the employee should have measurable goals such as giving presentations or restructuring meetings to ensure all voices are heard.[11] ●

team A group whose members work intensely with one another to achieve a specific common goal or objective.

Groups and teams can help an organization gain a competitive advantage because they can (1) enhance its performance, (2) increase its responsiveness to customers, (3) increase innovation, and (4) increase employees' motivation and satisfaction (see Figure 11.1). In this section we look at each of these contributions in turn.

Figure 11.1

Groups' and Teams' Contributions to Organizational Effectiveness

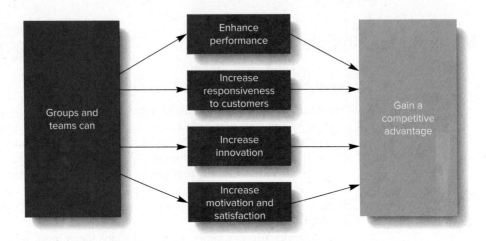

Groups and Teams as Performance Enhancers

synergy Performance gains that result when individuals and departments coordinate their actions.

One of the main advantages of using groups is the opportunity to obtain a type of synergy: People working in a group can produce more or higher-quality outputs than would have been produced if each person had worked separately and all their individual efforts were later combined. The essence of synergy is captured in the saying "The whole is more than the sum of its parts." Factors that can contribute to synergy in groups include the abilities of group members to bounce ideas off one another, to correct one another's mistakes, to solve problems immediately as they arise, to bring a diverse knowledge base to bear on a problem or goal, and to accomplish work that is too vast or all-encompassing for any individual to achieve alone.

To take advantage of the potential for synergy in groups, managers need to make sure that groups are composed of members who have complementary skills and knowledge relevant to the group's work. For example, at Hallmark Cards, synergies are created by bringing together all the different functions needed to create and produce a greeting card in a cross-functional team (a team composed of members from different departments or functions). For instance, artists, writers, designers, and marketing experts work together as team members to develop new cards.[12]

At Hallmark the skills and expertise of the artists complement the contributions of the writers and vice versa. Managers also need to give groups enough autonomy so that the groups, rather than the manager, are solving problems and determining how to achieve goals and objectives, as is true in the cross-functional teams at Hallmark. To promote synergy, managers need to empower their employees and to be coaches, guides, and resources for groups while refraining from playing a more directive or supervisory role. The potential for synergy in groups may be one reason why more managers are incorporating empowerment into their personal leadership styles (see Chapter 10).

Groups, Teams, and Responsiveness to Customers

Being responsive to customers is not always easy. In manufacturing organizations, for example, customers' needs and desires for new and improved products have to be balanced against engineering constraints, production costs and feasibilities, government safety regulations, and marketing challenges. In service organizations such as health care organizations, being responsive to patients' needs and desires for prompt, high-quality medical care and treatment has to be balanced against meeting physicians' needs and desires and keeping health care costs under control. Being responsive to customers often requires the wide variety of skills and expertise found in different departments and at different levels in an organization's hierarchy. Sometimes, for example, employees at lower levels in an organization's hierarchy, such as sales representatives for a software company, are closest to its customers and the most attuned to their needs. However, lower-level employees, like salespeople, often lack the technical expertise needed for new product ideas; such expertise is found in the research and development department. Bringing salespeople, research and development experts, and members of other departments together in a group or cross-functional team can enhance responsiveness to customers. Consequently, when managers form a team, they must make sure the diversity of expertise and knowledge needed to be responsive to customers exists within the team; this is why cross-functional teams are so popular.

In a cross-functional team, the expertise and knowledge in different organizational departments are brought together in the skills and knowledge of the team members. Managers of high-performing organizations are careful to determine which types of expertise and knowledge are required for teams to be responsive to customers, and they use this information in forming teams.

Teams and Innovation

Innovation—the creative development of new products, new technologies, new services, or even new organizational structures—is a topic we introduced in Chapter 1. Often an individual working alone does not possess the extensive and diverse skills, knowledge, and expertise required for successful innovation. Managers can better encourage innovation by creating teams of diverse individuals who together have the knowledge relevant to a particular type of innovation—as is the case with the U.S. Army's Futures Command teams described in the "Management Snapshot"—rather than by relying on individuals working alone.

Using teams to innovate has other advantages. First, team members can often uncover one another's errors or false assumptions; an individual acting alone would not be able to do this. Second, team members can critique one another's approaches and build off one another's strengths while compensating for weaknesses—an advantage of devil's advocacy discussed in Chapter 5.

To further promote innovation, managers can empower teams and make their members fully responsible and accountable for the innovation process. The manager's role is to provide guidance, assistance, coaching, and the resources that team members need, *not* to closely direct or supervise their activities. To speed innovation, managers also need to form teams in which each member brings a unique resource to the team, such as engineering prowess, knowledge of production, marketing expertise, or financial savvy. Successful innovation sometimes requires that managers form teams with members from different countries and cultures.

Groups and Teams as Motivators

Managers often form groups and teams to accomplish organizational goals and then find that using groups and teams brings additional benefits. Members of groups, and especially members of teams (because of the higher intensity of interaction in teams), are likely to be more satisfied than they would have been if they had been on their own. The experience of working alongside other highly charged and motivated people can be stimulating and motivating: Team members can see how their efforts and expertise directly contribute to the achievement of team and organizational goals, and they feel personally responsible for the outcomes or results of their work. This has been the case at Hallmark Cards.

The increased motivation and satisfaction that can accompany the use of teams can also lead to other outcomes, such as lower turnover. This has been Frank B. Day's experience as founder of Rock Bottom Restaurants Inc.[13] To provide high-quality customer service, Day organized the restaurants' employees into waitstaff teams, whose members work together to refill beers, take orders, deliver food to the tables, or clear off the tables. Team members share the burden of undesirable activities and unpopular shift times, and customers no longer have to wait until a particular server is available. Motivation and satisfaction levels in Rock Bottom restaurants seem to be higher than in other restaurants, and turnover has been less than experienced in other U.S. restaurant chains.[14]

Working in a group or team can also satisfy organizational members' needs for engaging in social interaction and feeling connected to other people. For workers who perform highly stressful jobs, such as hospital emergency and operating room staff, group membership can be an important source of social support and motivation. Family members or friends may not be able to fully understand or appreciate some sources of work stress that these group members experience firsthand. Moreover, group members may cope better with work stressors when they can share them with other members of their group. In addition, groups often devise techniques to relieve stress, such as telling jokes among hospital operating room staff.

Why do managers in all kinds of organizations rely so heavily on groups and teams? Effectively managed groups and teams can help managers in their quest for high performance, responsiveness to customers, and employee motivation. Before explaining how managers can effectively manage groups, however, we will describe the types of groups that are formed in organizations.

Types of Groups and Teams

To achieve their goals of high performance, responsiveness to customers, innovation, and employee motivation, managers can form various types of groups and teams (see Figure 11.2). Formal groups are those that managers establish to achieve organizational goals. The formal work groups are *cross-functional* teams composed of members from different departments, such as those at Hallmark Cards, and *cross-cultural* teams composed of members from different cultures or countries, such as the teams at global carmakers. As you will see, some of the groups discussed in this section also can be considered to be cross-functional (if they are composed of members from different departments) or cross-cultural (if they are composed of members from different countries or cultures).

Sometimes organizational members, managers or nonmanagers, form groups because they feel that groups will help them achieve their own goals or meet their own needs (e.g., the need for social interaction). Groups formed in this way are informal groups. For example, four nurses who work in a hospital and have lunch together twice a week constitute an informal group.

LO 11-2
Identify the different types of groups and teams that help managers and organizations achieve their goals.

formal group
A group that managers establish to achieve organizational goals.

Figure 11.2

Types of Groups and Teams in Organizations

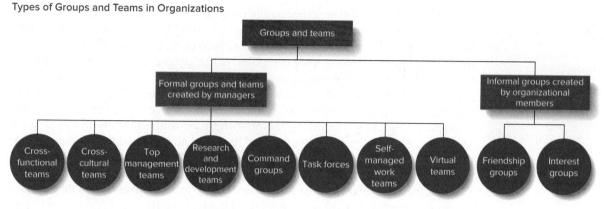

The Top Management Team

A central concern of the CEO and president of a company is to form a top management team to help the organization achieve its mission and goals. Top management teams are responsible for developing the strategies that result in an organization's competitive advantage; most have between five and seven members. In forming their top management teams, CEOs are well advised to stress diversity in expertise, skills, knowledge, and experience. Thus, many top management teams are also cross-functional teams: They are composed of members from different departments, such as finance, marketing, production, and engineering. Diversity helps ensure that the top management team will have all the background and resources it needs to make good decisions. Diversity also helps guard against *groupthink*—faulty group decision making that results when group members strive for agreement at the expense of an accurate assessment of the situation (see Chapter 5).

Research and Development Teams

Managers in pharmaceuticals, computers, electronics, electronic imaging, and other high-tech industries often create research and development teams to develop new products. Managers select research and development (R&D) team members on the basis of their expertise and experience in a certain area. Sometimes R&D teams are cross-functional, with members from departments such as engineering, marketing, and production in addition to members from the research and development department.

Command Groups

Employees who report to the same supervisor compose a command group. When top managers design an organization's structure and establish reporting relationships and a chain of command, they are essentially creating command groups. Command groups, often called *departments* or *units,* perform a significant amount of the work in many organizations. In order to have command groups that help an organization gain a competitive advantage, managers not only need to motivate group members to perform at a high level but also must be effective leaders.

Task Forces

Managers form task forces to accomplish specific goals or solve problems in a certain time period; task forces are sometimes called *ad hoc committees*. For example, Michael Rider, owner and top manager of a chain of six gyms and fitness centers in the Midwest, created a task force composed of the general managers of the six gyms to determine whether the fitness centers should institute a separate fee schedule for customers who wanted to use the centers only for exercise (and not use other facilities such as weights and swimming pools). The task force was given three months to prepare a report summarizing the pros and cons of the proposed change in fee schedules. After the task force completed its report and reached the conclusion that the change in fee structure probably would reduce revenues rather than increase them and thus should not be implemented, the task force was disbanded. As in Rider's case, task forces can be a valuable tool for busy managers who do not have the time to personally explore an important issue in depth.

Self-Managed Work Teams

Self-managed work teams are teams in which members are empowered and have the responsibility and autonomy to complete identifiable pieces of work. On a day-to-day basis, team members decide what the team will do, how it will do it, and which members will perform which specific tasks.[15] Managers can assign self-managed work teams' overall goals (such as assembling defect-free computer keyboards) but let team members decide how to meet those goals. Managers usually form self-managed work teams to improve quality, increase motivation and satisfaction, and lower costs. Often, by creating self-managed work teams, they combine tasks that individuals working separately used to perform, so the team is responsible for the whole set of tasks that yields an identifiable output or end product.

Managers can take a number of steps to ensure that self-managed work teams are effective and help an organization achieve its goals:[16]

- Give teams enough responsibility and autonomy to be truly self-managing. Refrain from telling team members what to do or solving problems for them, even if you (as a manager) know what should be done.

- Make sure a team's work is sufficiently complex so that it entails a number of different steps or procedures that must be performed and results in some kind of finished end product.

- Carefully select members of self-managed work teams. Team members should have the diversity of skills needed to complete the team's work, have the ability to work with others, and want to be part of a team.

- As a manager, realize that your role with self-managed work teams calls for guidance, coaching, and supporting, not supervising. You are a resource for teams to turn to when needed.

- Analyze what type of training team members need, and provide it. Working in a self-managed work team often requires that employees have more extensive technical and interpersonal skills.

Managers in a wide variety of organizations have found that self-managed work teams help the organization achieve its goals, as illustrated in the accompanying "Management Insight" feature.

Management Insight

Self-Managed Teams Key to Gore's Success

As a member of small R&D teams at DuPont, Bill Gore experienced firsthand how inspiring and motivating it can be to work on a self-managed team with the mission to create and develop innovative products—and the autonomy to do so. He reasoned that innovation and high motivation and performance would likely result when as many people as possible in an organization were working together and given the ability to manage their own work. And that is what he and his wife set out to do by founding W. L. Gore & Associates more than 60 years ago.[17]

Widely recognized for its diverse and innovative products, Gore has more than $3 billion in revenues and more than 9,500 employees (called associates) worldwide. Headquartered in Newark, Delaware, Gore's most widely recognized product is the waterproof and breathable fabric Gore-Tex. The company makes a wide array of products, including fabrics for outerwear, medical products used in surgeries, fibers for astronauts' space suits, and even Elixir strings for guitars. While Gore has thousands of products and more than 2,000 worldwide patents, most of its products are based on a very adaptable polymer (ePTFE), invented by the Gores' son in 1969.[18]

While Gore has a CEO (currently Jason Field) and four divisions (electronics, fabrics, industrial, and medical), there are very few managers, and associates do not have supervisors. The company is structured around a lattice of self-managed teams in which associates and their colleagues communicate directly with each other whenever the need or desire arises. Their mission is to innovate, to perform at a high level, and to enjoy their work.[19] For example, a team of empowered manufacturing associates realized that new manufacturing equipment was needed to produce products in the United States that had been previously made overseas, which had resulted in operational inefficiencies. The manufacturing team gathered information from other teams to develop specifications for the new machinery and negotiated with an outside supplier to build the $2 million worth of equipment.[20]

Using self-managed teams has helped Gore develop many innovative products, including Gore-Tex, its waterproof and breathable fabric. Ruaridh Stewart/ZUMA Press, Inc./Alamy Stock Photo

At Gore, associates recognize leaders who are especially adept at building great teams and accomplishing strategic goals, and the associates willingly become their followers. New hires are assigned into broad areas of the company, such as R&D, engineering, sales, technology, HR, and operations management, and assigned a sponsor. Sponsors are experienced associates who help newcomers learn the ropes, meet other associates, and become acquainted with Gore's unique culture and values centered around trust and motivation. Ultimately, sponsors help the new employees find a team for which they are a good fit. The teams are truly self-managing, so it is up to team members to decide whether they want newcomers to join them. Experienced associates are typically members of multiple self-managed teams.[21]

Because associates are responsible to each other and their teams, it should not be surprising to learn that associates and their performance are reviewed by their peers. Each year information is gathered from around 20 colleagues of each associate and given to a compensation committee within their work unit that determines relative contributions and compensation levels for members of the unit.[22]

One of the largest privately held U.S. companies, W. L. Gore is owned by company associates as well as the Gore family. Associates are awarded a percentage of their salary in shares of the company and participate in a profit-sharing program. The shares become vested after a certain period of time, and associates who leave the company can sell back their shares for cash payouts.[23]

Associates thrive in Gore's collaborative and team-based structure. Thus, it is not surprising to learn that Gore has received recognition for being a top employer year after year. The company has been on *Fortune* magazine's list of the "100 Best Companies to Work For" for 20 consecutive years—recognition shared only by 11 other companies.[24] ●

Sometimes employees have individual jobs but also are part of a self-managed team that is formed to accomplish a specific goal or work on an important project. Employees need to perform their own individual job tasks as well as actively contribute to the self-managed team so that the team achieves its goal.

Like all groups, self-managed teams can sometimes run into trouble. Members may be reluctant to discipline one another by firing members or withholding bonuses from members who are not performing up to par.[25] Buster Jarrell, a manager who oversaw self-managed work teams in AES Corporation's Houston plant, found that although the self-managed work teams were highly effective, they had a difficult time firing team members who were performing poorly.[26]

Virtual Teams

Virtual teams are teams whose members rarely or never meet face to face but, rather, interact by using various forms of information technology such as email, text messaging, collaborative software programs, videoconferences, and various meeting and management apps. As organizations become increasingly global, and as the need for specialized knowledge increases due to advances in technology, managers can create virtual teams to solve problems or explore opportunities without being limited by team members' needing to work in the same geographic location.[27]

Take the case of an organization that has manufacturing facilities in Australia, Canada, the United States, and Mexico and is encountering a quality problem in a complex manufacturing process. Each of its facilities has a quality control team headed by a quality control manager. The vice president for production does not try to solve the problem by forming and leading a team at one of the four manufacturing facilities; instead, she forms and leads a virtual team composed of the quality control managers of the four plants and the plants' general managers. When these team members communicate via email, the company's networking site, and videoconferencing, a wide array of knowledge and experience is brought together to solve the problem.

The principal advantage of virtual teams is that they enable managers to disregard geographic distances and form teams whose members have the knowledge, expertise, and experience to tackle a particular problem or take advantage of a specific opportunity.[28] Virtual teams also can include members who are not actually

Virtual teams enable managers to disregard geographic distances and form teams whose members have the knowledge and expertise to tackle a particular problem. Videoconferencing helps virtual teams stay connected. Andrey_Popov/Shutterstock

employees of the organization itself; a virtual team might include members of a company that is used for outsourcing. More and more companies, including SAP, Ultimate Software, and GE, are using virtual teams.[29]

Increasing globalization is likely to result in more organizations relying on virtual teams to a greater extent. One challenge that members of virtual teams face is building a sense of camaraderie and trust among team members who rarely, if ever, meet face to face. In fact, recent research suggests that the link between trust and team effectiveness was even stronger for virtual teams than for teams that work in the same location. This finding underscores the need for managers of virtual teams to focus on building trust among team members.[30] To address this challenge, some organizations schedule recreational activities, such as ski trips, so virtual team members can get together. Other organizations make sure virtual team members have a chance to meet in person soon after the team is formed and then schedule periodic face-to-face meetings to promote trust, understanding, and cooperation in the teams.[31] The need for such meetings is underscored by research suggesting that while some virtual teams can be as effective as teams that meet face to face, virtual team members might be less satisfied with teamwork efforts and have fewer feelings of camaraderie or cohesion. (Group cohesiveness is discussed in more detail later in the chapter.)[32]

Not surprisingly, members of successful virtual teams exhibit certain skills and abilities that help make these "long-distance" groups so effective. Researchers point out that leadership behaviors such as taking personal initiative and working independently are more beneficial to virtual teams than to teams that work face to face on a daily basis. In addition, studies point out that members' strong analytical and written communication skills provide competitive advantage to a company's virtual teams. These findings suggest that managers hiring employees for virtual teams might focus on some of these specific skills that have proved successful.[33]

Research also suggests that it is important for managers to keep track of virtual teams and intervene when necessary by, for example, encouraging members of teams who do not communicate often enough to monitor their team's progress and making sure team members actually have the time, and are recognized, for their virtual teamwork. Additionally, when virtual teams are experiencing downtime or rough spots, managers might try to schedule face-to-face team time to bring team members together and help them focus on their goals.[34]

Researchers at the London Business School, including Professor Lynda Gratton, studied global virtual teams to try to identify factors that might help such teams be effective. Based on their research, Gratton suggests that when forming virtual teams, it is helpful to include a few members who already know each other, other members who are well connected to people outside the team, and when possible, members who have volunteered to be a part of the team. It is also advantageous for companies to have some kind of online site where team members can learn more about each other and the kinds of work they are engaged in and, in particular, a shared online workspace that team members can access around the clock. Frequent communication is beneficial. Additionally, virtual team members should perceive their projects as meaningful, interesting, and important to promote and sustain their motivation.[35]

Today, members of virtual teams rely on many different technology tools to help them with their work activities, including Slack (a group chat and notifications app); Zoom (a videoconferencing/screen-sharing tool); World Time Buddy (a tool that allows workers to find optimal times to schedule calls and collaboration meetings with various remote team members); and Google Drive (an online collaborative document-sharing program).[36]

Friendship Groups

friendship group An informal group of employees who enjoy one another's company and socialize with one another.

The groups described so far are formal groups created by managers. Friendship groups are informal groups of employees who enjoy one another's company and socialize with one another. Members of friendship groups may have lunch together, take breaks together, or meet after work for meals, sports, or other activities. Friendship groups help satisfy employees' needs for interpersonal interaction, can provide needed social support in times of stress, and can contribute to people's feeling good at work and being satisfied with their jobs. Managers themselves often form friendship groups. The informal relationships that managers build in friendship groups can often help them solve work-related problems, because members of these groups typically discuss work-related matters and offer advice.

Interest Groups

interest group An informal group of employees seeking to achieve a common goal related to their membership in an organization.

Employees form informal interest groups when they seek to achieve a common goal related to their membership in an organization. Employees may form interest groups, for example, to encourage managers to consider instituting flexible working hours, providing on-site child care, improving working conditions, or more proactively supporting environmental protection. Interest groups can give managers valuable insights into the issues and concerns that are foremost in employees' minds. They also can signal the need for change.

Group Dynamics

How groups function and, ultimately, their effectiveness hinge on group characteristics and processes known collectively as *group dynamics*. In this section we discuss five key elements of group dynamics: group size, tasks, and roles; group leadership; group development; group norms; and group cohesiveness.

LO 11-3
Explain how different elements of group dynamics influence the functioning and effectiveness of groups and teams.

Group Size and Roles

Managers need to take group size, group tasks, and group roles into account as they create and maintain high-performing groups and teams.

GROUP SIZE The number of members in a group can be an important determinant of members' motivation and commitment and group performance. There are several advantages to keeping a group relatively small—between two and nine members. Compared with members of large groups, members of small groups tend to (1) interact more with each other and find it easier to coordinate their efforts; (2) be more motivated, satisfied, and committed; (3) find it easier to share information; and

(4) be better able to see the importance of their personal contributions for group success. A disadvantage of small rather than large groups is that members of small groups have fewer resources available to accomplish their goals.

Large groups—with 10 or more members—also offer some advantages. They have more resources at their disposal to achieve group goals than small groups do. These resources include the knowledge, experience, skills, and abilities of group members as well as their actual time and effort. Large groups also let managers obtain the advantages stemming from the division of labor—splitting the work to be performed into particular tasks and assigning tasks to individual workers. Workers who specialize in particular tasks are likely to become skilled at performing those tasks and contribute significantly to high group performance.

division of labor Splitting the work to be performed into particular tasks and assigning tasks to individual workers.

The disadvantages of large groups include the problems of communication and coordination and the lower levels of motivation, satisfaction, and commitment that members of large groups sometimes experience. It is clearly more difficult to share information with, and coordinate the activities of, 16 people rather than 8 people. Moreover, members of large groups might not think their efforts are really needed and sometimes might not even feel a part of the group.

In deciding on the appropriate size for any group, managers attempt to gain the advantages of small group size and, at the same time, form groups with sufficient resources to accomplish their goals and have a well-developed division of labor. As a general rule of thumb, groups should have no more members than necessary to achieve a division of labor and provide the resources needed to achieve group goals. In R&D teams, for example, group size is too large when (1) members spend more time communicating what they know to others than applying what they know to solve problems and create new products, (2) individual productivity decreases, and (3) group performance suffers.[37]

group role A set of behaviors and tasks that a member of a group is expected to perform because of his or her position in the group.

GROUP ROLES A group role is a set of behaviors and tasks that a member of a group is expected to perform because of his or her position in the group. Members of cross-functional teams, for example, are expected to perform roles relevant to their special areas of expertise. In our earlier example of cross-functional teams at Hallmark Cards, it is the role of writers on the teams to create verses for new cards, the role of artists to draw illustrations, and the role of designers to put verse and artwork together in an attractive and appealing card design. The roles of members of top management teams are shaped primarily by their areas of expertise—production, marketing, finance, research and development—but members of top management teams also typically draw on their broad expertise as planners and strategists.

Sometimes groups are too large to be effective—communication and coordination problems may prove to be a challenge in large groups trying to work together. Mark Bowden/123RF

In forming groups and teams, managers need to clearly communicate to group members the expectations for their roles in the group, what is required of them, and how the different roles in the group fit together to accomplish group goals. Managers also need to realize that group roles often change and evolve as a group's tasks and goals change and as group members gain experience and knowledge. Thus, to get the performance gains that come from experience, or "learning by doing," managers should encourage group members to take the initiative to assume additional responsibilities as they see fit and modify their assigned roles. This process, called role making, can enhance individual and group performance.

role making Taking the initiative to modify an assigned role by assuming additional responsibilities.

In self-managed work teams and some other groups, group members themselves are responsible for creating and assigning roles. Many self-managed work teams also pick their own team leaders. When group members create their own roles, managers should be available to group members in an advisory capacity, helping them effectively settle conflicts and disagreements. At Johnsonville Foods, for example, the position titles of first-line managers were changed to "advisory coach" to reflect the managers' role with the self-managed work teams they oversaw.[38]

Group Leadership

All groups and teams need leadership. Indeed, as we discussed in detail in Chapter 10, effective leadership is a key ingredient in high-performing groups, teams, and organizations. Sometimes managers assume the leadership role in groups and teams, as is the case in many command groups and top management teams. Or a manager may appoint a member of a group who is not a manager to be group leader or chairperson, as is the case in a task force or standing committee. In other cases, group or team members may choose their own leaders, or a leader may emerge naturally as group members work together to achieve group goals. When managers empower members of self-managed work teams, they often let group members choose their own leaders. Some self-managed work teams find it effective to rotate the leadership role among their members. Whether or not leaders of groups and teams are managers, and whether they are appointed by managers (often referred to as *formal leaders*) or emerge naturally in a group (often referred to as *informal leaders*), they play an important role in ensuring that groups and teams perform up to their potential.

Group Development over Time

As many managers overseeing self-managed teams have learned, it sometimes takes a self-managed work team two or three years to perform up to its capabilities.[39] As their experience suggests, what a group is capable of achieving depends in part on its stage of development. Knowing that it takes considerable time for self-managed work teams to get up and running has helped managers to have realistic expectations for new teams and to know that they need to give new team members considerable training and guidance.

Although every group's development over time is unique, researchers have identified five stages of group development that many groups seem to pass through (see Figure 11.3).[40] In the first stage, *forming,* members try to get to know one another and reach a common understanding of what the group is trying to accomplish and how group members should behave. During this stage, managers should strive to make each member feel that he or she is a valued part of the group.

In the second stage, *storming,* group members experience conflict and disagreements because some members do not wish to submit to the demands of other group

Figure 11.3

Five Stages of Group Development

members. Disputes may arise over who should lead the group. Self-managed work teams can be particularly vulnerable during the storming stage. Managers need to keep an eye on groups at this stage to make sure conflict does not get out of hand.

During the third stage, *norming,* close ties between group members develop, and feelings of friendship and camara-

During the norming stage of group development, team members develop close ties, and feelings of friendship typically develop.
Rawpixel.com/Shutterstock

derie emerge. Group members arrive at a consensus about what goals they should seek to achieve and how group members should behave toward one another. In the fourth stage, *performing,* the real work of the group is accomplished. Depending on the type of group in question, managers need to take different steps at this stage to help ensure that groups are effective. Managers of command groups need to make sure that group members are motivated and that they are effectively leading group members. Managers overseeing self-managed work teams have to empower team members and make sure teams are given enough responsibility and autonomy at the performing stage.

The last stage, *adjourning,* applies only to groups that eventually are disbanded, such as task forces. During adjourning, a group is dispersed. Sometimes adjourning takes place when a group completes a finished product, such as when a task force evaluating the pros and cons of providing on-site child care produces a report supporting its recommendation.

Managers should have a flexible approach to group development and should keep attuned to the different needs and requirements of groups at the various stages.[41] Above all else, and regardless of the stage of development, managers need to think of themselves as *resources* for groups. Thus, managers always should strive to find ways to help groups and teams function more effectively.

Group Norms

LO 11-4

Explain why it is important for groups and teams to have a balance of conformity and deviance and a moderate level of cohesiveness.

All groups, whether top management teams, self-managed work teams, or command groups, need to control their members' behaviors to ensure that the group performs at a high level and meets its goals. Assigning roles to each group member is one way to control behavior in groups. Another important way in which groups influence members' behavior is through the development and enforcement of group norms.[42] Group norms are shared guidelines or rules for behavior that most group members follow. Groups develop norms concerning a wide variety of behaviors, including working hours, the sharing of information among group members, how certain group tasks should be performed, and even how members of a group should dress.

group norms Shared guidelines or rules for behavior that most group members follow.

Managers should encourage members of a group to develop norms that contribute to group performance and the attainment of group goals. For example, group norms dictating that each member of a cross-functional team should always be available for the rest of the team when his or her input is needed, return phone calls as soon as possible, inform other team members of travel plans, and give team members a phone number at which he or she can be reached when traveling on business help to ensure that the team is efficient, performs at a high level, and achieves its goals. A norm in a command group of administrative assistants that dictates that assistants who happen to have a light workload in any given week should help out assistants with heavier workloads helps ensure that the group completes all assignments in a timely and efficient manner. And a norm in a top management team that dictates that team members should always consult with one another before making major decisions helps ensure that good decisions are made with a minimum of errors.

CONFORMITY AND DEVIANCE Group members conform to norms for three reasons: (1) They want to obtain rewards and avoid punishments. (2) They want to imitate group members whom they like and admire. (3) They have internalized the norms and believe they are the right and proper ways to behave.[43] Consider the case of Robert King, who conformed to his department's norm of attending a fund-raiser for a community food bank. King's conformity could be due to (1) his desire to be a member of the group in good standing and to have friendly relationships with other group members (rewards), (2) his copying the behavior of other members of the department whom he respects and who always attend the fund-raiser (imitating other group members), or (3) his belief in the merits of supporting the activities of the food bank (believing that is the right and proper way to behave).

Failure to conform, or deviance, occurs when a member of a group violates a group norm. Deviance signals that a group is not controlling one of its member's behaviors. Groups generally respond to members who behave deviantly in one of three ways:[44]

1. The group might try to get the member to change his or her deviant ways and conform to the norm. Group members might try to convince the member of the need to conform, or they might ignore or even punish the deviant. For example, in a Jacksonville Foods plant, Liz Senkbiel, a member of a self-managed work team responsible for weighing sausages, failed to conform to a group norm dictating that group members should periodically clean up an untidy interview room. Because Senkbiel refused to take part in the team's cleanup efforts, team members reduced her monthly bonus by about $225 for a two-month period.[45] Senkbiel clearly learned the costs of deviant behavior in her team.

2. The group might expel the member.

3. The group might change the norm to be consistent with the member's behavior.

This last alternative suggests that some deviant behavior can be functional for groups. Deviance is functional when it causes group members to evaluate norms that may be dysfunctional but are taken for granted by the group. Often group members do not think about why they behave in a certain way or why they follow certain norms. Deviance can cause group members to reflect on their norms and change them when appropriate.

Consider a group of receptionists in a hair salon who followed the norm that all appointments would be handwritten in an appointment book and, at the end of each day, the receptionist on duty would enter the appointments into the salon's computer system, which printed out the stylists' daily schedules. One day a receptionist decided to enter appointments directly into the computer system when they were being made, bypassing the appointment book. This deviant behavior caused the other receptionists to think about why they were using the appointment book at all. After consulting with the owner of the salon, the group changed its norm. Now appointments are entered directly into the computer, which saves time and reduces scheduling errors.

ENCOURAGING A BALANCE OF CONFORMITY AND DEVIANCE To effectively help an organization gain a competitive advantage, groups and teams need the right balance of conformity and deviance (see Figure 11.4). A group needs a certain level of conformity to ensure that it can control members' behavior and channel it in the direction of high performance and group goal accomplishment. A group also needs a certain level of deviance to ensure that dysfunctional norms are discarded and replaced with functional ones. Balancing conformity and deviance is a pressing concern for all groups, whether they are top management teams, R&D teams, command groups, or self-managed work teams.

The extent of conformity and reactions to deviance within groups are determined by group members themselves. The three bases for conformity just described are powerful forces that more often than not result in group members' conforming to norms. Sometimes these forces are so strong that deviance rarely occurs in groups, and when it does, it is stamped out.

Figure 11.4

Balancing Conformity and Deviance in Groups

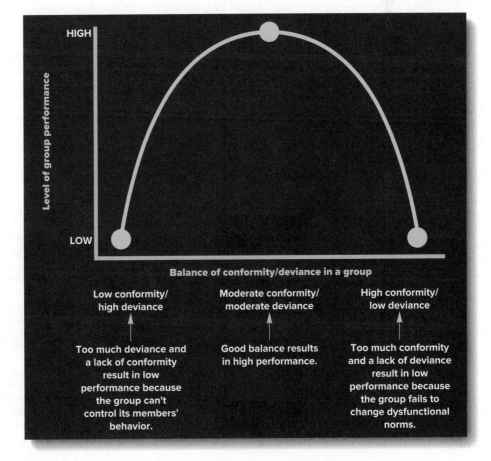

Managers can take several steps to ensure adequate tolerance of deviance in groups so that group members are willing to deviate from dysfunctional norms and, when deviance occurs in their group, reflect on the appropriateness of the violated norm and change the norm if necessary. First, managers can be role models for the groups and teams they oversee. When managers encourage and accept employees' suggestions for changes in procedures, do not rigidly insist that tasks be accomplished in a certain way, and admit when a norm they once supported is no longer functional, they signal to group members that conformity should not come at the expense of needed changes and improvements. Second, managers should let employees know that there are always ways to improve group processes and performance levels and, thus, opportunities to replace existing norms with norms that will better enable a group to achieve its goals and perform at a high level. Third, managers should encourage members of groups and teams to periodically assess the appropriateness of their norms.

Group Cohesiveness

group cohesiveness
The degree to which members are attracted to or loyal to their group.

Another important element of group dynamics that affects group performance and effectiveness is group cohesiveness, which is the degree to which members are attracted to or loyal to their group or team.[46] When group cohesiveness is high, individuals strongly value their group membership, find the group appealing, and have strong desires to remain a part of the group. When group cohesiveness is low, group members do not find their group particularly appealing and have little desire to retain their group membership. Research suggests that managers should strive to have a moderate level of cohesiveness in the groups and teams they manage because that is most likely to contribute to an organization's competitive advantage.

CONSEQUENCES OF GROUP COHESIVENESS There are three major consequences of group cohesiveness: level of participation within a group, level of conformity to group norms, and emphasis on group goal accomplishment (see Figure 11.5).[47]

Figure 11.5

Sources and Consequences of Group Cohesiveness

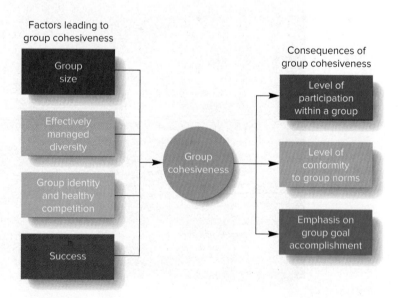

How much cohesiveness is too much? You can answer that question when you evaluate whether a group actually gets something done in its meetings or whether most of the conversation drifting out of the room consists of jokes, life experiences, or comparisons of the last company dinner's entrees. Glow Images/Getty Images

LEVEL OF PARTICIPATION WITHIN A GROUP As group cohesiveness increases, the extent of group members' participation within the group increases. Participation contributes to group effectiveness because group members are actively involved in the group, ensure that group tasks get accomplished, readily share information with each other, and have frequent and open communication (the important topic of communication is covered in depth in Chapter 13).

A moderate level of group cohesiveness helps ensure that group members actively participate in the group and communicate effectively with one another. The reason that managers may not want to encourage high levels of cohesiveness is illustrated by the example of two cross-functional teams responsible for developing new toys. Members of the highly cohesive Team Alpha often have lengthy meetings that usually start with nonwork-related conversations and jokes, meet more often than most of the other cross-functional teams in the company, and spend a good portion of their time communicating the ins and outs of their department's contribution to toy development to other team members. Members of the moderately cohesive Team Beta generally have efficient meetings in which ideas are communicated and discussed as needed, do not meet more often than necessary, and share the ins and outs of their expertise with one another to the extent needed for the development process. Teams Alpha and Beta have both developed some top-selling toys. However, it generally takes Team Alpha 30% longer to do so than Team Beta. This is why too much cohesiveness can be too much of a good thing.

LEVEL OF CONFORMITY TO GROUP NORMS Increasing levels of group cohesiveness result in increasing levels of conformity to group norms, and when cohesiveness becomes high, there may be so little deviance in groups that group members conform to norms even when they are dysfunctional. In contrast, low cohesiveness can result in too much deviance and undermine the ability of a group to control its members' behaviors to get things done.

Teams Alpha and Beta in the toy company both had the same norm for toy development. It dictated that members of each team would discuss potential ideas for new toys, decide on a line of toys to pursue, and then have the team member from R&D design a prototype. Recently, a new animated movie featuring a family of rabbits produced by a small film company was an unexpected hit, and major toy companies were scrambling to reach licensing agreements to produce toy lines featuring the rabbits. The top management team in the toy company assigned Teams Alpha and Beta to develop the new toy lines quickly to beat the competition.

Members of Team Alpha followed their usual toy development norm, even though the marketing expert on the team believed the process could have been streamlined to save time. The marketing expert on Team Beta urged the team to deviate from its toy development norm. She suggested that the team not have R&D develop prototypes but, instead, modify top-selling toys the company already made to feature rabbits and then reach a licensing agreement with the film company based on the high sales potential (given the company's prior success). Once the licensing agreement was signed, the company could take the time needed to develop innovative and unique rabbit toys with more input from R&D.

As a result of the willingness of the marketing expert on Team Beta to deviate from the norm for toy development, the toy company obtained an exclusive licensing agreement with the film company and had its first rabbit toys on store shelves in a record three months. Groups need a balance of conformity and deviance, so a moderate level of cohesiveness often yields the best outcome, as it did in the case of Team Beta.

EMPHASIS ON GROUP GOAL ACCOMPLISHMENT As group cohesiveness increases, the emphasis placed on group goal accomplishment also increases within a group. A strong emphasis on group goal accomplishment, however, does not always lead to organizational effectiveness. For an organization to be effective and gain a competitive advantage, the different groups and teams in the organization must cooperate with one another and be motivated to achieve *organizational goals,* even if doing so sometimes comes at the expense of the achievement of group goals. A moderate level of cohesiveness motivates group members to accomplish both group and organizational goals. High levels of cohesiveness can cause group members to be so focused on group goal accomplishment that they may strive to achieve group goals no matter what—even when doing so jeopardizes organizational performance.

At the toy company, the major goal of the cross-functional teams was to develop new toy lines that were truly innovative, that utilized the latest in technology, and that were in some way fundamentally distinct from other toys on the market. When it came to the rabbit project, Team Alpha's high level of cohesiveness contributed to its continued emphasis on its group goal of developing an innovative line of toys; thus, the team stuck with its usual design process. Team Beta, in contrast, realized that developing the new line of toys quickly was an important organizational goal that should take precedence over the group's goal of developing groundbreaking new toys, at least in the short term. Team Beta's moderate level of cohesiveness contributed to team members' doing what was best for the toy company in this case.

FACTORS LEADING TO GROUP COHESIVENESS Four factors contribute to the level of group cohesiveness (see Figure 11.5).[48] By influencing these *determinants of group cohesiveness,* managers can raise or lower the level of cohesiveness to promote moderate levels of cohesiveness in groups and teams.

Group Size As we mentioned earlier, members of small groups tend to be more motivated and committed than members of large groups. Thus, to promote cohesiveness in groups, when feasible, managers should form groups that are small to medium in size (about two to nine members). If a group is low in cohesiveness and large in size, managers might want to consider dividing the group in half and assigning different tasks and goals to the two newly formed groups.

Effectively Managed Diversity In general, people tend to like and get along with others who are similar to themselves. It is easier to communicate with someone, for example, who shares your values, has a similar background, and has had similar experiences. However, as discussed in Chapter 3, diversity in groups, teams, and organizations can help an organization gain a competitive advantage. Diverse groups often come up with more innovative and creative ideas. One reason cross-functional teams are so popular in organizations such as Hallmark Cards is that the diverse expertise represented in the teams results in higher levels of team performance.

In forming groups and teams, managers need to make sure the diversity in knowledge, experience, expertise, and other characteristics necessary for group goal accomplishment is represented in the new groups. Managers then have to make sure this diversity in group membership is effectively managed so groups will be cohesive (see Chapter 3). The "Focus on Diversity" feature describes how an assessment tool developed by Deloitte is helping organizations do this with regard to diverse work styles.

Focus on Diversity

Tapping into Team Members' Diversity

Anyone with teamwork experience has at times noticed another team member focus on what seems unimportant or seen a few team members dominate a meeting. In these situations, the team is not fully drawing upon every team member, so the organization is not fully benefiting from the team. Consultants at Deloitte wanted to address this problem. They believed they were seeing a failure to consider different work styles and perspectives. If team members could readily understand this diversity, they could treat it as a resource rather than an obstacle to cooperation.[49]

Deloitte built on research about brain chemistry to develop and test profiles of four primary ways that people work. The resulting system, named Business Chemistry, defines four styles: *Pioneers* inspire creativity; they look at the big picture and are open to new ideas, willing to take risks, and comfortable basing decisions on intuition. *Guardians* are cautious about risk and value stability; they want to learn from experience and look for detailed data to back decisions. *Drivers* care about results and winning; they get the team moving and want data so they can solve problems and tackle challenges. *Integrators* focus on relationships; they seek consensus and try to strengthen the team. This model assumes that teams need all of these perspectives at various times.[50]

Managing consulting firm Deloitte developed a profile of four different ways people work: Pioneers, Guardians, Drivers, and Integrators. Which profile do you fit and how can you use this style to work more effectively in a team setting? Adam Hester/Blend Images

Teams with diverse profiles should be creative, and their decisions should be well thought out. In practice, diversity poses challenges. For example, if a Driver opens the floor to debate an issue, an Integrator might hesitate to speak up and provoke an argument. If Guardians raise concerns about an idea, a Driver might feel frustrated about being slowed down, even though the concerns might be valid and significant. Team members who are unaware of these differences might work ineffectively. A Guardian might come prepared with pages of data that won't capture the imaginations of the team's Pioneers.[51]

Business Chemistry can help team members address these issues constructively. They can be aware of the strengths and limitations of their view and the views of others. They can practice imagining how people in other categories would think about situations. Also, team leaders can notice which kinds of perspectives aren't being addressed by the team and then seek out those perspectives. For example, if everyone is immediately excited about an idea, perhaps everyone is thinking like a Pioneer. The leader should pause and invite the team to consider what a Guardian-style team member would say about the idea.[52] ●

Group Identity and Healthy Competition   When group cohesiveness is low, managers can often increase it by encouraging groups to develop their own identities or personalities and engage in healthy competition. This is precisely what managers at Eaton Corporation's manufacturing facility in Lincoln, Illinois, did. Eaton's employees manufacture products such as engine valves, gears, truck axles, and circuit breakers. Managers at Eaton created self-managed work teams to cut costs and improve performance. They realized, however, that the teams would have to be cohesive to ensure that they would strive to achieve their goals. Managers promoted group identity by having the teams give themselves names such as "The Hoods," "The Worms," and "Scrap Attack" (a team striving to reduce costly scrap metal waste by 50%). Healthy competition among groups was promoted by displaying measures of each team's performance and the extent to which teams met their goals on a large TV screen in the cafeteria and by rewarding team members for team performance.[53]

If groups are too cohesive, managers can try to decrease cohesiveness by promoting organizational (rather than group) identity and making the organization as a whole the focus of the group's efforts. Organizational identity can be promoted by making group members feel that they are valued members of the organization and by stressing cooperation across groups to promote the achievement of organizational goals. Excessive levels of cohesiveness also can be reduced by reducing or eliminating competition among groups and rewarding cooperation.

Success   When it comes to promoting group cohesiveness, there is more than a grain of truth to the saying "Nothing succeeds like success." As groups become more successful, they become increasingly attractive to their members, and their cohesiveness tends to increase. When cohesiveness is low, managers can increase cohesiveness by making sure a group can achieve some noticeable and visible successes.

Consider a group of salespeople in the housewares department of a medium-size department store. The housewares department had recently been moved to a corner of the store's basement. Its remote location resulted in low sales because of infrequent customer traffic in that part of the store. The salespeople, who were generally evaluated favorably by their supervisors and were valued members of the store, tried various initiatives to boost sales, but to no avail. As a result of this lack of success and the poor performance of their department, their cohesiveness started to plummet. To increase and preserve the cohesiveness of the group, the store manager implemented a group-based incentive across the store. In any month, members of the group with the best attendance and punctuality records would have their names and pictures posted on a bulletin board in the cafeteria and would each receive a $50 gift certificate. The housewares group frequently had the best records, and their success on this dimension helped build and maintain their cohesiveness. Moreover, this initiative boosted attendance and discouraged lateness throughout the store.

Managing Groups and Teams for High Performance

Now that you understand why groups and teams are so important for organizations, the types of groups managers create, and group dynamics, we consider some additional steps managers can take to make sure groups and teams perform at a high level and contribute to organizational effectiveness. Before discussing these strategies, however, we highlight some of the traits and characteristics associated with high-performing work groups.

The concept of high-performing work teams is not new; it has been used by successful organizations for more than 20 years. High-performing work teams can be defined as groups that consistently satisfy the needs of customers, employees, investors, and other stakeholders and frequently outperform other teams that produce similar products or services.[54] Recent research into what constitutes a high-performing work group identifies several key factors that may contribute to the team's success, including a highly developed team culture, clearly defined norms that encourage effective behavior and high performance, and results-oriented meetings that include information sharing, problem solving, and decision making.[55]

Understanding what it takes to assemble and manage such top-performing groups is an ongoing challenge for any organization. Ways to create such high performance begin with two key strategies: (1) motivating group members to work toward achieving organizational goals and (2) reducing social loafing.

LO 11-5
Describe how managers can motivate group members to achieve organizational goals and reduce social loafing in groups and teams.

Motivating Group Members to Achieve Organizational Goals

When work is difficult, is tedious, or requires a high level of commitment and energy, managers cannot assume group members will always be motivated to work toward the achievement of organizational goals. Consider a group of house painters who paint the interiors and exteriors of new homes for a construction company and are paid on an hourly basis. Why should they strive to complete painting jobs quickly and efficiently if doing so will just make them feel more tired at the end of the day and they will not receive any tangible benefits? It makes more sense for the painters to adopt a relaxed approach, to take frequent breaks, and to work at a leisurely pace. This relaxed approach, however, impairs the construction company's ability to gain a competitive advantage because it raises costs and increases the time needed to complete a new home.

Managers can motivate members of groups and teams to achieve organizational goals by making sure the members themselves benefit when the group or team performs highly. For example, if members of a self-managed work team know they will receive a weekly bonus based on team performance, they will be motivated to perform at a high level.

Managers often rely on some combination of individual and group-based incentives to motivate members of groups and teams to work toward the achievement of organizational goals. When individual performance within a group can be assessed, pay is often determined by individual performance or by both individual and group performance. When individual performance within a group cannot be accurately assessed, group performance should be the key determinant of pay levels. Many companies that use self-managed work teams base team members' pay in part on team performance.[56] A major challenge for managers is to develop a fair pay system that will lead to both high individual motivation and high group or team performance.

Other benefits managers can make available to high-performing group members—in addition to monetary rewards—include extra resources such as equipment and computer software, awards and other forms of recognition, and choice of future work assignments. For example, members of self-managed work teams that develop new software at companies such as Microsoft often value working on interesting and important projects; members of teams that have performed at a high level are rewarded by being assigned to interesting and important new projects.

Reducing Social Loafing in Groups

social loafing The tendency of individuals to put forth less effort when they work in groups than when they work alone.

We have been focusing on the steps managers can take to encourage high levels of performance in groups. Managers, however, need to be aware of an important downside to group and team work: the potential for social loafing, which reduces group performance. Social loafing is the tendency of individuals to put forth less effort when they work in groups than when they work alone.[57] Have you ever worked on a group project in which one or two group members never seemed to be pulling their weight? Have you ever worked in a student club or committee in which some members always seemed to be missing meetings and never volunteered for activities? Have you ever had a job in which one or two of your coworkers seemed to be slacking off because they knew you or other members of your work group would make up for their low levels of effort? If so, you have witnessed social loafing in action.

Social loafing can occur in all kinds of groups and teams and in all kinds of organizations. It can result in lower group performance and may even prevent a group from attaining its goals. Fortunately, managers can take steps to reduce social loafing and sometimes completely eliminate it; we will look at three (see Figure 11.6).

1. *Make individual contributions to a group identifiable.* Some people may engage in social loafing when they work in groups because they think they can hide in the crowd—no one will notice if they put forth less effort than they should. Other people may think that if they put forth high levels of effort and make substantial contributions to the group, their contributions will not be noticed and they will receive no rewards for their work—so why bother?[58]

One way that managers can effectively eliminate social loafing is by making individual contributions to a group identifiable so that group members perceive that low and high levels of effort will be noticed and individual contributions evaluated.[59] Managers can accomplish this by assigning specific tasks to group members and holding them accountable for their completion. Take the case of a group of eight employees responsible for reshelving returned books in a large public library in New York. The head librarian was concerned that there was always a backlog of seven or eight carts of books to

Social loafing occurs when members of a group are not pulling their weight on projects and other tasks and are content to let others do the work. Albert Yuralaits/123RF

Figure 11.6

Three Ways to Reduce
Social Loafing

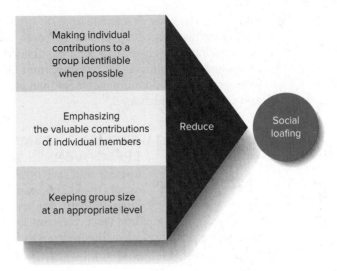

be reshelved, even though the employees never seemed to be particularly busy and some even found time to sit down and read newspapers and magazines. The librarian decided to try to eliminate the apparent social loafing by assigning each employee sole responsibility for reshelving a particular section of the library. Because the library's front desk employees sorted the books by section on the carts as they were returned, holding the shelvers responsible for particular sections was easily accomplished. Once the shelvers knew the librarian could identify their effort or lack thereof, there were rarely any backlogs of books to be reshelved.

Sometimes the members of a group can cooperate to eliminate social loafing by making individual contributions identifiable. For example, in a small security company, members of a self-managed work team who assemble control boxes for home alarm systems start each day by deciding who will perform which tasks that day and how much work each member and the group as a whole should strive to accomplish. Each team member knows that, at the end of the day, the other team members will know exactly how much he or she has accomplished. With this system in place, social loafing never occurs in the team. Remember, however, that in some teams, individual contributions cannot be made identifiable.

2. *Emphasize the valuable contributions of individual members.* Another reason social loafing may occur is that people sometimes think their efforts are unnecessary or unimportant when they work in a group. They feel the group will accomplish its goals and perform at an acceptable level whether or not they personally perform at a high level. To counteract this belief, when managers form groups, they should assign individuals to a group on the basis of the valuable contributions that *each* person can make to the group as a whole. Clearly communicating to group members why each person's contributions are valuable to the group is an effective means by which managers and group members themselves can reduce or eliminate social loafing.[60] This is most clearly illustrated in cross-functional teams, where each member's valuable contribution to the team derives from a personal area of expertise. By emphasizing why each member's skills are important, managers can reduce social loafing in such teams.

3. *Keep group size at an appropriate level.* Group size is related to the causes of social loafing we just described. As size increases, identifying individual contributions becomes increasingly difficult, and members are increasingly likely to think their individual contributions are not important. To overcome this, managers should form groups with no more members than are needed to accomplish group goals and perform at a high level.[61]

Summary and Review

GROUPS, TEAMS, AND ORGANIZATIONAL EFFECTIVENESS A group is two or more people who interact with each other to accomplish certain goals or meet certain needs. A team is a group whose members work intensely with one another to achieve a specific common goal or objective. Groups and teams can contribute to organizational effectiveness by enhancing performance, increasing responsiveness to customers, increasing innovation, and being a source of motivation for their members. [LO 11-1]

TYPES OF GROUPS AND TEAMS Formal groups are groups that managers establish to achieve organizational goals; they include cross-functional teams, cross-cultural teams, top management teams, research and development teams, command groups, task forces, self-managed work teams, and virtual teams. Informal groups are groups that employees form because they believe the groups will help them achieve their own goals or meet their needs; they include friendship groups and interest groups. [LO 11-2]

GROUP DYNAMICS Key elements of group dynamics are group size and roles; group leadership; group development; group norms; and group cohesiveness. The advantages and disadvantages of large and small groups suggest that managers should form groups with no more members than are needed to provide the group with the human resources it needs to achieve its goals and use a division of labor. A group role is a set of behaviors and tasks that a member of a group is expected to perform because of his or her position in the group. All groups and teams need leadership.

Five stages of development that many groups pass through are forming, storming, norming, performing, and adjourning. Group norms are shared rules for behavior that most group members follow. To be effective, groups need a balance of conformity and deviance. Conformity allows a group to control its members' behavior to achieve group goals; deviance provides the impetus for needed change.

Group cohesiveness is the attractiveness of a group or team to its members. As group cohesiveness increases, so do the level of participation and communication within a group, the level of conformity to group norms, and the emphasis on group goal accomplishment. Managers should strive to achieve a moderate level of group cohesiveness in the groups and teams they manage. [LO 11-3, 11-4]

MANAGING GROUPS AND TEAMS FOR HIGH PERFORMANCE To make sure groups and teams perform at a high level, managers need to motivate group members to work toward the achievement of organizational goals and reduce social loafing. Managers can motivate members of groups and teams to work toward the achievement of organizational goals by making sure members personally benefit when the group or team performs at a high level. [LO 11-5]

Management *in Action*

Topics for Discussion and Action

Discussion

1. Why do all organizations need to rely on groups and teams to achieve their goals and gain a competitive advantage? [LO 11-1]

2. What kinds of employees would prefer to work in a virtual team? What kinds of employees would prefer to work in a team that meets face to face? [LO 11-2]

3. Think about a group that you are a member of, and describe that group's current stage of development. Does the development of this group seem to be following the forming, storming, norming, performing, and adjourning stages described in the chapter? [LO 11-3]

4. Discuss the reasons that too much conformity can hurt groups and their organizations. [LO 11-4]

5. Why do some groups have very low levels of cohesiveness? [LO 11-4]

6. Imagine that you are the manager of a hotel. What steps will you take to reduce social loafing by members of the cleaning staff who are responsible for keeping all common areas and guest rooms spotless? [LO 11-5]

Action

7. Interview one or more managers in an organization in your local community to identify the types of groups and teams that the organization uses to achieve its goals. What challenges do these groups and teams face? [LO 11-2]

Building Management Skills

Diagnosing Group Failures [LO 11-1, 11-2, 11-3, 11-4, 11-5]

Think about the last dissatisfying or discouraging experience you had as a member of a group or team. Perhaps the group did not accomplish its goals, perhaps group members could agree about nothing, or perhaps there was too much social loafing. Now answer the following questions:

1. What type of group was this?

2. Were group members motivated to achieve group goals? Why or why not?

3. How large was the group and what group roles did members play?

4. What were the group's norms? How much conformity and deviance existed in the group?

5. How cohesive was the group? Why do you think the group's cohesiveness was at this level? What consequences did this level of group cohesiveness have for the group and its members?

6. Was social loafing a problem in this group? Why or why not?

7. What could the group's leader or manager have done differently to increase group effectiveness?

8. What could group members have done differently to increase group effectiveness?

Managing Ethically [LO 11-1, 11-2, 11-3, 11-4, 11-5]

Some self-managed teams encounter a vexing problem: One or more members engage in social loafing, and other members are reluctant to try to rectify the situation. Social loafing can be especially troubling if team members' pay is based on team performance and social loafing reduces the team's performance and, thus,

the pay of all members (even the highest performers). Even if managers are aware of the problem, they may be reluctant to take action because the team is supposedly self-managing.

Questions

1. Either individually or in a group, think about the ethical

implications of social loafing in a self-managed team.

2. Do managers have an ethical obligation to step in when they are aware of social loafing in a self-managed team? Why or why not? Do other team members have an obligation to try to curtail the social loafing? Why or why not?

Small Group Breakout Exercise [LO 11-1, 11-2, 11-3, 11-4, 11-5]

Creating a Cross-Functional Team

Form groups of three or four people, and appoint one member as the spokesperson who will communicate your findings to the class when called on by the instructor. Then discuss the following scenario:

You are a group of managers in charge of food services for a large state university in the Midwest. Recently, a survey of students, faculty, and staff was conducted to evaluate customer satisfaction with the food services provided by the university's eight cafeterias. The results were disappointing, to put it mildly. Complaints ranged from dissatisfaction with the type and range of meals and snacks provided, operating hours,

and food temperature to frustration about unresponsiveness to current concerns about healthful diets and the needs of vegetarians. You have decided to form a cross-functional team that will further evaluate reactions to the food services and will develop a proposal for changes to be made to increase customer satisfaction.

1. Indicate who should be on this important cross-functional team, and explain why.

2. Describe the goals the team should strive to achieve.

3. Describe the different roles that will need to be performed on this team.

4. Describe the steps you will take to help ensure that the team has a good balance between conformity and deviance and has a moderate level of cohesiveness.

Be the Manager [LO 11-1, 11-2, 11-3, 11-4, 11-5]

You were recently hired in a boundary-spanning role for the global unit of an educational and professional publishing company. The company is headquartered in New York (where you work) and has divisions in multiple countries. Each division is responsible for translating, manufacturing,

marketing, and selling a set of books in its country. Your responsibilities include interfacing with managers in each of the divisions in your region (Central and South America), overseeing their budgeting and financial reporting to headquarters, and leading a virtual team consisting of the top managers in

charge of each of the divisions in your region. The virtual team's mission is to promote global learning, explore new potential opportunities and markets, and address ongoing problems. You communicate directly with division managers via telephone and email, as well as written reports, memos, and text messages. When virtual team meetings are convened, videoconferencing is often used.

After your first few virtual team meetings, you noticed that the managers seemed to be reticent about speaking up. Interestingly enough, when each manager communicates with you individually, primarily in telephone conversations and emails, he or she tends to be forthcoming and frank, and you feel you have a good rapport with each of them. However, getting the managers to communicate with one another as a virtual team has been a challenge. At the last meeting, you tried to prompt some of the managers to raise issues relevant to the agenda that you knew were on their minds from your individual conversations with them. Surprisingly, the managers skillfully avoided informing their teammates about the heart of the issues in question. You are confused and troubled. Although you feel your other responsibilities are going well, you know your virtual team is not operating like a team at all; and no matter what you try, discussions in virtual team meetings are forced and generally unproductive. What are you going to do to address this problem?

Case in the News [LO 11-1, 11-2, 11-3, 11-5]

Adient Builds Better with Teams

When you slip behind the wheel of your Honda or Ford, you aren't sliding onto a seat made by those automakers. Almost certainly, the seats in your car or SUV were made by a company in an automaker's supply chain. Globally, the largest supplier of automotive seating is Michigan-based Adient. The company designs seat systems, including the fabric, springs, levers, and control technology, and builds them at 230 facilities around the world.

Despite its number-one position in terms of sales, Adient has struggled since it was spun off from Johnson Controls in 2016. In contrast to its competitors, it failed to generate a profit many quarters during that period, despite sales growth. Analysts identified the problem as a failure to operate efficiently enough for the slim profit margins that are typical for makers of auto components. This limits the company's future prospects, because automobile technology is poised for rapid advances in driverless vehicles, and profits would generate cash to invest in the seating needs for those new kinds of cars. In 2018, the company brought in a new CEO with a strong background in manufacturing. Douglas DelGrosso started his career in engineering and went on to management positions with Lear, Henniges Automotive, and Chassix (a maker of chassis systems). However, even as Adient was seeking the right expertise from its top managers, teams at individual locations were already making strides to improving efficiencies.

A notable example is the Adient factory in Lerma, Mexico. Adient Lerma leads the company in its systems for continuous improvement. It accomplishes this by assigning all of its employees to high-performance teams. All are required to learn not only a particular job but also the hundreds of manufacturing practices at the plant, principles of quality improvement, and safety standards. Every team meets weekly, bringing together employees handling different functions, to engage in problem solving. Topics under discussion are related to the facility's performance metrics in eight areas: efficiency, safety, quality, continuous improvement, scrap rates, total productive maintenance, the 5S system for organizing and maintaining workspaces, and empowerment of people (measured by turnover, absenteeism, and job rotation). As teams solve problems, they earn points that determine the size of a bonus for high performance. Many of the teams are self-managed as well as empowered to make improvement decisions.

The use of teamwork at Adient Lerma has made all the employees familiar with the company's performance objectives. Employees become experts in how to make the facility function better, and they personally care about improvement. In 2017 alone, the teams crafted more than 100 projects that cut costs by $1.38 million. That success positioned the company to win enough new sales and investment to announce a major expansion of the facility.

Meanwhile, in the UK city of Sunderland, the focus has been on efficiency through an embrace of the latest in automation and information technology. The so-called Industry 4.0 technologies include robotics, machine vision, and machine learning (an area of artificial intelligence). For example, software can analyze data to direct a robot where to spray steam on newly built seats. At Adient Sunderland, management put together a team of decision makers to expand the use of Industry 4.0 and make the facility a model for the rest of the company. The team identified the most significant problem areas, prepared a list of ideas, prioritized them, and implemented the 12 top-ranked ideas. The team most recently has focused on how to move data analysis from simply understanding past results toward being able to predict what will succeed in the future.

With these wins and Adient's dominance in market share, the company's management sees a profitable future. Executives predict they will benefit from customers' increasing focus on seating technology that delivers a great passenger experience; pursuing this effort offers potential for innovation and new products. Innovative products, in turn, give Adient an edge to compete on value, not just price. In addition, the company has been diversifying its mix of customers. For example, it recently entered a partnership arrangement with Boeing to develop and sell seating for aircraft. Those who fly in cramped seating will welcome the thought of improvements in this product line. For their part, Boeing and Adient expect airlines will welcome the chance to improve performance in a widely criticized area of passenger experience.

Questions for Discussion

1. In general, how can group norms help the teams at Adient Lerma achieve continuous improvement?

2. How does Adient Lerma motivate the members of its high-performance teams? What could the facility's managers do to discourage social loafing?

3. Do you think Adient Lerma's approach of putting all employees on empowered teams could also help the Sunderland facility achieve its goal of using Industry 4.0 technologies? Why or why not?

Sources: Adient corporate fact sheet, www .adient.com, accessed January 24, 2019; "Adient Names DelGrosso CEO, Succeeding Interim Chief Fritz Henderson," *Automotive News*, www.autonews.com, September 13, 2018; K. Nagl, "Assessing Adient's Future," *Crain's Detroit Business*, www.crainsdetroit. com, June 17, 2018; T. Hessman, "2017 IW Best Plants Winner: High Performance Teamwork and the Power of Collaboration at Adient Lerma," *Industry Week*, www.industryweek.com, March 23, 2018; A. Hand, "An Automotive Seat Maker's Drive to Industry 4.0," *Automation World*, www.automationworld.com, February 7, 2018; S. Chapman, "Boeing Partners with Adient to Manufacture Aircraft Seats," *Manufacturing Global*, www .manufacturingglobal.com, January 19, 2018.

Endnotes

1. R. Maze and G. Cavallaro, "Battling Bureaucracy: The Way Forward Requires Modernizing the Modernization Process," Association of the United States Army, www.ausa.org, February 22, 2018.

2. M. Myers, "Abrams: Army Units Will Be Tasked to Work on Each of Futures Command's Priorities," *Army Times*, www.armytimes. com, March 27, 2018; N. Martin, "Mark Esper: Army Forms Cross-Functional Teams to Support Tech Requirements Devt Process," *Executive Gov*, www.executivegov. com, December 11, 2017.

3. M. Pomerleau, "How a New Army Team Plans to Modernize the Network," *C4ISRNET*, www .c4isrnet.com, March 30, 2018.

4. J. Garamone, "Service Members Seeing First Fruits of Army Acquisition Changes," *DoD News (Department of Defense)*, www. defense.gov, April 18, 2018; M. Pomerleau, "In: Fast Solutions; Out: Drawn Out Development," *C4ISRNET*, www.c4isrnet.com, March 29, 2018.

5. J. Judson, "6 Questions with Army Under Secretary Ryan McCarthy," *Defense News*, www.defensenews. com, October 7, 2018; D. Parsons, "Army Speeds Up Fielding Artillery Missile by Five Years," *Defense Daily*, www.defensedaily.com, March 27, 2018.

6. T. M. Mills, *The Sociology of Small Groups* (Englewood Cliffs, NJ: Prentice-Hall, 1967); M. E. Shaw, *Group Dynamics* (New York: McGraw-Hill, 1981).

7. K. Casey, "How to Cultivate Soft Skills in Your IT Team," *The Enterprisers Project*, https:// enterprisersproject.com, February 12, 2018; T. Rahschulte, "Investing for Soft Skills: Build, Buy or Both," *Chief Learning Officer*, www.clomedia.com, January 3,

2018; M. Fouts, "Improve Team Collaboration with These Key Skills," *Forbes*, June 22, 2017, www .forbes.com.

8. Casey, "How to Cultivate Soft Skills"; Rahschulte, "Investing for Soft Skills."

9. M. Feffer, "HR's Hard Challenge: When Employees Lack Soft Skills," Society for Human Resource Management, www.shrm.org, accessed January 24, 2019.

10. G. Lewis, "The Most In-Demand Hard and Soft Skills of 2019," *LinkedIn Talent Blog*, https:// business.linkedin.com, accessed January 24, 2019; Fouts, "Improve Team Collaboration."

11. Rahschulte, "Investing for Soft Skills."

12. "Hallmark Fact Sheet," https:// corporate.hallmark.com, accessed January 24, 2019; R. S. Buday, "Reengineering One Firm's Product Development and Another's Service Delivery," *Planning Review*, March–April 1993, 14–19; J. M. Burcke, "Hallmark's Quest for Quality Is a Job Never Done," *Business Insurance*, April 26, 1993, 122; M. Hammer and J. Champy, *Reengineering the Corporation* (New York: HarperBusiness, 1993); T. A. Stewart, "The Search for the Organization of Tomorrow," *Fortune*, May 18, 1992, 92–98.

13. "CraftWorks Restaurants & Breweries," www .craftworksrestaurants.com, accessed January 24, 2019; A. Wallace, "Rock Bottom Founder Calls Decision to Sell 'Bittersweet,'" *Daily Camera*, www.dailycamera. com, accessed April 20, 2018.

14. S. Dallas, "Rock Bottom Restaurants; Brewing Up Solid Profits," *BusinessWeek*, May 22, 1995, 74.

15. J. A. Pearce II and E. C. Ravlin, "The Design and Activation of Self-Regulating Work Groups," *Human Relations* 11 (1987), 751–82.

16. B. Dumaine, "Who Needs a Boss?," *Fortune*, May 7, 1990, 52–60; Pearce and Ravlin, "The Design and Activation of Self-Regulating Work Groups."

17. "The Gore Story," www.gore.com, accessed January 24, 2019; G. Hamel, *The Future of Management*

(Boston: Harvard Business School Press, 2007).

18. "Our History," www.gore.com, accessed January 24, 2019.

19. "Our Beliefs & Principles," www .gore.com, accessed January 24, 2019.

20. R. E. Silverman, "Who's the Boss? There Isn't One," *The Wall Street Journal*, June 20, 2012, B1, B8.

21. "Working at Gore," www.gore.com, accessed January 24, 2019; Hamel, *The Future of Management*.

22. Hamel, *The Future of Management*.

23. "The Gore Story."

24. C. Zillman, "Secrets from Best Companies All Stars," *Fortune*, http://fortune.com, accessed January 24, 2019.

25. T. D. Wall, N. J. Kemp, P. R. Jackson, and C. W. Clegg, "Outcomes of Autonomous Work Groups: A Long-Term Field Experiment," *Academy of Management Journal* 29 (1986), 280–304.

26. A. Markels, "A Power Producer Is Intent on Giving Power to Its People," *The Wall Street Journal*, July 3, 1995, A1, A12; "AES Corporation/The Power of Being Global," www.aes.com/aes/ index?page5home, April 15, 2008.

27. W. R. Pape, "Group Insurance," *Inc.* (Technology Supplement), June 17, 1997, 29–31; A. M. Townsend, S. M. DeMarie, and A. R. Hendrickson, "Are You Ready for Virtual Teams?," *HR Magazine*, September 1996, 122–26; A. M. Townsend, S. M. DeMarie, and A. M. Hendrickson, "Virtual Teams: Technology and the Workplace of the Future," *Academy of Management Executive* 12, no. 3 (1998), 17–29.

28. Townsend et al., "Virtual Teams."

29. V. Maza, "Are Your Remote Workers Happy? How to Keep Teams Connected from Afar," *Forbes*, www.forbes.com, accessed January 24, 2019; D. DeRosa, "3 Companies with High-Performing Virtual Teams," *OnPoint Consulting*, www.onpointconsultingllc.com, accessed January 24, 2019.

30. C. Breuer, J. Hüffmeier, and G. Hertel, "Does Trust Matter More in Virtual Teams? A Meta-Analysis of Trust and Team Effectiveness Considering Virtuality and

Documentation as Moderators," *Journal of Applied Psychology* 101, no. 8 (2016), 1151–77.

31. Maza, "Are Your Remote Workers Happy?"

32. E. J. Hill, B. C. Miller, S. P. Weiner, and J. Colihan, "Influences of the Virtual Office on Aspects of Work and Work/Life Balance," *Personnel Psychology* 31 (1998), 667–83; S. G. Strauss, "Technology, Group Process, and Group Outcomes: Testing the Connections in Computer-Mediated and Face-to-Face Groups," *Human Computer Interaction* 12 (1997), 227–66; M. E. Warkentin, L. Sayeed, and R. Hightower, "Virtual Teams versus Face-to-Face Teams: An Exploratory Study of a Web-Based Conference System," *Decision Sciences* 28, no. 4 (Fall 1997), 975–96.

33. S. Krumm, J. Kanthak, K. Hartmann, and G. Hertel, "What Does It Take to Be a Virtual Team Player? The Knowledge, Skills, Abilities, and Other Characteristics Required in Virtual Teams," *Human Performance* 29, no. 2 (2016), 123–42.

34. S. A. Furst, M. Reeves, B. Rosen, and R. S. Blackburn, "Managing the Life Cycle of Virtual Teams," *Academy of Management Executive* 18, no. 2 (May 2004), 6–20.

35. L. Gratton, "Work Together . . . When Apart," *The Wall Street Journal* June 16–17, 2007, R4.

36. A. S. Hirsch, "How to Use Technology to Support Remote Teams," www.shrm.org, accessed January 24, 2019; M. DeFelice, "The Best Tech for Working Remote in 2018," *Forbes*, www.forbes.com, January 2, 2018.

37. A. Deutschman, "The Managing Wisdom of High-Tech Superstars," *Fortune*, October 17, 1994, 197–206.

38. J. S. Lublin, "My Colleague, My Boss," *The Wall Street Journal*, April 12, 1995, R4, R12.

39. R. G. LeFauve and A. C. Hax, "Managerial and Technological Innovations at Saturn Corporation," *MIT Management*, Spring 1992, 8–19.

40. B. W. Tuckman, "Developmental Sequences in Small Groups," *Psychological Bulletin* 63 (1965), 384–99; B. W. Tuckman and

M. C. Jensen, "Stages of Small Group Development," *Group and Organizational Studies* 2 (1977), 419–27.

41. C. J. G. Gersick, "Time and Transition in Work Teams: Toward a New Model of Group Development," *Academy of Management Journal* 31 (1988), 9–41; C. J. G. Gersick, "Marking Time: Predictable Transitions in Task Groups," *Academy of Management Journal* 32 (1989), 274–309.

42. J. R. Hackman, "Group Influences on Individuals in Organizations," in M. D. Dunnette and L. M. Hough, eds., *Handbook of Industrial and Organizational Psychology,* 2nd ed., vol. 3 (Palo Alto, CA: Consulting Psychologists Press, 1992), 199–267.

43. Hackman, "Group Influences on Individuals."

44. Ibid.

45. Lublin, "My Colleague, My Boss."

46. L. Festinger, "Informal Social Communication," *Psychological Review* 57 (1950), 271–82; Shaw, *Group Dynamics.*

47. Hackman, "Group Influences on Individuals in Organizations"; Shaw, *Group Dynamics.*

48. D. Cartwright, "The Nature of Group Cohesiveness," in D. Cartwright and A. Zander, eds., *Group Dynamics,* 3rd ed. (New York: Harper & Row, 1968); L. Festinger, S. Schacter, and K. Black, *Social Pressures in Informal Groups* (New York: Harper & Row, 1950); Shaw, *Group Dynamics.*

49. K. Christfort, "The Power of Business Chemistry," Deloitte, https://www2.deloitte.com, accessed January 24, 2019; K. Christfort and S. Vickberg, "Business Chemistry in the C-Suite," *The Wall Street Journal,* http://deloitte.wsj.com, November 2, 2017; S. M. Johnson Vickberg and K. Christfort, "Pioneers, Drivers, Integrators, and Guardians," *Harvard Business Review,* March–April 2017, 50–57.

50. T. Williams, "Business Chemistry: Are You a Driver, Guardian, Integrator, or Pioneer?," *The Economist,* https://exceed.economist.com, accessed January 24, 2019; Christfort and Vickberg, "Business Chemistry in the C-Suite."

51. Vickberg and Christfort, "Pioneers, Drivers, Integrators, and Guardians"; Christfort and Vickberg, "Business Chemistry in the C-Suite"; Christfort, "The Power of Business Chemistry."

52. Christfort and Vickberg, "Business Chemistry in the C-Suite"; A. Beard, "How Work Styles Inform," *Harvard Business Review,* March–April 2017, 58–59; Christfort, "The Power of Business Chemistry."

53. T. F. O'Boyle, "A Manufacturer Grows Efficient by Soliciting Ideas from Employees," *The Wall Street Journal,* June 5, 1992, A1, A5.

54. E. Kur, "The Faces Model of High Performing Team Management," *Leadership & Organizational Development Journal* 17, no. 1 (1996), 32–41.

55. D. D. Warrick, "What Leaders Can Learn about Teamwork and Developing High Performance Teams from Organization Development Practitioners," *Performance Improvement,* 55, no. 3 (2016), 13–21.

56. Lublin, "My Colleague, My Boss."

57. P. C. Earley, "Social Loafing and Collectivism: A Comparison of the United States and the People's Republic of China," *Administrative Science Quarterly* 34 (1989), 565–81; J. M. George, "Extrinsic and Intrinsic Origins of Perceived Social Loafing in Organizations," *Academy of Management Journal* 35 (1992), 191–202; S. G. Harkins, B. Latane, and K. Williams, "Social Loafing: Allocating Effort or Taking It Easy," *Journal of Experimental Social Psychology* 16 (1980), 457–65; B. Latane, K. D. Williams, and S. Harkins, "Many Hands Make Light the Work: The Causes and Consequences of Social Loafing," *Journal of Personality and Social Psychology* 37 (1979), 822–32; J. A. Shepperd, "Productivity Loss in Performance Groups: A Motivation Analysis," *Psychological Bulletin* 113 (1993), 67–81.

58. George, "Extrinsic and Intrinsic Origins of Perceived Social Loafing in Organizations"; G. R. Jones, "Task Visibility, Free Riding, and Shirking: Explaining the Effect of Structure and Technology on Employee Behavior," *Academy of Management Review* 9 (1984), 684–95; K. Williams, S. Harkins, and B. Latane, "Identifiability as a Deterrent to Social Loafing: Two Cheering Experiments," *Journal of Personality and Social Psychology* 40 (1981), 303–11.

59. S. Harkins and J. Jackson, "The Role of Evaluation in Eliminating Social Loafing," *Personality and Social Psychology Bulletin* 11 (1985), 457–65; N. L. Kerr and S. E. Bruun, "Ringelman Revisited: Alternative Explanations for the Social Loafing Effect," *Personality and Social Psychology Bulletin* 7 (1981), 224–31; Williams et al., "Identifiability as a Deterrent to Social Loafing"; Harkins and Jackson, "The Role of Evaluation in Eliminating Social Loafing."

60. M. A. Brickner, S. G. Harkins, and T. M. Ostrom, "Effects of Personal Involvement: Thought-Provoking Implications for Social Loafing," *Journal of Personality and Social Psychology* 51 (1986), 763–69; S. G. Harkins and R. E. Petty, "The Effects of Task Difficulty and Task Uniqueness on Social Loafing," *Journal of Personality and Social Psychology* 43 (1982), 1214–29.

61. B. Latane, "Responsibility and Effort in Organizations," in P. S. Goodman, ed., *Designing Effective Work Groups* (San Francisco: Jossey-Bass, 1986); Latane et al., "Many Hands Make Light the Work"; I. D. Steiner, *Group Process and Productivity* (New York: Academic Press, 1972).

Building and Managing Human Resources

Learning Objectives

After studying this chapter, you should be able to:

LO 12-1 Explain why strategic human resource management can help an organization gain a competitive advantage.

LO 12-2 Describe the steps managers take to recruit and select organizational members.

LO 12-3 Discuss the training and development options that ensure organizational members can effectively perform their jobs.

LO 12-4 Explain why performance appraisal and feedback are such crucial activities, and list the choices managers must make in designing effective performance appraisal and feedback procedures.

LO 12-5 Explain the issues managers face in determining levels of pay and benefits.

LO 12-6 Understand the role that labor relations play in the effective management of human resources.

Management Snapshot

Unilever CHRO Makes Talent Development Count

How Can Managers Effectively Manage Human Resources?

Leena Nair is the chief human resource officer (CHRO) of Unilever, which markets consumer products including popular brands such as Axe, Dove, and Lipton across the globe. She is responsible for planning the human resource needs of a 160,000-employee organization in about 190 countries. After joining Unilever as a management trainee in 1992, Nair worked her way up through a variety of HR positions before becoming the company's youngest CHRO as well as its first female and first Asian CHRO.[1]

According to Nair, these are challenging times for managing human resources. The trend toward replacing labor and decision making with robots and artificial intelligence has raised questions about the future value of people in organizations. In addition, this fast-changing business environment calls for flexibility and agility at all levels of an organization and a firm commitment to attracting and retaining a talented workforce. For Nair, these challenges just increase the importance of her role at Unilever. HR functions can no longer be content to create long-term career paths for employees, but instead need to equip people to contribute what humans uniquely can offer—a spirit of curiosity, a drive to innovate, and empathy for others both inside and outside the organization—especially in a global company where close to half of its workforce are millennials looking to make a difference and to have an impact on business initiatives.[2]

Nair's response to the challenge is Unilever's highly flexible approach to planning and operations. The initiative, called Connected 4 Growth, involves many different corporate initiatives, which include rewriting job descriptions and revising organizational structure to push decision making down to the employees closest to products and customers. Giving employees greater decision-making authority enables them to respond faster to customer needs using a flexible approach.[3]

Nair recognizes that employees can take on these responsibilities only if the company has properly identified the necessary skills, put people in positions they are prepared for, and created a system to develop the right kinds of talent. As CHRO, Nair takes a high-level view, looking at the key positions that influence business performance and ensuring the right skills are in place. For this fast-changing environment, training must be flexible and continuous. Getting a college degree is a starting point, not the end of learning. Unilever offers learning programs that Nair calls "snackable," meaning

Unilever's chief HR officer, Leena Nair, believes the company's flexible approach to planning, organizing, and developing talent has helped put decision-making authority in the hands of front-facing employees who can respond faster and better to customer needs.
Ritam Banerjee/Stringer/Getty Images

employees dip into learning resources often, adding skills as time and opportunity permit. The company spends more than $100 million on leadership development for its workforce around the globe.[4]

Finally, planning must be paired with measurement of results, so plans can be reinforced or changed. Nair uses metrics associated with business performance. For example, she wants Unilever to be "the number one employer of choice" among workers in the markets where the company operates. Where Unilever meets that objective, the company acquires better employees while spending less on recruitment. Nair's track record includes taking Unilever's employer brand to new heights—good news for the company's bottom line as well as its workforce.[5]

Overview

Managers are responsible for acquiring, developing, protecting, and utilizing the resources an organization needs to be efficient and effective. One of the most important resources in all organizations is human resources—the people involved in producing and distributing goods and services. Human resources include all members of an organization, ranging from top managers to entry-level employees. Effective managers, like Unilever's Leena Nair profiled in the "Management Snapshot," realize how valuable human resources are and take active steps to make sure their organizations build and fully utilize their human resources to gain a competitive advantage.

LO 12-1
Explain why strategic human resource management can help an organization gain a competitive advantage.

This chapter examines how managers can tailor their human resource management system to their organization's strategy and structure. We discuss in particular the major components of human resource management: recruitment and selection, training and development, performance appraisal, pay and benefits, and labor relations. By the end of this chapter you will understand the central role human resource management plays in creating a high-performing organization.

Strategic Human Resource Management

Human resource management (HRM) includes all the activities managers engage in to attract and retain employees and to ensure that they perform at a high level and contribute to the accomplishment of organizational goals. These activities make up an organization's human resource management system, which has five major components: recruitment and selection, training and development, performance appraisal and feedback, pay and benefits, and labor relations (see Figure 12.1).

human resource management (HRM) Activities that managers engage in to attract and retain employees and to ensure that they perform at a high level and contribute to the accomplishment of organizational goals.

Strategic human resource management is the process by which managers design the components of an HRM system to be consistent with each other, with other elements of organizational architecture, and with the organization's strategy and goals.[6] The objective of strategic HRM is the development of an HRM system that enhances an organization's efficiency, quality, innovation, and responsiveness to customers—the four building blocks of competitive advantage.

In today's highly competitive business environment, successful organizations understand that the HR function is no longer simply a part of the business that undertakes administrative tasks, sets employee-related policies, and hires and fires employees. Rather, many companies believe that the HR function is a critical

Figure 12.1

Components of a
Human Resource
Management System

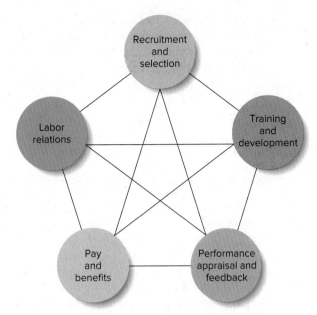

Each component of an HRM system influences
the others, and all five must fit together.

component of their strategic agenda and insist on HR managers not only understanding the critical tasks involved in running a business but also take an active role in helping senior management ensure that departmental strategies and goals align across the entire organization, that employee training and development remain a top organizational priority, and that the organization pursues a corporate culture that is competitive yet employee friendly.[7]

Overview of the Components of HRM

Managers use *recruitment and selection,* the first component of an HRM system, to attract and hire new employees who have the abilities, skills, and experiences that will help an organization achieve its goals. Microsoft, for example, has the goal of being one of the top cloud-computing tech companies in the world. To achieve this goal, managers at Microsoft realize the importance of hiring the best computer systems engineers: hundreds of highly qualified candidates are interviewed and rigorously tested. Microsoft has little trouble recruiting top computer engineering talent because candidates know they will be at the forefront of the cloud-computing industry if they work for Microsoft.[8]

After recruiting and selecting employees, managers use the second component, *training and development,* to ensure that organizational members develop the skills and abilities that will enable them to perform their jobs effectively in the present and the future. Training and development are an ongoing process, as is true at Unilever as described in the "Management Snapshot"; changes in technology and the environment, as well as in an organization's goals and strategies, often require that organizational members learn new techniques and ways of working. At Microsoft, newly hired program designers receive on-the-job training by joining small teams that include experienced employees who serve as mentors or advisers.

New recruits learn firsthand from team members how to develop computer systems that are responsive to customers' programming needs.[9] Another company that takes training and development seriously is Home Depot, as described in the "Management Insight" feature.

Management Insight

Strategic HRM Helps Build a Strong Future

For Home Depot, which operates home improvement stores and the fourth-largest e-commerce business in the United States, the trends shaping the retail and construction industries continue to bring tremendous challenges and opportunities to its CEO, Craig Menear, and his management staff.[10] The popularity of online shopping has led many other retailers to scale back and close stores. The construction industry feels the swings of the business cycle. During downturns, for example, homeowners put off remodeling old homes or having new ones built, so demand for building supplies tumbles. More recently, construction is booming, generating increases in sales. Home Depot, like the construction businesses it serves, is facing heavy competition for workers, with unemployment rates at their lowest levels in more than 15 years. Further complicating the picture, demand for workers in much of the country is seasonal, picking up in the spring and slowing as the weather turns cold.

With these challenges in mind, Home Depot has been following a strategy of using recessions as a time for investing in efficiency and growth to reap the benefits of delivering better service. During the last recession, company investments were targeted to improve the online shopping experience, renovate stores, and train workers, with the result that Home Depot stores were outselling Lowe's, a key competitor. A shorter-term challenge is to hire in a highly competitive labor market, where many workers are wary of retail jobs. For the past few years, Menear and his management team have set a hiring target of more than 80,000 seasonal workers.[11]

To compete in a tough labor market, Home Depot has tried to stand out as a superior employer. Like many employers after years of economic expansion, Home Depot has increased wages, and it recently announced one-time employee bonuses of $200 to $1,000, depending on years of service. Another way it does this is by simplifying the application process. The company offers an app that lets job seekers apply from their mobile devices, as well as a text-to-apply option. It reported that these options made applying faster and increased the number of applications by

Effective HR strategies have helped the Home Depot weather recessions as well as tight labor markets. Joe Raedle/Getty Images

50% over previous years. More recently, it has enhanced its job application app with a tool that lets the applicant schedule an interview at a store or distribution center. In the first few months after the self-scheduling tool was launched, more than three-quarters of applicants used it to set up interviews.[12]

Besides making job applications more accessible, Menear and his staff have made training more convenient for employees. Home Depot introduced what it calls its "PocketGuide," a training app for use on mobile devices. Employees use the app to look up product information and complete training activities. An early use of the app was to bring seasonal workers in the garden department up to speed quickly, which helps them succeed on the job and deliver better customer service.[13]

Looking to the future, Home Depot's charitable foundation has committed to supporting training programs for construction workers.[14] Partnering with the Home Builders Institute, the foundation has donated funds to train 20,000 construction workers over 10 years, preparing them for careers as carpenters, electricians, and plumbers. The program is available to veterans and to high school students in underserved communities. Support for preparing the next generation of construction workers not only boosts Home Depot's reputation as a business that cares about its workforce and the local community, but also builds a customer base for the years ahead. ●

The third component, *performance appraisal and feedback,* serves two purposes in HRM. First, performance appraisal can give managers the information they need to make good human resource decisions—decisions about how to train, motivate, and reward organizational members.[15] Thus, the performance appraisal and feedback component is a kind of *control system* that can be used with management by objectives (discussed in Chapter 8). Second, feedback from performance appraisal serves a developmental purpose for members of an organization. When managers regularly evaluate their employees' performances, they can give employees valuable information about their strengths and weaknesses and the areas in which they need to concentrate.

On the basis of performance appraisals, managers distribute *pay* to employees, which is part of the fourth component of an HRM system. By rewarding high-performing organizational members with pay raises, bonuses, and the like, managers increase the likelihood that an organization's most valued human resources will be motivated to continue their high levels of contribution to the organization. Moreover, if pay is linked to performance, high-performing employees are more likely to stay with the organization, and managers are more likely to fill positions that become open with highly talented individuals. *Benefits* such as health insurance are important outcomes that employees receive by virtue of their membership in an organization.

Last but not least, *labor relations* encompass the steps that managers take to develop and maintain good working relationships with the labor unions that may represent their employees' interests. For example, an organization's labor relations component can help managers establish safe working conditions and fair labor practices in their offices and plants.

Managers must ensure that all five of these components fit together and complement their company's structure and control systems.[16] For example, if managers decide to decentralize authority and empower employees, they need to invest in training and development to ensure that lower-level employees have the knowledge and expertise they need to make the decisions that top managers would make in a more centralized structure.

Each of the five components of HRM influences the others (see Figure 12.1).[17] The kinds of people the organization attracts and hires through recruitment and selection, for example, determine (1) the kinds of training and development that are necessary, (2) the way performance is appraised, and (3) the appropriate levels of pay and benefits. Managers at Microsoft ensure that their organization has highly qualified systems engineers by (1) recruiting and selecting the best candidates, (2) guiding new hires with experienced team members, (3) appraising performance in terms of their individual contributions and their teams' performance, and (4) basing pay on individual and team performance.

The Legal Environment of HRM

In the rest of this chapter we focus in detail on the choices managers must make in strategically managing human resources to attain organizational goals and gain a competitive advantage. Effectively managing human resources is a complex undertaking for managers, and we provide an overview of some major issues they face. First, however, we need to look at how the legal environment affects human resource management.

The local, state, and national laws and regulations that managers and organizations must abide by add to the complexity of HRM. For example, the U.S. government's commitment to equal employment opportunity (EEO) has resulted in the creation and enforcement of a number of laws that managers must abide by. The goal of EEO is to ensure that all citizens have an equal opportunity to obtain employment regardless of their gender, race, country of origin, religion, age, or disabilities. Table 12.1 summarizes some of the major EEO laws affecting HRM. Other laws, such as the Occupational Safety and Health Act of 1970, require that managers ensure that employees are protected from workplace hazards and that safety standards are met.

equal employment opportunity (EEO) The equal right of all citizens to the opportunity to obtain employment regardless of their gender, age, race, country of origin, religion, or disabilities.

In Chapter 3 we explained how effectively managing diversity is an ethical and business imperative, and we discussed the many issues surrounding diversity. EEO laws and their enforcement make the effective management of diversity a legal imperative as well. The Equal Employment Opportunity Commission (EEOC) is the division of the Department of Justice that enforces most EEO laws and handles discrimination complaints. In addition, the EEOC issues guidelines for managers to follow to ensure that they are abiding by EEO laws. For example, the Uniform Guidelines on Employee Selection Procedures issued by the EEOC (in conjunction with the Departments of Labor and Justice and the Civil Service Commission) guide managers on how to ensure that the recruitment and selection component of human resource management complies with Title VII of the Civil Rights Act (which prohibits discrimination based on gender, race, color, religion, and national origin).[18] Contemporary challenges that managers face related to the legal environment include how to eliminate sexual harassment (see Chapter 3 for an in-depth discussion of sexual harassment), how to accommodate employees with disabilities, and how to deal with employees who have substance abuse problems.

Table 12.1

Major Equal Employment Opportunity Laws Affecting HRM

Year	Law	Description
1963	Equal Pay Act	Requires that men and women be paid equally if they are performing equal work.
1964	Title VII of the Civil Rights Act	Prohibits employment discrimination on the basis of race, religion, sex, color, or national origin; covers a wide range of employment decisions, including hiring, firing, pay, promotion, and working conditions.
1967	Age Discrimination in Employment Act	Prohibits discrimination against workers over the age of 40 and restricts mandatory retirement.
1978	Pregnancy Discrimination Act	Prohibits employment discrimination against women on the basis of pregnancy, childbirth, and related medical decisions.
1986	Immigration Reform and Control Act	Prohibits discrimination on the basis of natural origin or citizenship, except for illegal immigrants, by employers having four or more employees.
1990	Americans with Disabilities Act	Prohibits employment discrimination against individuals with disabilities and requires that employers make accommodations for such workers to enable them to perform their jobs.
1991	Civil Rights Act	Prohibits discrimination (as does Title VII) and allows the awarding of punitive and compensatory damages, in addition to back pay, in cases of intentional discrimination.
1993	Family and Medical Leave Act	Requires that employers with 50 or more employees provide 12 weeks of unpaid leave for medical and family reasons, including paternity and illness of a family member.
1994	Uniformed Services Employment and Reemployment Rights Act	Requires rehiring of employees who are absent for military service, with training and accommodations as needed.
2009	Lilly Ledbetter Fair Pay Act	Allows employees to claim discriminatory compensation within a set time after receiving a discriminatory paycheck.

Recruitment and Selection

LO 12-2
Describe the steps managers take to recruit and select organizational members.

Recruitment includes all the activities managers engage in to develop a pool of qualified candidates for open positions.[19] **Selection** is the process by which managers determine the relative qualifications of job applicants and their potential for performing well in a particular job. Before actually recruiting and selecting employees, managers need to engage in two important activities: human resource planning and job analysis (see Figure 12.2).

Figure 12.2

The Recruitment and Selection System

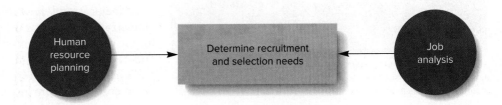

Human resource planning → Determine recruitment and selection needs ← Job analysis

Human Resource Planning

recruitment
Activities that managers engage in to develop a pool of qualified candidates for open positions.

selection The process that managers use to determine the relative qualifications of job applicants and their potential for performing well in a particular job.

human resource planning Activities that managers engage in to forecast their current and future needs for human resources.

outsource To use outside suppliers and manufacturers to produce goods and services.

Human resource planning includes all the activities managers engage in to forecast their current and future human resource needs. Current human resources are the employees an organization needs today to provide high-quality goods and services to customers. Future human resource needs are the employees the organization will need at some later date to achieve its longer-term goals.

As part of human resource planning, managers must make both demand forecasts and supply forecasts. *Demand forecasts* estimate the qualifications and numbers of employees an organization will need, given its goals and strategies. *Supply forecasts* estimate the availability and qualifications of current employees now and in the future, as well as the supply of qualified workers in the external labor market.

As a result of their human resource planning, managers sometimes decide to outsource to fill some of their human resource needs. Instead of recruiting and selecting employees to produce goods and services, managers contract with people who are not members of their organization to produce goods and services. Managers in publishing companies, for example, frequently contract with freelance editors to copyedit books that they intend to publish. Kelly Services is an organization that provides the services of technical and professional employees to managers who want to use outsourcing to fill some of their human resource requirements in these areas.[20]

Two reasons human resource planning sometimes leads managers to outsource are flexibility and cost. First, outsourcing can give managers increased flexibility, especially when accurately forecasting human resource needs is difficult, human resource needs fluctuate over time, or finding skilled workers in a particular area is difficult. Second, outsourcing can sometimes allow managers to use human resources at a lower cost. When work is outsourced, costs can be lower for a number of reasons: The organization does not have to provide benefits to workers; managers can contract for work only when the work is needed; and managers do not have to invest in training. Outsourcing can be used for functional activities such as payroll, bookkeeping and accounting, legal work, and the management of information systems.[21]

Outsourcing has disadvantages, however. When work is outsourced, managers may lose some control over the quality of goods and services. Also, individuals performing outsourced work may have less knowledge of organizational practices, procedures, and goals and less commitment to an organization than regular employees do. In addition, unions resist outsourcing because it has the potential to eliminate the jobs of some of their members. To gain some of the flexibility and cost savings of outsourcing and avoid some of its disadvantages, a number of organizations, such as Microsoft and IBM, rely on a pool of temporary employees to, for example, monitor cybersecurity threats.

A major trend reflecting the increasing globalization of business is the outsourcing of office work, computer programming, and technical jobs from the United States and countries in western Europe, with high labor costs, to countries such as India and

Human resource planning sometimes leads managers to outsource company functions such as accounting and customer service to other countries such as India. IndiaPictures/UIG/Getty Images

Malaysia, with low labor costs.[22] For example, computer programmers in India earn a fraction of what their U.S. counterparts earn. Outsourcing (or *offshoring*, as it is also called when work is outsourced to other countries) has also expanded into knowledge-intensive work such as engineering, research and development, and the development of computer software. According to a study conducted by The Conference Board and Duke University's Offshoring Research Network, more than half of U.S. companies surveyed have some kind of offshoring strategy related to knowledge-intensive work and innovation.[23] Why are so many companies engaged in offshoring, and why are companies that already offshore work planning to increase the extent of offshoring? While cost savings continue to be a major motivation for offshoring, managers also want to take advantage of an increasingly talented global workforce and be closer to the growing global marketplace for goods and services.[24]

Major U.S. companies often earn a substantial portion of their revenues overseas. For example, Hewlett-Packard, Caterpillar, and IBM earn over 50% of their revenues from overseas markets. And many large companies employ thousands of workers overseas. For example, Caterpillar has more than 52,000 workers in foreign countries; IBM employs close to 130,000 in India.[25] Key challenges for managers who offshore are retaining sufficient managerial control over activities and employee turnover.[26]

Job Analysis

job analysis
Identifying the tasks, duties, and responsibilities that make up a job and the knowledge, skills, and abilities needed to perform the job.

Job analysis is a second important activity that managers need to undertake prior to recruitment and selection.[27] Job analysis is the process of identifying (1) the tasks, duties, and responsibilities that make up a job (the *job description*) and (2) the knowledge, skills, and abilities needed to perform the job (the *job specifications*).[28] For each job in an organization, a job analysis needs to be done.

Job analysis can be done in a number of ways, including observing current employees as they perform the job or interviewing them. Often managers rely on questionnaires compiled by jobholders and their managers. The questionnaires ask about the skills and abilities needed to perform the job, job tasks and the amount of time spent on them, responsibilities, supervisory activities, equipment used, reports prepared, and decisions made. A trend, in some organizations, is toward more flexible jobs in which tasks and responsibilities change and cannot be clearly specified in advance. For these kinds of jobs, job analysis focuses more on determining the skills and knowledge workers need to be effective and less on specific duties.

After managers have completed human resource planning and job analyses for all jobs in an organization, they will know their human resource needs and the jobs they need to fill. They will also know what knowledge, skills, and abilities potential employees need to perform those jobs. At this point, recruitment and selection can begin.

External and Internal Recruitment

As noted earlier, recruitment is what managers do to develop a pool of qualified candidates for open positions. They traditionally have used two main types of recruiting, external and internal, which are now supplemented by recruiting over the Internet.

EXTERNAL RECRUITING When managers recruit externally to fill open positions, they look outside the organization for people who have not worked for the organization previously. There are multiple means through which managers can recruit externally: job postings on career websites, such as Indeed or Monster; job fairs in the local community; career fairs at colleges and universities; open houses for students and career counselors at high schools and on-site at the organization; recruitment meetings with local groups; and advertising on social media platforms and in local newspapers.

Many large organizations send teams of interviewers to college campuses to recruit new employees. External recruitment can also take place through informal networks, as occurs when current employees inform friends about open positions in their companies or recommend people they know to fill vacant spots. Some organizations use employment agencies for external recruitment, and some external recruitment takes place simply through walk-ins—job hunters going to an organization and inquiring about employment possibilities.

External recruiting has both advantages and disadvantages for managers. Advantages include having access to a potentially large applicant pool; being able to attract people who have the skills, knowledge, and abilities that an organization needs to achieve its goals; and being able to bring in newcomers who may have a fresh approach to problems and are up to date on the latest technology. These advantages have to be weighed against the disadvantages, including the relatively high costs of external recruitment. Employees recruited externally lack knowledge about the inner workings of the organization and may need to receive more training than those recruited internally. Finally, when employees are recruited externally, there is always uncertainty concerning whether they will actually be good performers. Nonetheless, managers can take steps to reduce some of the uncertainty surrounding external recruitment, with methods such as tests, temporary jobs, and internships.

INTERNAL RECRUITING When recruiting is internal, managers turn to existing employees to fill open positions. Employees recruited internally are either seeking lateral moves (job changes that entail no major changes in responsibility or authority levels) or promotions. Internal recruiting has several advantages. First, internal applicants are already familiar with the organization (including its goals, structure, culture, rules, and norms). Second, managers already know the candidates; they have considerable information about their skills, abilities, and actual behavior on the job. Third, internal recruiting can help boost levels of employee motivation and morale, both for the employee who gets the job and for other workers. Those who are not seeking a promotion or who may not be ready for one can see that promotion is a possibility in the future; or a lateral move can alleviate boredom once a job has been fully mastered and can be a useful way to learn new skills. Finally, internal recruiting is normally less time-consuming and expensive than external recruiting.

Given the advantages of internal recruiting, why do managers rely on external recruiting as much as they do? The answer lies in the disadvantages of internal recruiting—among them, a limited pool of candidates and a tendency among those candidates to be set in the organization's ways. Often the organization simply does not have suitable internal candidates. Sometimes even when suitable internal applicants are available, managers may rely on external recruiting to find the very best candidate or to help bring new ideas and approaches into their organization. When organizations are in trouble and performing poorly, external recruiting is often relied on to bring in managerial talent with a fresh approach.

lateral move A job change that entails no major changes in responsibility or authority levels.

Figure 12.3

Selection Tools

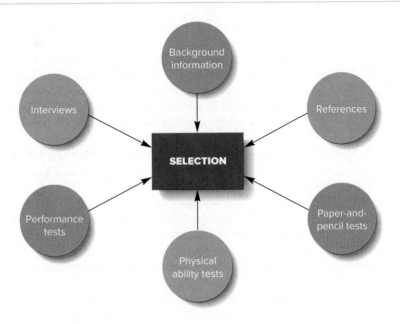

The Selection Process

Ideally, recruiting efforts have been broad enough and equitable enough to meet the standards of equal opportunity and provide a pool of applicants who meet basic qualifications. (For a discussion of seeking diverse candidates, see the following "Focus on Diversity" feature.) Managers then need to find out whether each applicant is qualified for the position and likely to be a good performer. If more than one applicant meets these two conditions, managers must further determine which applicants are likely to be better performers than others. They have several selection tools to help them sort out the relative qualifications of job applicants and appraise their potential for being good performers in a particular job. These tools include background information, interviews, paper-and-pencil tests, physical ability tests, performance tests, and references (see Figure 12.3).[29]

Focus on Diversity

Recruiting Practices That Promote Diversity

Many organizations have a policy of valuing diversity. Managers see advantages from including different perspectives, especially when employees reflect the diverse perspectives of the employer's customers and communities. Furthermore, a commitment to diversity widens the pool of potential talent, offering more ways to find the best people.[30]

A basic step is to review recruiting sources and messages. Recruiting in schools where many students are the same race or gender narrows the pool of candidates in terms of racial and gender diversity. Language also matters. Diversity-strategy consultant Joelle Emerson finds that women are less likely to respond to an ad looking for top performers described as "rock stars" than to an ad looking for someone who "seeks challenges." Daphne Wotherspoon, who helps companies find tech workers, makes a similar observation about the masculine appeal of a position described as "JavaScript ninja."[31]

Employers also should consider the image their recruiters and interviewers project. A survey of tax and accounting professionals found that most high-level managers in their organizations were white males. A person of color interviewed by these managers might doubt that the company values diversity. Conversely, Jessica Akue recalls that when she was the first black woman at a Canadian law firm, minority students would gravitate toward her at recruiting events, curious to know what it was like to work there. Employers also can set up panels of diverse interviewers. One interviewer may see and correct unintentional biases that a homogeneous panel would have overlooked.[32]

For the selection process, a useful control is to double-check one's opinions. Suppose the manager making a hiring decision likes a certain characteristic of a candidate. The manager can think, "Is this a preference, a tradition, or a job requirement?" Job requirements are essentials; preferences and traditions may be a plus, but they could limit selections to people who are so much alike that new ideas rarely surface.[33]

Similar issues arise with regard to physical or mental disabilities. Sean Casey, executive director of the Georgia Vocational Rehabilitation Agency, points out "everyone does things in life differently."[34] His point is that it is illogical as well as unjust to assume someone with a disability is less capable because he or she performs a task with accommodations. Casey adds that the person with a disability, simply by figuring out a way to adapt to the disability, has already demonstrated problem-solving skills. ●

BACKGROUND INFORMATION To aid in the selection process, managers obtain background information from job applications and from résumés. Such information might include the highest levels of education obtained, college majors and minors, type of college or university attended, years and type of work experience, and mastery of foreign languages. Background information can be helpful both to screen out applicants who are lacking key qualifications (such as a college degree) and to determine which qualified applicants are more promising than others. For example, applicants with a BS may be acceptable, but those who also have an MBA may be preferable.

Increasing numbers of organizations are performing background checks to verify the background information prospective employees provide (and to uncover any negative information such as crime convictions). In a recent study, nearly 96% of employers surveyed said their organization conducts one or more types of employment background screening.[35] According to ADP, an outsourcing company that performs payroll and human resource functions for organizations, more and more companies are performing background checks on prospective employees and are uncovering inaccuracies, inconsistencies, and negative information not reported on applications. According to ADP, more than half of applicants provide some form of false information about their employment history.[36]

INTERVIEWS Virtually all organizations use interviews during the selection process. Interviews may be structured or unstructured. In a *structured interview,* managers ask each applicant the same standard questions (such as "What are your unique qualifications for this position?" and "What characteristics of a job are most important

Some managers find situational interview questions useful in determining the right candidate for a specific job opening.
©Ariel Skelley/Getty Images

to you?"). Particularly informative questions may be those that prompt an interviewee to demonstrate skills and abilities needed for the job by answering the question. Sometimes called *situational interview questions*, these often present interviewees with a scenario they would likely encounter on the job and ask them to indicate how they would handle it.[37] For example, applicants for a sales job may be asked to indicate how they would respond to a customer who complained about waiting too long for service, a customer who was indecisive, and a customer whose order was lost.

An *unstructured interview* proceeds more like an ordinary conversation. The interviewer feels free to ask probing questions to discover what the applicant is like and does not ask a fixed set of questions determined in advance. In general, structured interviews are superior to unstructured interviews because they are more likely to yield information that will help identify qualified candidates, are less subjective, and may be less influenced by the interviewer's biases.

When conducting interviews, managers cannot ask questions that are irrelevant to the job in question; otherwise, their organizations run the risk of costly lawsuits. It is inappropriate and illegal, for example, to inquire about an interviewee's spouse or to ask questions about whether an interviewee plans to have children. Because questions such as these are irrelevant to job performance, they are discriminatory and violate EEO laws (see Table 12.1). Thus, interviewers need to be instructed in EEO laws and informed about questions that may violate those laws.

PAPER-AND-PENCIL TESTS The two main kinds of paper-and-pencil tests used for selection purposes are ability tests and personality tests; both kinds of tests can be administered in hard copy or electronic form. *Ability tests* assess the extent to which applicants possess the skills necessary for job performance, such as verbal comprehension or numerical skills. Autoworkers hired by General Motors, Chrysler, and Ford, for example, are typically tested for their ability to read and to do mathematics.[38]

Personality tests measure personality traits and characteristics relevant to job performance. Some retail organizations, for example, give job applicants honesty tests to determine how trustworthy they are. The use of personality tests (including honesty tests) for hiring purposes is controversial. Some critics maintain that honesty tests do not really measure honesty (i.e., they are not valid) and can be faked by job applicants. Before using any paper-and-pencil tests for selection purposes, managers must have sound evidence that the tests are actually good predictors of performance on the job in question. Managers who use tests without such evidence may be subject to costly discrimination lawsuits.

PHYSICAL ABILITY TESTS For jobs requiring physical abilities, such as firefighting, garbage collecting, and package delivery, managers use physical ability tests that measure physical strength and stamina as selection tools. Autoworkers are typically tested for mechanical dexterity because this physical ability is an important skill for high job performance in many auto plants.[39]

PERFORMANCE TESTS *Performance tests* measure job applicants' performance on actual job tasks. Applicants for administrative assistant positions, for example, typically are required to complete a keyboarding test that measures how quickly and accurately they type. Applicants for middle and top management positions are sometimes given short-term projects to complete—projects that mirror the kinds of situations that arise in the job being filled—to assess their knowledge and problem-solving capabilities.[40]

Assessment centers, first used by AT&T, take performance tests one step further. In a typical assessment center, about 10 to 15 candidates for managerial positions participate in a variety of activities over a few days. During this time they are assessed for the skills an effective manager needs—problem-solving, organizational, communication, and conflict resolution skills. Some of the activities are performed individually; others are performed in groups. Throughout the process, current managers observe the candidates' behavior and measure performance. Summary evaluations are then used as a selection tool.

REFERENCES Applicants for many jobs are required to provide references from former employers or other knowledgeable sources (such as a college instructor or adviser) who know the applicants' skills, abilities, and other personal characteristics. These individuals are asked to provide candid information about the applicant. References are often used at the end of the selection process to confirm a decision to hire. Yet the fact that many former employers are reluctant to provide negative information in references sometimes makes it difficult to interpret what a reference is really saying about an applicant.

In fact, several recent lawsuits filed by applicants who felt that they were unfairly denigrated or had their privacy invaded by unfavorable references from former employers have caused managers to be increasingly wary of providing any negative information in a reference, even if it is accurate. For jobs in which the jobholder is responsible for the safety and lives of other people, however, failing to provide accurate negative information in a reference does not just mean that the wrong person might get hired; it may also mean that other people's lives will be at stake.

reliability The degree to which a tool or test measures the same thing each time it is used.

THE IMPORTANCE OF RELIABILITY AND VALIDITY Whatever selection tools a manager uses need to be both reliable and valid. Reliability is the degree to which a tool or test measures the same thing each time it is administered. Scores on a selection test should be similar if the same person is assessed with the same tool on two different days; if there is quite a bit of variability, the tool is unreliable. For interviews, determining reliability is more complex because the dynamic is personal interpretation. That is why the reliability of interviews can be increased if two or more qualified interviewers interview the same candidate. If the interviews are reliable, the interviewers should come to similar conclusions about the interviewee's qualifications.

validity The degree to which a tool or test measures what it purports to measure.

Validity is the degree to which a tool measures what it purports to measure—for selection tools, it is the degree to which the test predicts performance on the tasks or job in question. Does a physical ability test used to select firefighters, for example, actually predict on-the-job performance? Do assessment center ratings actually predict managerial performance? Do keyboarding tests predict administrative assistant performance? These are all questions of validity. Honesty tests, for example, are controversial because it is not clear that they validly predict honesty in such jobs as retailing and banking.

Managers have an ethical and legal obligation to use reliable and valid selection tools. Yet reliability and validity are matters of degree rather than all-or-nothing characteristics. Thus, managers should strive to use selection tools in such a way that they can achieve the greatest degree of reliability and validity. For ability tests of a particular skill, managers should keep up to date on the latest advances in the development of valid paper-and-pencil tests and use the test with the highest reliability and validity ratings for their purposes. Regarding interviews, managers can improve reliability by having more than one person interview job candidates.

Training and Development

Training and development help to ensure that organizational members have the knowledge and skills needed to perform jobs effectively, take on new responsibilities, and adapt to changing conditions, as is the case at Unilever as described in the "Management Snapshot." Training focuses primarily on teaching organizational members how to perform their current jobs and helping them acquire the knowledge and skills they need to be effective performers. Development focuses on building the knowledge and skills of organizational members so they are prepared to take on new responsibilities and challenges. Training tends to be used more frequently at lower levels of an organization; development tends to be used more frequently with professionals and managers.

Before creating training and development programs, managers should perform a needs assessment to determine which employees need training or development and what type of skills or knowledge they need to acquire (see Figure 12.4).[41]

Types of Training

There are two types of training: classroom instruction and on-the-job training.

CLASSROOM INSTRUCTION Through classroom instruction, employees acquire knowledge and skills in a classroom setting. This instruction may take place within the organization or outside it, such as through courses at local colleges and universities or through online classes. Many organizations establish their own formal instructional divisions—some are even called "colleges"—to provide needed classroom instruction. For example, at Disney, classroom instruction and other forms of training and development are provided to employees at Disney University.[42]

Classroom instruction frequently uses videos and role-playing in addition to traditional written materials, lectures, and group discussions. *Videos* can demonstrate appropriate and inappropriate job behaviors. For example, by watching an experienced salesperson effectively deal with a loud and angry customer, inexperienced salespeople can develop skills in handling similar situations. During *role-playing*, trainees either directly participate in or watch others perform actual job activities in a simulated setting. At McDonald's Hamburger University, for example, role playing helps franchisees acquire the knowledge and skills they need to manage their restaurants.

Simulations also can be part of classroom instruction, particularly for complicated jobs that require an extensive amount of learning and in which errors carry a high cost. In a simulation, key aspects of the work situation and job tasks are duplicated as closely as possible in an artificial setting. For example, air traffic controllers are trained by simulations because of the complicated nature of the work, the extensive amount of learning involved, and the very high costs of air traffic control errors.

Margin notes

LO 12-3 Discuss the training and development options that ensure organizational members can effectively perform their jobs.

training Teaching organizational members how to perform their current jobs and helping them acquire the knowledge and skills they need to be effective performers.

development Building the knowledge and skills of organizational members so they are prepared to take on new responsibilities and challenges.

needs assessment An assessment of which employees need training or development and what type of skills or knowledge they need to acquire.

Figure 12.4   *Training and Development*

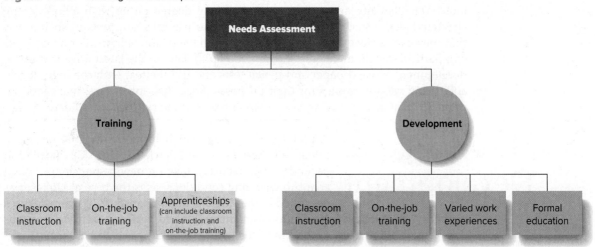

Technology continues to expand the concept of classroom instruction to include classes of trainees scattered across a variety of locations. With *distance learning,* trainees at different locations attend training programs online, using computers or mobile devices to view lectures, participate in discussions, and share documents and other information. Technology applications in distance learning may include videoconferencing, email, instant messaging, document-sharing software, and web cameras.

on-the-job training
Training that takes place in the work setting as employees perform their job tasks.

ON-THE-JOB TRAINING   In on-the-job training, learning occurs in the work setting as employees perform their job tasks. On-the-job training can be provided by coworkers or supervisors or can occur simply as jobholders gain experience and knowledge from doing the work. Newly hired servers in chains such as Chili's or the Olive Garden often receive on-the-job training from experienced employees. The supervisor of a new bus driver for a campus bus system may ride the bus for a week to ensure that the driver has learned the routes and follows safety procedures.

Managers often use on-the-job training on a continuing basis to ensure that their employees keep up to date with changes in goals, technology, products, or customer needs and desires. For example, Leading Real Estate Companies of the World (Leading RE), a Chicago-based firm, earned the top spot on *Training* magazine's 2018 list of the best training programs in the country. The company offers more than 350 online courses for managers, sales associates, and other staff, which are available 24/7 to accommodate busy schedules, can be used on mobile devices, and provide graphic-rich video and interactions to reinforce learning.[43]

Types of Development

Although both classroom instruction and on-the-job training can be used for development as well as training, development often includes additional activities such as varied work experiences and formal education.

VARIED WORK EXPERIENCES   Top managers need to develop an understanding of, and expertise in, a variety of functions, products and services, and markets. To develop executives who will have this expertise, managers frequently make sure

At many restaurants, new employees receive on-the-job training by shadowing more experienced servers as they go about their work. Reza Estakhrian/Photographer's Choice/Getty Images

that employees with high potential have a wide variety of job experiences, some in line positions and some in staff positions. Varied work experiences broaden employees' horizons and help them think about the big picture. For example, one- to three-year stints overseas are being used increasingly to provide managers with international work experiences. With organizations becoming more global, managers need to understand the different values, beliefs, cultures, regions, and ways of doing business in different countries.

Another development approach is mentoring. A *mentor* is an experienced member of an organization who provides advice and guidance to a less experienced member, called a *protégé*. Having a mentor can help managers seek out work experiences and assignments that will contribute to their development and can enable them to gain the most possible from varied work experiences.[44] Although some mentors and protégés create relationships informally, organizations have found that formal mentoring programs can be valuable ways to contribute to the development of managers and all employees. For example, 3M, Caterpillar, and insurance company USAA all have formal mentoring programs.[45]

Formal mentoring programs ensure that mentoring takes place in an organization and structure the process. Participants receive training, efforts are focused on matching mentors and protégés so meaningful developmental relationships ensue, and organizations can track reactions and assess the potential benefits of mentoring. Formal mentoring programs can also ensure that diverse members of an organization receive the benefits of mentoring. A study conducted by David A. Thomas, a professor at the Harvard Business School, found that members of racial minority groups at three large corporations who were very successful in their careers had the benefit of mentors. Formal mentoring programs help organizations make this valuable development tool available to all employees.[46]

When diverse members of an organization lack mentors, their progress in the organization and advancement to high-level positions can be hampered. In a recent survey of more than 1,000 professionals in North America, nearly three-quarters of the minority respondents said they participated in their companies' formal mentoring programs because they believed the mentoring experience can be a key tool to accelerating their careers and achieving professional growth. In addition, companies committed to attracting a diverse workforce find that mentoring programs help create a healthy corporate culture and retain top talent.[47]

Mentoring can benefit all kinds of employees in all kinds of work.[48] John Washko, a manager at the Four Seasons hotel chain, benefited from the mentoring he received from Stan Bromley on interpersonal relations and how to deal with employees; mentor Bromley, in turn, found that participating in the Four Seasons mentoring program helped him develop his own management style.[49] More generally, development is an ongoing process for all managers, and mentors often find that mentoring contributes to their own personal development.

FORMAL EDUCATION Many large corporations reimburse employees for tuition expenses they incur while taking college courses and obtaining advanced degrees. This is not just benevolence on the part of the employer or even a simple reward given to the employee; it is an effective way to develop employees who can take on new responsibilities and more challenging positions. For similar reasons, corporations spend thousands of dollars sending managers to executive development programs such as executive MBA programs. In these programs, experts teach managers the latest in business and management techniques and practices.

To save time and travel costs, some managers also rely on distance learning to formally educate and develop employees. Using videoconferencing technologies, business schools such as the Harvard Business School, the University of Michigan, and Babson College teach courses on video screens in corporate conference rooms. Business schools also customize courses and degrees to fit the development needs of employees in a particular company and/or a particular geographic region. Moreover, some employees and managers seek to advance their education through online degree programs.[50]

Transfer of Training and Development

Whenever training and development take place off the job or in a classroom setting, it is vital for managers to promote the transfer of the knowledge and skills acquired *to the actual work situation.* Trainees should be encouraged and expected to use their newfound expertise on the job.

Performance Appraisal and Feedback

LO 12-4
Explain why performance appraisal and feedback are such crucial activities, and list the choices managers must make in designing effective performance appraisal and feedback procedures.

The recruitment/selection and training/development components of a human resource management system ensure that employees have the knowledge and skills needed to be effective now and in the future. Performance appraisal and feedback complement recruitment, selection, training, and development. **Performance appraisal** is the evaluation of employees' job performance and contributions to the organization. **Performance feedback** is the process through which managers share performance appraisal information with their employees, give them an opportunity to reflect on their own performance, and develop, with employees, plans for the future. Before performance feedback, performance appraisal must take place. Performance appraisal could take place without providing performance feedback, but wise managers are careful to provide feedback because it can contribute to employee motivation and performance.

Performance appraisal and feedback contribute to the effective management of human resources in several ways. Performance appraisal gives managers important information on which to base human resource decisions. Decisions about pay raises, bonuses, promotions, and job moves all hinge on the accurate appraisal of performance. Performance appraisal can also help managers determine which workers are candidates for training and development and in what areas. Performance feedback encourages high levels of employee motivation and performance. It lets good performers know that their efforts are valued and appreciated. It also lets poor performers know that their lackluster performance needs improvement. Performance feedback can give both good and poor performers insight into their strengths and weaknesses and the ways in which they can improve their performance in the future.

performance appraisal The evaluation of employees' job performance and contributions to their organization.

performance feedback The process through which managers share performance appraisal information with employees, give them an opportunity to reflect on their own performance, and develop, with employees, plans for the future.

Types of Performance Appraisal

Performance appraisal focuses on the evaluation of traits, behaviors, and results.[51]

TRAIT APPRAISALS When trait appraisals are used, managers assess employees on personal characteristics that are relevant to job performance, such as skills, abilities, or personality. A factory worker, for example, may be evaluated based on her ability to use computerized equipment and perform numerical calculations. A social worker may be appraised based on his empathy and communication skills.

Three disadvantages of trait appraisals often lead managers to rely on other appraisal methods. First, possessing a certain personal characteristic does not ensure that the personal characteristic will actually be used on the job and result in high performance. For example, a factory worker may possess superior computer and numerical skills but be a poor performer due to low motivation. The second disadvantage of trait appraisals is linked to the first. Because traits do not always show a direct association with performance, workers and courts of law may view them as unfair and potentially discriminatory. The third disadvantage of trait appraisals is that they often do not enable managers to give employees feedback they can use to improve performance. Because trait appraisals focus on relatively enduring human characteristics that change only over the long term, employees can do little to change their behavior in response to performance feedback from a trait appraisal. Telling a social worker that he lacks empathy says little about how he can improve his interactions with clients, for example. These disadvantages suggest that managers should use trait appraisals only when they can demonstrate that the assessed traits are accurate and important indicators of job performance.

BEHAVIOR APPRAISALS Through behavior appraisals, managers assess how workers perform their jobs—the actual actions and behaviors that workers exhibit on the job. Whereas trait appraisals assess what workers *are like,* behavior appraisals assess what workers *do.* For example, with a behavior appraisal, a manager might evaluate a social worker on the extent to which he looks clients in the eye when talking with them, expresses sympathy when they are upset, and refers them to community counseling and support groups geared toward the specific problems they are encountering. Behavior appraisals are especially useful when *how* workers perform their jobs is important. In educational organizations such as high schools, for example, the numbers of classes and students taught are important, but also important is how they are taught or the methods teachers use to ensure that learning takes place.

Behavior appraisals have the advantage of giving employees clear information about what they are doing right and wrong and how they can improve their performance. And because behaviors are much easier for employees to change than traits, performance feedback from behavior appraisals is more likely to lead to improved performance.

RESULTS APPRAISALS For some jobs, *how* people perform the job is not as important as *what* they accomplish or the results they obtain. With results appraisals, managers appraise performance by the results or the actual outcomes of work behaviors. Take the case of two new car salespeople. One salesperson strives to develop personal relationships with her customers. She spends hours talking to them and frequently calls them to see how their decision-making process is going. The other salesperson has a much more hands-off approach. He is very knowledgeable, answers customers' questions, and then waits for them to come to him. Both salespersons sell, on average, the same number of cars, and the customers of both are satisfied with the service they receive, according to postcards the dealership mails to customers asking for an assessment of their satisfaction. The manager of the dealership appropriately uses results appraisals (sales and customer satisfaction) to evaluate the salespeople's performance because it does not matter which behavior salespeople use to sell cars as long as they sell the desired number and satisfy customers. If one salesperson sells too few cars, however, the manager can give that person performance feedback about his or her low sales.

OBJECTIVE AND SUBJECTIVE APPRAISALS Whether managers appraise performance in terms of traits, behaviors, or results, the information they assess is either *objective* or *subjective*. Objective appraisals are based on facts and are likely to be numerical—the number of cars sold, the number of meals prepared, the number of times late, the number of audits completed. Managers often use objective appraisals when results are being appraised because results tend to be easier to quantify than traits or behaviors. When *how* workers perform their jobs is important, however, subjective behavior appraisals are more appropriate than results appraisals.

Subjective appraisals are based on managers' perceptions of traits, behaviors, or results. Because subjective appraisals rest on managers' perceptions, there is always the chance that they are inaccurate. This is why both researchers and managers have spent considerable time and effort on determining the best way to develop reliable and valid subjective measures of performance.

objective appraisal
An appraisal that is based on facts and is likely to be numerical.

subjective appraisal
An appraisal that is based on perceptions of traits, behaviors, or results.

Who Appraises Performance?

We have been assuming that managers or the supervisors of employees evaluate performance. This is a reasonable assumption: Supervisors are the most common appraisers of performance. Performance appraisal is an important part of most managers' job duties. Managers are responsible for not only motivating their employees to perform at a high level but also making many decisions hinging on performance appraisals, such as pay raises or promotions. Appraisals by managers can be usefully augmented by appraisals from other sources (see Figure 12.5).

Figure 12.5
Who Appraises
Performance?

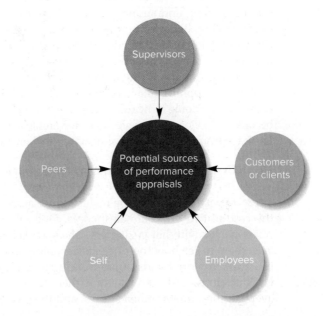

SELF, PEERS, EMPLOYEES, AND CLIENTS When self-appraisals are used, managers supplement their evaluations with an employee's assessment of his or her own performance. Peer appraisals are provided by an employee's coworkers. Especially when employees work in groups or teams, feedback from peer appraisals can motivate team members while giving managers important information for decision making. A growing number of companies are having employees appraise their managers' performance and leadership as well. And sometimes customers or clients assess employee performance in terms of responsiveness to customers and quality of service. Although appraisals from these sources can be useful, managers need to be aware of issues that may arise when they are used. Employees may be inclined to inflate self-appraisals, especially if organizations are downsizing and they are worried about job security. Managers who are appraised by their employees may fail to take needed but unpopular actions out of fear that their employees will appraise them negatively. Some of these potential issues can be mitigated to the extent that there are high levels of trust in an organization.

360-degree appraisal A performance appraisal by peers, employees, superiors, and sometimes clients who are in a position to evaluate a manager's performance.

360-DEGREE PERFORMANCE APPRAISALS To improve motivation and performance, some organizations include 360-degree appraisals and feedback in their performance appraisal systems, especially for managers. In a 360-degree appraisal a variety of people, beginning with the manager and including peers or coworkers, employees, superiors, and sometimes even customers or clients, appraise a manager's performance. The manager receives feedback based on evaluations from these multiple sources.

Companies in a variety of industries rely on 360-degree appraisals and feedback.[52] For 360-degree appraisals and feedback to be effective, there has to be trust throughout an organization. More generally, trust is a critical ingredient in any performance appraisal and feedback procedure. In addition, research suggests that 360-degree appraisals should focus on behaviors rather than traits or results and that managers need to carefully select appropriate raters. Moreover, appraisals tend to be more honest when made anonymously and when raters have been trained in how to use 360-degree appraisal forms.[53] Additionally, managers need to think carefully about the extent to which 360-degree appraisals are appropriate for certain jobs and be willing to modify any appraisal system they implement if they become aware of unintended problems it creates, such as comments that seem too subjective on the part of the person rating the individual manager or employee.[54]

Effective Performance Feedback

For the appraisal and feedback component of a human resource management system to encourage and motivate high performance, managers must give their employees feedback. To generate useful information to feed back to their employees, managers can use both formal and informal appraisals. Formal appraisals are conducted at set times during the year and are based on performance dimensions and measures that have been specified in advance.

formal appraisal An appraisal conducted at a set time during the year and based on performance dimensions and measures that were specified in advance.

Managers in most large organizations use formal performance appraisals on fixed schedules dictated by company policy, such as every six months or every year. An integral part of a formal appraisal is a meeting between the manager and the employee in which the employee is given feedback on performance. Performance feedback lets employees know which areas they are excelling in and which areas need improvement; it should also tell them *how* they can improve their performance. Realizing the value of formal appraisals, managers in many large corporations have committed substantial resources to updating their performance appraisal procedures and training low-level managers in how to use them and provide accurate feedback to employees.[55]

Formal performance appraisals supply both managers and employees with valuable information; however, employees often want more frequent feedback, and managers often want to motivate employees as the need arises. For these reasons many companies supplement formal performance appraisals with frequent **informal appraisals**, for which managers and their employees meet as the need arises to discuss ongoing progress and areas for improvement. Moreover, when job duties, assignments, or goals change, informal appraisals can give workers timely feedback concerning how they are handling their new responsibilities.

Managers often dislike providing performance feedback, especially when the feedback is negative, but doing so is an important managerial activity.[56] Here are some guidelines for giving effective performance feedback that contributes to employee motivation and performance:

informal appraisal
An unscheduled appraisal of ongoing progress and areas for improvement.

- *Be specific and focus on behaviors or outcomes that are correctable and within a worker's ability to improve.* Example: Telling a salesperson that he is too shy when interacting with customers is likely to lower his self-confidence and prompt him to become defensive. A more effective approach would be to give the salesperson feedback about specific behaviors to engage in—greeting customers as soon as they enter the department, asking customers whether they need help, and volunteering to help customers find items.

- *Approach performance appraisal as an exercise in problem solving and solution finding, not criticizing.* Example: Rather than criticizing a financial analyst for turning in reports late, the manager helps the analyst determine why the reports are late and identify ways to better manage her time.

- *Express confidence in an employee's ability to improve.* Example: Instead of being skeptical, a first-level manager tells an employee that he is confident that the employee can increase quality levels.

- *Provide performance feedback both formally and informally.* Example: The staff of a preschool receives feedback from formal performance appraisals twice a year. The school director also provides frequent informal feedback such as complimenting staff members on creative ideas for special projects, noticing when they do a particularly good job handling a difficult child, and pointing out when they provide inadequate supervision.

- *Praise instances of high performance and areas of a job in which a worker excels.* Example: Rather than focusing on just the negative, a manager discusses the areas her employee excels in as well as the areas in need of improvement.

- *Avoid personal criticisms and treat employees with respect.* Example: An engineering manager acknowledges her employees' expertise and treats them as professionals. Even when the manager points out performance problems to employees, she refrains from criticizing them personally.

- *Agree to a timetable for performance improvements.* Example: A first-level manager and his employee decide to meet again in one month to determine whether quality levels have improved.

Some companies have replaced annual performance reviews with more frequent, informal "check-ins" between managers and employees to provide feedback and discuss employee development. mavo/Shutterstock

Recent Trends in Performance Appraisal

Performance reviews have always been a source of stress for both managers and employees. It's difficult to look back on an employee's entire-year performance and come up with constructive feedback when situations or behaviors happened so far in the past.[57] When performance reviews take place on an annual basis, some employees are surprised and dismayed at some of the less-than-positive feedback they receive from supervisors, which may not have a positive impact on future employee performance.[58] In a recent Gallup survey, only 29% of employees strongly agreed that the annual evaluations they received were fair.[59]

Over the last several years, major organizations, such as GE, Microsoft, Adobe Systems, Netflix, and Accenture, have changed the way they evaluate employee performance—by doing away with annual performance reviews.[60] Instead, these companies have adopted a more informal and ongoing dialog between manager and employee as a way of discussing performance and providing feedback that can help shape future behavior.[61]

For example, Adobe's Check-in program requires managers and employees to meet at least once a quarter to discuss expectations, feedback, and growth and development. The discussion is informal (with no script), and there is no paperwork to fill out. Several years after companywide implementation, the Check-in program continues to work well: morale has increased significantly among employees and managers; fewer employees are leaving the company for jobs elsewhere; and involuntary departures (for people not meeting company expectations) have increased by 50%.[62]

Regardless of the approach they use, managers need to remember *why* they are giving performance feedback: to encourage high levels of motivation and performance. Moreover, the information that managers gather through performance appraisal and feedback helps them determine how to distribute pay raises and bonuses.

Pay and Benefits

Pay includes employees' base salaries, pay raises, and bonuses and is determined by a number of factors such as the characteristics of the organization and the job and levels of performance. Employee *benefits* are based on membership in an organization (not necessarily on the particular job held) and include sick days, vacation days, and medical and life insurance. In Chapter 9 we discuss how pay can motivate organizational members to perform at a high level, as well as the different kinds of pay plans managers can use to help an organization achieve its goals and gain a competitive advantage. As you will learn, it is important to link pay to behaviors or results that contribute to organizational effectiveness. Next we focus on establishing an organization's pay level and pay structure.

LO 12-5
Explain the issues managers face in determining levels of pay and benefits.

Pay Level

Pay level is a broad, comparative concept that refers to how an organization's pay incentives compare, in general, to those of other organizations in the same industry

pay level The relative position of an organization's pay incentives in comparison with those of other organizations in the same industry employing similar kinds of workers.

employing similar kinds of workers. Managers must decide if they want to offer relatively high wages, average wages, or relatively low wages. High wages help ensure that an organization is going to be able to recruit, select, and retain high performers, but high wages also raise costs. Low wages give an organization a cost advantage but may undermine the organization's ability to select and recruit high performers and to motivate current employees to perform at a high level. Either of these situations may lead to inferior quality or inadequate customer service.

In determining pay levels, managers should take into account their organization's strategy. A high pay level may prohibit managers from effectively pursuing a low-cost strategy. But a high pay level may be worth the added costs in an organization whose competitive advantage lies in superior quality and excellent customer service. As one might expect, hotel and motel chains with a low-cost strategy, such as Days Inn and Hampton Inns, have lower pay levels than chains striving to provide high-quality rooms and services, such as the Four Seasons.

Pay Structure

pay structure The arrangement of jobs into categories, reflecting their relative importance to the organization and its goals, levels of skill required, and other characteristics.

After deciding on a pay level, managers have to establish a pay structure for the different jobs in the organization. A pay structure clusters jobs into categories, reflecting their relative importance to the organization and its goals, levels of skill required, and other characteristics managers consider important. Pay ranges are established for each job category. Individual jobholders' pay within job categories is then determined by factors such as performance, seniority, and skill levels.

There are some interesting global differences in pay structures. Large corporations based in the United States tend to pay their CEOs and top managers higher salaries than do their European or Japanese counterparts. Also, the pay differential between employees at the bottom of the corporate hierarchy and those higher up is much greater in U.S. companies than in European or Japanese companies.[63]

Concerns have been raised over whether it is equitable or fair for CEOs of large companies in the United States to be making millions of dollars in years when their companies are restructuring and laying off a large portion of their workforces.[64] Additionally, the average CEO in the United States typically earns 312 times what the average hourly worker earns.[65] Is a pay structure with such a huge pay differential ethical? Shareholders and the public are increasingly asking this very question as well as asking large corporations to rethink their pay structures. Also troubling are the millions of dollars in severance packages that some CEOs receive when they leave their organizations. When many workers are struggling to make ends meet, people are questioning whether it is ethical for some top managers to be making so much money.[66]

Benefits

Organizations are legally required to provide certain benefits to their employees, including workers' compensation, Social Security, and unemployment insurance. Workers' compensation helps employees financially if they become unable to work due to a work-related injury or illness. Social Security provides financial assistance to retirees and former employees with disabilities. Unemployment insurance provides financial assistance to workers who lose their jobs due to no fault of their own. The legal system in the United States views these three benefits as ethical requirements for organizations and thus mandates that they be provided.

Other benefits such as health insurance, dental insurance, vacation time, pension plans, life insurance, flexible working hours, company-provided day care, and employee assistance and wellness programs have traditionally been provided at the option of employers. As of this writing, the Affordable Care Act signed into law by President Obama in 2010 still requires employers with 50 or more employees to provide them with health care coverage or face fines.[67] Benefits enabling workers to balance the demands of their jobs and of their lives away from the office or factory are of growing importance for many workers who have competing demands on their scarce time and energy.

In some organizations, top managers determine which benefits might best suit the employees and organization and offer the same benefit package to all employees. Other organizations, realizing that employees' needs and desires might differ, offer cafeteria-style benefit plans that let employees choose the benefits they want. Cafeteria-style benefit plans sometimes help managers deal with employees who feel unfairly treated because they are unable to take advantage of certain benefits available to other employees who, for example, have children. Some organizations have success with cafeteria-style benefit plans; others find them difficult to manage.

As health care costs escalate and overstretched employees find it hard to take time to exercise and take care of their health, more companies are providing benefits and incentives to promote employee wellness. According to a survey conducted by Fidelity Investments and the National Business Group on Health, close to 90% of organizations provide some kind of incentive, prize, or reward to employees who take steps to improve their health.[68] For working parents, family-friendly benefits are especially attractive. For example, access to on-site child care, the ability to telecommute and take time off to care for sick children, and provisions for emergency back-up child care can be valued benefits for working parents with young children.

Same-sex domestic partner benefits have been used to attract and retain valued employees. Gay and lesbian workers are reluctant to work for companies that do not provide the same kind of benefits for their partners as those provided for partners of the opposite sex. In recent years, however, after the U.S. Supreme Court in 2015 ruled that same-sex marriage was legal in all 50 states, many companies have reduced same-sex domestic partner benefits in favor of covering married partners of gay and lesbian employees.[69]

cafeteria-style benefit plan A plan from which employees can choose the benefits they want.

Labor Relations

Labor relations are the activities managers engage in to ensure that they have effective working relationships with the labor unions that represent their employees' interests. Although the U.S. government has responded to the potential for unethical and unfair treatment of workers by creating and enforcing laws regulating employment (including the EEO laws listed in Table 12.1), some workers believe a union will ensure that their interests are fairly represented in their organizations.

Before we describe unions in more detail, let's take a look at some examples of important employment legislation. In 1938 the government passed the Fair Labor Standards Act, which prohibited child labor and provided for minimum wages, overtime pay, and maximum working hours to protect workers' rights. In 1963 the Equal Pay Act mandated that men and women performing equal work (work requiring the same levels of skill, responsibility, and effort performed in the same kind of working conditions) receive equal pay (see Table 12.1). In 1970 the Occupational Safety and Health Act mandated procedures for managers to follow to ensure workplace safety. These are just a few of the U.S. government's efforts to protect workers' rights. State legislatures also have been active in promoting safe, ethical, and fair workplaces.

LO 12-6
Understand the role that labor relations play in the effective management of human resources.

labor relations The activities managers engage in to ensure that they have effective working relationships with the labor unions that represent their employees' interests.

Unions

Unions exist to represent workers' interests in organizations. Given that managers have more power than rank-and-file workers and that organizations have multiple stakeholders, there is always the potential for managers to take steps that benefit one set of stakeholders, such as shareholders, while hurting another, such as employees. For example, managers may decide to speed up a production line to lower costs and increase production in the hopes of increasing returns to shareholders. Speeding up the line, however, could hurt employees forced to work at a rapid pace and may increase the risk of injuries. Also, employees receive no additional pay for the extra work they are performing. Unions would represent workers' interests in a scenario such as this one.

Congress acknowledged the role that unions could play in ensuring safe and fair workplaces when it passed the National Labor Relations Act of 1935. This act made it legal for workers to organize into unions to protect their rights and interests and declared certain unfair or unethical organizational practices to be illegal. The act also established the National Labor Relations Board (NLRB) to oversee union activity. Currently, the NLRB conducts certification elections, which are held among the employees of an organization to determine whether they want a union to represent their interests. The NLRB also makes judgments concerning unfair labor practices and specifies practices that managers must refrain from.

Employees might vote to have a union represent them for any number of reasons.[70] They may think their wages and working conditions need improvement. They may believe managers are not treating them with respect. They may think their working hours are unfair or they need more job security or a safer work environment. Or they may be dissatisfied with management and find it difficult to communicate their concerns to their bosses. Regardless of the specific reason, one overriding reason is power: A united group inevitably wields more power than an individual, and this type of power may be especially helpful to employees in some organizations.

Although these would seem to be potent forces for unionization, some workers are reluctant to join unions. Sometimes this reluctance is due to the perception that union leaders are corrupt. Some workers may simply believe that belonging to a union might not do them much good while costing them money in membership dues. Employees also might not want to be forced into doing something they do not want to, such as striking because the union thinks it is in their best interest. Moreover, although unions can be a positive force in organizations, sometimes they also can be a negative force, impairing organizational effectiveness. For example, when union leaders resist needed changes in an organization or are corrupt, organizational performance can suffer.

The percentage of U.S. workers represented by unions today is smaller than it was back in the 1950s, an era when unions were particularly strong. In the 1950s, around 35% of U.S. workers were union members; in 2018, 10.5% were members of unions.[71] The American Federation of Labor–Congress of Industrial Organizations (AFL–CIO) includes 70 affiliated member unions representing close to 12.5 million workers.[72] Overall, approximately 14.7 million workers in the United States belong to unions. In general, the union membership rate of public-sector workers (ie, government workers) continues to be more than five times higher than that of private-sector workers (33.9% versus 6.4%).[73] Unions have made some inroads into other sectors of the workforce. In 2018, media employees of the *Los Angeles Times* and graduate students at Columbia, Yale, Tufts, and Brandeis universities all voted to join unions.[74]

Collective Bargaining

collective bargaining
Negotiation between labor unions and managers to resolve conflicts and disputes about issues such as working hours, wages, benefits, working conditions, and job security.

Collective bargaining is negotiation between labor unions and managers to resolve conflicts and disputes about important issues such as working hours, wages, working conditions, and job security. Sometimes union members go on strike to drive home their concerns to managers. Once an agreement that union members support has been reached (sometimes with the help of a neutral third party called a *mediator*), union leaders and managers sign a contract spelling out the terms of the collective bargaining agreement.

Summary and Review

STRATEGIC HUMAN RESOURCE MANAGEMENT Human resource management (HRM) includes all the activities managers engage in to ensure that their organizations can attract, retain, and effectively use human resources. Strategic HRM is the process by which managers design the components of a human resource management system to be consistent with each other, with other elements of organizational architecture, and with the organization's strategies and goals. [LO 12-1]

RECRUITMENT AND SELECTION Before recruiting and selecting employees, managers must engage in human resource planning and job analysis. Human resource planning includes all the activities managers engage in to forecast their current and future needs for human resources. Job analysis is the process of identifying (1) the tasks, duties, and responsibilities that make up a job and (2) the knowledge, skills, and abilities needed to perform the job. Recruitment includes all the activities managers engage in to develop a pool of qualified applicants for open positions. Selection is the process by which managers determine the relative qualifications of job applicants and their potential for performing well in a particular job. [LO 12-2]

TRAINING AND DEVELOPMENT Training focuses on teaching organizational members how to perform effectively in their current jobs. Development focuses on broadening organizational members' knowledge and skills so they are prepared to take on new responsibilities and challenges. [LO 12-3]

PERFORMANCE APPRAISAL AND FEEDBACK Performance appraisal is the evaluation of employees' job performance and contributions to the organization. Performance feedback is the process through which managers share performance appraisal information with their employees, give them an opportunity to reflect on their own performance, and develop with them plans for the future. Performance appraisal gives managers useful information for decision making. Performance feedback can encourage high levels of motivation and performance. Recent trends suggest that some organizations are moving away from the annual performance review for employees, instead taking a more informal approach to evaluating workers. This strategy includes specific, ongoing conversations between manager and employee on a regular basis to discuss expectations, performance feedback, and plans for growth and development. [LO 12-4]

PAY AND BENEFITS Pay level is the relative position of an organization's pay incentives in comparison with those of other organizations in the same industry employing similar workers. A pay structure clusters jobs into categories according to their relative importance to the organization and its goals, the levels of skill required, and other characteristics. Pay ranges are then established for each job category. Organizations are legally required to provide certain benefits to their employees; other benefits are provided at the discretion of employers. [LO 12-5]

LABOR RELATIONS Labor relations include all the activities managers engage in to ensure that they have effective working relationships with the labor unions that represent their employees' interests. The National Labor Relations Board oversees union activity. Collective bargaining is the process through which labor unions and managers resolve conflicts and disputes and negotiate agreements. [LO 12-6]

Management *in Action*

Topics for Discussion and Action

Discussion

1. Discuss why it is important for human resource management systems to be in sync with an organization's strategy and goals and with each other. [LO 12-1]

2. Discuss why training and development are ongoing activities for all organizations. [LO 12-3]

3. Describe the type of development activities you think middle managers are most in need of. [LO 12-3]

4. Evaluate the pros and cons of 360-degree performance appraisals and feedback. Would you like your performance to be appraised in this manner? Why or why not? [LO 12-4]

5. Discuss why two restaurants in the same community might have different pay levels. [LO 12-5]

Action

6. Interview a manager in a local organization to determine how that organization recruits and selects employees. [LO 12-2]

Building Management Skills

Analyzing Human Resource Management Systems [LO 12-1, 12-2, 12-3, 12-4, 12-5]

Think about your current job or a job you have had in the past. If you have never had a job, interview a friend or family member who is currently working. Answer the following questions about the job you have chosen:

1. How are people recruited and selected for this job? Are

the recruitment and selection procedures the organization uses effective or ineffective? Why?

2. What training and development do people who hold this job receive? Are the training and development appropriate? Why or why not?

3. How is performance of this job appraised? Does performance feedback contribute to motivation and high performance on this job?

4. What levels of pay and benefits are provided on this job? Are these levels appropriate? Why or why not?

Managing Ethically [LO 12-4, 12-5]

Some managers do not want to become overly friendly with their employees because they are afraid that doing so will impair their objectivity in conducting performance appraisals and making decisions about pay raises and promotions. Some employees resent it when they see one or more of their coworkers being very friendly with the boss; they are concerned about the potential for favoritism.

Their reasoning runs something like this: If two employees are equally qualified for a promotion and one is a good friend of the boss and the other is a mere acquaintance, who is more likely to receive the promotion?

Questions

1. Either individually or in a group, think about the ethical implications of managers'

becoming friendly with their employees.

2. Do you think managers should feel free to socialize and become good friends with their employees outside the workplace if they so desire? Why or why not?

Small Group Breakout Exercise [LO 12-1, 12-2, 12-3, 12-4, 12-5]

Building a Human Resource Management System

Form groups of three or four people, and appoint one member as the spokesperson who will communicate your findings to the class when called on by the instructor. Then discuss the following scenario:

You and your three partners are engineers who minored in business at college and have decided to start a consulting business. Your goal is to provide manufacturing process engineering and other engineering services to large and small organizations. You forecast that there will be an increased use of outsourcing for these activities. You discussed with managers in several large organizations the services you plan to offer, and they expressed considerable interest. You have secured funding to start your business and now are

building the HRM system. Your human resource planning suggests that you need to hire between five and eight experienced engineers with good communication skills, two clerical workers/administrative assistants, and two MBAs who between them have financial, accounting, and human resource skills. You are striving to develop your human resources in a way that will enable your new business to prosper.

1. Describe the steps you will take to recruit and select (a)

the engineers, (b) the clerical workers/administrative assistants, and (c) the MBAs.

2. Describe the training and development the engineers, the clerical workers/administrative assistants, and the MBAs will receive.

3. Describe how you will appraise the performance of each group of employees and how you will provide feedback.

4. Describe the pay level and pay structure of your consulting firm.

Be the Manager [LO 12-4]

You are Jennifer Boynton and just received some disturbing feedback. You are the director of human resources for Maxi Vision, a medium-size window and glass

door manufacturer. You recently initiated a 360-degree performance appraisal system for all middle and upper managers at Maxi Vision, including yourself, but excluding

the senior-most executives and top management team.

You were eagerly awaiting feedback about the new system from the managers who report directly to you. You recently implemented several important initiatives that affected them and their employees, including a complete overhaul of the company's appraisal system, which they would now be using to evaluate their own employees' performance. Conducted annually, performance appraisals are an important consideration in determining pay raises and bonus decisions.

You were so convinced the new performance appraisal procedures would be highly effective and well received that you hoped your own managers would mention them in feedback to you. And boy, did they!

You were amazed to learn that the managers and their employees thought the new performance appraisal system was unfair and a waste of time. In fact, several of the managers who report to you said their own performance was suffering based on the 360-degree appraisals they received from others in the organization. In addition, the managers told you their own employees hated the new appraisal system and partially blamed them for the new system because the employees viewed their bosses as part of the management team.

You couldn't believe the comments the managers conveyed as part of their own performance appraisals. You spent so much time developing what you thought was the ideal rating system for both managers and employees. Unfortunately, your enthusiasm for the new system wasn't shared by others in the company. Your own supervisor is aware of the complaints and told you it was a top priority for you to "fix this mess," which suggests she thinks you're responsible for creating a bad situation among employees and managers. What are you going to do?

Case in the News [LO 12-1, 12-2, 12-3, 12-4]

How Salesforce Sets Itself Apart in a Tight Labor Market

As its name suggests, San Francisco–based Salesforce .com started as a service to help companies sell better. Its first product, a computer system for customer relationship management (CRM), lets salespeople tap into company data to write quotes, prepare sales forecasts, generate bills automatically, share product information, and get reminders to follow up with particular clients about specific needs. If these capabilities sound obvious, that is a tribute to companies like Salesforce, because businesses formerly relied on their people to set up paper or computer processes to handle such information. The job of a salesperson could turn into an endless stream of paperwork, robbing time that could have been spent with customers. Salesforce's system became a hit, and today the company is

the top-selling provider of CRM. It continues to update the software, applying artificial intelligence to guide better decisions. The system has expanded to include tools for social media, online advertising and sales, app development, linking of customers' mobile devices, project collaboration, and more. The company has been growing rapidly, approaching its goal of $16 billion in revenues. Management is optimistic about the future. One reason is that companies see great potential in data analytics—delving deep into data to inform and make better decisions. Salesforce acquired MuleSoft, whose products enable companies to bring data from old computer systems into Salesforce's cloud-based system, making CRM potentially more valuable than ever.

The very success of Salesforce .com presents a human resource

management challenge. The demand for computer professionals to write, update, and debug software, plus those who can envision and create advances in the technology, is intense. Throughout the industry, companies struggle to find and keep talent. One way that Salesforce has addressed the difficulty is by offering its Lightning Web Components tools, which let clients and their technology providers develop their own apps that can access data in Salesforce and use the system's software. This takes some pressure off Salesforce to meet every client's industry-specific needs.

Nevertheless, Salesforce's demand for computer expertise remains, and the responsibility falls to Cindy Robbins, the company's president and chief people officer. Two signs of the significance of her role as HR chief are her position as company president and her reporting relationship directly to Salesforce co-CEO Marc Benioff. Benioff is considered Salesforce's visionary, while co-CEO Keith Block focuses on financial results. Robbins drew Benioff's attention when she and colleague Leyla Seka conducted an internal audit of pay at Salesforce and discovered that the company's female employees were being paid less than men doing the same work. Robbins insisted that the numbers were not to be disregarded, and she led an effort to bring women's pay in alignment with men's. She also ensured that future audits will be conducted to measure and maintain progress.

Herself a Latina and the first in her family to attend college, Robbins sees valuing diversity as an attitude that contributes to Salesforce's reputation as a great place to work. Her boss Benioff agrees. Benioff already had observed that women were underrepresented in the company's management, so he began requiring that 30% of attendees at quarterly executive meetings be women. The company also invites employees to set up groups called *ohana* groups dedicated to topics around shared interests (*ohana* is a Hawaiian word referring to a person's extended family, more broadly defined than just blood relations). The ohana groups build relationships across departments and office locations and have the potential to increase job satisfaction among employees.

A practical advantage of valuing diversity in a tight labor market is that it opens hiring managers' minds to locating talent in areas they might not otherwise consider. Employers tend to fall back on some image of an ideal candidate with a degree from a prestigious school and a personality resembling that of the company's current star performers. When employers do this, they miss out on talented people with other qualities, including the grit needed to overcome obstacles such as poverty and discrimination. Salesforce is among the companies trying to break away from that tendency and seek out talent where others are not looking. The company has partnered with the Year Up program, a one-year program that teaches technical and workplace skills to urban youth and helps them find internships (often leading to permanent jobs) with Salesforce and other organizations. The experience has been beneficial enough that Salesforce has built ties with other programs for "nontraditional" hiring strategies.

Questions for Discussion

1. In the information given, what evidence can you find that Salesforce.com is being strategic about human resource management?

2. The company's participation in Year Up is an example of external recruiting. Why would external recruiting be important for Salesforce to meet its hiring goals?

3. Suggest a few ways that Salesforce can use performance appraisals and pay to meet the challenge of attracting and keeping talent in a tight labor market.

Sources: Salesforce.com, "Products Overview," www.salesforce.com, accessed January 28, 2019; H. Draznin, "Salesforce President: Being an Introvert Is a Strength," *Boss Files* (CNN), www.cnn.com, accessed January 6, 2019; R. Miller, "Salesforce Keeps Rolling with Another Banner Year in 2018," *TechCrunch*, https://techcrunch.com, accessed January 6, 2019; A. Bridgwater, "Salesforce Aims to Ignite Web Developers with Lightning," *Forbes*, www.forbes.com, December 18, 2018; P. Thomas, "Backlog and Revenue Growth Power Salesforce Results," *The Wall Street Journal*, www.wsj.com, November 27, 2018; T. Walk-Morris, "Top Workplaces 2018, No. 1: Salesforce Focuses on Building Community during Period of Rapid Growth," *Chicago Tribune*, www.chicagotribune.com, November 2, 2018; M. Rosoff, "Salesforce's New Co-CEO Keith Block Explains How the Company Will Keep Growing," *CNBC Tech*, www.cnbc.com, August 8, 2018; Ellen McGirt, "Grit Is the New MBA," *Fortune*, February 1, 2018, 54–62.

Endnotes

1. Unilever, "About Us," www.unilever.com, accessed January 27, 2019; Rik Kirkland, "Talent Management as a Business Discipline: A Conversation with Unilever CHRO Leena Nair," McKinsey & Company, www.mckinsey.com, March 2018; WorkdayVoice, "Unilever CHRO Leena Nair: How to Thrive in an Upside-Down World," *Forbes*, www.forbes.com, December 4, 2017; "Most Influential 2017: Leena Nair, Chief HR Officer, Unilever," *HR* (United Kingdom), www.hrmagazine.co.uk, September 23, 2017.

2. A. Bryant, "Strategic CHRO: Leena Nair of Unilever on HR's Role: We Are the Business," *LinkedIn*, www.linkedin.com, October 22, 2018.

3. Alison Eyring, "Connected for Growth at Unilever" (Interview with Leena Nair), *People + Strategy*, Fall 2017, 49–50.

4. WorkdayVoice, "Unilever CHRO Leena Nair"; Kirkland, "Talent Management as a Business Discipline"; N. Singh, "CEOs Must Give 50% Time to People Issues," *Times of India*, https://timesofindia.indiatimes.com, July 6, 2018.

5. "Unilever to Use Mobile Gaming to Recruit Graduates," press release, www.unilever.com, accessed January 26, 2019; Kirkland, "Talent Management as a Business Discipline."

6. P. M. Wright and G. C. McMahan, "Theoretical Perspectives for Strategic Human Resource Management," *Journal of Management* 18 (1992), 295–320; J. E. Butler, G. R. Ferris, and N. K. Napier, *Strategy and Human Resource Management* (Cincinnati, OH: South-Western, 1991).

7. C. Day, "4 Reasons to Invite HR to Your Strategic Planning Meetings," *Fast Company,* www.fastcompany.com, accessed January 27, 2019.

8. A. Pressman, "Why Microsoft CEO Satya Nadella Is Tearing Up the Windows Business," *Fortune,* http://fortune.com, accessed January 26, 2019.

9. J. B. Quinn, P. Anderson, and S. Finkelstein, "Managing Professional Intellect: Making the Most of the Best," *Harvard Business Review,* March–April, 1996, 71–80.

10. W. Loeb, "Why Home Depot CEO Craig Menear Is the Retailer of the Year," *Forbes,* www.forbes.com, accessed January 26, 2019; L. Thomas, "Home Depot, Lowe's Embark on Spring Hiring Sprees as Labor Market Stiffens," *CNBC,* www.cnbc.com, February 14, 2018; P. Wahba, "Why Home Depot Is Spending an Extra $5.4 Billion on Stores and E-commerce in Next Three Years," *Fortune,* http://fortune.com, December 6, 2017.

11. Wahba, "Why Home Depot Is Spending an Extra $5.4 Billion."

12. "Home Depot Re-tools Interview Process in Latest Attempt to Attract New Hires," *Atlanta Business Chronicle,* www.bizjournals.com/atlanta, February 14, 2018.

13. Ibid.

14. S. McFarland, "Home Depot Giving $50M to Help Shore Up U.S. Labor Gap," *UPI,* www.upi.com, March 8, 2018.

15. C. D. Fisher, L. F. Schoenfeldt, and J. B. Shaw, *Human Resource Management* (Boston: Houghton Mifflin, 1990).

16. Wright and McMahan, "Theoretical Perspectives for Strategic Human Resource Management."

17. L. Baird and I. Meshoulam, "Managing Two Fits for Strategic Human Resource Management," *Academy of Management Review* 14, 116–28; J. Milliman, M. Von Glinow, and M. Nathan, "Organizational Life Cycles and Strategic International Human Resource Management in Multinational Companies: Implications for Congruence Theory," *Academy of Management Review* 16 (1991), 318–39; R. S. Schuler and S. E. Jackson, "Linking Competitive Strategies with Human Resource Management Practices," *Academy of Management Executive* 1 (1987), 207–19; P. M. Wright and S. A. Snell, "Toward an Integrative View of Strategic Human Resource Management," *Human Resource Management Review* 1 (1991), 203–25.

18. Equal Employment Opportunity Commission, "Uniform Guidelines on Employee Selection Procedures," *Federal Register* 43 (1978), 38290–315.

19. S. L. Rynes, "Recruitment, Job Choice, and Post-Hire Consequences: A Call for New Research Directions," in M. D. Dunnette and L. M. Hough, eds., *Handbook of Industrial and Organizational Psychology,* vol. 2 (Palo Alto, CA: Consulting Psychologists Press, 1991), 399–444.

20. "About Us," www.kellyservices.us, accessed January 26, 2019.

21. "What Should Your Business Outsource in 2018?," *Paychex,* www.paychex.com, March 20, 2018.

22. "ISG Research Identifies Top Markets for Outsourcing Growth and Service Delivery in 2018," *PR Newswire,* www.prnewswire.com, January 31, 2018.

23. "Report: Offshoring Evolving at Rapid Pace," https://today.duke.edu, accessed January 26, 2019; S. Minter, "Offshoring by US Companies Double," *Industry Week,* www.industryweek.com, accessed January 26, 2019.

24. D. Z. Morris, "How Outsourcing Tech Jobs Could Deepen Income Inequality in America," *Fortune,* http://fortune.com, accessed January 26, 2019.

25. "Average Number of Caterpillar Employees Worldwide from FY 2006 to FY 2017," *Statista,* www.statista.com, accessed January 26, 2019; "30 Amazing IBM Statistics and Facts (October 2018)," *DMR,* https://expanded ramblings.com, accessed January 26, 2019.

26. Deloitte, "The Risk Intelligent Approach to Outsourcing and Offshoring," www2.deloitte.com, accessed January 26, 2019.

27. R. J. Harvey, "Job Analysis," in M. D. Dunnette and L. M. Hough, eds., *Handbook of Industrial and Organizational Psychology,* vol. 2 (Palo Alto, CA: Consulting Psychologists Press, 1991), 71–163.

28. E. L. Levine, *Everything You Always Wanted to Know about Job Analysis: A Job Analysis Primer* (Tampa, FL: Mariner, 1983).

29. R. M. Guion, "Personnel Assessment, Selection, and Placement," in M. D. Dunnette and L. M. Hough, eds., *Handbook of Industrial and Organizational Psychology,* vol. 2 (Palo Alto, CA: Consulting Psychologists Press, 1991), 327–97.

30. C. Vargas, "Diversifying Tax Workforce Could Start with Hiring Practices," *Bloomberg BNA,* www.bna.com, March 22, 2018.

31. L. Stevens, "Small Changes Can Increase Corporate Diversity," *The Wall Street Journal,* www.wsj.com, March 13, 2018; Danielle Westermann King, "Unconscious Bias: Inside the Underbelly of Hiring," *Recruiting Trends,* www.recruitingtrends.com, April 2, 2018.

32. Vargas, "Diversifying Tax Workforce"; King, "Unconscious Bias."

33. King, "Unconscious Bias."

34. S. T. Casey, "From an Employer's View, Hiring Jobseekers with Disabilities," *Atlanta Business Chronicle,* https://www.bizjournals.com/atlanta, April 1, 2018.

35. J. Loffredi, "Before You Run an Employee Background Check You Need to Know These 6 Things,"

Inc., www.inc.com, accessed January 27, 2019.

36. T. C. Taylor, "Employee Background Check Best Practices to Protect Your Business," www.adp.com, June 6, 2018.

37. R. A. Noe, J. R. Hollenbeck, B. Gerhart, and P. M. Wright, *Fundamentals of Human Resource Management,* 8th ed. (Chicago: McGraw-Hill, 2020).

38. "What Is the Hiring Process in the Automotive Industry?," www.jobtestprep.com, accessed January 27, 2019.

39. D. Lechner, "Pre-Employment Physical Testing: What Skills Are You Looking For?," *Ergo Science,* http://info.ergoscience.com, accessed January 27, 2019.

40. N. Howe, "Putting Job Seekers to the Test," *Forbes,* www.forbes.com, September 18, 2017.

41. I. L. Goldstein, "Training in Work Organizations," in M. D. Dunnette and L. M. Hough, eds., *Handbook of Industrial and Organizational Psychology,* vol. 2 (Palo Alto, CA: Consulting Psychologists Press, 1991), 507–619.

42. B. Capodagli and L. Jackson, "Training Lessons from Disney," *Training,* www.trainingmag.com, accessed January 27, 2019; "Disney University 101—What It Is and Why You'll Love It," www.disneyfanatic.com, accessed January 27, 2019.

43. "Top 125 Award Winners," *Training,* www.trainingmag.com, January–February 2018, 50–51.

44. T. D. Allen, L. T. Eby, M. L. Poteet, E. Lentz, and L. Lima, "Career Benefits Associated with Mentoring for Protégés: A Meta-Analysis," *Journal of Applied Psychology* 89, no. 1 (2004), 127–36.

45. E. Moore, "7 Companies with Impressive Mentorship Programs," *Glassdoor,* www.glassdoor.com, accessed January 27, 2019.

46. P. Garfinkel, "Putting a Formal Stamp on Mentoring," *The New York Times,* January 18, 2004, BU10.

47. C. Emrich, M. H. Livingston, D. Pruner, L. Oberfeld, and S. Page, *Creating a Culture of Mentorship,* www.heidrick.com, accessed January 27, 2019.

48. Allen et al., "Career Benefits Associated with Mentoring"; L. Levin, "Lesson Learned: Know Your Limits. Get Outside Help Sooner Rather Than Later," *BusinessWeek Online,* www.businessweek.com, July 5, 2004; "Family, Inc.," *BusinessWeek Online,* www.businessweek.com, November 10, 2003; J. Salamon, "A Year with a Mentor. Now Comes the Test," *The New York Times,* September 30, 2003, B1, B5; E. White, "Making Mentorships Work," *The Wall Street Journal,* October 23, 2007, B11.

49. Garfinkel, "Putting a Formal Stamp on Mentoring."

50. "Executive Education," https://michiganross.umich.edu, accessed January 27, 2019; E. Brooks and R. Morse, "Methodology: Best Online MBA Programs Ranking," *US News,* www.usnews.com, January 8, 2018; J. A. Byrne, "Virtual B-Schools," *BusinessWeek,* October 23, 1995, 64–68.

51. G. P. Latham and K. N. Wexley, *Increasing Productivity through Performance Appraisal* (Reading, MA: Addison-Wesley, 1982).

52. J. S. Lublin, "Turning the Tables: Underlings Evaluate Bosses," *The Wall Street Journal,* October 4, 1994, B1, B14; S. Shellenbarger, "Reviews from Peers Instruct—and Sting," *The Wall Street Journal,* October 4, 1994, B1, B4.

53. C. Borman and D. W. Bracken, "360 Degree Appraisals," in C. L. Cooper and C. Argyris, eds., *The Concise Blackwell Encyclopedia of Management* (Oxford, England: Blackwell, 1998), 17; D. W. Bracken, "Straight Talk about Multi-Rater Feedback," *Training and Development* 48 (1994), 44–51; M. R. Edwards, W. C. Borman, and J. R. Sproul, "Solving the Double Bind in Performance Appraisal: A Saga of Solves, Sloths, and Eagles," *Business Horizons* 85 (1985), 59–68.

54. M. Buckingham, "The Fatal Flaws with 360 Surveys," *Harvard Business Review,* https://hbr.org, accessed January 27, 2019; J. Shriar, "The Pros and Cons of 360 Degree Feedback," *Office Vibe,* www.officevibe.com, May 1, 2017.

55. S. C. Twohill, "Make Performance Reviews Effective Again," *Workforce,* www.force.com, January 31, 2017.

56. S. E. Moss and J. I. Sanchez, "Are Your Employees Avoiding You? Managerial Strategies for Closing the Feedback Gap," *Academy of Management Executive* 18, no. 1 (2004), 32–46.

57. Quora, "Why Performance Reviews Are Way More Important Than You Think," *Inc.,* www.inc.com, accessed January 27, 2019.

58. A. Sarkar, "Is It Time to Do Away with Annual Performance Appraisal System? Benefits and Challenges Ahead," *Human Resource Management International Digest* 24, no. 3 (2016), 7–10.

59. B. Wigert and A. Mann, "Give Performance Reviews That Actually Inspire Employees," *Gallup Blog,* http://news.gallup.com, September 25, 2017.

60. K. Duggan, "Six Companies That Are Redefining Performance Management," *Fast Company,* www.fastcompany.com, October 20, 2015.

61. Sarkar, "Is It Time to Do Away with Annual Performance Appraisal System?"

62. "The Story of Check-in," www.adobe.com, accessed January 27, 2019; A. Smith, "More Employers Ditch Performance Appraisals," Society for Human Resource Management, www.shrm.org, May 18, 2018.

63. J. Flynn and F. Nayeri, "Continental Divide over Executive Pay," *BusinessWeek,* July 3, 1995, 40–41.

64. C. Kessler, "'Underpaid' CEOs Four Times More Likely to Lay Off Employees, Researchers Say," *Fortune,* http://fortune.com, August 21, 2018.

65. D. Rushe, "US Bosses Now Earn 312 Times the Average Worker's Wage, Figures Show," *The Guardian,* www.theguardian.com, August 16, 2018.

66. F. John Reh, "The Issues and Debates Surrounding CEO Compensation," *The Balance: Careers,* www.thebalancecareeers.com, accessed January 28, 2019.

67. "Affordable Care Act in 2019: What Do Employers Need to Know?," www.integrity-data.com, January 2, 2019.

68. A. Kohll, "What Employees Really Want at Work," *Forbes,* www.forbes.com, July 10, 2018; J. Wieczner, "Your Company Wants to Make You Healthy," *The Wall Street Journal,* www.wsj.com, April 8, 2013.

69. K. Hannon, "The Health Insurance Surprise Facing Some Same-Sex Couples," *Forbes,* www.forbes.com, accessed January 27, 2019.

70. S. Premack and J. E. Hunter, "Individual Unionization Decisions," *Psychological Bulletin* 103 (1998), 223–34.

71. Bureau of Labor Statistics, "Union Members—2018," www.bls.gov, January 18, 2019.

72. "Quick Facts (AFL–CIO)," www.unionfacts.com, accessed January 27, 2019; "Our Affiliated Unions," https://aflcio.org, accessed January 27, 2019.

73. "Union Members—2018."

74. A. Semuels, "Organized Labor's Growing Class Divide," *The Atlantic,* www.theatlantic.com, January 26, 2018.

PART 6

Tom Merton/age fotostock

Effective Communication

Learning Objectives

After studying this chapter, you should be able to:

LO 13-1 Explain why effective communication helps an organization gain competitive advantage.

LO 13-2 Describe the communication process.

LO 13-3 Explain the information richness of communication media available to managers.

LO 13-4 Describe the communication networks that exist in organizations.

LO 13-5 Describe important communication skills that managers need as senders and receivers of messages.

Management Snapshot

How Boston Consulting Group Promotes Better Communication

How Can Managers Encourage Effective Communication?

As a leading consulting firm focused on business strategy, Boston Consulting Group (BCG) has a culture that values learning. Its natural response to a problem or challenge is to investigate the situation, advance knowledge, and lead change. In recent years, BCG has used that approach to tackle two challenges related to communication within the organization.[1]

One challenge was triggered by plans to relocate BCG's New York office. Managing partner Ross Love was placed in charge of investigating what type of facilities would promote the kinds of interactions that promote innovation and problem solving. To find out what communication behaviors were already occurring, Love constructed an experiment. He signed up 115 employees to participate by wearing ID badges with sensors that tracked their locations and made a record of when and to whom the individual spoke (excluding the content of what they said) throughout the day over a four-month period. The initial data, which were anonymous, showed that people who engaged in more short, informal interactions spent less time in meetings—probably because they resolved more issues outside the meetings. This research guided plans to design facilities

that would attract people into shared spaces, where they would be likely to informally connect throughout the day.[2]

In the new location, BCG again measured traffic patterns and communications. It found that "collisions"—interactions of 15 minutes or less—occurred almost 20% more often in the new location. This was good news because of the association with less time in meetings, especially because the interactions often crossed team boundaries, thereby promoting more sharing of knowledge across the organization. In addition, more collisions at the new location crossed levels of the company's hierarchy, which for the junior employees is associated with feeling highly engaged. The greater variety of who is connecting with whom also is contributing to greater cohesion within teams and a move away from overreliance on a few individuals to convey information.[3]

Another communication challenge BCG addressed relates to the experiences of women. The firm found that women were leaving the company at an unacceptable rate and were more likely than their male colleagues to have low job satisfaction. Research showed that the problem was not the usual suspects, such as work–life balance. Rather, the women were less likely to feel supported and encouraged. With regard to communication, career development tended to involve mentors

Boston Consulting Group found that employees who engage in short, informal interactions with their colleagues spent less time in meetings because they were able to communicate effectively and resolve issues quickly, particularly in a shared office environment. Gary Burchell/ Getty Images

criticizing the women's communication style because it didn't match assumptions about how successful men communicate. In particular, mentors urged female employees to be more aggressive, on the assumption that this would strengthen their messages. Instead, the coaching was frustrating to hear and seldom was possible to implement. As one manager admitted, urging a female manager to "take up space" in the room felt like "encouraging her to grow 6 inches."[4]

BCG's talent development team reevaluated the program and determined that it would be more helpful to view effective communication as a broader set of skills that include not only asserting a point but also building rapport with the audience and interpreting feedback. With the revised training, mentors and mentees alike were pleased to see communication become more effective as people chose methods that suited their own strengths.[5]

Overview Even with all the advances in information technology that are available to managers, ineffective communication continues to take place in organizations. Ineffective communication is detrimental for managers, employees, and organizations and can lead to poor performance, strained interpersonal relationships, poor service, and dissatisfied customers. For an organization to be effective and gain a competitive advantage, managers at all levels need to be good communicators.

In this chapter we describe the nature of communication and the communication process and explain why all managers and their employees need to be effective communicators. We point out the communication media available to managers and the factors they need to consider in selecting a communication medium for each message they send. We then consider the communication networks organizational members rely on. Finally, we describe the communication skills that help managers be effective senders and receivers of messages.

Communication and Management

Communication is the sharing of information between two or more people or groups to reach a common understanding.[6] First and foremost, communication, no matter how electronically based, is a human endeavor and involves individuals and groups sharing information and coordinating their actions. Second, communication does not take place unless a common understanding is reached. Thus, if you try to call a business to speak to a person in customer service or billing and you are bounced back and forth between endless automated messages and menu options and eventually hang up in frustration, communication has not taken place.

LO 13-1
Explain why effective communication helps an organization gain competitive advantage.

communication The sharing of information between two or more individuals or groups to reach a common understanding.

The Importance of Good Communication

In Chapter 1, we described how in order for an organization to gain a competitive advantage, managers must strive to increase efficiency, quality, responsiveness to customers, and innovation. Good communication is essential for attaining each of these four goals and thus is a necessity for gaining a competitive advantage.

Managers can *increase efficiency* by updating the production process to take advantage of new and more efficient technologies and by training workers to operate the new technologies and expand their skills. Good communication is necessary for managers to learn about new technologies, implement them in their organizations, and train workers how to use them. Similarly, *improving quality* hinges on effective communication. Managers need to communicate to all members of an organization the meaning and importance of high quality and the ways to attain it. Employees need to communicate quality problems and suggestions for increasing quality to their superiors, and members of self-managed work teams need to share their ideas for improving quality with each other.

Good communication can also help to increase *responsiveness to customers.* When the organizational members who are closest to customers, such as salespeople in department stores and admission clerks in a health care facility, are empowered to communicate customers' needs and desires to managers, managers are better able to respond to these needs. Managers, in turn, must communicate with other organizational members to determine how best to respond to changing customer preferences.

Innovation, which often takes place in cross-functional teams, also requires effective communication. Members of a cross-functional team developing a new electronic game, for example, must effectively communicate with one another to develop a game that customers will want to play; that will be engaging, interesting, and fun; and that can potentially lead to sequels or derivative products. Members of the team also must communicate with managers to secure the resources they need for developing the game and to keep managers informed of progress on the project. Innovation, whether in products or processes, is most likely to occur in a culture where employees share ideas, rather than merely waiting for direction from above. To learn about a company that promotes this kind of communication, read the "Manager as a Person" feature.

Effective communication is necessary for managers and all members of an organization such as Boston Consulting Group, profiled in "Management Snapshot," to increase efficiency, quality, responsiveness to customers, and innovation and thus gain a competitive advantage for their organization. Managers therefore must have a good understanding of the communication process if they are to perform effectively.

Manager as a Person

Hyphen's Goal for Employees: Be Heard at Work

For Ranjit Jose and Arnaud Grunwald, the impetus to start their business came from their experiences as employees and managers. The two were friends and coworkers at the same company, which had grown rapidly. The two men noted that as teams grew larger and the corporate structure more complex, people found it harder to point out problems and share ideas. For many, the lack of a voice was frustrating—and came with the fear that if employees were bold enough to complain, there could be consequences. Jose and Grunwald proposed that their HR department conduct a survey of team members, but the department assured them they could wait for the annual survey, which was due in six more months.[7]

As the two men discussed the situation, they agreed that communication from employees to management was essential to business success. They also agreed that

Hyphen provides businesses with a technology platform that lets them gather and analyze anonymous communications from employees via their mobile devices. This strategy lets employees know their opinions matter. Ariel Skelley/Blend Images LLC

an annual survey in this age of Internet communication and computer analysis was sadly inadequate. And finally, they speculated that other growing businesses must have the same challenges, which suggested a need for a new business. Together, they planned the start-up of Hyphen. India-born Jose, who studied electrical and computer engineering in the United States, and Grunwald, who was born in France, attended the University of California, Berkeley, and managed global analytics, set up Hyphen with two headquarters, one in San Francisco and the other in Bangalore, India.[8]

Hyphen provides businesses with a technology platform that lets businesses gather and analyze anonymous communications from their employees. The purpose is to communicate to employees that their opinions matter and to make those opinions available quickly and easily, through a variety of methods. Employees can use mobile devices to reply to quick or more in-depth surveys. They can answer quick Pulse Polls containing weekly questions. And they can make anonymous comments using the Employee Voice tool. The computer system gathers the responses, analyzes them, and submits reports and alerts to management. For example, managers can gauge concerns about a new program or follow trends in employee satisfaction, both companywide and by division or team. Hyphen's founders see the enterprise as distinctive in the way it combines ease of use on mobile devices with powerful analysis to support decision making.[9]

While technology enables the product, the company's tagline best expresses the founders' vision for its customers' employees: "Be Heard at Work."[10] ●

The Communication Process

LO 13-2
Describe the communication process.

The communication process consists of two phases. In the *transmission phase,* information is shared between two or more individuals or groups. In the *feedback phase,* a common understanding is assured. In both phases, a number of distinct stages must occur for communication to take place (see Figure 13.1).[11]

Starting the transmission phase, the sender, the person or group wishing to share information with some other person or group, decides on the message, what information to communicate. Then the sender translates the message into symbols or language, a process called encoding; often messages are encoded into words. Noise is a general term that refers to anything that hampers any stage of the communication process.

Once encoded, a message is transmitted through a medium to the receiver, the person or group for which the message is intended. A medium is simply the

Figure 13.1

The Communication Process

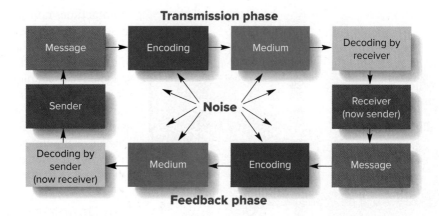

sender The person or group wishing to share information.

message The information that a sender wants to share.

encoding Translating a message into understandable symbols or language.

noise Anything that hampers any stage of the communication process.

receiver The person or group for which a message is intended.

medium The pathway through which an encoded message is transmitted to a receiver.

decoding Interpreting and trying to make sense of a message.

verbal communication The encoding of messages into words, either written or spoken.

nonverbal communication The encoding of messages by means of facial expressions, body language, and styles of dress.

pathway, such as a phone call, a letter, a memo, or face-to-face communication in a meeting, through which an encoded message is transmitted to a receiver. At the next stage, the receiver interprets and tries to make sense of the message, a process called decoding. This is a critical point in communication.

The feedback phase is initiated by the receiver (who becomes a sender). The receiver decides what message to send to the original sender (who becomes a receiver), encodes it, and transmits it through a chosen medium (see Figure 13.1). The message might contain a confirmation that the original message was received and understood or a restatement of the original message to make sure that it has been correctly interpreted; or it might include a request for more information. The original sender decodes the message and makes sure that a common understanding has been reached. If the original sender determines that a common understanding has not been reached, sender and receiver cycle through the whole process as many times as are needed to reach a common understanding.

The encoding of messages into words, written or spoken, is verbal communication. We also encode messages without using written or spoken language. Nonverbal communication shares information by means of facial expressions (smiling, raising an eyebrow, frowning, dropping one's jaw), body language (posture, gestures, nods, shrugs), and even style of dress (casual, formal, conservative, trendy). The trend toward increasing empowerment of the workforce has led some managers to dress informally to communicate that all employees of an organization are team members, working together to create value for customers.

Nonverbal communication can be used to back up or reinforce verbal communication. Just as a warm and genuine smile can back up words of appreciation for a job well done, a concerned facial expression can back up words of sympathy for a personal problem. In such cases, the congruence between verbal and nonverbal communication helps ensure that a common understanding is reached.

Sometimes when members of an organization decide not to express a message verbally, they inadvertently do so nonverbally. People tend to have less control over nonverbal communication, and often a verbal message that is withheld gets expressed through body language or facial expressions. A manager who agrees to a proposal that she or he actually is not in favor of may unintentionally communicate disfavor by grimacing.

If a picture is worth a thousand words, so too is nonverbal communication. Facial expressions, body language, posture, and eye contact all send powerful messages. Christopher Robbins/Digital Vision/Getty Images

Sometimes nonverbal communication is used to send messages that cannot be sent through verbal channels. Many lawyers are well aware of this communication tactic. Lawyers are often schooled in techniques of nonverbal communication such as choosing where to stand in the courtroom for maximum effect and using eye contact during different stages of a trial. Lawyers sometimes get into trouble for using inappropriate nonverbal communication in an attempt to influence juries.[12]

The Dangers of Ineffective Communication

Because managers must communicate with others to perform their various roles and tasks, managers spend most of their time communicating, whether in meetings, in telephone conversations, through email, or in face-to-face interactions. Indeed, some experts estimate that managers spend approximately 80% of their time engaged in some form of communication.[13] Effective communication is so important that managers cannot just be concerned that they themselves are effective communicators; they also have to help their employees be effective communicators. When all members of an organization are able to communicate effectively with each other and with people outside the organization, the organization is much more likely to perform highly and gain a competitive advantage. The "Ethics in Action" feature explores how this applies to the use of questions to foster effective communication.

When managers and other members of an organization are ineffective communicators, organizational performance suffers, and any competitive advantage the organization might have is likely to be lost. Moreover, poor communication sometimes can be downright dangerous and even lead to tragic and unnecessary loss of human life. For example, a recent study by Harvard University researchers found that changing how doctors communicate during shift changes reduced the risk of adverse events in patients by 30%. In addition, the researchers found that improving communication methods could also reduce the rate of medical errors by almost 25%.[14]

Ethics in Action

Questions Can Open the Door to Honest, Open Communication

Managers might assume that their most valuable communications deliver information and instructions. Research, however, supports the value of asking questions, listening to answers, and probing for details. Question-oriented communication builds trust and rapport, so it motivates employees, strengthens teamwork, and stimulates creativity. Even nonmanagement employees can gain power by asking questions, along with demonstrating respect and seeking opportunities to help. These behaviors build strong social networks, which become a source of opportunities for development and advancement. Thoughtful use

Asking questions as a form of communication builds trust and rapport, which can lead to motivated employees, effective teamwork, and increased creativity. Aleksandr Davydov/123RF

of questioning also is associated with greater effectiveness in personal selling.[15]

Some techniques improve the impact of questions. For getting people to share information, open-ended questions are more effective than multiple-choice or yes/no questions. Asking questions in a casual, conversational way causes people to open up. When questions aim to generate ideas, reassuring people that they can change their answers tends to free them to speak. Think of brainstorming sessions, where everyone is encouraged to toss out ideas. It may help to think of questions not as a debate with winners and losers, but as a dialog aimed at achieving a meeting of the minds, bringing the participants together on an idea, goal, or solution.[16]

Of course, the benefits of asking questions are achievable only with a person giving honest answers. Ideally, managers and employees function in an ethical environment that encourages honesty. But sometimes the context is competitive, as when negotiating a high-stakes deal with a counterpart trying to withhold information. In that case, honesty may be more likely with closed-ended questions and pessimistic assumptions—for example, in negotiating an acquisition, "Your sales growth has flattened out over the past two years, hasn't it?"[17]

A practice of asking questions and listening respectfully builds one's character because it demonstrates concern for others. Ken Sterling, executive vice president of BigSpeak, embraces questions as part of his policy of "radical candor," which involves caring about employees personally and challenging them directly. For the first objective, Sterling's meeting agendas include time for questions about employees' personal goals and concerns. The second objective, to challenge directly, involves offering honest feedback about what is and is not working. Here, too, Sterling asks questions in regular meetings. Specifically, he has teams identify areas of success, problems, and ideas for improvement. Making these questions routine teaches team members that questions are about problem solving, not criticism. This frees them to be honest.[18] ●

Information Richness and Communication Media

information richness The amount of information that a communication medium can carry and the extent to which the medium enables the sender and receiver to reach a common understanding.

To be effective communicators, managers (and other members of an organization) need to select an appropriate communication medium for *each* message they send. Should a change in procedures be communicated to employees in a memo sent through email? Should a congratulatory message about a major accomplishment be communicated in a letter, in a phone call, or over lunch? Should a layoff announcement be made in a memo or at a plant meeting? Should the members of a purchasing team travel to Europe to cement a major agreement with a new supplier, or should they do so through conference calls and email messages? Managers deal with these questions day in and day out.

There is no one best communication medium for managers to rely on. In choosing a communication medium for any message, managers need to consider three factors. The first and most important is the level of information richness that is needed. **Information richness** is the amount of information a communication medium can carry and the extent to which the medium enables the sender and receiver to reach a common understanding.[19] The communication media that managers use vary in their information richness (see Figure 13.2).[20] Media high in information richness are able to carry an extensive amount of information and generally enable receivers and senders to come to a common understanding.

The second factor that managers need to take into account in selecting a communication medium is the *time* needed for communication, because managers' and other organizational members' time is valuable. Managers at Curbstone Corporation, which develops and sells software for credit-card processing, drastically reduced the amount of time its staff spent traveling to make sales presentations and closing business by using videoconferencing and other web-based tools instead of face-to-face communication.[21]

The third factor that affects the choice of a communication medium is the *need for a paper or electronic trail* or some kind of written documentation that a message was sent and received. A manager may wish to document in writing, for example, that an employee was given a formal warning about excessive lateness.

Figure 13.2

The Information Richness of Communication Media

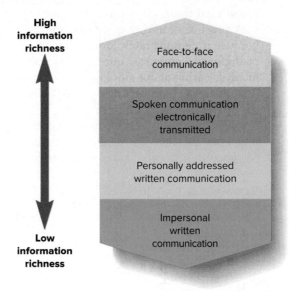

High information richness

Face-to-face communication

Spoken communication electronically transmitted

Personally addressed written communication

Impersonal written communication

Low information richness

In the remainder of this section we examine four types of communication media that vary along the three dimensions of information richness, time, and the availability of a paper or electronic trail.

Face-to-Face Communication

Face-to-face communication is the medium that is highest in information richness. When managers communicate face to face, they not only can take advantage of verbal communication but they also can interpret each other's nonverbal signals such as facial expressions and body language. A look of concern or puzzlement can sometimes tell more than a thousand words, and managers can respond to these nonverbal signals on the spot. Face-to-face communication also enables managers to receive instant feedback. Points of confusion, ambiguity, or misunderstanding can be resolved, and managers can cycle through the communication process as many times as they need to, to reach a common understanding.

management by wandering around A face-to-face communication technique in which a manager walks around a work area and talks informally with employees about issues and concerns.

Management by wandering around is a face-to-face communication technique that is effective for many managers at all levels in an organization. Rather than scheduling formal meetings with employees, managers walk around work areas and talk informally with employees about issues and concerns that employees and managers may have. These informal conversations provide managers and employees with important information and at the same time foster the development of positive relationships. With technology changing at breakneck speed and more employees working out of their homes or in remote locations, some experts suggest that in the late 2010s, management by wandering around has evolved into management by weekly check-in, which makes effective communication critical to an organization's success.[22]

Because face-to-face communication is highest in information richness, you might think that it should always be the medium of choice for managers. This is not the case, however, because of the amount of time it takes and the lack of a paper or electronic trail resulting from it. For messages that are important, personal, or likely to be misunderstood, it is often well worth managers' time to use face-to-face communication and, if need be, supplement it with some form of written communication documenting the message.

Advances in information technology are providing managers with alternative communication media for face-to-face communication. Like Curbstone Corporation mentioned earlier, other organizations use videoconferences to capture some of the advantages of face-to-face communication while saving time and money because managers in different locations do not have to travel to meet with one another.

In addition to saving travel costs, videoconferences sometimes have other advantages. Managers have found that decisions get made more quickly when videoconferences are used because more managers can be involved in the decision-making process and therefore fewer managers have to be consulted outside the meeting itself.

Taking videoconferencing one step further, Cisco and other companies have created web-based videoconferencing and collaboration systems that provide businesses with the opportunity

Despite the popularity of electronic communication, face-to-face communication is still the medium that is highest in information richness. Digital Vision/Getty Images

to not only see meeting participants but also enable the sharing of documents and other pertinent information with the group in real time. This technology provides managers and other organizational members with the tools to communicate with remote colleagues and other business professionals across the globe without spending time and money traveling to attend meetings in person.[23]

Spoken Communication Transmitted Electronically

After face-to-face communication, spoken communication transmitted over phone lines or via the Internet is second highest in information richness (see Figure 13.2). Although managers communicating over the telephone do not have access to body language and facial expressions, they do have access to the tone of voice in which a message is delivered, the parts of the message the sender emphasizes, and the general manner in which the message is spoken, in addition to the actual words themselves. Thus, telephone conversations have the capacity to convey extensive amounts of information. Managers also can ensure that mutual understanding is reached because they can get quick feedback over the phone and answer questions.

Video calling apps such as Skype and FaceTime enable people to communicate using voice and video over the Internet. They provide access to nonverbal forms of communication between sender and receiver, as well as enable individuals and businesses to conduct conference calls and interviews quickly and inexpensively. More and more companies are using Skype or FaceTime to interview potential candidates for job openings.[24]

Personally Addressed Written Communication

Lower than electronically transmitted verbal communication in information richness is personally addressed written communication (see Figure 13.2). One of the advantages of face-to-face communication and verbal communication electronically transmitted is that they both tend to demand attention, which helps ensure that receivers pay attention. Personally addressed written communications such as memos and letters also have this advantage. Because they are addressed to a particular person, the chances are good that the person will actually pay attention to (and read) them. Moreover, the sender can write the message in a way that the receiver is most likely to understand. Like voice mail, written communication does not enable a receiver to have his or her questions answered immediately, but when messages are clearly written and feedback is provided, common understanding can still be reached.

Even if managers use face-to-face communication, sending a follow-up in writing is often necessary for messages that are important or complicated and need to be referred to later. This is precisely what Karen Stracker, a hospital administrator, did when she needed to tell one of her employees about an important change in the way the hospital would be handling denials

Video calling apps such as Skype and FaceTime enable individuals and businesses to communicate quickly and inexpensively. More and more companies are also using these apps to interview potential candidates for job openings or to allow employees who work from home to communicate in real time with their colleagues in the office. Andrey_Popov/Shutterstock

of insurance benefits. Stracker met with the person and described the changes face to face. Once she was sure that the employee understood them, she handed her a sheet of instructions to follow, which essentially summarized the information they had discussed.

Email and text messages also fit into this category of communication media because senders and receivers are communicating through personally addressed written words. The words, however, appear on computer screens, laptops, or mobile devices rather than on paper. Email use in business is so widespread that some managers find they have to deliberately take time out from managing their email to get other work done, including taking action on business strategies and coming up with new and innovative ideas. According to the Radicati Group, a technology marketing research firm, by 2022 worldwide email traffic will reach 333 *billion* emails every day—including both business and consumer users.[25] To help employees manage their email effectively, many organizations provide in-house training programs or other guidance to help workers (and managers) use email as part of their daily work activities.[26]

The use of email has also enabled many workers and managers to become telecommuters, people employed by organizations who work out of their homes at least one day a week. According to recent statistics, at least 50% of the U.S. workforce telecommutes with some frequency. Many who work out of their homes indicate the flexibility of telecommuting enables them to be more productive while giving them a chance to be closer to their families and not waste time traveling to and from the office.[27]

Unfortunately, the widespread use of email has been accompanied by growing abuse of email. To avoid this abuse, managers need to develop a clear policy specifying what company email can and should be used for and what is out of bounds. Managers also should clearly communicate this policy to all members of an organization, as well as the procedures that will be used when email abuse is suspected and the consequences that will result when email abuse is confirmed.[28]

Impersonal Written Communication

Impersonal written communication is lowest in information richness and is well suited for messages that need to reach a large number of receivers. Because such messages are not addressed to particular receivers, feedback is unlikely, so managers must make sure that messages sent by this medium are written clearly in language that all receivers will understand.

Managers often find company newsletters useful vehicles for reaching large numbers of employees. Increasingly, companies are distributing their newsletters online and inviting employees to communicate through various channels with colleagues, customers, and others. For example, IBM's employee communications typically come through the company's intranet, known internally as W3, and it has led a transformation from professional to user-generated content within the company.[29]

Managers can use impersonal written communication for various types of messages, including rules, regulations, policies, newsworthy information, and announcements of changes in procedures or the arrival of new organizational members. Impersonal written communication also can be used to communicate instructions about how to use machinery or how to process work orders or customer requests. For these kinds of messages, the paper or electronic trail left by this communication medium can be invaluable for employees.

information overload A superabundance of information that increases the likelihood that important information is ignored or overlooked and tangential information receives attention.

Like personal written communication, impersonal written communication can be delivered and retrieved electronically, and this is increasingly being done in companies large and small. Unfortunately, the ease with which electronic messages can be spread has led to their proliferation. The electronic inboxes of many managers and workers are backlogged, and they rarely have time to read all the electronic work-related information available to them. The problem with such information overload is the potential for important information to be ignored or overlooked while tangential information receives attention. Moreover, information overload can result in thousands of hours and millions of dollars in lost productivity.

blog A website on which an individual, group, or organization posts information, commentary, and opinions and to which readers can often respond with their own commentary and opinions.

Some managers and organizations use blogs to communicate with employees, customers, investors, and the general public. A blog is a website on which an individual, group, or organization posts information, commentary, and opinions to which readers can often respond with their own commentary and opinions. Some top managers write their own blogs, and some companies, including Whole Foods, Chase Bank, and Disney, have corporate blogs.[30] Just as organizations have rules and guidelines about employee email and Internet use, a growing number of organizations are instituting employee guidelines for blogs.[31]

social networking site A website that enables people to communicate with others with whom they have some common interest or connection.

A social networking site, such as Facebook, Twitter, Instagram, or LinkedIn, enables people to communicate with others with whom they might have some common personal or professional interest or connection. Billions of people in the United States and around the world create custom profiles and communicate with networks of other participants via social networking sites. While communication through social networks can be work related, some managers are concerned that employees are wasting time at work communicating with their personal group of acquaintances through these sites. A recent study by Pew Research Center found that 27% of employees surveyed said they use social media at work to connect with family and friends.[32]

Communication Networks

Although various communication media are used throughout any organization, communication tends to flow in certain patterns. The pathways along which information flows are called communication networks.

Internal Communication Networks

LO 13-4
Describe the communication networks that exist in organizations.

An organizational chart may seem to be a good snapshot of an organization's communication network, but often it is not. An organizational chart summarizes the *formal* reporting relationships in an organization and the formal pathways along which communication takes place. Often, however, communication is *informal* and flows around issues, goals, projects, and ideas instead of moving up and down the organizational hierarchy in an orderly fashion. Thus, an organization's communication network includes not only the formal communication pathways summarized in an organizational chart but also informal communication pathways along which a great deal of communication takes place (see Figure 13.3).

communication networks The pathways along which information flows throughout an organization.

Communication can and should occur across departments and groups as well as within them and up, down, and sideways in the corporate hierarchy. Communication up and down the corporate hierarchy is often called *vertical* communication. Communication among employees at the same level in the corporate hierarchy, or sideways, is called *horizontal* communication. Managers cannot determine in

Figure 13.3

Formal and Informal
Communication
Networks in an
Organization

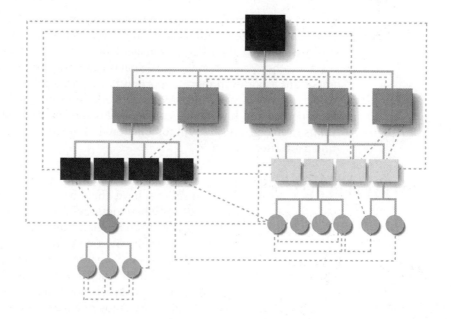

———— Formal pathways of communication summarized in an organization chart.

- - - - - Informal pathways along which a great deal of communication takes place.

advance what an organization's communication network will be, nor should they try to. Instead, to accomplish goals and perform at a high level, organizational members should be free to communicate with whomever they need to contact. Because organizational goals change over time, so do organizational communication networks. Informal communication networks can contribute to an organization's competitive advantage, because they help ensure that organizational members at all levels of the organization have the information they need when they need it to accomplish their goals.

grapevine An informal communication network along which unofficial information flows.

The **grapevine** is an informal organizational communication network along which unofficial information flows quickly, if not always accurately.[33] People in an organization who seem to know everything about everyone are prominent in the grapevine. Information spread via the grapevine can be about issues of either a business nature (such as an impending takeover) or a personal nature (such as the CEO's separation from her husband).

External Communication Networks

In addition to participating in networks within an organization, managers, employees, and those with work-related ties outside their organization often are part of external

The grapevine is an information communication network used by employees to convey both business and personal information.
Ingram Publishing

networks whose members span a variety of companies. For example, professionals in a local area often communicate in networks formed around common underlying interests, such as marketing, management, or human resources. For some managers and other professionals, participation in such interest-oriented networks is as important as, or even more important than, participation in internal company networks. Networks of contacts who are working in the same field or who have similar expertise and knowledge can be very helpful—for example, when an individual wants to change jobs, recruit top talent to her organization, locate new suppliers, or find a job after a layoff.[34]

Communication Skills for Managers

LO 13-5
Describe important communication skills that managers need as senders and receivers of messages.

Some of the barriers to effective communication in organizations have their origins in senders. Communication suffers when messages are unclear, incomplete, or difficult to understand; when they are sent over an inappropriate medium; or when no provision is made for feedback from the receiver. Sometimes, however, communication barriers have their origins in receivers. When receivers pay no attention to or do not listen to messages, or when they make no effort to understand the meaning of a message, communication is likely to be ineffective.

To overcome these barriers and effectively communicate with others, managers (as well as other organizational members) must possess or develop certain communication skills. Some of these skills are particularly important when *sending* messages; others are critical when *receiving* messages. These skills help ensure that managers can share information, possess the information they need to make effective decisions and take appropriate action, and have the ability to reach a common understanding with others.

Communication Skills for Managers as Senders

Organizational effectiveness depends on the ability of managers (as well as others in the organization) to effectively send messages to people both inside and outside the organization. Table 13.1 summarizes seven communication skills that help ensure that when managers send messages the information is properly understood, and the transmission phase of the communication process is effective. Let's see what each skill entails.

Table 13.1

Seven Communication Skills for Managers as Senders of Messages

- Send messages that are clear and complete.
- Encode messages in symbols that the receiver understands.
- Select a medium that is appropriate for the message.
- Use a medium that the receiver monitors.
- Avoid filtering and information distortion.
- Ensure that a feedback mechanism is built into messages.
- Provide accurate information to ensure that misleading rumors are not spread.

SEND CLEAR AND COMPLETE MESSAGES Managers need to learn how to send a message that is clear and complete. A message is clear when it is easy for the receiver to understand and interpret the information, and it is complete when the message contains all the information the sender and receiver need to reach a common understanding. In striving to send messages that are both clear and complete, managers must learn to anticipate how receivers will interpret messages and must adjust them to eliminate sources of misunderstanding or confusion.

Clear and complete messages include any nonverbal components. Messages are unclear if the tone of voice does not match the content of the words. Likewise, as described in the "Management Insight" feature, a person's nonverbal cues are very important when the manager first meets the person he or she is communicating with.

Management Insight

Making a Positive First Impression

Many business and daily life situations involve introducing yourself to others. Some examples are job interviews, first meetings with customers or clients, and presentations to a group including strangers. In these contexts, a first impression carries a great deal of weight. What the other person first observes in the first few seconds will shape how he or she interprets the communicator and the message.[35]

Managers cannot control every aspect of a first impression. They cannot overcome prejudices by changing their sex, race, or age, and they cannot change their facial features. But there are other ways to communicate a message of being trustworthy and agreeable.[36]

Making a good first impression carries a great deal of weight in both business and personal situations.
monkeybusinessimages/Getty Images

Facial expressions matter. A relaxed and smiling face is appealing. However, it is important to be consistent and sincere, not just flashing a smile when making eye contact. As for eye contact, it is necessary for building trust in a business context. Some experts suggest looking in the other person's eyes during 60% to 70% of the interaction. Those who are not used to making eye contact can practice by looking at the other person's eyebrows or space between the eyes until eye contact feels more natural.[37]

Posture and gestures make a difference as well. People tend to respond positively to erect but not stiff posture, with hands visible and arms uncrossed. Taking a minute to slow one's breathing, stand firmly, and think confident thoughts can help. Then, while talking, the speaker can increase trust by leaning in a little toward the other person. Also, researchers have found greater appeal in presentations where the presenters used more hand gestures to emphasize points. In the same vein, shaking hands firmly is a gesture that builds rapport.[38]

Clothing also plays a role. Those seeking to make a good first impression should, within their means, seek clothes that fit well in a flattering style and are suitable for the situation. At a minimum, it is essential to be clean and neat.[39]

First impressions include verbal communication, too. One way to make a positive and lasting impression is to greet people with questions that demonstrate a genuine interest. For example, if appropriate for the situation, a person might ask, "What has been the highlight of your day so far?" or "Has anything exciting been happening in your life?"[40] And then, of course, the questioner should listen carefully to the answer. ●

jargon Specialized language that members of an occupation, group, or organization develop to facilitate communication among themselves.

ENCODE MESSAGES IN SYMBOLS THE RECEIVER UNDERSTANDS Managers need to appreciate that when they encode messages, they should use symbols or language that the receiver understands. When sending messages in English to receivers whose native language is not English, for example, it is important to use common vocabulary and to avoid clichés that, when translated, may make little sense or are either comical or insulting. Jargon, specialized language that members of an occupation, a group, or an organization develop to facilitate communication among themselves, should never be used when communicating with people outside the occupation, group, or organization.

SELECT AN APPROPRIATE MEDIUM FOR THE MESSAGE As you have learned, when relying on verbal communication, managers can choose from a variety of communication media, including face-to-face communication in person, written letters, memos, phone conversations, email, voice mail, and videoconferences. When choosing among these media, managers need to take into account the level of information richness required, the time constraints, and the need for a paper or electronic trail. A primary concern in choosing the appropriate medium is the nature of the message. Is it personal, important, nonroutine, or likely to be misunderstood and in need of further clarification? If so, face-to-face communication is likely to be the best medium.

USE A MEDIUM THE RECEIVER MONITORS Another factor that managers need to take into account when selecting a communication medium is whether the medium is one that the receiver monitors. Managers differ in the communication media they pay attention to. Many managers simply select the medium they use the most and are most comfortable with. However, this choice can lead to ineffective communication. Managers who dislike telephone conversations and too many face-to-face interactions may prefer to use email, send many email messages per day, and check their own email often. Managers who prefer to communicate with people in person or over the phone may have email accounts but are less likely to respond to email messages. No matter how much a manager likes to use email, sending email to someone who does not respond to email is ineffective. Learning which managers like things in writing and which prefer face-to-face interactions and using the appropriate medium enhances the chance receivers will actually receive and pay attention to messages.

A related consideration is whether receivers have disabilities that hamper their ability to decode certain messages. A blind receiver, for example, cannot read a written message. Managers should ensure that employees with disabilities have resources available to communicate effectively with others.[41]

AVOID FILTERING AND INFORMATION DISTORTION Filtering occurs when a sender withholds part of a message because he or she mistakenly thinks the receiver does not need the information or will not want to receive it. Filtering can occur at all levels in an organization and in both vertical and horizontal communication. Rank-and-file workers may filter messages they send to first-line managers, first-line managers may filter messages to middle managers, and middle managers may filter messages to top managers. Such filtering is likely to take place when messages contain bad news or problems employees are afraid they will be blamed for. Managers need to hear bad news and be aware of problems as soon as they occur so they can take swift action to resolve the problem and limit the damage it may have caused.

Filtering sometimes occurs because of internal competition in organizations or because employees fear their power and influence will be diminished if others have access to some of their specialized knowledge. By increasing levels of trust in an organization, taking steps to motivate all employees to work together to achieve organizational goals, and ensuring employees realize that when the organization reaches its goals and performs effectively, they will benefit as well, this kind of filtering can be reduced.

Information distortion occurs when the meaning of a message changes as the message passes through a series of senders and receivers. Some information distortion is accidental—due to faulty encoding and decoding or a lack of feedback. Other information distortion is deliberate. Senders may alter a message to make themselves or their groups look good and to receive special treatment.

Managers themselves should avoid filtering and distorting information. But how can they eliminate these barriers to effective communication? They need to establish trust throughout the organization. Employees who trust their managers believe they will not be blamed for things beyond their control and will be treated fairly. Managers who trust their employees give them clear and complete information and do not hold things back—even if the information is bad news.

INCLUDE A FEEDBACK MECHANISM IN MESSAGES Because feedback is essential for effective communication, managers should build a feedback mechanism into the messages they send. They should either include a request for feedback or indicate how and when they will follow up on their message to make sure it was received and understood. When managers write memos or send emails, they can request that the receiver respond with comments or suggestions; schedule a meeting to discuss the issue; or follow up with a phone call. By building feedback mechanisms such as these into their messages, managers ensure they have been heard and understood.

filtering Withholding part of a message because of the mistaken belief that the receiver does not need or will not want the information.

information distortion Changes in the meaning of a message as the message passes through a series of senders and receivers.

rumors Unofficial pieces of information of interest to organizational members but with no identifiable source.

Managers can avoid information distortion by giving employees clear and complete information and establishing trust throughout the organization. LWA/Sharie Kennedy/Blend Images LLC

PROVIDE ACCURATE INFORMATION Rumors are unofficial pieces of information of interest to organizational members but with no identifiable source. Rumors spread quickly once they are started, and usually they concern topics that organizational members think are important, interesting, or amusing. Rumors, however, can be misleading and can harm individual employees and their organizations when they are false, malicious, or unfounded. Managers can halt the spread of misleading rumors by giving organizational members accurate information about matters that concern them and their work.

Providing accurate information is especially important in tough economic times like the recession in the late 2000s. During recessions, employees are sometimes laid off or have their working hours or pay levels cut back, and often experience high levels of stress. When managers give employees accurate information, this can help reduce their stress levels as well as motivate them to find ways to help their companies weather the tough times.[42] Moreover, when the economy does turn around, employees who receive accurate information from their bosses may be more likely to remain with their organizations rather than pursue other opportunities.

Communication Skills for Managers as Receivers

Managers receive as many messages as they send. Thus, managers must possess or develop communication skills that allow them to be effective receivers. We examine three of these important skills here in greater detail.

PAY ATTENTION Because of their multiple roles and tasks in an organization, managers often are overloaded and forced to think and deal with several things at once. Pulled in many different directions, they sometimes do not pay sufficient attention to the messages they receive. To be effective, however, managers should always pay attention to the messages they receive no matter how busy they are. When discussing a project with an employee, for example, an effective manager focuses on the project, not on an upcoming meeting with his or her own boss. Similarly, when managers are reading written communications, they should focus on understanding what they are reading—not being sidetracked into thinking about other issues.

BE A GOOD LISTENER Managers (and all other members of an organization) can do several things to be good listeners. First, managers should refrain from interrupting senders in the middle of a message so that senders do not lose their train of thought and managers do not jump to erroneous conclusions based on incomplete information. Second, managers should maintain eye contact with senders so that senders feel their listeners are paying attention; doing this also helps managers focus on what they are hearing. Third, after receiving a message, managers should ask questions to clarify points of ambiguity or confusion. Fourth, managers should paraphrase, or restate in their own words, the points senders make that are important, complex, or open to alternative interpretations. This is the feedback component that is so critical to successful communication.

Managers, like most people, often like to hear themselves talk rather than listen to others. Part of being a good communicator, however, is being a good listener—an essential communication skill for managers as receivers of messages transmitted face to face and over the phone.

BE EMPATHETIC Receivers are empathetic when they try to understand how the sender feels and try to interpret a message from the sender's perspective, rather than viewing the message from only their own point of view. Marcia Mazulo, the chief psychologist in a public school system in the Northwest, learned this lesson after interacting with Karen Sanchez, a new psychologist on her staff. Sanchez was distraught after meeting with the parent of a child she had been working with extensively. The parent was difficult to talk to, argumentative, and not supportive of her own child. Sanchez told Mazulo how upset she was, and Mazulo responded by reminding Sanchez that she was a professional and that dealing with such a situation was part of her job. This feedback upset Sanchez further and caused her to storm out of the room.

In hindsight, Mazulo realized that her response had been inappropriate. She had failed to empathize with Sanchez, who had spent so much time with the child and was deeply concerned about the child's well-being. Rather than dismissing Sanchez's concerns, Mazulo realized, she should have tried to understand how Sanchez felt and given her some support and advice for dealing positively with the situation.

Summary and Review

COMMUNICATION AND MANAGEMENT Communication is the sharing of information between two or more individuals or groups to reach a common understanding. Good communication is necessary for an organization to gain a competitive advantage. [LO 13-1]

THE COMMUNICATION PROCESS The communication process consists of two phases. In the *transmission* phase, information is shared between two or more individuals and groups. In the *feedback* phase, a common understanding is assured. In both phases, a number of distinct stages must occur for communication to take place. [LO 13-2]

INFORMATION RICHNESS AND COMMUNICATION MEDIA Information richness is the amount of information a communication medium can carry and the extent to which the medium enables the sender and receiver to reach a common understanding. Four categories of communication in descending order of information richness are face-to-face communication (including videoconferences); spoken communication transmitted electronically (including voice mail); personally addressed written communication (including email); and impersonal written communication (including corporate newsletters and blogs). [LO 13-3]

COMMUNICATION NETWORKS Communication networks are the pathways along which information flows in an organization. An organizational chart summarizes formal pathways of communication, but communication in organizations is often informal, including information transmitted through the grapevine. [LO 13-4]

COMMUNICATION SKILLS FOR MANAGERS There are various barriers to effective communication in organizations. To overcome these barriers and effectively communication with others, managers must possess or develop certain communication skills both as senders and receivers. As senders of messages, managers should send messages that are clear and complete; encode messages in symbols the receiver understands; choose a medium that is appropriate for the message and is monitored regularly by the receiver; avoid filtering and information distortion; include a feedback mechanism in the message; and provide accurate information to ensure that misleading rumors are not spread. Communication skills for managers as receivers of messages include paying attention; being a good listener; and demonstrating empathy. [LO 13-5]

Management *in Action*

Topics for Discussion and Action

Discussion

1. Why is face-to-face communication between managers still important in an organization? [LO 13-1, 13-2, 13-3]

2. What is the relationship between information systems and competitive advantage? [LO 13-3]

3. Which medium (or media) do you think would be appropriate for each of the following kinds of messages that an employee could receive from a boss: (a) a raise, (b) not receiving a promotion, (c) an error in a report prepared by the employee, (d) additional job responsibilities, and (e) the schedule for company holidays for the upcoming year? Explain your choices. [LO 13-3]

4. Do you think an organization's grapevine is an effective communication channel? Why or why not? [LO 13-4]

5. Why do some managers find it difficult to be good listeners? [LO 13-5]

6. Explain why employees might filter and distort information about problems and performance shortfalls when communicating with their bosses. What steps can managers take to eliminate filtering and information distortion? [LO 13-5]

Action

7. Interview a manager in an organization in your community to determine with whom he or she communicates on a typical day, what communication media he or she uses, and which typical communication problems the manager experiences. [LO 13-1, 13-2, 13-3, 13-4, 13-5]

Building Management Skills

Diagnosing Ineffective Communication [LO 13-1, 13-2, 13-3, 13-5]

Think about the last time you experienced very ineffective communication with another person—someone you work with, a classmate, a friend, a member of your family. Describe the incident. Then answer the following questions:

1. Why was your communication ineffective in this incident?

2. What stages of the communication process were particularly problematic and why?

3. Describe any filtering or information distortion that occurred.

4. How could you have handled this situation differently so communication would have been effective?

Managing Ethically [LO 13-1, 13-2, 13-3]

In organizations today, employees often take advantage of their company's communication systems, including email and access to the Internet. Email abuse is on the rise, and so is the amount of time employees spend surfing the Internet on company time—whether on their work computers or personal mobile devices. Recent statistics suggest that nearly 70% of the total amount of time spent surfing the Internet is company time.

Questions

1. Either by yourself or in a group, explore the ethics of using company communication systems for personal use. Should employees have some rights to use these resources? When does their behavior become unethical?

2. Some companies keep track of the way their employees use email and the Internet. Is it ethical for managers to read employees' private email or to record the sites that employees visit online?

Small Group Breakout Exercise [LO 13-1, 13-2, 13-3]

Using New Information Systems

Form groups of three or four people, and appoint one member as the spokesperson who will communicate your findings to the whole class when called upon by the instructor. Then discuss the following scenario:

You are a team of managing partners of a large firm of accountants. You are responsible for auditing your firm's communication systems to determine whether they are appropriate and up to date. To your surprise, you find that although your organization does have an email system in place and accountants are connected into a powerful network that includes opportunities for videoconferencing and use of collaborative software tools, most of the accountants (including partners) are not using this technology. You also find that the organizational hierarchy is still the preferred information system of the managing partners.

Given this situation, you are concerned that your organization is not exploiting the opportunities offered by new communication tools to obtain a competitive advantage. You have discussed this issue and are meeting to develop an action plan to get accountants to appreciate the need to learn, and to take advantage of, the potential of new technology.

1. What advantages can you tell accountants they will obtain when they use the new technology?

2. What problems do you think you may encounter in convincing accountants to use the new technology?

3. Discuss how you might make it easy for accountants to learn to use the new technology.

Be the Manager [LO 13-1, 13-2, 13-3]

A Problem in Communication

Mark Chen supervises support staff for an online company that sells furniture over the Internet. Chen has always thought that he should expand his staff. When he was about to approach his boss with such a request, the economy slowed, and other areas of the company experienced layoffs. Thus, Chen's plans for trying to add to his staff are on indefinite hold.

Chen has noticed a troubling pattern of communication with his staff. Ordinarily, when he wants one of his staff members to work on a task, he emails the pertinent information to that person. For the last few months, his email requests have gone unheeded, and his employees comply with his requests only after he visits with them in person and gives them a specific deadline. Each time, they apologize for the delay but say that they are so overloaded with requests that they sometimes stop reviewing and answering their emails. Unless someone asks for something more than once, they feel a request is not particularly urgent and can be put on hold.

Chen thinks this situation is dysfunctional and could lead to serious problems in the near future. He realizes, however, that his employees have no way of prioritizing tasks and that is why some very important projects were put on hold until he inquired about them. Knowing that he cannot add to his staff in the short term, Chen has come to you for advice. He wants to develop a system whereby his staff will provide some kind of response to requests within 24 hours, will be able to prioritize tasks, identifying their relative importance, and will not feel so overloaded that they ignore their boss's requests and ignore his emails.

Question

1. As an expert in communication, how would you advise Chen?

Case in the News [LO 13-1, 13-2, 13-3, 13-4]

How Netflix Aims to Make Communication Radically Honest

When Netflix CEO Reed Hastings hired Patty McCord as chief talent officer to build a company based on the then-innovative idea of renting DVDs by mail, his vision was to create the kind of company they both dreamed of working for. As they met to discuss what that company would be like, McCord pointed out that a list of corporate values would not be what achieved their vision; they needed to ensure that the values were practiced on a daily basis. So they focused instead on the kinds of behavior they wanted to see, and they began recording those on PowerPoint slides. After months of writing and discussing the ideas with Netflix managers, they had a big document that became known as Netflix's "culture deck."

Culture deck values include freedom coupled with responsibility, meaning employees have wide latitude for how they carry out their work, as long as they meet their performance objectives. For example, employees take paid time off at their own discretion, but they are expected to perform at a high level. Employees also are entrusted with types of information that many companies would keep confidential. They can look up measures of company performance, and managers can look up the salaries of all employees. Company announcements related to staffing give reasons for employees leaving, though more often they tell about hiring and promoting people within the organization.

In the early years of Netflix, when it was still a small company,

Hastings and McCord would use the culture deck as a tool for orientation of new employees. The two of them would gather 10 recent hires, show the slides, and lead a discussion of the behaviors and values they are meant to promote. Then Hastings learned of a service for posting presentations online, and he independently decided to post the Netflix culture deck for public viewing. Public access changed the purpose of the information. Tech workers would read the deck before they interviewed for a job. The result was that the interviewers and candidates were better able to identify who would embrace Netflix's culture of freedom and responsibility, versus who would better thrive at an organization with more structure. In this way, information sharing improved the company's recruitment and hiring results.

Sharing the culture deck supports a Netflix practice related to communication: radical honesty. The intent of radical honesty is to empower employees by giving them factual information about the company, including data about its performance, objectives, and desired behaviors and outcomes. In a radically honest environment, employees know what is expected of them, and they can tell whether they are succeeding. They also have input into performance appraisal, contributing to 360-degree feedback about managers' and coworkers' performance. Furthermore, they can choose which colleagues to review—even the CEO. And

they are expected to speak up when they see a problem or have an idea.

Hastings and McCord (who has since left the company and started a consulting practice) consider radical honesty to be a strength of Netflix's high-performance culture. The company continues to grow rapidly, adding 2,000 employees in a recent year to reach more than 6,000. It has survived the technological changes sweeping the entertainment industry and taken the leap into producing original content. Netflix recently reported an employee turnover rate of 11%, better than the 13% annual turnover among technology companies overall.

A major challenge of radical honesty is that some messages are bound to be disappointing or critical, so they are hard to receive. In particular, people tend to feel threatened by criticism, even if it is true and relevant. In practice, efforts to deliver radical honesty in performance feedback have sometimes come across as harsh. Other approaches to honest and open communication make a point to consider employees' emotions, while Netflix's culture and leaders have focused mainly on delivering accurate data. Consequently, employees whose manner of thinking is highly objective and fact driven are satisfied with this approach, while those who are more relationship-oriented risk feeling betrayed when a manager or coworker says their performance falls short. Ideally, employees are receiving ongoing and complete feedback, so they should not be surprised by such a message. In practice, however, some managers struggle to meet this standard for delivering feedback. As part of providing employees with full information, these situations, including firings, typically are disclosed to the whole team or workforce. Some employees respect the aim of openness, but it has the potential to shame those in the spotlight.

Questions for Discussion

1. What benefits do you think Reed Hastings and Patty McCord obtained from putting their vision for Netflix in writing in the culture deck? How effective do you think this medium was for this message?

2. What pros and cons do you see in managers following Netflix's practice of being radically honest about their employees' performance?

3. Would you want to work for an organization that practices radical honesty in communication as Netflix does? Why or why not?

Sources: J. Dunn, "The Feedback Paradox: Brutal Honesty, Radical Transparency, Radical Candor and Netflix," *Medium*, https://medium.com, November 3, 2018; S. Ramachandran and J. Flint, "At Netflix, Radical Transparency and Blunt Firings Unsettle the Ranks," *The Wall Street Journal*, www.wsj.com, October 25, 2018; "Learning from Netflix: How to Build a Culture of Freedom and Responsibility" (interview with Patty McCord), *Knowledge@Wharton*, http://knowledge.wharton.upenn.edu, May 29, 2018; R. Gray, "Being 'Radically Honest' in the Workplace," *HR*, www.hrmagazine.co.uk, February 23, 2018; K. Swisher, interview with Patty McCord, *Recode Decode*, full transcript, www.recode.net, January 10, 2018.

Endnotes

1. S. Apgar, "Designing for Collaboration: BCG's 'Collision Coefficient,'" *Urban Land*, https://urbanland.uli.org, December 4, 2017.

2. K. Gee, "The Not-So-Creepy Reason More Bosses Are Tracking Employees," *The Wall Street Journal*, www.wsj.com, March 21, 2017; R. Greenfield, "New Office Sensors Know When You Leave Your Desk," *Bloomberg Businessweek*, www.bloomberg.com, February 14, 2017.

3. Gee, "The Not-So-Creepy Reason"; "Amping Up the Collision Coefficient at BCG's New York Offices," http://structureone.com, September 7, 2017.

4. M. Stohlmeyer Russell and L. Moskowitz Lepler, "How We Closed the Gap between Men's and Women's Retention Rates," *Harvard Business Review*, https://hbr.org, March 19, 2017; A. Elejalde-Ruiz, "To Retain Women, Consulting Firm Targets Gender Communication Differences," *Chicago Tribune*, www.chicagotribune.com, September 9, 2016.

5. Russell and Lepler, "How We Closed the Gap"; Elejalde-Ruiz, "To Retain Women, Consulting Firm Targets Gender Communication Differences."

6. C. A. O'Reilly and L. R. Pondy, "Organizational Communication," in S. Kerr, ed., *Organizational Behavior* (Columbus, OH: Grid, 1979).

7. "About Hyphen," https://gethyphen.com, accessed February 15, 2019; S. Modgil, "How Engagement Startup Hyphen Enables Employees to Be Heard at Work," *People Matters*, www.peoplematters.in, April 6, 2018; S. Kashyap, "Hyphen Aims to Answer the Eternal Question: What Do Employees Want?," *YourStory*, https://yourstory.com, June 19, 2017.

8. Ibid.

9. "Get to Know Hyphen: The Real-Time Employee Engagement Platform," *YouTube*, www.youtube.com, accessed February 15, 2019.

10. Hyphen, "About Hyphen."

11. E. M. Rogers and R. Agarwala-Rogers, *Communication in Organizations* (New York: Free Press, 1976).

12. J. Romig, "Listening to Nonverbal Cues," *Listen Like a Lawyer* (blog), http://listenlikealawyer.com, accessed Februry 15, 2019.

13. N. Zandan, "How Much of Our Workdays Do We Spend Communicating?," *Quantified Communications*, www.quantifiedcommunications.com, accessed Februry 15, 2019.

14. S. Reinberg, "A Key Thing Doctors Can Do to Reduce Hospital Errors," *CBS News*, www.cbsnews.com, accessed February 15, 2019.

15. A. W. Brooks and L. K. John, "The Surprising Power of Questions," *Harvard Business Review*, May–June 2018, 60–67; S. Shellenbarger, "How to Gain Power at Work When You Have None," *The Wall Street Journal*, www.wsj.com, March 6, 2018.

16. K. Eikenberry, "The Mess of Discussion and the Magic of Dialogue," *TD*, January 2018, 48–53.

17. Brooks and John, "The Surprising Power of Questions."

18. Shellenbarger, "How to Gain Power at Work"; Ken Sterling, "How You Can Use Honesty to Be a Great Boss," *Inc.*, www.inc.com, April 16, 2018.

19. R. L. Daft, R. H. Lengel, and L. K. Trevino, "Message Equivocality, Media Selection, and Manager Performance: Implications for

Information Systems," *MIS Quarterly* 11 (1987), 355–66; R. L. Daft and R. H. Lengel, "Information Richness: A New Approach to Managerial Behavior and Organization Design," in B. M. Staw and L. L. Cummings, eds., *Research in Organizational Behavior* (Greenwich, CT: JAI Press, 1984).

20. R. L. Daft, *Organization Theory and Design* (St. Paul, MN: West, 1992).

21. Cisco WebEx, "Curbstone Corporation Case Study," http://try.webex.com, accessed February 15, 2019.

22. D. Hassell, "Management by Weekly Check-In Is the New 'Wandering Around,'" *Entrepreneur,* www.entrepreneur.com, June 9, 2016.

23. Cisco WebEx, "Accelerating Business with Online Collaboration," http://try.webex.com, accessed February 15, 2019.

24. D. Rogers, "How You Can Crush the Video Interview," *Monster,* www.monster.com, accessed February 15, 2019.

25. The Radicati Group, "Email Statistics Report, 2018–2022," www.radicati.com, accessed February 18, 2019.

26. "About Emailogic," www.emailogic.com, accessed February 18, 2019.

27. A. Muhammed, "10 Remote Work Trends That Will Dominate 2019," *Forbes,* www.forbes.com, accessed February 18, 2019.

28. A. Picincu, "Should Managers Monitor Employee Email & Internet Usage?," *Bizfluent,* https://bizfluent.com, October 16, 2018.

29. S. Rodenbaum, "IBM: Communication and Curation Go Hand in Hand," *Forbes,* www.forbes.com, accessed February 18, 2019.

30. M. Hendrickson, "Blog Your Way to an Awesome Reputation: The 10 Best Company Blogs," *DreamHost,* www.dreamhost.com, January 16, 2019.

31. Forbes Agency Council, "15 Practices for Your New Company Blog," *Forbes,* www.forbes.com, March 28, 2018.

32. S. Gausepohl, "Don't Let These Social Media Mistakes Ruin Your Career," *Business News Daily,* www.businessnewsdaily.com, December 2, 2016; C. Lampe and N. B. Ellison, "Social Media and the Workplace," www.pewinternet.org, June 22, 2016.

33. M. T. Wroblewski, "The Importance of the Grapevine in Internal Business Communications," https://smallbusiness.chron.com, November 6, 2018; O. W. Baskin and C. E. Aronoff, *Interpersonal Communication in Organizations* (Santa Monica, CA: Goodyear, 1989).

34. "The Power of Building an External Network," *Everwise,* www.geteverwise.com, accessed February 18, 2019.

35. C. Sun, "The Science of the First Impression: Five Elements of a Great First Impression," *Entrepreneur,* www.entrepreneur.com, March 13, 2018; S. Shellenbarger, "The Mistakes You Make in a Meeting's First Milliseconds," *The Wall Street Journal,* www.wsj.com, January 30, 2018; V. Van Edwards, "How to Hack a First Impression," *Entrepreneur,* May 2017, 46–48.

36. Shellenbarger, "The Mistakes You Make."

37. Van Edwards, "How to Hack a First Impression"; Sun, "The Science of the First Impression."

38. P. Petrone, "You Have 7 Seconds to Make a Good First Impression. Here's How to Do It," *The Learning Blog,* https://learning.linkedin.com, June 22, 2018.

39. Sun, "The Science of the First Impression."

40. Van Edwards, "How to Hack a First Impression"; Sun, "The Science of the First Impression."

41. K. Shih, "5 Easy Ways to Make Your Workplace Inclusive for Someone Who's Deafblind," www.perkins.org, accessed February 18, 2019.

42. Forbes Coaches Council, "12 Ways Managers Can Establish a Trusting Relationship with Employees," *Forbes,* www.forbes.com, April 28, 2017.

Tom Merton/age fotostock

14 Operations Management: Managing Operations and Processes

Learning Objectives

After studying this chapter, you should be able to:

LO 14-1 Explain the role of operations management in achieving superior quality, efficiency, and responsiveness to customers.

LO 14-2 Describe how information and technology help managers make better decisions.

LO 14-3 Describe what customers want, and explain why it is so important for managers to be responsive to their needs.

LO 14-4 Explain why achieving superior quality is so important.

LO 14-5 Explain why achieving superior efficiency is so important.

Management Snapshot

Efficiency Frees Kraft Heinz to Innovate

How Do Managers Ensure That Their Group's Activities Add Value to the Company?

For Bernardo Hees, chief executive of Kraft Heinz, the answer includes making sure the company operates efficiently and grows by adding new products that appeal to changing consumer tastes.

Kraft Heinz was formed in the 2015 merger of Pittsburgh-based Heinz with Kraft, headquartered near Chicago.[1] Its famous brands, along with Kraft cheese and Heinz ketchup, include Jell-O, Oscar Mayer, and Velveeta. While these are widely known and loved, they are attached to processed foods at a time when consumers are increasingly asking for freshness. The largest shareholder of the combined company is 3G Capital Partners, which appointed Hees to run the company.

When the merger was complete, Hees embarked on an effort to drive down any spending that wasn't contributing to the company's overall success.[2] This continued a pre-merger focus of Hees, who had led Heinz before the merger. He closed facilities located far from suppliers and customers, moving work to more centrally located facilities. He let executives know they would have more control over decision making but would do without offices and expensive perks. Such

efforts have enabled the company to increase its profit margin, a measure of revenues relative to costs. While some see 3G's focus on efficiency as ruthless cost cutting, Hees insists that it is primarily a way to build value by freeing up resources "to invest in our brands [and] . . . people."[3]

Indeed, the company has been pursuing ideas for new products. For example, observing that sales of Oscar Mayer hot dogs have been flat, management launched an investigation of whether the brand could become associated with healthy eating. The company developed an "all-natural" hot dog, which launched to a favorable response.[4] To build on its existing brands with a new breakfast food, the company developed Just Crack an Egg, a microwaveable serving-size cup containing a mixture of Kraft cheese, Ore-Ida potatoes, vegetables, and Oscar Meyer breakfast meat. The consumer stirs in an egg (for a fresh-food experience) and zaps the contents for a quick, protein-rich breakfast.[5]

These new product ideas are the result of responsiveness to customer wants and needs. Product managers at Kraft Heinz conduct research into what challenges consumers are facing related to their eating habits. They found that consumers want to do more of their shopping in the produce, meat, and dairy sections of the store, to get fresh, healthful options. But even as they want to eat well, they are pressed for time. A product such as Just

Implementing operational efficiencies has allowed Kraft Heinz CEO Bernardo Hees to invest in new products that address consumers' changing tastes.
Christopher Dilts/Bloomberg/Getty Images

449

Crack an Egg addresses all of these wishes, and for that reason, it was intentionally developed to contain no artificial colors or flavors.[6]

To keep up with changing tastes, Kraft Heinz cannot merely tweak its existing products; it needs to get involved with what is new and exciting. The company recently launched a business unit devoted to identifying opportunities and backing them financially.[7] The unit, called Springboard, focuses on natural, organic, craft, and specialty foods, looking for business ideas that could open up whole new categories. Start-up companies apply to Springboard for backing, and the ones selected will get coaching as well as access to Kraft Heinz's R&D facilities. If Springboard lives up to its name, it should launch Kraft Heinz on to a new growth trajectory.

Overview

As the "Management Snapshot" suggests, organizations must constantly evaluate their business practices in an effort to remain successful. Some organizations may adopt the latest technology and processes, while others use different strategies to stay competitive.

In this chapter we focus on operations management tools and techniques that managers can use to increase the quality of an organization's products, the efficiency of production, and the organization's responsiveness to customers. By the end of this chapter, you will understand the vital role operations management, information, and technology play in building competitive advantage and creating a high-performing organization.

LO 14-1
Explain the role of operations management in achieving superior quality, efficiency, and responsiveness to customers.

Operations Management and Competitive Advantage

Operations management is the management of any aspect of the production system that transforms inputs into finished goods and services. A production system is the system that an organization uses to acquire inputs, convert inputs into outputs, and dispose of the outputs (goods or services). Operations managers are managers who are responsible for managing an organization's production system. They do whatever it takes to transform inputs into outputs. Their job is to manage the three stages of production—acquisition of inputs, control of conversion processes, and disposal of goods and services—and to determine where operating improvements might be made in order to increase quality, efficiency, and responsiveness to customers and so give an organization a competitive advantage (see Figure 14.1).

Quality refers to goods and services that are reliable, dependable, or psychologically satisfying: They do the job they were designed for and do it well, or they possess some attribute that gives their users something they value.[8] *Efficiency* refers to the amount of inputs required to produce a given output. *Responsiveness to customers* refers to actions taken to meet the demands and needs of customers. Operations managers are responsible for ensuring that an organization has sufficient supplies of high-quality, low-cost inputs, and they are responsible for designing a production system that creates high-quality, low-cost products that customers are willing to buy.

operations management The management of any aspect of the production system that transforms inputs into finished goods and services.

Figure 14.1
The Purpose
of Operations
Management

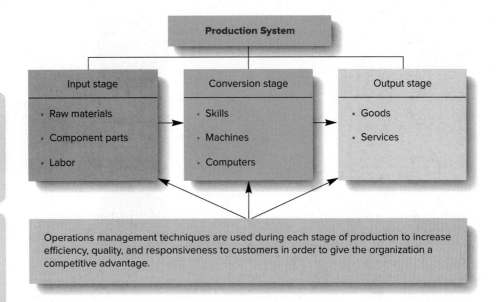

production system
The system that an
organization uses to
acquire inputs, convert
the inputs into outputs,
and dispose of the
outputs.

operations manager
A manager who
is responsible
for managing an
organization's
production system
and for determining
where operating
improvements might
be made.

One of the key components that can help all managers make sure their operations are efficient and capable of attracting and retaining loyal customers is the use of pertinent information to help make smart business decisions. We discuss the importance of information in the next section and point out some of the issues associated with collecting and utilizing information in the business environment.

Information and the Manager's Job

LO 14-2
Describe how
information and
technology help
managers make better
decisions.

data Raw, unsummarized, and unanalyzed facts.

information Data that are organized in a meaningful fashion.

Managers cannot plan, organize, lead, and control effectively unless they have access to information. Information is the source of the knowledge and intelligence that they need to make the right decisions. Information, however, is not the same as data.[9] Data are raw, unsummarized, and unanalyzed facts such as volume of sales, level of costs, or number of customers. Information is data that are organized in a meaningful fashion, such as in a graph showing changes in sales volume or costs over time. Alone, data do not tell managers anything; information, in contrast, can communicate a great deal of useful knowledge to the person who receives it—such as a manager who sees sales falling or costs rising. The distinction between data and information is important because one of the uses of information technology is to help managers transform data into information in order to make better managerial decisions.

Attributes of Useful Information

Four factors determine the usefulness of information to a manager: quality, timeliness, completeness, and relevance (see Figure 14.2).

QUALITY Accuracy and reliability determine the quality of information.[10] The greater its accuracy and reliability, the higher is the quality of information. Technology gives managers access to high-quality real-time information that they can use to improve long-term decision making and alter short-term operating decisions, such

Figure 14.2

Factors Affecting the **Usefulness** of Information

as how much of a particular product to make daily or monthly. Supermarket managers, for example, use handheld bar code readers that are wireless (using Bluetooth technology) or are linked to a server to monitor and record how demand for particular products such as milk, chicken, or bread changes daily so they know how to restock their shelves to ensure the products are always available.

TIMELINESS Information that is timely is available when it is required to allow managers to make the optimal decision—not after the decision has been made. In today's rapidly changing world, the need for timely information often means information must be available on a real-time basis—hence the enormous growth in the demand for mobile devices.[11] **Real-time information** is information that reflects current changes in business conditions. In an industry that experiences rapid changes, real-time information may need to be updated frequently.

real-time information
Frequently updated information that reflects current conditions.

Local transportation systems (e.g., buses, subway trains, commuter rail) use real-time information to help commuters track when they can expect their next transit ride. For example, the Transit app (available for Android and iOS devices) helps simplify daily commutes for people in 190 cities in more than 10 countries around the world, including the United States, Australia, Iceland, Canada, France, Germany, and the UK. The app updates arrival times of public transportation in your area (thanks to the locations setting/geotracking feature of your mobile device), monitors your walking speed, and tells you whether you're going to get to your ride on time. In addition, the app will suggest changing your transit connections based on detours or transportation delays to help you get to your destination on time. And it can even wake you up on your ride before you get to where you're going if you take a quick nap on your journey.[12]

COMPLETENESS Information that is complete gives managers all the information they need to exercise control, achieve coordination, or make an effective decision. Recall from Chapter 5, however, that managers rarely have access to complete information. Instead, because of uncertainty, ambiguity, and bounded rationality, they have to make do with incomplete information.[13] One function of technology is to increase the completeness of managers' information.

RELEVANCE Information that is relevant is useful and suits a manager's particular needs and circumstances. Irrelevant information is useless and may actually hurt the performance of a busy manager who has to spend valuable time determining whether information is relevant. Given the massive amounts of information that managers are now exposed to and their limited information-processing capabilities, a company's information systems designers need to ensure that managers receive only relevant information.

What Is Information Technology?

information technology (IT) The set of methods or techniques for acquiring, organizing, storing, manipulating, and transmitting information.

Information technology (IT) is the set of methods or techniques for acquiring, organizing, storing, manipulating, and transmitting information. A management information system (MIS) is a specific form of technology that managers select and use to generate the specific, detailed information they need to perform their roles effectively. Rapid advances in the power of technology—specifically the development of ever more powerful and sophisticated hardware and software—have had a fundamental impact on organizations and managers. Some recent developments, such as inventory management and customer relationship management (CRM) systems, contribute so much to performance that organizations that do *not* adopt them, or that implement them ineffectively, become uncompetitive compared with organizations that do adopt them. Today, much of the increasing productivity and efficiency of business in general has been attributed to the way organizations and their employees use advancing technology, including artificial intelligence, to improve their performance, as discussed in the "Management Insight" feature.

management information system (MIS) A specific form of technology that managers utilize to generate the specific, detailed information they need to perform their roles effectively.

Managers need information for three reasons: to make effective decisions, to control the activities of the organization, and to coordinate the activities of the organization. Next we examine these uses of information in detail.

Management Insight

With Butterfly, Software Becomes an Ever-Present Coach

How can technology enable managers to get better results? Imagine, for example, the challenges a fast-growing company faces in managing employees. When the company is small, a few people handle their area of expertise independently. As it grows, those people need help, individual projects become group projects, and someone familiar with the work becomes the manager. The demand for operating on a larger scale often outstrips the new managers' ability to pick up the people skills necessary for leadership, motivation, and control. The organization then wants to develop its managers, but doing so takes time, and training efforts can be difficult to target to the specific needs of a leader at a particular time.[14]

Information technology offers solutions, including software that applies *artificial intelligence*—typically software that has "learned," through massive amounts of trial and error, to analyze situations and propose responses that are associated with good outcomes. The more data the software processes, the better its recommendations become. An example is Butterfly, software that gathers anonymous data from an organization's instant messaging system and analyzes the data to identify situations calling for more active leadership. The three partners who founded Butterfly were inspired with their own difficulties in learning to lead their teams in prior jobs.[15]

Butterfly's creators describe their product as a management coaching system; the feedback from employees becomes the basis for defining the areas in which a manager needs to improve his or her leadership.[16] This analysis, in turn, becomes the basis of recommendations for improvement. The system also can be set up to deliver alerts when managers need additional support. Because the software uses artificial intelligence to improve its results based on experience, it is designed to increase in value as the company signs on more clients. In its early years, Butterfly has signed up notable clients including Citibank, Coca-Cola, and Ticketmaster. And the frequency of feedback—daily or weekly one-question surveys—also contributes to the pool of data. Cofounder Simon Rakosi says companies using Butterfly have measured increased productivity, decreased absenteeism, and higher levels of employee engagement.[17]

Managers are using Butterfly at Social.Lab, a social media marketing agency that is part of the advertising giant Ogilvy, where the software is part of the company's instant messaging system. The agency had been growing fast, and management was concerned about keeping employees engaged. Butterfly provided a way for managers to gather feedback easily without days of leadership training. Butterfly recommends a question to ask each time—say, asking employees to rate their level of stress. It analyzes the responses and then sends a report to managers, including customized tips and recommendations of articles to read about how to improve. Benjamin Snyers, who leads the North American operations of Social.Lab, says Butterfly has helped him identify problems and forced him to be "honest about the mood of the company." For example, at one point he learned that his team was feeling particularly stressed. Snyers learned to express his appreciation and motivate them by reinforcing the importance of their contributions.[18] ●

Information and Decisions

Much of management (planning, organizing, leading, and controlling) is about making decisions. For example, the marketing manager must decide what price to charge for a product, what distribution channels to use, and what promotional messages to emphasize to maximize sales. The manufacturing manager must decide how much of a product to make and how to make it so that the company makes a profit. The purchasing manager must decide from whom to purchase inputs and what inventory of inputs to hold. The human resource manager must decide how much employees should be paid, how they should be trained, what benefits they should be given, and when it makes sense to hire more workers. The engineering manager must make decisions about new product design. Top managers must decide how to allocate scarce financial resources among competing projects, how best to structure and control the organization, and what business-level strategy the organization should be pursuing. And regardless of their functional orientation, all managers have to make decisions about matters such as what performance evaluation to give to an employee.

To make effective decisions, managers need information both from inside the organization and from external stakeholders. When deciding how to price a product, for example, marketing managers need information about how consumers will react to different price points. They need information about unit costs because they do not want to set the price below the cost of production. And they need information about competitive strategy because pricing strategy should be consistent with an organization's overall business strategy. Some of this information will come from outside the organization (e.g., from consumer surveys and competitors) and some from inside the organization (information about production costs comes from manufacturing). As this example suggests, managers' ability to make effective decisions rests on their ability to acquire and process information.

BIG DATA The collection and analysis of large sets of data from consumers, competitors, employees, suppliers, and others has become a global industry, with the big data sector expected to top the $116 billion mark in the coming year.[19] *Analytics* is the process of examining all these data to uncover hidden patterns, unknown correlations, market trends, customer preferences, and the like, which can help managers make decisions that will advance the organization's business.[20] Analyzing data is no longer done by reviewing a spreadsheet and manually highlighting bits of information. Instead, powerful software can provide real-time information that assists managers at all levels of an organization in making faster, more effective decisions to help develop new products and services, while reducing costs.[21]

Information and Control

As discussed in Chapter 8, controlling is the process through which managers regulate how efficiently and effectively an organization and its members perform the activities necessary to achieve its stated goals.[22] Managers achieve control over organizational activities by taking four steps (see Figure 8.2): (1) They establish measurable standards of performance or goals; (2) they measure actual performance; (3) they compare actual performance against established goals; and (4) they evaluate the results and take corrective action if necessary.[23] UPS, for example, has a goal to deliver 99% of next-day packages by noon.[24] UPS has thousands of U.S. operating facilities that are responsible for the physical pickup and delivery of packages. UPS managers monitor the delivery performance of these facilities regularly; if they find that the 99% goal is not being attained, the managers determine why and take corrective action as necessary.

Although advances in technology have changed the way key data are shared with managers, the information is still critical to those responsible for making informed decisions in an organization.
Image Source Trading Ltd/Shutterstock

To achieve control over any organizational activity, managers must have information. To control the activities at UPS operating facilities, a UPS manager might need to know what percentage of packages each facility delivers by noon. To obtain this information, the manager uses UPS's own information systems; UPS is also a leader in developing proprietary in-house technology. All packages to be shipped are scanned with wireless scanners by UPS drivers who pick them up; then all this information is sent through UPS servers to its headquarters' mainframe computer. When the packages are scanned again at delivery, this information is also transmitted through the company's extensive computer network. Managers can access this information quickly to discover what percentage of packages were delivered by noon of the day after they were picked up, and also how this information breaks down facility by facility so they can intervene if delivery goals are not being met.

Management information systems are used to control all divisional and functional operations. In accounting, for example, information systems are used to monitor expenditures and compare them against budgets. To track expenditures against budgets, managers need information about current expenditures, broken down by relevant organizational units; software is designed to give managers this information. A twist on using technology to improve customer service is being used by several companies, including Disney World and Carnival cruise lines. Disney issues wristbands (called MagicBands) to visitors that work as hotel room keys, parking passes, and charge cards. The data collected when visitors tap the MagicBands throughout the theme park and resorts will help Disney zero in on guest preferences and provide better customer service.[25] Taking the wristband one step further, Carnival Corp. recently introduced Ocean Medallions, quarter-size, waterproof medallions that are encrypted and communicate with thousands of sensors on board and in port to enhance guests' travel experiences. Crew members on Carnival's Princess cruise line are able to access information about guests, family members can use the medallions to track each other, and touch screens throughout the ship will display recommended entertainment or dining options based on guests' information and their interests and activities.[26]

CYBERSECURITY Technology continues to evolve at a rapid pace. Although the results of such innovations have changed both business and daily life, these changes are not without challenges, particularly when it comes to controlling information. With advanced technology comes the need for *cybersecurity* to keep all of this information safe and protected against unauthorized use.[27]

In a recent survey conducted by *Security* magazine, 50% of the companies reported their information systems were attacked by hackers using malware to encrypt data, systems, and networks, essentially holding the information hostage until a ransom was paid. In the same survey, more than one-quarter of the companies see cyberattacks and ransom as their biggest threat in the near future.[28]

Another form of cybercrime—data breaches—has become commonplace as businesses collect large amounts of data from individuals. Over the past few years, data breaches have occurred in which information about millions of consumers has been stolen by cyber thieves who figured out how to infiltrate companies' so-called secure information systems. For example, in 2017 Equifax, one of three national credit reporting companies, suffered one of the biggest data breaches in history: Information for more than 145 million U.S. consumers (nearly half the country's population) was stolen.[29] Findings from a Senate investigation into the data breach revealed (1) Equifax's cybersecurity measures were weak; (2) the company ignored numerous warnings of risk to sensitive data, including a specific warning from the Department of Homeland Security about vulnerability in its systems; (3) the company failed to notify consumers, investors, and regulators in a timely manner about the massive breach; and (4) company assistance and information to affected consumers was inadequate. Recommendations from a Senate investigation include giving the Federal Trade Commission (FTC) supervisory authority to monitor credit reporting agencies going forward.[30]

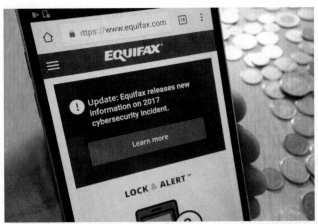

Cybersecurity has become a top priority for companies and managers trying to keep business and personal information safe. Credit-reporting firm Equifax found this out the hard way when its information system was breached by cyber thieves who stole the personal data of more than 145 million U.S. consumers.

Piotr Swat/Shutterstock

Small businesses, in particular, are vulnerable to cyberattacks because they typically do not employ a cybersecurity staff to monitor and protect company data and other vital information. According to the Information Security Forum, as real-time data collection via devices controlled by the Internet of Things (IoT) continues to play an important role in business operations, data leaks from industrial equipment and other digital products such as web cameras, alarm systems, and HVAC systems are easy targets for hackers.[31] The IoT is a network of devices, vehicles, home appliances, and other products embedded with electronics, sensors, and connectivity, which allow these "things" to collect and share data via the Internet.[32]

DATA PRIVACY Another aspect of controlling information within an organization concerns keeping data private and secure. While many companies are taking steps to make sure security measures outside the company's internal systems are solid, some firms do not use the same aggressive approach to keep their internal networks safe. Once a hacker infiltrates a company's internal networks, it may be difficult for the cyber thief to be detected.[33] In addition, some well-known tech companies seem to be in the news lately for security lapses when it comes to protecting consumers' private data. The "Ethics in Action" feature discusses how Facebook allowed personal data to be mishandled by outside consultants, which caused a serious backlash from users.

Ethics in Action

Users Quit Facebook over Privacy Issues

More than 200 million people in the United States are regular users of Facebook, the social networking platform created by Mark Zuckerberg and his Harvard classmates in 2004. Today Facebook has more than 2.2 billion monthly users around the globe who connect with friends and family, share personal stories and photographs, and follow selected national and international newsfeeds. Being active on Facebook has become a daily if not hourly routine for many people, most of whom assumed that their personal information was secure on the popular social platform.[34]

As a result of ongoing investigations into whether Russia interfered in the 2016 U.S. presidential campaign, Facebook became more than just a connection point for millions of users. News reports by *The New York Times, The Intercept,* and *The London Observer,* among others, revealed that over the last several years Facebook allowed a political data and voter-profiling firm, Cambridge Analytica, which was associated with the Trump presidential campaign, to harvest data from nearly 87 million users—without their knowledge.[35]According to reports, more than

300,000 Facebook users downloaded an app, which allowed Cambridge Analytica to use their personal information (as well as data from their Facebook friends) to create personality profiles for each user and then embed targeted ads and fake news stories based on personality types within their individual Facebook newsfeeds.[36] Some political observers suggest these ads and fake news influenced voters' decisions in the 2016 election.

After the news broke, Facebook stock price dropped nearly 20%, and CEO Zuckerberg was summoned to testify before Congress to explain the situation and resulting privacy issues. Zuckerberg apologized for the disinformation that appeared on Facebook, at one point saying that the company didn't do enough to keep users' data safe.[37] As a result of the data breach, many Facebook users quit the social media platform.[38] In response to the scandal, Facebook issued a link that appeared at the top of some users' newsfeeds to let them know they were among the members whose data were improperly harvested by Cambridge Analytica. But what about other Facebook users? Experts say all Facebook users should regularly check the social network's privacy settings to see which apps and websites have permission to access their Facebook data. In the meantime, Cambridge Analytica announced it was shutting down its business and filing for bankruptcy.[39] ●

Facebook CEO Mark Zuckerberg faced tough questioning when he testified before Congress about how personal data from more than 87 million Facebook users were accessed improperly by Cambridge Analytica. Yasin Ozturk/Anadolu Agency/Getty Images

Information and Coordination

Coordinating department and divisional activities to achieve organizational goals is another basic task of management. As an example of the size of the coordination task that managers face, consider the coordination effort necessary to prepare between 500,000 and 1 million meals for the people who visit Disney parks and resorts every day. Combine that type of volume with Disney's efforts to get food locally, and coordination gets complicated quickly. According to Lenny DeGeorge, executive chef for concept development at Walt Disney Parks & Resorts, the supply chain for the restaurants at the Disney parks and resorts worldwide—all 1,040 of them—depends on the location of the resort and what local growers and producers can provide. In Florida, for example, the company works with "Fresh from Florida" to find out what is in season and available. In Southern California, Disney has some local growers providing organic produce. DeGeorge and his Disney culinary colleagues now work in the Flavor Lab, an Orlando facility that provides professional and creative workspace for Disney food service employees to test new equipment, try out new recipes, and showcase best practices.[40]

Improving Responsiveness to Customers

Organizations produce outputs—goods or services—that are consumed by customers. All organizations, profit seeking or not-for-profit, have customers. Without customers, most organizations would cease to exist. Because customers are vital to the survival of most organizations, managers must correctly identify customers and promote organizational strategies that respond to their needs.

What Do Customers Want?

Given that satisfying customer demands is central to the survival of an organization, an important question is, What do customers want? To specify exactly what they want is not possible because their wants vary from industry to industry. However, it is possible to identify some universal product attributes that most customers in most industries want. Generally, other things being equal, most customers prefer

1. A lower price to a higher price.
2. High-quality products to low-quality products.
3. Quick service to slow service. (They will always prefer good after-sales service and support to poor after-sales support.)
4. Products with many useful features to products with few features.
5. Products that are, as far as possible, customized or tailored to their unique needs.

To meet those preferences, managers seek data and other information about customers' definitions of high quality and good service, so they can correct any problems and offer what is most valued. The "Managing Globally" feature describes how a company based in Finland is meeting those needs for customers around the world.

Managing Globally

HappyOrNot Helps Customers Keep *Their* Customers Happy

A frustrated teenager in Finland saw the need for HappyOrNot while trying to get help locating computer supplies in a store (during the 1990s, when computer users went to stores to buy disks). The shopper, Heikki Väänänen, wished he could easily send feedback to someone who cared about the store's performance. In college, he started a coding company; when a client bought it, he looked for a new business idea. No one had ever solved his shopping problem, so he and a colleague decided to try.[41]

Their solution was a terminal with a screen and four bright buttons labeled with four faces, happy to sad, green to red.[42] The screen invited customers to rate their experience. The first terminal, installed in a local grocery store, obtained more than 120 customer ratings in the first day. Besides giving shoppers a voice, the terminal solved a business problem: how to get feedback from large numbers of customers at an affordable cost. Survey responses are delayed and too time-consuming for many customers, and a sophisticated marketing research program is expensive. A set of HappyOrNot terminals delivers the right combination of features and price.

HappyOrNot had a strong launch in Finland, with government grants and a highly skilled labor force. But the founders needed help to spread the concept internationally. They hired a manager experienced in international sales, who introduced the terminals to London's heavily traveled Heathrow Airport in time for the 2012 Summer Olympics. Travelers saw the concept and became curious. They learned that the systems aren't just an easy-to-use gimmick but provide time-stamped data electronically in real time, so managers can pinpoint problems. A surge in complaints above a defined threshold triggers an alert, enabling a rapid response; for example, a spike in complaints about a restroom could signal a maintenance issue.[43]

Companies around the world have installed HappyOrNot terminals in business locations to gather customer feedback about their products and services. ©HappyOrNot Ltd.

As awareness has grown, Avis, McDonald's, UPS Stores, and other customers in more than 100 countries have installed HappyOrNot terminals. The company, now operating at a profit, has seen several years of doubling revenues. Besides the original terminals, it offers a touch screen version for gathering comments along with ratings and an online tool to collect feedback from customers of web-based businesses.[44]

One satisfied customer is the San Francisco 49ers, which installed HappyOrNot terminals around Levi's Stadium, linked to an app that lets managers monitor data within seconds of its entry. They can see, for example, which concession stands are performing well at which hours, displayed on a colorful map.[45] ●

Designing Production Systems to Be Responsive to Customers

Because satisfying customers is so important, managers try to design production systems that can produce the outputs that have the attributes customers desire. The attributes of an organization's outputs—their quality, cost, and features—are determined by the organization's production system.[46] Since the ability of an organization to satisfy the demands of its customers derives from its production system, managers need to devote considerable attention to constantly improving production systems. Managers' desire to attract customers with improved products explains their adoption of many new operations management techniques in recent years.

As an example of the link between responsiveness to customers and an organization's production system, consider how Southwest Airlines operates. One of the most consistently successful airlines in the United States, Southwest Airlines has been expanding rapidly. One reason for Southwest's success is that its managers created a production system uniquely tailored to satisfy the demands of its customers for low-priced, reliable (on-time), and convenient air travel. Southwest commands high customer loyalty precisely because its production system delivers products that have all the desired attributes: reliability, convenience, and low price.

Southwest's low-cost production system focuses not only on improving the maintenance of aircraft but also on the company's ticket reservation system, route structure, flight frequency, baggage-handling system, and in-flight services. For example, Southwest offers a no-frills approach to in-flight customer service. No meals are served on board, and there are no first-class seats. Southwest does not subscribe to the big reservation computers used by travel agents because the booking fees are too costly. Also, the airline flies only one aircraft, the fuel-efficient Boeing 737, which keeps training and maintenance costs down. All this translates into low prices for customers. In addition, Southwest is one of the few airlines that does not charge baggage fees. Passengers can check two bags for free.[47]

Southwest's reliability derives from the fact that it has the quickest aircraft turnaround time in the industry. A Southwest ground crew needs

A Southwest agent assists a customer. Southwest's operating system is geared toward satisfying customer demands for low-priced, reliable, and convenient air travel, making it one of the most consistently successful airlines in recent years. To help keep flights on schedule, Southwest's workforce has been cross-trained to perform multiple tasks.

Joseph Kaczmarek/AP Images

only 15 minutes to turn around an incoming aircraft and prepare it for departure. This speedy operation helps keep flights on time. Southwest has such quick turnaround because it has a flexible workforce that has been cross-trained to perform multiple tasks. Thus, the person who checks tickets might also help with other duties if time is short.

Customer Relationship Management

customer relationship management (CRM)
A technique that uses technology to develop an ongoing relationship with customers to maximize the value an organization can deliver to them over time.

One operations strategy managers can use to get close to customers and understand their needs is customer relationship management (CRM). CRM is a technique that uses technology to develop an ongoing relationship with customers to maximize the value an organization can deliver to them over time. By the 2000s most large companies had installed sophisticated CRM technology to track customers' changing demands for a company's products; this became a vital tool to maximize responsiveness to customers. A CRM system monitors, controls, and links each of the functional activities involved in marketing, selling, and delivering products to customers, such as monitoring the delivery of products through the distribution channel, monitoring salespeople's selling activities, setting product pricing, and coordinating after-sales service. CRM systems have three interconnected components: sales and selling, after-sales service and support, and marketing.

Suppose a sales manager has access only to sales data that show the total sales revenue each salesperson generated in the past 30 days. This information does not break down how much revenue came from sales to existing customers versus sales to new customers. What important knowledge is being lost? First, if most revenues are earned from sales to existing customers, this suggests that the money being spent by a company to advertise and promote its products is not attracting new customers and so is being wasted. Second, important dimensions involved in sales are pricing, financing, and order processing. In many companies, to close a deal, a salesperson has to send the paperwork to a central sales office that handles matters such as approving the customer for special financing and determining specific shipping and delivery dates. In some companies, different departments handle these activities, and it can take a long time to get a response from them; this keeps customers waiting—something that often leads to lost sales. Until CRM systems were introduced, these kinds of problems were widespread and resulted in missed sales and higher operating costs. Today the sales and selling CRM software contains *best sales practices* that analyze this information and then recommend ways to improve how the sales process operates.

When a company implements after-sales service and support CRM software, salespeople are required to input detailed information about their follow-up visits to customers. Because the system tracks and documents every customer's case history, salespeople have instant access to a record of everything that occurred during previous phone calls or visits. They are in a much better position to respond to customers' needs and build customer loyalty, so a company's after-sales service improves. Cell phone service providers like T-Mobile and Sprint, for example, require that sales reps collect information about all customers' inquiries, complaints, and requests, and this is recorded electronically in customer logs. The CRM module can analyze the information in these logs to evaluate whether the customer service reps are meeting or exceeding the company's required service standards.

A CRM system can also identify the top 10 reasons for customer complaints. Sales managers can then work to eliminate the sources of these problems and improve after-sales support procedures. The CRM system also identifies the top 10 best service and support practices, which can then be taught to all sales reps.

Finally, as a CRM system processes information about changing customer needs, this improves marketing in many ways. Marketing managers, for example, have access to detailed customer profiles, including data about purchases and the reasons why individuals were or were not attracted to a company's products. Armed with this knowledge, marketing can better identify customers and the specific product attributes they desire. Traditional CRM systems were organized by having salespeople input customer information. Now social CRM systems can track customers on social media and put them on a company's radar. For example, if a Twitter user posts frequently about a topic relevant to the company or about the company's products, a CRM system can bring the user to the attention of the company as an important connection or a potential customer. In addition, many companies use social CRM software to engage customers with their brands.[48] In sum, a CRM system is a comprehensive method of gathering crucial information about how customers respond to a company's products. It is a powerful functional strategy used to align a company's products with customer needs.

Improving Quality

As noted earlier, high-quality products possess attributes such as superior design, features, reliability, and after-sales support; these products are designed to better meet customer requirements.[49] Quality is a concept that can be applied to the products of both manufacturing and service organizations—goods such as a Toyota car or services such as customer service in a Citibank branch. Why do managers seek to control and improve the quality of their organizations' products?[50] There are two reasons (see Figure 14.3).

LO 14-4
Explain why achieving superior quality is so important.

First, customers usually prefer a higher-quality product to a lower-quality product. So an organization able to provide, *for the same price,* a product of higher quality than a competitor's product is serving its customers better—it is being more responsive to its customers. Often, providing high-quality products creates a brand-name reputation for an organization's products. In turn, this enhanced reputation may allow the organization to charge more for its products than its competitors are able to charge, and thus it makes even greater profits. For example, in 2019 Lexus ranked

Figure 14.3

The Impact of
Increased Quality
on Organizational
Performance

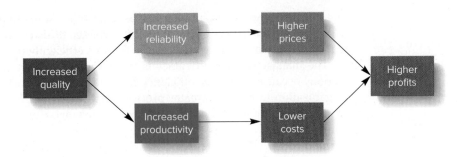

first on the J. D. Power list of the 10 most reliable carmakers for the eighth consecutive year.[51] The high quality and dependability of Lexus vehicles enable the company to charge higher prices for its cars than the prices charged by rival auto makers.

The second reason for trying to boost product quality is that higher product quality can increase efficiency and thereby lower operating costs and boost profits. Achieving high product quality lowers operating costs because of the effect of quality on employee productivity: Higher product quality means less employee time is wasted in making defective products that must be discarded or in providing substandard services, and thus less time has to be spent fixing mistakes. This translates into higher employee productivity, which means lower costs.

Improving Efficiency

LO 14-5

Explain why achieving superior efficiency is so important.

Another goal of operations management is to increase the efficiency of an organization's production system. The fewer the inputs required to produce a given output, the higher will be the efficiency of the production system. Managers can measure efficiency at the organization level in two ways. The measure, known as *total factor productivity*, looks at how well an organization utilizes all of its resources—such as labor, capital, materials, or energy—to produce its outputs. It is expressed in the following equation:

$$\text{Total factor productivity} = \frac{\text{Outputs}}{\text{All inputs}}$$

The problem with total factor productivity is that each input is typically measured in different units: Labor's contribution to producing an output is measured by hours worked; the contribution of materials is measured by the amount consumed (e.g., tons of iron ore required to make a ton of steel); the contribution of energy is measured by the units of energy consumed (e.g., kilowatt-hours); and so on. To compute total factor productivity, managers must convert all the inputs to a common unit, such as dollars, before they can work the equation.

Though sometimes a useful measure of efficiency overall, total factor productivity obscures the exact contribution of an individual input—such as labor—to the production of a given output. Consequently, most organizations focus on specific measures of efficiency, known as *partial productivity*, that measure the efficiency of an individual unit. For example, the efficiency of labor inputs is expressed as

$$\text{Labor productivity} = \frac{\text{Outputs}}{\text{Direct labor}}$$

Labor productivity is most commonly used to draw efficiency comparisons between different organizations. For example, one study found it took the average Japanese automobile components supplier half as many labor-hours to produce a part, such as a car seat or exhaust system, as it took the average British company.[52] Thus, the study concluded, Japanese companies use labor more efficiently than British companies do.

The management of efficiency is an extremely important issue in most organizations because increased efficiency lowers production costs, thereby allowing the organization to make a greater profit or to attract more customers by lowering its price. For example, in 1990 the price of the average personal computer sold in the United States was $3,000, by 1995 the price was around $1,800, and in 2019 it was around $350.[53] This decrease occurred despite the fact that the power and capabilities of the average personal computer increased dramatically during this time period (microprocessors became more powerful, memory increased, and multimedia capability was added).

Why was the decrease in price possible? Manufacturers of personal computers focused on quality and boosted their efficiency by improving the quality of their components and making PCs easier to assemble. This allowed them to lower their costs and prices yet still make a profit.

Facilities Layout, Flexible Manufacturing, and Efficiency

Another factor that influences efficiency is the way managers decide to lay out or design an organization's physical work facilities. This is important for two reasons. First, the way in which machines and workers are organized or grouped together into workstations affects the efficiency of the production system. Second, a major determinant of efficiency is the cost associated with setting up the equipment needed to make a particular product. Facilities layout is the operations management strategy whose goal is to design the machine–worker interface to increase production system efficiency. Flexible manufacturing is the set of operations management techniques that attempt to reduce the setup costs associated with a production system.

facilities layout The operations management strategy whose goal is to design the machine—worker interface to increase production system efficiency.

flexible manufacturing Operations management techniques that attempt to reduce the setup costs associated with a production system.

FACILITIES LAYOUT The way in which machines, robots, and people are grouped together affects how productive they can be. Figure 14.4 shows three basic ways of arranging workstations: product layout, process layout, and fixed-position layout.

In a *product layout,* machines are organized so that each operation needed to manufacture a product is performed at workstations arranged in a fixed sequence. Typically, workers are stationary in this arrangement, and a moving conveyor belt takes the product being worked on to the next workstation so that it is progressively assembled. Mass production is the familiar name for this layout; car assembly lines are probably the best-known example. It used to be that product layout was efficient only when products were created in large quantities; however, the introduction of modular assembly lines controlled by computers makes it efficient to make products in small batches.

In a *process layout,* workstations are not organized in a fixed sequence. Rather, each workstation is relatively self-contained, and a product goes to whichever workstation is needed to perform the next operation to complete the product. Process layout is often suited to manufacturing settings that produce a variety of custom-made products, each tailored to the needs of a different kind of customer. For example, a custom furniture manufacturer might use a process layout so that different teams of workers can produce different styles of chairs or tables made from different kinds of woods and finishes. Such a layout also describes how a patient might go through a hospital from emergency room to X-ray department, to operating room, to recovery,

Figure 14.4   Three Facilities Layouts

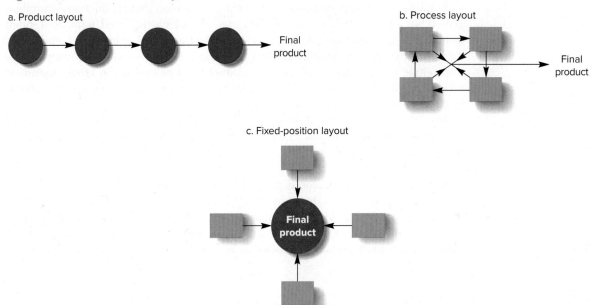

a. Product layout

Final
product

b. Process layout

Final
product

c. Fixed-position layout

Final
product

and so on. A process layout provides the flexibility needed to change a product, whether it is a PC or a patient's treatment. Such flexibility, however, often reduces efficiency because it is expensive.

In a *fixed-position layout*, the product stays in a fixed position. Its component parts are produced in remote workstations and brought to the production area for final assembly. Increasingly, self-managed teams are using fixed-position layouts. Different teams assemble each component part and then send these parts to the final assembly team, which makes the final product. A fixed-position layout is commonly used for products such as jet airlines, mainframe computers, and gas turbines—products that are complex and difficult to assemble or so large that moving them from one workstation to another would be difficult. Regardless of the layout, facilities need to be designed with efficiency in mind.

FLEXIBLE MANUFACTURING In a manufacturing company, a major source of costs is the costs associated with setting up the equipment needed to make a particular product. One of these costs is the cost of production that is forgone because nothing is produced while the equipment is being set up. For example, components manufacturers often need as much as half a day to set up automated production equipment when switching from production of one component part (such as a washer ring for the steering column of a car) to another (such as a washer ring for the steering column of a truck). During this half-day, a manufacturing plant is not producing anything, but employees are paid for this "nonproductive" time.

It follows that if setup times for complex production equipment can be reduced, so can setup costs, and efficiency will rise. In other words, if setup times can be reduced, the time that plant and employees spend actually producing something will increase. This simple insight has been the driving force behind the development of flexible manufacturing techniques.

Flexible manufacturing aims to reduce the time required to set up production equipment.[54] Redesigning the manufacturing process so that production equipment geared for manufacturing one product can be quickly replaced with equipment geared to make another product can dramatically reduce setup times and costs. Another favorable outcome from flexible manufacturing is that a company is able to produce many more varieties of a product than before in the same amount of time. Thus, flexible manufacturing increases a company's ability to be responsive to its customers.

To realize the benefits of flexible manufacturing, General Motors built a plant in Lansing, Michigan, in 2001 that can expand to meet demand. When it was first built, the company's Grand River Assembly plant was already more flexible than its other plants and was modeled after GM's innovative facilities overseas.[55] While some GM executives expressed concern that the site was too small to work well, the plant has received praise for its ability to manufacture a variety of car models as well as for its collaborative team management style and automation capabilities. In 2017, the company announced a multimillion-dollar investment in the Grand River plant for new tooling and equipment, as well as a major expansion of the facility's body shop.[56]

Just-in-Time Inventory and Efficiency

inventory The stock of raw materials, inputs, and component parts that an organization has on hand at a particular time.

just-in-time inventory system A system in which parts or supplies arrive at an organization when they are needed, not before.

Inventory is the stock of raw materials, inputs, and component parts that an organization has on hand at a particular time. Just-in-time (JIT) inventory systems play a major role in the process of identifying and finding the source of defects in inputs. When an organization has a just-in-time inventory system, parts or supplies arrive at the organization when they are needed, not before. Under a JIT inventory system, parts enter an organization's production system immediately; they are not warehoused for months before use. This means that defective inputs can be quickly spotted. Managers can then trace a problem to the supply source and fix it before more defective parts are produced.

JIT systems, such as Toyota's *kanban* system, were originally developed as part of the effort to improve product quality; they have major implications for efficiency. Toyota's system is based on the delivery of components to the production line just as they are needed. This leads to major cost savings from increasing inventory turnover and reducing inventory holding costs, such as warehousing and storage costs and the cost of capital tied up in inventory.[57]

Although companies that manufacture and assemble products can obviously use JIT to great advantage, so can service organizations. Walmart, the largest retailer in the world, recently modified its JIT process to one the company calls OTIF (on-time, in full). A recognized concept in supply chain management, OTIF simply means suppliers should deliver their products when and how the buyer needs them. Walmart expects food and consumable suppliers to deliver goods within a one-day window, while general merchandise or soft line suppliers must comply within a two-day period. If a delivery arrives early, late, or improperly packaged, a supplier could be fined a 3% penalty against invoice charges.[58]

By all measures of performance, JIT systems have been successful—inventory holding costs have fallen sharply and products are being delivered to customers on time. In addition, the design-to-product cycles for new products have dropped almost in half because suppliers are involved much earlier in the design process so they can supply new inputs as needed. Finally, as Walmart's OTIF process suggests,

Walmart recently modified its JIT process to OTIF (on-time, in full), which means suppliers should deliver products when and how the buyer needs them. If a Walmart delivery is early or late, the supplier could be fined by the company. Sergey Yechikov/Shutterstock

companies must continue to look for innovative ways to streamline global supply chains, especially because of the time pressures of e-commerce sales and deliveries.[59]

Self-Managed Work Teams and Efficiency

Another efficiency-boosting technique is the use of self-managed work teams (see Chapter 11). The typical team consists of from 5 to 15 employees who produce an entire product instead of only parts of it. Team members learn all team tasks and move from job to job. The result is a flexible workforce because team members can fill in for absent coworkers. The members of each team also assume responsibility for work and vacation scheduling, ordering materials, and hiring new members—previously all responsibilities of first-line managers. Because people often respond well to being given greater autonomy and responsibility, the use of empowered self-managed teams can increase productivity and efficiency. Moreover, cost savings arise from eliminating supervisors and creating a flatter organizational hierarchy, which further increases efficiency.

The effect of introducing self-managed teams is often an increase in efficiency of 30% or more. The introduction of self-managed teams at a GE Aviation plant in Durham, North Carolina, has produced year-over-year productivity growth, first time yield quality, and successful on-time delivery rates.[60]

Process Reengineering and Efficiency

process reengineering The fundamental rethinking and radical redesign of business processes to achieve dramatic improvements in critical measures of performance such as cost, quality, service, and speed.

Think of the major activities of businesses as processes that take one or more kinds of inputs and create an output that is of value to the customer. Process reengineering is the fundamental rethinking and radical redesign of business processes to achieve dramatic improvements in critical measures of performance such as cost, quality, service, and speed.[61] Customer relationship management can be thought of as a business process: Once a customer's order is received (the input), all the activities necessary to process the order are performed, and the ordered goods are delivered to the customer (the output). Process reengineering can boost efficiency because it eliminates the time devoted to activities that do not add value.

As an example of process reengineering in practice, consider how Ford Motor Company used it. One day a manager from Ford was working at its Japanese partner Mazda and discovered quite by accident that Mazda had only five people in its accounts payable department. The Ford manager was shocked, for Ford's U.S. operation had 500 employees in accounts payable. He reported his discovery to Ford's U.S. managers, who decided to form a task force to figure out why the difference existed.

Ford managers discovered that procurement began when the purchasing department sent a purchase order to a supplier and sent a copy of the purchase order to Ford's accounts payable department. When the supplier shipped the goods and

Managers at Ford Motor Company have used process reengineering to improve the efficiency of the company's procurement process. By simplifying the process, Ford has significantly reduced the time spent by accounts payable clerks to rectify complex vehicle orders that contain conflicting information. Robert Clay/Alamy Stock Photo

they arrived at Ford, a clerk at the receiving dock completed a form describing the goods and sent the form to accounts payable. The supplier, meanwhile, sent accounts payable an invoice. Thus, accounts payable received three documents relating to these goods: a copy of the original purchase order, the receiving document, and the invoice. If the information in all three was in agreement (most of the time it was), a clerk in accounts payable issued payment. Occasionally, however, all three documents did not agree. Ford discovered that accounts payable clerks spent most of their time straightening out the 1% of instances in which the purchase order, receiving document, and invoice contained conflicting information.[62]

Ford managers decided to reengineer the procurement process to simplify it. Now when a buyer in the purchasing department issues a purchase order to a supplier, that buyer also enters the order into an online database. As before, suppliers send goods to the receiving dock. When the goods arrive, the clerk at the receiving dock checks a computer terminal to see whether the received shipment matches the description on the purchase order. If it does, the clerk accepts the goods and pushes a button on the terminal keyboard that tells the database the goods have arrived. Receipt of the goods is recorded in the database, and a computer automatically issues and sends a check to the supplier. If the goods do not correspond to the description on the purchase order in the database, the clerk at the dock refuses the shipment and sends it back to the supplier.

Payment authorization, which used to be performed by accounts payable, is now accomplished at the receiving dock. The new process has come close to eliminating the need for an accounts payable department. In some parts of Ford, the size of the accounts payable department has been cut by 95%. By reducing the head count in accounts payable, the reengineering effort reduced the amount of time wasted on unproductive activities, thereby increasing the efficiency of the total organization.

In sum, managers at all levels have important roles to play in a company's effort to boost efficiency. Top management's role is to encourage efficiency improvements by, for example, emphasizing the need for continuous improvement or reengineering. Top management also must ensure that managers from different functional departments work together to find ways to increase efficiency. However, while top managers might recognize the need for such actions, functional-level managers are in the best position to identify opportunities for making efficiency-enhancing improvements to an organization's production systems. They are the managers who are involved in an organization's production system on a day-to-day basis. Improving efficiency, like quality, is an ongoing, never-ending process.

Operations Management: Some Remaining Issues

Achieving superior responsiveness to customers through quality and efficiency often requires a profound shift in management operations and in the culture of an organization. Many reports have appeared in the popular press about widespread disillusionment with JIT, flexible manufacturing, and reengineering. It is possible that many of the disillusioned organizations are those that failed to understand that implementing these systems requires a marked shift in organizational culture and a strong commitment to collecting pertinent information and data that can help managers make effective business decisions. None of these systems is a panacea that can be taken once, like a pill, to cure industrial ills. Making these techniques work within an organization can pose a significant challenge that calls for hard work and years of persistence by the sponsoring managers.

Managers also need to understand the ethical implications of the adoption of many of the production techniques discussed here. JIT, flexible manufacturing, and reengineering can all increase quality, efficiency, and responsiveness to customers, but they may do so at great cost to employees. Employees may see the demands of their job increase, or, worse, they may see themselves reengineered out of a job.

Is it ethical to continually increase the demands placed on employees, regardless of the human cost in terms of job stress? Obviously, the answer is no. Employee support is vital if an organization is to function effectively. What kinds of work pressures are legitimate, and what pressures are excessive? There is no clear answer to this question. Ultimately the issue comes down to the judgment of responsible managers seeking to act ethically.

Summary and Review

OPERATIONS MANAGEMENT AND COMPETITIVE ADVANTAGE To achieve high performance, managers try to improve their responsiveness to customers, the quality of their products, and the efficiency of their organization. To achieve these goals, managers can use a number of operations management techniques to improve the way an organization's production system operates. [LO 14-1]

INFORMATION AND THE MANAGER'S JOB Computer-based information systems are central to the operation of most organizations. By providing managers with high-quality, timely, relevant, and relatively complete data, properly implemented information systems can improve managers' ability to coordinate and control the operations of an organization and to make sound business decisions. In addition, information systems can help the organization gain a competitive advantage through their beneficial impact on productivity, quality, and responsiveness to customers. Unfortunately, collecting and utilizing pertinent data can also lead to issues of cybersecurity and data privacy, which managers must continue to address as part of their day-to-day responsibilities. [LO 14-2]

IMPROVING RESPONSIVENESS TO CUSTOMERS To achieve high performance in a competitive environment, it is imperative that the production system of an organization responds to customer demands. Managers try to design production systems that produce outputs that have the attributes customers desire. One of the central tasks of operations management is to develop new and improved production systems that enhance the ability of the organization to deliver economically more of the product attributes that customers desire for the same price. Techniques such as JIT, flexible manufacturing, and process reengineering are popular because they promise to do this. Managers should analyze carefully the links between responsiveness to customers and the production system of an organization. The ability of an organization to satisfy the demands of its customers for lower prices, acceptable quality, better features, and so on depends critically on the nature of the organization's production system. As important as responsiveness to customers is, however, managers need to recognize that there are limits to how responsive an organization can be and still cover its costs. [LO 14-3]

IMPROVING QUALITY Managers seek to improve the quality of their organization's output because it enables them to better serve customers, to raise prices, and to lower production costs. The attempt to improve quality requires an organization-wide commitment; managers emphasize a strong customer focus, find ways to measure quality, set quality improvement goals, solicit input from employees about how to improve product quality, and design products for ease of manufacture. [LO 14-4]

IMPROVING EFFICIENCY Improving efficiency requires one or more of the following: improve quality, adopt flexible manufacturing technologies, introduce just-in-time inventory systems, establish self-managed work teams, and use process reengineering. Top management is responsible for setting the context within which efficiency improvements can take place by, for example, emphasizing the need for continuous improvement. Functional-level managers bear prime responsibility for identifying and implementing efficiency-enhancing improvements in production systems. [LO 14-5]

Management *in Action*

Topics for Discussion and Action

Discussion

1. Why is it important for managers to pay close attention to their organization's production system if they wish to be responsive to their customers? [LO 14-1]

2. What is big data and how do managers use it to improve productivity? [LO 14-2]

3. What is CRM, and how can it help improve responsiveness to customers? [LO 14-3]

4. How can achieving superior quality help a company's bottom line? [LO 14-4]

5. What is efficiency, and what are some of the techniques that managers can use to increase it? [LO 14-5]

Action

6. Ask a manager how quality, efficiency, and responsiveness to customers are defined and measured in his or her organization. [LO 14-3, 14-4, 14-5]

7. Go into a local store, restaurant, or supermarket, and list the ways in which you think the organization is being responsive or unresponsive to the needs of its customers. How could this business's responsiveness to customers be improved? [LO 14-3]

Building Management Skills

Managing a Production System [LO 14-1, 14-3]

Choose an organization with which you are familiar—one that you have worked in or patronized or one that has received extensive coverage in the popular press. The organization should be involved in only one industry or business. Answer these questions about the organization:

1. What is the output of the organization?

2. Describe the production system that the organization uses to produce this output.

3. What product attributes do customers of the organization desire?

4. Does its production system allow the organization to deliver the desired product attributes?

5. Try to identify improvements that might be made to the organization's production system to boost the organization's responsiveness to customers, quality, and efficiency.

Managing Ethically [LO 14-1, LO 14-5]

After implementing efficiency-improving techniques, many companies commonly lay off hundreds or thousands of employees whose services are no longer required. And frequently, the remaining employees must perform more tasks more quickly—a situation that can generate employee stress and other work-related problems. In addition, these employees may experience "survivor's guilt" because they kept their jobs while many of their colleagues and friends were let go.

Questions

1. Either by yourself or in a group, discuss how to think through the ethical implications of using a new operations management technique to improve organizational performance.

2. What criteria would you use to decide what kind of technique is ethical to adopt and how far to push employees to raise the level of their performance?

3. How big a layoff, if any, would be acceptable? If layoffs are acceptable, what could be done to reduce their harm to employees?

Small Group Breakout Exercise [LO 14-1, 14-2, 14-3, 14-4, 14-5]

How to Compete in the Sandwich Business

Form groups of three or four people, and appoint one member as the spokesperson who will communicate your findings to the whole class when called on by the instructor. Then discuss the following scenario:

You and your partners are thinking about opening a new kind of sandwich shop that will compete head-to-head with Subway and ThunderCloud Subs. Because these chains have good brand-name recognition, it is vital that you find some source of competitive advantage for your new sandwich shop, and you are meeting to brainstorm ways of obtaining one.

1. Identify the product attributes that a typical sandwich shop customer wants the most.

2. In what ways do you think you will be able to improve on the operations and processes of existing sandwich shops and achieve a competitive advantage through better (a) product quality, (b) efficiency, (c) responsiveness to customers, and (d) big data?

Be the Manager [LO 14-1, 14-4]

How to Build Flat-Screen Displays

You are an operations management consultant who has been called in by the management team of a start-up company that will produce flat-screen displays for PC makers like Apple and HP. The flat-screen display market is highly competitive, so there is considerable pressure to reduce costs. Also, PC makers are demanding ever-higher quality and better features to please customers. In addition, they demand that delivery of your product meet their production schedule needs. Management wants your advice on how best to meet these requirements. The company is in the process of recruiting new workers and building a production facility.

Questions

1. What kinds of techniques discussed in the chapter can help these managers increase efficiency?

2. In what ways can these managers go about developing a program to increase quality?

3. What critical lessons can these managers learn from operations management?

Case in the News [LO 14-1, 14-2, 14-3, 14-4, 14-5]

How Brooks Brothers Redesigned Itself for a Brighter Future

At the start of this millennium, Brooks Brothers, a retailer of men's business apparel, was on shaky ground. The company had sold classic suits to most of the American presidents and was considered a style innovator, having introduced such concepts as ready-to-wear suits (in 1890), wash-and-wear shirts (1953), and no-iron cotton dress shirts (1998). But its reputation had been slipping, along with its revenues. In 1818, when Henry Sands Brooks founded the company, he did so with a mission: "To make and deal only in merchandise of the finest quality, to sell it at a fair profit and to deal with people who seek and appreciate such merchandise." Under the ownership of his sons, that mission continued. After the company was purchased by a retail conglomerate, it still grew. But when Marks & Spencer bought Brooks Brothers in 1988, the new owners tried to join the trend toward business casual, cutting prices and quality along the way. Consumers went elsewhere, and beginning in the late 1990s, the company operated at a loss with a market value below what Marks & Spencer had paid.

In 2002, Claudio Del Vecchio bought Brooks Brothers and became chief executive officer. Del Vecchio, from a wealthy Italian family, had revered the brand but saw what other former customers did: Fabrics and designs no longer were of high quality. His vision was to restore the company to its former greatness by reinforcing its culture and rebuilding its capacity to innovate and deliver great products, so Brooks Brothers and its reputation would outlast him.

Del Vecchio and the executives he hired worked with designers and suppliers, many from Italy, to upgrade specifications for the company's apparel. They improved tailoring and balance so the clothing would perform better. Along with business classics, they developed Golden Fleece and Red Fleece lines to appeal to younger customers. After about six months, they began shipping new items to stores, and within a year, the stores were fully stocked with better offerings. Designs included slim versions of shirts and suits to appeal to younger businessmen. Customers began returning, and by the following year, Brooks Brothers had begun reporting profits.

Part of the brand's appeal is its Made in America label. Its ties, made at a factory in Long Island City, New York, bear such a label. However, in choosing factory locations, managers consider a variety of factors. The company's top-selling no-iron shirts are made in Malaysia, where low wages keep the price moderate. But U.S. factories are ideal for customized and high-end products such as suits, and the majority of that work has been reshored, or moved back to the United States from other countries. For that purpose, Brooks Brothers purchased a Massachusetts garment factory and updated it to improve efficiency. As owner, the company can have its own managers enforce quality standards.

Brooks Brothers also has been increasing efficiency and responsiveness by modernizing processes for getting products to consumers. Instead of routing all products from factories to its warehouses to stores to consumers, it now fills orders with the nearest inventory, whether from factories, warehouses, or stores. Using stores to fill orders from customers who aren't near the company's two warehouses has shaved days off delivery times. Store employees use new software that lets them check inventory in their store and other stores, so they can quickly place orders and retrieve items for pickup. In addition, information technology is improving decisions about what to make and where to ship items. A new computer system helps managers rapidly adjust to sales patterns—for example, timing production so goods can be sent straight to the store that will sell them, bypassing time spent in a warehouse. The system also uses artificial intelligence to help predict what will sell where.

In 2018, when Brooks Brothers celebrated its 200th birthday, it was operating 50% more stores than in 2001 and was also selling in upscale department stores and on its retail website. It had built the brand in new markets, with 35% of revenues coming from sales in 50 countries outside the United States. E-commerce will be a key part of Brooks Brothers's future; online sales already account for the company's largest share of revenues and are growing faster than store retailing. E-commerce and store retailing drive growth together, because most Brooks Brothers's customers visit stores to get ideas and then complete purchases online. Together, these signs suggest that effective operations management is helping Del Vecchio realize his vision.

Questions for Discussion

1. What measures did Brooks Brothers take to improve product quality? Suggest one other method it could employ to further improve quality.

2. How is information technology helping Brooks Brothers improve responsiveness to consumers?

3. What benefits can Brooks Brothers obtain from reshoring operations (bringing production back into the United States from other locations)? Why is improving efficiency an important part of such moves?

Sources: A. Cheng, "How 200-Year-Old Brooks Brothers Is Embracing AI and Millennials—and Why It May Cozy Up to Amazon," *Forbes*, www.forbes.com, November 30, 2018; D. Parisi, "Inside Brooks Brothers' Big Bet on Artificial Intelligence," *Glossy*, www.glossy.co, November 30, 2018; J. E. Palmieri, "Brooks Brothers Institutes AI System," *WWD*, November 30, 2018, 6; H. Moser and S. Montalbano, "Quality Cost: The Number One Reason Companies Are Reshoring," *Quality*, October 2018, 36–39; J. Smith, "Brooks Brothers Refashions Its Supply Chain for Modern Retail," *The Wall Street Journal*, www.wsj.com, September 20, 2018; J. E. Palmieri, "Brooks Brothers Celebrates 200 Years of Style," *WWD*, April 25, 2018, 10–16; T. Agins, "With a Glance Backward, Brooks Brothers Looks to the Future," *The New York Times*, www.nytimes.com, April 21, 2018.

Endnotes

1. A. Gasparro, "Kraft Heinz's CEO on Cost-Cutting, Dealmaking and Oprah," *The Wall Street Journal*, www.wsj.com, May 16, 2017; B. Sweeney, "Kraft Heinz CEO: It's All about Long-Term Perspective, Not Ruthless Cost-Cutting," *Crain's Chicago Business*, www.chicagobusiness.com, September 12, 2017.

2. D. Gelles, "Bernardo Hees of Kraft Heinz: 'New Mistakes Are Welcome,'" *The New York Times*, www.nytimes.com, May 3, 2018.

3. A. Gasparro, "Tightfisted New Owners Put Heinz on Diet," *The Wall Street Journal*, www.wsj.com, accessed February 22, 2019.

4. Sweeney, "Kraft Heinz CEO."

5. D. Buss, "Customer-Led Innovation: Five Questions with Kraft Heinz's Greg Guidotti," *Brandchannel*, www.brandchannel.com, March 5, 2018; B. Kowitt,

"Why Kraft Heinz Is Betting Big on Eggs," *Fortune*, http://fortune.com, February 26, 2018.

6. Kowitt, "Why Kraft Heinz Is Betting Big on Eggs."

7. S. Bomkamp, "Processed-Food Stalwart Kraft Heinz Creates Unit to Go after Health-Conscious Consumers," *Chicago Tribune*, www.chicagotribune.com, March 7, 2018.

8. The view of quality that includes the concept of reliability goes back

to the work of W. Edwards Deming and Joseph Juran. See A. Gabor, *The Man Who Discovered Quality* (New York: Times Books, 1990).

9. N. B. Macintosh, *The Social Software of Accounting Systems* (New York: Wiley, 1995).

10. C. A. O'Reilly, "Variations in Decision Makers' Use of Information: The Impact of Quality and Accessibility," *Academy of Management Journal* 25 (1982), 756–71.

11. G. Stalk and T. H. Hout, *Competing Against Time* (New York: Free Press, 1990).

12. "About Transit" and "Regions," https://transitapp.com, accessed February 18, 2019; J. Rossignol, "Transit App Expands Real-Time Crowdsourced Data to 175 Cities," *MacRumors*, www.macrumors.com, August 17, 2018.

13. R. Cyert and R. March, *Behavioral Theory of the Firm* (Englewood Cliffs, NJ: Prentice-Hall, 1963).

14. K. Ang, "Companies Use AI to Help Managers Become More Human," *The Wall Street Journal,* www.wsj.com, April 29, 2018; S. F. Gale, "Robot Coaches: New Model for Leadership Training?," *Chief Learning Officer,* www .clomedia.com, August 25, 2017; J. Mannes, "Butterfly Nabs $2.4M Seed Round to Improve Managers with Targeted Tips," *TechCrunch,* https://techcrunch.com, October 6, 2017; H. R. Huhman, "Five Things the Best Leaders Do Every Day," *Entrepreneur,* www.entrepreneur. com, January 30, 2017.

15. Ang, "Companies Use AI to Help Managers"; T. Greenwald, "What Exactly Is Artificial Intelligence, Anyway?," *The Wall Street Journal,* www.wsj.com, April 30, 2018; C. Dessi, "This Startup Will Make You Unbelievably Happy at Work," *Inc.,* www.inc.com, April 25, 2016.

16. "Work of the Future: Butterfly a.i.," MIT–Solve, https://solve.mit.edu, accessed February 22, 2019.

17. Mannes, "Butterfly Nabs $2.4M Seed Round"; Gale, "Robot Coaches."

18. Ang, "Companies Use AI to Help Managers"; Dessi, "This Startup Will Make You Unbelievably

Happy"; Huhman, "Five Things the Best Leaders Do."

19. R. Whiting, "10 Data Analytics Companies to Watch in 2019," *CRN*, www.crn.com, accessed February 22, 2019.

20. "What Is Data Analytics?," https:// searchbusinessanalytics.techtarget. com, accessed February 22, 2019.

21. "Big Data Analytics: What Is It and Why It Matters," www.sas.com, accessed February 22, 2019.

22. S. M. Dornbusch and W. R. Scott, *Evaluation and the Exercise of Authority* (San Francisco: Jossey-Bass, 1975).

23. J. Child, *Organization: A Guide to Problems and Practice* (London: Harper & Row, 1984).

24. "Contract Logistics—Retail," www.ups-scm.com, accessed February 22, 2019.

25. "Unlock the Magic with Your MagicBand or Card," http:// disneyworld.disney.go.com, accessed February 22, 2019; "Big Data Meets Walt Disney's Magical Approach," https://datafloq.com, accessed February 22, 2019.

26. "OCEAN FAQs," www.princess. com, accessed February 22, 2019; "Princess Cruises Reports Ocean Medallion Activation Milestone," *Travel Agent Central,* www .travelagentcentral.com, October 1, 2018.

27. Cisco, "What Is Cybersecurity?," www.cisco.com, accessed February 22, 2019.

28. "50% of Companies Face Cyber-Attacks Motivated by Ransom," *Security* magazine, www.securitymagazine.com, accessed February 22, 2019.

29. G. Fleishman, "Equifax Data Breach, One Year Later: Obvious Errors and No Real Changes, New Report Says," *Fortune,* http:// fortune.com, September 8, 2018; B. Fung, "Equifax's Massive 2017 Data Breach Keeps Getting Worse," *The Washington Post,* www.washingtonpost.com, March 1, 2018.

30. "Bad Credit: Uncovering Equifax's Failure to Protect Americans' Personal Information," www.warren.senate.com, February 2018.

31. B. M. Egan, "3 Biggest Cybersecurity Threats Facing Small Businesses Right Now," *Entrepreneur,* www.entrepreneur. com, January 31, 2018.

32. S. Ranger, "What Is the IoT? Everything You Need to Know about the Internet of Things Right Now," *ZDNet,* www.zdnet.com, January 19, 2018.

33. KPMG Voice, "Perspectives: The Next Big Cybersecurity Threats Facing Businesses," *Forbes,* www.forbes.com, April 3, 2018.

34. "Our History," https://newsroom. fb.com, accessed February 22, 2019; Omnicore, "Facebook by the Numbers: Stats, Demographics & Fun Facts," www.omnicoreagency. com, January 6, 2019.

35. M. Rosenberg, N. Confessore, and C. Cadwalladr, "How Trump Consultants Exploited the Facebook Data of Millions," *The New York Times,* www.nytimes.com, March 17, 2018; M. Schwartz, "Facebook Failed to Protect 30 Million Users from Having Their Data Harvested by Trump Campaign Affiliate," https://theintercept.com, March 30, 2017.

36. D. Kurtzleben, "Did Fake News on Facebook Help Elect Trump? What We Know," *NPR,* www .npr.org, April 11, 2018; C. Press, "Facebook Data: How It Was Used by Cambridge Analytica (video)," *BBC,* www.bbc.com, April 9, 2018.

37. Bloomberg, "Facebook Cambridge Analytica Scandal: 10 Questions Answered," *Fortune,* http://fortune. com, April 10, 2018; Kurtzleben, "Did Fake News on Facebook Help Elect Trump?"

38. T. Hsu, "For Many Facebook Users, a 'Last Straw' That Led Them to Quit," *The New York Times,* www .nytimes.com, March 21, 2018.

39. L. Bruggeman, "Cambridge Analytica Shutting Down, Files for Bankruptcy," *ABC News,* https:// abcnews.go.com, May 2, 2018; J. Temperton, "Check If Your Facebook Data Was Shared with Cambridge Analytica," *Wired,* www.wired.co.uk, April 10, 2018.

40. D. Landsel, "The Most Fascinating Attraction at Disney World You Aren't Allowed to Visit,"

Food&Wine, www.foodandwine.com, accessed February 22, 2019; J. Clampet, "Skift Q&A: The Man Who Feeds More than 300,000 Guests a Day," *Skift,* http://skift.com, accessed April 27, 2015.

41. D. Owen, "Customer Satisfaction at the Push of a Button," *The New Yorker,* www.newyorker.com, February 5, 2018; G. Dickinson, "The Smiley Feedback Buttons at Airports Do Actually Work—and They Are Changing the Way We Travel," *(London) Telegraph,* www.telegraph.co.uk, February 16, 2018.

42. D. Eisen, "Customer Satisfaction Surveys Are Getting It All Wrong: There's a Better Way," *Hotel Management,* www.hotelmanagement.net, February 26, 2018.

43. Owen, "Customer Satisfaction at the Push of a Button"; Eisen, "Customer Satisfaction Surveys Are Getting It All Wrong."

44. HappyOrNot home page, www.happy-or-not.com, accessed February 22, 2019.

45. Owen, "Customer Satisfaction at the Push of a Button."

46. M. E. Porter, *Competitive Advantage* (New York: Free Press, 1985).

47. Company website, www.southwest.com, accessed February 22, 2019.

48. "What Is Social CRM?," www.salesforce.com, accessed February 22, 2019.

49. The view of quality as reliability goes back to the work of Deming and Juran; see Gabor, *The Man Who Discovered Quality.*

50. See also D. Garvin, "What Does Product Quality Really Mean?," *Sloan Management Review* 26 (Fall 1984), 25–44; P. B. Crosby, *Quality Is Free* (New York: Mentor Books, 1980); Gabor, *The Man Who Discovered Quality.*

51. J. Ryan, "J.D. Power Ranks Most Reliable Cars in America: Lexus Tops, Toyota and Porsche Tie," *Automobile Fanatics,* https://automobilefanatics.com, February 16, 2019.

52. J. Griffiths, "Europe's Manufacturing Quality and Productivity Still Lag Far behind Japan's," *Financial Times,* November 4, 1994, 11.

53. T. Brant, "The Best Budget Laptops for 2019," *PC Magazine,* www.pcmag.com, February 1, 2019.

54. P. Nemetz and L. Fry, "Flexible Manufacturing Organizations: Implications for Strategy Formulation," *Academy of Management Review* 13 (1988), 627–38; N. Greenwood, *Implementing Flexible Manufacturing Systems* (New York: Halstead Press, 1986).

55. L. VanHulle, "Lansing Grand River Plant's Milestone Means 'Confidence,'" *Lansing State Journal,* http://archive.lansingstatejournal.com, accessed March 30, 2018.

56. "Lansing Grand River Assembly Plant: Recent Major Investments," http://media.gm.com, accessed March 30, 2018.

57. "Just-in-Time—Philosophy of Complete Elimination of Waste," www.toyota-global.com, accessed February 22, 2019.

58. E. Lopez, "Behind the Scenes of Walmart's New On-Time, In-Full Policy," *Supply Chain Dive,* www.supplychaindive.com, October 17, 2017.

59. "The E-commerce Threat: CPG Supply Chains Need to Up Their Game," *Food Ingredients First,* www.foodingredientsfirst.com, January 26, 2018.

60. R. Jones, "Teaming at GE Aviation," *Management Innovation eXchange,* www.managementexchange.com, accessed February 22, 2019.

61. M. Hammer and J. Champy, *Reengineering the Corporation* (New York: Harper Business, 1993), 35.

62. Ibid.

Career Development

Managers face several challenges both in the course of their own careers and in facilitating effective career management for their employees. A career is the sum total of work-related experiences throughout a person's life.[1] Careers encompass all of the different jobs people hold and the different organizations they work for. Careers are important to most people for at least two reasons. First, a career is a means to support oneself and one's loved ones, providing basic necessities and opportunities to pursue outside interests. Second, a career can be a source of personal fulfillment and meaning. Many managers find that making a difference in an organization and helping improve organizational efficiency and effectiveness are personally as well as financially rewarding.

Career development is a concern for managers both in terms of how their own careers unfold over time and how careers are managed in their organizations. In the development of their own careers, managers seek out challenging and interesting jobs that will develop their skills, lead to future opportunities, and allow them the opportunity to do the kind of work that will be personally meaningful. Similarly, in motivating and leading employees, managers need to be attuned to employees' career development. When careers (of both managers and rank-and-file employees) are effectively managed in an organization, the organization makes the best use of its human resources and employees tend to be motivated by, and satisfied with, their jobs.

Both employees and managers play an important role in effectively managing careers. For example, employees need to understand themselves, the kind of work they find motivating and fulfilling, and their own future aspirations for their careers. Employees then need to proactively seek the education, training, and kinds of work experiences that will help them to have the careers they want. Managers can motivate employees to make meaningful contributions to organizations by providing them with work assignments, experiences, training, and opportunities that contribute to employees' career development.[2]

Ulta Beauty CEO Mary Dillon has served in different posts for an array of companies including U.S. Cellular, McDonald's Corporation, Quaker Foods, and PepsiCo. Michael L Abramson/Getty Images

Types of Careers

While every person's career is unique, the different types of careers that people have fall into four general categories: steady-state careers, linear careers, spiral careers, and transitory careers.[3]

steady-state career
A career consisting of the same kind of job during a large part of an individual's work life.

STEADY-STATE CAREERS A person with a steady-state career makes a one-time commitment to a certain kind of job that he or she maintains throughout his or her work life.[4] People with steady-state careers can become very skilled and expert at their work. A playwright who starts writing plays upon graduation from college and continues to write plays until retiring at age 70 has a steady-state career. So too does a dentist who maintains a steady dental practice upon graduation from dental school until retirement.

Some managers choose to have a steady-state career, holding the same kind of job during a large part of their work life, often becoming highly skilled and expert in what they do. A talented and creative graphic artist at a digital marketing company, for example, may turn down promotions and other "opportunities" so that he can continue to work on designing attractive layouts and illustrations, what he really likes to do. Similarly, some managers at Nordstrom have steady-state careers as area sales managers because they enjoy the direct supervision of salespeople and the opportunity to stay close to customers.

linear career
A career consisting of a sequence of jobs in which each new job entails additional responsibility, a greater impact on an organization, new skills, and upward movement in an organization's hierarchy.

LINEAR CAREERS A person who has a linear career moves through a sequence of jobs in which each new job entails additional responsibility, a greater impact on an organization, new skills, and upward movement in an organization's hierarchy.[5] The careers of many managers are linear, whether they stay with the same company or frequently switch organizations. A linear career traces a line of upward progress in the positions held.

Top managers in large corporations have moved through a series of lower-level positions in a variety of organizations before they became CEOs. Similarly, the assistant manager at the Red Lobster in College Station, Texas, started out in an entry-level position as a cashier. A linear career at Dillard's department stores may include the following sequencing of positions: sales associate, business manager, sales manager, assistant buyer, and corporate buyer.[6] Managers' employees also may have linear careers, although some employees may have other types of careers.

spiral career A career consisting of a series of jobs that build on each other but tend to be fundamentally different.

SPIRAL CAREERS A person who has a spiral career tends to hold jobs that, while building off of each other, tend to be fundamentally different.[7] An associate professor of chemical engineering who leaves university teaching and research to head up the R&D department of a chemical company for 10 years and then leaves that position to start her own consulting firm has a spiral career. Similarly, a marketing manager in a large corporation who transfers to a job in public relations and then, after several years in that position, takes a job in an advertising firm has a spiral career. Those three jobs tend to be quite different from each other and do not necessarily entail increases in levels of responsibility.

transitory career A career in which a person changes jobs and organizations frequently and in which each job is different from the one that precedes it.

TRANSITORY CAREERS Some people change jobs and organizations frequently and each job is different from the one that precedes it; this kind of career is a transitory career.[8] A middle school teacher who leaves teaching after two years to work as an administrative assistant in a consumer products company for a year and then moves on to do carpentry work has a transitory career.

Career Stages

Every person's career is unique, but there are certain career stages that people generally appear to progress through. Even if a person does not progress through all the stages, typically some of the stages are experienced. Each stage is associated with certain kinds of activities, hurdles, and potential opportunities. Regardless of the extent to which a person experiences each stage, and regardless of the exact number of the stages, about which there is some disagreement among researchers, here we discuss five stages (see Exhibit A) that are useful to understand and manage careers.[9]

These career stages apply to managers and nonmanagers alike. Thus, understanding the stages is important for managers both in terms of their own career development and in terms of the career development of their employees. Importantly, and increasingly, these career stages are experienced by most people in a variety of organizations. That is, while in the past, at least some people might have spent most of their careers in a single organization (or in just a few organizations), this is becoming increasingly rare. Rapid changes in technology, increased global competition, environmental uncertainty, outsourcing, and the layoffs many organizations resort to at one point or another to reduce costs are just some of the factors responsible for people's careers unfolding in a series of positions in a number of different organizations. Thus, a boundaryless career, or a career that is not attached or bound to a single organization, has become increasingly common, and most people have a variety of work experiences in multiple organizations throughout their careers.[10]

boundaryless career A career that is not attached to or bound to a single organization and consists of a variety of work experiences in multiple organizations.

PREPARATION FOR WORK During this stage, people decide what kind of career they desire and learn what qualifications and experiences they will need in order to pursue their chosen career. Deciding on a career is no easy task and requires a certain degree of self-awareness and reflection. Sometimes people turn to professional career counselors to help them discover the kinds of careers in which they are most likely to be happy. A person's personality, values, attitudes, and moods impact the initial choice of a career.[11]

After choosing a career area, a person must gain the knowledge, skills, and education necessary to get a good starting position. A person may need an undergraduate or graduate degree or may be able to acquire on-the-job training through an apprenticeship program (common in Germany and some other countries).

ORGANIZATIONAL ENTRY At this stage, people are trying to find a good first job. The search entails identifying potential opportunities in a variety of ways (such as researching job openings on various employment sites such as Monster or Indeed; attending career/job fairs; and mining personal contacts), finding out as much as possible about alternative positions, and making oneself an attractive candidate for prospective employers. Organizational entry is a more challenging stage for some kinds of careers than for others. An accounting major who knows she wants to work for an accounting firm already has a good idea of her opportunities and of how to

Exhibit A

Career Stages

Preparation for work → Organizational entry → Early career → Midcareer → Late career

make herself attractive to such firms. An English major who wants a career as an editor for a book publisher may find that entry-level positions that seem a good start to such a career are few and far between and may decide her best bet is to take a position as a sales representative for a well-respected publisher. More often than not, managers do not start out in management positions but rather begin their careers in entry-level positions in departments such as finance, marketing, or engineering.

EARLY CAREER The early-career stage begins after a person obtains a first job in his or her chosen career. At this stage there are two important steps: establishment and achievement. *Establishment* means learning the ropes of one's new job and organization—learning, for example, specific job responsibilities and duties, expected and desired behaviors, and important values of other organizational members such as the company's CEO. A person who has acquired the basic know-how to perform a job and function in the wider organization is ready to take the second step. *Achievement* means making one's mark, accomplishing something noteworthy, or making an important contribution to the job or organization.[12]

The achievement step can be crucial for future career progression. It is a means of demonstrating one's potential and standing out from others who are aspiring to become managers and are competing for desired positions. Downsizing and restructuring have reduced the number of management positions at many large companies, making it very important for individuals to manage the early-career stage effectively and thus increase their chances of advancement. By identifying where and how you can make a truly significant contribution to an organization, you can enhance your career prospects both inside and outside the organization.

Some people find that seeking out and gaining the assistance of a mentor can be a valuable asset for the early-career and subsequent stages. A mentor is an experienced member of an organization who provides advice and guidance to a less experienced worker (the *protégé*, or *mentee*). The help that a mentor provides can range from advice about handling a tricky job assignment, dealing with a disagreement with a supervisor, and what kind of subsequent positions to strive for, to information about appropriate behavior and what to wear in various situations. Mentors often seek out protégés, but individuals also can be proactive and try to enlist the help of a potential mentor. Generally, especially good potential mentors are successful managers who have had a variety of experiences, genuinely desire to help junior colleagues, and are interpersonally compatible with the would-be protégé. Research has found that receiving help from a mentor is associated with an increase in pay, pay satisfaction, promotion, and feeling good about one's accomplishments.[13]

mentor An experienced member of an organization who provides advice and guidance to a less experienced worker.

MIDCAREER The midcareer stage generally occurs when people have been in the workforce between 20 and 35 years. Different managers experience this stage in quite different ways. For some managers, the midcareer stage is a high point—a time of major accomplishment and success. For other managers, the midcareer stage is a letdown because their careers plateau.

Managers reach a career plateau when their chances of being promoted into a higher position in their current organizations or of obtaining a more responsible position in another organization dwindle.[14] Some managers inevitably will experience a career plateau because fewer and fewer managerial positions are available as one moves up an organization's hierarchy. In some organizations upper-level positions are especially scarce because of downsizing and restructuring.

career plateau A position from which the chances of being promoted or obtaining a more responsible job are slight.

Plateaued managers who are able to come to terms with their situation can continue to enjoy their work and make important contributions to their organization. Some plateaued managers, for example, welcome lateral moves, which give them the chance to learn new things and contribute in different ways to the organization. Some find being a mentor especially appealing and a chance to share their wisdom and make a difference for someone starting out in their field.

LATE CAREER This stage lasts as long as a person continues to work and has an active career. Many managers remain productive at this stage and show no signs of slowing down.

Effective Career Management

effective career management
Ensuring that at all levels in the organization there are well-qualified workers who can assume more responsible positions as needed.

Managers face the challenge of ensuring not only that they have the kind of career they personally desire but also that effective career management exists for all employees in their organization. Effective career management means that at all levels in the organization there are well-qualified workers who can assume more responsible positions as needed and that as many members of the organization as possible are highly motivated and satisfied with their jobs and careers. As you might imagine, effectively managing careers in a whole organization is no easy task. At this point, however, it is useful to discuss two important foundations of effective career management in any organization: a commitment to ethical career practices and accommodations for workers' multidimensional lives.

COMMITMENT TO ETHICAL CAREER PRACTICES Ethical career practices are among the most important ingredients in effective career management and, at a basic level, rest on honesty, trust, and open communication among organizational members. Ethical career practices include basing promotions on performance, not on irrelevant considerations such as personal friendships and ties, and ensuring that diverse members of an organization receive the career opportunities they deserve. Supervisors must never abuse their power to make career decisions affecting others and must never behave unethically to advance their own careers. Managers at all levels must abide by and be committed to ethical career practices and actively demonstrate this commitment; they must communicate that violation of these practices will not be tolerated; and they must make sure that organizational members who feel that they were not ethically treated can communicate their concerns without fear of retaliation.

ACCOMMODATIONS FOR WORKERS' MULTIDIMENSIONAL LIVES Effectively managing careers also means being sensitive to and providing accommodations for the multiple demands that many organizational members face in their lives. The dual-career couple is now the norm rather than the exception, the number of single parents is at an all-time high, and more and more midcareer workers need to care for family members who are sick or disabled. By limiting unnecessary moves and travel, adopting flexible work arrangements and schedules, providing on-site day care, and allowing workers to take time off to care for children or family members, managers make it possible for workers to have satisfying and productive careers while fulfilling their other commitments.

Careers are as important for managers' employees as they are for managers themselves. Understanding the many issues involved in effectively managing careers helps ensure that both managers and their employees will have the kinds of careers they want while helping an organization achieve its goals.

Endnotes

1. J. H. Greenhaus, *Career Management,* (New York: Dryden Press, 1987).

2. L. Lovelle, "A Payday for Performance" *Business Week,* April 18, 2005, 78–80.

3. M. J. Driver, "Careers: A Review of Personal and Organizational Research," in C. L. Cooper and I. Robertson, eds., *International Review of Industrial and Organizational Psychology* (New York: Wiley, 1988).

4. Ibid.

5. Ibid.

6. "Careers: Let's Build a Future Together," https://careers.dillards.com, accessed February 25, 2019.

7. Greenhaus, *Career Management.*

8. M. B. Arthur, "The Boundaryless Career: A New Perspective for Organizational Inquiry," *Journal of Organizational Behavior* 15 (1994), 295–306; M. B. Arthur and D. M. Rousseau, *The Boundaryless Career: A New Employment Principle for a New Organizational Era* (New York: Oxford University Press, 1996), 237–55; "Introduction: The Boundaryless Career as a New Employment Principle," in M. B. Arthur and D. M. Rousseau, eds., *The Boundaryless Career: A New Employment Principle for a New Organizational Era* (New York: Oxford University Press, 1996), 3–20; L. T. Eby et al., "Predictors of Success in the Era of the Boundaryless Career," *Journal of Organizational Behavior* 24 (2003), 689–708; S. C. deJanasz, S. E. Sullivan, and V. Whiting, "Mentor Networks and Career Success: Lessons for Turbulent Times," *Academy of Management Executive* 17, no. 4 (2003), 78–91.

9. N. Griffin, "Personalize Your Management Development," *Harvard Business Review,* March 2003, 113–19.

10. Driver, "Careers: A Review of Personal and Organizational Research."

11. J. L. Holland, *Making Vocational Choices: A Theory of Careers* (Englewood Cliffs, NJ: Prentice Hall, 1973).

12. Greenhaus, *Career Management.*

13. G. Dreher and R. Ash, "A Comparative Study of Mentoring among Men and Women in Managerial, Professional, and Technical Positions," *Journal of Applied Psychology* 75 (1990), 525–35; T. A. Scandura, "Mentorship and Career Mobility: An Empirical Investigation," *Journal of Organizational Behavior* 13 (1992), 169–74; D. B. Turban and T. W. Dougherty, "The Role of Protégé Personality in Receipt of Mentoring and Career Success," *Academy of Management Journal* 37 (1994), 688–702; W. Whitely, T. W. Dougherty, and G. F. Dreher, "Relationship of Career Mentoring and Socioeconomic Origin to Managers' and Professionals' Early Career Success," *Academy of Management Journal* 34 (1991), 331–51.

14. S. Vozza, "Three Things You Need to Do to Avoid Hitting a Career Plateau," *Fast Company,* www.fastcompany.com, February 21, 2019.

Glossary/Subject Index

A

Ability tests, 399
Accuracy, 187, 451
Achievement, 479
Achievement orientation, 143
ACHIEVEMENT ORIENTATION
A worldview that values assertiveness, performance, success, and competition, 143

Achievement-oriented behaviors, 335
Activity ratios, 263
Ad hoc committees, 242, 360
ADA (Americans with Disabilities Act), 99, 393
Adaptive cultures, 273–274
Adient Lerma, 381–382
Adjourning, 367
Administrative model, 160–161
ADMINISTRATIVE MODEL An approach to decision making that explains why decision making is inherently uncertain and risky and why managers usually make satisfactory rather than optimum decisions, 161

Age, 98
Age Discrimination in Employment Act, 98, 99, 393
Agile companies, 21
Aging of population, 98, 134
Agreeableness, 49
AGREEABLENESS The tendency to get along well with other people, 49

Alaska Air, 219–220
Allocating authority, 238–241
Alternative courses of action, 90, 164–165, 169
Alternatives
    assessing, 165–166
    choosing among, 167
    generating, 164–165
    implementing, 167
    learning from feedback, 167
Amazon, 121–122
Ambiguous information, 162
AMBIGUOUS INFORMATION
Information that can be interpreted in multiple and often conflicting ways, 162

Americans with Disabilities Act (ADA), 99, 102, 393
Annual meeting, 66
Annual planning cycle, 190
Artificial intelligence, 453

ASA (attraction-selection-attrition) framework, 62
Assessment center, 400
Attitudes, 52, 54–56
ATTITUDE A collection of feelings and beliefs, 54

Attraction-selection-attrition (ASA) framework, 62
ATTRACTION–SELECTION–ATTRITION (ASA) FRAMEWORK
A model that explains how personality may influence organizational culture, 62

Authority, 37, 238–241
AUTHORITY The power to hold people accountable for their actions and to make decisions concerning the use of organizational resources, 37, 238

Autonomy, 226

B

B2B network structures, 243–245
B2B NETWORK STRUCTURE
A series of global strategic alliances that an organization creates with suppliers, manufacturers, and distributors to produce and market a product, 243

Background checks, 398
Background information, 398
Backward vertical integration, 202
Balanced Scorecard, 270
BALANCED SCORECARD A management control system that takes a comprehensive look at an organization's overall performance using four measures: financial, customer service, internal business processes, and the organization's capability for strategic learning and growth, 270

Barriers
    distance and culture, 139–140
    trade and investment, 137–138
Barriers to entry, 129–131
BARRIERS TO ENTRY Factors that make it difficult and costly for an organization to enter a particular task environment or industry, 129

Bay of Pigs invasion, 168
Behavior appraisals, 405
Behavior control, 267–268
    bureaucratic control, 270–271

direct supervision, 268
    management by objectives, 268–270
Behavior model of leadership, 330–331
    consideration, 330
    initiating structure, 330–331
Belongingness needs, 294, 295
Benchmarking, 278
BENCHMARKING The process of comparing one company's performance on specific dimensions with the performance of other high-performing organizations, 278

Benefits, 410–411
Best Buy, 213–214
Big data, 455
Big five personality traits, 46–50
    agreeableness, 48, 49
    conscientiousness, 48, 49
    extraversion, 47–48
    negative affectivity, 49
    openness to experience, 48–50
Blog, 434
BLOG A website on which an individual, group, or organization posts information, commentary, and opinions and to which readers can often respond with their own commentary and opinions, 434

Body weight, 104
Bonus, 309–310
Boston Consulting Group (BCG), 423–424
Bottom-up change, 278
BOTTOM-UP CHANGE A gradual or evolutionary approach to change in which managers at all levels work together to develop a detailed plan for change, 278

Boundaryless career, 478
BOUNDARYLESS CAREER A career that is not attached to or bound to a single organization and consists of a variety of work experiences in multiple organizations, 478

Boundaryless organization, 244
BOUNDARYLESS ORGANIZATION
An organization whose members are linked by computers, email, computer-aided design systems, video teleconferencing, and cloud-based software, and who rarely, if ever, see one another face-to-face, 244

Bounded rationality, 161
BOUNDED RATIONALITY
Cognitive limitations that constrain one's ability to interpret, process, and act on information, 161

Brainstorming, 173
Brand loyalty, 129–131
BRAND LOYALTY Customers' preference for the products of organizations currently existing in the task environment, 129

Brooks Brothers, 472–473
Bureaucracy, 37
BUREAUCRACY A formal system of organization and administration designed to ensure efficiency and effectiveness, 37

Bureaucratic control
    definition, 271
    problems with, 271–272
BUREAUCRATIC CONTROL
Control of behavior by means of a comprehensive system of rules and standard operating procedures, 270

Bureaucratic red tape, 38
Bureaucratic theory, 37–38
Business, 192
Business case for diversity, 107–108
Business-level plan, 188
BUSINESS-LEVEL PLAN Divisional managers' decisions pertaining to divisions' long-term goals, overall strategy, and structure, 188

Business-level strategy, 197–200
    definition, 188
    differentiation strategy, 198–199
    focused low-cost and differentiation strategies, 199–200
    low-cost strategy, 199
BUSINESS-LEVEL STRATEGY A plan that indicates how a division intends to compete against its rivals in an industry, 188

C

Cafeteria-style benefit plans, 411
CAFETERIA-STYLE BENEFIT PLAN A plan from which employees can choose the benefits that they want, 411

O

Name Index

Company Index